STUDIES IN ECONOMIC HISTORY AND POLICY:
THE UNITED STATES IN THE TWENTIETH CENTURY

Edited by
LOUIS GALAMBOS & ROBERT GALLMAN

Crisis in the making
The political economy of New York State since 1945

Crisis in the making

The political economy of New York State since 1945

PETER D. McCLELLAND
ALAN L. MAGDOVITZ

Cambridge University Press

Cambridge
London   New York   New Rochelle
Melbourne   Sydney

Published by the Press Syndicate of the University of Cambridge
The Pitt Building, Trumpington Street, Cambridge CB2 1RP
32 East 57th Street, New York, NY 10022, USA
296 Beaconsfield Parade, Middle Park, Melbourne 3206, Australia

First published 1981

Printed in the United States of America
Typeset by Bi-Comp Inc., York, Pennsylvania
Printed and bound by The Book Press, Brattleboro, Vermont

Library of Congress Cataloging in Publication Data

McClelland, Peter D

Crisis in the making, the political economy of
New York State since 1945.

(Studies in economic history and policy)

Bibliography: p.

Includes index.

1. Finance, Public – New York (State) 2. New York
(State) – Economic conditions. 3. New York (State) –
Economic policy. I. Magdovitz, Alan L., joint author.
II. Title. III. Series.

HJ605.M33   336.747   80–24167
ISBN 0 521 23807 2

for
MATTHEW,
SETH,
and
MARNINA

Contents

vii

Editors' preface

The financial woes of New York, the state and the city, have been front-page news for a number of years now. Every newspaper editor in the country has had an opportunity to express his opinion about the revenues and expenditures of New York. Our U.S. senators and representatives have been forced to offer their conclusions – either by discussing the issue or by voting. What has been lacking in this public discourse, however, has been a thorough analysis of the underlying economic, fiscal, and legal issues, a historical perspective on the long-run developments involved, and a nonpartisan evaluation of who contributed to the crisis. The publication of this carefully researched volume by Peter D. McClelland and Alan L. Magdovitz meets these important needs, and we, as editors, are proud to have this book as the first in our series of Studies in Economic History and Policy: The United States in the Twentieth Century.

McClelland and Magdovitz untangle with great skill the factors that led to New York's long-run economic retardation and show how economic tendencies both constrained and were exacerbated by fiscal policies of the state and the city. They show the ways in which constitutional restraints on the issuance of debt were circumscribed to permit increased expenditures, in the absence of new revenues. The breakdown of controls on debt thus led both to fiscal excess and to the Balkanization of the public sector. Ironically, the withdrawal of major expenditure decisions from close public control was engineered by public figures known for their progressive stance on social issues and for their commitment to democratic principles.

McClelland and Magdovitz exhibit a high order of skill in economic and political analysis and in historical interpretation as they tell the story of the fiscal crisis in New York. *Crisis in the Making* should interest all those who are concerned with the evolution of American political economy.

Louis Galambos
Professor of History
Johns Hopkins University

Robert Gallman
Professor of Economics
University of North Carolina

Preface

This New York study had its origins in Michael Kammen's suggestion that I be included in the State Museum's bicentennial planning activities. My objections that I knew little about New York's history were overruled by a state official, who insisted that an absence of knowledge would contribute to a novel perspective. A paper prepared for these activities led to a request for a second, and then a third, and finally, to the editing of a book on New York's present-day economic problems. A growing sense of unease accompanied each task. The evidence pointed in ever starker terms to three unwelcome conclusions: New York's economy had been faltering for some time, retardation tendencies were getting worse, and little was being done to combat them. These apprehensions were intensified by the next request. The coordinator of a conference of New York historians asked for a paper reviewing the major fiscal developments of the state since 1945. I had anticipated that revenue, expenditure, and debt would show some tendency to rise. The explosions in all three were totally unexpected, particularly in a state encountering economic retardation that was becoming progressively more severe.

Here was a story in political economy that begged many questions, with few apparently interested in pursuing the answers. The problems and a proposal were therefore presented to George H. Hildebrand, then the Director of Cornell's Center for the Study of the American Political Economy. The resulting support, both in personal encouragement and in research funds, was nothing short of decisive. Without that support, this book would not have been written.

At this point, two research assistants were added to the project, whose contributions would also be critical.

One was Alan Magdovitz, then a Cornell junior. His main assignments were to dig through newspaper files and to interview politicians, bureaucrats, and newsmen throughout the state. To these tasks he brought an exuberance and concern, invariably infectious for many of those interviewed, that disguised a perceptiveness and a political astuteness remarkable in one so young. His humor, his unflagging zest for the job at hand, and his unshakable fair-mindedness in judging issues and personalities made all of our encounters as enjoyable as they were productive. It has been a privilege to know him as a colleague and a coauthor.

The other research assistant, John Scott Butler, was then a graduate student in Cornell's Department of Economics. A former accountant and a first-rate economist, "J.S.," as we came to know him, had, as his main assignment, unraveling the books of first New York State and then New York City. That was to be a far more formidable task than any of us anticipated. The bookkeeping practices of the state have been, to say the least, irregular, and those of the city were downright bizarre. With impeccable care and determination, J.S. put together the numerical fiscal fabric of this work. His other contributions ranged from scouring library sources to assessing legal cases to offering incisive criticisms and suggestions on a multitude of topics. Other demands subsequently diverted him from this New York project, but only after his contribution had been nothing short of monumental. It is a tribute to his exceptional integrity that he has resisted all pleas to accept joint authorship. To Alan and me, he will always have this status, along with that of respected colleague and valued friend.

Many others, in great and small ways, have helped us along the way to understand the politics and economics of the Empire State. Four should be singled out for special mention. To understand how the books were kept, we turned initially, and then with increasing regularity, to John J. O'Connor of New York State's Department of Audit and Control. Despite an overburdened schedule, he responded to all our requests with an Irish wit and an accountant's patience that belied the tediousness of the tasks. For guidance on constitutional matters, we relied partly upon Cornell's Law School faculty and library, but primarily upon Leon Edward Wein of Brooklyn Law School. As the reader will discover, Wein has been a voice in the wilderness, constantly attempting through legal action to force the politicians to abide by fiscal rules established in the law. For us, he was an expert guide through legal decisions and constitutional provisions that otherwise might have been an impenetrable maze. Many helped us to understand the problems of New York City, but two were outstanding for insightful generalizations combined with a mastery of detail: Raymond D. Horton of Columbia University, and Herbert J. Ranschburg of the Citizens Budget Commission.

The chapters on the economy were strengthened by consultations with, and comments from, economists in business, government, and academia: in particular, Regina Armstrong, Regional Plan Association;

Roy Bahl, Syracuse University; Karen Gerard, Chase Manhattan Bank; Amos Ilan, Port Authority of New York and New Jersey; Walter Isard, Cornell University; William J. Lawrence, Pace University; Robert A. Leone, Harvard University; George Roniger, Citibank; Marilyn Rubin, New York Office of Economic Development; Sidney Saltzman, Cornell University; Frans Seastrand, New York Department of Commerce; Sharon P. Smith, Federal Reserve Bank of New York; Thomas J. Spitznas, Chemical Bank; and Rona B. Stein, Federal Reserve Bank of New York.

We are also indebted to those who read all or part of the manuscript, correcting errors, eradicating vagueness, and appending vital information. The list includes Regina Armstrong, John Scott Butler, Donald H. Davenport, Lance E. Davis, Charles R. Holcomb, Amos Ilan, Walter Isard, Michael Kammen, Steven L. Kaplan, Peter J. Katzenstein, Walter F. LaFeber, William J. Lawrence, Patricia G. Leeds, Arthur Levitt, Edward A. Lutz, Duncan MacIntyre, Warren Moscow, John J. O'Connor, George H. Quester, Herbert J. Ranschburg, Marilyn Rubin, Frans Seastrand, Joel H. Silbey, Larry Silverman, Robert W. Smith, Thomas J. Spitznas, Rona B. Stein, Cushing Strout, Robert S. Summers, and Ruth C. Young.

In the final months of preparation, two undergraduates, Joseph Baumgarten and Margaret Forrence, were tireless assistants in tracking down references and aiding in other last-minute details.

For secretarial help at various stages I am indebted to Fran Brown, Linda Clasby, Lynn Rabenstein, and Verma McClary. The bulk of the final manuscript was assembled with the aid of Patricia Paucke, whose competence and patience remained unscathed, despite the drudgery of repeated additions and deletions.

These acknowledgments are perhaps appropriately closed with a personal reminiscence that bears obliquely upon many issues in the text. In the story that lies ahead will be found a cast of characters whose motives and actions are often less than admirable. Not all public servants, however, are unmindful of their obligation to serve the public. This was driven home to me when I met for the first time with Arthur Levitt to review the manuscript. The discussion began with incidental matters: anecdotes and personal insights that reflected his 24 years as New York State Comptroller. Quickly he turned to issues of consequence, particularly the pressures to which he had been subjected to use state employee pension funds to bail out New York City. Retirement had not tempered his indignation. As he recalled all of those who had sought to make him violate his fiduciary role as sole trustee of those funds, he became again their guardian in spirit if not in fact. His concern even then was an essay in dedication – so much so that his anger and apprehension began to impair his ability to speak. Almost with a note of apology, he rose and said, "I'm afraid I cannot continue." Within the hour, he had passed away. No New Yorker could ask for greater dedication.

Peter D. McClelland

Ithaca, N.Y.
Summer 1980

1

Introduction

March 10, 1831. The New York City audience awaited the principal speaker of the evening unsure what to expect. They had assembled that Saturday evening to honor the memory and achievements of Alexander Hamilton, long-time resident of New York and fiscal architect of the new republic. To breathe exhilaration and eloquence into subjects as dry as currency and public borrowing would be no mean achievement. Mindful of the difficulties, the program committee had given the task to one of the foremost orators of their generation or any other. Daniel Webster would not disappoint them. After a few ingratiating remarks about New York as "the commercial capital, not only of all of the United States, but of the whole continent also," Webster turned to the topic at hand. And what a topic it was, or more correctly, what a topic it became under the spell of Webster's rhetoric: how Hamilton built a fiscal infrastructure for a young and precarious nation. "He smote the rock of national resources, and abundant streams of revenue gushed forth. He touched the dead corpse of the Public Credit, and it sprung upon its feet."[1] That same public credit could of course be overstrained to the point of collapse, as New Yorkers of the future would repeatedly demonstrate. Excessive borrowing had, by 1842, brought the Empire State, in the words of its Comptroller, to "the very brink of dishonor and bankruptcy." Time and again the greatest city of the state would totter upon that same precipice: in 1915, in 1933, and most recently, in 1975. For Webster's commercial capital of a continent, this suggested a frailty as puzzling as it was ingrained.

The puzzles in recent years have multiplied. The state that was in 1950 a colossus in the industrial heartland of America had become by the 1970s an ailing economic hulk. The city that began the postwar era as the undisputed financial capital of America by 1975 could not borrow a dime in financial markets for itself. In that same year the credit rating of the Empire State was imperiled as it attempted to rescue New York City from bankruptcy. Only the last-minute intervention of the federal government averted fiscal chaos in what Webster termed, in the euphoria of that March evening, the "singularly prosperous State, which now is, and is likely to continue to be, the greatest link in the chain of the Union."

Crisis is an overworked word. But lurking in the difficulties just sketched is the threat of a fiscal crisis that, should it materialize, will be well deserving of the name. Federal intervention may now have become indispensable to propping up the financial structure of New York City. The merits of continuing such support will be reviewed by Congress in 1982. Should it be withdrawn, the great city could go under. In the financial maelstrom that would follow, a successful rescue operation almost surely could not be mounted from Albany. The state is much too weakened by economic retardation and overburdened with fiscal problems of its own. The financial burdens of the city, now running far into the billions, are much too great. Should the state therefore attempt to save the city on its own, the only question would be whether the state would go under too.

Problems of such magnitude and gravity invariably have a long and thought-provoking history. It is a history, however, that few have been anxious to write. New York historians, fascinated by the colonial period and enthusiastic about the nineteenth century, have at best a tepid interest in the modern era. Albany bureaucrats and politicians and reporters all have expert knowledge of a host of facts, but seldom elaborate a larger tapestry that weaves such facts into a unified and coherent pattern that makes the past explicable. Such men of affairs are also by instinct usually preoccupied with the present and the future. Yesterday is already ancient history in the hurly-burly world of framing laws and implementing budgets and reporting what is newsworthy. The prospect of continued neglect was a major moving force behind the writing of this book. The tale to be told is one of high finance and power politics, of gathering forces for economic retardation, coincident with an explosion in taxes, spending, and debt the likes of which the citizens of New York had never seen before. It is also a tale of personal ambitions given too much free rein by a political structure distinguished for its feeble checks and balances.

Nowhere was this feebleness more apparent than in the processes that led to the rapid escalation of the public debt. Excessive issuance of state debt had supposedly been blocked by a constitutional provision requiring that all increases in debt proposed by the legislature must be approved by voters in a statewide referendum. The rationale for this tight rein upon the politicians was spelled out by the Chairman of the Finance Committee when the provision was enacted in 1846. The requirement of a voter referendum, he noted, "was saying that we will not trust the legislature with the power of creating indefinite mortgages on the people's property . . . Whenever the people were to have their property mortgaged for a State debt . . . it should be done by their own voice, and with their consent."[2]

This constitutional provision was a breakwater against which the irresponsible and excessive borrowing schemes of politicians shattered for 114 years. In 1960, Nelson Rockefeller devised a way around it. Writing free verse, Robert Frost once observed, is like playing tennis with the net down. John D. Rockefeller's grandson Nelson had a marked aversion to playing with the net up in fiscal matters. For him, the need for continual voter approval of debt was an intolerable restraint. He therefore established public authorities, ramming the requisite legislation through a legislature with limited knowledge of what was being done and limited power to resist a determined governor. The public authorities then issued debt with the "moral obligation" backing of the state.[3] Because the debt was not that of the state, the public did not need to approve it in a referendum, or so the argument ran.

For 15 years the courts remained silent on a legal issue crying out for resolution: Did this fiscal gimmickry violate the Constitution? When the judges of the highest court of New York finally did speak, they answered no, but only by the narrowest possible margin of four to three. One of the four was subsequently subjected to disciplinary hearings, because at the time that he reached this momentous decision, he held better than $3 million in New York City notes. The result of these hearings was "censure and disapproval," but not removal from the bench. More important, the court decision was allowed to stand. A key constitutional provision – indeed, the only constitutional provision of consequence – inhibiting the excessive issuance of debt was thereby laid open to more Rockefeller-type end runs in the future.

New York City politicians took a different route to debt excesses. They had a different set of constitutional restraints to circumvent. The main provisions were a ceiling on the total of long-term city debt outstanding (10 percent of the value of taxable real estate), and requirements that short-term debt be issued only for a short term and long-term debt be issued only for the "probable useful life" of the project into which the borrowed funds were to be channeled.

The 10 percent ceiling was amended to death by repeated exceptions for different types of borrowing (water-supply facilities, docks, rapid transit facilities, low-rent housing, hospitals, and schools). It was also circumvented by public authorities issuing debt that did not count against the 10 percent ceiling. The restrictions upon the period during which debt could be outstanding were undermined primarily by two gimmicks. One was the repeated "roll-over" of short-term debt; that is, the retiring of one short-term issue with the proceeds of a new short-term issue. On close inspection, therefore, short-term debt was often outstanding for considerably longer than the short term. As for the issuance of what was officially long-term debt from the outset, the principal gimmick was for New York City politicians to propose, and Albany politicians to approve, various "probable useful lives" of a length that boggled the accountant's imagination. Long-term borrowing was, in effect, used to pay for a short-term benefit. Spending for vocational education, for example – by most accounting norms a current expense – was financed by a 30-year bond because the state legislature judged such spending to have a probable useful life of 30 years.

These manipulations were accompanied by several other fiscal curiosities. Revenue anticipation notes (RANS) were issued for amounts far in excess of revenues subsequently received. The deficiency was then often covered by the device noted: the short-term roll-over of what was ostensibly short-term debt. Bond anticipation notes (BANS) were supposed to be issued, as the name implies, to provide temporary funds until the bonds themselves would be issued and the notes retired with the proceeds of the bond sale. Instead, these BANS in the early 1970s were first issued and then repeatedly rolled over in anticipation of a fall in interest rates that never came.

At the center of a fiscal routine worthy of Houdini were two developments that foreshadowed doom. One was repeated borrowing to cover current operating expenses, well recognized by every responsible accountant as the height of fiscal folly. The other, associated in part with the financing needs of the first, was the repeated adding to, and rolling over of, short-term city debt. The structure finally collapsed in 1975, when the city was barred from further borrowing in the nation's capital markets.

The failure of the fiscal system of checks and balances in this instance was made painfully apparent by the only check of consequence coming not from the executive, or from the legislature, or from the courts, but from the financial community. Members of that community were the ones who finally reined in the city politicians. Their concern had to do not with constitutional propriety, but with fiscal procedures so ill-advised that the city was no longer deemed to be an acceptable credit risk. A crucial flaw in the existing system of checks and balances was that the courts could decide very little. The difficulty was an absence of clear-cut constitutional provisions that could be protected by the courts striking down clear-cut violations. Albany politicians decided what was the "probable useful life" of a project to be financed by long-term borrowing. If a decision appeared ludicrous to the concerned citizen, he or she had difficulty getting judicial review of what was essentially a fiscal judgment call. Albany politicians, by amending New York's Local Finance Law, eased the rules for issuing and rolling over short-term notes. Again there was a murkiness in the law that limited the possibilities of judicial review. With special legislation from Albany and debt shuffles in City Hall (one RAN retired, but a second issued whose receipts could be used to pay off the first), the roll-over possibilities had, in practice, no clear limit except the tolerance of the financial community.

One major theme of this book is the defects in this system of checks and balances in fiscal matters at both the state and the local level. If ever a fiscal structure was well suited to getting out of hand, this was it. But if the structure favored overdoing, why did the politicians in charge prove so amenable to the challenge?

The answer touches upon a second major theme. The starting point is a question that traditionally troubles undergraduates in introductory government courses: What is good government, and how can the behavior of politicians be influenced to serve the cause of such a government? (The question, of course, was no less troubling to the founding fathers of the republic.) Any speculation about the answer converges quickly on an issue that must be confronted squarely here. It is no less fundamental, controversial, and personal than one's views concerning the nature of man.

Much of subsequent analysis will be predicated upon a behavioral premise, self-evident to some and resisted by others as a slur upon humanity: namely, that most people most of the time pursue their own self-interest. This is not to deny the existence of more admirable human traits. Nor does it deny that for some individuals, the dominant driving force can be something other than self-interest. What is being claimed is a statistical generalization: that in any large assemblage of individuals, most will be found to pursue, throughout much of their professional careers, objectives that are in their own best interests.

Two conclusions follow concerning how a political system should be structured. One is the need to foster wherever possible a congruence between what is best for the politician and what is best for the public – what Jeremy Bentham called a juncture of duty and interest. When that congruence cannot be achieved, a system must be contrived such that (1) whenever the action of a public servant (or a group of them) threatens the public interest, a second individual will be in a position to oppose it, and (2) this second individual will not have a vested interest in suppressing his or her opposition, so that for this watchdog function, there will be a juncture of duty and interest. Such reasoning, unflattering though it may be, is at the very heart of why the founding fathers of the republic passionately argued for a system of checks and balances as indispensable to the functioning of good government.

The New York failures under this heading are legion. All reflect a clash between what was best for the public and what was best for the politician or bureaucrat who controlled the allocation of public funds. Three are particularly troubling because of unresolved problems they promise for the future.

First, the matter of debt. The politician all too frequently has a voracious appetite for more. If he can borrow now, spend the funds on pet projects, and leave office before the bills come due, the advantages to him are often overwhelming. The credit for the projects thereby funded he is quick to claim. The likelihood that the headaches of repayment will be his appears remote. The problem is as old as the capacity of elected officials to issue promissory notes upon the future. So are the dangers. Centuries before Rockefeller's spending spree, the philosopher David Hume warned that "it is very tempting to a minister to employ such an expedient, as enables him to make a great figure during his administration, without overburdening the people with taxes, or exciting any immediate clamours against himself. The practice, therefore, of contracting debt will almost infallibly be abused in every government."[4] The New York abuses have been sketched above. The citizens attempted to forestall such possibilities by constitutional restraints. The indifference of New York politicians to the popular will was then blatantly revealed by their persistent and successful efforts to circumvent these restraints contrived by the very people they were ostensibly elected to serve.

The second New York failure that bodes poorly for the future concerns the politicians' persistent slighting of the priorities of fostering growth and combating economic retardation. The gradualness and longevity of the processes at work make both of these long-run objectives. Elected officials generally serve only for a brief term. Their political ambitions therefore focus their attention upon short-run objectives that will enhance their reputation and their chances for reelection. The public too is usually preoccupied with short-run objectives, a preoccupation that most candidates for office willingly reinforce. The slighting of the priority of economic growth is therefore virtually assured.

This slighting in the New York case had particularly serious consequences. From 1946 on, the economies of New York City and New York State both became progressively weakened by the forces of economic retardation. The implied necessity for gradually scaling down fiscal objectives was ignored. Instead, the taxes, spending, and borrowing of the city and the state exploded. Most of the policies implemented by the politicians, instead of alleviating retardation, made it worse. They did little to prevent the deterioration of New York City's mass transit system, for example. They drove the city to the brink of bankruptcy, while raising state and local taxes to the point where New York was the most heavily taxed state in the union. For these and other reasons, the business climate became so poisoned that by 1975 a Fantus Company survey gave the Empire State undisputed last place for "attractiveness of business climate." Finally, and perhaps worst of all, the failure to adjust public services to the growing restraints implied by economic retardation persisted for so long, and the intervening fiscal excesses were so pronounced, that the present economic and fiscal adjustment problems are massive for the state and Herculean for the city. In the city's case, it is far from clear how solvable they are.

The third New York clash between self-interest and the public welfare involves primarily bureaucrats, not politicians. Again analysis begins with the behavioral premise of self-interest. Again it must be emphasized that this is not to deny the existence of public servants who are public spirited. But if most bureaucrats, like most politicians (and most of humanity) pursue their own self-interest throughout much of their professional careers, what behavior can one reasonably expect? At the lower echelons, one would not be surprised to encounter a bias for security of tenure, a bias which can lead to promotion rules that emphasize seniority over merit and thus tend to stifle incentive. The focus here, however, is higher up. The institutions in question are New York public authorities. The motivations that matter are those of the men who ran them. The charge to be examined is that certain authority chiefs implemented policies of questionable public merit, largely because an insulated bureaucratic structure gave too much free rein to their personal ambitions.

Public authorities, or "public benefit corporations," are quasi-governmental agencies established by an act of the legislature. By their very nature, such authorities are insulated from the political process. In the language of a New York commission established to review their powers,

> An authority may be in a better position than an agency of regular government to operate a public enterprise without regard for party politics, patronage, and party favoritism. If a public authority is responsible for the management of a public enterprise, then the entrepreneurial decisions necessary to the economical and efficient operation of a public enterprise may more likely be kept out of the political arena.[5]

The point to be emphasized – and it cannot be emphasized too strongly – is that authority policy is not independent of politics. It is merely subject to a different kind of politics. To insulate public authorities from pressures generated in the executive or the legislative branches of government is to remove from their operating procedures one set of checks and balances, and leave almost nothing in the way of other checks and balances. The heads of these organizations are thereby left relatively free to pursue their own ambitions, if so inclined.

In that pursuit, are they likely to serve the public well? The New York record does not suggest an encouraging answer. Precisely because public authorities are relatively immune from external intervention and often control the allocation of vast sums of money, the prospect of heading such an organization is viewed as highly desirable by men with a bias for bureaucratic power and for "getting things done" – a phrase that usually connotes a considerable expenditure of public funds, with little interference from, or consultation with, the public or its elected representatives. Nor is this absence of communication deemed undesirable by those whose biases are elitist to the core. If they believe that they know better than the public itself what the public needs, the less communication the better.

Such elitism merges easily with personal ambitions to build a bureaucratic empire. The careers of Robert Moses and Austin Tobin illustrate the process. The key to empire building is surplus funds. These can then be channeled into projects chosen not by the people, not by their elected representatives, but by the man who controls the authority generating such funds. One technique used by authority heads to generate a surplus was to levy tolls and other charges for using authority facilities far above costs – pricing policies that if encountered in business would be roundly condemned for doing what these did: generating monopoly profits. This same bias for generating surpluses encouraged these same bureaucratic chiefs to avoid whenever possible involving their authorities in strengthening the mass transit systems of New York's urban centers, particularly those in the New York City area. Mass transit systems are notorious for generating deficits. If surpluses were what these bureaucratic chiefs desired, they could hardly be expected to lend a hand in shoring up deteriorating transit systems, however urgent the need. The result for New York City was a transit system so starved for funds that by the 1970s, after decades of neglect and deterioration, it bordered upon a shambles. For a vital artery in the economic structure of a city grappling with serious economic decline, such defects signal a range of transit problems as serious as they are unresolved.

Last, but hardly least, was the contribution of public authority leaders to the circumvention of a constitutional ideal. The bureaucratic chief's ambition to control the allocation of money – a lot of money – meshed conveniently with Nelson Rockefeller's desire to avoid voter approval of increases in state debt, as mandated by the Constitution. Rockefeller projects were therefore shunted from the state to a public authority. The authority borrowed the funds, and thus financed the projects. The effect was a kind of disguised disenfranchisement of the electorate. A public that had the power to fend off direct attacks upon its purse by voting no to more state debt was helpless before an attack mounted through these authorities, whose actions in this context gave a certain dubious ring to their official title of "public benefit corporations."

Although public authorities in New York did not originate with Nelson Rockefeller, under his leadership they mushroomed in number and size throughout the state. During Rockefeller's last 12 years as governor, for example, public authority debt outstanding quadrupled in size. At $13.3 billion in 1973, it was almost four times the debt of the state itself. That same year (Rockefeller's last in office), a single New York public authority, the Housing Finance Agency, had surpassed the entire debt of the Empire State by almost 50 percent.

Why the public tolerated such developments is a third controlling theme of this work. Democracy is an old word, a tired word. It is also an important word. Whatever makes it work, one cornerstone is an educated and concerned public, knowledgeable about the issues and watchful of the actions of their elected representatives. This is the ultimate check in any system of checks and balances in any democracy worthy of the name. Through the ballot box the people can exact the ultimate penalty upon those who slight the public interest.

That is the theory. The New York reality in fiscal matters throughout the postwar era has been a tattered remnant of an old republican ideal. Partly the problem was that public authority policy, by and large, was beyond the power of the citizens to influence, either directly or indirectly. Partly the problem was the indifference and apathy of many New Yorkers toward those state and local fiscal policies that they might have influenced. They seldom clamored for more information, or penalized at the ballot box those who told them little. Indifference was also reinforced by a long-standing tradition favoring strong leadership in government, and by the public's rising expectations that seemed – at least superficially – to be well met by the expanded government programs advocated and implemented by their political leaders. The failures of the public, however, were not entirely of their own making. The complexity of modern fiscal processes defy ready understanding, even by an expert. The sums are huge, the accounts are many, and the dollar flows almost impossible to track. What was intrinsically difficult to understand, in turn, was often made completely unintelligible by accounting gimmicks devised by those in power to keep the layman (and not a few political opponents) ill-informed. The end result was a decision-making structure in fiscal matters that was elitist to the core. A knowledgeable and powerful few dominated most fiscal processes, and the few were not given to enlightening the many. This too is an old problem, as sometime New York Governor Grover Cleveland reminds us from the distant shadows of the nineteenth century. "I am convinced . . . that the perplexities and the mystery often surrounding the administration of State concerns grow, in a great measure, out of an attempt to serve partisan ends rather than the welfare of the citizen."[6]

The fourth and final theme of this work concerns the interaction of economic and political events. Although easy to specify in general form, these are difficult to document in detail. Causation tends to run both ways. As the growth of the economy slows down, for example, so does the growth in tax receipts. If the economy slumps sharply when the political unit (say, New York City) is already overextended in debt, the resulting shortfall in revenues can threaten fiscal chaos. Politics can also disrupt the economy. At the center of retardation is the exodus of business firms and people. Anything that intensifies this exodus tends to make retardation worse. This the politicians can do through, as it were, sins of commission – raising taxes, for example – or through sins of omission – allowing a deterioration in public services, or neglecting to keep the transportation network of a city (especially mass transit) in good working order. The potential for vicious circles is almost limitless. The exodus of firms, for example, cuts tax receipts. A fall in revenues can prompt a rise in tax rates or a decline in public services (or both), and these developments in turn prompt more businessmen to leave. Or to begin with the fiscal side, the threat of a fiscal collapse of the New York City variety can make businessmen more apprehensive about staying and more prone to leaving. Their exodus, in turn, by cutting into tax revenues, makes solving the ongoing annual deficits of the city more difficult. This in turn increases the probability that what is most feared will come to pass, namely, the actual bankruptcy of the metropolis.

The most notable features of the Empire State's fiscal developments in the postwar era were rapid expansions – pell-mell expansions – in taxes, spending, and debt by both New York City and New York State in the 1960s and early 1970s. The most notable economic features were three: (1) retardation was in evidence throughout the postwar era, (2) that sluggishness became suddenly far worse in the 1970s, and (3) these retardation tendencies, although pervasive throughout the state, were most pronounced in New York City.

Two facts are particularly striking. One is a geographical coincidence. Retardation was worst where fiscal excesses were worst: in New York City. The other is a coincidence in timing. Retardation accelerated sharply in the 1970s, hard on the heels of a range of government policies that, from the standpoint of promoting growth (and only from that standpoint) added toxic elements to what was already a frail economic situation. The forces of retardation, in evidence throughout the postwar era, were anchored in economic factors, not political developments. The Northeast in general and its inner cities in particular were losing out as more attractive alternatives drew from them some of their business firms and some of their productive laborers. Political developments in New York, however, made this outflow worse. Government was therefore more a part of the problem than a part of the solution. How could it have been otherwise? For reasons already cited, the priorities of promoting growth and combating retardation were sure to be slighted by politicians preoccupied with their own short-run objectives. The New York peculiarity is that this slighting was so pronounced, and the forces of economic retardation so powerful, that their interaction made the Empire State by the dawning of the 1980s both the weakest economic state of the Northeast and a potential fiscal cripple for the nation.

This book has two objectives. The first is relatively modest: to tell the story of New York's political and economic events since 1945, or at least to describe the highlights of what is ultimately a rambling and complex history in political economy. John Gunther claimed that there were two kinds of experts on Russia: those who had been there two weeks, and those who had been there twenty years. Any visit falling in between these two extremes fosters in the tourist a certain diffidence about the thoroughness of his knowledge. This book is also tailored to fall between these same extremes of casual encounter and exhaustive scrutiny. The end product ideally should be both a guide for the layman and a handbook for the expert. Wherever possible, technical matters have been relegated to footnotes and appendixes. For those who wish to hurry past economic details, the two lengthy chapters on the economy are preceded by a section labeled "Introduction and summary." It is designed to be a compressed and indispensable briefing for those whose major interests would otherwise prompt them to skip directly to chapters devoted to political events. For the expert, the hope is that the tables and technical descriptions will provide a useful reference source.

The second objective of this work is unashamedly ambitious. It is, in Jefferson's phrase, to ring a firebell in the night. If ever a set of political and economic problems threatened the welfare of the citizenry, those of New York City and New York State can justifiably claim that dubious distinction. Worse, the associated constitutional and economic issues, grave though they may be, have yet to be addressed in any thorough, determined, and comprehensive way. The hope is that by laying bare some of the defects of the past, this work will help to galvanize the citizenry to attack the flaws that still imperil the future.

An enterprise such as this at best can only partially succeed. Complexity cannot in every case be rendered into simplified description for the layman. The search for general patterns and broad overviews is sure to slight details and ignore exceptions regarded by the expert as essential to a thorough understanding of the past. The breadth of subject matter and the pervasiveness of blame assure that censure lurking in the pages to come will impinge upon the vested interests of many readers. The tempting reaction is not reappraisal but indignation, not reassessment of the public's needs but a personal defensiveness that will turn a deaf ear to any alarm, however clamorous. Such dangers would seem unavoidable in any work that seeks to scrutinize the political economy of what is still, for all its frailties, the Empire State.

Chapters 2, 3, and 4 examine the structure and the problems of first the economy and then the fiscal processes of the state. Chapter 5 details the political factors underlying the main developments in the regular fiscal activity of the state, that is, the tax changes and spending proposals initiated by one branch of government (usually the executive) and approved by the other (usually the legislature). Chapter 6 concerns irregular fiscal activities in the use of public funds – irregular in the sense that they were controlled, by and large, not by elected politicians but by the bureaucrats who ran the public authorities of the state. The reasons why fiscal excesses were possible in both processes, regular and irregular, are then examined in Chapter 7, under the heading "Of feeble checks and balances." All of these chapters, in turn, provide a useful background for broaching the topics of Chapter 8. Armed with such information, the reader can more readily understand the fiscal foolishness that came to dominate the procedures of New York City, and how the state became progressively more embroiled in that foolishness.

One shortcoming of the tale to be told should be noted at the outset. The reader will frequently sense a lurking presence whose role remains annoyingly ill-defined. The part played by the financial community in the political economy of New York is almost impossible to document in any thorough way. The phone calls, the private memos, the portfolio manipulations that mattered most are all part of a record that has largely disappeared, and what has not remains largely inaccessible to the public. Bits and pieces of evidence do suggest the obvious: that many of New York's fiscal developments of recent years – both city and state – were profoundly influenced by members of the financial community. They sat on the managing boards of public authorities that borrowed billions. They readily endorsed and vigorously peddled the many new debt instruments developed over these years, some of which were central to undermining constitutional restraints upon the issuance of debt by the city and the state. Their linkages to Nelson Rockefeller – or perhaps more correctly, his linkages to them – are legendary. Their role in the fiscal collapse of New York City is perhaps most controversial of all. What did the banks know, and when did they know it? Were they advising their clients to buy the bonds and notes of a city that they themselves doubted would remain fiscally sound? Little is known about the answers, but what is known is disquieting. The Securities and Exchange Commission produced a "damning" staff report in 1977 "that turned up numerous anomalies."[7] One of the few legal cases to come to trial revealed that Citibank persuaded a client, Alvin J. Brodsky, to buy New York City notes in March of 1975, when the managers of its own assets were "shunning" the issue. That revelation was made under cross-examination on a Friday. The following Monday, Citibank made an out-of-court settlement with Brodsky.[8] Questions of legal liability for devious investment procedures in 1975 are ultimately of secondary importance. What matters more is how the financial community has interacted with other powerful interest groups, particularly labor unions, to keep the city afloat since 1975, and the extent to which this shoring-up operation has enabled its members to clear out New York City obligations from their own portfolios. Here, too, our ignorance is massive, but likely to remain so.

The New York history about to be examined is, in one sense, not a peculiar aberration in political economy. The records of representative governments in this and other countries are shot through with examples of every single one of New York's major difficulties, from excessive debt to insulated bureaucracies to the distorting influences of self-interest upon the policies chosen by elected and appointed officials. Readers familiar with the recent experience of other American states, for example, are sure to be struck by the number of parallels to be found in the New York case. The Empire State experience, however, does seem to offer two distinctive aspects. One is a matter of degree. Its recent and pronounced economic retardation sets it apart from most other states in the union. Its fiscal excesses, particularly those of New York City, have few American parallels. The other distinctive aspect is the coincidence of economic slowdown with fiscal extravagance. This combination, fraught with dangers for the future, no other American state can begin to match in the postwar era.

Pressing and momentous challenges are, from another vantage point, opportunities for inventiveness and change. As New York has been in the vanguard of questionable innovations – particularly the emasculation of checks and balances and the evolution of a bureaucratic wilderness called public benefit corporations – so it might now take the lead among American states in devising new ways to remedy old problems, and thereby further the cause of good government (or at least the cause of better government) within the republic. No state can rival the challenges that the Empire State must now confront. Perhaps it can regain some of its lost luster by remedying in the future what it has tolerated for so long. But this is to get ahead of our story.

The New York City audience braced themselves for Daniel Webster's closing verbal cadenza. "There are two principles," he began, "strictly and purely American." More than this, he noted,

> they seem the necessary result of the progress of civilization and knowledge. These are, first, popular governments, restrained by written constitutions; and, secondly, universal education. Popular governments and general education, acting and reacting, mutually producing and reproducing each other, are the mighty agencies which in our day appear to be exciting, stimulating, and changing civilized societies. Man, everywhere, is now found demanding a participation in government, – and he will not be refused; and he demands knowledge as necessary to self-government. On the basis of these two principles, liberty and knowledge, our own American systems rest.[9]

For New Yorkers of the modern era, that has been a tenuous foundation. Ours is a story of limited participation and negligible general knowledge, of political smoke screens and the circumvention of constitutional restraints. Whatever else, it is a story that is sadly undemocratic. Had Webster glimpsed such a future on that March evening of 1831, his hand might not have raised so briskly the glass that signaled his closing toast: "Gentlemen . . . the City of New York; herself the noblest eulogy on the Union of the States."

2

Economic structure and economic problems: the setting

2.1. Introduction and summary

Easter Sunday, April 1977. In New York City's Cathedral of St. John the Divine, Bishop Paul Moore was castigating some of the local citizenry in a sermon that was hardly in keeping with the theme of resurrection. The corporations leaving New York City in its economic hour of need, he said, were like "rats leaving the sinking ship." Their executives were guilty of "betrayal."[1] The chairman of Mobil Corporation, for one, did not quite see it that way. Two months prior to the bishop's sermon his company had discovered that 80 percent of its employees were willing to work any place *but* New York City. "We can't get younger people who are really going to move up in the company to come to New York City," he complained.[2]

That this particular metropolis should have an economic hour of need, or be spurned by rising young executives, was, on the face of it, preposterous, at least from the vantage point of the years immediately following World War II. The city, as its enthusiasts never tired of pointing out, was "the Big Apple," "the hub," the center of cultural and financial activity in America. It had more theaters, museums, law firms, brokerage houses, and major banks than any other city in the nation – more by a wide margin. As for the prospects of serious economic decay, these appeared ludicrous to expert and layman alike in the surging optimism that followed the surrender of Japan. The Northeast was the heart of America's industrial might, New York State dominated the Northeast, and New York City dominated New York State. It was as simple as that.

But something clearly had gone awry by the 1970s. The colossus of the Northeast was showing unmistakable signs of decay. Advanced decay. Employment tumbled in the 1970s in almost every major industrial category. Manufacturing led the way with a loss of almost half a million jobs in six years. In New York City, manufacturing firms were going out of business at the *net* rate of nearly one a day. People were leaving too. Every week about 2,000 New Yorkers who would not be replaced packed their personal belongings and called for the moving

15

van. The result was the first absolute decline in the population of the Empire State since a group of Dutch immigrants settled at Fort Orange (now Albany) in 1624. Per capita income growth, perhaps the most comprehensive indicator of changing economic well-being, indicated a comprehensive slowdown. Throughout the 1970s, New York's annual growth rate was either close to last or dead last among the 50 states.

Admittedly, two national recessions in 1970 and 1974 had intensified the downward economic trends within the state. The basic problems, however, were far more fundamental than a regional reaction to national business cycles. The most compelling evidence of that was how New York responded when the nation slumped. The state's recessions began earlier, lasted longer, and were more severe than those experienced by the nation as a whole. Apparently the Empire State had acquired a new vulnerability that was becoming more apparent in the stresses created by cyclical downswings.

Admittedly, New York was not alone in its difficulties. Most older urban centers were encountering the problems of internal decay and suburban flight that bedeviled the cities of New York, particularly its largest city at the mouth of the Hudson. All of the older regions of the Northeast were confronting problems of sluggish local growth, but none of these could compare with the sluggishness of New York. In the metaphor of illness preferred by Governor Carey, the rest of the Northeast was suffering from "a common cold," but New York "had a case of pneumonia."[3] How was such a shattering transformation possible? Why had the colossus of the Northeast become an ailing hulk?

The answer cannot be broached without some understanding of what it was that was being transformed, and when the turning point occurred.

"Retardation" is a relative word. It suggests a failure relative to some norm. The norms that matter most to economists assessing regional retardation are usually the average *national* growth rates in measures of aggregate economic performance: population, total output, total employment, and the like. The Empire State's economic performance, when checked against such norms, was clearly surging at the start of the twentieth century and lagging badly by the 1970s. The turning point appears to have been the period between World Wars I and II. This interwar shift from a surging to a slumping region was masked, in part, first by the Great Depression, which inhibited business relocation because of excess capacity and depressed markets, and second by World War II, during which plant relocation was inhibited by wartime scarcities in materials and labor. By the time that V-J Day brought chaotic celebration to Times Square, however, the die was cast.

In the postwar era, three developments are particularly striking. From the very first, the growth of the New York economy lagged behind that of the nation: in population, in employment, and in per capita income. Second, this retardation accelerated sharply in the 1970s as total employment actually declined and population growth turned negative. Third, all of these developments were particularly marked in New York City. If the state, in Carey's colorful phrasing, had a case of pneumonia, its greatest metropolis was threatened with collapse of the lungs. Nor were New York's economic problems entirely echoed in the neighboring states that, with New York, constituted the older industrial heartland of the Northeast. In the immediate postwar era, most of these neighbors suffered from a similar sluggishness, but none could begin to match the dramatic acceleration in retardation that engulfed New York in the 1970s. In the early years, therefore, the Empire State was an average runner in a slow crowd. In the 1970s, it dropped – quickly and decisively – to the rear of the pack.

The growing weakness in New York City was especially worrisome. Outside observers (and not a few New Yorkers) tend to forget both the degree to which the state is dependent upon nonagricultural pursuits (less than 2 percent of the state's labor force is in agriculture) and the extent to which a single great metropolis dominates most nonagricultural activities. In the New York City area can be found 6 out of every 10 manufacturing jobs in the state, 7 out of every 10 nonmanufacturing jobs, and almost two-thirds of the state's entire population, who receive better than two-thirds of its total personal income.[4] The corollary of this single-city dominance is the relative unimportance of the upstate region as a leading force for aggregate economic growth within the state. Strikingly barren of high-income counties, the upstate region's per capita income has lagged far behind that of the downstate area throughout the postwar era. Half of total upstate manufacturing employment is concentrated in three cities: Buffalo, Rochester, and Syracuse. These three aside, the cities of upstate New York, if ranked by either population or manufacturing employment, begin at levels that are comparatively unimportant even by Buffalo standards, and rapidly decline to levels that are miniature dots on any state population or employment map. The inescapable conclusion – somewhat unexpected and certainly ominous – is that, more than any other state in the union, New York in the modern era has hitched its economic fate to the fortunes of a single metropolis. And that metropolis in the postwar era was encountering grave economic difficulties. But why?

The easy part of the answer is to identify what the problem was not. It was not primarily the product of particular difficulties in a handful of manufacturing industries, such as apparel and printing and publishing. These industrial sectors had their problems, to be sure. But by the definition of retardation advanced earlier – a failure relative to national norms – every single sector of consequence in the state's entire economy was lagging when compared with national growth rates for that industry. This was as true for finance, insurance, and real estate as it was for manufacturing, as true for banking as it was for apparel. The distinctive feature of New York's manufacturing sector was that its absolute decline in employment began earlier (the mid-1950s) and was more pronounced than was the case in other sectors. That is the first point. The second is that whatever the cause of this laggard performance, it was not a poor industrial mix. The state did not have, in the postwar era, an unduly high proportion of industries whose national growth rates were comparatively slow. In fact, it had a mildly favorable mix. If the employment growth rate in each New York industry had matched the average national growth rate for that industry, total New York employment in the postwar years would have expanded at a rate slightly above (rather than far below) the average growth rate of employment for the nation as a whole. This is equivalent to saying that, say, the average height of dogs in New York is below the national average, not because the state has an unduly high percentage of dachshunds and Pekingese, but because each breed within the state is, by national standards, somewhat stunted.

So much for what the problem was not. To diagnose what it was, a useful first approach is to identify why New York has been losing an exceptionally large number of firms. There are three possibilities: a high death rate for firms, a low birth rate, or an exceptionally high rate of firm net outmigration. The rate at which established New York firms have been dying off is roughly equivalent to the national death rate for firms, which in turn is similar to the firm death rate in neighboring states of the Northeast. The surprising conclusion is that whatever has been causing New York's exceptionally severe retardation, it is not the result of an atypically high proportion of business enterprises being killed off every year. The birth rate of firms in New York has been roughly equivalent to the birth rates in all of its immediate neighbors, including the New England states. These birth rates, however, have been well below that of the nation as a whole. Further, data on manufacturing firms suggest that much of the differential (New York versus the nation) is to be explained by a below-average birth rate for branches. Finally, the net rate at which firms have been migrating out of New York has been extraordinarily high relative to both national norms and the migration rates of other northeastern states.

These rather pedestrian quantitative observations allow us to zero in on what seems to be the central economic difficulty of the Empire State. Employment growth has been sluggish because firm growth has been sluggish. The abnormal rate of disappearance of firms from the state appears to be largely the result of (1) a below-average birth rate, particularly for branches, and (2) an extraordinarily high net outmigration of firms. Notice the apparent similarity in the decision-making process that leads to firm outmigration on the one hand, and to low firm birth rates, particularly low branch birth rates, on the other. Both kinds of decisions require a comparison of location options. The first of these is a decision to leave, based upon an unfavorable comparison between a present and a prospective location. The second is a decision not to enter, based upon similar comparisons. A new firm refuses to be "born" in New York, or in the case of branch creation, the parent company refuses to establish its newest offspring in the Empire State. The central problem to be explained therefore is why in the postwar era in general (and in the 1970s in particular) so many firms left and so few entered.

Part of the answer has a long history, as noted previously, dating from the interwar period and linked to factors making for diffusion out of most of the older metropolitan areas of the Northeast. Some of these factors caused firms to get out. Others caused people to leave, and various firms to follow them in pursuit of the markets and the labor supplies these people promised when relocated.

The initial exodus of firms was partly fostered by changing production technologies that intensified the need of certain firms for low-cost space. A second factor contributing to diffusion was the growing popularity of the truck, which tended to undermine many of the previous advantages of concentrated urban production. The outward drift of city dwellers to the suburbs, and the general westward drift of the American population, also pressured market-oriented firms to pull up stakes and go.

The exodus of people was linked to different factors: the rising popularity of the automobile, improvements in mass transit, and rising incomes and improved availability of mortgage funds, which for an ever larger cohort of Americans made the dream of a home in the suburbs a reality. Relative to other cities in the Northeast, New York City suffered disproportionately from a legal change and a geographic peculiarity. The National Origins Immigration Act of 1924 sharply curtailed foreign immigration, thereby depriving the city of the huge injections of humanity that in the past had swelled its labor force and its markets. As the native population drifted toward the suburbs, that drift took many former New York City residents beyond the borders of the state. The city had the peculiar disadvantage of being squeezed in between Connecticut and New Jersey. Metropolitan diffusion into the suburbs therefore brought in its wake not merely losses for New York City – in potential incomes to tax and potential markets to service – but often losses for the state as well.

All of these developments can be detected in the interwar years. Following World War II, they tended to intensify. The population exodus to the suburbs (and to the West) was further stimulated by such factors as government subsidies for highways and for housing, rising per capita incomes, and rising family formation. Also in the postwar era came a growing list of urban ills that made the cities of the Northeast less attractive for their residents: rising crime, increasing pollution, and a deterioration in many public services. Nowhere were these more in evidence than in the largest metropolis of the Northeast, squeezed into narrow confines at the mouth of the Hudson River. Last but hardly least were the problems associated with being an early leader in American industrialization. Capital equipment was now getting older, and more prone to deterioration and technological obsolescence.

Compounding these general problems were a host of specific factors that have been cited by various writers as the major causes of New York's special economic ills. Almost all of these (and certainly any of major importance) can be grouped under 11 headings. Three are specific to New York City, namely:

1. Its defective transportation system
2. The high cost of space in the city
3. Its poor "quality of life," a vague phrase designed to capture everything from pollution to the threat of violent crime

The remaining eight causes refer to statewide problems, namely:

4. State and local taxes far above the national average
5. The high cost of energy in New York
6. The high cost of labor (and the obstreperous tendencies of unions)
7. The changing composition of the population (an influx featuring the poor, the unskilled, and the uneducated, and an outflow featuring the wealthy, the skilled, and the better educated)
8. Environmental laws restricting business activity in the state

9. Federal policies that took out of New York more dollars than they gave back
10. The increasing attractiveness to firms and to people of other regions in the United States, particularly in the South and Southwest
11. The defective "business climate" of the state, another vague phrase referring to businessmen's perceptions of many factors, including those just listed, but with special emphasis upon the attitudes and policies of labor in general, unions in particular, and government officials, both state and local

The ideal way to attack such a list is to formulate a model of firm location decision making, incorporate into the model the causal factors noted, and then (with the aid of such a model) estimate how much of a difference each of the 11 made to the actual relocation decisions that have been central to New York's slumping economic performance. This option is unfortunately not feasible. A scarcity of data, the apparent imprecision of the decision-making process, and a lack of knowledge about how relocation decisions actually were made all preclude what is instinctively the economist's first choice.

The alternative is a retreat from analysis in the direction of description. Much of Chapter 3 therefore attempts to establish which of the 11 factors appear to have been important to firm relocation. Two conclusions emerge from this exercise. The first is linked to the finding that none of the major causes of New York's retardation is likely to improve in the immediate future, and not a few are likely to get worse. It follows that a major resurgence of the New York economy – or a major reversal of retardation tendencies – is highly unlikely. That conclusion, in turn, will prove to be a central premise for the fiscal forecasts attempted in later chapters. Second, on the matter of the puzzle noted at the outset – why New York retardation accelerated so sharply in the 1970s – the answer, or much of it, appears to be closely linked to a range of political decisions. Into a state combating retardation for decades were injected, primarily in the 1960s and early '70s, a multitude of government policies that were, from the standpoint of fighting retardation (and only from that standpoint), the worst possible decisions at the worst possible time. New York State, long an ailing colossus of the Northeast because of economic forces it neither initiated nor desired, received from politicians in the postwar years little that could be counted as remedial medicine, and much that came to outright economic poison. In short, government was more a part of the problem than a part of the solution. Why?

Partly the answer was that, to some extent, the gravity of the economic problem for a long time was difficult to detect. Partly the confidence – some might say the overconfidence – of many New Yorkers dulled their sensitivity to gathering signs of weakness. Finally, and most critical of all, political and bureaucratic structures within the state made far too easy the pursuit by politicians and bureaucrats of their own short-run goals, even when those goals clashed head on with the long-run economic needs of New York City and New York State. The result was a rash of fiscal excesses for the state, and near bankrupty for the city. How this came to pass is the controlling issue for remaining chapters.

2.2. Economic retardation: problems of definition

"Retardation," as noted, is a relative word. It suggests a failure relative to some norm. But relative to what? If New York unemployment is worse than the national average, that is certainly suggestive. But is unemployment, a cyclical measure, an adequate indicator of retardation, a long-run or secular problem? Before the "relative to what?" question can be addressed, the nature of what it is that is being retarded must be settled.

Economic retardation suggests a failure of performance at the most comprehensive level within a region. The problem is not that a few industries are having difficulties, but that a slowdown is evident in the most general measures of the economic performance of a geographic area, such as total output or total employment. But what rate of growth in employment constitutes a slowdown? If all of the United States is in a slump, as it was for example in the mid-1970s, one is hardly surprised to find national trends mirrored in the Empire State. This returns to center stage the question of relative performance with which the discussion began. What is the norm against which the achievements of the New York economy should be measured?

One way to approach the question – perhaps the best way – is to view regions as competing to attract and hold factors of production, particularly labor and capital. If profitable opportunities start to disappear in region A while improving in region B, factors will move from A to B. If returns to labor and capital in, say, the Brooklyn area start to fall below returns available in adjacent states, labor and capital will tend to migrate toward the area of higher prospective returns.

As labor and capital leave, signs of economic decay may spread. Firms close their doors, employment opportunities fall, unemployment rises, and would-be workers who had not previously planned to move are compelled to look for greener pastures. As some firms move, other firms that service their needs tend to follow. For example, as corporate headquarters shift from Manhattan to southern Connecticut, firms that specialize in office interior decorating are drawn in that direction. Similarly, as people move, firms that service their needs are also drawn in the same direction: supermarkets, gas stations, department stores, and so on. And as people move away, the pool of labor available to local firms contracts, thereby adding yet another incentive to ignore New York as a possible place to locate a new firm or a new branch.

This very movement admittedly may help to remove part of the differential in returns that caused the movement in the first place. As labor migrates from region A to region B, labor becomes relatively more scarce in A (thereby creating upward pressures on the wages in A) while at the same time it becomes relatively more abundant in B (thereby creating downward pressures on the wages in B). A movement of capital should have a similar effect upon rates of return to capital in the two regions.

These tendencies for the migration of productive factors to equalize factor returns in different regions must be hedged with qualifications that need not concern us here.[5] The points that do concern us, to review, are these: (1) regions compete for productive factors, (2) competition is largely based upon prospective returns, (3) if a region starts to lose in that competition, it will experience an outflow of labor and capital, (4) those initial outflows can set in motion certain cumulative processes that cause further outflows of capital and labor, and finally (5) the exodus of capital and labor, if it occurs in a significant volume, is sure to produce the symptoms of economic retardation, namely, a slowing down (or possibly even a decline) in the growth rates of such aggregate measures of regional economic activity as total output and total employment.

It might be objected that a national focus is too narrow, that if a foreign country experiences a boom, American capital will be drawn in that direction too. As legitimate as that wider focus is for capital flows, it has only limited relevance for labor, and negligible relevance for that third productive factor emphasized by economists: land or natural resources. Labor can move across international borders only with difficulty, and the fertile soils of Iowa are quite immobile, however immigration laws are drafted. For this reason – the relative immobility of factors of production among nations – our focus will be national rather than international.

Once that focus is accepted, the question noted at the outset can be answered with comparative ease. New York has experienced economic retardation whenever it has failed to grow as fast as other regions within America. Notice what is not implied. This does not necessarily mean that output and employment must be falling in New York while they are rising in the nation as a whole. This certainly would be symptomatic of serious retardation, but these are not the most common symptoms of retardation. The most common symptoms are for New York growth rates in measures of aggregate economic activity – such as total output and employment – to lag significantly behind national growth rates. By such norms, the Empire State has been in the throes of economic retardation for half a century or more. Recent experience is distinctive only in that this retardation has showed signs of intensifying at a time when fiscal excesses have made the penalties of a further economic slowdown serious for New York State and nearly catastrophic for New York City.

2.3.   New York retardation: problems of timing

The best indicators of economic retardation, as noted, are measures of relative growth rates (the region versus the nation) in either total output or total inputs used to create that output. For output growth rates, ideally one might compare the growth in America's Gross National Product with that of New York's Gross Regional Product. A series combining the growth of all inputs would be rather treacherous to construct, not the least of reasons being the difficulty of measuring each series (particularly capital) and the difficulties in combining them. As an alternative, one could focus upon the growth rates of the single input labor by scrutinizing employment trends.

Already we have a sense of misgiving. The best measures of retardation are not easily derived. Worse, for much of New York's history, the basic data inputs for constructing even the series noted are not available. The one series that is available is population. All is not lost, however, if the process of retardation is reconsidered.

The basic idea is that flows of productive factors are responsive to differentials in prospective returns. A movement of labor, of course, is also a movement of people. As some workers also move their families, the movement of people will undoubtedly exceed the movement of the actual laborers. Thus, if a region is developing more rapidly than its neighbors, it will attract relatively more people. Its population growth rate should therefore exceed the national average. Conversely, a slower-than-average growth rate in population signals a waning of the region's economic strength relative to competing regions. This does *not* assume that individuals migrate only for economic reasons, but it does assume that trends in the aggregate movement of people are symptomatic of trends in relative economic strength. Put another way, the implicit theory relates to statistical tendencies that are not disproved by isolated instances to the contrary.[6]

The movement of people is admittedly not a perfect indicator of economic surge or retardation, but it is a comprehensive measure, closely tied to the search of labor for better economic opportunities. It can also provide the key to dating the rise and fall of New York's economic strength.

If one calculates the rate of increase of population over each decade between 1790 and 1970 for New York (see Table 2.1, line 2) and divides each calculation by the growth rate of the American population in the same decade (line 1), the resulting pattern (line 3) suggests that the fortunes of the state have waxed and waned twice since confederation. A period of strong relative growth between 1790 and 1830 was followed by a loss of strength until 1890, at which point a resurgence occurred and persisted (with the exception of the war years) until the 1930s. Thereafter, the state's ability to attract and hold population again declined. This same pattern is suggested by the data on net migration into the state (line 4). The Empire State therefore seems to have experienced two long cycles of growth and retardation over two centuries.

This assertion, on close inspection, must be restructured, because the demographic data must be restructured. If the population of the state is divided into "New York City residents" and "Other," and once again the same comparisons are made between state and national growth rates (Table 2.1, lines 6 and 8), the general pattern gives way to two quite distinct developments:

1. The relative drawing power of New York City was extraordinary between 1790 and 1930 with two exceptions, both – perhaps predictably – associated with wartime disruptions (1810–20 and 1860–70). After 1930, the drawing power of the city declined dramatically.
2. The drawing power of the rest of the state has been somewhere between weak and undistinguished for the past two centuries except for the earliest years (1790–1830) and the most recent years (1940–70).

These patterns must be modified by one further bit of disaggregation. An obvious puzzle is: Where were the rapid population growth areas between 1940 and 1970? Of the total state population increase outside New York City of 4.3 million over this time period, more than half occurred in counties immediately adjacent to New York City,[7] and

Table 2.1. *National and New York State demographic trends, 1790–1970*

	1790–1800	1800–10	1810–20	1820–30	1830–40	1840–50	1850–60	1860–70
Decade pop. growth (%)								
1. National	35	36	33	34	33	36	36	27
2. N.Y. State	73	63	43	40	27	28	25	13
3. N.Y. growth as % of U.S. growth ([2] ÷ [1])	209	175	130	118	82	78	69	48
4. Migration rate into N.Y. State[a]	N.A.	7.9	2.4	3.5	1.6	3.5	−4.0	−0.1
Decade pop. growth (%) New York City[b]								
5. Growth	50	45	25	51	62	75	64	26
6. As % of U.S. growth ([5] ÷ [1])	143	125	76	150	188	208	178	96
Rest of state								
7. Growth	78	66	46	38	21	18	14	7
8. As % of U.S. growth ([7] ÷ [1])	223	183	139	112	64	50	39	26

[a] Decade net migration as a percentage of mid-decade population.

[b] Bronx, Kings, Queens, New York, Richmond counties.

Sources: Migration data from Stanley Lebergott, "Migration in the U.S., 1800–1960: Some New Estimates," *Journal of Economic History* XXX (December 1970), 846. Population data calculated from U.S., Bureau of the Census, *Historical Statistics of the United States: Colonial Times to 1970* (1975), I, 8, 32; New York [State], Department of Commerce, *A Century of Population Changes in Counties of New York State,* Research Bulletin

a further 18 percent is explained by the growth rates of three counties encompassing three urban centers: Buffalo, Rochester, and Syracuse.[8] The apparent resurgence of upstate New York after World War II suggested by Table 2.1 (line 8) is therefore, by and large, a statistical mirage. The dominant pattern in the postwar years remained one of population growth in the immediate vicinity of New York City and limited growth elsewhere (with three exceptions, all of which were urban rather than agrarian developments).

The first conclusion, then, is that the timing of New York's present economic retardation dates from the interwar period. It was then that the state's population growth began to drop below national growth rates. By the 1940s, it was clearly marked as a laggard – a designation it has retained to the present day. The trend in the state's per capita income suggests the same conclusion. From the moment that such data first became available (1929) until the outbreak of World War II, New York's average per capita income fell from 165 percent of the national average to 147 percent – a staggering decline in barely more than a decade.[9] This tendency persisted in the postwar years, so that by the late 1970s the gap was narrowed to a slender 6 percent, and even that edge in favor of New York would probably disappear if adjustments were made in order to take into account the higher cost of living in the New York City area (see Table 2.2).[10]

1870–80	1880–90	1890–1900	1900–10	1910–20	1920–30	1930–40	1940–50	1950–60	1960–70
26	26	21	21	15	16	7	14	19	13
16	18	21	25	14	21	7	10	13	9
61	69	100	119	93	131	100	71	68	69
1.8	8.4	10.5	14.7	5.7	10.6	3.6	1.9	1.3	N.A.
29	31	37	39	18	23	8	6	−1	1
112	119	176	186	120	144	114	43	—	8
9	10	10	13	10	19	6	15	30	15
35	38	48	62	67	119	86	107	158	115

no. 15, March 1966, p. 32; New York [State], Division of the Budget, *New York State Statistical Yearbook*, 1977, p. 48. Figures for New York City population prior to 1860 based upon county totals reported in J. H. French, *Gazetteer of the State of New York* (Syracuse: R. D. Smith, 1860), 151. The population of Bronx County for this period was estimated to be the same percentage of the combined populations of two counties (Bronx and Westchester) as it was when data for those two counties were first made available (1860).

The second conclusion is that retardation hit New York City particularly hard. Part of the blow was softened by downstate diffusion. The city's loss was sometimes a neighboring county's gain. But not always. If the focus is broadened to include the entire downstate area, all of the measures of aggregate economic strength suggest the same conclusion. Relative to the rest of New York State, the downstate area was slumping badly. Its growth rates were slower – in population, employment, and per capita income – and its losses were more pronounced in people and jobs and firms: the bone and sinew of any region's economy.

The third conclusion is that New York retardation – city and state – became progressively worse after 1945. This acceleration became particularly marked in the 1970s. Prior to that decade, New York's economy had always weathered particularly well any postwar slump in the national economy. Beginning in 1970, a new vulnerability became apparent. Compared to national downturns, as noted previously, the region's recessions began earlier, lasted longer, and disappeared more gradually. One symptom of growing problems was a surge in New York unemployment rates to levels far above the national average (see Table 2.3). Another was the plunge in the state's per capita income from 120 percent of the national average in 1970 to a scant 106 percent by 1977.

Table 2.2. *New York and national per capita personal income,*
1948–77 (constant 1967 $)

Year	U.S.A.	N.Y. total	Downstate N.Y.		Upstate N.Y.[c]
			Total[a]	N.Y.C.[b]	
1948	1,989	2,494	2,724	2,644	2,069
1949	1,945	2,459	2,709	2,625	2,000
1950	2,082	2,598	2,865	2,786	2,141
1951	2,130	2,590	2,785	2,656	2,184
1952	2,184	2,600	2,826	2,722	2,226
1953	2,255	2,670	2,876	2,759	2,321
1954	2,220	2,692	2,903	2,775	2,284
1955	2,345	2,847	3,077	2,969	2,380
1956	2,432	2,943	3,227	3,129	2,509
1957	2,432	2,957	3,279	3,178	2,540
1958	2,395	2,883	3,253	3,172	2,435
1959	2,481	3,031	3,454	3,376	2,511
1960	2,502	3,091	3,476	3,351	2,519
1961	2,532	3,131	3,465	3,312	2,536
1962	2,619	3,226	3,587	3,424	2,592
1963	2,683	3,286	3,651	3,510	2,643
1964	2,790	3,426	3,784	3,645	2,787
1965	2,934	3,550	3,891	3,760	2,939
1966	3,073	3,675	4,006	3,881	3,078
1967	3,167	3,822	4,186	4,077	3,175
1968	3,295	3,978	4,363	4,267	3,293
1969	3,374	3,942	4,287	4,108	3,333
1970	3,392	3,960	4,305	4,098	3,353
1971	3,420	4,006	4,342	4,104	3,418
1972	3,602	4,132	4,490	4,220	3,516
1973	3,758	4,178	4,506	4,231	3,617
1974	3,689	4,114	4,433	4,163	3,572
1975	3,640	4,044	4,360	4,105	3,512
1976	3,768	4,064	4,367	4,109	3,557
1977	3,904	4,143	4,446	4,188	3,637

Note: Current dollar figures deflated by the Consumer Price Index.
[a] New York City plus Nassau, Suffolk, Putnam, Rockland, and Westchester counties.
[b] Bronx, Kings, New York, Queens, and Richmond counties.
[c] All counties not listed in notes *a* and *b*.
Sources: Personal income data from U.S., Bureau of the Census (1975), I, 224; U.S., Bureau of the Census, *Statistical Abstract of the United States*, 1978, p. 449; New York [State], Department of Commerce, *Personal Income in Areas and Counties of New York State*, Research Bulletin no. 9, March 1965; ibid., no. 42, August 1976*a*; ibid., no. 46, November 1978*a*; ibid., no. 47, August 1979*b*;. Consumer Price Index from U.S., Bureau of the Census (1975), I, 210; U.S., Bureau of the Census, *Statistical Abstract*, 1978, p. 490.

Table 2.3. *New York and national unemployment rates, 1947–78 (percentages)*

Year	U.S.A.	New York State	
		Total	N.Y. City
1947	3.9		
1948	3.8		
1949	5.9		
1950	5.3		
1951	3.3		
1952	3.0		
1953	2.9		
1954	5.5		
1955	4.4		
1956	4.1		
1957	4.3	4.0	
1958	6.8	6.3	6.1
1959	5.5	5.4	5.3
1960	5.5	5.0	5.0
1961	6.7	6.0	5.6
1962	5.5	5.2	5.0
1963	5.7	5.4	5.3
1964	5.2	5.1	4.9
1965	4.5	4.6	4.6
1966	3.8	4.2	4.2
1967	3.8	3.9	3.7
1968	3.6	3.5	3.2
1969	3.5	3.5	3.1
1970	4.9	4.5	4.8
1971	5.9	6.6	6.7
1972	5.6	6.7	7.0
1973	4.9	5.4	6.0
1974	5.6	6.4	7.2
1975	8.5	9.5	10.6
1976	7.7	10.3	11.2
1977	7.0	9.1	10.0
1978	6.0	7.7	8.9

Note: The calculation of unemployment rates has changed over time. Any use of these data to make comparisons across time should therefore be approached with caution. The main use of these data in this study is to compare rates across regions at a point in time.

Sources: U.S.A.: to 1970, U.S., Bureau of the Census (1975), I, 137; thereafter, U.S., Bureau of the Census, *Statistical Abstract*, 1975, p. 350; ibid., 1978, p. 409. N.Y.: to 1970, New York [State], Department of Labor, *Employment Statistics*, vols. VI and X; thereafter, data supplied by New York State Department of Labor.

Trends in employment[11] also indicate accelerating retardation, particularly in the 1970s, and particularly in the downstate area. The most revealing calculation is one similar to that made for population, comparing relative employment growth rates (New York versus the national average).[12] The first step is to calculate, for four postwar periods, the percentage growth rate in New York State employment (see Table 2.4, line 2). The second step is to make similar employment growth rate calculations for the United States as a whole (line 1). If each New York rate is then divided by the comparable national rate (line 8), the results suggest an ominous pattern. For each of three periods – 1947–52, 1952–60, and 1960–70 – the growth rate in New York employment was roughly half the national average. In the 1970s, while national employment continued to grow, New York employment actually fell – about as sinister a sign of accelerating retardation as one can imagine.

If separate employment growth rate calculations are made for upstate and downstate New York (Table 2.4, lines 3 and 4), and these rates are divided by national growth rates (lines 9 and 10), it becomes apparent that retardation, while a statewide phenomenon, is particularly marked in the downstate area. Here throughout the postwar era the employment growth rate slid further and further behind the nation's performance, culminating in an absolute decline in total employment in the 1970s.

Similar calculations for neighboring states help to assess the once popular claim that New York's problems are the same as those experienced by all of the states in the older industrial heartland of the Northeast. That suggestion is wrong. If employment growth rates are calculated for the New England states, and for New Jersey and Pennsylvania (Table 2.4, lines 5, 6, and 7), and these rates are expressed as a percentage of national growth rates (lines 11, 12, and 13), several patterns emerge. First, New York growth rates roughly matched those of the New England states until the 1960s, when a sharp divergence occurred. The New England states first surged ahead in the 1960s, and then fell back in the 1970s to a level similar to what they had achieved in the late 1940s and '50s (about half that of the national growth rate). Second, New Jersey employment growth rates remained exceptional by standards of the Northeast until the 1970s, when they dropped to levels roughly equivalent to those of New England. Third, Pennsylvania employment growth rates lagged badly in the 1940s and '50s, recovered in the 1960s, and then slumped in the 1970s; but that slump, unlike New York's, did not involve an absolute decline in employment. In short, while employment advanced elsewhere in the Northeast, jobs within the Empire State were actually disappearing. Eco-

Table 2.4. *Employment trends, United States and selected states, 1947–77*

	1947–52	1952–60	1960–70	1970–77
Total employment growth (%)				
1. U.S.A.	11.19	11.06	30.80	16.05
2. New York State: total	5.62	6.07	15.74	−4.29
3. upstate[a]	N.A.	5.64	20.23	5.09
4. downstate[b]	N.A.	6.27	13.70	−8.79
5. New England States	5.55	6.29	22.84	8.41
6. New Jersey	14.45	12.68	29.35	9.05
7. Pennsylvania	1.07	1.25	17.08	4.67
State growth rate as % of U.S. growth rate (%)				
8. New York State: total ([2] ÷ [1])	50	55	51	N.C.
9. upstate ([3] ÷ [1])	N.A.	51	66	32
10. downstate ([4] ÷ [1])	N.A.	57	44	N.C.
11. New England States ([5] ÷ [1])	50	57	74	52
12. New Jersey ([6] ÷ [1])	129	115	95	56
13. Pennsylvania ([7] ÷ [1])	10	11	55	29

Note: Data are for employees on nonagricultural payrolls. N.A. = not available; N.C. = no calculation possible.

[a] All counties not listed in note *b*.

[b] For 1952–71, New York City plus Nassau, Suffolk, Westchester, and Rockland counties; thereafter data include Putnam County as well.

Sources: Pa. and N.J. data from U.S., Bureau of the Census, *Statistical Abstract,* 1950, p. 178; ibid., 1952, p. 189; ibid., 1978, p. 413. N.Y. and U.S.A.: See Tables C.1 and C.2, Appendix C.

nomic retardation had thus been a long time in the making, but by the 1970s its symptoms were becoming severe.

2.4. New York retardation: problems of causation

2.4.a. The setting

Four economic characteristics, all of them somewhat surprising, are central to understanding the economy of New York State.

The first is massiveness. Typical comparisons emphasize an American focus: for example, that with only 1.4 percent of the nation's total land area, the Empire State has 9 percent of the nation's population, generates 10 percent of the nation's employment, and receives 10 percent of its personal income. International comparisons are perhaps more instructive for putting such achievements in perspective. The value of goods and services annually created within New York's borders (Gross State Product) is larger than the Gross National Product of Great Britain, larger than the GNP of all of the Scandinavian countries combined, and barely fails to match the combined GNP of America's neighbors to the north and south: Canada and Mexico.[13]

The second characteristic of note is irregular topography and poor soil. The agricultural area officially classified as "Fair to Good: large farms, well managed, should compete reasonably well in the state and national economy" consists, by and large, of a narrow corridor across the center of the state, beginning at the Hudson River, running down the Mohawk Valley, and terminating in the Buffalo–Niagara area.[14] Thus, despite a land area that compares quite favorably in size with that of many of the breadbasket states to the west, agriculture in New York is a minor sector in the state's economy. Even "minor" is perhaps too flattering an adjective for a sector that employs less than 2 percent of the state's total labor force.

With less than 2 percent of the work force in agriculture, it follows that more than 98 percent is employed in nonagricultural pursuits, which brings us to the third dominant characteristic of the state. The concentration of much of this employment in the New York City area comes as no surprise. What is surprising is the extent of that concentration. The point can be made in several ways. Maps invariably highlight what is too easily forgotten: that downstate New York is little better than a southeastern appendage to a political entity whose major land mass sprawls from Pennsylvania's northern border to the Great

Lakes. Maps also underscore that downstate New York, although trivial in geographic dimensions, fairly overwhelms all other areas of the
state in population concentration, income generation, and manufacturing employment (see Maps 2.1 and 2.2 and Figure 2.1). Regional
aggregates tell the same story. In the New York City area[15] can be
found almost two-thirds of the state's entire population, who receive
better than two-thirds of its total personal income. In the same restricted territory could be found (as of the mid-1960s) 6 out of every 10
manufacturing jobs in the state, and 7 out of every 10 nonmanufacturing jobs.

Simple subtraction yields the fourth and final point. If the downstate
area dominates to this extent, the upstate area, although relatively
massive in land area, must be surprisingly unimportant to the economy
of the state. Again a scrutiny of maps is instructive. The upstate area is
strikingly barren of high-income areas, except for the counties encompassing Buffalo, Rochester, and Albany (see Map 2.3). Not surprisingly, upstate per capita income on the average has lagged well behind that of downstate New York throughout the postwar years (see
Figure 2.2). Large manufacturing centers are similarly scarce in the
upstate region. Half of total upstate manufacturing employment is
concentrated in three cities: Buffalo, Rochester, and Syracuse (see
Figure 2.3). Other than these three, the urban centers of the upstate
area appear as comparatively unimportant dots on any state map
scaled to indicate relative size of population or employment (see Maps
2.1 and 2.2).

The inescapable conclusion – somewhat unexpected and certainly
alarming – is that, more than any other state in the union, New York in
the modern era has hitched its economic fate to the fortunes of a single
metropolis. And that metropolis in the postwar era was encountering
grave economic difficulties. But why?

2.4.b. A diffused phenomenon?

From one perspective, New York's retardation is centered in New
York City, and confined to a handful of industries. In the period 1960–
74, for example, most of the absolute decline in employment occurred
in manufacturing, almost three-quarters of that manufacturing decline
was accounted for by falling employment in four industries (apparel,
food, leather, and printing), and eight out of every nine jobs lost by
these four industries were lost in New York City.[16] These four were
also among the four largest manufacturing industries in the state (see
Figure 2.4). The tempting conclusion is that New York retardation is a

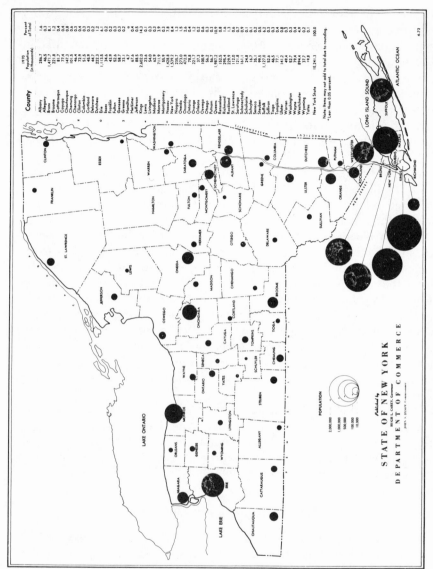

Map 2.1. Concentrations of population in New York State, 1970. *Source:* U.S. Bureau of the Census.

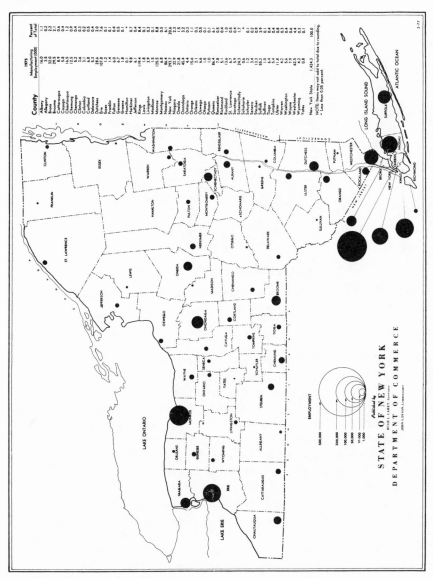

Map 2.2. Industrial concentrations in New York State, 1975 (as measured by number of manufacturing employees covered by unemployment insurance). *Source:* New York State Department of Labor.

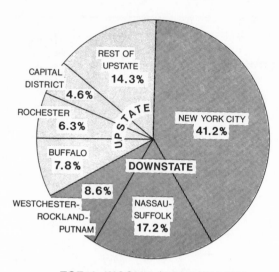

TOTAL INCOME: $134.8 BILLION

Figure 2.1. Percentage distribution of total personal income by economic area, 1977. *Source:* U.S. Department of Commerce.

localized phenomenon. Explanations of retardation, by this interpretation, should therefore feature the specific difficulties of specific industries. A lot of the job loss has been in the apparel industry, for example, and much of apparel's difficulties can be traced to improved technology permitting the use of less skilled and lower-paid workers who were more readily available elsewhere. Added to these labor problems have been such factors as the rising traffic congestion in the garment district that has slowed deliveries and increased costs.

This parochial approach will not do. As noted in Section 2.2, retardation is a relative concept, and relative to national norms, every single industry of consequence in the state has been suffering from retardation. In the period 1960–74, for example, the cost to the Empire State of this listless performance *was of the order of 2 million jobs:* some 300,000 actually lost in three sectors (mining, manufacturing, and transportation and public utilities) plus the 1.7 million jobs that should have been created but were not, because New York industries failed to keep pace with the national growth rate of their own industry.[17]

The image of selective decline in a handful of industries based in New York City is therefore a gross distortion of the facts. The state has experienced a massive retardation across a whole range of industries,

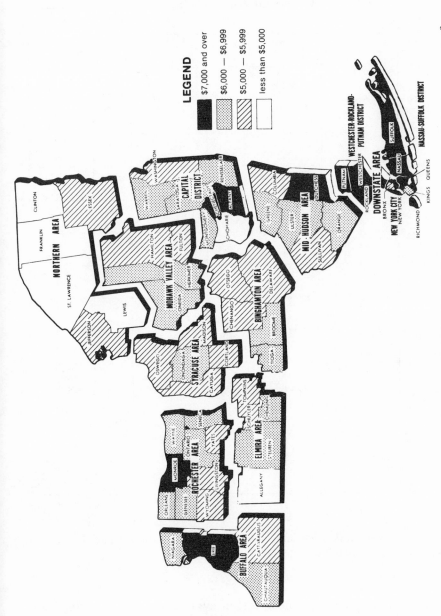

Map 2.3. Personal income per capita in counties of New York State, 1977. *Source:* U.S. Department of Commerce.

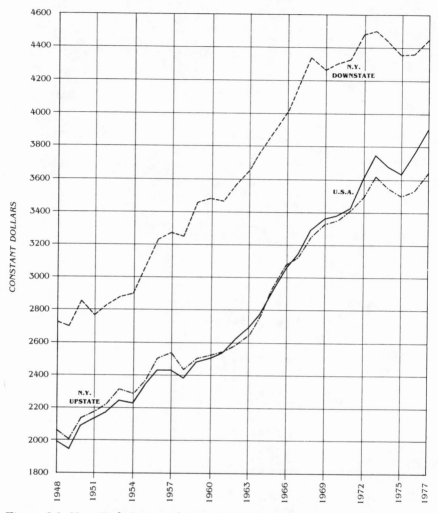

Figure 2.2. New York State and United States: per capita personal income, 1948–77. *Source:* See Table 2.2.

the effects of which have been felt in every corner of the state. One way to illustrate the diffused nature of the state's retardation is to plot various indexes of employment.[18] If previous assertions about the state's retardation are correct, two tendencies should be apparent. Any New York index of employment should fall ever further behind the comparable national index (indicating relatively slow state growth), and any downstate index should fall below the comparable upstate

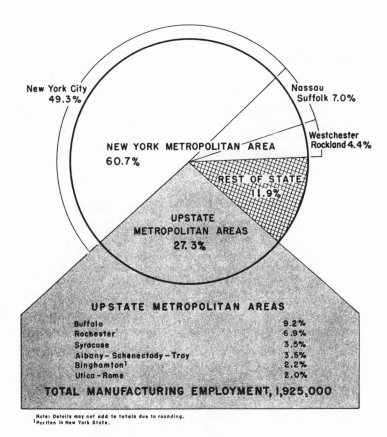

Figure 2.3. Manufacturing employment in metropolitan areas of New York State, 1965. *Source:* U.S. Bureau of the Census.

index (indicating even worse retardation in the New York metropolitan region). With minor qualifications, this will be found to be the case.

The first point to be made using index comparisons is that New York retardation predated the beginning of the absolute decline in the state's manufacturing employment in the mid-1950s. Manufacturing data alone make this clear. If United States and New York indexes of manufacturing employment are compared (see Figure 2.5), New York's performance can be seen to have been lagging behind that of the nation from 1946 onward.[19] New York manufacturing employment actually peaked in 1953 and fell thereafter, whereas national employment (with minor interruptions) continued to grow. The result is an

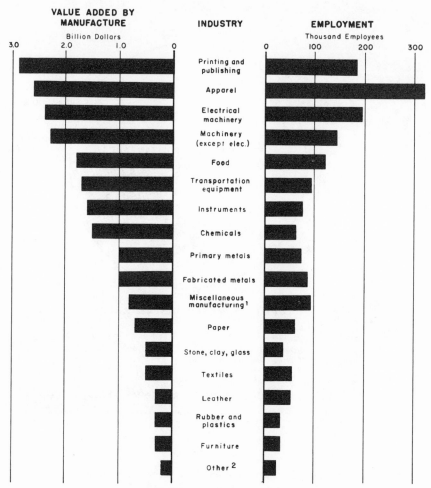

Figure 2.4. Rank of major industry groups in New York State, 1965. *Source:* U.S. Bureau of the Census.

ever widening gap between the two indexes. That gap, however, was apparent long before, 1953.

Second, retardation was pervasive throughout both manufacturing and nonmanufacturing industries. If the indexes of nonmanufacturing employment[20] for the nation and for New York's two regions are compared, a gap is evident between downstate and national growth performances from the early 1950s,[21] and between upstate and national growth performances beginning in the early 1960s (see Figure 2.6).

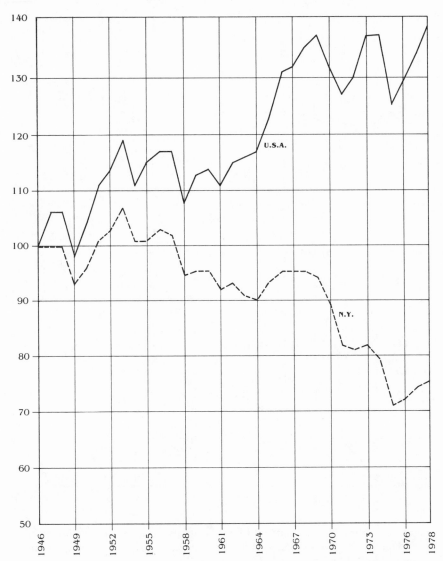

Figure 2.5. New York State and United States: index of manufacturing employment, 1946–78 (1946 = 100). *Source:* See Table C.2, Appendix C.

Third, downstate growth performance has been significantly worse than upstate performance. This is evident in the tendency of the gap in nonmanufacturing indexes (upstate versus downstate) to widen in the postwar era (see Figure 2.6). Manufacturing indexes show a more complicated pattern. The rate of decline in upstate employment actu-

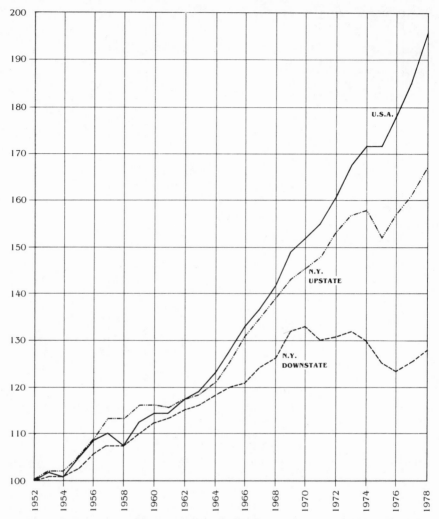

Figure 2.6. New York regions and United States: index of nonmanufacturing employment, 1952–78 (1952 = 100). Data exclude government employment. *Source:* See Tables C.3 and C.4, Appendix C.

ally exceeded that of the downstate area in the late 1950s and early 1960s. (Note in Figure 2.7 how the downstate line remains above the upstate line until 1965.) Beginning in 1964, the upstate region surged ahead for two years and then slumped gradually thereafter. Downstate employment was relatively static through the late 1960s and then plummeted in the 1970s. If secular trends in the two indexes of manufac-

Figure 2.7. New York regions and United States: index of manufacturing employment, 1952–78 (1952 = 100). *Source:* See Tables C.3 and C.4, Appendix C.

turing employment are considered for the period as a whole, the overall impression is of gradual decline in one (upstate) and precipitous decline in the other (downstate).

Fourth and last, these indexes illustrate how retardation became more pronounced in the 1970s. In that decade, in all employment indexes plotted, the gap between the United States index and comparable New York indexes became noticeably worse. This was the result of national growth persisting while New York employment changes featured either slower growth or faster decline than had previously been the case.

A final word should be added about the importance of grasping from the outset that the retardation problem of the state extends well beyond the single sector of manufacturing. Declines in that sector have been the most dramatic, and partly for that reason, its problems have captured much of the attention of the news media. But if that were all there was to New York's economic plight, the gravity of the situation would be far less than it actually is, because manufacturing is a sector of only modest size in the state's total economic structure.

Employment data illustrate the point. In the 1970s, between a fifth and a quarter of total state employment was in manufacturing (see Table C.2 in Appendix C). In New York City, where retardation has been most pronounced, the same sector accounts for less than 20 percent of employment and output (see Tables 2.5 and C.4).

Manufacturing has not dominated even the export activity of New York City. The concept of an "export" industry is important to regional economics. The term refers to those industries that sell their products (or most of them) to buyers located outside the borders of the region. Their special importance stems from the fact that they bring in their wake other industries to service their needs and the needs of their employees – cleaning services, interior decorating firms, shopping centers, gas stations, and so on. A surge in export industry activity will therefore have a multiplied effect on regional income and employment.[22] As John F. Kennedy observed in another context, a rising tide lifts all boats. By the same token, a receding tide lowers the fleet. One of New York City's problems has been the slow growth or absolute decline in a range of export industries. But the problem has affected far more than the manufacturing sector. By one estimate,[23] manufacturing in the late 1970s accounted for less than one-seventh of export production in New York City, well behind "Services" and "Finance, Insurance, and Real Estate," which together accounted for better than half (see Table 2.6). *All* of these export industries of the city – manufacturing and nonmanufacturing alike – have been growing at rates far below comparable national rates. In short, the answer to the question posed in the heading of this section is a resounding yes: New York's economic retardation is a diffused phenomenon.

2.4.c. The wrong industrial mix?

One possible explanation for the relatively slow growth of employment in New York State in the postwar era is that New York was cursed

to have poor acceleration, because most Mexicans own Volkswagen beetles.

As logical as the explanation might appear, for New York it is totally without foundation. The Empire State did not have an unfavorable mix of industries. Rather, it had a mildly favorable mix. If the employment growth rate in each New York industry had matched the average national growth rate for that industry, total New York employment in the postwar years would have expanded at a rate slightly above (rather than far below) the average growth rate for the nation as a whole.[24] In short, the sluggishness of New York growth reflected the failure of almost every single one of its industries to match the national growth rate for that industry. To return to our car analogy, this is equivalent to saying that cars on New York roads have poor acceleration, not because New Yorkers own a disproportionately high percentage of underpowered models, but rather because all makes of cars operated in the state have, by national standards, rather sluggish engines.

2.4.d. The disappearance of New York firms: births, deaths, and migrations

A useful approach to the problem of explaining New York's retardation is to ask why firms have disappeared. The answer can be broken down into three parts. The *net* change in the number of firms in a region over any period of time is the combined result of the death of old firms, the birth of new firms, and the migration of existing firms into, or out of, the state. As unsurprising as that partitioning process is, it allows us to identify a surprising characteristic of New York's economic problems.

The best available data on this firm-generation process suggest three conclusions:[25]

1. The death rate of firms has been roughly constant in recent years for all regions throughout America. The New York rate accordingly has not been very different from death rates elsewhere.[26]
2. The birth rate of firms in New York State has been roughly equivalent to the birth rates in all of its immediate neighbors, including the New England states (see Table 2.7).[27] New York's birth rate has admittedly been significantly below that of the nation as a whole, but data on manufacturing firms suggest that much of this differential is to be explained by a below-average birth rate for branches (see Table 2.8).
3. The pattern of firm migration into, and out of, New York sets the state apart from all other states, including those of the Northeast.[28] More particularly, its rate of inmigration

Crisis in the making

Table 2.7. *Rates of closure, birth, in- and outmigration of firms by state in the North and South, 1969–74 (percentages)*

State	Closure rate	Birth rate	Inmigration rate	Outmigration rate
North	33	20	0.02	0.07
New England	33	22	0.22	0.09
Connecticut	33	23	0.69	0.24
Maine	34	22	0.20	0.08
Massachusetts	32	21	0.17	0.19
New Hampshire	37	29	0.65	0.22
Rhode Island	33	21	0.24	0.36
Vermont	36	23	0.20	0.11
Middle Atlantic	33	18	0.05	0.17
New Jersey	33	19	1.05	0.27
New York	35	19	0.11	0.59
Pennsylvania	29	16	0.12	0.22
East North Central	33	22	0.05	0.08
Illinois	33	24	0.17	0.26
Indiana	33	20	0.16	0.20
Michigan	34	25	0.08	0.10
Ohio	33	20	0.11	0.15
Wisconsin	30	19	0.13	0.09
South	35	29	0.10	0.03

Note: Migration rates for a region are significantly below migration rates for individual states in that region insofar as there has been significant intraregional movement captured by the state measure but ignored by the regional measure.

Source: Carol L. Jusenius and Larry C. Ledebur, *Documenting the "Decline" of the North,* U.S. Department of Commerce, Economic Development Research Report, June 1978, p. 4.

has been relatively low, while its rate of outmigration has been astronomically high.

We have therefore arrived at a proximate explanation for much of New York's economic retardation. Employment growth has been sluggish because firm growth has been sluggish. The latter was *not* the result of an unduly high death rate of firms. Despite its pronounced retardation, New York does not appear to have been killing off business enterprises at a faster rate than any other region. The abnormal disappearance of firms from the state appears to be largely the product of two factors: a below-average birth rate and an extraordinary outmigration of firms.

Table 2.8. *Birth rate and employment creation rate for major manufacturing establishments, New York State and United States, 1969–76 (percentages)*

	N.Y.	U.S.A.
Birth rate for firms[a]		
Total	16	26
Single-establishment births	9	11
Headquarters births	2	2
Branch births	3	11
Subsidiary births	1	2
Employment creation rate in new establishments[b]		
Total	20	26
In new single establishments	6	5
In new headquarters	2	2
In new branches	10	17
In new subsidiaries	2	2

Note: Major manufacturing establishments are defined as those with 20 or more employees in SIC codes 20, 22–39, 48, and 73.
[a] Calculated by dividing firm creation (1969–76) by number of major manufacturing establishments in 1969.
[b] Calculated by dividing employment created by new firms (1969–76) by total employment in 1969.
Source: Calculated from data compiled using Dun and Bradstreet tapes for a forthcoming study, *Regional Growth: Interstate Tax Competition,* Advisory Commission on Intergovernmental Relations, Washington, D.C.

Notice how these assertions all but bury the notion that New York's problems are mainly the result of firms being killed off during the cyclical downturns of the 1970s. If that assertion were true, New York death rates would have been disproportionately high during that period, which they were not. Notice further that relative to Pennsylvania, New Jersey, and the New England states, New York has neither an unusually high death rate nor an unusually low birth rate: Its distinctive feature is its net outmigration rate. Notice finally the apparent similarity in the decision-making processes that led to firm outmigration on the one hand and to low firm birth rates, particularly low branch birth rates, on the other. As noted previously, both involve location (or relocation) decisions based upon a comparison of the Empire State with attractive alternatives. Much of subsequent analysis will therefore focus upon the migration decision of firms, more particularly, upon factors making New York a less attractive place to be for those contemplating location or relocation of a business enterprise. But why in the postwar era in general – and why in the 1970s in particular – did so many leave and so few enter?

2.5. The migration process

2.5.a. Early beginnings: the interwar years

The broad outlines of New York City's progress from colonial seaport to modern metropolis are well known, and need only be reviewed briefly here. In the early nineteenth century perhaps the city's greatest advantages were linked to water – the Erie Canal to tap the interior and a deep-water, ice-free harbor to attract foreign and domestic commerce. By mid-century, New York was a mercantile city of the first importance. Thereafter, it underwent an astonishing transformation in size and economic complexity. Its early lead in finance contributed to its later domination of America's capital markets and the associated services of banking, insurance, and trading in stocks, bonds, and commodities. To water linkages were added a railroad network that favored, among other things, the concentration of production by manufacturing firms that clustered close to railway terminals. Also stimulating manufacturing growth in New York City was its huge market, made ever larger by massive injections of immigrants. The new arrivals also swelled the region's labor supply, skilled and unskilled.[29] Although the details of the nineteenth-century transformation of this urban center are familiar – from seaport town to mercantile city to industrial and commercial giant – how and why that transformation was accomplished are topics that, at best, are only partially understood. Whatever obscurities remain about causation, however, one fact remains undisputably clear: By the outbreak of World War I, New York City was an American urban colossus.

With the return to peace in 1918 came a range of factors destined to erode that preeminence. The erosion involved both the migration of people and the migration of business firms.

The movement of people in interwar America included three major developments. One was the sharp curtailment of foreign immigration by the National Origins Immigration Act of 1924, a development that struck particularly hard at New York City. No longer would it be the recipient of huge injections of foreigners, enhancing its labor supplies and expanding its local markets. Within the United States, the black population began its trek from rural South to urban North. The resulting influx into New York City in the interwar years, however, remained comparatively minor, with limited economic consequences. While the City was gaining a few more black Americans and many fewer foreigners, it was also losing some of its native residents to surrounding suburbs – a trend in evidence in all of the older cities of the Northeast. Partly this reflected rising real incomes and the availability of mortgage money. Partly it was the result of changing transportation technology. Automobiles and improved roads altered the options of would-be commuters. So did the rise of commuter railways and subways. New York City was in the vanguard of such developments. In 1900 the construction of its first subway began. The network proliferated: across the Harlem River to the Bronx, across the East River to Brooklyn and Queens, with other linkages forged by tunnels under the Hudson and a network of bridges over various water barriers. Railroads also facilitated ease of access to the suburbs: the Delaware, Lackawanna and Western to East Orange, the New York Central (by express service) to Scarsdale and White Plains, the New Haven to Pelham. By modern standards the resulting exodus of humanity was modest in size and confined largely to upper-income groups for whom the costs of housing and commuting were not serious deterrents. But the exodus had begun.

So had the exodus of firms. Factory layouts were changing, particularly for firms that manufactured durable goods. The multistory building was being replaced by the single-level, land-intensive layout, which avoided costly up-and-down movements. This trend was in evidence long before the Roaring Twenties, but it gained momentum in that era. Again transportation developments were crucial. The roads and tunnels and bridges that were proliferating in and around the great metropolis, in concert with the growing popularity of the truck, were undermining the previous advantages of concentrated urban production. Also making for dispersion of manufacturing in general was the westward dispersion of the American population. The exodus of firms from New York City, like the exodus of people, was more of a trickle than a torrent. But here too, the exodus had begun.

This redeployment of business firms was somewhat inhibited by both the Great Depression and World War II. The first created excess capacity, thereby dampening incentives to build anew elsewhere. The second all but froze the geographical distribution of industrial and commercial activity because of wartime scarcities that complicated any relocation. When the war was over, however, it was apparent that diffusion tendencies of the past would become intensified in the future. What remained obscure was the magnitude of prospective outflows and the economic strains that would accompany such losses.

2.5.b. *The postwar exodus: some characteristics*

In the postwar era, earlier migration tendencies became more pronounced. The population shift to the suburbs accelerated as incomes rose, transportation networks improved, family units multiplied, and mortgage money became more readily available. The factors slowing inner-city business growth in New York also intensified. As the American population drifted west, so did markets. In the wake of growing urban concentration came a growing list of urban ills that for many business executives translated into higher firm costs and a less congenial place to work. Throughout the Northeast, the advantages of being an early leader in industrialization now brought the disadvantage of a capital stock that was older and more prone to deterioration and technical obsolescence.

To this point one might object that the discussion has been somewhat myopic in its focus upon New York City. It is the state's retardation (not just the city's) that is the central problem to be explained. A focus upon the city would nevertheless seem warranted, because it was there that the migration problems were centered, particularly in the early stages. Recall the point made in Section 2.4.a: that in terms of commercial and industrial centers within the state, New York has one giant and three modest upstate centers (Buffalo, Rochester, and Syracuse), and thereafter the gradient of size slips quickly down from modest to minute. It should therefore come as no surprise that the gathering forces making for outmigration from all major cities of the Northeast struck particularly hard at the one huge metropolis of the Empire State.

That metropolis also had a serious geographic handicap (see Map 2.4). Wedged in between New Jersey and Connecticut, the New York metropolitan region suffered from the peculiarity that normal metropolitan diffusion would take many of its people and its firms beyond the borders of the state. The associated suburban growth was often into neighboring Connecticut and New Jersey, particularly the latter. The precariousness of the situation should be immediately apparent. New York State's economy, as emphasized in Section 2.4.a., was peculiarly dependent upon the success of a single city. As outward diffusion from this city set in, the state would lose many of the migrating individuals and firms because of the proximity of political boundaries at the mouth of the Hudson River. Weakness at the very center of what had been the state's greatest economic strength therefore seemed virtually assured in the postwar era.

Other factors besides conventional diffusion from an older city would intensify that weakness. Before these are considered in detail, a

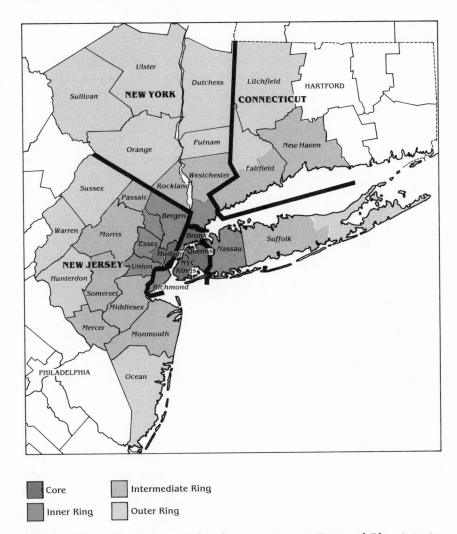

Map 2.4. The region's rings of development. *Source:* Regional Plan Association, "The State of the Region: 1977," *Regional Plan News,* no. 101, November 1977, p. 5.

few characteristics of the migration of firms from New York should be clarified. (The migration patterns of people will be discussed at length in Section 3.2.) All remarks on this topic must be prefaced with a warning. Even the most comprehensive of available data on firm migration from New York are far from complete, and many of the related series cover only manufacturing firms. Further, the question of the

Crisis in the making

Table 2.9. *Migration from New York State and subareas to major destination states: number of reports and employment loss, 1961–73*

	Statewide reports		Statewide employment loss[a]		N.Y.C. reports		N.Y.C. employment loss[a]	
	No.	% dist.	No.	% dist.	No.	% dist.	No.	% dist.
Total moveouts	1,054	100	144,551	100	733	100	98,658	100
To: New Jersey	516	49	56,678	39	467	64	53,226	54
Pennsylvania	91	9	11,512	8	50	7	6,647	7
Connecticut	110	10	16,106	11	81	11	12,175	12
N. Carolina	34	3	5,163	4	11	2	1,761	2
Massachusetts	34	3	2,867	2	16	2	1,271	1
Ohio	31	3	5,609	4	14	2	2,516	3
Florida	22	2	4,510	3	11	2	1,740	2
S. Carolina	12	1	1,677	1	1	—	271	—
Tennessee	13	1	2,615	2	7	1	1,880	2
Virginia	17	2	2,762	2	8	1	1,702	2
California	18	2	5,825	4	7	1	1,200	1
Illinois	16	2	1,930	1	7	1	530	1
Texas	10	1	4,655	3	5	1	3,990	4
All other states	130	12	22,642	16	48	7	9,749	10

Note: Data for 1973 apply to the first 10 months of the year.
[a] For reports in which employment was supplied.
[b] Nassau, Suffolk, Westchester, and Rockland counties.

typicality of the data that have been collected cannot be answered. The trends about to be discussed are therefore merely beacons in a great darkness, but they cast the only light available.[30]

The postwar migration of firms out of New York State appears to have had the following characteristics:

1. In terms of employment loss, small firm movement was probably more important than the movement of large corporations.[31]
2. The destination of these firms was predominantly adjacent states, a tendency that was particularly marked for firms leaving New York City.
3. Smaller firms have been more inclined to remain in close proximity to New York City than have larger ones.
4. Total firm outmigration appears to have accelerated in the 1970s.

	Suburbs of N.Y.C.[b] reports		Suburbs of N.Y.C.[b] employment loss[a]		Upstate reports		Upstate employment loss[a]	
	No.	% dist.	No.	% dist.	No.	% dist.	No.	% dist.
Total moveouts	138	100	17,856	100	183	100	28,037	100
To: New Jersey	35	25	2,784	16	14	8	668	2
Pennsylvania	13	9	1,013	6	28	15	3,852	14
Connecticut	18	13	2,940	16	11	6	991	4
N. Carolina	7	5	1,750	10	16	9	1,652	6
Massachusetts	5	4	555	3	13	7	1,041	4
Ohio	4	3	1,150	6	13	7	1,943	7
Florida	9	7	2,420	14	2	1	350	1
S. Carolina	4	3	155	1	7	4	1,251	4
Tennessee	1	1	150	1	5	3	585	2
Virginia	4	3	185	1	5	3	875	3
California	8	6	935	5	3	2	3,690	13
Illinois	3	2	116	1	6	3	984	4
Texas	1	1	60	—	4	2	605	2
All other states	26	19	3,643	20	56	31	9,550	34

Source: New York [State], Select Committee on the Economy, *Industry in New York: A Time of Transition,* Legislative Document no. 12, 1974, p. 85.

   5. Also in the 1970s, the exodus to southern states, while still
      a comparatively minor part of total migration, showed
      signs of increasing.

The tendency to move to adjacent states is particularly marked, although hardly surprising given the geographic squeezing of New York City between Connecticut and New Jersey. In the period 1961 to 1973, for example, one study of New York manufacturing firms leaving the state found that almost half went to New Jersey, and better than two-thirds went to New Jersey, Connecticut, and Pennsylvania (see Table 2.9). A similar study for 1975 found a similar propensity to migrate to the same three states (see Table 2.10). Another striking feature of these moves was the relative insignificance of migration to the South. The 1961–73 study, for example, found that only 12 percent of existing firms went to southern states. These findings will prove to be particularly useful in assessing the importance of the various causes of migration – a topic to which the discussion must now turn.

Table 2.10. *Migration from New York State by destination: major manufacturing closings and contractions planned, under way, or completed, 1975*

	Number	Employment loss[a] (no.)	Size loss[b] (sq. feet)
Total moveouts	97	9,306	4,348,900
To: New Jersey	36	2,565	1,399,400
Pennsylvania	17	1,867	1,114,200
North Carolina	5	855	434,000
Texas	5	383	102,000
Connecticut	4	515	43,000
Kentucky	3	500	211,300
Illinois	3	345	86,000
Tennessee	3	150	N.A.
Ohio	2	321	176,000
Massachusetts	2	155	40,000
Florida	2	125	63,000
Mississippi	1	230	200,000
Out of United States	2	480	50,000
All others	12	815	430,000

[a] Represents employment loss for 95.9 percent of the closings and contractions that involved moves out of state.
[b] Represents size loss for 76.3 percent of the closings and contractions that involved moves out of state.
Source: New York [State], Department of Commerce, "A Statistical Profile of Industrial Migration in New York State: 1975," unpublished paper, 1978*b*, p. 27.

2.6. Causes of New York retardation: the list of major contenders

The list of factors explaining New York's retardation, at first glance, appears to be horrendous. If every cause suggested by every writer were enumerated, the result would be an endless litany of woes that would dull the mind and leave even the most determined reader more confused than enlightened. Some of these emphasize various government policies that encouraged suburban flight: for example, the road-building subsidies that improved commuting possibilities and the housing subsidies that made more attainable for many a home in the outskirts. These are not, however, peculiar to New York State, nor do they seem particularly crucial in explaining firm migration. And it is

New York retardation in general and firm exodus in particular that are our special concerns. Other explanations feature technical change creating special difficulties for certain New York industries, especially those located in New York City. Containerization of water cargo, for example, shifted port activity to New Jersey, where space required for container operations was more readily available. The airplane displaced the ocean liner for most transatlantic travelers, a development that also cut into Port of New York activity.[32] The web offset press in printing increased that industry's need for space. Technological changes in apparel production speeded standardization, making individual skills less important and the availability of low-cost, unskilled workers more important: synthetic fibers, steam forming, computer-directed pattern making, faster and more specialized sewing machines that required less oiling. As important as each change was for each specific industry, the list of technical changes is relatively short, whereas the list of lagging sectors in New York is almost as broad as the state's economy. The answer to our problem must ultimately be far more general than these.

In the profusion of factors cited as causes of New York's retardation, almost all of them (and certainly any of major importance) can be grouped under the eleven headings noted previously.[33] Two sorts of questions come immediately to mind. The first type concerns whether the charges lurking in each item on the list are justified. Have New York taxes, for example, been well above those of most other states? Was labor unduly expensive in New York? Has the federal government continually drained dollars from the state? These are questions of fact, and the answer in each case is as straightforward as getting the facts straight. The second type of question is more complex. Once the facts have been established, what contribution did each of the eleven causes make to retardation in general and to firm migration in particular? For example, if New York taxes were atypically high (they were), how many of the firms that left the state departed for that reason?

Notice what is at stake. The answers to the first set of questions will let us decide which causes mattered. But they will not let us decide how much each one contributed to overall retardation. The economist will recognize a familiar distinction. The first calls for a list of inputs for a model, while the second can be answered only by the construction of a model. Into these murky waters the discussion must now plunge, if only momentarily.

2.7. Of models and methodology

The economic retardation of New York State, as noted, was distinguished for the predominant role played by the exodus of some firms, and the refusal of others to enter. How are these propensities to be explained?

The migration of economic activity has been a subject of study in economics for more than a century. Contemporary theory, by and large, portrays the location decision of firms as a geographical extension of neoclassical microeconomics.[34] The objective is to maximize profits. Firms therefore choose that location where profits are maximized. To discover why so many firms spurned New York, the obvious solution is to construct a model of the decision-making process – a model that will indicate which factors mattered and how sensitive migration decisions were to changes in those factors.

This model-building ambition collides with four empirical problems. The first is the disaggregated nature of the process. Apparel firms did not leave for the same reasons as did corporate headquarters. What is required, therefore, is not one model, but a multitude of models, one for each type of firm, with types of firms identified by the similarity of the forces that determined their migration. Second, at this level of disaggregation, there is a pronounced scarcity of relevant data and a scarcity of information about how firms actually reached the decision to migrate. Consider the case of dress manufacturing. The firm that left New York City for North Carolina almost surely compared the relative wage rates in the two locations. But which wage rates mattered most and what those wage rates actually were is extremely difficult to discover. Third, even the migrating firms lack precise information on certain relevant costs. The question is not just whether wages or taxes or utility costs are presently lower in prospective location A than in present location B. More important is the likely trend in those costs in areas A and B over the next few years and the next few decades. The firm contemplating migration is therefore forced to forecast the trend in all relevant costs (and also in prospective sales in different locations), with all of the attendant uncertainties that invariably accompany such forecasts. Fourth, the obvious cost considerations are sometimes not central to the migration decision. This appears to be particularly true, for example, for corporate headquarters. A 1976 survey of corporate headquarters located in New York City found that three-quarters of them believed that their operating costs were higher in their present location, but still they remained in that location.[35] Nor is this surprising. Clerical costs and rents are a small part of the firm's aggregate budget.[36] If operating costs are not crucial to the location decision, what is? The answer, or at least a large part of the answer, appears to be the ability to attract and hold top executives. That ability, in turn, is critically dependent upon the "quality of life" in the New York City area – as noted, a catchall phrase whose ingredients include such diverse elements as crime, pollution, commuting problems, the cost of suburban housing, and the quality of local schools. This is not a variable that lends itself to precise analysis. Location decisions influenced by such considerations are therefore fraught with imprecision, even when company executives attempt to explain why they moved. A top executive of Richardson-Merrell, for example, noted that the decision of his firm to leave New York City was "a subjective judgment that we would be more comfortable and more productive in an atmosphere that was – how shall I put this? – less stressful."[37]

Despite the vagueness that pervades much of our knowledge about how decisions are made, several generalizations about the relocation process do seem defensible. First, most firms do not continuously scour the country for superior locations. Considerable inertia must be overcome before a move is seriously contemplated. Partly this reflects the time, energy, and costs inherent in the search for a new location. Often it reflects an emotional attachment to the present location, founded upon familiarity and memories from long acquaintance. Establishing a totally new facility in a totally new location can also be an expensive operation. Analyzing the business migration of recent years, *Dun's Review* noted: "It's [often] cheaper to expand or rebuild a plant than start one from scratch. Available buildings offer in-place roads and utilities, fewer problems with permits and zoning, and in some cases, a ready-made labor force."[38] The corporate executive, this line of argument suggests, is not unlike Hamlet: he would prefer to bear those ills he knows than fly to others that he knows not – or at the very least, the process of flight requires considerable prodding. Second, the decision to migrate from New York (especially from New York City) appears typically to be a two-stage process. The first step is the decision to leave; the second, the decision where to go. The president of a New York consulting firm specializing in company relocation found that his clients' decisions to relocate resulted "from a desire to escape a negative situation in their operating environment."[39] The negative elements, as noted, could vary wildly among firms, from economic costs to the quality of life in the firm's present location. The factors conditioning the second step – the search for alternatives – were similarly diverse. From these observations comes a final, if rather obvious, generalization: that no explanation emphasizing a single cause for the flight of firms from New York will do. The process is far too complex and the accompanying reasons are far too diverse.

Despite these efforts at clarification, the migration of firms from New York remains, at best, a dimly understood process. The firm itself confronts uncertain cost and sales data, in part because its forecasts of geographic trends in costs and sales have inescapable elements of uncertainty. Costs alone are seldom the only consideration, and sometimes not the paramount consideration. The more imprecise the variables that matter – such as business climate or quality of life – the more imprecise becomes the decision-making process concerning relocation. Finally, the external observer seldom knows much about how this mixture of precise and imprecise information is evaluated in the board room when top executives confront the hard choice of whether to relocate, and if so, where.

The methodological implications of this lack of knowledge and lack of precision in the choice procedure are unfortunate. The discussion began with the observation that if the problem was to explain the relocation of firms, the ideal solution was to model that decision-making process. This ambition seems doomed to failure.[40] Notice that the costs of failure run high. If the decision making involved could be modeled with accuracy and precision, then the numerical parameters of that model would indicate the sensitivity of the location decision for a given type of firm to changes in the variables included in the model. (For example, how many fewer firms would leave if the corporate tax were cut by 10 percent?) That measure of sensitivity is what the politician and the planner desperately need. With such measures in hand, they could forecast the likely change in firm migration – and the associated change in New York employment – that would result from different possible changes in government policies. All that would be required would be to specify how a given policy, such as lower taxes, would affect each of the variables in the model. Finding the implied impact on (say) employment would then be as simple as cranking these revised numbers through the model.[41] A more useful tool for evaluating different prospective policies aimed at fighting retardation is difficult to imagine. When no such device is available, estimating the likely impact of any government policy on the net migration of firms from the state becomes a matter of guesswork. With so much at stake, the retreat from models and precision to back-of-the-envelope speculation is hardly welcome.

3

The causes of New York retardation

3.1. The road behind and the road ahead

Before the causes of retardation are considered in detail, a review of the terrain already covered would seem in order.

Relative to national averages of employment and population growth, the Empire State has been confronting retardation for decades. The turning point was the interwar period, a turning point disguised in part because of constraints on relocation that occurred during the Great Depression and World War II. From 1946 onward, the state by any comprehensive economic measure failed to match the average pace of national expansion. These laggard tendencies persisted through the 1950s and 1960s, and then intensified sharply in the 1970s. Weakness in the state's economy penetrated every major industrial sector and every production center of consequence from the Bronx to Buffalo. For all this diffusion of retardation, weakness was particularly pronounced in New York City, a phenomenon that was especially ominous, given the peculiarly dominant role that this city has played throughout the twentieth century in the aggregate economic performance of the state.

The proximate causes of New York's retardation are primarily two: a low birth rate of new firms, particularly new branches, and a high rate of net outmigration by firms. Both reflect relocation decisions that can only be explained by an unsatisfactory state of affairs within New York. But which affairs were particularly unsatisfactory? The list of major causes of New York's retardation reduces to 11 factors, 8 of them referring to statewide conditions, and 3 peculiar to New York City. How are these 11 to be approached?

The option of model building is not a possibility for reasons noted. A scarcity of data, the apparent imprecision of the decision-making process, and a lack of knowledge about how relocation decisions actually were made all preclude what is instinctively the economist's first choice.

Several options remain. The first is to get the facts straight. This chapter is therefore devoted primarily to description, not analysis. The extent to which taxes were high or energy was costly or New York

61

City's transit system was defective – these are the kinds of questions that will dominate the text. A second task is to attempt a forecast for the future. Without a precise model to generate such a forecast, the economist might reasonably wonder how such an assignment can be broached at all. The key to the technique used is what might be termed the pervasiveness of gloom, or perhaps more cheerfully, the absence of radiant sunshine. If a detailed examination of each of the 11 major causes of retardation suggests that not one of them is likely to improve significantly in the future (and not a few are likely to get worse), it follows that a major resurgence of the New York economy – or a major reversal of retardation tendencies – is highly unlikely. As modest as that conclusion seems to be, it is a central premise vital to making the fiscal forecasts that will be attempted in future chapters.

A final puzzle for this chapter concerns a question as yet totally unexamined: Why did New York's retardation accelerate in the 1970s? A central thesis of this book is that this acceleration, or much of it, was closely linked to political decisions. Why this was so – why so little was done to combat retardation and so much was done to exacerbate it – will be a controlling topic for subsequent chapters. The task of this chapter is to examine the causes of retardation in detail.

3.2. Population and migration

February 1971. Michael Burke, president of the New York Yankees, was threatening to take the Yankees out of New York. "We have a problem," he noted, "and we have to find some way to improve our stadium . . . or find another place to play."[1] The Brooklyn Dodgers and baseball Giants had already left. The football Giants were pondering the merits of New Jersey. (For most baseball fans, the threatened loss of the latter was far less serious than the impending exodus of the club of Ruth and Gehrig, DiMaggio and Mantle. Football, they noted, had hardly any statistics worth memorizing.) The Yankees would be persuaded to stay – the price would be the renovation of Yankee Stadium – but many others had gone or would go: not renowned athletes, most, but for all this lack of luster, no less important to the economic life of the metropolis.

The sheer magnitude of the ebb and flow boggled most imaginations (see Table 3.1). In a scant two decades between 1950 and 1970, *net* migration (immigrants minus emigrants) included an influx of almost half a million blacks into New York City and an exodus of better than a million and a half whites. In the next five years (1970–75), the flow of blacks reversed, the white exodus continued, and their combined net

Table 3.1. *Net migration from New York City and New York State,
1940–75 (thousands)*

	1940–50	1950–60	1960–70	1970–75
White				
New York City[a]	−322	−977	−814	−387
Rest of state[b]	316	905	176	−314
Total state	−6	−72	−638	−701
Nonwhite				
New York City	252	129	320	−122
Rest of state[b]	24	153	76	182
Total state	276	282	396	60

[a] Calculated as the difference between total migration and black migration. These data are therefore distorted by the inclusion of Hispanic migration. Puerto Rican migration to New York City has been estimated as an inflow at 214,576 for the decade 1950–60, and an outflow of 16,238 for the decade 1960–70. (New York [City], Mayor's Policy Committee, "Agenda for Economic Development," February 3, 1975, p. A 33.)
[b] Calculated as the difference between the total for the state and the total for New York City.
Sources: State data from U.S., Bureau of the Census, *Statistical Abstract of the United States,* 1964 and 1978; city data from New York [City], Temporary Commission on City Finances, *Economic and Demographic Trends in New York City: The Outlook for the Future,* Thirteenth Interim Report, May 1977*b*, pp. 66, 85.

outmigration totaled another half million. Over a quarter of a century, therefore, the city has witnessed comings and goings of more than two and a half million people – a flow twice the size of the entire population of Houston, or four times that of Boston or Cleveland or San Francisco.

The pattern for the rest of the state was sharply different. For much of the 1940s and 1950s, the loss of white population in New York City was roughly matched by gains in the rest of the state. In the 1960s, those gains fell far behind the city exodus, leading to a net state loss of 638,000. In the first half of the 1970s, the trend became more alarming. Departures from the city continued unabated, but now the rest of the state also experienced a net loss of its white population that almost matched that of the city. The combined effect for the state was staggering: almost three-quarters of a million people (net) had disappeared beyond its borders within five years (1970–75). Trends in upstate black migration also offer the unexpected. In the 1940s, the influx to the city was almost equivalent to the influx to the state. In the 1950s, city and upstate regions shared almost equally a total net influx of 282,000. In the 1960s, upstate inmigration again became inconsequential, as the city captured better than 80 percent of the total state influx of almost 400,000. The trends of the 1970s did not fit any of these patterns. Upstate regions gained, the city lost (for the first time in the twentieth century), and the combined effect was a negligible addition for the state (60,000).

The prevalence of movement in the postwar era is hardly surprising. The republic has always been a nation in flux. According to the Census Bureau, each year one in five Americans will move to a new address. Most of the migration patterns of New York City and New York State are symptomatic of larger national trends. For much of this century, the white population has been fleeing the center city of every city of consequence. (The population of Manhattan, for example, peaked in 1910.) It has drifted first from the inner city to suburbia, and more recently, from the suburbias of the North and East to those of the South and West. In the period 1960 to 1975, for example, all of the major cities of the north lost population, and the rate of loss for the largest one of all, New York City, was actually far below that of any of the rest (see Table 3.2). For much of this century, the black population has gravitated from South to North, from rural America of the cotton and tobacco belts to urban America in the industrial heartland east of the Mississippi and north of the Mason-Dixon line. Between 1900 and 1970, the proportion of the nation's blacks living in urban areas rose from 23 to 81 percent. The proportion living in the South fell from 90 to 53 percent.[2] Once in the cities of the North, the black population showed no tendency to match the white population's drift to the suburbs. To the "center cities" they came, and in the center cities they tended to remain. Nowhere is this tendency more apparent than in the Empire State. Throughout the postwar era, the percentage of nonwhites has risen sharply in every single metropolitan area of consequence. In every case, that population change has been confined almost exclusively to the central city region of each urban area (see Table 3.3.).[3]

For all this echoing of national trends, the postwar migration patterns of the Empire State have featured several peculiarities, particularly in the state's minority influx. The surge of black immigration in the 1950s was in keeping with national trends. The acceleration of that surge in the 1960s, however, contrasted sharply with the slowing down in the national flow from rural to urban centers. Throughout the postwar era, the city has been a magnet for Puerto Rican migrants as no other urban center of America has been.[4] Combined with the high rate of

Table 3.2. *Twelve largest cities in the Northeast: population trends, 1960–75*

City	1960 population	1970 population	Average annual change (%), 1960–70	1975 population	Average annual change (%), 1970–75	Aggregate change (%), 1960–75
New York	7,781,984	7,895,563	+0.1	7,472,500	−1.1	− 4.0
Chicago	3,550,404	3,369,357	−0.5	3,099,391	−1.6	−12.7
Philadelphia	2,002,512	1,949,996	−0.3	1,815,808	−1.4	− 9.3
Detroit	1,670,144	1,514,063	−0.9	1,335,085	−2.4	−20.1
Baltimore	939,024	905,787	−0.4	851,698	−1.2	− 9.3
Cleveland	876,050	750,879	−1.4	638,793	−3.0	−27.1
Washington, D.C.	763,956	756,668	−0.1	711,518	−1.2	− 6.9
St. Louis	750,026	622,236	−1.7	524,964	−3.0	−30.0
Milwaukee	741,324	717,372	−0.3	665,796	−1.4	−10.2
Boston	697,197	641,071	−0.8	636,725	−0.1	− 8.7
Pittsburgh	604,332	520,089	−1.4	458,651	−2.4	−24.1
Buffalo	532,759	462,768	−1.3	407,160	−2.4	−23.6

Note: Not adjusted for annexations.
Source: U.S., Department of Commerce, Bureau of the Census.

Table 3.3. *Population and nonwhite percentage in Standard Metropolitan Statistical Areas (SMSAs), 1940–70*

	Population (thousands)				Nonwhite population as % of total			
	1940	1950	1960	1970	1940	1950	1960	1970
United States	131,669	151,326	179,323	203,184	10.5	10.7	11.2	12.4
New York State	13,479	14,830	16,782	18,241	4.4	6.5	8.9	13.2
All SMSAs	11,811	13,037	14,811	16,099	5.0	7.2	9.8	14.6
Central cities	9,149	9,639	9,441	9,386	5.6	8.7	13.5	22.0
Outside central cities	2,662	3,399	5,370	6,713	2.7	2.8	3.3	4.3
Albany–Schenectady–Troy	531	589	658	722	1.1	1.7	2.6	3.7
Central cities	288	299	279	257	1.5	2.8	5.5	8.6
Outside central cities	243	290	379	465	0.5	0.5	0.6	1.0
Binghamton[a]	193	215	250	268	0.5	0.5	0.7	1.3
Central city	78	81	76	64	1.0	1.0	1.7	2.6
Outside central city	115	134	174	204	0.2	0.2	0.2	0.9
Buffalo	959	1,089	1,307	1,349	2.5	4.4	6.8	8.8
Central city	576	580	533	463	3.2	6.5	13.8	21.3
Outside central city	383	509	774	886	1.5	2.0	2.0	2.3

Elmira	74	87	99	102	1.6	2.2	2.7	3.6
Central city	45	50	47	40	2.6	3.6	5.4	8.1
Outside central city	29	37	52	62	0.1	0.3	0.3	0.7
New York	8,707	9,556	10,695	11,576	6.1	8.9	12.0	18.0
Central city	7,455	7,892	7,782	7,896	6.4	9.8	14.7	23.4
Outside central city	1,252	1,664	2,913	3,680	4.6	4.5	5.0	6.4
Poughkeepsie	121	137	176	222	3.6	4.1	5.8	7.2
Central city	41	41	38	32	3.5	4.5	9.6	18.8
Outside central city	80	96	138	190	3.7	3.9	4.7	5.2
Rochester	557	615	733	883	0.9	1.6	4.0	7.0
Central city	325	332	319	296	1.1	2.4	7.6	17.6
Outside central city	232	283	414	586	0.7	0.7	1.2	1.7
Syracuse	406	465	564	636	0.9	1.4	2.6	4.4
Central city	206	221	216	197	1.1	2.3	5.7	12.0
Outside central city	200	244	348	439	0.6	0.7	0.7	1.0
Utica–Rome	263	284	331	341	0.4	0.9	1.6	2.5
Central cities	135	143	152	142	0.6	1.6	3.1	5.4
Outside central cities	128	141	179	199	0.2	0.2	0.3	0.5
Outside SMSAs	1,669	1,793	1,971	2,142	1.2	1.3	1.9	2.5

Note: Data are for SMSAs as defined in 1971.

[a] New York State portion only; excludes Susquehanna County, Pennsylvania.

Source: New York [State], Council of Economic Advisers, *Annual Report*, 1974, p. 23.

natural increase of those already in New York City, this influx expanded the Puerto Rican population from 62,000 in 1940 to almost a million in 1975, from less than 1 percent of the city's population to more than 12 percent (see Table 3.4). The migration flows of this minority group have contrasted sharply with those of the black population. In the 1960s, for example, while black migration to the city more than doubled, Puerto Rican migration was cut in half. In the 1970s, both groups have been inclined to quit the city. The outflow of blacks has been more than matched by gains elsewhere in the state, but the evidence suggests a dispersion of Puerto Ricans to other states and back to their native island.[5]

Why did they come? And why did they leave?

The literature on migration will never yield a definitive answer for all who move. At the center of almost every explanation of American population movements of this century however is a single and compelling premise: that for most of the migrants most of the time, the primary motivation has been the opportunity for economic advancement.[6] The response of whites and blacks alike, should they be asked the causes of their move to and from this or any other state, would therefore probably bear a marked resemblance to the dominant response of Oregon settlers a century ago, who noted simply that they had headed west "to better their condition."

If this is the general explanation for migration, has New York's generous welfare system played a special role? The literature on black migration to the state has featured an attempt – in some cases, more vigorous than reasoned – to demonstrate that welfare payments had nothing to do with the influx. That statement is correct on one count, misleading on a second, and possibly downright wrong on a third. Studies do suggest that the welfare-seeking migrant is, by and large, a myth.[7] Few migrants apply for welfare immediately. Of those who migrated to New York and subsequently received welfare, roughly 15 percent received AFDC (Aid to Families with Dependent Children) payments during their first year in the state,[8] and the lapse between migrating and applying for welfare (for those who did both) has averaged about three years. What is perhaps too often ignored in such discussions, or at the very least skimmed over in considerable haste, is the probable role that New York's generous welfare schemes had in retaining the impoverished. For the poor, any interstate move is costly and hazardous. A job may not be found, or found quickly, at the end of the journey. For the poor, the glow of greener pastures is sure to pale before the certainty of a welfare check in hand. And New York City could justifiably claim that it had one of the most generous welfare packages in the country: subsidized public housing and rent control on

Table 3.4. Composition of the Hispanic population in New York City, 1900–75 (thousands)

Year	Total Spanish origin	Puerto Rican origin					Other Spanish origin
		Total	Puerto Rican birth or parentage	Puerto Rican birth	Puerto Rican parentage	Other Puerto Rican origin	
1900	—	0.3	0.3	0.3	[a]	—	—
1910	—	0.6	0.6	0.6	[a]	[a]	—
1920	—	7.4	7.4	7.4	[a]	[a]	—
1930	—	44.9	44.9	44.9	[a]	[a]	—
1940	—	61.5	61.5	61.5	[a]	[a]	—
1950	—	246.0	246.0	187.6	58.4	[a]	—
1960	—	613.0	613.0	429.7	183.3	[a]	—
1970	1202.3	846.7	812.0	482.0	330.0	34.7	355.6
1975	1387.0	941.0	N.A.	N.A.	N.A.	N.A.	446.0

[a] Data not available, but the figures are believed to be minimal.
Source: New York [City], Temporary Commission on City Finances (1977b), 88.

privately owned buildings, extensive Medicaid benefits, welfare schemes that included Aid to Dependent Children, Home Relief and Veteran Assistance, Supplemental Security Income, Day Care, Mental Health Services, a Human Resources Program, and a Youth Services Agency[9] – not a list easily matched by any other city or state in the union. The final point – almost totally ignored in the literature – is that because migrants coming to New York did not rush to get welfare immediately, it does not follow that the presence of welfare possibilities was irrelevant to their influx. New York City became in the 1960s "a highly visible showcase for the antipoverty programs of the Johnson Administration."[10] For those of limited means, a long-distance move is always a risk. They have few assets. If employment income ceases, the economic result can be catastrophic if no welfare options are available. The generous welfare options of New York, therefore, must have represented to many an underwriting of the risk of movement – a promise that economic catastrophe would not ensue, should the harsh realities of the city's job market temporarily thwart their employment ambitions. It is surely not a coincidence that black migration to the city surged in the 1960s while falling elsewhere, at exactly the same time that New York was becoming, in the language cited previously, "a highly visible showcase" of antipoverty programs.

Notice what the argument is not. The question at stake is not whether the poor deserve welfare, or whether New York City and State should sponsor welfare programs that are, by national standards, comparatively generous. The point at issue is a puzzle: Why did so many blacks come to, and then remain in, a city and a state that whites were scrambling to leave? The complete answer is no doubt complex, shrouded in speculations about how, in the minds of blacks, New York contrasted with their place of residence before they migrated to the Empire State, and how similar contrasts in the minds of whites led so many to quit the same state. The single certainty is that New York has been far more successful at retaining its black population than at retaining its white population throughout the entire postwar era. Even now, the upstate gains more than compensate for city losses of black population, whereas the white exodus appears to be accelerating from both areas. Whatever the complete explanation of this contrast, it seems wildly improbable that it is totally unrelated to New York's welfare schemes, which compare so favorably with those available elsewhere.

The economic consequences of this massive movement of humanity are easy to list and difficult to document in detail. From the earliest days of the American republic, its migrants have usually featured the younger and more energetic cohort of the resident population left behind. New York's postwar migration is no exception. From the southern states and Puerto Rico came predominantly younger people in search of better opportunities. Largely rural in background, these new urban arrivals demonstrated a marked capacity to grapple successfully with the many adjustment problems of life in America's largest city. The black immigrants, for example, appear to have been less prone to poverty than the black population they joined, and very much their equals in overcoming personal disadvantages.[11] One expert even speculates that "it may be that the black rural–urban migrant brings to the city a more constructive set of attitudes toward school and work than those of the urban native he joins."[12]

The difficulty is that relative to the white population, the nonwhite population as a whole has fewer skills, less education, and a greater incidence of poverty. And the white population has been leaving first the city, and then the state, in droves. In short, although the qualities of minority immigrants may have bolstered the economic potential of the minority population they joined, these immigrants did not begin to compensate for the economic losses associated with the exodus of whites. That is simple arithmetic: If the income potential of those who leave exceeds that of the new arrivals, the average income potential of the resident population must go down. The phenomenon is apparent in the city and the state. Between 1950 and 1974, for example, state per capita income fell from 125 percent to 113 percent of the national average; that of the city fell from 143 percent to 116 percent (see Table 3.5).[13]

This population shuffle, then – minorities in and whites out – has brought a downward pressure on the income-generating potential of the region. The associated shift in age structure has had a similar effect. Despite the much-publicized departure of white retirees, New York migration data indicate what most migration data indicate: that if an area is losing population – and with white exodus far exceeding minority influx, New York City has been losing population for better than a quarter of a century – the predominance in that flow of younger people will bias the age distribution of the population left behind toward those who are older, less productive, and more service dependent.[14] In every decade since 1950, New York City has increased its population aged 65 or older, and lost population in the productive age cohort of 25 to 64 (see Table 3.6). This means that fewer people of working age must now support more people who are not of working age.

To forecast what the future demographic trends will be requires speculation about what is, for most, an unexciting race among three uninteresting variables: birth rates, death rates, and rates of net migra-

Table 3.5. *Changes in family income distribution by race and ethnicity in New York City, 1960–74 (families in thousands)*

Year	Total	Nonwhite	Hispanic	Puerto Rican
1960				
Below regional median	1,180	203	N.A.	120
Above regional median	900	61	N.A.	20
Total	2,080	264	N.A.	140
1970				
Below regional median	1,211	294	241	172
Above regional median	848	101	53	29
Total	2,059	395	294	200
1974				
Below regional median	1,288	356	260	N.A.
Above regional median	702	100	50	N.A.
Total	1,990	456	310	N.A.

Note: Median family income for the New York region was $6,696 in 1960, $11,169 in 1970, and $13,099 in 1974.
Source: New York [City], Temporary Commission on City Finances (1977b), 98.

tion. One of these is relatively uncomplicated. No change of consequence is expected in the death rate. The trick is to forecast the birth rate and estimate prospective migration – both highly tenuous exercises.

One point is abundantly clear: If trends of the recent past persist into the immediate future, the result can only be further sharp declines in the population of the city and the state. The boom in birth rates immediately following World War II was replaced in the 1960s by falling fertility rates for all populations: white, black, and Puerto Rican.[15] In the 1970s, migration trends have also shifted sharply against the state. More whites have left in the five years 1970–75 than left in the previous decade. For the first time this century, black migration in the 1970s also became negative for the city, and barely positive for the state. At the same time, Puerto Rican inmigration slowed, and movement back to the island has almost doubled.[16] Should these trends continue (stable death rates, falling birth rates, and rising outmigration),[17] the result can only be a further drop in population. The only question is whether that decline will be large or small.

If decline persists, several further implications seem highly probable. The population will feature a falling percentage of whites and a

Table 3.6. *Percentage change in New York City population by age, 1910–75*

Age	1970–75	1960–70	1950–60	1940–50	1930–40	1920–30	1910–20
Under 5	−23	−9	+3	+54	−19	−5	+11
5–17	−5	+13	+16	−10	−8	+16	+15
18–24	+6	+23	−14	−12	−4	+27	+2
25–34	+13	−1	−19	−6	+3	+24	+18
35–44	−19	−17	−18	+1	+14	+34	+23
45–64	−11	−10	+3	+20	+36	+33	+38
65 and over	+4	+17	+35	+46	+57	+50	+30
Total	−5	+0.3	−1	+6	+8	+23	+18

Source: New York (City), Temporary Commission on City Finances (1977b), 77.

rising percentage of nonwhites, partly because whites are quitting the state at a more rapid rate, and partly because the rate of natural increase of those whites who stay behind is far below that of the non-white population.[18] The age structure will also shift, if the increasing predominance of younger people in the exodus of recent years continues into the future.[19] These trends are likely to be more pronounced in all of New York's inner cities, from New York City to Syracuse to Rochester to Buffalo. (In Rochester, for example, the white population of the inner city fell by 23 percent between 1970 and 1977.)[20]

New York enthusiasts can find in these demographic trends a number of cheery implications for the economy. As city population falls, so will urban crowding. As fewer children are born, the need for educational expenditures will decline, initially in elementary schools, and thereafter throughout the educational system. Falling birth rates of the past promise fewer youths injected into the labor market in the future, thereby easing the pressures upon unemployment, particularly teenage unemployment. Some analysts even speculate that the loss of laborers will outpace the loss of jobs, thereby improving the labor market for all participants. That market will also feature, particularly in New York City, a better-educated cohort than in the past, as the open enrollment policies of the City University of New York enable more minority students to achieve a higher level of education.[21]

But surely such thoughts are too colored by wishful thinking and too little influenced by the facts. A tighter labor market, for example, implies rising wages that could discourage the inmigration of some firms and encourage the departure of others. This is not, however, the central weakness in the previous reasoning. The critical question is this: Who is the city or the state likely to lose? The city, for example, will gain if outmigration of the future is dominated by the old, the poor, and the service dependent. It will lose if that migration is dominated by the young, the able, and the wealthy. The lower the percentage of the population working, and the higher the percentage on welfare, the more limited are the opportunities to raise tax dollars, and to divert those dollars from welfare payments to upgrading other public services. The critical question is not whether crowding in the city will decline as population declines, but whether that reduction will be accompanied by improvements in the quality of life within the city, particularly less dirt, better schools, improved commuting facilities, and a lower incidence of crime. These all take money: money that must be raised from somewhere, and the most obvious source is from the residents themselves. In the case of New York City, the possibility of increased dollars for such activities is made extremely unlikely by its precarious fiscal position (see Chapter 8). But fiscal problems are likely to be compounded by the demographic trends just discussed, with the wealthy and the young more likely to exit than the poor, the old, and the service dependent.[22] The exodus of young people has eroded the ratio of those who work to those who do not work. This has been reinforced in a troubling way in New York City by a falling participation rate within the work force that remains. While the national female labor force participation rate has been rising, that of the city has been falling. While the national male labor force participation rate has been declining, that of the city has fallen even faster, and from a lower starting point.[23]

The pessimism lurking in the preceding paragraph hinges critically upon the prospect of continued outmigration and the probable characteristics of those destined to leave. This gloom might be dispelled and the outflow stemmed if the regional economy could rebound smartly. Fewer would leave as better opportunities became available locally.[24] Further retardation, on the other hand, would intensify migration, and intensify the loss of the young, the skilled, and the well-to-do. Which prospect – rebound or further retardation – is more likely? In a sense, this entire chapter is directed to that question. The answer lurking in all that has gone before and all that is to come is not encouraging.

3.3. The labor market

High up on the list of important costs for most businesses is the cost of labor. High up on the list of complaints of many New York businessmen is the unsatisfactory state of the New York labor market.[25] That does not augur well for a state that would reverse business exodus.

The complaints are primarily two: high wages and poor labor attitudes.

"Attitude" is a treacherous concept, particularly when applied to such a large and diverse collection of humanity as the Empire State work force. The facts of the case, however, are less important than businessmen's perceptions of those facts. Perceptions condition choices, and businessmen choose which plants will be located where. In the mild phrasing of a legislative commission, the prevailing view in the business community is that "labor attitudes in New York leave something to be desired."[26] To hear the businessmen tell it, they leave a lot to be desired. Whenever their opinions are candidly expressed on the topic of New York labor in general and unions in particular, one is sure to encounter all the synonyms for "obstinate" and much less charitable adjectives as well: recalcitrant, obstreperous, intransigent, militant, and even piratical.

Antagonism between labor and management is hardly peculiar to New York. The state nevertheless does seem to have been wracked by a hostility peculiar in degree if not in kind. Three features of the local labor market appear to be central to this turbulence. One is an odd provision in the state's unemployment insurance law. New York is one of two states[27] that authorizes the payment of unemployment insurance benefits to employees on strike. To most businessmen, this is tantamount to a strike subsidy, fostering mulishness and prolonging walkouts.[28] Their reactions to the law therefore tend to range from indignation to outrage. A related feature of the New York labor market that also provokes business hostility is the strength, the reputation, and the actions of many of the unions throughout the state. With a long history of union activity, New York is among the leading states in percentage of the work force in unions.[29] The problem is not so much the pervasiveness of union membership as the reputation that New York labor has earned – fairly or unfairly – through the various unrelated actions of various unrelated unions. The bellicose demands and illegal strikes of public employee unions; the manning requirements imposed by printing unions upon that industry, which, according to management, made "expensive labor even more costly";[30] the strikes of typographers that helped to destroy four of New York City's seven daily newspapers – these are but skirmish reports from a landscape that appears to the profit-seeking executive to be far too belligerent for his own good. The third factor clouding the labor picture is a suspicion, often suppressed but possibly pervasive, that the work ethic has been corroded by the liberal benefits available to those who do not work. In the forthright phrasing of a businessman who moved his family-owned business to New Jersey in 1968, the firm's high absentee rate in New York City was "directly related" to employee incentives not to work, including "the State's liberal workman's compensation regulations and unemployment insurance payments, and the high public assistance payments."[31]

Notice two points. The first is that attitude is more important than fact. The accuracy of businessmen's characterizations is not at issue here. If they believe that workers in New York have a poor attitude – because of strong unions, a law that subsidizes strikes, and generous benefits for not working – that belief will color the decisions in the board room the next time the question is raised where to locate a new plant or relocate an old one. Second, about one fact (and perhaps only one) there can be little debate: The belief that "labor attitudes in New

Table 3.7. *Average hourly wages in selected industries: New York City as a percentage of national average, 1960–78*

Industry	1960	1965	1970	1975	1978
Foods and kindred products					
Dairy products	133	144	142	155	N.A.
Bakery products	117	123	119	115	102
Apparel					
Men's overcoats[a]	120	120	113	118	109
Men's furnishings[b]	139	131	131	130	126
Women's outerwear[c]	136	130	133	138	129
Dresses	137	133	134	144	N.A.
Women's undergarments[d]	118	116	124	129	124
Printing					
Newspapers	133	133	147	169	179
Bookbinding[e]	102	112	116	117	110

[a] Men's, youths', and boys' suits, coats, and overcoats.
[b] Men's, youths', and boys' furnishings, work clothing, and allied garments.
[c] Women's, misses', and junior outerwear.
[d] Women's, misses', children's, and infants' undergarments.
[e] Blank books, loose-leaf binders, and bookbinding and related work.
Sources: Calculated from wage data in U.S., Department of Labor, *Employment and Earnings, United States, 1909–1978*, Bulletin 1312–11; New York [State], Department of Labor, *Employment Statistics*, vol. X, August 1973. New York data for 1975 and 1978 supplied by New York State Department of Labor.

York leave something to be desired" has been, and still is, a pervasive phenomenon in the business community. In survey after survey, the kinds of charges noted above are repeated, not infrequently in emotional language conveying hostility and frustration. In short, under one labor market heading – the attitude of labor – the Empire State clearly has a problem.

Under the other major labor market heading – high wages – the issue is less clear-cut.

The complaint that New York wages are "high" is, curiously enough, almost impossible to verify. Consider the wage data of New York City, the very heart of the region's manufacturing activity. The average hourly earnings of most workers in most industries appear to be well above the national average – from one-third to one-fifth higher in most cases (see Table 3.7). Or consider more disaggregated data. The aver-

Table 3.8. *Interarea pay comparisons in selected manufacturing groups, 1969–70 (percentages of New York City pay)*

Metro areas	Office clerical	Machinists (maintenance)	Unskilled plant
New York City	100	100	100
Buffalo	99	96	103
Albany	N.A.	92	92
Paterson, N.J.	96	91	95
Newark, N.J.	98	97	104
Allentown, Pa.	100	93	95
Scranton, Pa.	82	76	79
Philadelphia, Pa.	95	89	97
Charlotte, N.C.	N.A.	74	67
Greenville, S.C.	81	65	65
Raleigh, N.C.	N.A.	65	66

Note: Figures are based upon either average weekly salary or average straight-time hourly earnings.
Source: New York [State], Select Committee on the Economy, *Industry in New York: A Time of Transition,* Legislative Document no. 12, 1974, p. 37.

age hourly wages of various white-collar workers – secretaries, draftsmen, clerks, keypunch operators – also tend to be higher in New York City than in other major American urban centers.[32] Much of the evidence for blue-collar workers suggests the same conclusions. A 1971 survey of the women's dress industry, for example, found that New York City had the highest average (straight time) hourly wage in the industry.[33] (For evidence on other blue-collar wages, see Table 3.8.)

What, then, is the problem? If workers are paid more, surely labor is overpriced. The difficulty is that workers may be paid more because they produce more. Consider again those high wages of workers in the New York City dress industry. Are they paid more because unions have inflated their wages, or because they have superior skills? Notice in passing that the labor unions cannot have it both ways. To claim that all of the higher wage is due to superior worker skill is to acknowledge that none of it is due to unions. By this interpretation, unions have done very little for their workers. Alternatively, if much of the higher wage is attributable to unions forcing wages well above what skill considerations alone would dictate, then labor unions have helped to generate a wage gap that has stimulated the exodus of industries from the city and the state.

Which view is correct? Are workers actually more expensive in New York City, or are the observed high wages merely a reflection of superior productivity? A state legislative committee gave the answer, as unwelcome as it is definitive: "No credible proof could be found that New York State workers are or are not more productive than workers in other states."[34] They were forced to accept that conclusion because of the inability of research – however detailed and sophisticated – to determine how much of high wages can be attributed to worker skills, to superior capital equipment, to superior plant organization, and so on. In short, efforts to disentangle the productivity question have collided with a brick wall.

A second approach to the question using not wage data but migration data is more revealing. New York, particularly New York City, has a significant proportion of industries whose location and relocation decisions are particularly responsive to the relative costs of labor. These industries, such as apparel, are among the vanguard of those leaving the state. In explaining their exodus, the businessmen who made the decisions have repeatedly cited labor market conditions: for example, the investment company that moved to Baltimore with the expectation of saving "up to 25 percent in labor costs";[35] the Buffalo company that shifted 400 jobs to a northern New England state because of "high wage costs, as well as problems with rigid union work rules and regulations";[36] the American Can executive who noted after a move to Canaan that his firm "found it easier to assemble a work force and keep employees on the job in Connecticut than in New York."[37] ("That is not measurable," he added, "but I'm sure it added a few years to the sum of our lives.")

The apparel industry illustrates both the general problem and the complexity of the process. Unskilled labor appears to have been significantly cheaper elsewhere. Firms heavily dependent upon such labor have therefore been inclined to leave. Skilled workers are a different story. Readily available in New York City and often less available elsewhere, they do not appear to have been overpriced – or overpriced in a major way – for most of the apparel firms still located in New York City. The bias not to leave is accordingly strong. As one industrial survey noted: "More than one company that had moved a labor-intensive division to another state said it would not consider moving its high quality, highly skilled lines out of New York."[38]

All this suggests that the city and the state have experienced a classic economic adjustment, difficult to detect in wage data but more apparent in migration data and the accompanying explanations of those who made the move. Labor has been cheaper elsewhere for many firms, particularly for those using predominantly unskilled workers. Many of these have migrated from the state primarily in search of cheaper labor. (Secondarily, many sought out and found a more amicable labor environment that included right-to-work laws, lower union membership, and the opportunity to write a fresh set of work rules.) Migration, however, helps to slow subsequent migration. The departure of firms from New York should ease the demand for labor and thereby reduce the upward pressures on wages within the state. Their influx elsewhere should create more labor demand and thus intensify the upward pressures on the wages in the receiving states. Although somewhat tentative, evidence can be marshaled to suggest that the gap in wages – particularly the gap between New York City and regions competing for its industries – is not widening, and may be narrowing.[39] To the extent that this sharply modifies the wage differential for unskilled workers, firms dependent upon such labor will be less inclined to leave. Those relying upon highly skilled labor have always been far more prone to stay, in part because of the extensive labor pool available to them, and in part because skilled labor does not appear to be much cheaper in other localities.

The tempting inference is that the worst is over: that whatever labor market conditions have contributed to business exodus in the past, they will contribute less in the future. Three unresolved puzzles obfuscate whatever rays of sunshine are lurking in such a forecast. One is the likely course of technological change. Consider for one last time the labor market of the apparel industry. Technological progress in the past has fostered standardization in the production process.[40] The more standardized the process, the less the need for highly skilled labor. If the trend to standardization persists in the future, for every garment firm affected by the process, New York City's skilled labor force will become progressively less important, and the availability of cheap, unskilled labor will become progressively more important. In short, technological change could erode some of the drawing power of one of the region's biggest assets: a large, concentrated, and highly skilled work force. A second unknown is the extent to which the members of that work force will leave the city and the state, leaving behind a residual that is, as a collective entity, progressively less skilled. The final puzzle is the extent to which labor's attitude will influence the plant location decisions of executives inside and outside the state. The present crisis atmosphere has sparked a number of cooperative ventures by labor and management at various levels of aggregation throughout the state. (There is nothing like the prospect of the rowboat being swamped to foster a certain harmony among the rowers.) Widely publicized as these ventures are, none seems destined to change substantially the factors cited previously. Consider for example the legal provision granting unemployment insurance benefits to strikers. The prospects for an honest reappraisal of what is both a New York curiosity and a festering sore in the imaginations of businessmen is virtually nil. To repeal the law, or even to discuss possible repeal, would invariably generate a hurricane of union indignation that no politician would dare confront. Albany legislators are therefore quick – one might even say lightning quick – to shove this issue back into the drawer or the wastebasket or the closet. Finally, and most important of all, the most optimistic of likely scenarios under both headings – wages and labor attitudes – is hardly grounds for rejoicing. The wage gap making the state a relatively high-cost labor area for some industries may narrow, but only gradually.[41] The attitude of labor in general and unions in particular may become less bellicose and more conciliatory, less piratical and more cooperative, but again, only gradually. This means that, with respect to labor market developments, these negative factors may lose some of their potency, but – and this is the point – they are almost sure to remain negative. Here, too, then the Empire State cannot expect to find a bracing tonic to fortify its flagging economic vigor. The best that it can hope for is a diminution in the toxic ingredients that have proven to be so poisonous in the past.

3.4. Energy

Throughout the postwar era, New York has had an energy problem. That statement is curious, given the tourist's imagery of the raging Niagara and a massive St. Lawrence Seaway development. Surely hydro power is abundant and electricity cheap in a state so well endowed with water resources. In fact, hydro power is relatively scarce and energy costs are relatively high. And that is the problem.

Surprisingly, only about 5 percent of the energy generated within New York State comes from hydro sources (see Table 3.9). Nuclear power, although more in use in this state than in most others, generates less than 15 percent of the power produced by the local electric utility industry. The remaining possibilities are coal, gas, and oil. New York does not have any deposits of consequence for any of these three.[42]

Large coal deposits are relatively close by in neighboring Appalachian states,[43] but environmental regulations inhibit the burning of coal in major population centers, and the crumbling railroad network of the Northeast complicates delivery where it can be used.

Virtually all gas must also be imported. In the early 1970s, supply was limited, prices were kept artificially low, and rationing was re-

Table 3.9. *Generation of electricity by the seven largest privately owned utility companies in New York State, 1967–78*

Year	Steam generation Billions of kwh	Steam generation %	Nuclear generation Billions of kwh	Nuclear generation %	Hydro generation Billions of kwh	Hydro generation %	Other generation[a] Billions of kwh	Other generation[a] %	Total generation Billions of kwh	Total generation %
1978	66.47	80.6	12.03	14.6	3.49	4.2	0.50	0.6	82.49	100.0
1977	66.52	80.4	11.16	13.5	3.91	4.7	1.10	1.3	82.69	100.0
1976	65.11	81.8	8.41	10.6	4.50	5.7	1.59	2.0	79.61	100.0
1975	65.89	79.7	10.94	13.2	4.06	4.9	1.78	2.2	82.67	100.0
1974	63.95	78.9	9.91	12.2	4.06	5.0	3.18	3.9	81.10	100.0
1973	67.05	80.6	7.14	8.6	4.09	4.9	4.95	5.9	83.23	100.0
1972	64.29	78.7	6.73	8.2	4.35	5.3	6.29	7.7	81.66	100.0
1971	63.87	81.3	6.87	8.8	3.71	4.7	4.09	5.2	78.54	100.0
1970	66.49	88.0	3.99	5.3	3.55	4.7	1.51	2.0	75.54	100.0
1969	64.19	92.0	1.74	2.5	3.76	5.4	0.10	0.2	69.79	100.0
1968	60.84	91.1	1.51	2.3	3.53	5.3	0.88	1.3	66.76	100.0
1967	57.48	91.7	1.62	2.6	3.43	5.5	0.12	0.2	62.65	100.0

Note: Excludes electricity generated by the Power Authority of the State of New York (PASNY).
[a] Other generation comprised largely of gas turbines and diesel engines.
Source: New York [State], Department of Public Service.

quired. The initial allocation policy of the Public Service Commission favored established industries over new industries and residential users over both – not a happy situation for a state desperately in need of industrial expansion. By the late 1970s, gas prices had risen steeply and the allocation policy of the commission (now slightly modified) became less crucial.[44] In the interim, a number of plant expansions were discouraged or terminated by the scarcity of this low-cost fuel.[45]

The major source of energy within the state – again, perhaps surprisingly – is oil. Much of it is imported, with dependence upon imported oil particularly striking in the southeastern portion of the state, which is also the manufacturing center of the state.[46]

The inevitable result is a state in which energy costs are well above the U.S. average. A few comparisons suggest how pervasive the problem is. Gas is a relatively cheap fuel. Petroleum is relatively expensive. American manufacturing gets 53 percent of its energy needs from gas and only 14 percent from petroleum. New York manufacturing gets 23 percent of its energy needs from gas and 33 percent from petroleum.[47] Four points about energy costs should be emphasized. First, the variations in costs within the state are enormous, with downstate prices tending to exceed upstate prices by a wide margin.[48] Second, much of New York manufacturing is centered in and around New York City, the high-cost area. Third, energy costs within New York City have always been higher than those in other major cities throughout the postwar era (see Table 3.10). Fourth, energy costs in general have shot up in recent years, and this trend is likely to be accompanied by even higher costs in the New York City area, mainly because of rising oil prices and rising New York City taxes (see Figure 3.1).[49]

Has high-priced energy driven industry from the state? The evidence is mixed. In some of the surveys of businessmen who have left or of those who have remained, energy costs are placed high on the list of detrimental factors, although well behind taxes and labor market conditions.[50] In other surveys, energy costs receive far less prominence.[51] Occasionally, they are not mentioned at all.[52] Alone and in isolation, the present level of energy cost differentials do not appear to have been a decisive factor in driving any given firm out of New York to a low-cost energy region.[53] Precisely because the state has been a relatively high-cost energy region for so long, its industrial structure is dominated by firms requiring below-average amounts of energy, such as apparel, printing, and instruments (see Table 3.11). If the cost of a relatively unimportant input goes up, the impact upon total costs – and therefore upon the decision to relocate – is marginal. Schaefer Breweries illustrate the arithmetic. The company did leave Brooklyn for Pennsylvania in 1976. In discussing the move, a company execu-

Table 3.10. Cost of 500 kilowatt-hours of electricity in selected U.S. cities, 1965–76

	1965	1966	1967	1968	1969	1970	1971	1972	1973	1974	1975	1976
Actual annual cost[a]												
New York City	$174	$175	$181	$183	$185	$191	$217	$241	$279	$414	$449	$476
Boston	168	166	163	162	161	163	178	185	192	275	299	301
Chicago	150	151	151	153	154	160	171	186	192	218	243	261
Los Angeles	116	116	116	117	121	129	138	157	174	225	242	256
Atlanta	105	105	105	105	108	109	114	125	134	163	217	223
Houston	N.A.	127	125	131	133	133	142	144	148	159	180	214
Relative annual cost												
New York City	100%	100%	100%	100%	100%	100%	100%	100%	100%	100%	100%	100%
Boston	97	95	90	88	87	85	82	76	69	66	67	63
Chicago	87	86	84	83	83	84	79	77	69	53	54	55
Los Angeles	67	66	64	64	65	68	64	65	62	55	54	54
Atlanta	61	60	58	58	58	57	53	52	48	40	48	47
Houston	N.A.	73	72	72	72	70	66	60	53	38	40	45

[a] Figures are rounded to nearest dollar.

Source: U.S., Department of Labor, Bureau of Labor Statistics, "Retail Prices and Indexes of Fuels and Electricity," monthly reports.

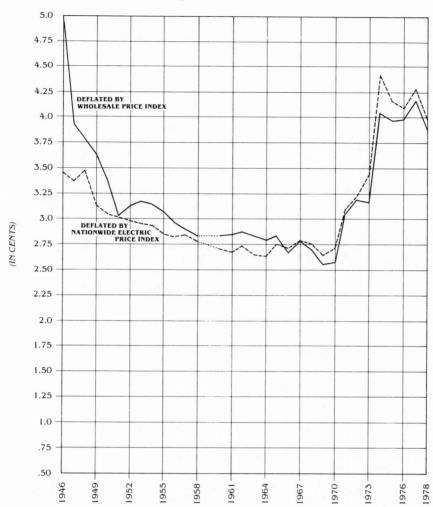

Figure 3.1. Consolidated Edison: revenue per kilowatt-hour for commercial–
industrial customers, 1946–78. *Source:* See Table C.5, Appendix C.

tive noted that, as a result, electricity costs per barrel were cut in half.
He hastened to add, however, that "electricity represented only 1 or 2
percent of total brewing costs here [in Pennsylvania] and could hardly
be decisive for a company."[54] One should be suspicious of the inference that because energy costs are unimportant for some, they are
therefore unimportant for all. Clearly, high-cost energy has been a
negative factor in the past as companies pondered any extensive list of
pros and cons for New York State.

Table 3.11. *Purchased fuels (excluding electric energy) used in manufacturing: New York State and United States, 1971*

	Share of manufacturing value added (%)		Total fuel[a]		Petroleum[a]		Natural gas[a]		Petroleum plus natural gas[a]	
	United States	New York State	United States	New York State	United States	New York State	United States	New York State	United States	New York State
All manufacturing	100.0	100.0	10.6	4.2	1.40	1.26	6.23	1.14	7.63	2.40
Food	10.9	7.9	7.8	5.6	1.08	1.61	4.25	1.95	5.33	3.56
Tobacco	0.8	—	1.8	—	0.50	—	0.47	—	0.97	—
Textiles	3.2	2.1	8.2	4.6	2.00	2.16	3.06	0.64	5.06	2.80
Apparel	4.0	10.9	1.1	0.7	0.16	0.08	0.35	0.08	.51	0.16
Lumber	2.2	0.5	8.5	4.1	1.63	0.45	3.19	1.20	4.82	1.65
Furniture	1.7	1.3	2.7	3.0	0.32	0.62	1.09	0.60	1.41	1.22
Paper	3.7	2.8	30.0	18.2	9.97	10.74	12.38	1.62	22.35	12.36
Printing and publ.	5.8	14.2	1.2	0.6	0.13	0.09	0.64	0.17	0.77	0.26
Chemicals	9.4	6.9	24.3	8.5	2.05	2.20	14.71	1.46	16.76	3.66
Petroleum	1.8	0.3	78.9	12.0	4.50	3.69	71.36	0.59	75.86	4.28
Rubber and plastics	3.0	1.6	5.4	6.2	0.98	1.28	2.44	1.79	3.42	3.07
Leather	0.9	1.2	3.0	2.3	0.81	0.53	0.90	0.34	1.71	0.87
Stone, clay, glass	3.4	2.5	33.2	18.0	3.21	5.60	19.85	5.73	23.06	11.33
Primary metals	6.7	3.4	28.2	18.3	3.12	4.42	15.82	7.66	18.94	12.08
Fabricated metals	7.0	4.7	3.8	4.2	0.39	0.68	2.17	1.21	2.56	1.89
Machines ex. elec.	9.8	8.6	2.8	2.5	0.34	0.48	1.47	0.98	1.81	1.46
Electrical equip.	8.9	9.1	2.0	2.1	0.33	0.73	1.17	0.82	1.50	1.55
Transp. equipment	11.1	7.2	2.5	2.4	0.34	0.85	1.23	1.01	1.57	1.86
Instruments	2.7	10.8	2.0	2.6	0.38	0.48	0.57	0.33	0.95	0.81
Ordnance and misc.	3.3	3.7	2.4	2.2	0.55	0.57	1.19	0.47	1.74	1.04

[a] Kilowatt-hour equivalent per dollar of value added.

Source: New York [State], Council of Economic Advisors, *Annual Report*, 1974, p. 19.

Will it continue to be a negative factor in the future? If heavy dependence upon oil is the central problem, the obvious solution is to develop alternative energy sources. This the power companies propose to do with an expansion plan that is at least optimistic, if not downright rambunctious. With the price tag running to billions, they propose to build 10 new generating plants, 8 of them nuclear and 2 coal-fired.[55] At the outset of the 1980s, this is an ambitious plan going nowhere in a hurry. Ten to 15 years are required to license and build a new generating plant, or so the power companies estimate.[56] The actual process may take far longer. The problem is to get the license. Opposition comes primarily from two quite different groups. One emphasizes the environmental degradation that will accompany, or may accompany, the building of a new plant, particularly a nuclear plant. (After the accident at Three Mile Island, nuclear plants have raised for many the prospect of environmental degradation in a rather extreme form.) The other major opposition group questions the need for more plants, independent of environmental considerations. They note the presence of excess capacity at the moment,[57] and emphasize the likelihood that growth in future demand will be sluggish because the growth performance of the state as a whole is likely to be so sluggish.

To the experts will fall the task of debating these technical issues. However they are resolved, two forecasts can be made with considerable assurance. One is that they will not be resolved in a hurry.[58] The other is that the protracted nature of the debate will assure the continued heavy reliance upon oil as a major energy source within the state. This in turn will mean that New York will continue to be, in the remaining decades of this century, a relatively high-cost energy area.[59] The unfortunate inference is that, once again, the Empire State must look elsewhere for fulcrums for economic growth to combat the present retardation.

3.5. Environmental protection laws

Up and down Wall Street several years ago a fictitious tale was circulated that involved a communiqué to Moses from the Almighty. "There is some good news and some bad news," it read. "The good news is that your enemies will be assailed by hail, fire, and a plague of locusts that will devour every herb of the land and every fruit of the tree. The bad news is that you have to prepare the environmental impact statement." The story is symptomatic of hostility, turbulent and deep-rooted, that lashes out at environmental protection laws as a

major deterrent to economic progress. Senator Daniel Patrick Moynihan can lash with the best of them:

> I would assert . . . that when environmental laws prohibit us
> from building . . . a plant; when they place over our cities
> standards that we do not always meet in the heart of our
> forests; when they tell us that we cannot have new factories
> because our old buildings are crumbling; then we begin to see
> that the economy of the City and of the State are as much
> affected by these laws as by the laws of economics.[60]

What are the laws, and has their impact upon New York been as catastrophic as Moynihan suggests?

The laws in question date primarily from a movement in the late
1960s and early 1970s that culminated in a burst of legislation designed to modify American priorities. According to the head of the
Environmental Protection Agency (hardly an unbiased spectator), it
was nothing less than "a revolution in the way we approach problems
and make decisions."[61] The revolution was simply to insert environmental considerations – sometimes subtly and sometimes forcibly –
into decision making that usually involved the use of economic resources. The legislation fairly tumbled forth from Washington, including the Coastal Zone Management Act, the Resource Conservation and
Recovery Act, the Clean Air Act, and the Federal Water Pollution
Control Act, the last two making the federal government a major force
in setting air and water pollution standards. Perhaps the most widely
publicized of the lot, and certainly one of the most vigorously
applauded and denounced, was the 1969 National Environmental Policy Act (NEPA). Among its provisions was the requirement that all new
federal projects "significantly affecting the quality of the human environment" be accompanied by a detailed analysis of both the probable
environmental impact and the feasible alternatives.[62] Many of the
states were quick to pass similar laws ("mini-NEPAs") requiring similar statements for state and local projects, and for private projects requiring government authorization.

New York was not among the pioneers. Partly this reflected the
power of vested interest groups to stem what they regarded as a catastrophic tide of red tape. Partly it reflected the priorities of Governor
Rockefeller. He had a mania for building – by the state, by its agencies, and by public authorities. He did not view with enthusiasm the
prospect of inhibiting this construction process with environmental
priorities. Rockefeller's admirers would be scandalized by such a suggestion. Was this not the man, they would demand, who was the guiding force behind the Pure Waters Program and the Adirondack Park

Legislation? He was.[63] The first, however, involved primarily sewage treatment and water-supply projects. The second was designed mainly to prevent large second-home developments within the park noted. Neither threatened Rockefeller's building plans in a major way. When those plans did clash with environmental interests, the Governor made his preferences clear. He supported, for example, a Consolidated Edison plan to build a giant hydroelectric plant in the scenic highlands of Storm King Mountain despite the thunderous disapprovals of environmentalists. ("An imaginative, large-scale attempt to relieve the power shortage," Rockefeller noted with approval.)[64] He fought to build a six-lane expressway on the east bank of the Hudson despite the protests of such groups as the Sierra Club and the Citizens Committee of the Hudson Valley. He attempted to bulldoze through the legislature a plan to build two bridges across Long Island Sound, despite the objections of every conceivable citizens' committee and environmental group. This was not a governor to lead the charge – or even to follow the charge – that would extend to state and local projects federal NEPA assessment procedures.[65]

That assignment would fall to Governor Carey. He began by misunderstanding the issues. While advocating the establishment of environmental impact analysis, Carey hastened to add: "This does not mean that we will lose construction jobs within this state."[66] The main point of economists and environmentalists alike is that there is often an inescapable trade-off between economic gains and environmental costs.[67] If, for example, automobile emissions pollute the air, society can have *either* the associated increase in smog and grime *or* better emission controls that raise the price of cars. By the same token, emission controls for smokestacks raise the cost of steel, and effluent controls raise the costs of all those firms that otherwise would dump untreated refuse into the rivers and lakes adjoining their factories. In short, more stringent environmental regulations almost invariably raise producers' costs, and thus the prices paid by consumers.

Which higher costs are worth incurring? To ask the question is to concede the environmentalists' central point: that the question should be asked. Under Governor Carey, the New York Legislature passed a law to foster the inquiry process. Modeled on the 1969 federal NEPA, New York's State Environmental Quality Review Act (SEQR) requires environmental impact statements for many proposed projects originating with either the state or local governments, and proposals of private developers whose projects require government approval.[68]

That was a bold step in 1975 by politicians confronted with economic retardation. Perhaps predictably, they later dragged their feet with amendments and delays. Only on November 1, 1978, did the

SEQR provisions become fully operative. Its probable impact remains
unclear, in part because enforcement can proceed only through litigation, and to date the courts have not been confronted with many cases.

What was the total impact of all the New York acts and programs
designed to improve the environment or to inhibit its degradation –
not just the Environmental Quality Review Act, but a host of others,
including the Mined Land Reclamation Act, the Tidal Wetlands Regulatory and Management Program, and the Freshwater Wetlands Regulatory and Management Program? Assessing their impact on much of
past retardation is comparatively easy. The state's economic difficulties throughout most of the postwar years have been totally unrelated
to environmental protection laws for the simplest of reasons: For most
of those years, there were no laws of consequence to impinge upon the
development process. The future is more cloudy. No one can estimate
with much confidence the net impact of present laws upon a multitude
of future projects that, if unconstrained, would foster economic
growth – with one exception. Whatever the size of that net impact, it is
sure to be negative. To the extent that laws in other states are modified
to match more closely those of New York, however, these negative
influences will be diminished. Firms for whom environmental costs
loom large will be less inclined to leave in search of more liberal
restrictions. Notice what the implications are, and what they are not.
These considerations do not imply that environmental laws should be
repealed or enforced in a lax way. The citizens and their elected representatives must decide which trade-offs are worth making between
environmental priorities and growth priorities, particularly of the
short-run variety. The point here is that there is a trade-off. That being
the case, the only change in environmental laws that might be used to
combat economic retardation in a major way is wholesale repeal, and
that is not about to happen. The inescapable conclusion is that future
fulcrums for economic development, if they can be found, must be
found elsewhere.

3.6. Taxation and business exodus

From the earliest intrusions of government officials into the citizen's
pocketbook, taxation has been recognized as having a powerful influence upon economic activity. Perhaps most often quoted in this context is John Marshall's observation that the power to tax involves the
power to destroy. Al Smith made the same point, but with the politician's gusto: "Now, there is such a thing as drying up the sources of
taxation. You can finish anything with too much taxes; it doesn't make

any difference what it is, it can't last."[69] The New York tax problem is more subtle than either Smith or Marshall would suggest. The central question is not whether taxes can destroy, but whether they have forced businesses to leave the Empire State – admittedly a destruction of sorts. That there should be any doubt about the answer may strike the average citizen as absurd. Obviously taxes are a cost of relevance in deciding where to locate a new plant. Obviously those who make that decision are not indifferent to the prospects of paying higher personal taxes themselves. And yet scholastic conclusions on the subject are painfully cautious. A typical example is the following: "While the precise impact of local taxes on the economic decline of [New York City] cannot be identified, comparative data suggest strongly that the impact has been more than inconsequential."[70] That sentence, when unsnarled, simply asserts that high taxes have made a difference to economic decline. But how much?

The comparatively high level of New York taxes is cited as a detrimental factor in the struggle to attract new firms and hold old ones by every single study with any claim to thoroughness and competence.[71] Similarly, every systematic survey of New York business opinion reveals that high taxes are viewed as an important factor contributing to the industrial exodus of recent years.[72] Not surprisingly, individual businessmen often echo those sentiments when commenting upon their own intentions to leave or their doubts about staying.[73]

With such pervasive evidence of dissatisfaction, the charges must have some substance to them. But how much of the exodus of the past can be attributed to the availability of lower taxes elsewhere? That question actually has two quite distinct aspects:

1. How large was the actual tax differential in favor of other locations outside New York?
2. What difference did that differential make to the corporate executives who decided where to locate a new plant or relocate an old one?

Curiously enough, there are few competent attempts to answer the first question, and none whatsoever to answer the second[74] – a level of ignorance that is at least remarkable, and possibly disgraceful, given that firms have been leaving for a long time, exodus is central to the state's retardation, and taxes are one of the few devices available to Albany politicians to stem that exodus, if they had some clear idea how different prospective tax changes might affect the location decisions of different types of business enterprises.

Concerning the first question – how New York taxes compare with those of other states – all comparisons are complicated by the complex differences among the various state and local tax systems, by the interactions among different state and local taxes, and by the interactions between these two and the federal structure (for example, a larger state income tax payment permits a larger federal income tax deduction).

For all these intricacies, a few general observations can be made. First and possibly foremost, New York's tax image is terrible. Among the 50 states, it is generally believed to have one of the highest tax structures, if not *the* highest. The reality only partly justifies the image. New York does have the highest state and local per capita tax rate in the country.[75] That rate, however, is actually a composite figure, the result of both personal and business taxes, and it is personal taxes that largely account for New York's dubious preeminence as the most heavily taxed region in America.

The corporate tax structure is muddied by endless specifics. Taxes vary across companies, as does their importance to company decision making. Occasionally – and only occasionally – a tax change does have a clear impact. Perhaps the most notorious New York example was the response of security firms to a 1975 hike in taxes on stock and bond transactions. So immediate and pronounced was the migration of brokerage firms to New Jersey[76] (a scant five-minute subway ride from Wall Street) that the taxes were repealed within the year.[77]

This one example aside, the general complexity of the corporate tax structure defies any easy linkage from a tax change to company migration out of the state. Case studies do suggest that the corporate taxes paid by most New York firms located outside New York City are competitive with the taxes imposed at alternative sites outside the state.[78] This is not true for most firms located in New York City, to no small degree because of the additional income tax levied by the city. Even in the latter case, however, for most firms the suspicion is that tax differentials are not especially wide, and that it takes a wide differential to prompt a move. Armchair theorizing supports that belief. Any difference in corporate taxes, when passed through to shareholders, almost invariably reduces to pennies a share (if that) – not a situation to spark a call for heads on a platter at the annual stockholders' meeting, and not much of a threat to the personal fortunes of corporate executives who control the decision whether to stay or to move. Empirical evidence supports this theorizing. As noted previously, most New York City firms pay higher taxes to remain there, and most firms do remain.[79] In sum, for the State of New York, the corporate tax picture is hardly sunny, but (with a few notable exceptions), it is not catastrophically bleak either.

State officials are not above suppressing the negative tax aspects entirely, while accentuating only the bright spots: the absence of personal property taxes, the presence of tax credits for capital improvements, the generous carry-over provisions for net operating losses (back three years and then forward five).[80] As a valid assessment of the aggregate tax structure of the state, such pitches are as much to the point as praise for a dilapidated lifeboat with no leaks in one end. The overall condition of the tax structure aimed at business enterprises is, at the very least, in need of considerable repair. That portion aimed at individuals is an unmitigated disaster.

New York State and its localities impose the highest personal tax burdens in the nation. For residents of New York City, those burdens are even worse, largely because of the highest city income tax in the nation. One study released in 1974 even presumed to suggest that New York had no untapped tax capacity left.[81] (Albany politicians quickly disposed of that notion by raising taxes even further in 1975. For details of the taxes in question see Table 3.12.) Any comparison of individual tax rates is therefore sure to cast a pall upon the merits of remaining in the Empire State. Of the states immediately adjacent to New York (Connecticut, New Jersey, and Pennsylvania), all have sharply lower personal taxes, and two do not tax earned income at all.[82] For top corporate executives contemplating a move out of New York City, this translates into a prospective saving in total personal taxes *of better than 60 percent.*[83]

Do differentials of this magnitude matter? More carefully put, do differentials in the prospective tax bills of corporate executives affect their decision making about where to locate or relocate their businesses? The poverty of our knowledge about the answer has already been emphasized. The evidence is clear that tax differentials make some difference, but how big a difference remains a matter of conjecture. For some, those conjectures emphasize the probability that wide differentials, particularly in prospective personal tax payments, have been a factor of the first importance in driving industry from the city and the state. Although the precise causal links are far from clear, it is perhaps worth noting in this context the propensity of New York City firms to flee to the three adjacent states. For example, as noted previously: (1) of the manufacturing firms leaving New York City in the 1961–73 period, 82 percent went to Connecticut, New Jersey, and Pennsylvania,[84] and (2) of the 21 firms in *Fortune's* top 500 who moved their headquarters out of New York City in the period 1959–75, almost two-thirds went to either New Jersey or Connecticut.[85]

Discussions of future New York tax trends tend to focus less upon prospective politics than upon the feasibility of tax cuts. Optimists emphasize that as incomes rise, tax revenues will also rise, and the surpluses thereby generated will give the fiscal leeway for substantial tax reductions. Pessimists are not convinced. Forecasts of rising revenues, they note, assume a generous rise in state incomes.[86] This prospect appears limited for two reasons. New York developments in the

Table 3.12. *Major tax changes increasing revenues of New York State budget funds, 1956–76*

1956   None
1957   None
1958   None
1959

  Cigarette tax – from 3¢ to 5¢ per pack

  Estate tax – from 1%–20%, to 2%–21%

  Gas tax – from 4¢ to 6¢ per gallon; diesel fuel tax, from 6¢ to 9¢ per gallon

  Personal income tax – 3 new brackets; withholding instituted

  Tobacco products tax – 15% wholesale price (repealed in 1961)

1960   None
1961

  Insurance taxes – 2% tax on gross premiums received by foreign and alien title insurers added

1962

  Bank and insurance taxes – due dates for payments advanced (some were later decelerated under 1974 legislation)

  Corporation franchise and corporation and utilities taxes – same

1963

  Alcoholic beverage control licenses – fees increased by 25% to 50%; additional fees charged; gallonage fees imposed on liquor (75¢ per gal.), beer (1⅛¢ per gal.), liquor 24% or less alcohol (16⅔¢ per gal.), and wines (6⅔¢ and 13⅓¢ on sparkling)

1964   None
1965

  Cigarette tax – from 5¢ to 10¢ per pack

  Motor vehicle fees – passenger vehicle registration fees raised by 50%

  Pari-mutuel tax – breakage raised to dime and state share at flat tracks increased

  Sales and use tax – new 2% tax imposed

1966

  Stock transfer tax – temporary 25% surtax added (made permanent in 1968)

1967

  State lottery adopted

1968

  Bank tax – to 6% net income; 2% of first 3% of dividends

  Cigarette tax – from 10¢ to 12¢ per pack

  Corporation and utilities taxes – rates generally increased by about 30%

  Corporation franchise tax – from 5½% to 7% net income

  Highway use tax – a fuel use tax added

  Insurance taxes – rate on ocean marine underwriting profits increased to 6½%

  Gas tax – from 6¢ to 7¢ per gallon

  Pari-mutuel tax – takeout increased, with state share raised at harness tracks

  Personal income tax – four brackets added

  Unincorporated business tax – from 4% to 5½%

  Real estate transfer tax adopted

1969

  Sales and use tax – from 2% to 3%

Table 3.12. (*cont.*)

1970
   Partial conformity to Federal Tax Reform Act of 1969: minimum income tax
     for individuals; new unrelated business income tax
   Pari-mutuel tax – state sharing in OTB; harness track takeout and tax revised
1971
   Bank tax – from 6% to 8% net income; and from 2% of first 3% of dividends
     to 2% of first 3½% of dividends
   Corporation franchise tax – from 7% to 9% net income
   Corporation and utilities taxes – raised by 15.4%
   Pari-mutuel tax – flat track takeout raised; state share increased for Finger
     Lakes track only
   Sales and use tax – from 3% to 4%; base extended to meals under $1.00
1972: 2nd Special Session of 1971
   Alcoholic beverage tax – liquor over 24% alcohol, from $2.25 to $3.25 per
     gallon; liquor 24% or less alcohol, from 66⅔¢ to 80¢ per gallon
   Cigarette tax – from 12¢ to 15¢ per pack
   Gas tax – from 7¢ to 8¢ per gallon; diesel fuel tax, from 9¢ to 10¢ per gallon
   Gift tax imposed
   Personal income tax – additional bracket, minimum tax rate doubled; capital
     gains taxability increased (50% to 60%); temporary (5-year) 2½% surcharge
     imposed; percentage depletion disallowed
1973   None
1974   None
1975   None in regular session
1975: Special Session
   Bank tax – from 8% to 12% net income; plus 30% surcharge on bank tax
     liability for 1975 and 1976 taxable years
   Corporation franchise tax – from 9% to 10% net income; alternative taxes
     increased comparably (but minimum tax, $150 to $250); plus one-year
     20% surcharge on tax for 1975 calendar-year and 1976 fiscal-year
     corporation liability
   Sales and use tax – changed from quarterly to monthly remittance of sales
     tax by vendors with taxable quarterly receipts, etc., of $300,000 or more;
     estimated payment of March liability required, as well as regular payment
     due that month (effective 3/1/76); requirement extended to vendors with
     taxable receipts of $100,000 or more, effective 9/1/77 [*Note:* Provisions
     partially revised by subsequent 1976 legislation, but the revisions did not
     affect these requirements.]
1976
   Corporation and utilities taxes – public utilities and transportation and
     transmission companies required to make tax payments on an estimated
     basis for taxable years ending on or after December 31, 1976; reporting
     period changed to calendar year
   Personal income tax – 2½% surcharge extended through March 31, 1977

Source: New York [State], Governor, *Governor's Five-Year Projection of Income and Expenditures, General Fund, Fiscal Years 1977–78 through 1981–
82,* February 17, 1977*b*.

short run are closely linked to national economic trends. National growth, in turn, must combat in the 1980s such factors as declining productivity and rising Arab oil prices. A second and ultimately more important reason for a pessimistic view of state revenue prospects concerns the likelihood of retardation persisting in New York, accompanied by a further outmigration of firms that generate income and of people who have above-average earning capabilities.

The case for gloom is only half complete. The rest concerns the likelihood that expenditure increases will roughly match whatever gains are made in revenue, thereby ruling out any large surplus that could provide the basis for a major tax cut. Many expenditures are difficult to control, much less reverse: public employee compensation, debt service, pension obligations, energy-related costs. Others are loaded with political peril for any politician who proposes major reductions: welfare, Medicaid, school aid, and local revenue sharing. Also lurking in the wings and as yet not seriously addressed are the future spending needs implied by a deteriorating capital infrastructure: water and sewer lines, public buildings, roads and bridges and mass transit networks.[87] Many areas of the older Northeast of course confront such capital replacement problems, but they are much in evidence in New York State and downright prominent in New York City. The fiscal implications, as the pessimists are quick to emphasize, are perhaps best captured by a single adjective: "grim."[88]

Which scenario is more likely: the optimistic world of rising revenues enabling major tax reductions, or the pessimistic world in which sluggish revenues and rising expenses make unfeasible any major relief for New York's overburdened taxpayers? The best guide to the future is probably the immediate past. The record is not encouraging.

Tax cuts admittedly were achieved in the latter part of the 1970s, perhaps most notably in personal income taxes (the first permanent reduction in the personal income tax in the history of the state, the Governor's 1977–78 budget message proudly announced). The critical question is not whether some reductions have been made, but whether these cuts have altered significantly the relative position of New York as a heavily taxed state. The answer appears to be no. A detailed survey in 1979, for example, concluded that "there would appear to be some convergence in tax burdens between New York State and the nation. But . . . the narrowing of the gap between New York and other states is almost unrecognizable."[89]

The final point, about as unwelcome as those preceding it, is that the state government is responsible for only a part of New York taxes, and developments at the local level show no signs of dramatic improvement.[90] Nowhere is this more apparent than in New York City, where retardation and exodus are most pronounced. The city's problem is not one of generating a surplus that can be translated into tax cuts. Its problem is somehow to eradicate a huge and continuing deficit between revenues and operating expenses – a problem that both city and state politicians have yet to solve decisively.[91] The prospect for major tax cuts in the locality where they are probably most needed is therefore almost nonexistent (barring a huge infusion of federal funds).

Perhaps the best summary judgment about the future was lurking in Governor Carey's initial budget pronouncement of the 1980s. For all his assurances of tax cuts to come, the Governor was forced to concede that "the challenge now is to show we can hold spending while revenues decrease."[92] It was a statement singularly barren of promise for those who hope for major tax reductions just over the horizon.

3.7. Government and the business climate

"We're not giving business the business any more," proclaimed a New York Commerce Department slogan. "We're giving it a break."[93] One clear implication was that heretofore what business had been getting from the state government was less than a break. Commerce Commissioner John Dyson readily conceded the point: "For over ten years now New York State has built up a bad taste in a lot of mouths. And I realize better than anyone else we have no one to blame but ourselves. Too long we took business for granted."[94] The reference to 10 years the business community might regard as a far too shallow characterization of a long-standing problem. The point about bad taste in a lot of mouths – their mouths – was very much to the point.

Business climate is an amorphous concept: a tenuous characterization of the moods and perceptions of a multitude of executives, owners, and entrepreneurs. However elusive the idea, something was very wrong with the New York reality by the 1970s. All of the surveys confirmed it.[95] One of the most comprehensive was one of the least flattering. Under the heading "Locational factors unfavorable for operating a business in New York State," business respondents listed the attitudes of state government leaders, state legislators, state department officials, and local government leaders.[96] This is doubly curious. In a state traditionally dominated by Republicans, the expectation is, at the very least, a favorable rapport between the business community and elected officials. In a state fighting retardation for decades, one would expect an aggressive wooing of business interests to stem the exodus of some firms and encourage the influx of others. Neither wooing nor rapport were much in evidence by the early 1970s. In their stead was a catalogue of charges as diverse as the community from which they sprang. At the center of this pervasive disaffection was a

short list of major grievances: excessive taxation, inefficient government, inaccessible officials, mountains of red tape, laws often friendly
to labor (such as that authorizing the payment of unemployment benefits to strikers) and unfriendly to business (such as environmental
regulations), and above all, an attitude throughout the corridors of
power that was at best indifferent, and at worst hostile to the needs of
business. In the crisp phrasing of the chairman of the Bulova Watch
Company, "We . . . feel that we are overtaxed and underserved."[97]

Many analysts agreed. Commissioner Dyson conceded that "there
are more laws and rules impeding business here than in any other
state."[98] A New York City group of business and labor leaders led by
David Rockefeller called for "a crackdown on bureaucratic idiocy"
and the proliferation of red tape.[99] The staff director of New York City's
Temporary Commission on City Finances characterized tax policy as
"too often . . . made on the back of an envelope without sufficient
thought."[100] Even Assembly Speaker Duryea conceded that the state's
economy had been imperiled by "slap-dash, now-you-see-it-now-
you-don't, make-shift fiscal policies."[101] And, as noted previously, the
Commerce Department was willing to concede that somebody had
been giving business the business.

Any knowledgeable bureaucrat could counter such charges with a
near endless list of tax incentives and development agencies tailored
to do what businessmen claimed was not being done, namely, encourage industry and commerce within the state.

The development agencies are designed primarily to help with business financing. Their main technique is to use their tax-exempt status
as public organizations to borrow funds at low interest rates, and then
pass along the funds and the interest rate savings to would-be private
borrowers. Of the many state and local agencies designed to accomplish this dollar shuffle, three should be singled out for particular mention.

Job Development Authority (JDA). A public authority established in
1962, the JDA makes low-interest, long-term second mortgage loans to
help finance "the construction, acquisition, rehabilitation or improvement of industrial or manufacturing plants, research and development
facilities, or other eligible business facilities."[102] It may also help to
finance the purchase of machinery and equipment.[103] By selling its
own (state-guaranteed) bonds,[104] the Authority raises dollars that are
then funneled to businesses via nonprofit local development corporations. The latter, often established specifically to aid in this funneling,
request the dollars and supervise the details of the financing.

Industrial development agencies (IDAs). The State Industrial Development Agency Act of 1969 permits the state legislature to authorize
communities to form industrial development agencies. Not to be con-

fused with local development corporations (the conduits for JDA loans), these agencies can issue their own revenue bonds "for the purpose of acquiring, constructing, equipping and furnishing industrial, manufacturing, warehousing, commercial, pollution control, horse breeding, research and recreation facilities."[105] The local agency, of course, has no interest in keeping for itself any of the aforementioned facilities. It acquires them at the request of a local firm, and then transfers the facility through a lease-purchase agreement. The local agency issues its own revenue bonds, uses the proceeds to buy (say) a building, then leases that building to a firm (whose desire to acquire that building initiated the entire procedure). The rental payment is fixed to recover the cost of principal and interest on the initial bond issue.[106] When the bonds are paid off, title passes to the firm in question. The major advantage gained is tax-exempt financing. As a quasi-government agency, each local development agency can issue tax-exempt bonds at appropriately low interest rates. These savings are then passed along to the leasing firm in the form of lower rental payments (which are really lower principal and interest payments in disguise).[107] There is also a second tax advantage. Because ownership of the property in question belongs to the local development agency (until the bonds are paid off), technically that property is also exempt from property taxes. In practice, some property tax payments are usually included as part of the negotiation with the firm seeking the lease-purchase arrangement.

Urban Development Corporation (UDC). Established in 1968, this public authority can come to the aid of business in a variety of complex ways because of the extraordinary range of its powers. It can, for example, engage in lease-purchase agreements similar to those noted above, and with similar tax advantages. On its own, it may create industrial parks, rehabilitate old factories, or build new ones with no clear buyer standing in the wings. No other state has a comparable agency empowered to use public funds to build or develop on its own account, for sale or lease to private users. UDC can also assist companies and local communities in obtaining government grants for economic development.

Along with the carrot of low-interest agency-supported financing, the state can dangle before prospective New York businessmen a range of tax incentives, including property tax exemptions, capital investment credits, tax-exempt financing for industrial pollution control facilities, and special credits for firms that raise local employment.[108] Understanding the structure of the tax break and its implications for the cost structure of a given firm requires a lawyer's eye and an accountant's care. The point to be emphasized here – most easily grasped by reference to Table 3.13 – is that tax incentives derive their

Table 3.13. *Incentives offered to industry in selected states, as of May 1973*

Incentive	N.Y.	N.J.	Pa.	Conn.	Va.	N.C.	S.C.	Tenn.	Total states in U.S.
For establishing industrial plants in areas of high unemployment									
By state	X[1]		X						10
By locality	X[1]	X[2]	X						6
Income tax exemption									
Corporate	X[1,3,4]			X[5]					18
Personal	X[3]	X[6]	X					X	19
Tax exemption									
Land, buildings	X[1]						X	X[7]	17
Equipment, machines	X[8]		X[9]	X[10]			X	X[7]	26
Sales/use tax exemption on new equipment	X	X	X[9]		X	X[11]	X	X[11]	28
Accelerated depreciation of industrial equipment					X[12]			X[13]	20
Inventory tax exemption on goods in transit	X[8]	X[14]	X[15]	X		X[14]	X	X	40
Tax exemption on manufacturing inventories	X[8]	X	X[15]	X			X	X	30
Tax exemptions on raw materials used in manufacturing	X[8]	X	X[9]	X[16]	X[17]	X[18]	X	X	43
Excise tax exemption		X	X						10
For encouraging research and development	X[4]	X	X		X[16]		X		6

Notes to Table 3.13

1. In low-income areas, a reduction in corporate, business, or personal income taxes, and at local option, abatement of property tax, both up to 10 years.
2. Cities have authority to grant tax abatements in blighted areas for development.
3. Reduction in corporate, business, or personal income tax for new buildings and equipment.
4. Treatment of costs for new research and development facilities as current expenses.
5. Corporate income tax credit only for pollution-control equipment.
6. New York or Pennsylvania citizens employed in New Jersey not exempt.
7. Applicable at local level only.
8. Personal tangible and intangible property not subject to ad valorem taxes.
9. Exclusion from sales and use taxes on industrial purchases used directly in industrial production and research.
10. Equipment and machinery acquired after 1973 assessment date exempt from local property tax.
11. New equipment taxed at lower rate.
12. Allowable depreciation conforms closely with federal income tax law.
13. Amortization not allowed for emergency equipment.
14. Applicable to goods stored in bonded warehouses.
15. Tangible personal property excluded at local level.
16. Local governments may tax tangible personal property of R&D firms at lower rates.
17. Exempt from sales/use tax, but not business capital tax.
18. Leaf tobacco is allowed exemption of 60% of tax rate; bales of cotton, 50%; peanuts, 20%.
Source: New York [State], Select Committee on the Economy (1974), 78.

importance only within a comparative framework. The presence of such incentives means little. The critical question is whether the incentives in question are better than those being offered by other regions competing for the same industry. The competition is fierce, and by no means limited to tax breaks and subsidized financing through development agencies.

A Pennsylvania-based aluminum firm illustrates the infighting. In 1971 a New York manufacturer acquired this firm, intending to move it to upstate New York. The local New York Industrial Development Agency was contacted, as was the county economic coordinator and the state Commerce Department representative. To house the new plant an abandoned aircraft plant was found in upstate New York. The local IDA offered to finance its acquisition through low-interest tax-exempt bonds. While these negotiations were in progress, the new owner of the aluminum plant received a telephone call from the Governor of South Carolina. The owner remembers the conversation. "He [the Governor] said he had heard that I was trying to locate a plant, and he wondered if he could fly up in his personal jet, pick me up, and fly me down to South Carolina to show me what they had to offer."[109] What South Carolina had to offer included (1) a plant in Spartanburg that was 30 years newer than the New York aircraft plant, and available at one-fifth the cost, and (2) a 10-year moratorium on most taxes that reduced the prospective tax bill on the Spartanburg plant to $2,000 a year. (The prospective tax bill on the New York property was $79,000 a year.) The State of South Carolina also offered to pay the cost of moving the company from Pennsylvania, and the costs of training all workers hired. The company moved to South Carolina.

The example illustrates that corporate decision making about plant location and relocation is often not the exclusive product of free market forces. The incentives brandished by state governments can also be a factor of the first importance. In that rivalry, New York State throughout the Rockefeller era was little better than an impotent and inept competitor. The ineptness was indicated by the absence of long-range planning, the indifference to business climate, and the near total absence, at every level of government, of the kind of information vital to plant location decisions, such as potential labor supplies, transportation and warehousing facilities, and computer services. No bureaucrat or politician of consequence seemed to care, or to care very much, whether business came or went. A legislative commission in the early 1970s discovered that of 279 "industrial prospects" in the files of the Commerce Department – new firms that might enter the state or old ones that might leave – the records of 102 had simply disappeared.[110] It also discovered that 70 percent of the industries that moved out of New York between 1968 and 1973 "were not contacted in a timely manner by the Department of Commerce or any other industrial development agency."[111] The impotence of the state was indicated by the frailty of its development agencies and the niggardliness of its tax incentives. The Job Development Agency, for example, loaned on the average less than $5 million a year, and had, in the opinion of the State Comptroller, an ongoing propensity "to overstate its accomplishments."[112] The handful of tax incentives – none outstanding relative to those available in other states – could not begin to counteract the reputation of New York as a heavily taxed region.[113]

With the exit of Rockefeller and the entrance of Carey, with the demise of confidence and the growing recognition that economic retardation had New York by the throat, came a new determination at all levels of government to do better. The new Governor appointed commissions and boards to study the problem and suggest solutions. The list included (but was by no means confined to) the Economic Development Board to devise long-run strategies, the Council on the Economy to coordinate the activities of all groups concerned with improving the state's economy, and the Job Retention Board to review state bids and to allocate government contracts to in-state firms, provided the lowest local bid did not exceed the lowest out-of-state bid by more than 10 percent. Taxes could not be slashed – there was too little room to maneuver on the expenditure side – but they could be marginally reduced at the state level. The surcharges on the corporation franchise tax and the bank tax were allowed to expire. The insurance tax was lowered, as was the personal income tax. Legislation was also passed to phase out two taxes that businessmen particularly condemned: the stock transfer tax (by 1981) and the unincorporated business tax (by 1982).

Whether these and other actions can breathe new warmth and vigor into the New York business climate remains to be seen. Certainly the business community should be heartened by a new awareness and a new activism within government. The state renowned for Madison Avenue is finally attempting to sell itself. Old-fashioned boosterism has become the chosen assignment of a range of government officials and private citizens, often organized into commissions, agencies, or councils for that specific purpose. Nowhere is this more evident than in New York City, with its Economic Development Administration, Industrial and Commercial Incentive Board, Business Marketing Corporation, Business–Labor Working Group, and many other groups with similar objectives.

The rhetoric has accordingly improved dramatically. The slogan "I Love New York" has become the watchword in board rooms and on bumper stickers from Long Island to Lake Ontario. The accompanying government actions, however, remain relatively modest. Its ability to offer tax and other incentives is constrained by a tight fiscal situation in Albany and a near disastrous fiscal situation in New York City. The ability of government agencies to extend low-cost loans to businesses is constrained by the public's vetoing of expanded lending power for the Job Development Agency, and by the capping of other kinds of "moral obligation" borrowing by public authorities.[114] If development agencies cannot borrow a lot more, they cannot lend a lot more. New York laws that have particularly antagonized the business community – especially environmental protection laws and the payment of unemployment benefits to strikers – are not now under consideration for overhauling or repeal, nor are they likely to be. In short, the politicians of New York appear to be severely constrained in what they can do to amend the business climate and combat economic retardation. Nor is it clear that they have the determination to use what tools they do command in a decisive and persistent manner. Economic development is a long-range goal. As one pessimistic businessman observed, "Politicians seek votes and are only interested in the short term."[115] There is therefore a persistent danger that the recent whirlwind of appointments and pronouncements in Albany and elsewhere, in the words of an old Indian saying, will be little more than wind upon the buffalo grass. Herbert Bienstock put it differently. As New York Regional Director of the U.S. Bureau of Labor Statistics, he was asked to serve on Governor Carey's Economic Development Task Force. By his own admission, Bienstock attended only one meeting: "It was a waste of time . . . No one has ever put together a group of economists to work on New York City. Really put them to work – with resources and dollars – and said 'Here, don't come out with a study, come out with a set of policy recommendations.' All that comes out now is bullshit."[116]

The language is abrasive, but the judgment is a not unreasonable characterization of many government actions in the 1970s ostensibly designed to fight the newly recognized problem of business exodus and economic retardation. The challenge for the future is clear. Recommendations must be predicated upon expert study and then translated into policy. Whether either will be possible remains a critical and largely unanswered question for the 1980s.[117]

3.8. Drumbeats from Dixie

Retardation, as noted, is a relative concept. The basic notion is that region A is lagging behind region B. It follows that the causes of retardation are *both* the factors slowing A down *and* the factors speeding B up. Or to drop the A and B and substitute N and S, the retardation of the Northeast (N) is partly to be explained by the rise of the Sunbelt region (S) – a collection of some 15 states stretching south from Virginia and west to California (or at least to the southern part of California).[118] This the popular press has occasionally headlined as a new war between the states. The war is not particularly new. Competition among regions to attract and hold factors of production and producing factories is as old as the 13 colonies. It is endemic to any capitalist system comprised of diverse regions operating within a given set of national boundaries. What is new is the recent surge in economic strength of an American region heretofore considered relatively weak (the South), while the economic energies of the region heretofore considered the strongest in the nation (the Northeast) appear to be flagging. Part of New York's difficulties can therefore be traced to the rising competitive strength of southern states. What are the origins of this intensified competition from an unexpected quarter?

Explanations of southern resurgence have tended to focus upon a handful of reasons why the Sunbelt has become a more attractive location for industry. Foremost in almost every list are the following:[119]

1. The rise of air conditioning
2. The presence of governments more friendly to business and the absence of high taxes
3. The expanded markets and expanded labor pools that have resulted from increased migration to the area[120]
4. The comparative cheapness of labor and the relative absence of strong unions
5. The abundance of low-cost space
6. The disproportionate share of federal spending (particularly military spending) that has been allocated to southern states

Some of these reasons are of questionable relevance, at least when expressed in this oversimplified form. The need for more space, for example, helps to explain why certain manufacturing industries are getting out of cities. It does not explain why those industries should seek out less congested areas in the Sunbelt rather than in the Frostbelt. The argument about the flow of federal dollars is suspect for a different reason. Certainly the South does have a disproportionate share of military bases, partly for reasons of climate, partly because of odd space requirements (a missile testing range requires a lot of room), and partly because of southern dominance of congressional committees that have been influential in the allocation of military spending and installations. (When Mendel Rivers of South Carolina chaired the House Armed Services Committee, for example, the fear was expressed in Washington that if Charleston should receive another naval

base it would sink.) The flow of federal dollars, however, is not confined to bolstering military bases. And about the regional distribution
of the aggregate flow of all federal dollars we know comparatively
little (see Section 3.9).

Pared down in this way, these reasons reduce to an even shorter list
of generalizations singularly lacking in analytical precision. We do
know that the South is viewed by many businessmen as an attractive
region in which to locate. What we do not know is which factors contributed to each location or relocation decision, and how much they
contributed. A subsidiary of Dun and Bradstreet, for example, suggested in 1976 that of the 48 contiguous states, Texas was the most
attractive place to do business, in part because it had "no corporate or
personal income taxes, weak unions, low government debt, and low
workmen's compensation costs."[121] Which of these or other factors
were responsible for business actually pulling up stakes and moving to
Texas remains very much an unknown.

What of the future? Economic theory leads one to expect that many
of the initial advantages of the South will be eroded by the process of
migration and growth. Population density will rise, pollution and congestion will get worse, wage differentials (the South versus the North)
should narrow, and so should the differentials in prospective returns to
venture capital. Offsetting these tendencies to erode the South's competitive advantage may be gains associated with economies of scale.
The popular press has often stressed this theme. The lurking metaphor
resembles a nuclear reactor: Once various thresholds have been
crossed – in the density of business services, in the size of the local
market, in the available pool of skilled labor, and so on – growth becomes an accelerating, interacting process, at least in the short run.
Typical of this line of argument is *Business Week's* explanation of the
recent quickening in southern economic expansion: "Perhaps the most
important factor that seems to have been overlooked is that at some
point around the late 1960's, Southern growth achieved a critical mass,
turning orderly migration into a flood. Growth became self-sustaining
as the South's industrial base broadened and deepened."[122]

Tentative evidence suggests that the migration of New York firms to
the South, while still comparatively minor, has risen somewhat in
recent years.[123] Whether the drawing power of the South will increase
or decrease in the immediate future is unclear. What does seem clear is
that no radical and quick decline in the South's attractiveness seems
likely in the 1980s. This in turn implies that developments external to
New York are unlikely to assist in any major way the Empire State's
attempts to combat the forces of retardation.

3.9. Federal dollar allocation: prime mover of retardation?

The *Village Voice* headline read "Regional Robbery." Senator Daniel Patrick Moynihan of New York, who viewed himself as more than the voice of the village, spelled out the theft: "The overall pattern of Federal taxation and expenditure has the effect of systematically deflating the economy of New York. In effect, national prosperity is traded for New York's decline. Government statistics conceal the incredible gap between the aggregate Federal taxes levied in New York and the expenditures returned to it."[124]

Here was an explanation of New York's economic difficulties with guaranteed down-home appeal. While shunting the blame down the Hudson and up the Potomac, it fairly sparkled with optimism and indignation. If the federal government was to blame, presumably the local politicians were not. If the main cause of the region's retardation was the misallocation of federal dollars, the solution was as simple as a reallocation of those dollars. All that was needed was to make the decision makers in Washington see the error of their ways. As a straight-from-the-shoulder, no-nonsense political accusation, it was the stuff of reelection campaigns. As an accurate description of the facts, the accusation was hardly in the no-nonsense category.

The accusation itself was anchored in federal data that seemed above reproach. Three conflicting estimates, however, indicated hidden difficulties in the calculation procedure. A Dreyfus Corporation estimate agreed with Senator Moynihan that New York was being drained by federal taxation. For every dollar paid in taxes, Dreyfus estimated that only 47 cents was returned to New Yorkers.[125] The Tax Foundation found the opposite: For every dollar paid, $1.32 was returned. Into this numerical fray the *National Journal* charged with assurances that all previous disputes would be laid to rest. Dreyfus Corporation and Moynihan, the *Journal* concluded, were right as to direction but wrong as to magnitude. For every dollar paid in taxes, New Yorkers received back 89 cents.[126]

Something was apparently befuddling the simple process of adding and subtracting. Senator Moynihan's original estimate illustrates the problem. For the year 1976, he noted that federal outlays received by New York totaled $40.6 billion, whereas net collections from New York by the Internal Revenue Service totaled $33.7 billion. New York residents therefore apparently received a surplus from Washington of $6.9 billion. This Moynihan converted into a deficit of $7.4 billion by claiming that receipts should exclude $13.3 billion in "Interest on the

Public Debt" and a further $1 billion for "Foreign Economic and Financial Assistance." If 40.6 is reduced by these two figures (13.3 + 1.0), the revised receipt total (26.3) minus tax payments (an unrevised 33.7) implies that New Yorkers were being drained of a net of $7.4 billion.[127]

The arithmetic is impeccable. The logic behind the arithmetic is not. The heart of the conversion from surplus to deficit is the exclusion of interest payments from receipts.[128] Moynihan's reasons for that subtraction are compelling. A large portion of these payments (not all of them, but better than 50 percent) are paid initially to the Federal Reserve Bank of New York City, and from that bank to Federal Reserve branches throughout the country. As officially recorded, these payments are somewhat arbitrarily allocated to the three areas serviced by the New York City Fed: New York, New Jersey, and Connecticut.[129] If these allocations are spurious – if, in Senator Moynihan's wording, interest payments in reality "went every which way"[130] – one solution is to ignore the allocation completely: the solution chosen by Moynihan, Dreyfus Corporation, and the *National Journal* to derive their deficit estimates.

Moynihan was on the right track, but failed to pursue his own procedure to its logical conclusion. Are there other dollars arbitrarily allocated to regions that in fact go "every which way"? Consider the case of defense. The example is far from trivial. The *National Journal* was quick to concede that "spending for defense accounts for nearly all the federal spending discrepancies among the Northeast, Midwest, South and West."[131] The largest part of the defense budget is defense procurement. This spending is recorded according to the location of the prime contractor. Many of the dollars spent, however, do not go to that geographic region. Part of the difficulty is that official data "frequently list contracts by headquarters location of the company instead of the site of production."[132] The main difficulty is that the prime contractor may be only a minor contributor to the production process. The usual defense procurement contract is filled partly by subcontracting, so much so that subcontracting "accounts for a major portion of procurement expenditures."[133] The result is that a billion-dollar contract for a supersonic fighter allocated to, say, a firm located in Washington State may result in increased orders for a multitude of plants scattered throughout the country. If interest payments should be ignored because they cannot be traced, presumably defense procurement expenditures should be dropped for the same reason.[134] But if both of these numerical series are thrown out because the dollars "go every which way," what is left of the ambition to estimate the net federal surplus or deficit of each state, including New York State? Very little.

This was made painfully apparent to Moynihan's friend, Paul Volcker, then president of the New York Federal Reserve Bank, when he asked his staff to scour the data for the truth. They reported back that "the data were insufficient to support Moynihan's contention."[135] Other experts agree. Perhaps the most intelligent and balanced review of the problem concluded that all of the published estimates "too readily incorporate elements of the Federal budget whose geographic incidence (who really pays and benefits) is in reality impossible to determine."[136] If the allocation cannot be determined, the regional net surplus or deficit resulting from that allocation also cannot be determined. In short, no one, including Senator Moynihan, has the foggiest idea whether the federal government takes more dollars from New Yorkers than it returns to them.

The question, of course, is far from trivial: How do federal policies help and hurt the regional economy of New York? The relevant issues for addressing that question range far beyond the flows of expenditures and receipts. For example, federal loan subsidies, environmental policies, tariff decisions, and price regulations for transportation and energy are hardly irrelevant. Also contributing to pressures on state and local budgets have been the many federally mandated programs not completely covered by federal grants. To assess the impact of all such policies, however, requires a far more sophisticated model of national and regional development than is presently available. It also would require far more accurate data on interregional dollar flows than we apparently now possess.

3.10. Space, crime, and the "quality of life" in New York City

March 20, 1976. The nation's second-largest chemical manufacturer, Union Carbide, had just announced that it was moving its 3,500 employees from Park Avenue to a 144-acre site near Danbury, Connecticut. In a letter to its staff, the company explained why: "While we recognize that New York City does have many advantages, the long-term quality-of-life needs of our headquarters employees were the overriding factors in arriving at this conclusion."[137] "Quality of life" was a fortunately vague phase. It had nothing specific to offend anyone – except that there was something offensive enough to convince Union Carbide executives that, as a place to live and work, the Big Apple was also the Tarnished Apple. They were not alone. A 1977 survey of city residents revealed that two-thirds considered New York City to be a "fair" or "poor" place to live.[138] A nationwide poll in the same year indicated that only 6 percent of Americans gave New York City a "good" or "excellent" rating as a prospective residence.[139] That external opinion was particularly crucial. Again and again the management of corporations headquartered in New York echoed the same complaint: that they could not attract talented young executives to the city. Repeatedly they cited that difficulty as their companies packed up and moved: Continental Can to Chicago, Mobil Oil to the Washington area, Texasgulf, Inc., to southern Connecticut, General Telephone and Electronics to Stamford – and then Union Carbide.[140] "People are the most important resource we or any other company have," explained a Union Carbide official.[141] A senior vice-president put the case in the bluntest possible terms. "[Prospective recruits] tell us that they don't want to live in that jungle. And they don't like the alternative either: a home in an expensive suburb that may be an hour and a half travelling time from our offices."[142]

Was it really a "jungle"? Had the cultural and financial center of America come to such a sorry pass that it evoked only images of savagery in the imaginations of those who contemplated living there? The image for many outsiders was no doubt a distortion of the reality. But the reality did have its seamy side. The city's deteriorating fiscal position (described in Chapter 8) had contributed to a deterioration in public services, such as sanitation and schools. The charges of polluted air, dirty streets, and filthy subways sullied by graffiti were not without foundation. Heading the list of concerns of both those within the city and those without who were contemplating an inward move were three particular shortcomings: crime, a scarcity of space, and the high cost of living within America's largest and most congested city.

Crime is a cantankerous skeleton that refuses to stay in the city's closet. Time and again executives who are moving out of the city or contemplating such a move note the prevalence of the phenomenon and its importance in terms of the thefts of merchandise, the expenses of security, and the unwillingness of employees to work late.[143] Nor can this skeleton be dismissed by noting certain favorable comparisons with other major American urban centers: that New York, for example, ranks twelfth in murders and eighteenth in forcible rape.[144] Relative to Boston or San Francisco, life in the Big Apple may not be all that perilous. The difficulty is that relative to Danbury, Connecticut, there is no contest. And it is to these more pastoral settings that much of the city's industry has taken flight. The tirades of business leaders make clear as nothing else can the grip that this factor has upon the consciousness of those who assemble in the board room to consider relocation: for example, the Ingersoll-Rand executive vice-president who complained, as his company headed for Woodcliffe Lake, New Jersey, that "we don't consider the streets downtown safe at night";[145] the

Seagram officials who viewed with a jaundiced eye "the increasing number of prostitutes along Lexington Avenue [which] has made . . . executives reluctant to show off [the area] to visiting businessmen";[146] the Union Carbide executive who noted with dismay the mugging of a Carbide executive as he walked from Pennsylvania Station to the company offices, causing "head injuries serious enough to require hospitalization:"[147] the plant manager of a recreational equipment company who cited as a reason for moving to eastern Pennsylvania that "increasingly his work force was fearful of being victims of crime around the plant."[148]

The odds are admittedly low that any given executive or employee will be subjected to any crime in a given month or year. Odds are perhaps less important in this instance than isolated instances of brutality. What matters in the fears of many is not the probability coefficient associated with a violent crime, but the prospective violence should the crime occur. Indicative of how widespread such apprehensions are were the responses to a *New York Times* survey of top executives of 95 industrial giants with headquarters in the city – about as hardheaded a collection of humanity as the urban community could boast. The leading question was, "What proposals for building the strength of New York City's economy would be most helpful to your company?" In third place behind lower taxes and improved government efficiency was, "Develop new and better ways to reduce crime."[149]

The story of relative living costs is quickly told. With more than 7 million residents packed into a space about one-quarter the size of Rhode Island, the city understandably is noted for its high living costs in general and the high cost of space in particular. Budget studies suggest that the cost of living in New York City compared to other cities is only marginally worse for low-income families – roughly 2 to 8 percent above the all-urban average (see Table 3.14). For middle- and upper-income groups, however, the comparison is far worse, New York living costs outdistancing the average for American cities by 10 to 26 percent. Part of the difference may be explained by the fact that rent control probably benefits low-income groups more than those at higher levels. For all groups taken collectively, New York City in the late 1970s was still the fourth most expensive city in America, behind Boston, Honolulu, and Anchorage, Alaska.[150]

The cost of space, as noted previously, is partially obscured by the presence of rent control. The scarcity of space, however, is everywhere in evidence. In a city built upon an island, it could hardly be otherwise. Few corporations have benefited greatly from rent controls. Much of their space tends to be priced at market value, and that value runs high. Industries have tried to economize on the use of this high-

Table 3.14. *Four-person family budget for New York City area, 1967–78*

Year	Lower living standard		Intermediate living standard		Higher living standard	
	Total	As % of U.S. average[a]	Total	As % of U.S. average[a]	Total	As % of U.S. average[a]
1967	6,021	102	9,977	110	14,868	114
1968	N.A.	N.A.	N.A.	N.A.	N.A.	N.A.
1969	6,682	102	11,247	112	17,101	117
1970	7,183	103	12,134	114	18,545	120
1971	7,578	105	12,585	115	19,238	121
1972	7,841	106	13,179	115	20,165	122
1973	8,661	106	14,448	114	21,999	121
1974	9,852	107	16,648	116	25,470	123
1975	10,266	107	17,498	114	27,071	121
1976	10,835	108	18,866	116	29,677	125
1977	11,155	106	19,972	117	31,655	126
1978	12,063	104	21,587	116	34,252	125

Note: New York City area is defined as the New York City–northeastern New Jersey region.

[a] Average for urban United States.

Source: U.S., Department of Labor, Bureau of Labor Statistics, annual news releases. For a description of how budgets are calculated, see Jean C. Brackett, "New BLS Budgets Provide Yardsticks for Measuring Family Living Costs," *Monthly Labor Review* XCII (April 1969), 3–16.

cost input in a variety of ways. Manufacturing firms are smaller – about half the national average[151] – and often use a vertical working style rather than a horizontal one. Technological progress favoring the horizontal style has created predictable pressures for certain industries to quit the city. Printing now requires more layout space, particularly after the advent of the web offset press. Many facets of the apparel industry now function more efficiently in the typical modern horizontal plant. A study of manufacturing companies that left New York City between 1961 and 1973 found that, on the average, they almost doubled their square footage.[152] Not surprisingly, the scarcity of space is often featured in the explanations of why they left. Some note the high rents of the city; others, the drop in rents achieved by moving; still others, the role of "inadequate space" in prompting their departure. [153]

Again, what of the future? Optimists note with enthusiasm that the Consumer Price Index for New York City has risen more slowly than the U.S. average in the late 1970s (see Table 3.15). This same search for rays of hope has unearthed the changing relative price of office space, with that of the city now more competitive with office rents of other urban centers. The good news unfortunately is not very relevant news. Consumer Price Index comparisons do not adequately portray the relative budget expenses of upper- and middle-income groups. [154] By no stretch of the imagination are prices in the great city about to rise so slowly (or fall so precipitously) that New York will become anything but a high-cost area for high-priced executives. And it is the inability to attract young and rising executives that is a recurring theme in the exodus refrain of various corporations. Nor are other trends in the quality of life likely to improve significantly in the decade ahead. Further deterioration in the city's public services, including sanitation, school, and crime fighting, seems virtually assured by the city's fiscal plight, as precarious as it is unresolved. As for the assertion that city office rents are now more competitive, that statement is rapidly being qualified by rising demand, and even were that not the case, the statement is only partly to the point. A building boom in the late 1960s and early 1970s (see Table 3.16) did create excess office space and slumping rents in the mid-1970s, a trend that now shows signs of reversing. More importantly, office rents have never been a key cost factor in the location decision of most *non*manufacturing firms, especially the kind of service industries and corporate headquarters that dominate the city's economic landscape. This helps to explain why the space problem was totally ignored in a survey that documented the dissatisfactions of top executives of 40 giant corporations headquartered in New York.[155] That indifference contrasts sharply with the ongoing worry of executives of manufacturing firms,

Table 3.15. *Consumer price comparisons: New York City and other urban centers, 1950–78*

Year[a]	(1) U.S. city average[c]	(2) New York City[d]	(3) N.Y. as % of city average ([2] ÷ [1])
	Consumer price index[b]		
	(1935–39 = 100)		
1950	175.6	172.4	98
1951	187.4	183.0	98
1952	190.9	186.0	97
	(1947–49 = 100)		
1953	115.4	113.3	98
1954	114.5	112.6	98
1955	114.9	112.4	98
1956	116.2	113.9	98
1957	120.2	117.6	98
1958	123.5	121.1	98
1959	124.6	122.8	99
	(1957–59 = 100)		
1960	103.1	103.9	101
1961	104.2	104.8	101
1962	105.4	106.4	101
1963	106.7	108.7	102
1964	108.1	110.4	102
1965	109.9	112.2	102
1966	113.1	116.0	103
1967	116.3	119.0	102
1968	121.2	124.1	102
1969	127.7	131.8	103
	(1967 = 100)		
1970	116.3	119.0	102
1971	121.3	125.9	104
1972	125.3	131.4	105
1973	133.1	139.7	105
1974	147.7	154.8	105
1975	161.2	166.6	103
1976	170.5	176.3	103
1977	184.0	187.3	102
1978	199.1	197.7	99

[a] Average for year, except 1950–55 (for October) and 1978–79 (for September).
[b] All items.
[c] Average for 46 cities to 1962, for 50 cities to 1965, for 56 cities thereafter.
[d] New York City to 1962; New York City–northeastern New Jersey area thereafter.
Source: U.S., Department of Labor, Bureau of Labor Statistics, *Monthly Labor Review.*

Table 3.16. *Office completions in Manhattan business district by location, 1947–76*

Year	Number of buildings	Rentable space (thousands of square feet)			
		Total	Midtown	Downtown	Misc. [a]
1947–49	8	1,220	995	—	225
1950–54	38	9,489	8,462	652	375
1955–59	72	23,387	16,706	5,563	1,118
1960–64	64	28,618	22,821	5,470	327
1965	10	3,741	2,245	1,496	—
1966	5	1,195	1,195	—	—
1967	10	5,306	3,636	1,670	—
1968	4	4,980	3,260	1,720	—
1969	15	11,908	8,167	3,741	—
1970	17	8,659	4,242	4,417	—
1971	18	14,869	8,082	6,648	139
1972	11	15,790	11,222	4,568	—
1973	7	5,949	3,398	2,550	—
1974	3	4,215	1,530	2,685	—
1975	5	2,900	1,500	1,400	—
1976	2	520	170	350	—

[a] Includes districts that contain some office buildings, e.g., Greenwich Village, Madison Square, Upper East and West Sides.
Source: Emanuel Tobier, "Manhattan's Central Business District: Key to New York City's Future," *City Almanac* XII (October 1977), 8.

particularly firms in which changing technology is giving the edge to large horizontal structures. For them, the relevant rent comparison is not one among major cities, but one that pits New York City spatial costs against those available in more suburban or even rural settings. By such norms, the costs of space in America's most populous city are sure to remain strikingly unfavorable, because the relative density of that urban center is not likely to be modified substantially. In short, for the many stimuli to exodus buried in the catchall phrase that heads this section – space, crime, and the quality of life – improvement for most appears less likely than further deterioration, and dramatic improvement for any seems well beyond the realm of possibility.

3.11. Mass transit in and around the Big Apple

The same absence of dramatic improvement appears to be the most likely scenario for the city's mass transit system. Congestion has always been a problem, but never more so than in the modern era – spilling into the city streets; backing up into tunnels, throughways, and bridges; slopping down into subways that threaten mayhem every rush hour. All cities of any size, of course, grapple with similar problems. The New York City battle, however, has been peculiar in degree if not in kind. An island with nowhere to expand but up, it has a population density – roughly 40 persons per acre – that no other American city can begin to match. Only five other cities have densities in excess of 20 persons per acre, and the worst of the lot (Jersey City) has, by Big Apple standards, a modest 26 per acre.

The associated mass transit needs are huge. "Monstrous" might be a better word. Five other American cities have a substantial commuter rail service (Boston, Philadelphia, Chicago, Washington, and San Francisco), but none can begin to approach the New York City total transit volume of 3 to 4 million rides per day – a movement of humanity roughly equivalent to the entire population of Chicago, and almost 100 times the total daily passenger traffic of Amtrak.[156] To move this mass of humanity by any other means is unthinkable. To cite but one example, the automobiles required to transport the equivalent of a single trainload of commuters is estimated to require about four acres of parking space, which is eight times the area of the main concourse at Grand Central Terminal.[157]

The city fathers therefore had before them in the postwar years a challenge of the first importance if the economic arteries of the metropolis were to flourish. By and large, they bungled the job. By the 1960s, the evidence was multiplying of a transit system careening toward collapse. Private commuter railways cried out for subsidies, and then justified their pleas by repeated bankruptcies – the Hudson and Manhattan Railroad, the New Haven Railroad, the Long Island Rail Road, to mention only those of crucial importance to New Yorkers. Commuters became increasingly accustomed to cancellations, breakdowns, overcrowding, and long delays. The inner transit system of New York City was in a state that most riders characterized as somewhere between shabby and shocking. Graffiti and grime got worse, so did the perceived risk of crime, cars deteriorated along with services, and the noise level was probably worse than that of any other subway in the world.[158] Something was drastically wrong. But what?

The challenge of mass transit has two aspects: the movement of people and the movement of goods. Neither was to be accomplished in the New York City area with much proficiency. The average speed of a motor vehicle in the central business district is currently about 9 miles per hour. The average speed of a horse-drawn vehicle on city streets in 1907 was 11.5 miles per hour. For business firms, one obvious consequence has been slower and more costly deliveries. Typical of complaints is that of a Manhattan printing firm:

> New York City loft buildings generally have poor loading facilities, and so trucks frequently load or unload from the street or sidewalks. New York City police, para-police and metermaids are creating havoc among our truckers – ticketing and forcefully moving our trucks before they can even make their deliveries or pick up. The cost of traffic tickets alone is becoming a huge overhead factor in our industry. Delays in delivery are even worse, for they are doubling and tripling our delivery costs while creating massive delays in delivery that already are responsible for major job delays and lost customers.[159]

If goods have moved in a sluggish manner, so have the people. That linkage is not inevitable. Mass transit railways could have whisked commuters in and out, while city subways moved the bulk of people underground, with neither flow impinging upon the highways and byways so vital to delivery vehicles. They could have. Instead, the subways have been plagued by breakdowns, delays, and filthy stations. Worse, bands of youths and those with criminal inclinations now add a perilous aspect that, in the imagination of most commuters, overshadows the merely distasteful features of a prospective journey, particularly a journey after dark. The rail linkages, although relatively safe, have become notorious for delays and inefficiencies. The Long Island Rail Road, the nation's largest and busiest commuter line, has justifiably earned the nickname of the Long Island Snail Road. (When the American Gas Association announced plans to move its headquarters out of New York City, one executive snorted, "If I needed any push it was that [expletive deleted] Long Island Rail Road.")[160] Other rail links to the city have a track record that varies from fair to miserable.[161] But why this abysmal record of inefficiency and neglect in a sector so vital to economic health and quality of life in the great city?

From the economist's vantage point, mass transit is a venture usually deserving of a subsidy. The better the transit system, the greater the number of riders. Increased usage of the transit system lowers surface traffic congestion, thereby fostering speedier and less costly deliveries. The downtown business community should benefit from higher sales. Property owners in the inner city should benefit from higher property

values. The fiscal problem is that the transit authority which creates
these benefits cannot charge businessmen and property owners for
benefits created. (In the economist's jargon, these are "externalities":
benefits from a decision – in this case, to improve the mass transit
system – that accrue to others, but that cannot be captured by those
who make the decision.) The solution has two parts: (1) keep fares
down and run the transit system at a deficit, and (2) cover the deficit by
a tax on those who benefit, with the tax of course not to exceed the
monetary value of the benefits in question.[162] In short, the economist
would usually have the politician subsidize the development and
maintenance of any mass transit system.

This the New York politicians did, but never adequately. The key
financial problems of New York City's mass transit are easy to summarize and difficult to solve. Operating expenses have risen, fares have
failed to keep pace, government subsidies have also lagged, and the
resulting shortage of funds is largely responsible for inadequate
maintenance and the failure to upgrade the capital stock. The problem
of controlling costs has been complicated in many cases by sloppy
management, poor worker productivity, and intransigent unions.[163]
More recently, inflation has fueled the tendencies of costs to rise. Between 1966 and 1976, for example, operating costs of the New York
transit system tripled.

The politicians were only too willing to restrain the rise in city
transit fares, thereby intensifying the need for subsidies. Fare increases have high political visibility, and the fear was ever present that
commuter indignation over a price increase could lead to negative
results at the ballot box. But the politicians were also consistently
unwilling to provide sufficient subsidies to prevent the deterioration of
the mass transit system. Part of the reason during the early postwar
years was the widely held belief that the private automobile was the
commuting device of the future, with mass transit relegated to a distant second. Part of the problem was that when those perceptions
clashed head on with the mounting traffic chaos of New York City in
the 1960s, a new willingness to subsidize was repeatedly thwarted by
a scarcity of revenues. The city by then already had a budget
hopelessly overstretched. The economics of deterioration also favored
the politics of underfunding. The very gradualness of the wearing-out
process of transit facilities – cars and tracks and stations – meant that
politicians who did little were unlikely to be penalized severely at the
ballot box. Mass transit was therefore a natural to receive too little and
too late.

Exacerbating all these difficulties was the persistent decline in ridership (see Figure 3.2). One formidable influence making for decline

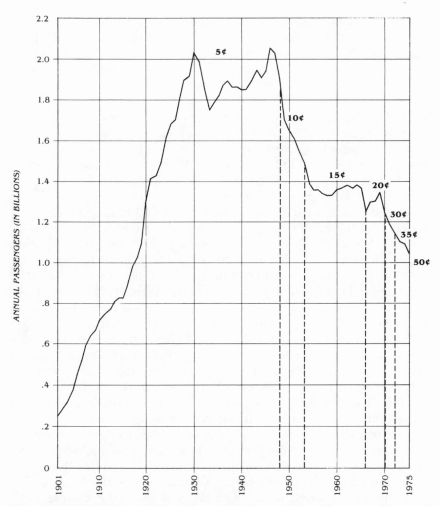

Figure 3.2. New York City Transit Authority: annual rapid transit rides (and subway fares), 1901–75. *Source:* Regional Plan Association, "The State of the Region, 1977," *Regional Plan News,* no. 101 (November 1977), p. 24.

was the growing popularity of the automobile, a trend that the government persistently encouraged through its subsidies to road construction. Rising fares also tended to discourage would-be users. More recently, ridership has suffered because of falling employment in the city, particularly in Manhattan.[164] Last but hardly least, the New York transit system, as noted, had acquired an unenviable reputation for filth and graffiti; for crime, especially in the evening hours; for noisy cars and deteriorating services. The result was a vicious circle. Ridership declined because of deterioration in mass transit services. Operating expenses did not fall proportionately as ridership declined. Revenues were therefore squeezed. One tempting response was to let services deteriorate even further. This did not augur well for a system whose services were already described even by cautious academics as "woefully inadequate."[165] The only way to break out of such a vicious circle is through a massive injection of funds. But from where?

In the 1960s and '70s, New Yorkers attacked the problem of inadequate funding mainly in two ways. One involved more state participation. The other attempted to divert surplus funds generated by certain city transit facilities – notably the tolls on bridges and tunnels – to offset the deficits generated by subways and commuter trains. The increased role of the state was heralded by a $2.5 billion bond authorization in 1967 for the purpose of improving highways and public transit. (The highway funds went quickly. The mass transit dollars appear to have been doled out more gradually.) The first major reorganization of the transit system was initiated in 1965 with the creation of the Metropolitan Commuter Transportation Authority, primarily to acquire the financially sagging Long Island Rail Road. This authority in turn was absorbed in 1968 into the newly created Metropolitan Transportation Authority (MTA), a sprawling behemoth that controlled subways, railways, bus systems, and airports that operated in and around New York City (see Figure 3.3). One key old authority absorbed into this new super-authority was the Triborough Bridge and Tunnel Authority. Charging toll fees well above its costs, the Triborough Authority had long been famous, if not notorious, for generating surplus funds. Now these could be used to ease the deficits of other elements in the mass transit system. The key old authority not included in this reorganization was the Port Authority of New York and New Jersey. Its exclusion was, on the face of it, surprising. Like the Triborough Bridge and Tunnel Authority, it had long charged prices for the use of its facilities well above costs, and thereby generated huge surpluses. Not only could the Port Authority have helped, but it should have helped: Its charter made the improvement of mass transit an appropriate target for those surplus funds. And yet this authority had repeatedly shied away from assisting in such improvements. Why? The answer can hardly be found in the politics of the legislative process. The Port Authority, as an authority, was relatively immune from those politics. That immunity, curiously enough, was the central problem. Port Authority policy for much of the postwar era was firmly in the grip of its executive director, Austin Tobin, who consistently opposed the cause of mass transit in the city – this despite the crying need, and despite

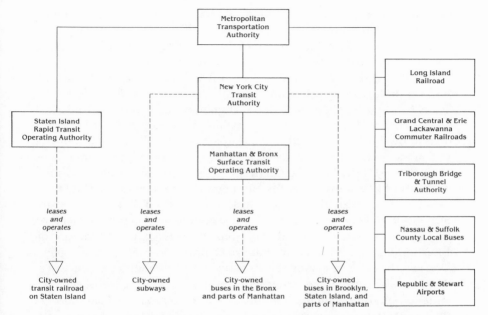

Figure 3.3. Organization of public transit in the New York City area. *Source:* Edward S. Seeley, Jr., "The Financial Outlook for the New York City Transit Authority," *City Almanac* XIV (June 1979), 9.

the fact that, as a public authority, the Port Authority was ostensively designed to serve the public, and not Austin Tobin. How this absurdity came to pass will be explored in more detail in Chapter 6.[166]

These, then, were the main state and local efforts to combat the underfunding of New York City's transit system: more state subsidies and an organizational restructuring to enable certain surpluses from bridge and tunnel tolls to be diverted to deficit sectors such as subways and commuter railroads.

It was not enough. Not nearly enough. The surpluses of the Triborough Bridge and Tunnel Authority were on the order of $50 to 60 million, while annual deficits for the entire transit system ran to hundreds of millions. State voters were infrequently asked to authorize more state borrowing to aid mass transit, and almost as frequently said no. The federal government tried to help in a modest way. Beginning in 1964 it provided some support for capital improvements, but nothing like the massive injections needed to upgrade and overhaul an entire system suffering from decades of neglect. Congress resisted aid formulas that would have given to New York City an exceptionally large share of the funds available. New Yorkers grumbled that their share was exceptionally small. (The Transit Authority, for example, carries some 40 percent of the nation's riders while receiving only about 17 percent of federal operating subsidies).[167]

The best indicator of repeated underfunding in the 1970s was the limited progress made in improving the system. The New York City Transit Authority, the heart of the system, has been repeatedly accused of "a shocking decline in maintenance" that included nothing less than allowing cars "literally to fall apart."[168] The Transit Authority's various schemes for subway expansion and car improvement have come to very little. What began in the early 1970s as a promise to build 40 miles of new subway routes had been whittled down by 1980 to 15 miles or less, with the major construction project – the Sixty-third Street line to Queens – years behind schedule and more than twice as expensive as once estimated. The plan to install air conditioning on Interborough Rapid Transit trains has progressed at a snail's pace. Delivery of modern cars is running far behind schedule, and many of those received have had major flaws in design. Even if all of the construction plans now on the drawing board were put in place tomorrow, the associated changes would be unlikely to alter New Yorkers' perceptions of an unsafe, unclean, and uncomfortable transit system.

The future does not appear to offer much chance for remedying these deficiencies in any major way. The MTA, using cost estimates that are undoubtedly too conservative, has forecast rising deficits in the years immediately ahead.[169] The central problems are variations on the same old theme. Expenses are forecast to rise rapidly while revenues are expected to lag behind. Labor costs, a large element in total expenses, are sure to increase as powerful unions demand more and labor productivity remains notoriously poor. Revenue increases can come from three sources: higher fares, more riders, or larger subsidies. Fares were raised in 1980, but despite that increase, the MTA was still forecasting a huge deficit in 1981, a deficit that could get even larger if higher fares discourage some riders. Total passenger traffic may benefit from rising gasoline prices that should force more automobile riders to consider the mass transit alternative. Offsetting this tendency for growth, however, will be all of the factors that have made for declining ridership in the past, particularly deteriorating services and population exodus from, and job reductions in, the Manhattan area. The remaining possibility for closing the deficit gap is a government subsidy. The city can do little with its precarious fiscal position. The state, as noted in Section 3.6, also has limited room for fiscal maneuvering as it grapples with rising expenditures and the need to cut taxes. Its most recent effort to provide roughly $200 million to the MTA by taxing the gross receipts of oil companies is unlikely to survive a court challenge.[170] Even if the tax does survive, the associated revenues will make only a modest contribution to an overwhelming need. Assistance from the federal government has been increasing, but the added dollars seem unlikely to be sufficient to close the MTA deficits of the future without a radical revamping of Washington policy.[171]

If MTA deficits cannot be covered by some combination of higher fares, more riders, and larger subsidies, the inescapable implication for the future is the same as it has been in the past: further cuts in services and further cuts in maintenance. Worse, closing the deficit gap of the MTA is ultimately a secondary goal. The major requirement is not to find a few hundred million dollars a year to cover an excess in operating expenditures. The major requirement in the 1980s is the same as it was in the 1970s, or the 1960s, or the 1950s: to provide a massive injection of dollars to overhaul and upgrade a system that has been allowed to deteriorate for decades. Where are such riches to be found? Mayor Koch was quick to volunteer the answer. "That's a decision for the Congress and the President."[172] The Mayor had a point. Given the mountainous subsidies needed and the clear inability of city or state to come up with the dollars, the only possibility is the federal government. Officially estimated in the mid-1970s at *$50 billion*,[173] the requisite funds far exceed the capabilities of a city on the verge of bankruptcy and a state combating pervasive economic retardation.[174]

New Yorkers therefore confront yet another problem that borders on the intractable. Economic arguments concerning the external benefits generated by a transit system can always be marshaled in favor of subsidizing the city's transit system. The striking feature of the ongoing New York transit problem has been the inadequacy of the political response to meet obvious needs. In the early postwar era, when city and state governments might have generated adequate subsidies, they did not. The resulting decades of neglect produced a severely deteriorated system just when improvements were desperately needed. To combat accelerating retardation in the 1970s, particularly in the inner city, a massive overhauling of the transit system had much to recommend it. But fiscal excesses of the past, and fiscal pressures generated by accelerating retardation in the 1970s, made both the state and the local government – separately or in concert – totally incapable of meeting that challenge. And it is far from clear that Washington will be willing to clean up the mess created by decades of neglect at the state and local level.

3.12. Government policies: why so little and so late?

The foregoing has sketched a tension that, in some senses, is remarkable – a tension between the growing need to counteract the faltering tendencies of the economy and the absence of any coherent and determined effort by politicians to meet that need. Indeed, many government policies made a difficult situation worse. In short, government was more a part of the problem than a part of the solution. Why?

Problems of retardation were slow to be addressed, in part because they were difficult to detect in earlier stages. Cyclical booms kept obscuring secular slowdown. The turning point for the state, as noted, seems to have been centered in the 1920s and 1930s. In the early 1940s, the winds of war swept down upon a nation largely unsuspecting and unprepared, and in the process pushed productive capacity to the limit while inhibiting the interregional migration of industry. In the immediate postwar era, the general consensus seemed to be that little of consequence had changed in the economic structure of the entire Northeast. The region was now simply an updated version of its old superior, bustling self. Even the manufacturing sector, already sluggish and destined for rapid deterioration, was given a clean bill of health by most observers. A Resources for the Future study commissioned in the late 1950s, for example, concluded that "the most striking feature in the history of American manufacturing is the enduring strength of the Northeast . . . Even today the great industrial belt of the Northeast continues to dominate the regional structure of American manufactures much as it did at the beginning of this century."[175]

New York City and State were also given a clean bill of health. In the year (1960) in which the economic muscle of the Northeast was being lauded for its continued "domination" of the nation, Raymond Vernon published *Metropolis 1985: An Interpretation of the Findings of the New York Metropolitan Region Study.*[176] The findings were largely optimistic, as were Vernon's forecasts to 1985. As late as the mid-1960s – a full decade after manufacturing employment had begun to decline absolutely in the state – that refrain was substantially unchanged. In January of 1965, for example, Mayor Wagner told a gathering of bankers that "New York City is in more vigorous, dynamic and robust condition, both economically and socially, than any other great metropolis in this country or in the world."[177]

This view was almost immediately reinforced by events well beyond the borders of the city. Once again cyclical boom obscured secular trends.[178] Once again wartime demands were at the center of that boom, but this time the conflict was not global, but instead confined to an obscure corner of Southeast Asia whose very name, Vietnam, was heretofore little known to any save stamp collectors and State Department officials. The timing was ideally suited to obscure the gathering forces of secular retardation. For present-day analysts who disparage the myopia of that era, confident that their hindsight now would have been foresight then, it is instructive to browse through a 1970 publication entitled "Area Indexes of Business Activity: New York State, 1957–1969."[179] The trend in almost every single measure of economic activity for every region in the state, when graphed, appears to be upward, even reassuringly upward. For those who cared to check – and almost no one did – the Vernon forecasts for *Metropolis 1985* also appeared to be pretty well on track as of 1969.[180] State officials did check, and emerged with buoyant optimism:

> New York State's economy in the seventies will reach record levels, spurred on by the coming of age of the postwar generation, rising incomes and the continuing emergence of new growth industries. The state's economy, undoubtedly the most advanced, complex and mature economy in the nation (and possibly the world) will continue to set the pace for the nation.[181]

By the late 1960s, however, it was *not* setting the pace for the nation. It had not done so for decades.

Even after retardation had been thrust to center stage by events of the early 1970s, many were slow to diagnose the long-run nature of the difficulties. The present downturn was a momentary phenomenon, they reasoned, brought on by a national recession. As a national downturn had caused the problem, so a national upturn would solve it. Governor Rockefeller's Council of Economic Advisors, for example, observed in 1972 that "the current economic problems of the State are traceable in large part to recession in the national economy. The recession will not last forever, and State conditions will improve as the national economy picks up momentum."[182] As something of an ominous afterthought, they did note "the possibility that the temporary slump . . . may have masked more basic structural changes in the economy of New York State."[183] The point was well taken, but the logic was upside down. What had masked the structural changes was the previous boom. The present slump would reveal them for what they were: serious, pervasive, and with a history spanning decades.

New Yorkers were slow to address their problems, not only because they were difficult to detect, but because their self-confidence and optimism dulled their ability to assess the gravity correctly once the problems were detected. The people who brandished such labels as the Big Apple and the Empire State were not likely to be receptive to the notion that their colossus of the Northeast was now in a state of secular decline. It was therefore not surprising that throughout the gathering storm, and indeed well into some of the early downpours, the more determined optimists (often politicians and bureaucrats) continued to accentuate the positive while ignoring the negative. Their praise for the state had a way of quickly narrowing to praise for that single city whose economic might was so central to the state's success. In New York City's achievements, past and present, there was much that was impressive, and not a little that was awesome. A few examples:

1. The city is the undisputed leader among American urban centers in total production and total population.
2. It is a transportation focal point, with air terminals, rail terminals, bus and truck terminals, and the busiest harbor in the United States.
3. The city has the largest concentration of major corporate headquarters in America, more than three times as many as its nearest urban competitor.
4. Headquartered in the city are six of the "big eight" accounting firms that audit most of the giant corporations of the country.
5. The city has one-third of all large law firms in America, more than double the number of its nearest urban rival, and nearly as many as the next three cities combined.
6. In addition to a concentration of accounting and legal services, the city has a heavy concentration of marketing, management, and other business consulting services, whose receipts are two-and-a-half times those of second-ranked Chicago.
7. New York is the undisputed financial capital of America. It can claim 6 of the 10 largest commercial banks in the country, which collectively hold almost two-thirds of the deposits of those 10 largest banks, and better than a quarter of the deposits of the 200 largest banks. It dominates the transactions in securities and commodities with its many exchanges: the New York Stock Exchange, American Stock Exchange, International Commercial Exchange, New York Cocoa Exchange, New York Coffee and Sugar Exchange, and New York Cotton Exchange.
8. The city has a leading position in international business and trade, with more than half of the headquarters of all foreign corporations operating in America, over one-third

of all international law firms, and better than twice the annual U.S. customs collections of its nearest rival, Los Angeles.

9. As a cultural and entertainment center, the city is unrivaled in America, with more than 60 museums, 50 institutions for the performing arts, 36 Broadway theaters, and some 500 other theaters.

The business community has long recognized the advantages of proximity to this extraordinary concentration of enterprise, talent, and services. A 1976 survey of executives of New York's giant corporations, for example, asked them to explain why their companies were located in the city.[184] The responses emphasized the easy access to business leaders, the financial community, worldwide travel connections, a huge labor pool, an extensive market, and a range of business services, including legal, accounting, and advertising.

And yet this understates the case. The great metropolis to many executives is more than a collection of services and institutions. For them it has a special magnetism difficult to put into words. Occasionally business leaders try:

Edgar F. Bronfman, president of Distillers Corporation–Seagram Limited: "There's an electricity about New York, the beat, the pace, the pulse. It's eyeball to eyeball and that's what it's all about."[185]

F. Ross Johnson, president of Standard Brands: "The place for a company serving the world market is at the center, and the center today is New York City."[186]

Jack Cunningham, president of Gourmet Poultry Specialties: "Look, I'm a New Yorker, I want to stay here. I mean, how could I move to Maryland and root for Baltimore? My team is the Yankees."[187]

Michael Burke, president of the Yankees: "I've often said that I'd rather be a lamppost in New York than a millionaire in any other city."[188]

Irving L. Rousso, executive vice president of Russ Togs, Inc.: "New York, after all, is still the hub."[189]

Hub the city may have been throughout the postwar era, but it was a deteriorating hub. Accentuating the positive by itself seldom does much to eliminate the negative. A patient suffering from tuberculosis derives few medical benefits from compliments on his superb eyesight. The metaphor of illness is instructive. Optimism can be destructive insofar as it encourages indifference to problems of growing severity. Throughout the 1960s and 1970s, the propensities of New York enthusiasts to stress the satisfactory elements in the economy of the city and the state were somewhat misguided, insofar as they diverted attention from the severity of the economic ailments and the urgency of finding a cure, or at the very least arresting the spread of the infection.

The difficulty in detecting problems and an optimism that favored glossing over those detected are only part of the explanation why so little was done by politicians to combat retardation in its early or more advanced stages. The issue here is not just the sins of omission – not just the failure to evolve long-run strategies for combating a long-run problem. Many government policies made economic retardation worse. The repeated escalation of taxes, the tightening of environmental restrictions, the underfunding of mass transit in New York City, the souring of New York's business climate by intransigent bureaucrats and unsympathetic politicians – these are but highlights from a long list. Collectively, they suggest a disturbing hypothesis.

Why did New York's retardation, long in the making, accelerate sharply in the 1970s? One is struck by the coincidence of timing. Most of the policies and problems discussed in previous sections either were centered in the 1960s or early 1970s or became much more pronounced in those years. One is also struck by the apparent vagueness of the businessmen's decisions to relocate. Was the key development of the 1970s that location and relocation decision making was suddenly shifted because so many businessmen had been pushed across an ill-defined threshold roughly labeled "being fed up" – not with any single factor, but with a vast array that ranged from higher taxes to declining public services, from more costly energy to more stringent environmental regulations, from intransigent labor to unresponsive politicians? Recall the statement quoted earlier by the president of a New York consulting firm specializing in company relocation: that his clients' decisions to relocate resulted "from a desire to escape a negative situation." Was New York's central problem in the 1970s that it had become "a negative situation" in the minds of too many businessmen, both those within the state who heretofore had not considered getting out and those outside the state to whom the task had fallen of deciding where to locate a branch or firm? The suspicion – and it can never be more than that – is that in those imaginations the image of New York turned sharply negative over a narrow span of years, and for reasons often closely linked to what the politicians had done, and what they had failed to do.

Notice what the argument is not. New York's retardation was long in the making, and for reasons primarily beyond the politicians' ability to control. The puzzle here is why that retardation accelerated in the 1970s, and how much of that acceleration can be attributed to political acts. Notice further that nothing in this chapter suggests that increased tax dollars failed to buy benefits for some one, or that increased environmental restrictions were inadvisable. The question is one of priorities. The challenge for politicians is to reconcile conflicting priorities. The goal of fighting economic retardation in many cases clashed with other spending plans or regulations favored by those in power. The issue is not why fighting retardation lost out in these clashes, but why it was almost totally ignored. Did ignoring that priority reflect the wishes of the people, channeled through their elected representatives? Or were most of the important decisions little related to the long-run needs of the populace, and more closely related to the short-run ambitions of those who made the decisions? If the answer to the latter question is yes, the slighting of economic retardation as a serious priority ceases to be a puzzle. Economic growth is a long-run goal. Politicians traditionally favor short-run, highly visible achievements to enhance their records. As a collective group, they were therefore singularly ill suited to be the guardians of New York's economic fate in the postwar era, unless their own self-interest was supplanted by higher goals. But was it? These will be the controlling issues for the remainder of this book.

4

Fiscal structure and fiscal problems

4.1. The puzzle in outline

On a grey morning in the late spring of 1976 two graphs were scrutinized with dismay (Figures 4.1 and 4.2). They had just been plotted. As much as any single factor, that scrutiny – and that dismay – led to the writing of this book. The project of plotting them seemed routine enough. All they portrayed were the total expenditure and debt of New York State since 1946. The conclusions of the previous chapter were already known. That spending and debt should be on the rise was hardly news. The fantastic explosions apparent from the graphs, however, were totally unexpected. The economic might of the state had been weakening since the interwar period. Through the decades of growing retardation, expenditures and indebtedness had not grown cautiously (or even retrenched), but rather had skyrocketed. In their wake came a bombardment of tax increases the likes of which the state had never seen before (see Table 3.12). It was as if a patient progressively weakened by advancing years were now being subjected to ever more vigorous body blows. As economic therapy goes, it was hardly the route to revitalized health.

Something must have gone awry in the political economy of the state. At the very least, something was downright curious. How could New York have plunged simultaneously into prolonged retardation and a spending spree the likes of which the state had never seen before? How could such fiscal actions make economic sense? And if they did not make economic sense, what was their rationale? Finally – and disturbingly – what dangers lay ahead if economic retardation continued unabated while expenditures and debt rushed pell-mell for the upper stratosphere?

4.2. The puzzle in detail

The story begins with the two graphs noted: Figures 4.1 and 4.2. Expenditures, of course, are the heart of the story. The fate of this item

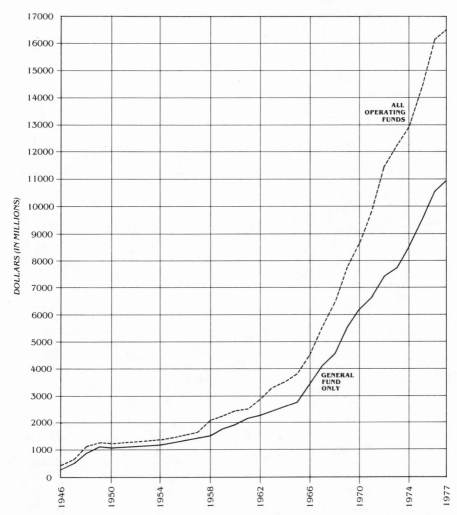

Figure 4.1. New York State expenditures, 1946–77. *Source:* See Table C.12, Appendix C.

tends to exert a controlling influence on the rest of state finance for the simplest of reasons: If more dollars are to be spent, they must be rounded up from somewhere, by increasing taxes or by more borrowing or by some combination of the two.[1] Small wonder, then, that the explosion in spending was accompanied by similar explosions in tax increases and total debt outstanding.

This image of explosion, however, will not quite do, at least not as the numbers appear in Figure 4.1. Two rather tedious corrections are

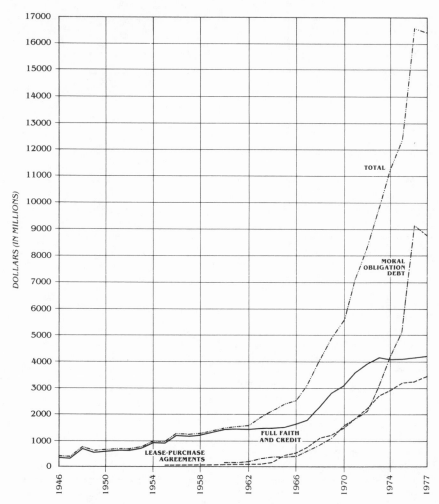

Figure 4.2. New York State total debt and debtlike commitments, 1946–77.
Source: See Table C.13, Appendix C.

unavoidable. The first is to correct for inflation. If state spending
should double while the price level also doubles, then "real" (or constant dollar) state spending will not have risen at all. The expenditure
data of Figure 4.1 must therefore be deflated by a price index to correct for this phenomenon. Second, under which governor did spending
increase the most? The question seems absurd. The answer is as obvious as it is well known: under Nelson Aldrich Rockefeller. But is it
really all that obvious? Harriman was governor for four years; Wilson,
for one year; Rockefeller, for fifteen. Which one accelerated spending

Table 4.1. *New York State spending under five governors: average annual growth rates, 1946–77*

Governor	General Fund only		All Operating Funds	
	Current $	Constant $	Current $	Constant $
Dewey (1946–55)	14.1	5.8	14.6	6.3
Harriman (1955–59)	9.2	4.9	10.4	6.0
Rockefeller (1959–74)	10.9	5.0	12.6	6.6
Wilson (1974–75)	12.3	5.2	10.8	3.7
Carey (1975–77)	7.2	−0.8	11.8[a]	3.2[a]
Average, 1946–77	11.4	4.8	12.8[a]	6.2[a]

Note: Dates shown are for fiscal years ending March 31.
[a] Excludes 1977.
Source: New York (State), Office of the Comptroller, *Annual Reports;* Table C. 16, Appendix C. All nominal data deflated by price index for state and local governments. See Appendix A.3.

the most? The answer can only be found by converting the deflated (or constant dollar) spending totals into an average annual growth rate for each of five governors. The results appear in Table 4.1. They are totally unexpected. If one focuses upon spending from the General Fund only (that is, spending totals as reported in the Executive Budget), Rockefeller's annual growth rate places second behind Dewey's and barely ahead of Harriman's. If instead one used the more comprehensive spending totals reported under All Operating Funds,[2] the picture is not radically revised. The annual growth rate under Rockefeller does exceed that of both Dewey and Harriman, but only by a narrow margin.

This would seem to make no sense at all. How can one reconcile the image of explosion in Figure 4.1 with the assertion that, on the average, total state spending increased under Rockefeller at about the same rate as under his two predecessors? The answer is that any numerical series which grows at a constant rate, when plotted on arithmetic scale, will appear to explode. This has sobering implications for those who would stigmatize John D. Rockefeller's grandson Nelson as a profligate spender. He did not, it seems, revamp New York State government spending. He merely carried forward a tradition of rising (real) annual expenditure of about 6 percent per annum. That conclusion, however, is also wrong.

Surely, the reader must protest, the numbers do not lie. But they do, and for two quite different reasons.

4.3. The defects in the numbers

The numbers in question are the annual spending totals for the state. One of the "distortions" – to use a softer word than "lies," which most accountants would endorse – is comparatively minor. The other is nothing short of a grotesque distortion of the fiscal truth.

State expenditure data have been continually distorted in a minor way by a range of fiscal gimmicks with a single objective: to shunt expenditures and revenues out of the actual year in which they occurred and into some other fiscal year. For example, the cash-basis accounting system[3] used by the state permits certain kinds of expenditure commitments made this year to appear as dollars actually spent next year. Similarly, what appears as a short-term loan called a "first instance appropriation" is often not a loan at all, but an outright gift (or a loan never to be collected, which comes to the same thing).[4] The associated spending at the outset is not entered under expenditure at all, but rather under loans, only to reappear as expenditure when the loan is written off as uncollectible, often many years after the original transaction.

The inescapable implication is that *all* expenditure data as reported annually by the state comptroller are nothing more than first approximations to the truth. As approximations go, however, they seem at first glance not to be hopelessly at variance with the facts. Manipulations of the sort just described do cause reported spending totals to be off by as much as 5 or 6 percent. Thus, Republican critics complain about "what the (Democratic) governor gets away with," but the sin in question is simply an announced spending total of $12.7 billion, when the "true" total is "closer to $13.5 billion," if items funneled into off-budget funds are added in.[5] The implied gap of $800 million, while not trivial, is hardly of the chasm variety.

Except there is a chasm. It is not the result of shuffling expenditure items between fiscal years. It is the result of making expenditure items totally disappear. The dominant motivation for this disappearance is to subvert two constitutional principles of the state: legislative control over money matters and voter approval of any proposed increase in state debt. This is the primary reason why the numerical conclusion ventured in the preceding section is dead wrong: that Nelson Rockefeller did not revamp New York State government spending, but merely carried forward a tradition of rising (real) annual expenditure of about 6 percent per year. He did considerably more than that. Perhaps his greatest coup was to wrench a large portion of expenditure out of the Executive Budget – and therefore away from regular legislative review – and place it in the hands of a peculiar institution called a public authority: the Hydra of New York's fiscal history – alarming, largely overlooked, and growing.

4.4. Public authorities: the institution that obscures

Public benefit corporations, more commonly called public authorities, will be discussed more fully in Chapter 6. At this juncture, only four points need to be emphasized. Public authorities in New York State are huge. They are growing rapidly. They are relatively independent. And in that independence can be found the key to their astonishing growth in the past two decades.

First, the matter of size. Through the coffers of several hundred statewide public authorities pass gross receipts that amount to several billion dollars annually. (In 1977, they totaled \$2.4 billion.)[6] Their combined debt now exceeds the total debt of the state itself by a factor of roughly four. A single public authority, the Housing Finance Agency, has a total debt outstanding that exceeds the debt of New York by almost 50 percent.[7] Another authority, the Municipal Assistance Corporation, has even more debt outstanding then the Housing Finance Agency, and is presently marching toward a debt ceiling of \$10.0 billion[8] – a magnitude that few states in the union have ever contemplated, never mind approximated, in their fiscal operations.

Second, the matter of growth. The origin of the public authority in New York dates from the 1920s, but the era of phenomenal expansion has largely coincided with the Rockefeller era. In 1962, Rockefeller's fourth year as governor, there were 125 public authorities in the Empire State, 26 of them statewide authorities, with a combined debt of \$3.3 billion. By his last year in office (1973), there were over 230, 41 of them statewide, with a combined debt that had quadrupled to \$13.3 billion.

Third, the matter of independence. All public authorities are created by the legislature, and as such, are ultimately subject to the control of the elected representatives of the people – at least in theory. In practice, these institutions have two critical areas of independence. One concerns daily operation. Once they have been established by the legislature, their functioning is seldom or never closely scrutinized by the legislature. Policy is dictated by top management, who usually are appointed by the governor. As such, they may be responsive to the will of the chief executive (and in Rockefeller's regime, they usually were). Their fiscal operations, however, are seldom a subject of legislative scrutiny, or even legislative approval, with two notable exceptions.

Frequently (but not always) the legislature specifies a debt ceiling for the public authority. Not infrequently, authorities with such ceilings petition the legislature to raise them. With or without a debt ceiling, many petition for what amounts to loans or gifts from the state (especially first instance appropriations). Seldom if ever do these petitions provide the occasion for any semblance of a thorough legislative review. Daily operations have therefore remained by and large outside the purview of the elected representatives of the people, partly because of information withheld, and partly because of the legislators' considerable indifference to being informed.

The second crucial aspect of independence for public authorities is their exemption from certain constitutional provisions governing the state's fiscal processes. All debt increases of the state proposed by the legislature must be approved by the voters in a referendum. No debt increase of any public authority requires such approval. The temptation – in Rockefeller's years, the overwhelming temptation – was to circumvent the need for voter approval of state debt by shunting capital projects into the arms of public authorities. The latter could then borrow the money, proceed with the project, and ignore the public's views on the matter. In short, at the heart of the recent ballooning of these public corporations was a motivation that was undemocratic in spirit and undemocratic in effect. What became relegated to insignificance in the creation of billions upon billions of debt was that which the Constitution had deliberately inserted into the state's debt-creation process: the will of the people as expressed in a statewide referendum.

If this was the strategy, what were the tactical devices that made it all possible?

Broadly speaking, there were two: moral obligation bonds and lease-purchase agreements. The first amounts to a moral (but not a legal) guarantee given by the state to back the bonds issued by a public authority. With such a guarantee in hand, the authority can borrow more money, and at cheaper rates. The second is a variant of a commercial lease-purchase agreement. In the case of a building, for example, the public authority borrows the funds, erects the building, and leases it to the state. The rental payments are set at a level sufficiently high to pay the principal and interest on the bonds initially sold to raise the construction money. When the bonds have been retired, title to the building will pass from the authority to the state.

Both of these gimmicks are described in more detail in Chapters 6 and 7. What matters here are the threats that they bring to the New York citizenry. Two in particular are worrisome. One fairly springs from the page. The Constitution intended for the voters of New York to have a say in all debt expansion precisely because the state's past history illustrated – viciously – the capacity of politicians to overissue debt if not constrained.[9] That intention has been undermined not in a small way, but in a staggering way. Second, the undermining now encompasses a debt escalation that could – repeat, could – imperil the fiscal fabric of the state itself. To the extent that public authorities issue debt in anticipation of future receipts that are sure to pour in – for example, borrowing to build a bridge that will subsequently be paid for by tolls – to that extent the state is risking little by offering its own "moral" guarantee to back up such debt. But should the debt be huge, and the funds not roll in, what then? The state would have thrust upon it two unpleasant options. It could honor its moral guarantee, and attempt to round up the needed dollars by extensive borrowing. But that borrowing could be so large in total, and the merits of bailing out the penniless public authority so suspect in the eyes of the financial community, that the state's own ability to borrow could be imperiled. Alternatively, the state might renege on its moral guarantee. In that case, however, the investment community (holding billions in public authority debt carrying a similar guarantee) might panic, and that panic could also imperil the state's access to financial markets: access without which the state could not long survive given its ongoing credit needs. But surely, the reader must be saying, such a scenario is nothing more than the calamitous flight of the academician's fancy. Surely the politicians would never risk such a fate.

They would, and they have. The suspect public authority is the Municipal Assistance Corporation, or MAC. In the late spring of 1975, when New York City was denied further access to financial markets, MAC took over the task of borrowing the funds needed by the city. There are, broadly speaking, four troubling aspects. First, the city's need for more borrowed funds has been voracious, primarily because it has shown no sign of bringing a deficit budget into balance. (MAC's outstanding debt has risen from $3.8 billion in 1976 to $6.2 billion in 1980, apparently en route to its present debt ceiling of $10.0 billion.)[10] Second, all of that debt carries the moral obligation backing of the state. Third, federal support has been crucial to preventing the city from going bankrupt. Fourth, this federal support is, at present, due to be withdrawn in the early 1980s. No fiscal wizardry is needed to see the menace. If the city does not balance its budget, MAC must continually borrow more. If the federal government at some point refuses to be a party to this debt escalation, can the state alone shore up what is, at bottom, a gargantuan and ongoing deficit enterprise? And if it cannot, what then?

Not a pleasant topic, and one that almost all of the parties most likely to be affected are scrupulously avoiding. Contingency planning for fiscal Armageddon has seldom been a passion of politicians. The details whereby the folly of city and state politicians led to the creation of MAC will be the topic of Chapter 8. The future of that creation, of the city, and of the state will be the topics of Chapter 9. At this juncture a final word would seem required about the road behind and the road immediately ahead.

4.5. The central problem reexamined

This chapter began with three surprising revelations. The first two were the explosions in expenditure and debt in the postwar years – this despite the secular retardation of the state's economy dating from the interwar period. The third was that the rate of growth of spending under Rockefeller was not appreciably different from the growth rates under his two predecessors, Dewey and Harriman. Rockefeller was not such a big spender after all, or so the implication seemed to be. This inference was tempered in a minor way by the realization that the state's bookkeeping practices tend to obscure the true totals for spending in any given year, or at least the totals that would be recorded by conventional accounting practices. The same inference was tempered in a major way – indeed, utterly destroyed – by the realization that a lot of state-related activity was not included in the reported totals of state spending. It is time to attempt to remedy this oversight.

Corrective action cannot come by the obvious route: adding public authority spending to reported state spending to get a better estimate of the dollar flows that annually go into state-related activity. An annual spending total for public authorities (corrected for state transfers) is impossible to construct. The alternative is to focus upon debt. Here the data are available, and the story is overwhelming.

First, the matter of annual growth rates under the different governors. To the regular debt of the state (called "full faith and credit" debt) must now be added all debtlike commitments of the state (lease-purchase agreements and moral obligation-backed authority debt). These appear in Table 4.2. Debt escalation under Rockefeller far outstripped that under his two predecessors.[11] The staggeringly large growth rate under Carey reflects the creation of the Municipal Assistance Corporation, and its spewing forth of billions in moral obligation debt in its first year of operation.

The second issue concerns the absolute level to which indebtedness soared under Rockefeller, with public authority debt now added to the picture. By 1976, the bicentennial year of the republic, New York State had reached indebtedness levels not merely without precedent in its own history, but quite unmatched by any other state in the union. (See

Table 4.2. *New York State tax revenues and debt under five governors:*
average annual growth rates, 1946–77

	Tax revenues		Debt[a]	
Governor	Nominal (%)	Real (%)	Nominal (%)	Real (%)
Dewey (1946–55)	6.9	1.5	10.4	4.8
Harriman (1955–59)	7.2	4.5	10.6	7.8
Rockefeller (1959–74)	11.7	8.2	14.8	11.3
Wilson (1974–75)	8.9	0.9	10.7	0.7
Carey (1975–77)	8.3	1.0	34.0[b]	22.6[b]
Average, 1946–77	9.4	5.0	13.4[b]	8.8[b]

Note: Dates shown are fiscal years terminating in March 31.
[a] All debt, including debtlike commitments.
[b] Excludes 1977.
Source: See Table 4.1. All data deflated by GNP implicit price deflator. See Appendix A.3.

Table 4.3. If total debt figures are converted to a per capita basis, these conclusions are only slightly modified: See Table 4.4.) Only 22 percent of that total New York debt was in the form of regular (or full faith and credit) debt instruments issued by the state. The rest consisted of debtlike commitments, primarily to public authorities, most of it either moral obligation guarantees (55 percent) or lease-purchase agreements (20 percent).[12] As for New York public authorities, their total indebtedness by America's two-hundredth anniversary registered a mind-boggling $14 billion.[13] To be precise, $14,149,954,000. No other state could begin to match such a total, not even when each state's regular debt was augmented by the addition of debtlike commitments of the New York State variety. Two numbers drive the message home. The total debt of (statewide) public authorities of New York exceeded the total debt of the most indebted state (California) by more than a factor of 2, and the average indebtedness of all of the states by a factor of almost 10.[14] Something had gone berserk in the debt-issuing process of the Empire State. But what and why? And what was the linkage of this increase to the rise in spending by both the state and its public authorities?

The search for an answer must proceed along two distinct paths. Part of the story concerns the rise of regular state spending, and with it, the escalation of taxes and regular (full faith and credit) state debt. These are the topics of Chapter 5. Part of the story concerns the changing

Table 4.3. *Changes in state debt, 1956–75 ($ millions)*

State	1956 debt	1975 debt	Net increase	Increase in short term	Increase in long term	
					Guaranteed	Nonguaranteed
N.Y.	1,939	14,635	12,696	1,995	2,623	8,078
Calif.	943	6,470	5,527	0	4,791	736
Pa.	1,245	5,360	4,115	−1	2,686	1,429
Mass.	934	3,941	3,007	848	1,345	814
N.J.	884	3,886	3,002	311	1,139	1,552
Conn.	478	2,922	2,444	71	2,053	321
Ill.	699	2,798	2,099	245	716	1,138
Ohio	591	2,662	2,071	79	1,493	499
Ky.	70	1,965	1,895	0	361	1,533
Tex.	213	1,943	1,730	1	617	1,111
All others[a]	4,894	25,545	20,651	783	9,699	10,171
	12,890	72,127	59,237	4,332	27,523	27,382

[a] Includes Alaska and Hawaii, which were territories in 1956. These contributed $1.9 billion of the 1975 total of $59.2 billion.

Source: U.S., Bureau of the Census, *State Government Finances,* 1956 and 1975.

Table 4.4. *Changes in state debt per capita, 1956–75 ($ per person)*

State	1956 debt	1975 debt	Net increase	Increase in short term	Increase in long term	
					Guaranteed	Nonguaranteed
Vt.	18	978	960	4	528	428
Conn.	217	943	726	2	646	77
N.Y.	121	810	689	110	137	441
Del.	357	1,024	667	42	490	135
Oreg.	102	734	632	0	632	0
Ky.	23	580	557	0	107	450
Mass.	196	678	482	146	207	130
W.Va.	139	591	452	16	308	128
R.I.	79	494	415	20	219	175
N.J.	166	530	364	42	135	186
All states[a]	79	339	260	20	120	119

[a] Excludes Alaska and Hawaii, which were territories in 1956. In 1975, they had the highest per capita debt of all states: $1,945 and $1,342, respectively.

Sources: U.S., Bureau of the Census, *State Government Finances*, 1956 and 1975; U.S., Bureau of the Census, Current Population Series, P–25, no. 646, February 1977, table 2, p. 3.

institutional structure of public authorities, why such changes were made, and how they affected state indebtedness. These are the topics of Chapter 6. Finally, and perhaps most important of all, is the question posed at the outset of this chapter: How could New York have plunged simultaneously into secular retardation and a spending spree the likes of which the state had never seen before? Why did the elected representatives of the people approve it? Why did the courts condone it, when so much was financed by moral obligation debt, which seemed to fly in the face of the constitutional provision prohibiting the state from extending its credit to public authorities? The American system of checks and balances was apparently providing very little check and not much balance in New York fiscal matters, especially in the Rockefeller years. The reasons for this limited restraint will be considered in Chapter 7. All of these attempts to explain the fiscal developments of the state leave unanswered the question why New York City budgeting went so awry, and how that festering sore may yet imperil the fiscal viability of the state itself. To these issues the discussion will return in Chapter 8.

5

The political economy of the governors

5.1. Introduction

The 1960s are still referred to in Albany corridors as the "Go-Go years." They were more than that. "Watershed" is a word that the historian uses at his peril. Few periods in history are characterized by such discontinuities that this formidable label can be applied to them with confidence. And yet something did happen – something quite dramatic – between Franklin Roosevelt's largest peacetime budget of $10 billion and Jimmy Carter's budget of $500 billion; between the government's groping response to many of the social problems of the Great Depression and the thrusting social activism of the '60s and '70s; between the 1950s budgets of the Department of Health, Education, and Welfare of less than $2 billion and its present-day budget of almost 100 times that figure.[1] Whatever that something was – whatever the appropriate characterization and explanation of this momentous shift in the nation's priorities concerning the appropriate roles of government in the economy – that movement was national in scale and centered in the 1960s. New York's fiscal developments in the postwar era are variants of these larger currents within the nation. The cautiousness that typified the fiscal initiatives of Dewey and Harriman, the aggressive expansionism under Rockefeller, were all in step with the times. But this is to understate the case. However much the fiscal activism of the '60s within the Empire State was echoed elsewhere, it was almost invariably a fainter echo. Few states could rival New York's explosion of revenue, expenditure, and debt in the Rockefeller years. And no state could begin to match that deadly combination of fiscal chaos and economic retardation that came hard upon the heels of the "Go-Go years."

The numbers of Tables 5.1 and 5.2 constitute the controlling focus of this chapter. Consider the problem. If the task is to disentangle the political linkages between the governor's mansion and the dollars spent, which linkages are worth disentangling? The list of possible contenders is horrendous. Almost every expenditure item tended to increase in the postwar years. A detailed listing of every expenditure

Table 5.1. *New York State: Shared Taxes and expenditures from All Operating Funds allocated into thirty categories for selected years, 1946–77 (constant 1972 dollars, in millions)*

Category	Fiscal year ending March 31					
	1946	1955	1959	1974	1975	1977
1. Higher Education	21.9	50.4	65.4	993.2	982.2	904.7
2. Aid to Public Schools	301.1	522.4	814.9	2380.9	2234.9	2271.6
3. Other Education[a]	19.0	60.1	90.5	649.9	760.8	738.0
4. Health	25.1	85.1	92.3	252.6	265.6	252.9
5. Mental Hygiene	135.0	239.4	310.3	799.3	855.9	800.9
6. Medicare/Medicaid – State	0.0	0.0	0.0	500.4	460.1	564.9
7. Medicare/Medicaid – Federal	0.0	0.0	0.0	1036.4	849.4	1006.7
8. Aid to Dependent Children – State[b]	15.2	48.2	47.2	298.6	221.4	150.9
9. Aid to Dependent Children – Federal[b]	14.2	60.1	91.7	715.6	459.4	502.1
10. Old Age Assistance – State[b]	45.7	37.5	43.9	22.8	16.8	11.5
11. Old Age Assistance – Federal[b]	59.4	67.3	60.6	59.4	35.0	38.3
12. Aid to the Blind – State[b]	1.1	2.3	2.1	1.1	1.1	0.7
13. Aid to the Blind – Federal[b]	1.9	3.0	2.9	2.8	2.3	2.5
14. Aid to the Disabled – State[b]	0.0	20.1	19.2	49.8	37.4	25.5
15. Aid to the Disabled – Federal[b]	0.0	25.8	26.3	118.6	77.5	84.7
16. Local Public Assistance – State[c]	0.0	24.5	30.1	189.3	142.2	163.0
17. Local Public Assistance – Federal[c]	0.0	23.3	26.9	348.0	374.7	279.7
18. Other Social Services[d]	42.2	74.7	103.8	−26.4[e]	612.7	664.6
19. Transportation[f]	64.8	268.8	508.2	786.4	774.0	575.3
20. Correctional Services	36.1	52.1	60.1	142.6	157.9	183.2

144

21. Housing – Local Assistance	8.0	15.7	22.9	66.0	96.9	62.2
22. Legislature	7.5	7.9	12.1	27.7	29.0	34.5
23. Judiciary	14.2	14.2	18.5	43.6	49.9	46.3
24. General Purpose Local Assistance[g]	289.0	176.9	174.7	574.2	554.0	569.6
25. Conservation	10.2	19.3	22.4	125.0	135.8	134.1
26. Subsidies to UDC[h]	0.0	0.0	0.0	1.8	53.5	65.2
27. Subsidies to HFA[i]	0.0	0.0	0.0	32.5	30.8	34.8
28. Subsidies to MTA[j]	0.0	0.0	0.0	0.0	0.0	21.0
29. Debt Service	131.6	129.3	113.8	526.2	531.5	625.0
30. All other[f,k]	211.2	477.6	619.7	1596.1	1593.8	1542.1
31. Total	1,454.3	2,506.3	3,380.7	12,314.5	12,396.6	12,356.6

Note: Shared Taxes are taxes collected by the state but passed directly to local governments without appropriation or any guarantee of the amount to be passed. In 1946 all General Purpose Local Assistance was of this type. Now it is only a small part. Shared Taxes are included here to improve the comparability of the figures. Expenditures include all state expenditures for which reimbursement is received (in whole or in part) from the federal government. This inclusion is dictated in part by conceptual considerations. If reimbursement is received, the state is almost invariably involved in the decision making, and such expenditures thus reflect state expenditure priorities. In the case of Medicare, for example, the state is involved in establishing eligibility criteria, although the expenditure is totally reimbursed. Inclusion is also dictated by pragmatic considerations. Again, in the case of Medicare, the state comptroller reports only a total for "Medicare/Medicaid." In this and many other instances, disentangling reimbursed expenditures would be next to impossible.

All data deflated to constant 1972 dollars using the GNP deflator. The dollar totals in this table were used to calculate the changes in dollar totals in Table 5.2.

[a] Includes such items as professional licensing, museums, and motion picture censoring.
[b] In fiscal years after 1974, Federal and State Income Maintenance, which is no longer itemized into these categories, is split as follows:

Aid to Dependent Children	80.0%
Old Age Assistance	6.1%
Aid to Disabled	13.5%
Aid to Blind	0.4%

Notes to Table 5.1 (*cont.*)

These were estimated from the following table:

Fiscal year	State				Federal			
	ADC	OAA	AD	AB	ADC	OAA	AD	AB
1974	80.2%	6.1%	13.4%	0.3%	79.8%	6.6%	13.2%	0.3%
1973	72.6	8.8	18.2	0.4	78.2	7.6	13.9	0.3
1972	75.8	9.3	14.5	0.4	79.5	9.8	10.3	0.4
1971	78.5	9.8	11.3	0.4	81.0	10.7	7.9	0.4
1970	79.0	10.3	10.3	0.5	82.3	10.9	6.4	0.4

Sources: New York [State], Office of the Comptroller, *Annual Report* (hereafter *Annual Report of the Comptroller*), 1974, pt. II, pp. 42–3, 1973, pp. 78–9, 1972, pp. 78–9, 1971, pp. 74–5, 1970, pp. 84–5.

c The heading in the comptroller's report is "Local Administration." These funds are used primarily for "Public Assistance and Care," i.e., for social programs other than those listed in lines 6 through 15. See *Annual Report of the Comptroller*, 1970, p. 81.

d Estimated by subtracting the twelve categories above it from the total social services spending.

e Although the calculations are done the same way for each year, the year 1974 (and only 1974) seems to have a negative residual. The comptroller's office could not explain why this negative entry resulted from a residual method. In nominal (undeflated) terms the results are:

Fiscal year	All other social services
1977	888.9
1976	679.0
1975	713.3
1974	-28.0
1973	389.9
1972	465.8
1971	380.8
1970	359.3
1969	350.5
1968	243.7
1967	189.3
1966	165.9
1965	117.0
1964	102.2

Source: Annual Report of the Comptroller, 1977, pt. I, pp. 15, 17; pt. II, pp. 40–1; 1976, pt. I, pp. 16, 17; pt. II, pp. 40–1; 1975, pt. I, pp. 12, 14; pt. II, pp. 42–3; 1974, pt. I, pp. 11, 13; pt. II, pp. 42–3; 1973, pp. 10, 12, 78, 79; 1972, pp. 10, 11, 78, 79; 1971, pp. 10, 11, 74, 75; 1970, pp. 12, 13, 84, 85; 1969, pp. 13, 14, 88, 89; 1968, pp. 13, 14, 72, 73; 1967, pp. 17, 74, 75; 1966, pp. 19, 70, 71; 1965, pp. 12, 92, 93; 1964, pp. 18, 86, 87.

147

Notes to Table 5.1 (*cont.*)

[f] Transportation expenditures after 1963 are available from the comptroller in the "Expenditures" section of "Part 1: Narrative" in the *Annual Report* for each year. Three subtotals, corresponding to State Purpose Local Assistance, and Capital Construction, must be combined. Prior to 1964, "Transportation" consists of the following items: (1) expenditures from the Capital Construction Fund on highways, parkways, and grade crossings, and (2) estimated expenditures by the Department of Public Works for transportation. (In 1967 this department became the Department of Transportation.) In 1944, 54.57% of this department's expenditures went for "Transportation" and 45.43% for "All Other," as classified here. These expenditures are not broken down by purpose after 1944. Those percentages are therefore used to allocate the total spending of the Department of Public Works in the years 1946 to 1963, inclusive. (See *Annual Report of the Comptroller*, 1944, vol. I, p. 66.)

[g] Now called State–Local Revenue Sharing.

[h] Urban Development Corporation.

[i] Housing Finance Agency.

[j] Metropolitan Transportation Agency.

[k] Estimates of All Operating Funds prior to 1964 include an inflation procedure described in note *a* of Table C.12, Appendix C. This increment for the years 1946, 1955, and 1959, converted to constant 1972 dollars, amounts to $11.8 million, $24.8 million, and $33.6 million, respectively.

Source: Annual Report of the Comptroller, 1977, pt. I, pp. 15, 17, 20; pt. II, pp. 40, 41, 101; 1975, pt. I, pp. 12, 14, 17; pt. II, pp. 42, 43, 106; 1974, pt. I, pp. 11, 13, 14; pt. II, pp. 42, 43, 106; 1959, pp. 40, 56, 57, 83, 93, 96, 105; 1955, pp. 26, 42, 43, 59, 69, 79, 82; 1946, pp. 18, 19, 27, 45, 99.

Table 5.2. Spending changes under five New York State governors: Changes in the annual totals of Shared Taxes and expenditures from All Operating Funds allocated into thirty categories (constant 1972 dollars, in millions)

	Changes in annual spending totals for fiscal year ending March 31				
Category	1946–55 (Dewey)	1955–59 (Harriman)	1959–74 (Rockefeller)	1974–75 (Wilson)	1975–77 (Carey)
1. Higher Education	28.5	15.0	927.8	−11.0	−77.5
2. Aid to Public Schools	221.3	292.5	1566.1	−146.1	36.8
3. Other Education[a]	41.2	30.4	559.4	110.9	−22.8
4. Health	60.0	7.2	160.3	13.0	−12.7
5. Mental Hygiene	104.4	70.9	489.0	56.6	−55.0
6. Medicare/Medicaid – State	0.0	0.0	500.4	−40.3	104.8
7. Medicare/Medicaid – Federal	0.0	0.0	1036.4	−187.0	157.2
8. Aid to Dependent Children – State[b]	33.0	−1.0	251.4	−77.2	−70.5
9. Aid to Dependent Children – Federal[b]	46.0	31.6	623.9	−256.2	42.7
10. Old Age Assistance – State[b]	−8.2	6.4	−21.1	−5.9	−5.3
11. Old Age Assistance – Federal[b]	8.0	−6.8	−1.2	−24.3	3.2
12. Aid to the Blind – State[b]	1.3	−0.2	−1.0	0.0	−0.4
13. Aid to the Blind – Federal[b]	1.1	−0.1	0.0	−0.5	0.2
14. Aid to the Disabled – State[b]	20.1	−0.9	30.6	−12.5	−11.9
15. Aid to the Disabled – Federal[b]	25.8	0.5	92.2	−41.1	7.2
16. Local Public Assistance – State[c]	24.5	5.7	159.2	−47.1	20.8
17. Local Public Assistance – Federal[c]	23.3	3.7	321.1	26.7	−95.0
18. Other Social Services[d]	32.5	29.1	−130.3	639.2	51.9
19. Transportation[f]	204.0	239.4	278.3	−12.5	−198.7
20. Correctional Services	16.0	8.0	82.5	15.3	25.3

Table 5.2 (cont.)

21. Housing – Local Assistance	7.7	7.1	43.1	30.9	-34.7
22. Legislature	0.4	4.2	15.6	1.4	5.4
23. Judiciary	0.1	4.2	25.1	6.3	-3.6
24. General Purpose Local Assistance[g]	-112.1	-2.2	399.5	-20.2	15.7
25. Conservation	9.1	3.1	102.6	10.8	-1.7
26. Subsidies to UDC[h]	0.0	0.0	1.8	51.7	11.7
27. Subsidies to HFA[i]	0.0	0.0	32.5	-1.7	4.1
28. Subsidies to MTA[j]	0.0	0.0	0.0	0.0	21.0
29. Debt Service	-2.2	-15.5	412.3	5.3	93.5
30. All other[f,k]	266.4	142.2	976.4	-2.3	-51.8
31. Total	1,052.0	874.4	8,933.8	82.1	-40.1

Note: For notes, see Table 5.1.
Source: See Table 5.1.

category of the New York State government would itself fill a book (and annually does, in the form of the comptroller's *Annual Report*). To reduce this unwieldy mass to manageable dimensions seemed to require three steps:

1. All dollars spent by the state in a given year were calculated from official sources for each major expenditure category listed in Table 5.1.[2]

2. These current dollar figures were deflated to adjust for the general price inflation that has been so endemic to the postwar years.

3. The deflated figures were then used to compare the total annual spending in a given category during the last year in which a particular governor was in office with what the annual spending level was in that same category during the last year of his predecessor.[3]

The difference between the two annual spending amounts is what appears in Table 5.2. Under Governor Harriman, for example, the figure of 239.4 opposite "transportation" indicates that $239.4 million *more* dollars were spent on transportation during Harriman's last year in office than during Dewey's last year.[4]

This procedure would, of course, fail to identify expenditures that surged rapidly under a particular governor and then (before that governor left office) fell back to previous levels. This possibility is of little significance for the era under consideration for one obvious reason: The dominant trend of almost every major expenditure category almost all of the time was up, not up and then down.

Which spending categories emerge from this procedure as central to the explosion of total state spending in the postwar years? Under Dewey, two increases in particular catch the eye: aid to public schools (+$221 million) and transportation (+$204 million). Between them they account for almost half of the total rise in annual state spending that occurred between the end of World War II and Dewey's departure from the governor's mansion. The same two categories dominate expenditure increases under Dewey's successor, this time accounting for roughly two-thirds of the total rise in annual state spending under Harriman of $874 million. All of these figures pale before the Rockefeller onslaught. First, the matter of totals. Annual spending by the state rose by roughly $1 billion under both Dewey and Harriman. Under Rockefeller *it rose by almost 9 times that figure* (with all data already corrected for inflation). A marked shift in emphasis was apparent away from transportation. Not that the amount spent for transportation was significantly less – far from it. The increase under Rockefeller of more than $200 million in this category compares quite favorably with increases under Dewey and Harriman. In the Rockefeller regime, however, a rise of $200 million was no longer a claim to distinction. Indeed, that order of magnitude borders on the insignificant when compared with the truly staggering increases that occurred in other categories. The three education categories,[5] for example, rose by a total of just over $3 billion, half of that going for aid to public schools and a third for higher education. The main health categories[6] rose by just over $2 billion, 70 percent of which represented federal and state spending for Medicare and Medicaid. Under the heading of social services the dominant gains were in federal and state Aid to Dependent Children (+$874 million) and to local communities for social services (+$480 million).[7] Last, but certainly not least, was debt service, which rose by over $400 million. In total, these nine categories – three health, three education, two social services, and debt service – accounted for almost 80 percent of the entire increase in annual state spending under Rockefeller of $8.9 billion. It is both a sign of the times and a signal of Rockefeller's priorities that all save the last are captured by the modern phrase "health, education, and welfare."

And yet something is missing. Those with even a passing knowledge of the state's history will be inclined to ask with indignation: Where are all those Rockefeller construction projects? What happened to expenditure for housing by the Housing Finance Agency? Where is that fiscal fiasco, the Urban Development Corporation? Were not hundreds of millions of dollars spent on "Rocky's Folly," the Albany Mall? The questions are symptomatic of the fiscal sleight of hand that for years has plagued the accounting procedures of the state. The dollar figures in Table 5.2 refer only to the annual expenditures in All Operating Funds. Excluded from Table 5.2 – and excluded from the governor's budget and largely hidden from review by both the legislature and the public – are the millions upon millions of dollars spent annually by public authorities within the state. (The Albany Mall presents a special variant of the fiscal end run to be considered in Chapter 6, Section 6.4.) Only part of the Rockefeller story is therefore considered in this chapter. The ballooning of expenditures by public authorities, how these suited the Governor's purposes, and why this multimillion dollar flow proceeded largely independent of public knowledge or legislative scrutiny will be the topics of Chapter 6. The focus here is confined to the numbers in Table 5.2, representing as they do the most comprehensive accounts of total state spending published by the state comptroller. Our task is to outline, for the Dewey–Harriman–Rockefeller era, at least the main political forces behind the major expenditure increases in All Operating Funds.

5.2. Dewey and Harriman: cautious innovations on a small scale

5.2.a. Introduction

The gubernatorial years of Dewey (1942–54) and Harriman (1955–58) are singularly barren of high fiscal drama. But then an absence of drama was, for that era, typical fiscal fare. The limited programs and expenditures undertaken in capital construction illustrate the conservative tenor of the time, and for that reason are the topic of the next section. A few beginnings, however, remain worthy of note because of the larger programs they foreshadowed. Three especially should be singled out: state subsidies for middle-income housing, increased aid for primary and secondary education, and the expansion of a state university system. A separate discussion of each in the Dewey–Harriman years therefore follows the section on capital construction.[8] All four are but strands in a larger tapestry of fiscal change well captured by the data of Table 5.2.

At first glance, the role of Governor Dewey in initiating and implementing any and all programs undertaken during his regime appears to be decisive. A Republican in an era when Republicans continually controlled both houses of the New York State legislature, Dewey had at his command the powerful leverage inherent in party discipline and gubernatorial clout, with the latter clearly exceptional compared to gubernatorial powers in other states.[9] Harriman, by contrast, had only one of two. The powers of the governor were obviously his to command. The difficulty was that the legislature remained in the control of the Republicans, and Harriman was a Democrat. Worse, his relationship with the leadership in both houses was at best mildly cool, and at worst downright frigid. Oswald Heck, the Assembly Leader, generally maintained a posture of reticent cordiality toward the Governor, but Senate Majority Leader Walter Mahoney disliked Harriman and made no secret of the fact. With party discipline among Republicans still strong, Harriman was constantly confounded in his efforts by opposition from a hostile legislature. Most political observers were unsurprised at the resulting tendency to inertia. Alan Hevesi's description is typical: "Harriman was faced with the fierce opposition of a decisive legislative majority, and so could choose only between continuous yielding and compromise, or else, fervid but unproductive partisanship on his own part."[10] A hostile legislature, however, was only part of the problem. Harriman had the instincts and the training of an international statesman, with limited knowledge of – and limited interest in – New York State affairs. From first to last his controlling priority was to gain the presidency, with the governor's mansion in Albany viewed mainly as a way station on the road to 1600 Pennsylvania Avenue.

In the popular mind, these two contrasting descriptions tend to summarize the role of these two governors in New York's fiscal developments between 1942 and 1958: decisive, almost authoritarian, control and direction under Dewey; inertia, drift, and negligible leadership under Harriman. Although not entirely wide of the mark, these caricatures appear somewhat overdrawn when measured against the political events of the period.

5.2.b. Capital construction

Few politicians can stand a surplus, and Dewey was no exception. He was handed one on the proverbial silver platter because of a peculiar constellation of events over which he had little control. The tax structure of New York siphoned off a booming wartime economy far more money than could be spent given wartime shortages. These surpluses led to the establishment in 1944 of the Postwar Reconstruction Fund (renamed the Capital Construction Fund in 1949). By the close of World War II it could boast a balance of some $457 million – no mean sum when one realizes that, converted to 1972 dollars, that $457 million would become almost $1.2 billion.

The stated purpose of the Postwar Reconstruction Fund, as its title suggests, was to finance in the immediate postwar era such projects as highways, public housing, parks, and parkways. For Albany politicians, the fiscal situation was as close to ideal as they were likely to get. Most of the spending assignments had high political visibility, and the available surplus permitted their construction with negligible borrowing or taxation.[11] The net result was a rash of projects, modest in magnitude by Rockefeller standards, which by the time Dewey left office had all but dissipated the entire $457 million.[12]

Only one construction project in the Dewey–Harriman years approached the grand scale typical of the 1960s: the New York Thruway. Once the scale was candidly appraised, it became apparent that the Postwar Reconstruction Fund could not finance it. For nickels and dimes – for modest projects planned and executed on a modest scale – this was a till into which Dewey could continually reach for the requisite funds. The New York Thruway was quite a different matter.

The idea of an expressway across the Empire State did not originate with Dewey. For years a concept on the drafting board of planners, it was placed on the official state highway maps as early as 1942. When construction finally did begin in the late 1940s, it was long overdue. The road network of the state had become, in the postwar era, both outmoded and badly overloaded. The resulting traffic pressures, in the colorful phrasing of the Thruway Authority, "threatened the lives and economic welfare of its citizens, the safety and comfort of its millions of motorists."[13]

That something would be done during Dewey's administration was therefore almost a foregone conclusion. But why not use the Postwar Reconstruction Fund to finance this much-needed postwar construction project? The answer was insufficient funds. To build a 535-mile expressway from New York City to Albany and westward to Buffalo and the Pennsylvania border would require, according to initial estimates, $202 million. Skyrocketing costs in the immediate postwar years quickly revised this figure to $500 million – more than the entire balance of the Postwar Reconstruction Fund at its peak.[14] Where, then, would the dollars – half a billion of them – come from?

The answer was somewhat curious on two counts: the use of a public authority to control the project, and the use of state backing for the bonds sold by that authority to raise initial construction funds. From the outset, the New York Thruway was envisioned by many as a toll road. This reflected the conventional notion of user charges paying for a specific public project. In the case of an expressway, those who benefited from its use should be the ones to pay for its construction and maintenance, or so the argument ran. But why should financing, construction, and maintenance be turned over to a public authority rather than to a state agency? As noted elsewhere,[15] almost none of the conventional arguments favoring the creation of public authorities will withstand close scrutiny. Sadly, this critical issue of whether to create an authority was almost completely buried in the political infighting over whether to build a highway. Voting in the legislature for the Thruway Bill tended to follow strict party lines, the Republicans in favor, the Democrats against, and neither side winning any laurels for cogent justification of their position.[16] Senator Elmer F. Quinn was among the few who saw the jurisdictional issues for what they were: critical. Noting the example of how the New York Port Authority had extended its powers and operations far beyond the confines envisioned by its legislative founders, he asked whether the state was unwittingly about to create another "super authority." "Who will the three members of the authority be responsible to?" Quinn wanted to know.[17] To which he might have added – and nobody thought to add – what guarantees are there that the bureaucrats controlling this public authority will make decisions in the best interests of the public? The answer to the latter question, as spelled out in more detail in Chapter 6, is less than reassuring.

If financing a highway through a public authority was somewhat curious, backing the bonds of that authority with the "full faith and credit" of the state was downright atypical. It was also illegal, unless specific steps were taken to modify the law. The reasons for seeking such backing were financial: With this backing the bonds of the Thruway Authority could be marketed at significantly lower rates of interest.[18] The Constitution of New York specifically prohibits the state from extending its credit (or its full faith and credit backing) to a public authority. The state could therefore extend its fiscal backing to Thruway bonds only if a constitutional amendment authorizing that extension received voter approval in a referendum. The issue was accordingly put before the voters in November 1951. To judge by the overwhelming public support – almost four to one in favor – the Thruway was an idea whose time had come. It did not follow that other highway proposals would be similarly embraced. The voters' tolerance for highway spending proved to be rather low, as demonstrated by their rejection of a proposed $750 million bond issue in 1955. Their tolerance for housing bonds was similarly constrained, as Harriman was to discover. Rockefeller rediscovered the same fact, and then found a way around it. But this is to get ahead of our story. The point at issue at this juncture is how Harriman's discovery was initially made.

5.2.c. Housing

The passage of the Mitchell–Lama housing bill in 1955 is often cited as inaugurating New York State's active participation in housing projects. This statement is correct if the word "housing" is preceded by the phrase "middle-income." State concern with low-income housing is at least as old as the 1893 Tenement House Act, which attempted to regulate building standards, particularly in the slums of New York City.[19] Almost half a century would pass before the state indicated a willingness to use its own dollars to alleviate a growing problem that bordered on a national scandal. The point was hammered home by Governor Lehman at the very outset of 1938: a seminal year in New York's political history for many reasons:

> The United States is one of the most backward countries of the world in providing decent housing. This state, because of its highly urbanized centers of population, is one of the worst sufferers. In the city of New York, for example, over 500,000

families live in seventeen square miles of squalid unhealthy slums. I am convinced that government can best contribute toward the stimulation of business in this period of recession by promoting a far flung program of public low-cost housing.[20]

Other New York notables gave nods of approval to the same point, including Wagner, LaGuardia, and most of those who attended the 1938 Constitutional Convention. Before the year was out, the legislature had passed and the voters approved a $300 million bond issue for loans to municipalities for slum clearance and low-income housing. For any who still had doubts about the pressing need for such a program, Governor Lehman gave a ringing (if somewhat predictable) endorsement: "The expenditure of state funds for decent housing, in addition to providing decent homes and living conditions for thousands of its citizens and decreasing crime within slum areas, will save human misery and public expenditure in treating the social evils which come with dilapidated, unsanitary, and dangerous housing."[21]

Despite the compelling nature of the rationale, despite widespread support among politicians and the public, almost nothing was done. The task was admittedly complicated by the brief time span – only three years – between voter approval and December 7, 1941. But by January 1947, $272 million of the $300 million – more than 90 percent of the original authorization – remained untapped. For once, Dewey abandoned his usual conservative stance on public spending issues. The $300 million, he decided, was unequal to the task. Three times he asked first the legislature and then the voters to expand the State Public Housing Loan Fund. Three times his requests were granted. By 1955 the state had been authorized to borrow nearly a billion dollars to assist in slum clearance and low-income housing (see Table 5.3).[22] Actual spending in the period 1948 to 1955 amounted to $305 million, or roughly one-third of the total authorized.[23]

In a nation only gradually expanding its social welfare programs, the figures are impressive, and at first glance, somewhat curious. From first to last Dewey was, by present-day standards, a fiscal conservative. Why should a low-income housing program be pursued with such vigor during his administration? Part of the answer was a blatant mismatch between supply and demand. In the immediate postwar years, New York had a housing shortage that was nothing less than acute, and construction of any housing had much to recommend it. (The rule that one could not stay in a New York City hotel for more than five days is but one indicator of how severe that shortage was.) A second reason for Dewey's support – perhaps equally compelling – was the politics of trying to stop what others had initiated. As noted previously, the initial

Crisis in the making

Table 5.3. *Approval and issuance of New York State housing debt,*
1939–60 ($ millions)

Fiscal year ending March 31	During the year		Cumulatively	
	Debt approved	Debt issued	Debt approved	Debt issued
1960	0.0	55.1	935.0	528.1
1959	0.0	49.0	935.0	473.1
1958	0.0	0.0	935.0	424.1
1957	0.0	40.4	935.0	424.1
1956	0.0	50.7	935.0	383.7
1955	200.0	0.0	935.0	333.0
1954	0.0	61.0	735.0	333.0
1953	0.0	62.7	735.0	272.0
1952	0.0	0.0	735.0	209.2
1951	0.0	58.3	735.0	209.2
1950	300.0	43.3	735.0	150.9
1949	0.0	51.5	435.0	107.6
1948	135.0	28.2	435.0	56.1
1947	0.0	0.0	300.0	27.9
1946	0.0	0.0	300.0	27.9
1945	0.0	0.0	300.0	27.9
1944	0.0	8.3	300.0	27.9
1943	0.0	0.0	300.0	19.6
1942	0.0	0.0	300.0	19.6
1941	0.0	19.6	300.0	19.6
1940	0.0	0.0	300.0	0.0
1939	300.0	0.0	300.0	0.0

Source: Annual Report of the Comptroller, 1960, p. 114; 1959, p. 101; 1958, p.
87; 1957, p. 87; 1956, p. 87; 1955, p. 87; 1954, p. 87; 1953, p. 87; 1952, p. 87;
1951, p. 87; 1950, p. 91; 1949, p. 83; 1948, p. 91; 1947, p. 67.

plan dated from the immediate prewar years, and reflected to no small
degree the liberal philosophy of Governor Lehman. Lehman's efforts
to implement the program almost immediately ran afoul of the shortages in building materials and manpower that accompanied World
War II. His successor, Dewey, therefore confronted in the postwar era
not only a crushing shortage of almost every kind of housing, but also a
legacy favoring public support for low-income housing, complete with

plans and the expectation that they would be carried out. To sabotage such an enterprise would have been to risk political mayhem. Conservative instincts therefore bowed to liberal pressures because any other course of action appeared to be the height of folly. Under Harriman, expenditure continued, but at a reduced pace – $140 million in four years – bringing the total outlay for low-income housing under New York's two postwar governors to a total of almost half a billion. Even by the norms of spending to come, this was an impressive magnitude.

Unlike low-income housing, New York State support for middle-income housing was a postwar idea. As will be argued in Section 5.3.g, it could hardly have been otherwise. Among the many oddities concerning the inauguration of this program, two in particular stand out. The first is Harriman's vigorous endorsement of an idea clearly not his own; the second, the peculiar nature of the official explanation for undertaking what quickly became a multibillion dollar enterprise.

Early beginnings can be traced to 1950, when Senator MacNeil Mitchell and Assemblyman Alfred J. Lama proposed that the state authorize $100 million in debt to aid in the construction of "no profit and middle-income housing."[24] Their proposal was based upon a three-year study by the Joint Legislative Committee on Housing, of which Mitchell was chairman and Lama secretary. The idea fell on deaf ears, but only temporarily. In 1955 it resurfaced as a $50 million proposal drafted by the same Joint Legislative Committee. Passage by the legislature was comparatively easy, but subsequent ratification by the voters was a close thing – so close that it was initially thought to have failed. (The final count showed a squeaking 24,700 majority in its favor.) Harriman then attempted to climb on a bandwagon which turned out to be little more than a pushcart, at least until Rockefeller arrived to overhaul the vehicle from top to bottom. Making the cause of middle-income housing his own, Harriman proposed in early 1956 a further $200 million "to enable the state to lend money to regulated private housing companies for middle-income housing."[25] The Republican legislature reacted to the Democratic Governor's suggestion with typical obstreperousness. Harriman's proposal was voted down and in its stead the legislators substituted a proposal of their own, which, on close inspection, was the same idea with a reduced price tag of $100 million. This time the requisite referendum failed, but again the margin was narrow: 46 percent for, 54 percent against.[26] Undaunted by both snubs, Harriman returned to do battle with a scaled-down proposal of his own. If $200 million was too much for the legislature and $100 million was too much for the voters, would $50 million do? The answer was no. (The legislature buried the entire proposal.) That would have ended the matter for a less determined man. Harriman would champion the cause one last time in 1958. It was to be his final year as Governor and his final fling at New York housing. If scaling down the price tag could not elicit more support, perhaps a sharply higher price tag would. However strange the logic, it worked. Admittedly, the Governor's proposal of $100 million for middle-income housing was packaged with a second $100 million proposal for low-income housing, and the latter type of proposal, as previously noted, had been repeatedly successful in the state. The legislature passed both, but shrewdly divided them to give voters the opportunity of accepting one and not the other. Perhaps to everyone's surprise, they accepted both, although by comparatively slim margins.

For all this leadership and initiative generated by the executive, the roots of state support for middle-income housing were to be found, as noted, with the Joint Housing Committee of both legislative houses and the two members whose names were to be so closely linked with housing projects in New York. Significantly, both Senator Mitchell (Republican, Manhattan) and Assemblyman Lama (Democrat, Brooklyn) were from New York City, where the middle-income housing problem was centered. But what was the problem? When the original bill was framed and passed in 1955, the Joint Legislative Committee on Housing and Multiple Dwellings attempted to provide the answer:

> A commendable job has already been done by the Government in providing public housing for the lowest income families and in clearing slums. Private enterprise with some public aid has also done a good job in housing high-income families. But middle-income families in ever-increasing numbers are still found living in substandard housing. Ordinarily, families in that category would be considered too well off to be entitled to public aid; yet many are unable to afford truly adequate housing without such aid. Mainly they are white-collar workers in urban areas throughout the State who do not want to be public dependents, but who would welcome Government aid which helps private enterprise supply their housing needs. [27]

For a political statement almost devoid of content, this was a masterpiece. The argument reduces to the observation that, with respect to housing within the state, the poor were already being helped, the rich could take care of themselves, and therefore the middle-income group deserved a hand because their housing, for reasons never given, was judged to be inadequate, by criteria never specified.[28] Pursued to its logical conclusion, this line of argument could justify state support for almost any middle-income purchase of almost any product. Something was creating a propensity to vagueness, and that something was at the heart of the middle-income housing problem. Just what it was, why politicians shied away from spelling it out, and how Rockefeller attacked the effects while ignoring the cause will be the subject of Section 5.3.g.

5.2.d. Primary and secondary education

The trend in state spending on aid for primary and secondary education in the Dewey–Harriman years is rather startling. In every year between 1948 and 1958 the numbers increased, sometimes dramatically: this despite the fiscal caution that typified much of the Dewey and Harriman administrations. How was it all possible?

The central driving force, of course, was the postwar baby boom. This radical upward revision in the birth rate also guaranteed a new and much-expanded generation of pupils, all of whom had to be taught, somehow, within the halls of learning of the Empire State. Year after year the *New York Times* noted the rise in state aid to education, and singled out as the primary cause "increased enrollment."[29]

There were three exceptions. On three separate occasions the politicians stepped in and revised the formula for state aid, in each case making the resulting payments more generous. For all their pontifications on the subject, the legislators from first to last appear to have been more preoccupied with their own political survival than with the needs of students. The public was ready for change – demanding change – and woe to the politician who chose to fight this rising sentiment for increased state support for education. Through it all, Dewey remained a reluctant, almost a coerced, participant, while Harriman was largely a spectator of events controlled by others.

The first clash was a victory for Dewey and fiscal conservatism. The setting was 1948. Senator Fred Young and Assemblyman Wheeler Milmoe, both Republicans, had the audacity to propose a revision in state aid for schools with a price tag of $103 million. Dewey countered with a proposed $30 million increase, a suggestion deemed so niggardly that it sparked a near rebellion among Republican legislators who feared voter reprisals at the polls. When the final vote came in the Senate and the Assembly, however, despite expressions of support during the debate for the more liberal Young–Milmoe bill, party disciplines prevailed and the Governor's proposal carried the day.

Dewey may have won the battle, but he was almost immediately threatened with an unacceptable loss of troops. In the subsequent November election, the Republican majority in the Senate fell from 40–15 to 31–25, and the Republicans' hold on the Assembly was reduced from 107–42 to 87–63.[30] In January of 1949, in a special message to the legislature, the Governor proposed that state aid to education should be increased by $40 million over the amount required by the existing formula. The *New York Times* explanation for this rapid about-face was unabashedly political:

> Mr. Dewey's recommendations are calculated to win the approval of most of the Republican majority in the legislature. They have been urging such a step upon him ever since the election last November in which a number of Republican candidates seeking reelection were defeated partly as a result of their support of the administration's refusal to allocate more funds for education last year.[31]

Assemblyman Milmoe finally had his day. The proposal to increase state aid and revise the formula for apportionment became known as the Feinberg–Milmoe bill. To no one's surprise, it sailed effortlessly through both houses (receiving unanimous support en route) and was signed into law in April of 1949. Dewey's fiscal conservatism had clashed head on with the public's demand for more, with little room for doubt about the victor:

> The law approved today represents the culmination of six years of effort by educators, school boards and others to have the state aid for education formula, originally enacted in 1925, revised to meet modern conditions . . . It is the first Dewey administration proposal on education to have the support and backing of teacher and education groups. Heretofore, all Dewey education bills have been criticized as inadequate.[32]

Five years later the winds of change again propelled a reluctant Dewey into a comprehensive reexamination of the issue and the formula. In January of 1954 he announced his intention to establish a Temporary State Commission on Education Finance. Popularly known as the Heald Commission after its head, Chancellor Henry Heald of NYU, this appointed body took two years to formulate a report, by which time Dewey was no longer Governor. His successor was hardly a dynamo on education matters. The riptides of public sentiment were nevertheless lashing at Albany doors, and if a Republican governor was incapable of turning them aside, a Democratic governor was unlikely to quell their energies.

Nothing less than a wholesale revision in state aid to education was advocated by the Heald Commission. Most of its proposals, incorporated into a variety of bills in 1956, passed with little opposition. The accompanying debate was notable only for the scramble it precipitated among politicians to augment what was already in the process of being increased. When the relevant act was finally passed, the basic formula for aid had been substantially revised. One measure of how substantial that revision was is the $123 million increase in state aid for education in 1956.[33]

It would rise once more at the initiative of politicians before Harriman left office. In 1958, in a curious reversal of their conventional role of reining in the Democrats, the Republican legislators augmented the Governor's proposed aid to education package by $22 million. The *New York Times* was once again less than charitable in its characterization of the motives behind the move:"Politically, today's decision was based on the theory that more political benefit would accrue to Republicans in next fall's state campaign from raising state aid than from continuing the temporary income tax cuts."[34] With the backing of the party that controlled both houses of the legislature, the proposed increase in aid could hardly fail. When the bill was finally signed into law, Assembly Speaker Oswald Heck and Senate Majority Leader Walter Mahoney felt compelled to labor the obvious: "The bill was conceived by Republicans, drafted by Republicans, and passed by Republicans."[35] Harriman's office was relatively silent on the subject, but then it had much to be silent about.

5.2.e. Higher education

The origins of New York's current state university system can be traced not so much to the initiatives of any single politician as to the marked deficiencies in the state's higher education facilities in the closing years of World War II. In a statement capturing the sentiments of most New Yorkers, Governor Dewey noted that "a million young men will come home to this state at the end of the war. Our duty to them, second only to winning the war, is the highest duty of all."[36] When it came to the duty of providing these men with a publicly supported college education, the Empire State was singularly ill-prepared. Virtually every state in the union, with the exception of New York, had a state university system.[37] In terms of per capita spending for higher education, New York ranked a dismal forty-seventh.

That something would be done at the close of the war was therefore a foregone conclusion. Dewey broached the problem in the conventional way. In August of 1946 he appointed a commission comprised of 30 prominent New York legislators and civic leaders, headed by Owen D. Young. In the subsequent political infighting over competing proposals, two distinct approaches emerged. The first, relatively narrow in conception, favored the conversion of an existing university to a state university, with Syracuse frequently cited as perhaps the most obvious choice. The second approach, more sweeping in conception and more demanding of dollars and concrete, called for the establishment of a system of community colleges in various parts of the state. The evidence suggests that Governor Dewey favored the more limited version. One variant of that constrained approach was advanced by his budget director, with members of his administration actively endorsing that variant. The broader conception apparently originated with the opposition. Irwin Steingut, Democratic Minority Leader of the Assembly, was a dominant figure in formulating a plan that advocated a state-operated system of colleges, medical schools, dental schools, and schools of nursing. The Young Commission unanimously endorsed a similar if somewhat more modest approach that called for a series of community colleges in various parts of the state, at least two medical centers, and other professional schools. The bills incorporating the major ideas of the Young Commission swept effortlessly through the legislature, and were signed into law by Dewey on April 4, 1948. The Governor took advantage of the occasion to observe, "I am very proud that in my administration the foundation has been laid."[38]

It was a cautious statement regarding who had laid that foundation, and rightly so. In the initial planning, Dewey appears to have been more a necessary adjunct than a dominant and guiding hand. In subsequent implementations of the Young Commission proposals, he was anything but vigorous. As late as 1955 – almost coinciding with Dewey's departure from the governor's mansion – the *New York Times* observed with some dismay that "the state university system has not fulfilled its promise of low cost college and professional education . . . Only one liberal arts college at Binghamton, known as Harpur College, has been established."[39] The *Times* went on to point out that Harpur's tuition of $400 per year was more than twice the average fee of other publicly supported colleges and roughly equal to the tuition charged by private liberal arts colleges.

This tradition of modest initiatives was to persist during Harriman's administration. At the request of the State University trustees, and with the support of Republican legislative leaders Oswald Heck and Walter Mahoney, a $250 million bond issue for expansion of the State University system successfully navigated the tricky waters of two rounds of legislative approval and the necessary voter referendum.[40] More money was now available, but Harriman, who had little to do with acquiring it, was not in any rush to spend it. When he finally did clear out his Albany desk to make way for his successor, the statesman turned governor could justifiably point out that total annual spending by the state for higher education had risen from less than $30 million under Dewey to $43 million in the final year of his administration.[41] By the final year of Rockefeller's administration, the number would read $1,052 million.[42]

In summary, and in retrospect, several judgments are easily made and one remains obscure in assessing the role of these two governors in New York's evolving system of higher education. What Dewey's contribution was in the formulation of the original plan is difficult to detect. At best, he appears to have helped facilitate the inevitable, establishing the obvious commission to originate a plan, and subsequently signing into law the resulting recommendations, which had overwhelming popular support. At worst, he was initially sympathetic to a much narrower conception of a single state university, and subsequently dragged his feet in implementing the 1948 bill, thereby scaling down accomplished fact to match more closely his narrower conception of what a state university system should be. If the final judgment on Dewey's contribution is in doubt, that concerning Harriman is not. As with so many developments during his four-year term in Albany, Harriman remained largely a spectator of events whose unfolding reflected little creative imagination or political initiative generated from within the governor's mansion. Also patently obvious is the minor role of both governors in putting into place the system that now exists within the state. Massive blueprints, massive construction, and massive spending – these were hardly typical of their gubernatorial years. As of 1959, however, rolling into Albany by way of Rockefeller Center and Pocantico Hills was a new governor whose thoughts instinctively ran to grandeur.

5.2.f. Looking back, wistfully

How undistinguished it all seemed in November of 1958 – how patently innocuous. Looking back over 13 years of postwar fiscal activity within the Empire State, New York taxpayers might single out a spending program or two to complain about, perhaps the odd state tax deserving of a jaundiced eye. But nothing massive. Nothing grotesque. Above all, nothing blatantly irresponsible or constitutionally suspect. To be sure, a few early storm warnings were in evidence, but nothing ominous: a housing project here, a thruway there, the unpretentious beginnings of a state university system, a vigorous but by no means lavish program of state aid for primary and secondary education. Through it all – the initiatives of the politicians and the proddings of the public – the controlling ethos was one of fiscal viability: Spending had to be matched by taxes, or when it was not, as in the case of

Mitchell–Lama housing or the New York Thruway, borrowings now would be repaid later by receipts sure to be generated once the structure that prompted the borrowing was in place.

How could it have been otherwise? The cautious fiscal course navigated by the ship of state in these postwar years reflected conservatism in the wheelhouse, combined with the modest ambitions of a legislative crew distinguished neither for their powers nor for their rambunctiousness. Confidence was the watchword of the day. The freshening winds that foreshadowed the social activism of the 1960s were snapping at the halyards, but regardless of what lay ahead, the awesome craft that was the Empire State was expected by one and all to meet the challenge of its motto: Excelsior.

And then the hurricane struck.

5.3. Nelson Rockefeller: grandiose schemes, grandiose price tags

5.3.a. Introduction

The transformation was staggering. When Rockefeller took the governor's oath for the first time, the citizens of New York had never witnessed a budget from the chief executive in excess of $2 billion. This benchmark was surpassed in his second year in office. By the time Rockefeller left for good, total annual spending from all operating funds had zoomed to a mind-boggling $13 billion. Total increases in real expenditure under Dewey and Harriman *combined* ($1.9 billion) came to barely one-fifth of the increase recorded in the Rockefeller years ($8.9 billion).[43] Taxes were pushed to the limit, but the resulting flow of dollars that cascaded into Albany was not enough. Not nearly enough. When Rockefeller turned the handle to the chief executive's office for the first time, the state owed $1.1 billion. When he closed the door for the last time, it owed $3.4 billion. (Public authorities of the state owed an additional $12 billion.)[44] Because this particular chief executive was so central to this transformation, a brief biographical sketch would seem to be in order.

5.3.b. Of extravagance and ambition

"The very rich," F. Scott Fitzgerald once remarked, "are different from us." One reason for that difference is the environment through which the children of the wealthy pass en route to adult life. Compared to American norms of the day, the Rockefeller upbringing was, in Fitzgerald's understated term, different.

Nelson and his brothers of course were not alone in being raised within a household characterized by luxury. As names like Vanderbilt, DuPont, and Astor readily attest, a family dynasty anchored in abundance is a not infrequent phenomenon within American society. There was nonetheless about the Rockefeller upbringing an aura of massive opulence that few could match. Their nine-story house on West Fifty-fourth Street in New York City included an infirmary, gymnasium, playground, and squash court. So crammed did it become with art treasures that the house next door had to be acquired to accommodate the overflow. Summer vacations were usually spent at the family cottage at Seal Harbor, Maine. "Cottage" is perhaps a misnomer for an estate that included a playhouse, formal gardens, stables, miles of trails, a small lake, and almost every recreational device young boys might want, including a bowling alley and a squash court. All of these facilities paled in comparison with Pocantico Hills. Located 30 miles up the Hudson River near Tarrytown, the 3,500-acre estate – 10 times the size of Monaco – cost half a million dollars a year simply to maintain. Its aura of deliberate magnificence was echoed in "The Playhouse" built especially for the boys. A gymnasium comprised of two stories, the structure housed basketball and squash courts, indoor and outdoor tennis courts, an indoor swimming pool, billiard room, and bowling alley.

Many biographers of the Rockefellers emphasize the lessons of industry and frugality that John D. Junior attempted to instill into his sons: the allowance variously reported as 25 or 30 cents per week, part of which was to be saved and part donated to charity; the supplementary earnings available from such tasks as shining boots (10 cents a pair), trapping mice (5 cents each), or hoeing the garden (10 cents per hour). The whimsical blends too easily into connotations of normalcy. The Rockefeller boys learned the value of a dollar just like any other American youth, the hidden implication seems to be. Whatever they gained from these experiences with dimes and nickels, Nelson and his brothers quickly learned that no one ever asked that question so all-important to less well-funded families: Can we afford it? For any project deemed worthwhile, however large or small, the funds were always there, and effortlessly so: to build a fully equipped darkroom when Nelson became interested in photography, or to provide a $2,500 reward for abstaining from cigarettes and alcohol until the age of 21. (Nelson was one of three family members to earn this particular bonus.) At bottom, money was not something to be acquired for any of the Rockefellers. It was something to be spent.

If money was not a problem, neither was social standing. The right contacts, the relevant experts, were always there when needed. Much has been made of the democratic influence of Lincoln School on Nelson's thinking. Funded by the Rockefeller Foundation, Lincoln was designed to test some of the educational theories of John Dewey under the supervision of Teachers College of Columbia University. For the Rockefeller boys who enrolled, the school did provide contact with students from a variety of ethnic, social, and economic backgrounds. Its leveling influence, however, was hardly reinforced by much that typified their daily lives outside Lincoln. Here the tone was elitist; the pervasive sense, of privileged position. Merely to cruise up the Nile was not the family's style. For intellectual stimulation they brought along Charles Breasted, one of America's foremost Egyptologists. Trips to the Museum of Natural History were made more interesting by the frequent viewing of new acquisitions not yet on public display, with the museum's director often acting as guide and commentator. Brother David's interest in insect collecting was furthered by two summers at the insect farm of Dr. Frank E. Lutz, curator of the Museum of Natural History and a renowned entomologist. To encourage Nelson's interest in travel and exploration the family arranged for him to accompany Sir Wilfred Grenfell's expedition to Antarctica. From experiences such as these the Rockefeller offspring could not help but gain a sense of privileged position: that the very best was at their beck and call, and call they should whenever the occasion demanded.

Elitism, grandeur, and abundance – what had been so characteristic of childhood days invariably conditioned young Nelson's approach to college, and ultimately to life itself. How unsurprising it therefore was that his first action upon arriving at Dartmouth as a freshman was to drop in on President Ernest Martin Hopkins. As John D., Jr., noted with approval, Hopkins was a family friend whom Nelson liked. And how typical was Nelson's response, on the eve of graduation, to classmates' questions about the future: "My job will be to take the wealth that will come under my direction and use it to do the greatest good for the greatest number."[45] His audience no doubt believed that the wealth to be so tapped and channeled was Rockefeller in its origins. Citizens of New York State would find out otherwise, and with a vengeance, in the 1960s. In that single decade they would witness a dazzling proliferation of social programs, accompanied by an explosion of revenue, expenditure, and debt totally without precedent in the history of the Empire State. Small wonder that traditional Republicans (and not a few Democrats) would view the process with amazement. Their surprise, however, was hardly justified. For those who cared to look – and almost no one did – the proclivities of Nelson Rockefeller that would bring these developments in their wake were clearly evident in all that had preceded his gubernatorial tenure. Four were particularly crucial. He was a spender first, a social activist second, and a would-be presidential candidate from start to finish. And despite the smiles, the winks, and the affability, he proved to be one of the most ruthless politicians of his day.

All his life, Nelson Rockefeller would be a spender. As a boy, he almost invariably dissipated his allowance quickly, despite his father's lectures on frugality. While an undergraduate at Dartmouth, he was forever broke, apparently covering short-term deficits by infrequent jobs, frequent borrowing from classmates, and, on at least one occasion, a secret advance from his mother.[46] Access to public funds, if anything, intensified these tendencies. His first federal position was as head of the Office for Coordination of Commercial and Cultural Relations between the American Republics.[47] The man who gave him the job in 1940, President Roosevelt's special assistant, James Forrestal, cautioned Rockefeller that his annual budget would be $3.5 million plus "whatever else he could wheedle from Congress."[48] Four years later young Rockefeller had exceeded Forrestal's preliminary estimate by a factor of ten, spending a total of $140 million in the interim. It was only the opening salvo. The decimal point was moved over several places when, as Special Assistant for Cold War Strategy under Eisenhower, he evolved a master plan with a price tag of $18 billion to be spread over six years. (In his last six years as governor of New York, he would exceed this figure by more than 300 percent.) By the middle of the 1950s, proposals and policies such as these had earned him a reputation for lavishness that would cost him dearly in Washington. His prospective appointment as Deputy Secretary of Defense under Eisenhower was blocked by Treasury Secretary George Humphrey. In Rockefeller's own words, "George told the President I'd wreck the budget with my spending."[49]

Thwarted in his efforts to rise within the Eisenhower administration, Rockefeller shifted his attention to New York, the governor's mansion, and the prospects of storming the Oval Office by way of downtown Albany. En route he would establish a record for social activism that would puzzle some Republicans and enrage others.[50] None, however, should have been astonished.

Humanitarian programs were a vibrant and continuing strand of Nelson Rockefeller's activities from the first moment that he had the opportunity to unleash his energy and imagination as a social activist. Wherever his influence was felt, there almost surely one would find a profusion of programs for the needy. As Undersecretary of the

Department of Health, Education, and Welfare under Eisenhower, for example, he helped to frame legislation on child welfare, vocational education, social security benefits for widows, and more federal–state construction of chronic-disease hospitals. The same general priorities were much in evidence a decade earlier in his Latin American ventures. While acting as Coordinator of Inter-American Affairs during the war years, Rockefeller set up the Institute of Inter-American Affairs, a federal agency designed "to aid and improve the health and general welfare of the people of the Western Hemisphere in collaboration with their governments." In the immediate postwar era, similar humanitarian concerns were part of the motivation prompting Rockefeller, as a private citizen, to establish two private organizations to assist less-developed nations, one nonprofit (the American International Association for Economic and Social Development), and one unabashedly a profit-making venture (the International Basic Economy Corporation).[51] Between the two, they fostered such diverse enterprises as mobile health clinics, the dissemination of improved farming techniques, the development of hybrid corn seeds in Brazil, and the expansion of pasteurized milk facilities.

Invariably planned and executed on a grand scale, these ventures in less-developed nations also demonstrated a capacity to fail on a grand scale: examples are the farm equipment that sank in marshy grounds, the fishermen who used newly acquired motorized fishing boats for smuggling, the crops that rotted on the ground because nobody made arrangements to transport them to market. As one associate observed, "Nelson likes big, broad ideas and large-scale action. He knows how to get things done in a big way – and when he makes a mistake, it's likely to be a whopper too."[52]

Through it all – the triumphs and the catastrophes – Rockefeller remained an incurable optimist, confidently eyeing the next project. Behind that optimism, however, lay something of a more sinister nature. A fiercely competitive spirit[53] brought up in an environment of opulence and elitism is not likely to suffer gracefully any opposition to getting his own way, however great or small the stakes. Symptomatic of Rockefeller's approach to life was his car-driving style in wartime Washington. As summarized by a fellow commuter, "He drove as if he were piloting a Paris taxicab. He seemed to be paying no attention to the traffic. He drove too fast. He drove too close to other cars. The rest of us were always cringing and mentally putting on the brakes. He didn't seem to give a damn."[54] Whether behind a wheel or behind a desk, young Rockefeller approached the world with all the deference of a runaway locomotive. The presumption, of course, was that all of humanity would give way or step aside. When they failed to do so, they encountered – often to their surprise – a ruthlessness that seemed widely at variance with the charm, the ebullience, and the effusive good fellowship for which the man was known.

Like his humanitarian instincts, the strands of ruthlessness were much in evidence from Rockefeller's earliest adult years. In the 1930s they were blatantly apparent in his attempts to lease out space in Rockefeller Center. So aggressive were his tactics that one real estate agent instituted a suit for $10 million,[55] while another likened Nelson's methods to those of "John D., Sr., at his roughest." A decade later the same traits were apparent in Rockefeller's efforts to get his own way at the United Nations Conference in San Francisco. His actions were so single-minded and aggressive that one State Department official accused him of acting "as if he were a separate delegation."[56] From a less-committed vantage point, Walter Lippmann characterized his behavior as "riding roughshod through a world conference with a bloc of twenty votes."[57] In the decades of political activity that lay ahead, opponents would frequently have difficulty disentangling the charm from the ambition, the affability from the aggressiveness. When they did see the Juggernaut for what it was – usually after the fact and from the prostrate position of defeat – they tended to label Rockefeller, as T. H. White observed, "simply the most ruthless man in politics."[58] Given the briskness of competition in that arena, such judgments suggest a propensity as intemperate as it was ingrained.

This, then, was a man of multiple crosscurrents: energetic and optimistic, affable and yet ruthless, a doer more than a thinker, a Republican social activist with – of all things for a Republican – a flair for the massive, a spender preoccupied with prospective benefits with little attention to costs, a steamroller in the guise of the good Samaritan.

But to what end? What were his ambitions? For those New Yorkers who think of Nelson Rockefeller as "their" governor devoted to problems of the Empire State, the most salutary corrective is a close reading of a biography of the man. Almost any biography will do. What is sure to emerge is the impression of a politician whose ambitions, from first to last, remained fixed upon 1600 Pennsylvania Avenue. His chosen route in pursuit of that address was eminently conventional. Neither senator from New York nor mayor of New York City would do. (When the possibility of running for mayor was raised in 1949, one of his aides snapped, "He doesn't want to be Mayor, he wants to be Pope.")[59] The stepping-stone that caught Rockefeller's fancy from the first was governor of New York: a route to the presidency that many had tried, and that two Roosevelts and Grover Cleveland had exploited with success.[60]

At what point the young Rockefeller became determined to be president is understandably vague. By his own admission, he "never wanted to be vice-president of anything,"[61] but rather took it for granted that someday he would gain the highest political office in the land. "It was always there, in the back of my head," he confided to one of his biographers.[62] When asked by a newsman when he first thought of being president, he replied, "Ever since I was a kid." With typical candor – and just a trace of arrogance – he added, "After all, when you think of what I had, what else was there to aspire to?"[63]

How reasonable those aspirations seemed in the halcyon days of his first gubernatorial campaign. His resources, personal and financial, were awesome: good looks, vigorous health, the Rockefeller wealth, and a staff of experts forever at his beck and call. Equally important, the people loved him. Or more cautiously, many of the people were captivated by him. Never was this more apparent than in his first gubernatorial race. One of the early competitors for the Republican nomination in that race, Leonard Hall, was quickly deterred by the Rockefeller charisma: "The guy's got magic. All politicians get to be pretty good smilers and handshakers – that's our stock-in-trade. But when Nelson goes upstate and shakes hands with some leader's wife, she gets weak in the knees, like he was some damned prince or something."[64] Upstate politicians tended to agree: "They come out to see whether he's for real, and then, Bang, he's got 'em. I don't know what's doing it, that grin or the winks he throws around or just that he looks so goddamn regular they believe in him. I guess he surprises them. Whatever it is, it's dynamite."[65]

In his own way, Rockefeller loved the people. For the gregarious humanitarian, the cheering and applause, the affection and admiration were always heady wine. As his son Steven put it, "He's always loved the street, the crowd, shaking hands, dealing with hecklers. He just eats it up. Going to the people is his thing; he loves the applause."[66] The final phrase is particularly revealing. Beneath Rockefeller's caring for humanity (which was genuine enough) lay the need to gratify his ego with their awe and admiration. "Nelson was addicted to having people around him," an associate of wartime years observed. "It was as though he had to see his reflection in their faces."[67]

In later years, many would be surprised that the cruel winds of presidential politics could buffet into oblivion many of Rockefeller's humanitarian instincts. Two quotations that span the years of his presidential efforts suggest the sad transition of the man. To Theodore H. White, writing of the 1960 presidential race, Nelson Rockefeller was "one of the sunniest, most expansive and outgoing personalities of American politics . . . his constant smile is genuine, his great bear hug an authentic expression of delight in meeting people."[68] A scant decade later, William Farrell, former *New York Times* Albany bureau chief, would write, "Nelson is a true democrat. He has contempt for *everyone* regardless of race, color, creed, religion or anything else."[69] Behind such observations can be found a radical shift in personality that depressed so many of his followers. By Rockefeller's final year as governor of New York, he had become more the cynic than the Samaritan, less ebullient and more crafty, less gregarious and more quarrelsome. The moving forces behind these changes were many, but first and foremost was the souring experience of repeated failures to gain the presidency.

But this is to get ahead of our story. The year was 1959. The sunny Rockefeller had swept triumphantly into the governor's mansion in Albany. A few scant months after his first day in office he would establish in New York City a base of operations to pursue the 1960 Republican nomination. Almost immediately that operation would achieve such a pitch and efficiency that T. H. White would dub the contemporaneous organization of John F. Kennedy "a Montana roadshow" by comparison.[70] But for the moment, at least in form if not totally in spirit, Nelson Rockefeller was the chief executive of New York. What lay in store for its legislators and citizenry seems almost predictable from all that had gone before. Spending soared, and so did taxes. The first outran the second, with the inevitable ballooning of debt. The dollars fairly cascaded into state coffers. The ends they would be directed toward under Rockefeller were chiefly health, education, and social welfare programs. And building. He had a mania for building.

5.3.c. Primary and secondary education

Aid to primary and secondary education in New York under Rockefeller was not unlike United States defense spending at the height of Cold War hostilities. A caldron of popular sentiment was boiling in favor of "more," and the vapors penetrated Albany corridors, legislator's offices, and the governor's mansion in such a way that even the least perceptive politician knew he opposed this particular cause at his peril. No one of consequence did oppose it. The need for "more" was almost overwhelming, although how much more was an open question. During Rockefeller's tenure, the baby boom of postwar years continued to strain the educational facilities of the state, particularly the high schools, as the tiny tots of returning soldiers became the teenagers of the 1960s. The result was an ongoing challenge for New York to meet its constitutional obligation to provide "a system of free common schools, wherein the children of this state may be educated."[71]

If much was demanded, much was given. Total state aid for primary and secondary education, a scant $113 million in 1946, and $538 million by 1958 (Harriman's last year in office), soared to $2,522 million by 1973.[72] In the same three years, aid per pupil increased from $61 to $205 to $726 – a jump by a factor of almost 12 in a single generation.[73]

At first glance, Nelson Rockefeller seems only peripherally involved with this surge in spending. The education budget is formulated not by the governor of New York, but by the Regents of the state. Appointed for 15 years[74] by the legislature (*not* the governor), this body is presumed to direct the educational policy of the state, by and large, quite independent of executive influence. At least in theory. In practice, this apparent autonomy is tempered by the governor's role in the budgetary process. All budget proposals of the Regents are forwarded to the governor and subsequently incorporated into the latter's budget. "Incorporated" can include a multitude of manipulations reflecting the preferences of the chief executive and not the educators. It is therefore no surprise that a survey of educational groups in the state revealed a common view emphasizing the importance of the governor in the formulation of educational policy.[75] These perceptions simply reflect an insight at least as old as colonial scuffles with imperious agents of the crown: that control of the purse strings invariably brings with it a determining influence in any policy involving money. For the Regents of Rockefeller's day, as for the colonists of yesteryear, the purse was almost always linked to important policy issues. In the blunt wording of one of the Regents, "We've never been autonomous. All our major decisions involve money."[76]

With a grip this firm in the hands of a man as grasping as Rockefeller, the limited degree to which the Governor appears to have influenced aid to primary and secondary education comes as something of a surprise. The typical scenario was for Rockefeller's original proposal, however generous, to be subsequently modified upward by the legislature. Faced with the prospect of even higher spending, the Governor, like the girl in the Broadway musical *Oklahoma*, could seldom say no.

The events of 1960 illustrate the process. Rockefeller initially proposed an increase in aid for primary and secondary education that was subsequently countered by a proposal originating in the legislature for more than twice what the Governor had in mind. Popular support was instantly marshaled for the higher figure ($75 million). Rank-and-file legislators caucused with their leaders, the leaders caucused with the Governor, and the net result was that the higher figure (shaved by a mere $5 million to $70 million) carried the day. Subsequent changes in state aid for primary and secondary education during Rockefeller's administration were mainly variations on this script: the Governor's initial figure being raised at legislative initiative, with the final compromise inevitably in favor of more – often a lot more. The increases of 1962, for example, were "an amalgam of the [Joint Legislative] Committee recommendations and changes proposed by the Governor and the Republican legislative leaders."[77] Again, in 1964, Rockefeller's proposed hike was amended upward by the legislature, and again Rockefeller accepted the larger figure. That the entire process reeked of politics is suggested by Eugene Samter's findings that since 1950, 71 percent of the increases in state aid occurred in the twelve statewide election years.[78]

But why should Nelson Rockefeller, justly famous for his lavish spending, always be – to reverse Nathan B. Forrest's Civil War saying – firstest with the leastest? The answer is at least partially apparent in the infighting over education spending in 1969. The case is special in that Rockefeller for once began the struggle from a posture of overt restraint.

The Regents began by asking for the moon, or so many political observers thought at the time: an increase in the state's share from 49 to 54 percent, coupled with an increase of $140 million in the ceiling for state aid. Rockefeller countered with austerity proposals in an austerity budget. Impending financial difficulties, he argued, called for a 5 percent cutback in all state spending as well as a hike in the sales tax to balance the budget. Even aid for primary and secondary education – that most sacred of fiscal cows – did not escape the threat of the axe. The Governor proposed cutting the state's share of aid from 49 to 46 percent, with a complementary cut in operating aid (which would affect all districts), although some increases were to be allowed for special programs and special districts.

The last of these was initially interpreted as a face-saving gesture: "While many schools would get less aid the governor could claim credit for having continued to help education in a year of austerity."[79] The controlling motivation was undoubtedly more complex. Rockefeller's proposals were but the opening salvo in a tussle waged with educators and the legislature. Republicans initially pledged their support for his main suggestions. Democrats predictably opposed them, indicating an unwillingness to consider either less spending on education or more taxes. Intense lobbying followed from such education interests as the Educational Conference Board and the State Teachers Association. With a time-honored cause and well-established channels for exerting pressure, the advocates were optimistic. "Education will do alright," observed a member of the Assembly. "Education is seen as being of special importance by both the speaker and minority leader."[80] It had had that special importance for more than two decades, and the cause was not about to falter now. If cuts in education were to be restored, however, the legislators faced the unwelcome choice either of making offsetting cuts in other programs or of voting for more taxes. When the problem was put in those terms – and the structure of Rockefeller's budget tended to control the terms in which subsequent alternatives could be put – the opposition to the proposed hike in the sales tax disintegrated. The final compromise that the two legislative leaders worked out with the Governor modified some education cuts and postponed other reductions for a year. Before that year was out, the most significant of these delayed cuts were thrown out in favor of more.[81]

Education, as the Assembly member noted, would do all right. The strategy by which it did all right Milstein and Jennings summarized as follows:

> The strategies and processes in school aid policy-making observed in the 1969 session are not unusual for New York State. The governor proposes a program and a budget to which all others in the process react. His central purpose is to obtain passage of this budget. Given a legislative majority of his own party, he can usually expect a minimum of difficulty. At the outset the governor can accept or reject the recommendations of the regents as suits his purposes without fear of any differences between them becoming a rallying point for opposition in the legislature. His next task is to meet any counterdemands in the legislature by the opposition party, dissidents in his own party, or the educational interest groups. The governor's strategy is one of letting the legislative leadership gauge the pressures and advise him on necessary modifications. At the same time, however, the legislative leadership realizes that modifications leading to additional taxes or offending a large proportion of the electorate will be blamed on the legislature.[82]

This is surely only part of the story. Another part – a critical part – was Rockefeller's structuring of the horse trading. Confident that the cause of primary and secondary education would continually be championed by legislators, and with a sharp sense of how public pressure would readily convert the suggestions of the few into the proposals of the many, Rockefeller maneuvered to insure that much of what was almost sure to be spent anyway would be requested by the Assembly and the Senate. He who requests must be prepared to trade, at least in the political arena. And Nelson Rockefeller was never at a loss for fiscal items that he wanted but was having difficulty wresting from the legislature. By this interpretation, the curious reticence of Rockefeller to advocate spending for a popular cause becomes much more explicable. His strategy seemed to be to let others up the ante and then exact a price for giving in. He had other fish to fry where fewer hands were grappling for the pan.

5.3.d. Higher education

The active participation of New York State in higher education, advocated by the legislation of 1948, had amounted to very little in the decade prior to Rockefeller's arrival in Albany. Dewey's conception of the appropriate role for the state, whether intrinsically small-minded or not, was modest to a fault when it came to dollars spent. Harriman added little to a tradition that bordered on inertia. And then came Nelson Rockefeller.

The beginning was conventional enough. In his first year, Rockefeller appointed a three-man task force to determine "how the state can assure a college education for every qualified student."[83] The credentials of its members were impeccable, as illustrated by those of its chairman, Henry T. Heald: President of the Ford Foundation and former Chancellor of New York University. Rockefeller did not wait for the commission's report to reveal his own hand. In October of 1960 he stated publicly that higher education was, among pending projects, "the biggest remaining unattacked area," adding that New York's public and private college facilities should be doubled within the decade.[84] One month later the Heald Commission concurred. In a report entitled "Meeting the Increasing Demand for Higher Education in New York State," it spelled out over 100 proposals, including the Rockefeller notion that enrollment should be doubled in a decade.[85] Also included in the proposed agenda were expansion and strengthening of the State University of New York (SUNY) by establishment of two comprehensive university centers and by conversion of teachers colleges to liberal arts colleges, a sharp expansion in community college enrollments, conversion of agricultural and technical colleges to community colleges, and finally, a strengthening of private universities through a system of state aid tied to the number of degrees granted.

This was the stuff of which expenditure revolutions could be made. Rockefeller had two obvious points of attack – private colleges and public colleges – and two obvious financing problems – dollars for construction and dollars for operating expenses. The Heald Commission never specified how its many proposals were to be financed. The controlling premise was simply that the state could afford whatever was required. Both the premise and the proposals were enthusiastically embraced by Rockefeller. In his usual fiscal style, he would finance much of the enterprise by building now and paying later – often much later, after he was gone, possibly to the White House.

State assistance for operating expenses was provided primarily by direct appropriations and by an unprecedented program of scholarships, grants, and loans. These were put in place by getting legislative approval for certain programs, after which the dollars tended to flow each year in a relatively automatic way from the state to the student to the higher education institution where the student was enrolled. The programs thereby implemented comprise a lengthy and (for most) somewhat tedious list: the Scholar Incentive Plan and the plunge into the alphabet soup tradition of government agencies that gave educators of the state such new labels to disentangle as SEEK, FOP, EOP, and HEOP.[86] These are merely highlights from a complex and aggressive drive that resulted in a deluge of state dollars to support a massive expansion in the operating expenditures of higher education institutions throughout the state.

Funds for construction required more deft maneuvering. Extensive building projects can proceed only if accompanied by extensive borrowing. The Constitution required that any proposed increase in state debt be approved by the voters in a referendum. The implied necessity for ongoing popular endorsement of his plans Nelson Rockefeller found intolerable. The voters were unlikely to say yes to everything, and might say no to a lot. The alternative – how obvious it seems in retrospect – was to issue debt through some organization other than the state. In broad outline, the evasion tactic consisted of having a public authority issue the necessary debt and channel the funds so raised into construction projects on a multitude of campuses, public and private. (The state's credit was indirectly involved through its "moral obligation" backing of this debt, described in more detail in Chapter 6, Section 6.4.) Details of the actual financing are complex, as one public authority frequently relied upon a second public authority to market its bonds. From first to last, Rockefeller was firmly in control of the process. If it required the creation of a new public authority, he would tailor the enabling act and guide the bill through the legislature. Whether old authority or new, he was the man who appointed the top executives, and he tended to choose those whose loyalties to himself and to his expansionist programs were well established. Authority policy was Rockefeller policy, at least when it came to multiplying campus buildings.

Three authorities were crucial. One was not new: the New York State Dormitory Authority. Established in 1944, it had since 1955 designed, financed, and constructed SUNY facilities. Now in Rockefeller's first year as governor it was empowered to do the same for private institutions. That assured expansion of college residences. The expansion of other SUNY academic facilities was attacked by establishing in 1962 the State University Construction Fund (SUCF). This public authority would raise its funds through a second public authority created two years previously by Rockefeller, the Housing Finance Agency (HFA). With the dollars so generated, SUCF would design and construct facilities for the State University system. (Prospective tuitions and fees were expected to assist in subsequent repayments.)

This took care of SUNY. The City University of New York (CUNY) was another story. Officially created in 1961, CUNY was a reorganization and expansion of four quasi-independent city colleges originally founded as Free Academy more than a century earlier. The word "free" was all important. It signaled the policy of free tuition that would become a serious bone of contention in the mid-1960s. By that time, CUNY was comprised of four senior colleges (Brooklyn, City, Hunter, Queens) and six two-year community colleges, plus a College of Police Science and a Graduate Center. It was also by then a college with a crisis. The baby boom of postwar years had become the teenager boom of the '60s. Like so many universities at that time, CUNY was about to be inundated. Its facilities were already pressed to the limit, but so was its authorized borrowing under the debt limitations of New York City. If it could not borrow, it could not build. If it could not build, the impending torrent of promising young freshmen would have to be reduced to a trickle. And that prospect seemed grossly unfair, particularly given the booming construction program then in progress on the many campuses of the SUNY system.

The resulting fight featured a predictable alignment. Advocating more state aid were Democrats, especially downstate Democrats. Aligned against them were Republicans, especially upstate Republicans, who anchored most of their arguments in two demands: If CUNY was to become more dependent upon state aid, it should become part of SUNY, and free tuition should be replaced at CUNY by tuition charges equivalent to those at SUNY ($400 per student).[87] The second of these evoked a roar of protest from CUNY alumni, many of whom were now in positions of influence throughout the state. The policy of free tuition and stiff academic requirements, they argued, had produced an outstanding student body – a "proletarian Harvard" as some of them chose to phrase it.

Into this fracas Nelson Rockefeller charged with a policy stance that was as curious as it was unsuccessful. For once he was not to be on the side of the angels in the cause of higher education. Perhaps Rockefeller's passion for control made especially attractive the prospect of absorbing CUNY into the SUNY system. He was the man who appointed the 15-member Board of Trustees who ran SUNY. The mayor of New York City appointed the 21-member Board of Higher Education that governed CUNY. Perhaps he saw CUNY as a prize to be captured to strengthen the academic respectability of his pet project in higher education. (SUNY was long on construction dollars, but short on prestige.) Whatever his motivation, he made a series of opening moves that seemed to assure amalgamation. In November of 1965, he announced a proposal to establish five colleges in New York City – one per borough – as an extension of the SUNY system.[88] At the same time he indicated that he did not oppose the free tuition policy of CUNY, provided that the city could find the funds to finance necessary expansion. This was coupled with a statement insisting that the state's share of CUNY operations should not exceed 50 percent. The catch was that the state was already paying 50 percent of CUNY capital costs. As for the chances of CUNY raising construction funds of any consequence (with or without matching dollars from the state), this avenue was effectively blocked because CUNY was already bumping against the debt ceiling noted previously. The implication was obvious. Faced with inadequate facilities, inadequate funds, a prospective flood of students, and Nelson Rockefeller's threat to build SUNY competitors in the city, CUNY officials would have to capitulate.[89] The *New York Times*, for one, saw the Rockefeller threat to build in the city for what it was: "It was difficult not to interpret this as political pressure to help the city's higher education leadership to make up its mind to join the state's fold voluntarily."[90] Senator Manfred Ohrenstein (D, Manhattan) was more blunt. It was, he claimed, "nothing more than a bald maneuver by the Governor to bludgeon the City University to submit to state control in return for state fiscal aid."[91]

As a bludgeoning attempt, it was a dismal failure. Ohrenstein had a few maneuvers of his own. The critical ones took the form of two legislative proposals framed by the Joint Legislative Committee on Higher Education, which Ohrenstein chaired. One was that the state's share of CUNY's operating expenses be raised over a five-year period to 65 percent. The other advocated a $400 million bond issue to finance construction and improvements at CUNY. This, in turn, was to be backed by a special fund (outside the city's debt limit), with the city and the state to share equally the costs of interest and bond redemptions. The two proposals were made public in late April of 1966. By early May, the Governor made known his opposition to both of them.[92]

Ohrenstein now received help from an unexpected quarter. In early May the Chancellor of CUNY, Albert H. Bowker, announced that unless construction funds were immediately forthcoming, 2,278 prospective freshmen would have to be turned away the next fall. In that curious way of American politics, abstract complexities became transformed into a concrete reality that dominated subsequent debate. The thorny issues of administrative structure and financing, little noted and less understood by most, became compressed and transformed in the popular imagination into those 2,278 bright young minds about to have the door to higher education slammed in their faces. This was something that the voters could understand. It was also something that the legislators could understand. "This is outrageous," thundered Senate Minority Leader Joseph Zaretski. "Someone ought to be in jail."[93] Rockefeller attempted to discount the relevance of Chancellor Bowker's announcement, labeling it an attempt to forge "a dramatic lever" by those who wanted more state aid.[94] The public was not to be so easily diverted. Neither were the Democrats. In a brilliant if obvious move, Assembly Speaker Anthony Travia (D, Brooklyn) combined the two Ohrenstein proposals into a single bill. The Governor would therefore not have the option of supporting more aid for operating expenses while killing the crucial construction proposal.

Rockefeller was suddenly in a corner. This was an election year. The polls that spring showed him to be trailing badly. New York City was sure to be a key battleground in the coming election, particularly in areas where parents depended heavily upon CUNY to educate their children. The indignation of many prospective voters had been focused and intensified by the prospective denial of admission to 2,278 deserving teenagers, apparently because of some reluctance on the part of state officials to lend CUNY a hand. Rockefeller therefore faced the unpleasant prospect that if he scuttled the Travia bill, he would probably be branded as the man who was strangling CUNY and the chances of the city's youth for higher education.

That was a bullet that Rockefeller was not about to bite. In a dramatic reversal, the Governor sought a compromise with Travia in late May. By mid-June, they had fashioned a revised bill that Rockefeller publicly endorsed. Its key provisions were:

1. Emergency funds were to be made available to guarantee admission for the 2,278 who otherwise would have been rejected by CUNY that fall.
2. A CUNY construction fund was to be established, with the city and the state sharing equally the cost of debt service and amortizing the bonds.[95]
3. The state's share of CUNY's operating budget was to be fixed at 50 percent.

The bill swept through both houses of the legislature, but not without a certain rancor, and with the fate of the freshmen in waiting still occupying a curious position of importance in the debate. (Senate Majority Leader Earl Brydges, for one, announced that the only reason he was voting yes was his unwillingness "to personally stand in the way of the education of these children.")[96] A certain rancor also swirled about the governor's mansion. Rockefeller conceded publicly that he was "pretty sore," claiming that the main reason was the "unjust criticism" directed at him – unjust, he suggested, given his efforts "to help this university [CUNY] grow."[97] He was also pretty sore because he had lost the battle to make CUNY part of SUNY.

If the Governor had lost in the struggle over administrative control, he was not about to capitulate completely in the struggle for construction dollars. In that particular arena, the dominant beneficiary was clear. By the early 1970s, a special legislative committee noted the tendency for CUNY projects to be delayed.[98] By the time Rockefeller left office, the state-sponsored debt of CUNY totaled $274 million; that of SUNY, $1,979 million, or more than seven times that of its big-city rival.[99]

The aggregate impact of all these programs upon annual state spending is best revealed by dollar totals. State outlays for higher education rose from $43 million in Harriman's last year to $1,052 million in Rockefeller's last year, or by a multiple of 24 in 15 years.[100] From a system that, in the Dewey and Harriman era, was not much better than a handful of public institutions with little coherence and less direction, the state and city university systems had become, by 1973, the first and third largest systems of higher education in the country. New York was not just first. It was first *and* third. The legacy of debt from this catapulting of the state into educational prominence was no less formidable than the annual dollar flows required to keep the two systems going. From New York City to Buffalo, dormitories, libraries, laboratories, and other buildings now dotted campus landscapes in a profusion unthinkable in Harriman's regime. By the time of Rockefeller's exodus from office in 1973, the unpaid bills from this proliferation of glass and concrete totaled more than $2 billion.[101] The fiscal premise has always been that these would be paid off from university receipts: tuitions, fees, dormitory charges, and the like. The lurking problem soon to dominate the stage was a fall in total student enrollment at institutions of higher education within New York. From a peak of 549,374 in 1975, undergraduate enrollment is expected to fall by one-third in the next two decades.[102] Fewer students imply smaller receipts, which in turn suggest the likelihood that higher education facilities will join the long line of fiscal cripples in need of additional state support in future years. In a word, Rockefeller overdid, and left the bills to be sorted out by those who would succeed him. But Nelson

Rockefeller usually overdid, and one of the costs of his overdoing was almost invariably a pile of unpaid bills.

Just how the Governor brought about this revolution in the state's higher education is not entirely clear. The battle plan was obvious enough. Experts generally concede that the Heald Commission Report provided the blueprint for the expansion of higher education in New York during the Rockefeller years.[103] The fiscal tactics were also clear: state-funded programs to aid with operating expenses, public authorities to aid with construction. What remains obscure is the nature of the political infighting that accompanied this radical revamping of higher education facilities. One is struck by the almost total absence of vigorous controversy, despite the radical nature of the transformation. A scanning of the pages of the *New York Times* during Rockefeller's tenure, for example, yields almost no details of titanic battles won and lost in Albany back rooms and legislative chambers. To be sure, a few ripples can be detected from time to time: scuffles over whose district should get a new educational facility; tensions lest aid to private institutions violate the traditional separation of church and state; squabbles over administrative structure; uneasiness lest support for more dollars for higher education bring in its wake higher taxes, cutbacks elsewhere, or both. But these were little more than tempests in a teapot, totally predictable, and singularly short of wind velocity.

Perhaps the most vigorous scuffling over state aid for higher education accompanied Rockefeller's third move to bolster private educational facilities in the state (as distinct from his many moves to bolster SUNY). His first move was to expand the building priorities of the Dormitory Authority in 1959 to include private institutions as well as SUNY institutions. His second move came as part of the Heald Commission's recommendation, noted earlier, that state aid be granted to private institutions in proportion to number of degrees granted. Nothing happened for seven years. As the opening salvo of a third assault on the problem, Rockefeller appointed in 1967 a special committee of five leading educators to "advise the governor and the board of regents on how the state can help preserve the strength and vitality of privately financed universities."[104] The struggle was rigged from the outset by the charges given to the committee and the members chosen. They responded by giving Rockefeller what he wanted, which, on close inspection, was merely the Heald Commission suggestion, right down to the idea of tying state aid for private universities and colleges to the number of degrees granted. Many legislators were unhappy with this suggestion. Some argued that the money would be better spent on the state university system. Others expressed fears that tying aid to diplomas granted would turn many private colleges into di-

ploma mills. (Their fears proved to be only too well founded.)[105] Many
were concerned lest the traditional separation of church and state be
imperiled by the system of aid adopted. All objections, however, reduced to arguments over detail. No one – or no one of consequence –
challenged the fundamental premise that the state should do more for
higher education. The factions that fought the Governor over the details of his 1968 proposal tended to be relatively weak and diffuse.
Despite their frailty, Rockefeller left nothing to chance. A frequent
advocate of the iron fist in the mailed glove, he rammed the requisite
bill through the legislature on the very last day of the 1968 legislative
session. Thus was a system inaugurated whereby private institutions
received $400 per bachelor's or master's degree granted and $2,400
per doctoral degree.[106] Legislators failed to notice that these dollar
figures were totally without accompanying rationale. In the blur that
was the final day for legislative action in that year, they are perhaps to
be forgiven for their oversight. Whether the Governor should be forgiven for deliberately instituting a whirlwind ratification process that
guaranteed oversights is quite another matter.

Why at no time during Rockefeller's tenure did proposed bills to aid
higher education in the state encounter major opposition? Three factors would seem to be particularly relevant. The first was the attitude
of the public. If the cause of primary and secondary education was
almost sacred, that of higher education was not far behind in the postwar, post–baby boom, post-Sputnik era. As for vested interests, few
were threatened and many stood to gain. Construction unions in particular, always a powerful lobby in these years, were delighted at the
prospect of an expansion that called for annual construction contracts
that would ultimately total to billions. The second reason explaining
legislators' reluctance to lead a charge against the cause of higher
education was the attitude of Rockefeller. As much as any single enterprise within the state, this was the Governor's pet project. He had
said so when he campaigned in 1958. He had said so when he became
governor.[107] And for any legislators still in doubt, his ramrod tactics,
typified by events of 1968, conveyed a message that was crystal clear.
The wavering few might also garner reassurance from the 1963 report
commissioned by the legislature (not the Governor) that vigorously
endorsed the recommendations of the Heald Commission made three
years earlier. Finally, the legislators did not have much to say about
many of the dollars spent. Their supervisory role as elected representatives of the people in many instances fell victim to that most classic of
all Rockefeller razzle-dazzles: the issuance of moral obligation debt by
public benefit corporations. The state did not borrow and build; au-

thorities did – the Dormitory Authority, the State University Construction Fund (with the help of the Housing Finance Agency), the City University Construction Fund (with the help of the Housing Finance Agency). The borrowing was therefore not subject to legislative approval or to popular approval. (The intent of the Constitution is unmistakable: it should have been approved by both.) Chairman Mao was once asked what it would take for China to capture Hong Kong. His reply: "Just a phone call." The suspicion is that this was usually all that it took to ensure that a New York public authority would launch a construction project on a New York campus: a phone call from the governor's office to those whom Rockefeller had placed at the head of public benefit corporations empowered to borrow and build whatever seemed necessary to carry forward the surge in higher educational facilities within the state – a project considered to be so urgent in the 1960s, and yet destined to produce excess capacity by the 1980s.

5.3.e. Health care

Health, education, and welfare – these three summary labels that captured much of the social activism of the 1960s also signaled many of the priorities of New York's leading social activist of that era. Nelson Rockefeller had served under Eisenhower as undersecretary of that department whose very initials – HEW – helped to fuse the three in the popular imagination. The first was by no means the least of Rockefeller's concerns. Long an advocate of improved health care for the nation, he urged the state he now directed to upgrade its manpower and facilities in almost every conceivable area: massive expansion in health insurance coverage, particularly for the elderly; improved research and dissemination of knowledge; new medical schools and the enlargement of existing ones; and a full-scale assault upon mental illness, including a network of hotels for the mentally retarded.[108]

It was a bold plan, typical of the man. The problem of marshaling dollars he broached in the typical way. New construction was to be financed primarily by the issuance of debt by public authorities, particularly by that mushrooming conglomerate so central to so many of Rockefeller's plans, the Housing Finance Agency. From the federal government came the centerpiece of expanded health care for the needy. Its name was Medicaid. New York fairly elbowed other states out of the way in its scramble to exploit this program to the maximum in dollars spent and health care offered. The cost of scrambling for preeminence came high. An undistinguished $266 million in 1958, annual health care spending by New York had, by 1973, reached a level of $2,742 million.[109] The course of construction was no less remarkable. In the Rockefeller years, the Empire State put in place 23 new state mental health facilities, created 2 new state medical schools and provided financial aid to existing medical schools permitting enrollment expansion equivalent to 2 more medical schools, gave state aid for constructing or expanding 109 voluntary and municipal hospitals and nursing homes, and provided hundreds of millions of dollars in long-term, low-interest loans for public or nonprofit health facility construction through the sale of bonds by the State Housing Finance Agency.[110]

In this meteoric rise to fiscal prominence, 1965 was the critical year. Not that health care was a novelty in the Empire State before then – far from it. As Rockefeller was quick to point out, New York had a well-established tradition of providing medical care for those receiving welfare relief as well as those who were medically indigent.[111] As originally conceived, local governments paid all medical costs for needy persons, with subsequent reimbursements by the state covering all expenditures except in-patient hospital care (which was eventually added in 1965).[112] All of these forms of medical assistance paled in significance before the onslaught of the mid-1960s. In retrospect, much of that onslaught had an aura of the inevitable. President Johnson's Great Society idea had captured the imaginations of many Americans, and the votes of many congressmen. Improved health care was but a part of a larger effort to overhaul, from top to bottom, the social services of one of the world's wealthiest nations.

In 1965 two new programs were inaugurated through changes in the federal Social Security Act, with far-reaching implications. Commonly known as Medicaid and Medicare, they were instantly confused in the public's mind, and have been ever since. With two labels of such marked similarity, confusion was hardly surprising.

The program that caught much of the publicity at the time was Medicare. Introduced as Title XVIII of the Social Security Act, it offered a national health insurance program for the aged (primarily for Social Security beneficiaries), administered by the federal Social Security Administration.[113] About all that this program had in common with Medicaid was a concern over national health and a similarity in name. The first premise of the Medicaid program was that medical care for the needy (as distinct from care for the aged in particular) should be the responsibility of government. The second premise was that states would determine the extent of their participation, with federal funds complementing state contributions according to a complex formula tied to per capita income.[114] Finally, the questions of determining who were needy and which medical services to provide were left to the states (subject to certain limiting federal criteria).[115]

In short, New Yorkers had no option concerning Medicare in 1965. It was a federal program for which the states had no responsibility. Medicaid was the problem. Should the Empire State participate at all, and if so, under what terms? The issue of participation was never in doubt. Nelson Rockefeller led the charge, or so he thought. Long an advocate of state support for health care programs, and quick to reach for federal dollars to complement state programs, he had a third reason for favoring New York participation that had little to do with the welfare of the citizenry. The upcoming gubernatorial election promised to be the fight of his political life, with all statewide polls indicating in early 1966 that he was trailing his potential challengers – in fact, trailing badly. What better issue to garner votes than a health care scheme with obvious benefits for millions of New Yorkers? What was obvious to the Governor, however, was also obvious to other politicians. At this juncture in Rockefeller's career, the Democrats for the first time controlled the Assembly, and were therefore a more decisive influence in the legislative process. For once they decided not only to outspend the Governor, but to outspend him in the grand style more commonly associated with his name than theirs. Led by House Speaker Anthony Travia, the Democrats countered Rockefeller's health care schemes with a bill that offered higher eligibility criteria (a $6,700 income ceiling for a family of four, instead of $4,700), to be administered by a different agency (the State Health Department rather than the Board of Welfare).[116]

The resulting infighting bore a marked resemblance to that which repeatedly developed over aid for primary and secondary education. Nelson Rockefeller proposed a lot, and the legislature proposed more. Subsequent squabbles focused only upon details. Larger questions concerning the appropriate role of government in this expenditure were never raised. As with primary and secondary education, the implicit premise was that public support for "more" was overwhelming. The only issue was how much more. Two differences, however, were apparent. The first was that Rockefeller seems to have been genuinely caught off guard by the legislators' beneficence. The second was that what was proposed by Travia and company – and ultimately accepted by the Governor – was so blatantly beyond the capabilities of the state that the legislators quickly tried to reduce what had been granted in a moment of mindless generosity. What Rockefeller labeled "the greatest social program in three decades"[117] was destined for the paring knife in a matter of months. Former U.S. Secretary of Health, Education, and Welfare Marion B. Folsom labeled New York's income eligibility levels "too high and out of reach of the state's resources."[118] Momentarily, they were out of reach for the federal government, too.

On June 2, 1966, the Secretary of HEW revealed that Congress had appropriated only $155 million for Medicaid to be distributed to all states in 1966. New York's programs alone would require, by the bill just passed, $217 million. The *New York Times* estimated that between 5.5 and 7 million New Yorkers – more than one-third of the state's population – would be affected by the legislation passed in 1966. One estimate put the impending *annual* cost at more than a billion and a half dollars.[119]

Retrenchment became the order of the day, as impending costs – an issue masterfully avoided by the legislators when framing the bill for medical assistance – came home with a vengeance. A scant two months after the initial statute was passed, eligibility requirements were tightened. In 1968 and again in 1969 and 1971 the New York legislature lowered the income eligibility levels. They were not alone in being aghast at prospective costs. Congress in 1967 also cut income eligibility levels, with further modifications in favor of more modest spending in 1969 and 1972.[120] As Rockefeller had led the charge, so he led the retreat, only to be outdistanced once again by legislative leaders proposing to cut even more. It was not a process that the Governor was inclined to resist vigorously. Present commitments were clearly too high, something had to be cut back, and if other hands were more visible upon the paring knife, so much the better.[121]

Despite repeated efforts to make benefits less generous, Medicaid expenditures in New York, like Topsy, demonstrated a remarkable capacity for growing (see Table 5.4). Three factors have been central to sustaining that process. First, New York's programs, despite all the cuts, remain atypically generous relative to those in other states. Eligibility criteria are exceptionally high and benefits are exceptionally broad. By Rockefeller's final year in office, for example, only one other state (Minnesota) matched New York in providing every one of 17 optional medical services for both the medically needy and all welfare recipients.[122] Second, utilization has expanded as the public has become more aware of the possibilities. Third, costs have skyrocketed, partly because of inflation and partly because of fraud and mismanagement. The last of these borders on a state scandal. Repeated investigations have unearthed excessive medical charges and payments to the ineligible. (First prize for fraud should perhaps go to the dog that managed to be certified for Medicaid not once but twice by the New York City Department of Social Services.)[123] These failures, in turn, are symptomatic of an absence of control that would be laughable were it not so expensive. By one estimate, the loss from "ineligibility errors, fraud and abuse" exceeds one million dollars *a day*.[124] There is not merely a failure to control, but no serious pretense to achieving con-

Table 5.4. *New York State
expenditures for Medicaid, 1967–77
($ millions)*

Year	Total spending
1967	606.7
1968	1,036.7
1969	1,028.7
1970	1,030.8
1971	1,590.9
1972	1,828.6
1973	1,902.8
1974	2,120.8
1975	2,772.2
1976	2,919.9
1977	2,670.9

Sources: For 1967–73, New York [State], Temporary Commission to Revise the Social Services Law, *The Administration of Medicaid in New York State*, Interim Study Report no. 6, Albany, February 1975, p. 7; for 1974–77, Norma W. Wedlake, Temporary State Commission to Revise the Social Services Law of the State of New York, private communication.

trol. Thus, for example, New York remained the only state lacking a centralized computer-based Medicaid system a decade after Medicaid began. The maze of overlapping and poorly coordinated bureaucracies responsible for the program is so impenetrable that when the state's chief Medicaid officer resigned in 1976 she felt obliged to point out, with a modesty as exceptional as it was accurate, "I am not the director of Medicaid. No one is."[125] The bottom line – or the top line, as the case may be – was provided by the Temporary Commission charged with investigating the administration of Medicaid in New York State in the mid-1970s. The program, it concluded, was "uncontrollable, unmanageable, and unaccountable."[126]

How typical these labels are of so much that emerged during the Rockefeller years. The entire assault upon health care in New York State under his leadership was quintessential Rockefeller. Spending exploded, construction projects mushroomed, the associated debt ran to billions, and the associated controls – on building, on implementation, and on management – were minimal. New York was once again to be first in disbursements and last in coherent supervision. The aid program that was initially lavish to the point of idiocy was subsequently cut back to being merely generous. The building program was quickly shunted into the welcoming arms of public authorities controlled by Nelson Rockefeller's lieutenants. While legislators scuffled with the governor over billions in aid, they would say little about billions being channeled into construction, primarily because the associated decision making had been wrenched from their hands.[127]

Overbuilding was also part of the tradition. By the time Rockefeller left office, estimates of the surplus of hospital beds in New York State ran as high as 20 percent.[128] Within a decade that surplus was expected to be cut roughly in half, not so much because of rising demand as because of a shakedown of supply through hospital closings and decertifications.[129]

5.3.f. Welfare

Under the heading of welfare, the popular image of Nelson Rockefeller is one of a wild reversal from lavish liberal to tight-fisted conservative, from emphasis in his early years on "enlightened care and assistance for needy individuals, families and children,"[130] to emphasis by the time of his vice-presidential hearings on the need to "root out welfare frauds" and make "employable recipients . . . take available jobs or job training, or else lose welfare benefits."[131] In 1960 he vetoed a bill that would have imposed a one-year residency requirement for welfare recipients, "because of my belief in the preservation of human dignity."[132] Three times before he left the govenor's mansion, he would attempt to institute residency requirements.[133] The young Rockefeller was known for his vigorous endorsement of such welfare causes as day-care support, subsidized housing, legal services for the poor, and a guaranteed minimum income. The aging Governor became associated in the popular mind with such unpopular policies as lower benefits, more stringent work requirements, and tougher eligibility standards – and even the suggestion that a fund be established to send poor newcomers back to their home state.[134] While hardly fair, it was perhaps inevitable that the man who was undoubtedly the greatest advocate of welfare spending in New York's history should be accused before he left office of selling out the poor and, with his emphasis upon the need for residency requirements, even of attempting "to make scapegoats of blacks and Puerto Ricans for all of the economic and social problems of [the] State."[135]

The most common explanation for this changing Rockefeller posture has usually emphasized political opportunism, particularly the desire to gain conservative support for one last try at the White House. (Unlike Henry Clay, the disenchanted liberals argued, Rockefeller would not rather be right. He would rather be president.) Other relevant strands in what is undoubtedly a complex web of motivations include the Governor's growing awareness that costs were getting out of hand and his growing suspicion that welfare was undermining the initiative and independence of at least some of its beneficiaries.[136]

Untangling which of these factors mattered most is not important here. What does matter is the recognition that, as reversals go, Rockefeller's was a modest retreat. Five points in particular are worth underscoring. First, welfare aid (both state and federal) was distributed predominantly in the form of dollars funneled to local governments, with evolving state and federal requirements progressively eroding the discretion of local authorities. Second, in real dollar terms, total *annual* welfare spending under Rockefeller rose by $1,325 million, a figure five times as large as the increase recorded under Dewey and Harriman combined.[137] Third, benefit levels remained exceptionally high. By one estimate made on the eve of Rockefeller's departure, New York welfare standards were among "the highest in the country," offering to a family of four benefit levels equivalent to a gross income of $7,000 per year.[138] Fourth, the bulk of welfare support in the 1960s and 1970s went for a single purpose: Aid to Families with Dependent Children (AFDC), a program that still overshadows all other state welfare activities (see Table 5.5).[139] Finally, the rise of AFDC spending under Rockefeller raises a puzzle that has almost totally escaped analysis.

At first glance, there appears to be no puzzle whatsoever. If AFDC payments are converted to constant (1972) dollars, and the annual growth rate in the resulting totals is calculated for the gubernatorial years of Dewey, Harriman, and Rockefeller, the striking fact is the absence of sharp divergence among the results (see Tables 5.6 and 5.7). Annual growth rates under Dewey, for example, averaged a bare percentage point less than those recorded under Rockefeller (11.4 percent and 12.8 percent, respectively). If the Rockefeller years are disentangled, however, a curiosity becomes immediately apparent. Sandwiched in between an average growth rate in the early years and a slumping growth rate in the later years is a tremendous surge in the period 1965–68. But which of these years were particularly crucial? Table 5.8 supplies the answer. In 1967 and again in 1968 the number of recipients fairly exploded.[140] In the second of these years, average monthly payments also recorded a remarkable surge. The combined effect was

Table 5.5. *New York State expenditures for State-Aided Public Assistance and Services Programs, 1976 ($ millions)*

Class of expenditure	Subtotals	Totals
Total expenditure		7,179
Source of funds		
Federal aid		3,300
State aid		2,092
Local aid		1,787
Application of funds		
Supplemental Security Income (federal administered)		669
State-administered Public Assistance & Services		
Programs		587
Locally administered Public Assistance & Services		
Programs		5,923
Locally administered Public Assistance & Services Programs: program analysis		
Medical assistance		2,920
Income maintenance		2,138
Aid to aged, blind & disabled[a]	2	
Aid to dependent children[b]	1,755	
Emergency assistance to families	15	
Home relief	354	
All other programs	12	
Services		287
Day care[c]	118	
Foster care[d]	114	
Other purchased services	44	
Work incentive programs	11	
Local administration		555
Service administration costs	151	
Income maintenance administration costs	302	
Medical assistance administration costs	94	
Training	9	
Food on the table[e]		23
Total		5,923

[a] Consists of retroactive adjustments of AABD payments and Emergency Assistance to Adults costs for 1976.
[b] Includes AFDC–Foster Care Maintenance assistance.
[c] Non-WIN Day Care only.
[d] Excludes AFDC–Foster Care maintenance assistance.
[e] Includes administrative costs only.
Source: New York [State], Department of Social Services, *Statistical Supplement to Annual Report for 1976*, no. 1053, p. 1.

to make total (real) payments in 1968 a staggering 83 percent higher than they had been just two years previously. Why? What had prompted such an explosion, and what role, if any, had Nelson Rockefeller played in this dramatic change in New York's most basic income maintenance program?

A scanning of Rockefeller's public statements sheds little light upon the answer. The Governor did note that total payments increased sharply in these years, but his explanations were confined to citing the increase in numbers and the rising costs per case.[141] These are not causes, but effects to be explained.

An official of New York's Department of Social Services has suggested at least part of the answer, and raised several intriguing possibilities.[142] The basic needs allowances were raised three times between September 1966 and January 1968, for a combined increase of almost 10 percent.[143] As the standard of need was raised, the number of potentially eligible persons increased, and with higher benefits, the program became more acceptable. Also fostering respectability, according to the state Board of Social Welfare, were two other factors: "The entry of the whole community into the active aspects of welfare policy-making and the recognition that welfare benefits for the eligible are now a matter of legal right, not of paternalistic privilege."[144]

This was reinforced in an unexpected way by the advent of Medicaid in 1966. Medicaid applicants were provided with information on public assistance programs (including the AFDC program), and public assistance recipients were automatically eligible for Medicaid. The Medicaid program was publicized throughout the state, and low-income persons needing assistance for medical care were encouraged to apply. Publicity increased participation. Publicity plus rising participation helped to erode application inhibitions in general and the "welfare stigma" in particular. The application process for one program (Medicaid) generated more applications for another (public assistance), both because of information gained while applying and because inhibitions against accepting welfare were eroded by the very process of the initial application. By this interpretation, the publicity and procedures that accompanied the initiation of Medicaid in New York State were a central driving force raising the number of participants in the AFDC program.[145] And it was the ballooning in the number of recipients of the latter that was the central puzzle to be explained.

There is another factor of relevance to the soaring enrollment of the 1960s, apparently crucial and yet difficult to document. The suspicion is that enforcement of eligibility requirements became more lax. In theory, the procedures for determining eligibility required a full field investigation of any potential recipient.[146] Practice was another story.

Table 5.6. *Aid to Families with Dependent Children in New York State: selected data on expenditures and recipients, 1945–76*

Calendar year	Total expenditures[a] (millions of constant dollars)[b]	Monthly average number of recipients (thousands)	Average monthly payment per recipient (constant dollars)[b]	Recipients as a % of total state population
1976	1,311.9	1,231.4	88.79	6.81
1975	1,137.5	1,217.2	77.88	6.73
1974	1,131.1	1,176.7	80.11	6.50
1973	1,114.0	1,232.1	75.35	6.76
1972	1,213.9	1,289.7	78.43	7.02
1971	1,190.5	1,266.2	78.35	6.88
1970	1,036.6	1,127.0	76.64	6.17
1969	917.6	1,014.0	75.40	5.60
1968	869.3	886.9	81.68	4.91
1967	611.9	721.7	70.65	4.02
1966	476.3	596.3	66.56	3.34
1965	429.1	548.0	65.25	3.09
1964	371.5	497.0	62.29	2.83
1963	313.6	440.8	59.27	2.52
1962	272.7	383.6	59.25	2.22
1961	237.9	328.3	60.39	1.92
1960	200.5	273.3	61.15	1.62
1959	194.9	265.4	61.20	1.59
1958	183.8	256.0	59.84	1.54
1957	151.8	223.3	56.63	1.36
1956	147.1	205.5	59.62	1.28
1955	145.6	198.4	61.18	1.24
1954	132.0	177.9	61.80	1.22
1953	120.4	164.7	60.89	1.06
1952	128.6	178.6	60.02	1.17
1951	131.0	185.3	58.86	1.22
1950	136.1	197.4	57.46	1.32
1949	137.5	176.3	64.99	1.18
1948	111.2	151.4	61.21	1.04
1947	100.0	132.2	62.98	0.95
1946	70.6	99.3	59.21	0.74
1945	50.0	68.0	61.36	0.54

[a] These totals are larger than those appearing in Table 5.1 because the latter excludes AFDC payments by New York City.

Table 5.7. *Aid to Families with Dependent Children in New York State: annual rates of change in payments and number of recipients for selected periods, 1945–76*

Period	Governor	Annual rate of change[a] in		
		Number of recipients (%)	Real average monthly payment[b] (%)	Real total AFDC expenditures[b] (%)
1945–54	Dewey	11.3	0.1	11.4
1955–58	Harriman	9.5	−0.8	8.6
1959–73	Rockefeller	11.0	1.6	12.8
1974	Wilson	−4.5	6.3	1.5
1975–76	Carey	2.3	5.3	7.7
	Rockefeller:			
1959–64	early	11.7	0.7	12.5
1965–68	middle	15.6	7.0	23.7
1969–73	late	6.8	−1.6	5.1
1945–64		11.0	0.1	11.1
1965–76		7.9	3.0	11.1
1945–76		9.8	1.2	11.1

[a] Rates of change are an annual average between the year before the governor assumed office and the governor's last year in office; or from the year before the period shown to the last year of the period shown, except that 1945 is the base year when it appears.
[b] All data deflated by the GNP deflator (1972 = 100).
Source: Calculated from the data in Table 5.6.

Notes to Table 5.6 (*cont.*)

[b] Deflated to constant dollars using the GNP deflator (1972 = 100).
Sources: New York [State], Department of Social Services, *Statistical Supplement to Annual Report for 1976*, table 11, p. 11; ibid., 1969, table 20, p. 23; New York [State], Department of Social Services, "Monthly Average Number of Recipients and Annual Expenditures in the Public Assistance Programs: New York State, 1945–1958," a table dated May 29, 1959. Population estimates are from U.S., Bureau of the Census, Current Population Series, P–25, no. 47, March 9, 1951, p. 3; no. 164, October 15, 1957, p. 6; no. 304, April 8, 1965, p. 10; no. 460, June 7, 1971, p. 8; no. 640, November 1976, p. 21; no. 464, July 1, 1976, pp. 2, 3.

Table 5.8. *Aid to Families with Dependent Children in New York State: annual change, 1965–70*

	Annual rate of increase in		
Year	Number of recipients (%)	Real average monthly payment (%)	Real total AFDC expenditure (%)
1965	10.3	4.8	15.5
1966	8.8	2.0	11.0
1967	21.0	6.1	28.5
1968	22.9	15.6	42.1
1969	14.3	−7.7	5.6
1970	11.1	1.6	13.0

Source: See Table 5.6.

In the guarded phrasing of a government report, "There are some indications that beginning about the mid-1960s, those procedures were not strictly followed."[147] Partly this reflected the investigator's growing reluctance to push his or her luck in a hostile neighborhood. Partly it reflected changing mores within the agency charged with enforcement. Concern with the problems of discrimination tended to modify attention to the letter of the law, and rigor gave way to permissiveness. A former Director of the New York City Department of Social Services put it more discreetly, if the phenomenon of ignoring the law can ever be put discreetly: "Early in the 1960's the focus of the department changed from establishment of eligibility to the provision of services. Increasingly, throughout the 1960s, there developed an attitude of indifference among staff in regard to eligibility encouraged by top administration."[148]

Timing, of course, is all important. Were the effects of this change in attitude and enforcement centered in the three-year period under consideration? No definitive answer seems possible. At the very least, however, relaxed enforcement of eligibility standards was clearly reinforcing the increased publicity and the declining stigma of welfare associated with the advent of Medicaid.

As noted previously, if Rockefeller is to be accused of attacking welfare, the accusations must be as modest as the attack. Throughout much of the 1960s, the basic Rockefeller tactic was for "further study" of the problem: a commission here; a citizens' committee there; a conference with business, labor, and community leaders "to consider new approaches to welfare."[149] By the close of the decade, however, the handwriting was on the wall – in red ink – that spending was getting out of hand, and possibly fraudulent practices already were out of hand. New York's Governor responded with a two-pronged attack that emphasized employment of welfare recipients and tighter administration of the program.[150]

The major restructuring of work incentives dates from 1971,[151] when the Governor made three proposals: one designed to reward certain kinds of activity, such as training and employment (Incentives for Independence); a second, requiring AFDC mothers for whom private employment could not be found to work in public service jobs (Public Service Opportunities); and a third, requiring all AFDC recipients to report biweekly to pick up their welfare checks and receive counseling. The first was never put into effect, the third was not implemented until 1973 because of a court challenge, and the second was quickly superseded by a new federal law requiring all AFDC mothers to work once their youngest child had reached school age.[152]

The net result was hardly a Rockefeller triumph. To cite but one example, employable persons receiving public assistance are required to report semimonthly to the local branch of the state's Employment Service office to pick up their welfare checks and possibly to be referred to employment. A review of the program's operation in 1975 by a Legislative Commission uncovered the following:[153]

1. Two-thirds of the offices visited provided no interviews to welfare clients to assist with job placement. ("The program is almost non-existent in New York City.")[154]
2. Of welfare applicants reporting, only 8 percent were referred to any job.
3. Less than one-quarter of those referred took jobs as a result.
4. Less than one-third of those placed in jobs remained in those jobs for more than three months.

Combining these results suggests that less than one-half of 1 percent of welfare recipients were successfully placed in jobs by the Employment Service office.[155] Given the objective of getting the welfare recipient back into the work force, such evidence suggests a program that is somewhere between a failure and a fiasco. A leading expert on New York's welfare problems put it more gently: "In all candor, it must be said that the program has not succeeded in placing huge numbers of welfare clients in jobs in the private sector of the economy."[156]

Rockefeller's attempt to tighten welfare administration was more successful, but only moderately so. The issue of welfare cheating and the associated problems of deficient administration the Governor approached with caution in the 1960s, and with indignation in the 1970s. To a midwestern audience in 1968 he soft-pedaled the entire notion: "I know some think that if we could get the bums and cheats off welfare rolls, that would solve the problem. Frankly, that's not the problem."[157] By the time he left office, he looked back with pride upon his innovations of the 1970s designed "to get the cheats and chiselers off the taxpayer's back."[158] Once again 1971 was the pivotal year. A scant three years after assuring midwesterners that getting "bums and cheats off the welfare rolls" was not the critical problem, Rockefeller reorganized the Department of Social Services, proposed for all welfare recipients a more detailed application form and periodic face-to-face recertification, and established the Office of Welfare Inspector General "to root out welfare frauds."[159] What the newly appointed Inspector General rooted out with a series of spot checks was evidence of fraud and inefficiency as grotesque as it was controversial. A more careful and comprehensive survey of the problem was subsequently attempted after responsibility for audits was transferred from local departments to the state level. The resulting statewide review in 1972 uncovered a statewide ineligibility rate of 17.6 percent among AFDC cases. This finding, in turn, sparked a tightening of procedures that was little more than the implementation of Rockefeller's 1971 suggestions. Applicants were now obligated to complete an 11-page form requiring "documentation and verification," and all recertification was to be done by face-to-face interviews. These more stringent requirements did result in "the first major decline in [New York] welfare rolls since World War II," as Rockefeller proudly noted on the occasion of his vice-presidential hearings.[160] That decline, however, hardly signaled the achievement of perfection in administration. The 1975 Legislative Commission noted earlier, for example, found that in a number of instances, those who should have been dropped from the welfare rolls were not, and of those who were dropped for good reason, one-third managed to get back on the rolls promptly.[161]

In retrospect, the course of welfare in the state would seem to mirror the trend in AFDC payments of Table 5.7: explosion in the 1960s, followed by a plateau in the early 1970s. The upsurge of the '60s was centered in the years 1967–68, and appears at first glance to be little related to the initiatives of Rockefeller. The central force appears to have been the advent of Medicaid and all that came in its wake, particularly a growing awareness of welfare possibilities and a diminished sense of stigma from exploiting them to the full. Not that the Governor was totally irrelevant to these developments: He pushed for Medicaid in Congress, led the charge for liberal Medicaid benefits in his own state, and set a tone throughout the '60s – an aura that swirled out of the governor's mansion to penetrate every Albany nook and cranny –

that favored activism and generosity in all government responses to the problems of the needy. His subsequent reversal in the 1970s was not unlike his Medicaid retreat. The attack upon payment levels and lax administration did not mark a new churlishness, but rather reflected the fact that spending, even by Nelson Rockefeller's generous norms, was getting out of hand. His efforts to institute work requirements met with negligible success. His efforts to tighten administration and remove the ineligible from the welfare rolls did help to convert a frenzied upward trend into a plateau. The associated payment levels for the eligible, however, remained generous by national standards. The bottom line, in annual bills to pay, had risen by almost a billion dollars[162] between his first year as governor and his last. If he was not, for once, a prime mover in a spending surge, he was most assuredly a contributing factor.

5.3.g. *Housing*

It all seemed so innocent at the start, so unconnected at the end: the advent of rent control during World War II, the push for middle-income housing subsidies in the 1950s, the mushrooming debt of the Housing Finance Agency in the 1960s, the marked signs of deterioration in New York City housing by the 1970s. The deterioration made clear, as nothing else could, that something had gone alarmingly awry. By the 1970s, the problem was not merely in evidence: It bordered on a crisis. The signs were everywhere that the stock of housing in the great city was in a state of decay, and getting worse. Maintenance was being neglected, apartments were being abandoned at the rate of 30,000 to 40,000 *per year*,[163] and as buildings were abandoned, real estate tax receipts – that centerpiece of the city's fiscal structure – were falling into arrears by hundreds of millions of dollars. A tour of the worst areas was enough to make one wonder who had won World War II:

> Vast stretches of real estate in at least three of five boroughs have decayed beyond the point of no return. Ancient tenements and (until recently) quite habitable buildings alike stand empty, boarded up and stripped, vandalized and blackened by fire. Some no longer stand at all except in piles of broken brick and rubble. Whole blocks of Brooklyn and the Bronx have been compared (by expert witnesses) to the bombed-out ruins of London and Berlin.[164]

Small wonder that, by the mid-1970s, three civic associations were warning of the possibility of "the virtual collapse of the housing inventory of New York City."[165] Small wonder that a civic court judge, having agreed to inspect the problem first hand, called off the tour after three hours, saying, "I'm so depressed, I don't want to see anything more."[166] What had gone wrong? And what did New York City decay have to do with Mitchell–Lama Housing and Nelson Rockefeller?

The story really begins in 1943, when (four months after the rest of the country) federal rent controls went into effect in New York City. When peace returned, the rest of the country quickly abandoned this and other forms of price controls. New York City retained rent control, with responsibility for its administration passing first to the state (1950) and then to the city (1962).

The effects that followed were the result of economic mechanisms that are the essence of simplicity. If the government puts a ceiling on (say) the retail price of chickens, and that price is well below the market price, farmers will be quick to complain that they cannot take a "fair" return from investing in chickens. "Fair" is something of a loaded word, but in this context it simply refers to what farmers could make if they invested in some activity other than chickens. Suppose that their pleas fall upon deaf ears? Farm investment will then be diverted away from chickens into other activities, and fewer chickens will be raised. Supply will decline, and housewives will bemoan the scarcity of chickens at the supermarket. (They will also be delighted with its low price on those rare occasions when they can find it.)

Apartments are not unlike chickens in their responsiveness to the basic laws of supply and demand. Any rent control policy is equivalent to a price ceiling. Its immediate effect is to cut the receipts of owners of apartment buildings. Its longer-run effect is to erode supply. Unlike the case of chickens, this supply response may require some time to become apparent. The available stock of chickens can be reduced rather abruptly by more slaughtering and less breeding. The supply of apartment buildings will be changed more gradually by two processes. First, owners of buildings will cut back on maintenance expenditures. In justifying this move, they will undoubtedly refer to the low rate of return they are receiving on their investment because of low rents. Nor are they likely to be forced to reverse this poor maintenance policy by a flight of tenants. Apartments will be too scarce, and the policy of poor maintenance will be too widespread. Second, would-be builders of new apartments will frequently be dissuaded from that enterprise by the prospect of low rents, and hence low returns on their investment. The existing stock of apartments therefore will deteriorate in quality, while additions of new buildings to that stock are held back. Precisely because a building is such a durable asset, the associated problems may take a long time to surface in an extreme form. If rent control persists long enough, however, deterioration may become so bad that abandonment becomes preferable to retaining ownership and paying taxes. This tendency is reinforced if rents lag well behind rising operating costs, especially the costs of fuel, electricity, and repair services.

There are two, and only two, ways to combat this shrinkage in supply. Rent controls can be removed, with the hope that the resulting rise in rents will attract more private capital into maintenance and new construction. The other possibility is to retain rent controls and have the government subsidize activities that private capital will not undertake on its own. The first of these, from first to last, has been politically unthinkable in New York City. The second has been attempted through middle-income housing subsidies that date from the Mitchell–Lama bill of 1955 (see Section 5.2.c). The nature of the problem helps to explain the silence of the legislators concerning the main reason for needing the subsidy program. Reluctant to advocate abandonment of rent controls, they were no more anxious to single out rent controls as the major reason why a government stimulus to supply was now required.

Rockefeller maintained the tradition of silence,[167] but radically restructured the subsidy process. By the time he became Governor, the Mitchell–Lama program initiated in 1955 under Harriman was, in Rockefeller's phrasing, "virtually at a standstill."[168] What he failed to add was the reason why it was at a standstill: This was what the voters wanted. They had said so by voting down proposals to expand state debt for this purpose. Never one to take no for an answer, Rockefeller now proposed to set up a public authority to accomplish what the voters had recently turned down. His first step was to establish a task force to study housing, headed by Otto Nelson, Jr., a vice-president of New York Life Insurance Company. His second step was to take the key recommendation of the task force and whisk it through the legislature. The proposal in question was to establish a public authority, the Housing Finance Agency (HFA), whose primary function would be to subsidize middle-income housing in New York. Under the old Mitchell–Lama program,[169] the state borrowed the money and funneled it into subsidized middle-income housing projects. Under the scheme now proposed by Rockefeller, the Housing Finance Agency would do the same thing. The critical difference was that increases in HFA debt did not require voter approval.

Given the obvious intention of circumventing voter disapproval, the absence of popular outcry against the scheme is remarkable. The negligible commentary in the press was in keeping with the monumental indifference of the legislators.[170] The enabling act sailed through the

Assembly on March 11, 1960, as one of 49 bills, without so much as a ripple of discontent. Two weeks later the Senate gave its blessings with only 5 negative votes, and those from upstate Republicans traditionally opposed to any form of public housing.

It was as if the largest battleship in the fleet had been launched unnoticed in the night. Within four years, HFA had financed more than twice as much middle-income housing as had been funded under the old Mitchell–Lama law.[171] Within a decade and a half, its total debt outstanding exceeded its original authorized debt ceiling by a factor of 10. At $5.7 billion, it also exceeded by more than 50 percent the entire full faith and credit debt of New York State itself.[172] What had begun as a modest maneuver to circumvent voter disapproval of middle-income housing subsidies had become, by the time Nelson Rockefeller left office, a colossus that financed university and mental hygiene facilities as well. As its functions were multiplied and its debt limit was repeatedly raised, the legislature gave no more evidence of disapproval than they did when HFA was initially created. When Rockefeller attempted a similar gimmick to stimulate low-income housing, however, opposition was immediately ferocious, and almost decisive. Almost.

The year was 1968: a year of presidential aspirations and racial tensions which somehow became linked to a set of blistering phone calls from Atlanta to Albany that would once again restructure New York State's approach to subsidized housing. This time the problem was low-income housing. Like middle-income housing in the early 1960s, it was in danger of grinding to a halt, primarily for want of funds. Voters had repeatedly turned down debt proposals designed to channel more state money in this direction. Private developers were also reluctant to undertake many new projects because of soaring costs and endless red tape.[173] State agencies lacked the authority to initiate such developments on their own. The Rockefeller solution was to establish yet another public authority, the Urban Development Corporation (UDC), with two distinct advantages: First, it could borrow without requiring voter approval for expansion of its debt, and second, it would have extensive powers to initiate housing projects on its own.

The circumvention of voter disapproval implicit in the first provoked surprisingly little commentary. It was the second that proved to be the bone of serious contention. Edward Logue, the man destined to head UDC, informed Rockefeller that success depended critically upon the public authority's having the power to override local zoning and local building codes. This evoked a storm of protest from all of those who saw – correctly – that home rule was thereby seriously imperiled. A secondary concern had, for some, an undercurrent of racial tensions. Suburban areas in general and their legislators in particular were apprehensive that the establishment of UDC "would lead to low-cost housing for minority groups in the suburbs."[174]

All of these objections Rockefeller thought he had hammered into silence by early April, or at least enough of them to assure passage of the relevant bill. With the expectation of success, he left Albany to march in the funeral procession of Dr. Martin Luther King, Jr., in Atlanta. On April 9, at the conclusion of that march, he learned that in his absence the Assembly had voted down his UDC proposal, 85 to 45. Rockefeller was furious. In a series of calls to Albany henchmen, he threatened to unleash every single weapon in the governor's arsenal if that vote were not promptly reversed. His henchmen, in turn, scoured the corridors of power with promises of punishments the likes of which the legislators had seldom seen. The effect was remarkable. The Assembly that had voted no on UDC that afternoon by 11:30 that night voted yes, 86 to 45. Many remained angered by both the tactics and the results. Not a few linked the actions of Governor Rockefeller to the presidential aspirations of candidate Rockefeller. ("Which progress are we promoting here?" William Passannante (D, Manhattan) wanted to know: "The governor's progress from Albany to Washington?")[175] Anger gave way to smiles, however, when the Governor subsequently signed a bill (passed the day after the UDC reversal) dramatically raising legislators' pensions. Rockefeller denied "categorically" that the two events were related. As for his strong-arm tactics in ramming UDC down various reluctant throats, he merely observed, somewhat philosophically, that "one has to use whatever authority one has when something of major importance to the people comes before you."[176]

That wording was a masterpiece of misdirection. The implication seemed to be that the Governor was simply acting on behalf of the populace, who had judged the establishment of UDC to be "of major importance." The signals given by the populace were just the opposite. Proposals to increase state debt to subsidize low-income housing had been repeatedly voted down in statewide referenda. The elected representatives of the people had voted no by almost two to one when asked to approve the establishment of a public authority to undertake low-income housing outside regular state channels. There was little doubt who had judged the creation of UDC to be "of major importance," and there was little doubt who had got his way.

There was also little doubt about the awesome nature of UDC's powers. It could override local zoning and local building codes. In the words of one expert commentator, it was "unique in the breadth and depth of its power to initiate, finance, construct, and supervise the management of residential, commercial, industrial and civic facilities."[177] The construction of low-income housing was accordingly shifted from near stagnation to full speed ahead. Within five years, UDC would build more than 30,000 housing units in 100 developments across the state. Within eight years, it would default on its notes. But that is another story.[178]

5.3.h. Taxes

The New York State government, unlike national governments, cannot print its own money. This means that every single dollar spent must first be raised through either taxes or borrowing. Even if the New York government was willing to go into debt – and Rockefeller was more than willing to undertake a debt expansion the likes of which the state had never seen – the resulting funds were insufficient to finance the helter-skelter expansion in expenditure that characterized the Rockefeller years. The inescapable conclusion was that taxes would also have to be raised. For any chief executive to persuade legislators to approve substantial increases despite their fears of voter reprisals requires the exercise of deft political maneuvering. To persuade voters in subsequent gubernatorial elections not to vent their hostility on the politician most responsible for higher taxes requires nothing less than a masterful sleight of hand. Rockefeller was more than equal to the challenge.

In the repeated escalation of state taxes during Nelson Rockefeller's years as governor,[179] the changes of 1959 and 1965 are particularly noteworthy for the magnitude of the increases wrenched from the legislators and imposed upon the public. The first of these typified a boldness that would have done credit to Genghis Khan. In office for less than a year, with negligible experience in state politics, the new governor of New York had the audacity to request a $277 million tax increase to balance the state's first $2 billion budget. (How trivial that sum appears today.) Legislators facing reelection in 1960 were predictably unenthusiastic. The leaders of both houses were still smarting from personal defeat at the hands of Rockefeller. Both Senate Majority Leader Walter Mahoney and Assembly Speaker Oswald Heck had coveted the governor's post in 1958. Both ambitions had been quashed by the man now seeking their support.

Rockefeller attacked the problem at several levels. Party politicians far below the Governor brought the usual pressures to bear upon reluctant legislators in ways inevitably difficult to document: the brandishing of rewards and threats involving political appointments, campaign support, or backing for a favorite local bill. The Governor himself remained aloof from most of the arm twisting,[180] preferring instead to voice his arguments to the public and let the pressures build upon the legislators indirectly. Thus on two successive nights in February he made an impassioned plea on television for his tax proposals, blaming his predecessor, Harriman,[181] for the prospective deficit that he now faced, and championing the cause of fiscal conservatism:

> We have got to stop this big borrowing because we have got to stop fooling ourselves. Do you realize that every time we use a dollar of borrowed money that it costs the taxpayer a dollar and fifty cents by the time they pay it back because of interest charges . . . unpleasant as it is, we have got to face the facts squarely. We have got to get back on a pay-as-you-go basis.[182]

Given the deluge of debt to come, this smacked of King Henry VIII advocating low cholesterol diets.

However curious the words from Rockefeller's lips, the policy advocated would ultimately carry the day in a smashing success for the new governor. Admittedly, in the pitch and sway of catering to legislators' discontents a few concessions had to be made. For example, Rockefeller's proposal to cut the personal tax exemption (to a standard $600) was revised upward in exchange for the legislature's dropping a proposed $40 million budget cut. What emerged from trades such as this was the original budget only slightly the worse for wear, and trivially scaled down in prospective dollars to be raised.

How it survived so well is still a puzzle. The pressures of party politics undoubtedly played a part. So did the legislators' reluctance to lock horns with a rising political star whose charisma and popular appeal had so recently been demonstrated at the polls. Finally, the very magnitude of the tax increase – the largest ever voted by a New York State Legislature – made the prospective voter backlash difficult to gauge. For many who failed to gain reelection in 1960, the threat clearly had been underestimated.

The 1965 tax increases were variations on these same themes of executive initiative and legislative reluctance, with several crucial differences. Now it was Nelson Rockefeller who faced reelection in the following year. (In 1959 he could count on three intervening years to dull the taxpayers' indignation.) It was also Nelson Rockefeller who had failed so miserably in 1964 to gain the presidency. Finally, control of the New York legislature had passed from Republicans to Democrats as part of the 1964 Democratic landslide. Embittered by the immediate past and uncertain about his political future, bursting with unsatisfied spending plans and anxious to get the jump on a new Democratic legislature sure to make spending suggestions of its own, the Governor proposed the largest Executive Budget in New York's history – approximately $3.5 billion worth – with a potential deficit of $300 to $500 million, to be eradicated by tax increases, especially a 2 percent sales tax.

Daring as this fiscal proposal was, it hardly compared with that of 1959. This time Rockefeller had in his favor almost three-quarters of a decade of experience in state politics, in building that network of personal contacts and favors owed, of patronage granted and withheld, which in the hands of the master politician turned governor of New York can exert such prodigious pressures on the politics of the state. And Rockefeller was fast becoming a master. Also in his favor was the confused state of the opposition. Will Rogers once quipped: "I am not a member of any organized political party. I am a Democrat." That remark was a fair characterization of New York's Democrats in the wake of their 1964 election triumphs. Symptomatic of their lack of party unity was the struggle over the leadership in both houses of the New York legislature. For speaker of the Assembly the main contestants were Stanley Steingut and Anthony Travia; for leadership of the Senate, Jack E. Bronston and Joseph Zaretski. Mayor Wagner of New York City was among those who championed the cause of Travia and Zaretski. Sensing opportunity in a deadlock that persisted for almost six weeks (the opportunity was rather hard to miss), Rockefeller offered to use his influence in support of Wagner's candidates in exchange for Democratic support for his 1965 budget, including its proposed tax increases.[183] To this maneuver Rockefeller added the 1959 strategies of horse trading over minor items and appeals to his constituency. The New York City sales tax, for example, was cut by 1 percent to gain support from that quarter. Once again the Governor went on statewide television to plead his case, but now he buttressed this general approach by having his office contact directly local government offices, business associations, and contractor groups, "pointing out the jobs and money that will be lost unless the budget goes through as proposed."[184] Finally, a new and devastating tactic was added, a form of brinkmanship that amounted to nothing less than a breakdown of state payments. Rockefeller refused to make any major concessions in his tax package, and refused to pass any expenditure bills until that package was passed. With a new fiscal year at hand and no new budget as yet approved, there was no money – literally – to pay the salaries of state employees (or for anything else). "Notes of intention" were used to pay employees, and local banks agreed to honor them, but apprehensions ran high. With the 1959 experience behind them, legislators could better gauge the likely voter backlash from a large tax hike, but ultimately they were incapable of mustering serious opposition to Rockefeller. Both newly elected leaders in the state legislature owed him. Mayor Wagner owed him. Legions of Republicans throughout the state, great and small, now owed him, too. Finally, the Governor's determination to have his way culminated in a fiscal tactic that transfigured the final hours of debate into a seeming choice between capitulation and chaos. The Governor got his way.

In 1971, Nelson Rockefeller had his last grand fling at escalating taxes. In a budget that called for a 20 percent increase in expenditure – a staggering figure even by Rockefeller's standards – he included a tax hike of $1.1 billion.

From the outset of the 1971 budgetary process, there was something curious, something not quite right. The memory of the golden 1960s was fading fast amid the realities of the recession of the early 1970s. Conservative Republicans such as Perry Duryea and John Hughes led a charge to slash the Executive Budget to ribbons. Many Democrats joined in, particularly those who traced their loss of control of the legislature to Democratic support of the 1965 tax increase. Most puzzling of all was the absence of vigorous support for the Governor's budget from the Governor himself. The threats and rewards brought to bear with such vigor in 1965 were barely visible. The *New York Times* even presumed to suggest that rather than leading a charge to get budget cuts restored, "Rockefeller led the fight to get his reduced budget passed."[185] Why should New York's Governor ask for so much at a time of growing economic difficulties? And why did he give way so readily to cuts initiated by the legislature, when giving way was hardly Rockefeller's style?

Part of the answer concerns the purposes for formulating such an overblown budget in the first place. The main audience to which it was directed apparently resided in Washington. A revenue sharing plan was being advocated by President Nixon, with Rockefeller acting as chief lobbyist for the interests of the states. The stakes were high: some $10 billion in federal aid, of which a large percentage could reasonably be expected to be captured by New York. By this interpretation, the Rockefeller budget was consciously designed to emphasize to Washington decision makers the dire straits of all the states, with particular emphasis on the dire straits of the Empire Sate. And of course, other things being equal, the larger the New York budget, the larger the expected flow of revenue-sharing dollars from Washington to Albany.

Another element in the tax scenario of 1971 would seem to involve the philosopher's puzzle of whether a glass is half empty or half full. The legislative assault upon Executive Budget was viewed by many as leaving that document in ribbons, a slender shadow of its initial silhouette, with $625 million slashed from the requested tax increase of $1.1 billion.[186] This kind of knife work, the murmurs ran, had never been seen before, at least not under Nelson Rockefeller. The arithmetic of subtraction, however, is instructive. If $625 million of a desired $1.1 billion was denied, then $475 million was granted – hardly a trivial figure by Rockefeller standards, and one that measured up admirably to the tax increases of 1959 and 1965. About the legitimacy of labeling these earlier tax hikes "large" the public and the legislature had no doubts. A retreat from the massive to the merely sizeable, as Rockefeller well knew, invariably leaves a handsome increment to be spent.

It therefore seems highly probable that the Governor was playing a double game, and playing it rather well. The initial budget, unreasonable by any standards, was framed with Washington publicity in mind. The subsequent legislative cuts were expected to leave that publicity relatively unscathed, and also leave – for all the hacking – a dramatic increase in state taxes. If the drama of that increase was disguised by a scenario of excessive proposals subsequently reduced, so much the better. Last, but hardly least, the Governor was not through with his tax demands for 1971.

Those who viewed the spring paring as a Rockefeller rout were forced to rethink their position before the year was out. On December 5 the Governor called for a special session of the legislature to begin on December 27. The state, it seemed, had spent itself into a hole, the prospective deficit was $1.5 billion, and to close the gap the Governor was demanding tax hikes that, on close inspection, bore a striking resemblance to many of the tax proposals voted down the previous spring. By delaying the legislative session until the last possible moment, Rockefeller prevented any formulation of a comprehensive alternative plan. To mount pressures upon the legislators, he used the old tactic of going to the people with a list of dire results should his proposals not be passed: closings of mental hospitals, colleges, and correctional facilities and severe cuts in school payments and welfare aid. To woo New York City Democrats, he linked the success of his tax proposals to a prospective $100 million state loan to the Metropolitan Transportation Authority, without which transit and commuter fares would have to be radically increased.[187] (This particular ploy was labeled by Assemblyman Richard M. Gotfried (D, Manhattan) as the "crudest and most blatant form of political blackmail.")[188] After six days of frantic cajoling, bickering, and horse trading, the legislature authorized a $407 million increase in taxes. Added to the $475 million gained the previous spring this gave a total of $882 million, which was 80 percent of a number that almost everyone had forgotten: the original tax hike proposal of $1.1 billion. Nelson Rockefeller had not forgotten.

How had Rockefeller survived? One is almost tempted to ask, how on earth had Rockefeller survived? He compiled one of the worst records for repeated tax increases[189] since Sir George Grenville devised a stamp tax for the American colonies, and yet time and again the voters had returned him to the governor's mansion.

Part of the answer, of course, was his wealth. The Rockefeller dollars tended to inundate all challengers. In 1962, he spent five times as much as his opponent; in 1966, ten times as much. He always had the money – for private polls, for his own cameramen and film crews, for media blitzes that incessantly bombarded New Yorkers concerning the merits of Nelson Rockefeller and the demerits of his opponent. (The media budget alone for his 1970 campaign totaled $3.2 million. "It was estimated that this effort reached 95 percent of the television homes in the state and that the average New York City family saw 9.4 Rockefeller television commercials in that year.")[190] Part of the answer was that although tax increases may have offended some, expenditure increases won the hearts, or at least the votes, of others. With his mania for building, Rockefeller could anchor much of his campaign in visual accomplishments: highways and hospitals, housing projects and campus buildings. The Teachers' Union, a growing power in the 1960s and 1970s, viewed Rockefeller as a friend. The construction unions viewed him as something of a gubernatorial Santa Claus, and rightly so. No one, they correctly argued, had done more for the cause of public construction in the state. Welfare recipients viewed him as a champion of their cause, at least through the 1960s, and that in turn helped this liberal Republican to make inroads into many Democratic strongholds in urban ghettos. His election tactics were always the same: Capture as much as possible of the Democratic vote in New York City, and then win big in upstate returns. Disillusioned Republicans had nowhere else to turn except to the Democratic candidate, and that, for most, was unthinkable. The Democrats, for their part, had the ongoing problem that the Governor was forever undercutting their claims to represent the cause of liberal spending. Finally, Rockefeller's longevity in office, combined with his wealth, his gubernatorial powers, and his contacts, gave him a grip – for the most part, an iron grip – upon a party structure that was being radically transformed during his years in office. The turning point was the Supreme Court's 1962 decision in favor of "one man, one vote" (*Baker* v. *Carr*). Previously, New York seats had been apportioned by counties, giving power to the party's county boss and cohesiveness to the party's structure. Now with constant reapportionment in response to demographic shifts, new districts often crossed county lines. Bosses were no longer certain from one election to the next what would remain within their domain. Legislators who were victorious in one election remained uncertain which geographic area would comprise their district in the next election. The power of the local boss was accordingly eroded, and the power of special interest groups grew apace. Would-be candidates now looked less to the county boss and more to organizations such as the Teachers' Union for campaign workers and campaign funds.[191] This transformation little affected the growing powers of the Governor. If he had the right contacts within the party, he usually had the right contacts with special interest groups as well. He could always claim an organization of his own, with a cohesiveness, a patronage history, and a financial base that could marshal power when it counted – a lot of power. His repeated successes at the polls were proof of that.

5.4. The hurricane in review

How splendid the list of achievements must have seemed to Rockefeller as he bade farewell to Albany politics. The greatest advocate of welfare spending in the state's history had urged in his first inaugural address that New York "help to lead America toward new horizons of well being and equal opportunity for all citizens."[192] Now, as he crossed the threshold of the governor's office for the last time, he could justifiably claim to have backed that vision to the hilt. During his regime, spending for health, education, and welfare had been radically transformed. The state's university system, a paltry 38,000 students on 28 campuses in 1958, could now boast 246,000 students on 71 campuses.[193] New York's welfare benefits were among the highest in the country. So were its Medicaid benefits. Above all, new buildings erected in the name of health, education, and welfare had fairly mushroomed up and down the state, from Long Island to the St. Lawrence, from the Bronx to Buffalo: medical schools and mental health facilities, hospitals and nursing homes, libraries and dormitories, laboratories and low-income housing.

These achievements, however, were not without their drawbacks. Tax increases that helped to pay for them had also helped to drive industry from the state, thereby shrinking the tax base and employment possibilities. The very generosity of welfare benefits had helped to hold within New York a growing welfare class, thereby augmenting welfare payments of the future. As the dollars multiplied and the bureaucracy grew, control was frequently a shambles. The state's main welfare program, AFDC, when finally investigated thoroughly, was found to have a scandalous ineligibility rate of 17.6 percent (better than one in six). Planning was, at best, tenuous, and at worst, totally absent. When Nelson Rockefeller took over, he championed the cause of planning: "To generate a new era of progress, we need not only to focus on the problems of our time, but to anticipate the problems of the future as well. We need to chart courses which will achieve basic solutions."[194] That was the dream. The reality reeked of failure. With no sense of the secular retardation in the state's economy that had been in evidence for years, he did much to offend established businesses and little to attract new ones. With no sense of the demographic shifts that were sure to shrink student enrollments, in evidence since the mid-1960s, he drove his SUNY expansion program relentlessly forward. By the late 1970s, excess capacity was rampant throughout the state's higher educational system. Indicative of overbuilding of a different sort, excess capacity was also prevalent in the state's hospitals. Rockefeller's professed objective of charting "courses which will achieve basic solutions" was seldom met. In housing, for example, the Governor had claimed in 1968 that the state would "have to build new low-income and middle-income housing at a rate at least six times the rate we are building it now."[195] By his final year in office, Rockefeller was forced to concede: "It's obvious that we haven't had a solution to the housing problem . . . private money has to be attracted back into it."[196]

Shortly after Rockefeller's death in 1979, his record was reviewed by former Governor Malcolm Wilson in an article entitled "Nelson A. Rockefeller: Man of Balance."[197] A fitting tribute from an old friend, it was hardly a fitting characterization of the facts. Whatever Nelson Rockefeller's claim to a place of prominence in the state's history, it can scarcely rest upon a claim to balance. This was a man with a propensity for overdoing, for triumphs on a grand scale, and for failures on a grand scale. Impatient when constrained and impetuous when not, a spender more than a planner, a doer more than a thinker, he prodded, cajoled, and bullied the state into a spending spree that, in retrospect, was often as intemperate as the man.

Not that Rockefeller always got his way. In the rise of spending for welfare, for Medicaid, and for primary and secondary education, he appears to have been more a contributing factor than a decisive influence, with one important qualification. He set a tone and style that favored at least a liberal, if not a lavish, approach to all state problems. For Democrats bent upon social legislation, it proved infectious. For conservative Republicans, it was difficult to counteract. The Governor, they knew, was almost always in favor of more.

In some instances, he did not just contribute. He took control. A powerful man in a powerful position, he became progressively more deft at getting his way, at maneuvering all of the many levers at his disposal. Or, as some Democrats chose to put it on the occasion of his retirement, he was "a consummate politician whose use of patronage and power would make an old-line Tammany boss proud."[198] Taxes were a case in point. So was SUNY. Confronted with a flagging system that had little tradition and an uncertain future, he gave it a massive blueprint and a massive injection of dollars, thereby converting it by the time he left office into the largest system of higher education in the country. Housing was also a case in point. What was a modest building program running out of steam in the late 1950s had become a multibillion dollar enterprise by the early 1970s.

There was, moreover, a darker side to these achievements, blatantly undemocratic and even constitutionally suspect. Most of the building – for SUNY and CUNY, for low- and middle-income housing, for hospitals and mental health facilities – was wrenched from the hands of the legislature and transferred to public authorities; and authority debt expansion required no voter approval. Frequently it required nothing more from the legislature than the authorization of a debt ceiling. The authorizations that came to matter most were in the hands of one man – the Governor – and the lieutenants he appointed to run public authorities. The resulting explosion of debt and construction spending hardly reflected the wishes of the people. In fact, in some instances the people had expressed the opposite wish by voting down a proposed increase in state debt to finance a project that was subsequently financed by a public authority. Indeed, that negative vote was the key reason for transferring the construction project in question to the jurisdiction of a public authority. Decision making by the elected representatives of the people in the legislature thus tended to give way to decision making by the chief executive and his bureaucratic appointees. The wishes of the people were thus superseded, by and large, by the wishes of one man. Nelson Rockefeller was a better judge of what the people needed, or so he apparently believed. Whatever his strengths, Rockefeller was not a democrat in the broadest sense of that word, as many of his contemporaries repeatedly emphasized. John Lindsay's characterization is typical: "He just doesn't believe in local participation, in the common sense of ordinary people. He thinks he knows what's best for everyone. So he walks right in and builds things, big things. He's a colonialist."[199]

This was hardly a man of balance. Moreover, what he threatened – and ultimately subverted by this process – was the very spirit of the Constitution that had been encapsulated in that provision requiring voter approval of all proposed increases in state debt. The threat was hardly new. Justice Brandeis, for one, had sounded a warning decades earlier: "The greatest dangers to liberty lurk in insidious encroachments by men of zeal, well-meaning but without understanding."[200] There have been encroachments. They have been insidious. In his own way, Rockefeller was well-meaning. He cared about social welfare programs, but insisted on defining for himself how and when they were to be attacked. He may or may not have been, in Brandeis's phrase, "without understanding" when it came to judging the needs of New Yorkers. When it came to subverting a constitutional principle to get his way, he understood too much. The vehicle whereby he got his way involved an old institution – the public authority – and a new financial gimmick – the moral obligation bond. How these two led to that accomplishment, and what dangers presently exist because of the staggering dimensions of that accomplishment, are therefore the subjects of the next chapter.

6

Public authorities in New York State: the evolution of bureaucratic giants

6.1. The nature of the problem

Arthur Levitt was worried. The year was 1972. State expenditures and debt had been exploding at unprecedented rates in the past decade. So had public authorities. And that was one of the developments that had the State Comptroller worried. With typically guarded phrasing, he summarized his concerns in November of that year as follows:

> These quasi-governmental agencies [public authorities] have been operating on a scale so massive that, in some instances, they overshadow the fiscal operations of the State itself. Moreover, authorities now perform many public benefit activities once accomplished within the regular framework of State government. Since authority operations are not subject to the same degree of public scrutiny to which regular State activities are subjected, this trend tends to obscure the overall scope of public activities, as well as the fiscal impact of public sector services within the State.[1]

But what exactly was a public authority? What dangers lay in their being relatively free of "public scrutiny"? And why were they now operating – for the first time in the state's history – on a scale so massive that they threatened to overshadow nothing less than the fiscal operations of the state itself?

About the massiveness there could be little debate. In 1962, Rockefeller's fourth year as governor, there were 125 public benefit corporations in New York, 26 of them statewide authorities, with a total outstanding debt of $3.3 billion. By the time Rockefeller left office, there were over 230, 41 of them statewide, with a total debt outstanding of $13.3 billion. One measure of their impact upon the state's economy is the magnitude of the dollar flows they annually took in and reallocated: almost $2 billion in gross receipts by 1974. It was their debt, however, that staggered the imagination. It had quadrupled in 12 years. At $13.3 billion, it was almost four times the entire full faith and credit debt of the state itself.[2] A single authority, the Housing Finance

Agency, *had surpassed the entire Empire State in debt outstanding by almost 50 percent.*[3] A second empire, it seems, was in the making. Small wonder that Arthur Levitt spoke of the public authorities' tendency to "overshadow" the fiscal operations of the state. Nor was there another state in the union where this explosion of authorities was seriously echoed.[4] Many had witnessed the expansion of public benefit corporations in the 1960s and early 1970s, but nothing like the proliferation of leviathans that now sprawled across the landscape from the Hudson to Lake Erie. They were huge. They were largely beyond public control. And in that tenuous control were dangers of the first magnitude.

6.2. The nature of the beast

Characterizing a public authority is not an easy task. Nowhere in either the statutes or the Constitution of New York is the term defined. Even the use of the name "authority" is no sure guide to which institutions count. The Housing Finance Agency, for example, is a public authority despite its name, whereas the State Liquor Authority is not (being a regulatory agency with none of the attributes of a public authority). For all this legal and semantic vagueness, the basic nature of the institution is relatively clear-cut. Public authorities are public benefit corporations, the name of the latter signifying in no uncertain terms whose benefit these entities are designed to serve. In more formal terms, the latter is defined in the law as "a corporation organized to construct or operate a public improvement wholly or partly within the State, the profits from which enure to the benefit of this or other States, or to the people thereof." This merely reiterates in a more complicated way the fundamental point to be kept ever to the fore in subsequent discussion: that public authorities are corporate bodies designed to serve the public – not the bureaucrat, not the politician, but the public. As corporate bodies, they possess many of the characteristics of private corporations, such as the right to hold and acquire real estate and the right to enter into contracts.[5]

The interesting question is what sets a public authority apart from a regular state agency. That something sets it apart is clear: "In brief, the public authority is a corporate body authorized by the Legislature to function outside the regular structure of the State or local government. By virtue of its corporate attributes, authorities have autonomous characteristics not available to 'regular' governmental agencies."[6] The characteristic that seems to be all important is financial. State and local governments can transfer money to public authorities just as easily as to regular government agencies. But what public authorities escape – and state agencies cannot avoid – are the constitutional limitations on the issuance of debt. This key difference helps to explain why many public authorities were created in the first place.

The classic New York study detailing the reasons for creating public authorities is still William Ronan's 1956 *Staff Report on Public Authorities under New York State.*[7] In a rambling and somewhat repetitious manner, this report spells out roughly a dozen reasons why public authorities exist. What is remarkable is that few if any of the reasons advanced give any justification whatsoever for the existence of public authorities.

Ronan's main economic argument is that public authorities offer a means of accomplishing specific tasks (such as the construction of roads, bridges, or tunnels) by charging users of the resulting facilities. The users of the New York Thruway, for example, pay for its construction and maintenance through cash surrendered at its toll booths. This admittedly is an argument for one form of financing over another (user charges instead of taxes), which in many instances appeals on grounds of equity. Those who benefit directly should be those who pay, seems to be the rationale. This does not explain why a public authority rather than a state agency should build the structure and collect the tolls. Ronan offers three principal justifications for preferring the former over the latter. None will stand up under close scrutiny.

The first reason is couched in terms of fiscal necessity. The state Constitution limits the amount of debt that can be incurred by a locality to a percentage of the assessed valuation of real estate.[8] It also requires that any issuance of debt by the state itself be approved by a voter referendum.[9] The public authority, as Ronan notes, "offers the distinct advantage" of being able to borrow outside these debt limitations.[10] But distinct advantage for whom? The question becomes all the more critical when one realizes – as Ronan realizes[11] – that the desire to circumvent these constitutional provisions has been the major reason for the development of the public authority device in New York State.

Consider the matter of voter referendum on new state debt. In the 1950s the state asked the voters to approve an increase in debt to finance the development of subsidized housing for middle-income groups. The proposal was voted down. Presumably that negative vote reflected the public's judgment concerning the desirability of the project. Enter the public authority. If one of these quasi-independent agencies could be set up to float its own debt, and the proceeds used to initiate the middle-income housing in question, the negative attitude of the public could be thwarted. And thwarted it was. The public authority in question became known as the Housing Finance Agency. Its borrowing tended to be backed by the moral obligation of the state (described in Section 6.4), thereby assuring two things: Its bonds could be sold to the financial community at a relatively low interest rate, and the voters of the state would have nothing whatsoever to say about the appropriateness of any of its debt, because none of that debt would be subject to a voter referendum.

In sum, the argument that a public authority permits the circumvention of constitutional limitations upon the issuance of debt is certainly an explanation (and a key explanation) of why public authorities have been resorted to so frequently in New York State.[12] That explanation, however, is hardly a justification. Indeed, it cuts the other way. If this has been the primary motivation for initiating so many public authorities, then all of them are prima facie suspect.

But what kinds of arguments might justify their existence? Ronan suggests two possible answers.

One reason advanced is political convenience: the "desire to establish a buffer between the political administration and the public so that elective officials may avoid direct responsibility for actions which might be a source of political embarrassment."[13] This may help to explain why public authorities are created by politicians, but, once again, it hardly justifies their existence. The concept of a "buffer" Ronan tends to defend on somewhat different grounds: "The autonomy of the public authority is believed to lessen the dangers of partisan interference with long-range capital enterprises."[14] This is both deficient in theory and wrong in fact. Any passing knowledge of the operation of public authorities in New York State suggests that their creation and operation is hardly free from party politics. The more important question, however, is why independence is presumed to be an unmitigated good. The controlling issue is the extent to which the actions of public authorities do or do not reflect the interests of the people. Ronan's premise seems to be that insulated bureaucrats will always be more responsive to those interests than bureaucrats subjected to pressure, monitoring, and control from the executive and the legislature – this despite the fact that the same legislature and executive are the elected representatives of the people, and are therefore subject to the discipline of the ballot box.

The same point can be made by standing another Ronan quotation on its head. Along the same general theme, he argues that "an authority may be in a better position than an agency of regular government to operate a public enterprise without regard for party politics, patronage, and party favoritism. If a public authority is responsible for the management of a public enterprise, then the entrepreneurial decisions necessary to the economical and efficient operation of a public enterprise may more likely be kept out of the political arena."[15] This is essentially an argument in the negative: that public authorities are to be preferred because of what they avoid. But – to repeat the key question – why is the end result presumed to be superior? Why should the public interest be better served by bureaucrats insulated, or at least partly insulated, from "the political arena"? What will undoubtedly be better served are the vested interests of the bureaucrats. In serving those interests, however, the heads of public authorities do not have an enviable record for acting on behalf of the populace at large.

They do not even have an enviable record for efficiency. The Comptroller of New York, for example, noted in 1972 that audits conducted by his staff have amply demonstrated that "this form of government operation is not inherently more efficient than the regular structure of State government."[16]

Efficiency, however, is not the central issue. Let us be quite clear about what is. None of the arguments advanced thus far demonstrates that state agencies are superior to public authorities. In deciding which is better, however, the electorate should be equally skeptical of both. In particular it should view with a jaundiced eye arguments favoring "insulation." The plea to make decision making free of political influence at bottom is an argument that expresses a profound distrust of the democratic process. Not only does it imply that neither the people nor their elected representatives can be entrusted with any influence over certain kinds of decisions, but the hidden premise is that bureaucrats will serve the public interest better than its elected representatives. There is absolutely no reason in theory why this should be the case. What the facts suggest is that the heads of public authorities are often motivated by their own self-interest much of the time. To insulate them from the political process is to remove from the structure of their decision making a critical form of checks and balances, and *leave almost nothing in the way of other checks and balances.* What the theory and facts therefore indicate is that there should be no presumption whatsoever that the resulting bureaucratic structure will serve the public well, or serve the public better than a system more responsive to the political process.[17]

This leaves only one item on Ronan's list of possible reasons for establishing a public authority instead of a state agency. Certain projects, such as the building of a bridge between New York and Canada, raise multiple jurisdiction problems. Other examples are bridges between states, or in the case of the Port Authority of New York and New Jersey, harbor and port facilities involving more than one state. To deal with such projects through normal government agencies, as Ronan points out, would involve "elaborate inter-jurisdictional arrangements."[18] These difficulties are neatly sidestepped by the creation of a public authority, such as the Buffalo and Fort Erie Public Bridge Authority, or the Lake Champlain Bridge Commission. To the advantages of simplifying jurisdictional arrangements Ronan adds the virtues of continuity and flexibility that are presumed to accompany the establishment of control in the hands of an appointed executive whose members serve for a designated term. He concludes with a cautionary note: "It [the public authority] can be responsibly controlled if its powers are carefully delineated and there is a periodic and systematic review of its activities."[19]

Under both headings – delineation of powers and systematic review – actual developments within the state do not make for a happy story. The extent to which the activities of public authorities are subject to "periodic and systematic review" will be taken up in Section 6.5. Public control of public authorities will be found to be minimal or nonexistent. But that is only half of the problem. The other half concerns the means whereby an old objective – the "careful delineation" of powers and responsibilities of public authorities – was radically altered in the course of half a century as the result of restructuring the associated notions of what a public authority was designed to do and how it was supposed to do it. The main architects of this restructuring were Robert Moses and Nelson Rockefeller. The public and their elected representatives were almost never consulted on the merits of these changes. Worse, they were continually deceived, misled, or misinformed, in order to minimize their interference in the transformation process. In this manner, the desires of the few were little affected by the wishes of the many. The tale of what resulted has much to do with power politics and ambitious bureaucrats; with the proliferation of highways, parks, and buildings; with bond indebtedness now running into billions. It has very little to do with democracy.

6.3. Robert Moses: architect of unintended immortality

On March 6, 1978, Robert Moses addressed an invited audience at the National Portrait Gallery, apparently on the premise that his portrait would some day hang there. He was 89. Aside from glasses and a cane, there was no sign that time had softened the man who, in *New York Times* phrasing, had "terrorized generations of public officials, and whose monuments no New Yorker can miss."[20] Those monuments were duly noted by the man who introduced Moses – 416 miles of

Table 6.1. *Major public authorities controlled at some point by Robert Moses*

Authority	Length of term	Removable by
Appointed by the mayor of New York City		
Triborough Bridge and Tunnel Authority[a]	6 years	Mayor
New York City Parks Department[b]	At pleasure of mayor	Mayor
Marine Parkway Authority[c]	At pleasure of mayor	Mayor
Henry Hudson Parkway Authority[c]	At pleasure of mayor	Mayor
New York City Housing Authority[d]	At pleasure of mayor	Mayor
Appointed by the governor of New York State		
Long Island State Park Commission	6 years	Governor
New York State Council of Parks[e]	6 years	Governor
Jones Beach State Park Authority[f]	6 years	Governor
Bethpage State Park Authority[f]	6 years	Governor
New York State Bridge Authority	5 years	Senate[g]
New York State Power Authority	5 years	Senate[g]
Appointed by the executive of Nassau County		
Nassau County Bridge Authority	3 years	County executive

[a] The Triborough Bridge Authority (controlled by Moses) merged with the New York City Tunnel Authority in 1946. Moses controlled the combined authority.

[b] Moses served as commissioner.

[c] Consists of one member, the New York City Commissioner of Parks. Both the Marine Parkway Authority and the Henry Hudson Parkway Authority subsequently merged with the Triborough Bridge Authority.

[d] Controlled by Moses indirectly. (See for example Robert Caro, *The Power Broker: Robert Moses and the Fall of New York* [New York: Vintage Books, 1975], 706.)

[e] The president of the Long Island State Park Commission, Moses, served as an automatic member. Moses was chairman.

[f] Board consists of Long Island State Park Commissioner.

[g] Upon recommendation of the governor.

Sources: Caro (1975); *Legislative Manual of New York State*, various years; *The Greater New York Charter*, Laws of 1901, Chapter 466; *McKinney's Consolidated Laws of New York State, Annotated*, vol. XLII (Public Authorities) and other volumes; Thelma G. Smith (ed.), *Guide to Municipal*

parkways and 25 million acres of state parks, to cite only two items from a long list. That Moses should have any monuments at all is something of a puzzle. How could one man, never elected to a single political office of consequence, spend so much of the public's money? The key to his success was his ability to wheedle, maneuver, and threaten his way to the top of a bureaucratic empire that was quite without precedent in the history of the Empire State. Its main components were the dozen-odd public authorities that politicians, for various reasons, allowed him to control (see Table 6.1).[21] On paper, Moses was usually the chief executive in a structure of managing boards or committees. In practice, he ran every last one of them with an iron fist that tolerated few suggestions and little opposition.

And yet the question remains: How could a single bureaucrat amass such power?[22] From the beginning of his rise to prominence, Moses was threatened with the prospect that the public authorities he controlled would be funded into oblivion. Take for example the Triborough Bridge Authority. The legislators who voted this public authority into existence structured the enabling law so that it could float bonds, use the proceeds to build a bridge, and then pay off the bonds with toll receipts. When the bonds were paid off, both the toll booths and the Authority would cease to exist. This was in keeping with the conventional notion of public authorities: that their corporate life should terminate when the initial cost of a specific project (in this case a bridge) had been recovered through user charges. The original act therefore included a clause stating that the Triborough "board and its corporate existence shall continue only for a period of five years and thereafter until all its . . . bonds have been paid in full."

Winston Churchill once remarked that he had not become the Queen's First Minister to preside over the dissolution of the British Empire. Robert Moses was no more enthusiastic about the prospective disappearance of his empire. Unlike Churchill, he found the means to stop dissolution dead in its tracks.[23] The key was to be found in the legal phrasing cited above. If the Triborough Bridge Authority would cease to exist when all of its bonds had been paid in full, all that was necessary to preserve the Authority was some device to prevent retirement of all of its bonds. Moses found his opportunity when he was

---

Notes to Table 6.1 (*cont.*)

Government of the City of New York; New York [State], Temporary State Commission on Coordination of State Activities, *Staff Report on Public Authorities under New York State,* by William Ronan, Legislative Document no. 46, March 21, 1956 (hereafter *Public Authorities under New York State*); *Laws of New York 1934,* Chapter 2.

charged with drafting a new bill for the Triborough Authority. But which device? And how could it be hidden from legislators whose intentions were the exact opposite of his own? The solution was embarrassingly simple. To disguise its true intent, Moses buried the solution far inside the act, and couched the requisite wording in terms well calculated to confuse even the most attentive reader. In a subdivision that apparently had nothing whatsoever to do with the longevity of the Authority was a single sentence: "The authority shall have power from time to time to refund any bonds by the issuance of new bonds, whether the bonds to be refunded have or have not matured, and may issue bonds partly to refund bonds then outstanding and partly for any other corporate purpose."[24] That did it. The Triborough Bridge Authority would cease to exist when all of its bonds were paid off. But if every time its bonds were about to mature they were refunded (*before* maturing) into new bonds, then the Authority would achieve a new longevity bordering on immortality. With a stroke of the pen, Moses thereby transformed what was intended to be a temporary institution into a near-permanent New York fixture.

Two problems remained for the empire builder. The first was money and what to do with it. If the bonds of the Authority were, in effect, never paid off, and toll receipts kept pouring in, what could be done with the surplus? Maintenance of the Triborough Bridge itself was a trivial expenditure, and the spending of toll receipts for other purposes was severely constrained by the terms of the Triborough Act. The original legislation creating the authority had explicitly authorized it to construct only a single, specific project: two bridges and their "approaches." Again Moses' ambitions clashed with a basic notion of a public authority: in this case, the notion that it was created to accomplish a single, specified objective. That particular idea he relegated to the ash can by yet another provision in the revised Triborough Act that he was drafting.

The new terms stated that the Authority could acquire land for, and construct, "new roads, streets, parkways or avenues connecting with the approaches" to its bridges. The key work is "connecting." As every New York cab driver knows, the Triborough Bridge can be reached from virtually any road in the metropolis. Put another way, virtually all roads in the city can be viewed as "connecting" with this bridge (or with any other bridge for that matter). This unsurprising observation meant that, by the new law, the Authority was empowered to build almost anything that could be termed a "road, street, parkway or avenue" in a geographic area that was both vast and unspecified. Into that unspecified domain Robert Moses charged with a passion for construction – and power – that rivaled even the inclinations of Nelson Rockefeller.

He could gratify both only if one final problem could be solved. What the legislature had granted unwittingly the legislature could take away. The last challenge was to devise a means of insulating his powers from such attacks. Again the solution was embarrassingly simple, although no one saw it except Moses. An authority floats bonds. Bonds are a legal contract between seller and purchaser, the terms of which cannot be violated by any one – not even by the legislature of New York. All that was required therefore was to write into the bond contracts the key powers initially granted to him (or to his office) by the legislators. And this is exactly what Moses did.

Even if the powers became insulated, surely the man remained vulnerable, or so one might expect. He was appointed to his various bureaucratic positions by politicians, usually the governor of the state or the mayor of New York City. The same politicians could usually remove him "for cause," which generally meant, in the wording of the Public Authority Law of New York, "for inefficiency, neglect of duty, or misconduct in office."[25] Even if forced removal was unlikely – the process was almost sure to be cumbersome and politically embarrassing – Moses remained vulnerable, given the limited tenure associated with all of his bureaucratic positions (usually five or six years; see Table 6.1). Politicians might hesitate to throw him out, but would they not resist his amassing of power by failing to reappoint him when his terms expired? The answer was unambiguously in the negative. From Al Smith to Nelson Rockefeller, Robert Moses was reappointed again and again – and again.[26] The story of how this was achieved is both shabby and complex, and not of critical importance to the arguments developed here.[27] Its main ingredients were a mixture of the admirable and the appalling: an ability "to get things done" (mainly, to get bridges, parks, and highways built); an unrivaled knowledge of the legal and institutional structure of the state; a carefully cultivated public image assuring popular support; and a network of political influence, obligations, and intimidation that even included the hiring of " 'bloodhounds' to dig up facts about an opponent that could induce him to cease his opposition."[28] As his biographer observed, Robert Moses "was a pioneer in McCarthyism twenty years before McCarthy."[29]

He was a pioneer in much more than that. Emerson once observed that an institution is the lengthened shadow of one man. In the evolution of the structure of public authorities in New York, this is perhaps too flattering an image for Robert Moses. His shadow nevertheless fell heavily upon that institution, leaving an imprint that has proven to be distressingly durable. Before his rise to power, public authorities were generally viewed as temporary entities. Empowered to accomplish a specific task, they should cease to exist when the task was done, or so the argument went. This notion about what an authority should be has largely been obliterated. The modern variant not infrequently has powers, purposes, and a life-span all of which remain ill-defined. And with that lack of definition has come a bureaucracy awesome in its jurisdictional dimensions, awesome in the public funds that it controls, and answering to almost no one, or to very few – and faintly.

The second Moses legacy is nothing less than a tradition of monopoly profits, extracted from the public, and allocated by and large at the whim of bureaucratic chiefs. Recall the problem of tolls on the Triborough Bridge. The revenues thereby received quickly matched the construction costs of what the Authority was supposed to build. In this and many other similar instances, however, the tolls continued to be charged and the funds thereby assembled were diverted to other tasks not intended to be accomplished by the authority in question – or certainly not intended by the legislators whose votes set up the Authority in the first place. Monopoly profits, roundly condemned when encountered in the private sector, are possible only when prices are charged well in excess of costs. And yet just such prices continue to be charged by a host of public authorities, with the surplus thus amassed redirected to other "public" projects. Note that this implies nothing whatsoever about whether those other public projects are good or bad in themselves. The central argument tendered here is that decisions on how much money to take from the public, and what projects to finance with the resulting funds, should be decided *not* by bureaucrats but by the elected representatives of the people. If taxes levied or projects funded are subsequently judged by the public to be unwise, they can express their dissatisfactions either directly to the politicians or indirectly through the ballot box. This of course does not guarantee a perfect link between the public's interests and the actions of their elected representatives. But a system with some linkages, however imperfect, is surely preferable to one with no linkages whatsoever. The latter would seem to be the world of New York public authorities, or at least much of that world.

If ever the career of a single man illustrated the premise that a bureaucratic chief can be motivated primarily by self-interest, it is the empire building of Robert Moses. One controlling theme of this book can be couched as a question: If bureaucrats are so motivated, what prevents their pursuit of self-interest from operating to the detriment of the public interest? As the actions of Moses suggest, the answer may often be "very little." The same question of course should be asked of politicians. Here too the answer is discouraging, as the career of Nelson Rockefeller demonstrates. His role in the transformation of public authorities within New York State is part of that demonstration.

6.4. Nelson Rockefeller: the stunting of fiscal viability and the rise of moral obligation bonds

April 3, 1938. For the eighth time in New York State's history, a Constitutional Convention was about to assemble to consider appropriate revisions in the state's most fundamental document. With a sense of the importance of their mission, the delegates trickled into Albany – 168 in all, including a well-tanned Al Smith, sporting his familiar brown derby.

Among their various concerns were the "many problems [that] have arisen in connection with the mushroom growth of authorities."[30] What may have been a mushrooming by the standards of 1938 came to little more than a handful of toadstools by the standards of the postwar era. In terms both of numbers created and (more importantly) of dollars controlled, the era of the giants lay largely in the future (see Tables 6.2, 6.3, and 6.4). For all that, the delegates remained concerned, and with good reason. The problems emphasized in the previous section were even then apparent:

> [Public authorities] bring sharply to the fore the question of popular responsibility. In the final analysis, all these authorities perform governmental functions, and have tremendous financial powers, but they are responsive to the control of the voters only in that the members of the authority are appointed by a popularly elected executive, be he mayor or governor. But once the authority is established, it is almost self-perpetuating. Sometimes the activities of an authority transcend in financial scope the activities of a whole town or village, but they have none of the elements of popular control which accrue as a matter of course to the town or village.[31]

"Elements of popular control" – this above all else was the critical issue, even in 1938. Under that particular heading, the worst was yet to be (see Sections 6.5 and 6.6).

The same was true for almost every major concern that the delegates brought to the question of the appropriate means for establishing and operating public authorities in the state. Take the matter of finance, and the appropriate fiscal linkages between the state and any authority

Table 6.2. *A chronological list of statewide public authorities created in New York State*

Authority, commission, or corporation	Year created
Port Authority of New York and New Jersey[a]	1921
Albany Port District Commission[b]	1925
Lake Champlain Bridge Commission	1927
Niagara Frontier Bridge Commission[c]	1929
Whiteface Mountain Bridge Commission[d]	1929
Power Authority of the State of New York[e]	1931
New York State Bridge Authority	1932
American Museum of National History Planetarium Authority	1933
Bethpage Park Authority[f]	1933
Buffalo and Fort Erie Public Bridge Authority	1933
Central New York Regional Market Authority	1933
Industrial Exhibit Authority	1933
Jones Beach State Parkway Authority	1933
Lower Hudson Regional Market Authority[g]	1933
Pelham–Portchester Parkway Authority[h]	1933
Saratoga Springs Authority[i]	1933
Thousand Islands Bridge Authority	1933
Triborough Bridge Authority[j]	1933
Henry Hudson Parkway Authority[k]	1934
Marine Parkway Authority[k]	1934
New York State World War Memorial Authority[h]	1934
Albany Light, Heat, and Power Authority[h]	1935
Albany Regional Market Authority[h]	1935
Queens–Midtown Tunnel Authority[l]	1935
Rockland, Westchester Hudson River Crossing Authority[h]	1935
New York City Tunnel Authority[j]	1936
New York City Parkway Authority[m]	1938
Niagara Frontier Authority[n]	1943
Dormitory Authority	1944
Whiteface Mountain Authority[o]	1944
Triborough Bridge and Tunnel Authority	1946
New York State Thruway Authority	1950
Ogdensburg Bridge Authority	1950
Genesee Valley Regional Market Authority	1951
New York City Transit Authority	1953
Niagara Frontier Port Authority	1955
Oswego Port Authority	1955
Brooklyn Sports Center Authority[h]	1956
Higher Education Assistance Corporation[p]	1957
New York State World War Memorial Authority[h]	1957
East Hudson Parkway Authority	1960
New York State Housing Finance Agency	1960
Adirondack Mountain Authority	1960
New York State Job Development Authority	1961

Table 6.2 (*cont.*)

Authority, commission, or corporation	Year created
New York State Atomic Research and Space Development Authority[a] (Energy Research Development Authority)	1962
Manhattan and Bronx Surface Transit Operating Authority	1962
State University Construction Fund[r]	1962
Mental Hygiene Facilities Inpatient Fund[r]	1963
Metropolitan Commuter Transportation Authority (Metropolitan Transportation Authority)	1965
Long Island Rail Road[s]	1966
Niagara Frontier Transportation Authority	1967
Battery Park City Authority	1968
United Nations Development Corporation	1968
Urban Development Corporation	1968
Rochester–Genesee Regional Transportation Authority	1969
Environmental Facilities Corporation	1970
State of New York Mortgage Agency	1970
Capital District Transportation Authority	1970
Central New York Transportation Authority	1970
New York Municipal Bond Bank Agency	1972
Medical Care Facilities Finance Agency[r]	1973
Municipal Assistance Corporation	1975
Project Finance Agency	1975

Note: "This classification of authorities is based upon the participation of the Governor in appointments to Authority boards." New York [State], Office of the Comptroller, *Annual Report* (hereafter *Annual Report of the Comptroller*), 1972, p. 23.

[a] Called the Port of New York Authority until 1972.

[b] Not classified as a public authority in *Public Authorities under New York State*. See ibid., pp. 603–4 for an explanation; it is considered there to be a district corporation.

[c] Superseded by the Niagara Frontier Authority in 1943.

[d] Superseded by the Whiteface Mountain Authority in 1944.

[e] Lobbied in New York State's interest for the joint United States–Canada development of the St. Lawrence River until 1951.

[f] Dissolved in 1975.

[g] Dissolved in 1968.

[h] Never activated.

[i] Dissolved in 1961.

[j] Merged into the Triborough Bridge and Tunnel Authority in 1946.

[k] Merged into the New York City Parkway Authority in 1938.

[l] Merged into the New York City Tunnel Authority in 1936.

[m] Merged with the Triborough Bridge Authority in 1940.

[n] "Terminated" in 1956. (See *Public Authorities under New York State*, p. 29).

[o] Merged with the Adirondack Mountain Authority in 1960.

Table 6.3. *Outstanding bonds and notes of public authorities
in New York State, 1960–76 ($ millions)*

Fiscal year ending in calendar year	Total bonds and notes outstanding	"Moral obligation" debt	Battery Park City Authority	Dormitory Authority	Housing Finance Agency	Municipal Assistance Corporation
1976	18,913.0[a]	9,173	200.0	1,939.0	5,203.5	3,676.0[a]
1975	14,150.0	5,197	200.0	1,889.5	5,245.7	0.0
1974	13,253.4	4,246	200.0	1,685.2	5,042.3	—
1973	12,058.5	3,079	200.0	1,438.2	4,699.7	—
1972	10,589.0	2,149	200.0	1,332.0	4,053.1	—
1971	8,874.5	1,596	0.0	1,187.1	3,091.5	—
1970	7,357.2	968	0.0	1,033.9	2,312.5	—
1969	6,502.2	843	0.0	828.1	1,901.0	—
1968	6,161.0	663	—	698.3	1,677.4	—
1967	5,108.3	462	—	573.2	1,216.0	—
1966	4,662.6	418	—	393.0	938.8	—
1965	4,536.1	410	—	258.7	846.0	—
1964	4,198.4	333	—	171.3	622.9	—
1963	3,742.0	254	—	133.0	286.4	—
1962	3,267.8	60	—			—
1961	3,131.0	60	—			—
1960	2,920.6	0	—			—

[a] The Municipal Assistance Corporation and Project Finance Agency are included here, but not in the *Annual Report*.
Source: Annual Report of the Comptroller, 1977, pt. I, pp. 28, 37; 1976,

---

Notes to Table 6.2 (*cont.*)
[p] Now the Higher Education Services Corporation.
[q] Later called the Atomic and Space Development Authority.
[r] Acts for the New York State Housing Finance Agency.
[s] Part of the Metropolitan Transportation Authority.
Source: Annual Report of the Comptroller, 1961, p. 54, and various subsequent years; *Public Authorities under New York State,* pp. 13–39, 583–4, 697; New York [State], Office of the Comptroller, *Public Authorities in New York State: A Financial Study,* Comptroller's Studies for the 1967 Constitutional Convention, Study no. 4, June 1967, pp. 5–49.

N.Y.S. Mortgage Agency	N.Y.S. Thru-way Au-thor-ity	N.Y.S. Urban De-velop-ment Cor-pora-tion	Port Au-thority of N.Y. and N.J.	Power Au-thority of the State of N.Y.	Proj-ect Fi-nance Agency	Tri-borough Bridge and Tunnel Au-thority	All others
362.6	762.2	1,252.8	2,021.7	2,402.3	302.2[a]	256.0	534.7
384.4	780.0	1,167.4	1,964.6	1,640.2	0.0	276.5	601.7
156.3	814.9	1,167.3	1,955.5	1,407.9	—	294.8	529.2
47.6	833.7	770.0	2,029.9	1,221.3	—	315.4	502.7
49.7	776.7	397.5	1,796.8	1,243.4	—	331.2	408.6
41.2	789.6	250.2	1,711.7	1,147.7	—	326.5	329.0
—	811.6	0.7	1,470.7	1,064.5	—	318.1	345.0
—	835.4	0.0	1,377.6	953.9	—	310.3	295.7
—	860.4	—	1,389.5	980.3	—	337.2	217.9
—	888.5	—	906.5	973.1	—	354.3	196.4
—	905.8	—	832.8	1,021.5	—	376.1	195.0
—	934.8	—	855.9	1,060.7	—	392.5	187.4
—	941.1	—	806.1	1,077.5	—	408.6	170.5
—	953.1	—	739.5	1,079.8	—	419.3	130.9
—	—	—	—	—	—	—	
—	—	—	—	—	—	—	
—	—	—	—	—	—	—	

p. 41; 1975, p. 33; 1974, p. 28; 1973, p. 24; 1972, p. 23; 1971, p. 23; 1970, p. 24; 1969, p. 25; 1968, p. 23; 1967, p. 31; 1966, p. 28; 1965, p. 28; 1964, p. 21; 1963, p. 30; 1962, p. 48; 1961, p. 53.

with ostensible independence. Although somewhat difficult to marshal, the evidence of the day suggested that in many cases, public authorities were the recipients of indirect subsidies from the state. About the merits of such fiscal funneling, the delegates had no doubts whatsoever: "Sometimes authorities are indirectly subsidized by the State in a manner which has been called dangerous, because by its very nature the subsidy is not immediately apparent . . . Such a subsidy, of course, violates the principle of complete self-support which is one of the basic virtues of the authority mechanism."[32] Nelson Rockefeller thought otherwise. What was in 1938 a trickle of indirect aid to

Table 6.4. *Financial data for statewide authorities in New York State, 1977 ($ thousands)*

	Total assets	Bonds out-standing	Notes out-standing	Excess of assets over liabilities and reserves	Gross revenues
Transportation					
Buffalo and Fort Erie Public Bridge	18,126	2,370	—	14,713	3,683
Capital District Transportation	12,061	—	—	9,867	5,192[a]
Central New York Regional Transportation	12,552	—	—	11,558	4,482[a]
East Hudson Parkway[b]	97,153	—	—	39,959	6,009
Jones Beach State Parkway[c]	92,294	4,501	—	60,154	14,018
Lake Champlain Bridge[d]	2,621	—	—	2,571	409[e]
Long Island Railroad[f]	243,664[g]	—	—	102,584	137,832[e]
Manhattan and Bronx Surface Transit Operating[f]	5,442[h]	—	—	(16,550)	128,238[e]
Metropolitan Transportation[i]	479,115[g]	51,940	—	223,434	41,399[a]
New York City Transit[f]	223,395[h]	50,605	33,500	(354,883)	650,951
New York State Bridge	78,881	22,220	—	55,468	8,665[e]
New York State Thruway	1,350,762	724,608[j]	—	434,379	139,598
Niagara Frontier Transportation	89,254[g]	—	—	73,231	24,334[a]
Ogdensburg Bridge and Port	28,017[g]	860	120	4,463	1,272
Rochester-Genesee Regional Transportation[b]	22,420	—	—	20,056	7,799[a,e]
Staten Island Rapid Transit[f]	1,686	—	—	(848)	2,135[e]
Thousand Islands Bridge[k]	5,307	—	—	4,929	1,859
Triborough Bridge and Tunnel[f]	985,482	233,900	—	737,039	197,632
Port development					
Albany Port District	19,396	3,209	—	12,628	1,151
Port Authority of New York and New Jersey[l]	4,396,559	1,821,923[m]	205,000[n]	1,883,782	552,563
Port of Oswego	4,601[g]	—	—	(163)	595

230

Commerce and development					
NYS Energy Research and Development	24,046[g]	9,390	—	(6,382)	4,099
Environmental Facilities Corporation	21,466	3,202	9,043	4,403	703
Industrial Exhibit	3,942	—	—	1,513	—
New York State Job Development	90,532	89,075[o]	—	287	1,015[e]
Power Authority of the State of New York	3,575,020	2,299,441	240,000	941,370	439,284
United Nations Development Corporation	57,823	55,000	—	(2,324)	9,052
Finance and housing					
Battery Park City	208,361	200,000	—	—	—
Community Facilities Project Guaranty Fund[b]	—	—	—	—	—
Dormitory Authority	2,849,887	1,745,114	297,560	800,607	3,983
Facilities Development Corporation[a]	126,334	—	—	1,488	50,693
Higher Education Services Corporation[r]	25,496	—	—	4,895	94,739
Housing Finance Agency	5,860,025	4,646,257	761,405	21,834	4,917
Municipal Assistance Corporation[s]	—	—	—	—	—
Medical Care Facilities Finance Agency[t]	211,483	62,000	140,990	—	15[e]
Municipal Bond Bank[t]	—	—	—	(40)	—
Project Finance Agency[t,u]	—	—	—	—	—
State of New York Mortgage Agency	381,702	350,013	—	15,629	30,202
State University Construction Fund[v]	—	—	—	—	—
Urban Development Corporation[w]	1,452,576	1,042,183	177,695	(169,204)	74,796
Market centers					
Central New York Regional Market	1,189	123	—	777	295
Genesee Valley Regional Market	2,284	1,070	—	(1,133)	424
Totals	23,060,954	13,419,004	1,865,313	4,932,091	2,644,033

Note: This classification of authorities is based upon the participation of the governor in appointments to authority boards and their engagement in statewide or regional activities.

[a] Does not include revenues from operating assistance programs.

[b] Financial statements have been recast in 1977.

231

Notes to Table 6.4. (*cont.*)

c Terminated as of July 1, 1978, after its bonds were paid and New York State advances were forgiven. Responsibility for operation of the theater will be transferred to the Office of Parks and Recreation.

d A bi-state authority serving New York and Vermont.

e Total expenses (less depreciation) exceeds gross revenues.

f Activities are coordinated by the Metropolitan Transportation Authority.

g Cost less depreciation of certain facilities.

h Does not include cost of facilities to New York City.

i Does not include investment in Long Island Railroad, which is shown separately.

j $359 million are state guaranteed.

k An international authority serving the United States and Canada.

l A bi-state authority serving New York and New Jersey. Does not include the Commuter Car Program being financed under state-guaranteed bonds. At December 31, 1977, this program has assets of $104.2 million, including $100.5 million invested in commuter cars. Outstanding bonds totaled $78.4 million.

m Of which $78.38 million are state guaranteed.

n Loans payable.

o Of which $84.45 million are state guaranteed.

p This authority has not issued financial statements because it is inactive.

q These figures do not include fees for the care of patients, which are returned to the Mental Hygiene Services Fund.

r These figures are for the Guaranty Student Fund only. No financial statements were provided for the Tuition Assistance Program (TAP), Regents', Scholarship, or Fellowship programs.

s MAC is a special purpose authority whose financial statements do not lend themselves to this schedule. It has assets of $468.3 million, and liabilities of $4.2 billion (of which $4.1 billion are bonds outstanding). Its bonds outstanding have a first call on and the net funding deficit is offset by amounts to be provided from the proceeds of future taxes (sales and stock transfer) and certain state aid otherwise allocable by the state to New York City.

t Activities are supervised by the Housing Finance Agency.

u PFA is a special purpose authority whose financial statements do not lend themselves to this schedule. It has assets of $474.3 million, liabilities of $454.4 million (of which $233.7 million are bonds outstanding, and $197.2 million of contingent liabilities), and a restricted fund balance of $19.9 million.

v This agency does not include financial statements with its annual report.

w Financial statements have been recast for the past two years.

Source: Annual Report of the Comptroller, 1978, p. 38.

authorities under his leadership became a torrent, and the more disguised from public view the better. But this is to get ahead of our story.

Rockefeller wanted two things. One was a massive expansion in construction. Low-income housing, middle-income housing, college dormitories, mental health facilities, the renovation of downtown Albany – these are but lead items in a lengthy and expensive shopping list that was largely his creation. Second, he wanted a device to quell popular opposition whenever it threatened to interfere with his construction ambitions. The threat that mattered most was the constitutional provision requiring that any increase in the state's debt be approved by the voters. Massive construction would require a massive expansion in debt to finance it. The public might say no, and thereby scuttle the entire enterprise, or at least large parts of it. If the Constitution allowed voters to approve increases in one kind of debt, could not other kinds be devised that would deprive them of a voice? The answer was yes. It came in two parts. One was a lease-purchase agreement, the most flagrant example of which was a deal with Albany County to finance the rebuilding of downtown Albany, a financial shell game to be described in more detail later in this section. The other was a state guarantee of public authority debt with a name that reeked of rectitude: the moral obligation bond. The nature of both was briefly sketched in Chapter 4. It is time to scrutinize these fiscal gimmicks in more detail.

Consider Rockefeller's problem at the outset of his tenure as governor. He wanted, among other things, a rapid expansion in middle-income housing. Voters had said no to a proposed debt issue for that purpose. They would probably say no again. If a way to circumvent that negative vote could be found, the implications were staggering: The same device could be used to thwart their wishes *any* time the voters threatened to say no to *any* debt proposal. The solution had two parts. The first was to establish a public authority to finance the middle-income housing in question: the Housing Finance Agency (HFA). The second was to get it funds. If the Authority simply borrowed in its own name, that would avoid the necessity of voter approval. The one catch was that investors might be reluctant to lend it sums – or at least huge sums – particularly in the early stages of its operation. And Rockefeller wanted huge sums.

This reluctance to lend could be overcome by having the state guarantee the Authority's debt. The form of that guarantee, however, would have to be chosen with infinite care. It could not be in the form of a full faith and credit backing: The Constitution prohibited such credit extensions by the state to any public benefit corporation.[33] The debt, however, might be guaranteed "indirectly." The trick was to have the public authority – in this case, the Housing Finance Agency – make all principal and interest payments on its debt from a specified fund. Should any shortfall occur in that fund, the enabling legislation specified that the state "shall annually apportion" to that fund whatever is needed to cover the shortfall. That harmless looking phrase – "shall annually apportion" – is, in effect, a brilliant constitutional dodge. By New York laws, no legislature of the present can bind a legislature of the future to apportion funds. Any law passed now that includes the above phrase is therefore not legally binding, but only "morally" binding. Future legislatures may decide to honor the commitment (by apportioning funds to cover a shortfall), but they may not. It follows that if the guarantee is only moral and not legal, the state is not violating the constitutional prohibition against extending credit support to public authorities.[34] Or so the advocates of this new contrivance argued.

As a constitutional end run, the moral obligation bond was a masterpiece. Rockefeller could ram through the state legislature the necessary act to create a public authority, and the authority could then build what Rockefeller wanted. He saw to that because as governor he appointed the men who ran the authority. The requisite funds could be borrowed from the public through the sale of authority bonds that carried the moral obligation backing of the state. Investors took that guarantee seriously, and this was all that was necessary to extract billions from them. The voters, of course, were disenfranchised. They were supposed to vote on the merits of construction projects by voting for or against the debt needed to fund those projects. If the borrowing was done by a public authority issuing bonds that carried the moral obligation backing of the state, their votes were never taken.

The moral obligation bond was one of two gimmicks used by Nelson Rockefeller to thwart the constitutional requirement that all increases in state debt be subject to voter approval. The other was the lease-purchase agreement. The most notorious example of the latter was the lease-purchase agreement with that most improbable of state financiers, Albany County. The price tag would be in excess of one billion dollars.

The problem was downtown Albany. When Rockefeller first bustled into the governor's mansion, that setting was hardly to the liking of a man whose tastes ran to the magnificent. As an urban center, the capital of the Empire State was not merely unglorious. It was positively shabby.

Rockefeller attacked with typical gusto. Apparently to strive to create the most beautiful capital in America, or even North America, was too modest an ambition. His goal was nothing less than "the most spectacularly beautiful seat of government in the world."[35] From the drafting boards of experts came plans for a multitude of office buildings, legislative, administrative, and judicial, most of them connected by a five-level underground plaza structure housing meeting centers, cafeterias, shops, and parking facilities. (At the opening in 1973, Rockefeller would note that, "If there is anything more satisfying than dedicating a new building, it is dedicating eight new buildings.")[36] The watchwords were lavishness and haste in an enterprise that became variously known as "Rocky's Folly," "Instant Stonehenge," and "Rocky's Edifice Complex." Technicians dubbed it the Albany Mall. Almost two million square feet of marble would be used. (Rockefeller chose it himself, and he chose the best.) Seventy prime contractors and 270 subcontractors would literally stumble over one another in the feverish scramble to finish enough of the structure to justify a dedication before the great man left office. To Arthur Levitt and any other responsible citizen who knew the facts, the entire project appeared to be "extravagant, inefficient, and consistently off schedule."[37] To no one's surprise, the end result was not a triumph of spatial efficiency. Construction costs per square foot of usable space were estimated to vary between $94 and $230 at a time when that cost for other public buildings in the Albany area ranged between $35 and $46 – one-half to one-fifth (or less) of Mall costs.[38]

But whose dollars? Where could the funds be found – ultimately almost $2 billion – to erect this contrived pantheon of marble in a state wrestling with economic retardation? The voters surely would have none of it, and the voters would have their say. The Constitution guaranteed that by granting to them the right of referendum for any proposed increase in state debt, and this exercise in architectural megalomania would obviously require extensive borrowing. In this instance, the key suggestion apparently originated with the Mayor of Albany, but it was Rockefeller who seized it and made it policy.[39] How simple the idea was. If the problem was that voters might say no, the solution was to prevent them from expressing any opinion. Albany County[40] would borrow the funds, construct the buildings, and rent the structures to the state under a lease-purchase agreement. The state would pay in rent a sum sufficient to retire the principal and interest on the associated debt over 40 years, at the end of which time title to the buildings would be transferred to the state. That the state would end up owning the buildings seemed only fair. It would build them under the direction of the state superintendent of Public Works. It would pay for them under the guise of a lease-purchase agreement. Indeed, the only reason that investors would be willing to lend Albany County the hundreds of millions required was the assurance that the state was underwriting the entire enterprise through its rental payments. The least that the state could expect from such an arrangement was ownership of what was to be built. The least that the voters might have expected was a voice in the authorization of the project. They never got it.

The above is more than the tip of the iceberg, but not the whole iceberg. Two processes were at work under Rockefeller. One involved the circumvention of voter approval of proposed increases in state debt through lease-purchase agreements and moral obligation bonds. The other was the progressive undermining of the old ideal of the fiscally independent public authority. Both had the single objective of getting more dollars to projects that Rockefeller wanted. The net effect was a radical transformation in the nature of New York public authorities and in the norms that came to be fashionable in deciding what a public authority ought to be.

In terms of alarming implications for the future, the most ominous development in the demise of fiscal independence was the particular transformation embodied in the Urban Development Corporation, and subsequently perfected in the Municipal Assistance Corporation. Nothing less than the credit rating of the entire state would ultimately hang in the balance.

The undermining of fiscal independence did not begin with the creation in 1968 of the Urban Development Corporation (UDC),[41] but it was perhaps the most blatant case of wholesale abandonment of the priority of fiscal independence. The underlying motivation was once again a compulsion to build: in this case, to build low-income housing. That phrase "low income" had a troubling fiscal ring to it. It suggested that a gap was likely to emerge between what the Authority paid out and what it was likely to receive back. These difficulties were lurking in Rockefeller's observations on his approach to housing for low-income families: "I was unable to obtain public approval of State bond issues to finance low-income housing. We therefore devised an innovative approach whereby the State can lease up to 50 percent of the apartments in a middle-income project to rent them to low-income families on a subsidy basis."[42] Notice first the aura of unconscious arrogance and fiscal gimmickry. The public would not approve, but if that disapproval could be circumvented, apparently this was supposed to reflect well on the man who devised a way to thwart their wishes. The centerpiece of the fiscal thwarting, of course, was the use of moral obligation bonds by the Urban Development Corporation to raise much of the necessary capital. Notice second the word "subsidy." Who would pay for it? Ideally (at least from the standpoint of New Yorkers) the answer would be the federal government. The creators of

operating revenues. That was the theory. Rockefeller remolded it to suit his purposes, and his purposes required millions.

Outright subsidies were no longer made merely to enable the struggling young authority to get started. Millions were now given annually by the state to enable faltering old authorities to survive. The Urban Development Corporation, for example, received endless state support almost from its inception, much of it to cover operating expenses. The legislature has granted millions upon millions to various well-established transportation authorities as an outright subsidy to mass transit.[48] These are but two instances of a general trend that, by 1974, prompted an outburst from State Comptroller Levitt: "To an increasing extent, these appropriations have served to assist the authorities to meet their continuing cash needs because they have not become economically viable. In addition, some of the appropriations have been made for the purpose of undertaking activities which might otherwise have been performed by State agencies."[49] More bluntly put, the old concept of seed money for the novice authority has given way to the fiscal mores of "anything goes."

What went, of course, were hundreds of millions of the taxpayers' dollars. Some were funneled through first instance appropriations. Part of that funneling was hidden from view by the interest-free aspect of these loans. In 1974, for example, the outstanding state loans to public authorities totaled $276 million.[50] That same sum lent at, say, 6 percent – a conservative figure for 1974 – would have earned for the taxpayers of New York more than $16 million. *Any* interest-free loan to a public benefit corporation is therefore equivalent to a state subsidy equal to the interest payments that the authority would otherwise have to ante up for borrowed funds.

The old premise that these loans would be short term has also fallen by the wayside. In its stead can be found examples of repeated loan extensions, or worse, the practice of writing the loan off as a bad debt. The first encourages perpetual reliance upon state funding. The second is equivalent to an outright subsidy, momentarily disguised as a loan that, on close inspection, is not a loan at all. It is a gift. In the eight-year period 1964–72, for example, New York State loaned a total of $309 million to its public authorities, while writing off $154 million as uncollectible.[51] Nor was it clear how much of the remaining loans outstanding would ever be collected. The Metropolitan Transportation Authority, for example, owed $101 million by the end of 1974, but had already been "forgiven" a further $92 million. The Urban Development Corporation owed $48 million, with no prospect of repayment, as its default in 1975 would demonstrate. Perhaps the most flagrant case is the least known: the Ogdensburg Bridge and Park Authority. Conceived in the late 1950s, this Authority was to receive an initial loan of $16 million from the state, to be paid off by some combination of bond sales to the public and operating revenues of the Authority within a year and a half of the bridge opening. The bridge opened in 1960; the Authority ran a deficit in every year thereafter, never sold a single bond, and has no prospect of such sales given its miserable earnings record. And yet, when Rockefeller left office, it was entered on the state's books under "accounts receivable" as owing $21 million.[52] In terms of likely repayment, that debt ranked with Confederate bonds. Small wonder that Comptroller Levitt concluded in the early 1970s that "there has been no improvement in the collectibility of the first instance advances," adding that with the passage of time the original concept of the "first instance appropriation" was being "further abused."[53] From anyone else, that would have been a gentle rebuke. From Arthur Levitt, it was a scathing denunciation.

In all of these fiscally suspect developments of the 1960s – the escalation of state loans and the multiplication of state subsidies to ostensibly independent authorities – the influence of Nelson Rockefeller varied from important to decisive. His were the hands upon the reins whenever budgetary matters were at stake, and as his tenure progressed, those hands became more powerful and more grasping. To be sure, his control was not absolute. The legislators had a vote. Their leaders in the Assembly and the Senate were important parties to a bargaining process in which the chief executive's budget proposals were tinkered with by legislators who often knew little, controlled little, and said little (see Chapter 7, Section 7.2). But woe to the politician who defied any fiscal proposal that Nelson Rockefeller cared about deeply. And Rockefeller cared deeply about public authority expansion. He spurned from the outset the older notion of a single-purpose, fiscally independent public authority designed to self-destruct when its single task was done. He openly defied the constitutional provision that gave to citizens of the state the right to approve proposed increases in state debt. Moral obligation debt ballooned, lease-purchase agreements ballooned, and the flow of state aid to public authorities swelled to a torrent. Much of the authority debt was created to finance projects that the public would have turned down, had they been given a chance to express their opinions. Had such a future been revealed to those assembling in Albany on that warm April day in 1938, it would surely have provoked a storm of verbal outrage and fist shaking. It might even have been enough to make Al Smith doff his brown derby in wonderment at the machinations of modern state finance.

6.5. Performance and control: some general problems

These, then, were the three main transformations forged over half a century that reshaped public authorities in the Empire State. All but obliterated was the old ideal of a single-purpose, fiscally independent authority designed to disappear when that purpose was accomplished. The new breed – many of them gargantuan and growing – are almost all montrosities when measured against older norms, bristling as they are with multiple purposes and near immortality, and progressively more dependent upon state handouts for survival.

If the breed is new, is the performance worse? The question admits to no easy resolution. Three points, however, are absolutely clear. The first is that a multitude of purposes has confounded evaluation and control. The second is that the demise of fiscal independence should have brought, and has not brought, the demise of authority independence. If ongoing state support is required for ongoing survival, the end product should be relabeled a state agency and its control restructured accordingly. Third, under the headings of objectives pursued and efficiency achieved, by even the most liberal of performance criteria, the new breed is riddled with defects.

First, the matter of objectives. At first glance, these appear to be one of the strong points of a public benefit corporation. Comparatively insulated from party politics, the public authority, with its managing board of public-spirited citizens, should bring to policy decisions an Olympian view well calculated to serve the populace at large. Planning should take into account all of the costs and benefits of a proposal: environmental as well as economic, regional as well as local. Measured against such aspirations, the facts are nothing short of shocking.

Assume for the moment that, by and large, public benefit corporations are controlled by bureaucrats, and that bureaucrats are motivated primarily by their own self-interest. What policy choices would one predict for most of New York's public authorities most of the time? The answer presumably is that set of policies which best serves the bureaucrats in control. Prestige and power tend to vary with the size of empire under their jurisdiction. The dominant drive, therefore, is empire expansion. The key to expansion is money: money generated by profitable ventures of the authority, and money borrowed from the public. This drive would therefore bias authority choices in favor of lucrative projects and against those likely to incur a deficit, whatever the associated benefits and costs might be to the public. The more net revenue generated, the more dollars available to expand the authority's domain. The same priorities would favor monopoly pricing to achieve monopoly profits whenever the authority operated in an insulated market. Tolls would seldom be reduced, and never voluntarily eliminated, even long after the bridge or tunnel generating them had been paid for. To preserve and enhance the possibilities of commanding borrowed funds, the authority would favor minimizing investor risk in choosing its new projects – a policy that meshes nicely with the priority of pursuing projects likely to yield a surplus rather than a deficit.

The two premises noted and the inferences derived from them are, depressingly, an all-too-accurate description of much of the functioning of many public authorities within the Empire State. The one major qualification that must be added is the influence of Nelson Rockefeller. His ambitions also demanded empire building by public benefit corporations. Their growth and proliferation during his regime were therefore characterized by an unfortunate harmony of self-interests between the politician who controlled so much and the bureaucratic chiefs who wanted to control more. Whether authorities operated largely inside or outside Rockefeller's sphere of influence, most of the decision makers who directed them little noted nor long remembered that a public benefit corporation is also a public trust. The associated slighting of the public's interest is apparent in monopolistic prices in monopolized markets; in the persistence of tolls on bridges long since paid for; in the overbuilding of college dormitories; in the wealthy Port Authority's slighting of crucial mass transit projects likely to yield a deficit, while pouring more than a billion dollars into a 110-story edifice called the World Trade Center.

If defective performance has been anchored in defective priorities, has that performance at least been characterized by efficiency? The evidence is not encouraging. Insulated from the salutary prods of competitive markets, and relatively immune from public scrutiny or the probings of its elected representatives, public authorities can hardly be expected to be paragons of proficiency and economy. The New York Comptroller's audit reports of public authorities in the state are shot through with charges of questionable procedures and outright incompetence:[54] The Capital District Psychiatric Center (built by the Facilities Development Corporation), whose construction problems included "leakage in the main building and parking structure, problems in the operation of the air conditioning system, and a gymnasium floor which cannot be used"; 143 automobiles provided by the New York State Thruway Authority to its personnel, judged to be "both unnecessary and wasteful of Authority resources"; the marketing of bonds by the Housing Finance Agency through private negotiation rather than competitive bidding;[55] the New York State Bridge Authority's failure to invest $279,293, causing a sacrifice of $21,000 in foregone income; a similar failure by the Metropolitan Suburban Bus Authority, resulting in "larger than necessary bank balances" (one check for $116,232 was not deposited at all for nine months); the willingness of the New York City Transit Authority to tolerate an explosion in overtime pay in the final 12 months of employment, sharply raising the pension benefits of retiring personnel – these are but straws in the wind from a barnyard in disarray, with the jumbles and bungling largely hidden from public view.

What was the control problem? Why, for example, should a public official complain that the Triborough Bridge and Tunnel Authority should not be a "wandering goose dropping its golden eggs as it pleases"?[56] The golden eggs were the dollars generated by monopolistic tolls well in excess of costs. The man who, for years, determined where they would be dropped was Robert Moses. But why was the Triborough Authority experience so typical? The answer, in a nutshell, was that most authorities had, in Jefferson's phrase, "wormed out of the elective principle." This was partly by accident, partly by design, and partly because of legislative incompetence.

The legislature, of course, was where control should have begun. All New York State public authorities are created by special legislative act.[57] In that creation process, elected representatives have their best opportunity to exert their influence by specifying such things as objectives to be pursued, funding techniques to be used, procedures to be followed, and information to be reported annually to the legislature (including a thorough audit of the books). In practice, debate is usually perfunctory, and the resulting legislative terms are lax. The provisions governing the ability to borrow, for example, are all-important.[58] Here should be found a critical constraint on size in terms of an authorized debt limit, as well as a determining influence upon authority policy buried in the provisions spelling out the kinds of borrowing that can and cannot be undertaken. Longevity is also linked to debt, insofar as most authorities terminate only when their bonds and notes are paid off. Seldom is there any provision compelling the use of surplus funds to eliminate outstanding debt. (Seldom is there any provision specifying any use whatsoever for surplus funds, including distribution back to where they came from: the pockets of the public.) Amazingly, some New York authorities have been created with no debt limit whatsoever.[59] Others began small, but found that repeated requests to raise their debt limit met with little resistance and less scrutiny. The Housing Finance Agency, for example, began with a debt limit of $525 million. Seventeen years later its total debt *outstanding* exceeded that original authorization by a factor of 10. The Urban Development Corporation, as documented at length in Section 6.6.b, requested an increase in its authorized debt limit just prior to defaulting on its notes. Legislative ignorance was so pervasive that the increase was effortlessly achieved and the subsequent default was a complete surprise. The four blind men of the Indian fable made foolish judgments about the nature of an elephant because each believed that the part of the anatomy he held was typical of the whole. The lawmakers of New York went them one better, allowing the beast to saunter through the legislative chambers with no pretense of inspection whatsoever.

The executive might have done better, but usually did not. Here too the failures were both structural and personal. The structural problems concern the nature of the appointment and removal process for those destined to direct public authorities. For state authorities, the top level of management, usually a board of directors and an executive director, is almost always appointed by the governor with the advice and consent of the Senate. Removal of the person who matters most, the executive director, is generally a power granted to the governor. Here surely is a channel of influence from elected politician to a bureaucrat in charge. The power to appoint and to remove should bring in its wake a sensitivity of authority policy to the governor's wishes. In practice, that sensitivity was typical during Rockefeller's reign, in part because his own longevity in office meant that most top officials were his appointees,[60] in part because his phenomenal connections with the financial community made his displeasure dangerous to risk by those who borrowed millions every year, in part because many authorities required ongoing financial support from the state and needed Rockefeller's blessings to get the dollars.

This imagery of authority responsiveness to the governor's wishes is sullied by three depressing qualifications.

The first is that even when authorities were responsive to the chief executive's desires, the results often flew in the face of what the public wanted. In 1961 a proposal to guarantee bonds designed to further the development of higher education facilities was defeated *for the fourth time*. In 1962, Rockefeller created the State University Construction Fund, a public authority designed to provide academic buildings, dormitories, and other facilities for higher education. In 1965 the voters rejected *for the fifth time* a bond proposal to fund low-income housing. In 1968, Rockefeller established the Urban Development Corporation to build low-income housing. These were hardly policies of the people, by the people, and for the people.

Second, even with the possibility of tight control, Rockefeller tended to give his top bureaucrats the freedom to pursue whatever policies they desired, consistent with the Rockefeller aim of "more." The result was a set of public institutions often autocratic in structure and arrogant in their slighting of any pleas for help or information from any quarter save the governor's mansion. When William Ronan took over the Metropolitan Transportation Authority, for example, "he ignored MTA's operational and management problems, showed no interest in cost control, and pursued new projects with near abandon."[61] The sensitivity of the end result to public needs is suggested by the nickname it soon acquired of "Holy Ronan Empire," or its secular variant, "Wholly Ronan Empire."

Third, executive control of public authority policies has tended to be more tenuous than the Rockefeller experience would suggest. This results, in part, from an absence of any close match between the governor's term of office and the appointment terms of the heads of public authorities. A new governor inherits a set of authority officials appointed by his predecessor. They may remain loyal to the old, thwart the new, and thereby undercut the electorate's call for change implicit in the changeover of administration. Rockefeller's successor, Carey, for example, complained bitterly about the unresponsive bureaucracy that he inherited:

> The way [Rockefeller] set up the authorities, boards, and commissions with term appointments, it's almost beyond the reach of a governor to effectuate policy because he has these overlapping directorships in so many ways that their policy – which used to be his policy – becomes state policy without the intervention of the public. To call it a dynasty is one thing, but it's feudal.[62]

The governor could of course remove these top bureaucrats, but only for "inefficiency, neglect of duty, or misconduct in office." In practice, such charges are difficult to prove. More important, the issue is not misconduct. The issue is conduct insensitive to changing public priorities. Interestingly enough, Robert Moses saw the problem and offered the solution long before he became an empire builder on his own. Responsibility to elected officials, he argued, was the key. Appointed officials should therefore have a term of office coincident with that of the governor, and be removable by him if they fail to follow his orders: "If New York wants . . . efficient government, it must make someone responsible who can be held to account and give him power commensurate with his obligations. There is no other way."[63] It is ironic that the man who had the no-nonsense solution to the problem would subsequently build an insulated empire that fended off responsibility to anyone save Robert Moses.[64]

Control, of course, is partly a function of information available. Public authorities have therefore tended to reveal a minimum. In this they are assisted by their privileged position. Their tax-exempt status assures immunity from inspection by the Internal Revenue Service. Their major source of funds, the municipal bond market, is little affected by Securities and Exchange Commission regulations. The minutes of their board meetings – ostensibly the critical forum of debate for policy proposals – are often curiously devoid of content, with little compulsion to make them more revealing. Even control of the books, that most basic control of all, is exercised imperfectly. Some authorities, such as the Port Authority of New York and New Jersey, simply refuse to make financial information available on the flows of funds among their several parts (see Section 6.6.a.). Of the 11 largest New York public authorities, 5 are not subjected to any pre-audit whatsoever, and 2 have only their maintenance and operating expenses pre-audited, but not their payrolls.[65] In other words, the Comptroller's Office has virtually no way of monitoring, on an ongoing basis, the spending of about half of the largest public authorities in the state. When inefficiencies and other defects are detected, the comptroller has no way of compelling the authority in question to adopt his recommendations. Prior to 1977, he could not even compel a response in writing justifying why no action had been taken.[66] To be sure, copies of all authority audits, with their suggestions, are forwarded by the comptroller to a host of public officials in the executive and the legislature, but these are pearls cast before those who lack the interest or the power to insist upon change. And so the inefficiencies tend to remain.

6.6. Performance and control: examples of failure

The shattering implications for the public's welfare are too easily lost in the muted phrases of generalities. Only examples can make the associated perils clear. The two that follow are merely symptomatic of a sickness, chronic and ulcerous, which pervades these so-called public benefit corporations of the Empire State.

6.6.a. The Port Authority and mass transit

The oldest authority in America is the Port Authority of New York and New Jersey. Established in 1921, and modeled after the London Port Authority, its stated purpose was "a better coordination of the terminal, transportation and other facilities of commerce in, about, and through the port of New York."[67]

Three points are crucial to subsequent discussion. First, the Authority is massive. It employs over 8,000 people, has annual gross revenues of roughly half a billion, and has assembled over the years fixed assets now valued at more than four billion.[68] Secondly, the ancient principle of a single-purpose authority was torpedoed long ago. Soon after its inception, this public benefit corporation became multipurpose in focus and in fact, using profits from stronger ventures to support less fiscally viable enterprises. Indicative of its multiple objectives is the heterogeneous collection of assets that the Port Authority now controls: four bridges, two tunnel complexes across the Hudson, a rapid transit line linking New Jersey to downtown Manhattan, two bus terminals, two truck terminals, eight marine terminals, four airports, two heliports, the World Trade Center, and trade development offices in nine cities. Third, last, and worst, the Port Authority has operated largely beyond public scrutiny or public control, with the unsurprising result that it has frequently failed to serve that public well. These failures at bottom have been the result of planning and priorities heavily conditioned by the perceptions of its bureaucratic chief and little affected by the needs of the people, particularly the needs of inner-city residents and the priorities of urban planning. Nothing better illustrates this process than the Port Authority's persistent refusal to attack the problems of mass transit, despite its surplus funds, despite the pressing needs in that sector, and despite the terms of its charter, which clearly authorized Authority activity in this area. Why?

Part of the answer concerns the Port Authority's control structure. It provides a case in point for all that is worst in the undemocratic operation of public benefit corporations.[69] In theory, policy is controlled by an executive director and a board of directors (or commissioners). In practice, the board does little more than rubber stamp the proposals brought before it. The executive director is the man who molds and manipulates what will and what will not be done. At least that was the story as long as Austin Tobin was at the helm, and he remained there for 30 years (1942–72). A bureaucrat to rival Robert Moses in the insulated empire he controlled, Tobin wanted little except approval from his Board of Directors. The composition of the Board furthered that objective. Heavily weighted with members of the financial community, it gave little or no representation to elected officials, to representatives of community organizations, or to representatives of the industries vitally dependent upon the Authority's facilities (such as railroads, airlines, and bus companies). Board meetings were rigged in the conventional way. Tobin's staff controlled the proposals made and the supporting data. Board members did not have the time, the staff, or the expertise to make independent appraisals for themselves. Small wonder that their meetings earned a reputation for being "lifeless, cut and dried affairs."[70] The Executive Director was determined to drain from them any trace of controversy or inquiry.[71]

The public was kept at bay by two conventional devices. The first was secrecy. This went beyond the usual process of disclosing a minimum. Not that this aspect was missing. Financial data, for example, were published only in consolidated form to disguise the flow of funds among the Authority's many enterprises. What was perhaps special about the Port Authority's pursuit of secrecy was the lengths to which it would go to conceal information. A congressional committee investigating the Port Authority's activities in the 1960s discovered that many major decisions did not appear at all in the minutes of the Board meetings. When the House Judiciary Committee asked for better documentation, the Authority refused in such a blunt and sweeping way that Tobin stood trial for contempt – this despite the fact that as an interstate authority, the Port Authority had been created by congressional legislation.[72] In this same spirit of pigheaded paranoia, the Port Authority in 1973 withdrew its application for a rate increase for its Trans-Hudson transit line rather than respond to the all-too-reasonable request that it provide financial data for the operation of each of its facilities, including the Trans-Hudson line. A public authority may be a public trust, but the people apparently were not to be trusted with enlightening information concerning the operation of *their* corporation.

When the public's priorities threatened to intrude through the actions of elected representatives, Austin Tobin had another line of defense. The first was secrecy. The second was covenants. The lengthened shadow of Robert Moses once again casts a darker hue upon a landscape not his own. His was the twisted genius that first devised the gimmick of insulating bureaucratic powers and policies from legislative intervention by writing those powers and policies into bond contracts. Tobin merely followed in his footsteps. The end result was devastating for the cause of improving mass transit facilities in the New York City area.

In August of 1955, in a pamphlet entitled "Dynamic Planning for the Metropolitan Region," Austin Tobin made plain his vision for the transportation future of the City: "Our own planning in the field of arterial highways for the New York metropolitan area accepts the fact that the structure of our surging metropolitan area today is being shaped almost entirely by the motor vehicle. In airport planning we make the basic assumption that air transportation will become the dominant means of long distance travel."[73] The use of "Our" was perhaps too generous. The vision was primarily Tobin's, as were the plans. Notice the absence of any reference to mass transit. The omission was not accidental. Almost from its inception the Port Authority has consistently fended off requests to aid in the development of mass transit facilities in the New York City area. This became harder to do as the years wore on and mass transit facilities degenerated from inadequate to pathetic. Following World War II, pressures for the Port Authority to take a hand in improving these facilities became almost irresistible. Almost. For three decades the public and their elected representatives would battle the Port Authority to divert some of its surplus revenues into improving mass transit. They would lose. More correctly, with one trivial exception, they would lose. In winning that exception, the legislators made one concession that lost the war.

Tensions between transit needs and Port Authority recalcitrance erupted into open conflict in 1959. The state legislatures of New York and New Jersey in that year proposed that the Port Authority finance a commuter railroad improvement. Tobin rejected the idea, claiming that to link his Authority's activities to such a deficit operation would imperil the Port Authority's ability to borrow money. Almost no one took that argument seriously, but Tobin mounted such an effective campaign against the proposal in financial and political circles that the proposal was dropped. Three years later the Port Authority again came under pressure. This time the proposal involved its acquisition of the Hudson and Manhattan rail line (renamed PATH).[74] Tobin ultimately agreed, but only on condition that a new bond covenant[75] be authorized for Port Authority debt, which in effect limited Port Authority support of deficit operations of mass transit facilities to the probable deficit of the single railroad it was now taking over. The covenant in question "prohibited commitment of Port Authority revenues or reserves to any other rail transportation projects unless the deficits generated by such projects and PATH together amounted to less than one-tenth the amount in the General Reserve Fund (excluding the other reserve funds) or 1 percent of total bonded debt."[76]

With a single clause, Tobin dealt a devastating blow to the cause of mass transit in New York City for years to come. It took the legislators some time to understand how comprehensive their capitulation had been. In 1971, they authorized construction of rail links to Kennedy and Newark airports. A year later, the governors of New York and New Jersey announced the inclusion of these rail links in a larger transit agreement with Port Authority Commissioners that included the extension of several rail lines,[77] all designed to improve mass transit access to the city. No one seemed to notice that the 1972 proposals violated the 1962 covenant limiting the support given by the Port Authority to a minuscule dollar figure (roughly the annual deficit of the railroad taken over in 1962). Austin Tobin noticed. The publicity accompanying the new proposal he characterized as a "grandstand play." The plan, he added, had little chance of implementation. The law was on his side. He had, after all, deliberately maneuvered to contrive legal provisions that would stop a proposal such as this one dead in its tracks. The legislators counterattacked with two assaults, the first of which was futile and the second, unconstitutional.

Their first action was to pass amendments that in effect made the 1962 covenant inapplicable to any bonds issued after mid-1973. The difficulty was that bonds had already been issued with that covenant, the last of which would not be retired until the year 2007. This legislative change therefore implied nothing whatsoever about new Port Authority freedom to undertake the 1972 proposal – at least not before 2007. Realizing after the fact the futility of this approach, the legislators in 1974 repealed all statutory protection heretofore created under the 1962 covenant. This was challenged in the courts as a violation of the provision in the federal Constitution prohibiting states from passing laws that impaired contracts. Robert Moses understood what the legal outcome must be. So did Austin Tobin. They had both tailored their bond contracts with an eye precisely to this provision of the federal Constitution. In 1977 the Supreme Court handed down the predictable decision that the law repealing the 1962 covenant protection was unconstitutional. Austin Tobin by that date had resigned as executive director of the Port Authority. Absent in the flesh but present in the provisions of old laws, he still had Authority policy firmly by the throat, or at least that policy which minimized Authority participation in mass transit improvement. The city, with its economy in secular decline, could ill afford this continued boycott by an authority flush enough to make a desperately needed contribution to its transportation infrastructure. The people knew it. The legislators of New York and New Jersey knew it. But one man said no, and made it stick.

What was the Port Authority doing with its surplus revenues? If mass transit was a cause to be shunned, what causes did it embrace? The funds it had to allocate for new projects bordered on the lavish. With a virtual monopoly of Hudson River crossings and air travel facilities in the New York City area, the Port Authority could charge, and has charged, monopoly prices well above costs. The resulting profits have annually poured into its coffers *net* receipts in excess of $100 million.[78] In recent years a large portion of this revenue has been used to build the World Trade Center, a project with a prospective cost in excess of a billion dollars.[79] (You could buy a lot of commuter rail line for a billion dollars.) Was *this* in the public interest? Was a twin-towered, 110-story office complex more vital to city development than mass transit improvement? Data on the Trade Center's occupants suggest an answer in the negative. Many of its 110 floors are occupied by state agencies, not by private businesses vital to the city's economy. More importantly, if the city needs more office space, rents will rise and private capital will respond to those needs by constructing more buildings. If the city needs mass transit improvements, private capital on its own can be expected to do nothing.

As the building's existence is a tribute to warped priorities, so its construction has been illustrative of the secrecy and inefficiencies that can blight public authority operation. A Comptroller's audit in 1978 revealed, among other shortcomings, (1) the absence of competitive bidding in the awarding of many contracts, (2) in one instance, the approving of two different contracts for the same work, and (3) a tradition of preparing the minutes approving World Trade Center construction contracts *before* the actual meeting of the Board of Commissioners.[80] "And who picks up the tab for all these grandiose schemes?" the president of Trailways Bus Company demanded to know, and then supplied his own answer: "The commuters and the bus riders, people who constantly find themselves at the mercy of the autocratic, monopolistic functionings of the Port Authority."[81] Although the focus is too narrow, the outrage is to the point. Commuters are only one class of contributors to the building of the World Trade Center. Every user of a Port Authority facility contributes directly through tolls or indirectly through transportation fares inflated by Authority rental and other charges levied upon airlines, bus companies, and other private firms that use its facilities. By no stretch of generosity can Authority surpluses so generated be construed as indicative of enviable efficiency. They are indicative of monopoly pricing well above costs, a policy that has given to this public benefit corporation monopoly profits to channel into other public ventures.

The details examined here suggest that the Port Authority of New York and New Jersey has violated almost every single criterion of consequence by which a public benefit corporation should be judged. It does not have a single purpose, but many, and has deliberately consolidated published data to hide the fiscal interactions of its several parts. It has not matched user charges with actual costs, but has used its monopoly power to extract monopoly profits from its consumers. The funds so generated it has channeled into projects that reflected not merely an insensitivity to public needs, but a determination to defy public demands. The only major criterion for public benefit corporations that it has met successfully is fiscal viability. The other New York authority to be examined could not claim even that.

6.6.b. The Urban Development Corporation and default

Nothing better illustrates the tenuous nature of executive and legislative control of public authorities than the experience of the Urban Development Corporation. The financing of UDC proceeded in such a

pell-mell and ill-conceived manner that ultimately it faced bankruptcy, and in the process imperiled the state's access to financial
markets. If errors of this magnitude cannot be diagnosed early and
remedies instituted by the elected representatives of the people, what
hope is there for successful monitoring and correction of lesser sins?
Moreover, the opportunities of those elected representatives to inter-
vene in the operation of a public authority were exceptional in the
case of UDC, because the authority repeatedly asked the state government for funds and for an increase in its debt limit. Even with these
expanded opportunities, the legislature saw little, and did less.

The prevailing ignorance in the Senate and the Assembly was nothing short of massive. Even the leaders were apparently ill-informed
until the crisis was upon them. Assemblyman Steingut testified to the
Moreland Commission that "he had no knowledge of UDC's financial
difficulties until he met with Governor Carey on January 8, 1975."[82]
The same was apparently true for Senate Majority Leader Warren Anderson: "Until mid-1974 he had heard nothing of UDC's problems,
and . . . until January 1975 his communications with both the Governor and the financial community concerning UDC were minimal."[83] If
Anderson's communications were minimal, those of the typical legislator were nonexistent. How was this possible? When the UDC legislation was initially passed, surely the elected representatives of the
people scrutinized the terms of the bill for possible dangers. Senator
Anderson tells a different story:

> Q. Was there any focus in the legislative discussions or
>   debates about the possibility that UDC's bonds would
>   be riskier and would have to be picked up by the State
>   because it was going into ghetto housing or because
>   UDC was acting as a developer and not just as a
>   lender?
> A. I don't think the Legislature focused on that . . . I
>   think that people had the feeling that perhaps some of
>   it might not be self-sustaining but in the total of it, it
>   would be.
> Q. But I take it nobody ever sat down and said, "What are
>   we going to do if this doesn't pay off?"
> A. No, that's true.[84]

Inattentive at the outset, the legislators were no better guardians of the
public's interest when UDC sought further appropriations from them.
This was as true for the Assembly as it was for the Senate, as Steingut's
testimony made painfully clear:

> Q. Do you recall any discussion of the problems of the
>   kinds of practices that UDC had undertaken or the

problems of the rapid rate of growth during the
discussions at any of these appropriations?

A. Not to my recollection.[85]

As legislators had missed the smoke, so they ignored the fire. Their chance came in 1973. At the close of the previous year, UDC requested an increase in its debt limit from $1.0 to $1.5 billion. By the time the issue came before the legislature, an audit of UDC had been published that was so bad that the underwriters were dismayed. One of them characterized the accompanying financial statements as "a disaster, there were terrible problems, it was one of the worst financial statements that I had ever seen."[86] The legislators were not dismayed because they remained blissfully ignorant of the audit report. They approved the request for a hike in the debt ceiling, which was not unlike approving the funds to buy a more powerful car for a driver whose alcoholic tendencies were a matter of public record.

The reasons for this lack of legislative scrutiny are primarily two. The first concerns a scarcity of staff to sift through the mountains of data that inevitably accompany the modern fiscal process. The second was Rockefeller's propensity to ramrod legislation through, often on the last day permitted under the Constitution. In the case of the request to raise UDC's debt ceiling, for example, Assemblyman Steingut observed that the bill was presented "suddenly," and that "the Legislature had very little opportunity to study the bill."[87]

But if the Governor was part of the problem, he should also have been part of the solution. To begin with, he appointed the top officials with the advice and consent of the Senate. In the case of UDC, this included[88] a nine-member Board of Directors comprised of (1) a chairman who served at the pleasure of the Governor, (2) four members appointed for a specified term, and removable by the Governor for "inefficiency, neglect of duty, or misconduct in office," and (3) four ex-officio members. As the Moreland Commission pointed out, "The power to appoint and remove is an important mechanism of gubernatorial supervision and control. It permits and indeed obliges the Governor to monitor management performance."[89] Nelson Rockefeller felt no such obligation. Admittedly he did receive information constantly on various UDC operations from such officials as the Director of the Budget, the Secretary to the Governor, and the President of UDC, Edward Logue. But rather than closely monitor the activities of any public authority, Rockefeller preferred instead to set up a team and give them "virtually total freedom"[90] to run the organization as they saw fit.

If the first line of defense failed, so did the second. The Governor's watchdog for detecting imprudent and devious fiscal practices was the

Division of the Budget. Because of its repeated requests for state funds, UDC presented the Division with an exceptional chance to monitor the financial activities of a public authority. In practice, the Division monitored very little. Part of the problem was a tradition of neglect. (Until the 1975 fiscal crisis associated with UDC, the Division, by its own admission, "virtually ignored public authorities.")[91] Part of the problem was the nature of the information received from UDC. According to Budget Division officials,

> Frequently . . . the Division did not receive budget submissions from UDC in sufficient time to analyze the data or formulate recommendations to the Governor. Moreover, they found that UDC's submissions were often inadequate and that the necessary data were not readily accessible to the Division. Finally, the submissions explained in detail only the need for, and proposed uses of, the requested appropriations and generally did not provide much information except in summary form, on UDC's overall capital budget.[92]

Defective reporting, initiated by one government agency, was thereby tolerated by another as regular policy. (The Budget Division, after all, could always have elicited more information with the threat of saying no to requests for financial aid.)[93]

The one serious scrutiny of UDC by another government agency was the infrequent auditing conducted by the Comptroller's Office. Section 28 of the UDC Act authorizes the Comptroller to examine from time to time, but not less than once every five years, "the books and accounts of the corporation including its receipts, disbursements, contracts, reserve funds, investments and any other matters relating to its financial standing." As a result of two audits (1972 and 1974), the Comptroller made a series of recommendations concerning UDC financial practices.[94] Recommendations are one thing. Implementation is another. Not only did the Comptroller's Office lack the power to have its recommendations implemented, but it did not even have the means to coerce this authority to report what action had been taken in response to its recommendations. To be sure, copies of the audit reports were sent to the Governor, the Budget Director, the Chairman of the Senate Finance Committee, and the Chairman of the Assembly Ways and Means Committee. Such circulation guarantees that all of the Comptroller's suggestions reached those who could implement change. Every indication suggests, however, that the recommendations in question fell upon deaf ears.[95]

In sum, when it came to closely monitoring this public authority to prevent excesses and errors, the Governor would not, the legislature could not, and the Division of the Budget maintained a posture of cultivated ignorance. Who then was left? Assemblyman Steingut thought he had the answer:

Q. Do you have any view as to how perhaps the banking industry on its part might have looked to see or might have assumed who was tending the store?

A. I would assume, and I do not pretend to be a financier in any manner, shape or form, but I would assume that as a bank makes a loan, they look after it to see if they are well protected . . .

Q. So you might have looked at them as one of the checks and balances?

A. Absolutely.[96]

What is disturbing about this belief is not that events would prove it to be wrong. What is crucial is that it signals both a desperate poverty of supervision and control in the right hands – the elected representatives of the people – and the absurd hope for a disciplining force in the wrong hands – the financiers who stood to gain so much from the millions of dollars of public authority borrowing that annually were funneled through their organizations. The issue of consummate importance is *not* whether a given public authority has so violated the basic canons of sound finance that it is brought to the very brink of bankruptcy. That does matter, but in the larger scheme of public authority regulation, such behavior is comparatively rare. The nub of the issue can be phrased as a question: What checks and balances help to insure that public authorities act in the interest of the public, as opposed to acting in the interests of politicians, bureaucrats, and various vested interest groups in the business community? To presume that the defensible answer will give a place of prominence, or any place at all, to "the banking industry" is not unlike assuming that the best guardians of automotive safety are used car salesmen.

6.7. Darwinian dynamics gone wrong

In 1859, Charles Darwin staggered the scientific world with an idea as simple as it was novel. Species, he argued, are not fixed and immutable, but evolve over time. Evolution is the result of the interaction between changing environmental possibilities and the differing capacities of species to respond. Some have characteristics that allow their possessors to function more efficiently in the struggle for survival. The edge which they have in that struggle, and their ability to transmit the key characteristics to their offspring, will result in their gradual predominance over similar species lacking those characteristics. Or as Darwin preferred to put it, they will come to dominate through the process of natural selection.

Institutions also evolve. In the changing environment of the twentieth century, the public benefit corporation of New York State has progressed from microorganism to giant in a scant half century, barely a flicker of the eyelash in Darwin's time scale. The rapidity of the mutation reflects human control of the processes of change. The resulting selection was also natural, insofar as it reflected, in the main, desires of the powerful few to reshape the institution to suit their personal needs and ambitions. The public, to be sure, also tried to condition the evolutionary process, primarily through provisions enacted at various constitutional conventions. Their influence, however, was repeatedly undermined. Such constraints as they placed upon the growth and powers of the beast were destroyed, one by one, as the few who were the dominant architects of transformation multiplied its strengths. The species as it now exists is, by and large, unfettered by popular control, and only moderately responsive to the commands of their elected representatives. Not that it has become progressively more independent on every count – quite the contrary. As unresponsiveness to electoral command has become more ingrained, so dependence upon state subsidies, disguised and undisguised, has increased to the point where, for some, such ongoing support is indispensable for survival.

By any democratic norm, it was absurd. How could the public remain so silent in the face of such developments?

Part of the answer – a large part – is ignorance and indifference. Part of the answer was the gradualness of change. "Habit is habit," wrote Mark Twain, "and not to be flung out the window by any man, but coaxed downstairs a step at a time."[97] A mere handful, led by Moses and Rockefeller, had managed to coax the electorate downstairs, one undemocratic step at a time, until they now accepted what should have been offensive in the extreme. In short, these few accomplished a revolution – or at least an evolution – second only to taxation without representation in its fiscal implications, without so much as a placard of protest appearing on the streets.

If the end result was undemocratic in form, was it really all that bad in operation? Was the public welfare that much imperiled by these transformations from single purpose to multiple purpose, from fiscal independence to fiscal dependence, from finite life to indefinite existence? The question is insidious, because it encourages the reader to take to the issue of evaluation the wrong frame of reference. At bottom, the issue *is* form, not operation. The question to be asked is *not* whether middle-income housing or college dormitories or the World Trade Center are "good things." Obviously each has its own utility, but the important question in this arena is *relative* usefulness: What could the public have had for its money had its dollars not been channeled in these directions? If this judgment is indispensable for the evaluation of public authorities, they are certain to escape unscathed in the smoke of unresolved debates. The question of what might have been and what should be must be attacked from a different quarter.

The starting point is motivation. What moved the few who molded the institution into its present form? The evidence is overwhelmingly in favor of an answer dominated by a single word: self-interest. Not that a concern for the public was entirely absent in the likes of Austin Tobin and Robert Moses. But the drive that dominated, the drive that determined most of the policy choices most of the time, would seem to have been what was best for number one, often harnessed to the unexamined premise that the resulting choices would be best for all. Superficial benevolence blended with self-interest and elitism usually produces unconscious arrogance: that a single person can better judge what the people need than the people can themselves – that what is good for Robert Moses is also best for the citizens of New York, whether or not they can appreciate what is foisted upon them.

But surely, one might argue, the crassness of the motivational fabric of those in control need not imply a flood of undesirable results. After all, in Mandeville's phrasing, private vices might be public benefits. Or as Adam Smith preferred to put the matter, the pursuit of self-interest may be the key to advancing public welfare. The missing piece that sends this argument crashing to the ground is a system of checks and balances to encourage the desirable and discourage the pernicious. The key to good government is *not* to get rid of the bad guys and put in the good guys. The key is to devise a structure of incentives and constraints that bring to the fore the best that the participants have to offer, while reining in hard the unattractive tendencies lurking in all of us. In this enterprise, New Yorkers have long been threatened by a kind of terminal naïveté. Too many still cling to the childlike belief that a public servant is likely to be dominated by a desire to serve the public. Precisely because of the dangerous passivity such faith encourages, that psychological premise should be jettisoned by the adult mind. The central difficulty with public authority decision making is that it is allowed to proceed largely beyond any system of checks and balances, political or economic. The disciplining force of competitive markets tends to have a minimal impact upon most of them. They are largely insulated from popular control, and respond sluggishly if at all to the expressed concerns of elected representatives in the legislature. This insulation has been deliberately contrived to minimize the influence of what has been variously termed "partisan politics," "legislative meddling," or "the whims of the public." The first point to understand is that the resulting decision making by public authorities is not free of politics. It is merely the product of a different brand of politics. The second point is that these politics, precisely because of that insulation, cannot be presumed to operate in the best interests of the public. How could they, when the public's voice is deliberately stifled, and the self-interest drives of the ruling elites are little tempered by the need for legislative approval?

James Madison saw the dangers even if he failed to foresee the New York public authority as a likely vehicle for abuse: "I believe there are more instances of the abridgment of the freedom of the people, by gradual and silent encroachments of those in power than by violent and sudden usurpations."[98] Freedoms have been abused. The mutation called moral obligation bonds, for example, was deliberately contrived to frustrate the provision of the state Constitution requiring voter approval of all prospective increases in state debt.

As the public's freedom to decide how their dollars would be spent has been abridged, so the magnitudes involved have risen to stupendous heights. Annually, more than $2.3 billion pass through statewide authorities alone. This is equivalent to a single person and his heirs spending more than a million dollars a year from the founding of Christianity to the present. The debt of these same authorities now exceeds $14.9 billion.[99] The dollars borrowed and spent by public benefit corporations consume economic resources to create bridges, tunnels, highways, airports, railroads, parks, housing, dormitories, port facilities, and parking lots. In their impact upon inputs used and goods and services produced within the state, public authority operations rival the activities of the state itself. And yet this ebb and flow, massive and growing, is the product of decisions that are little influenced by the people of New York or by their elected representatives in Albany.

The solution is also obvious. No one saw that more clearly than Arthur Levitt: "The inherent evil in the excessive use of the authority structure is obvious: there is a loss of public control and of legislative understanding. Control must be restored if our democratic process is to remain meaningful."[100] Restoration of control should include – must include – converting a large number of public benefit corporations to state agencies and superimposing upon the rest extensive new restrictions.

The conversion of many public authorities into state agencies will be resisted by three lines of argument. None will withstand close scrutiny.

First, in contrast to state agencies, a public benefit corporation is supposed to be more efficient, flexible, and innovative. The evidence does not bear out such claims. They are not more efficient. No less an authority than the New York State Comptroller has emphasized that point, and in no uncertain terms.[101] Nationwide they are not more flexible and innovative than regular government agencies, as a recent study has documented in depressing detail.[102]

Second, public benefit corporations are ostensibly to be preferred to state agencies because they escape many of the personnel policies of the civil service, and can therefore hire the able and fire the incompetent with greater ease. This smacks of designing a new car engine that is relatively unresponsive to either accelerator or brake because of a certain sluggishness in the old engine. The question largely unexplored is whether a rejuvenation of the more governable model is not possible. If the key problem is defective personnel policies of the state, it is high time that those defects were assailed directly, as difficult as that may be.

Third, and most subtle of all, is a claim echoed up and down the halls of every public authority of consequence in the state that these authorities are superior to state agencies because their extensive independence enables them to attract more highly motivated top executives, who are willing to forego the rewards of private enterprise for the opportunity to leave their mark upon the state. The causal statement is correct but the inference is wrong. The highly motivated are drawn to top positions in public authorities because of the freedom of decision making that accompanies those positions. But it is precisely this freedom that is the problem. What Austin Tobin, Robert Moses, and William Ronan would call a desirable latitude in policy making every other New Yorker should label as a reprehensible absence of popular control. Is it worth crippling mass transit in New York City to preserve the services of an Austin Tobin? Is it worth the gamble of UDC's default to give free rein to an Edward Logue? Obviously not. As long as public authorities in New York State are sufficiently insulated to make them, by and large, the playthings of their top executives, they will continue to attract to those positions those who enjoy playing with the public's money – a lot of money. It is high time that the public had more to say in that game, and by implication, time that the likes of Austin Tobin and Robert Moses had less.

For those public authorities not destined to be converted into state agencies, the desirable change is easy to specify in general terms and difficult to document in detail. Every last one of them should become, as State Comptroller Levitt noted, more amenable to popular control and legislative understanding. The specific legal changes required to effect this transformation will require expert study, and may well vary across different types of authorities. As a first approximation, however, a number of general modifications in design are suggested by the previous discussion.

First, the matter of controlling policy. As the younger Robert Moses pointed out, if the governor is to be responsible, the governor must have the authority to say what policies should and should not be carried out. At a minimum, the minutes of the meetings of the managing board of each public authority should require gubernatorial approval. The practice of fabricating the minutes in advance of the actual board meeting should also be replaced by an accurate and comprehensive account of what actually went on. (The governor can hardly control what he cannot monitor.) The chief executive should also be able to appoint and remove the top executives of public benefit corporations with considerably greater ease than is now the case. At a minimum, the terms of these executives and that of the governor should correspond, so that a newly elected chief executive will not be hamstrung, as Carey was hamstrung, by the loyalty of authority officials to that predecessor who appointed them. Longevity in office is also a danger, as the autocratic tendencies of Robert Moses and Austin Tobin have made abundantly clear. Reappointment of top executives should therefore be limited to one or two terms. This may well sacrifice expertise, but it should remove the threat that a power-seeking bureaucrat such as Moses will get a viselike grip upon state authorities in the future.

Second, and all-important, is budgetary control. The legislature should have restored to it at least some of its conventional powers over money matters. This should include for most authorities, and possibly for all, approval of annual budgets and approval of proposed debt issues. Authority pricing should be tightly regulated. If monopoly prices are to be charged, the legislature and not the bureaucrats should specify how the resulting surplus is to be spent. The public should have restored to it what Rockefeller snatched away. Moral obligation bonds either should be dispensed with or, if they are to be used, should be subject to voter approval in a referendum. If the state is to provide the backing, the electorate should sanction the process.[103]

Finally, the flow of information from authorities to everyone – the governor, the legislature, and the people – should be increased and made more intelligible. At best, authority reports tend to strike even the informed reader the same way *Pilgrim's Progress* struck Huck Finn: "The statements was interesting but tough." At worst, information is suppressed and often deliberately withheld, as the Port Authority has demonstrated repeatedly. The time for tolerating such recalcitrance is past. The time is at hand for the resurgence of popular control, to be complemented by an outpouring of information designed to inform, not obscure; to enlighten, not confuse.

The task is somewhat more delicate, and somewhat more important, than the above might be taken to imply. To stamp out undesirable unresponsiveness of public authorities while preserving the energy and imagination of those who direct them is a complicated task admitting to no easy solution. There is a fine line between controlling and stifling. There is a linkage between independence and creativity. Finding the optimal way to proceed is therefore a demanding task to be predicated upon exhaustive study. But that study must surely be undertaken, because a wholesale restructuring must surely be undertaken. For too long New Yorkers have assumed that public benefit corporations are superior to state agencies, largely because of the known defects of the latter. They are like judges in a beauty contest, anxious to give first prize to the second candidate on the strength of inspecting only the first candidate. It is time for a symmetry of skepticism to be directed toward both.

The importance of the task of reexamination and restructuring is far broader than the state. New York has led many other states into the bureaucratic wilderness. It should take a hand in leading them out. The Empire State has repeatedly set precedents that other states have followed. Its Housing Finance Agency, for example, became the national model for a public authority turned financial intermediary, with its debt boasting a quasi-guarantee from the state, such as moral obligation backing. By 1975, Moody's Investment Service listed 79 such authorities in 30 states.[104] An association of state HFAs had even been created, with 35 members and its own Washington lobby. The best indication that *all* of the problems of tenuous control and warped bureaucratic priorities are national in scope is the conclusion of a recent and comprehensive survey of public benefit corporations throughout America. It paints upon a larger canvas a picture similar in bleakness to that of New York State:

> It is the thesis of this book that public authorities that are supposed to act in the general interest of a state, region, or city frequently do not. Because of their insulation, they overemphasize financial returns and reflect or accept the viewpoints of banking and business participants. They bias government investment in favor of physical infrastructures for short-term economic return. Ideologies of laissez-faire, localism, autonomy, and limited politics converge to limit the forms and ambitions of public enterprise, to preserve the power of groups with

narrow and specialized aims, and to relieve the enterprises
themselves of obligations to respond to broader interests.[105]

Public authorities are not just a New York problem. They are a national
problem.

The reader at the present juncture is surely less than satisfied. The
suspicion probably remains that this description of an undemocratic
structure must be somewhat overdrawn for public benefit corporations,
at least within New York State. After all, they are created by the legislature. Their debt limits, including all revisions, must be approved by
the legislature. Insofar as they are reliant upon ongoing state subsidies
through loans and gifts, these too must be approved by the elected
representatives of the people in the Assembly and the Senate. This
must be a system in which the executive's ability to push through
authority legislation and the authority's ability to be independent of
the legislature are far more circumscribed than this chapter would
lead one to believe. Lurking behind these concerns is the question of
relative power in budgetary matters, in particular, the issue of the
extent to which the governor calls the tune and the legislators dance to
the strains that annually accompany the chief executive's budget.
These questions are therefore major topics of the next chapter.

7

Of feeble checks and balances

7.1. Checks and balances: guardians of the public good

Economists believe that, in matters economic, most people are motivated by self-interest most of the time. They also have a theory, dating from Adam Smith, which suggests that under certain conditions, this pervasive drive on behalf of self will tend to work for the benefit of all. That improbable conversion is accomplished, by and large, by the disciplining force of competitive markets, Smith's principal guardian of the public good. If one producer will not supply what consumers are demanding, another will. After all, there is profit to be made from expanding sales. If two or more producers attempt to limit output and raise prices, other producers are sure to undercut their inflated prices in pursuit of their own profits. As long as competition rules in the marketplace, Smith argued, the end result should be the goods consumers want at reasonable prices.

The validity of Smith's theorizing need not concern us here. The relevance of his behavioral premise in the realm of politics is all-important. What is the appropriate view of man that should condition how a political system should be structured? Attempts to provide an answer usually include two dominant themes. One emphasizes a clash of values. Some citizens, for example, would give greater emphasis to the priority of equality; others, to the priority of freedom. Differences in ideals often lead to clashes over policies. The second theme, and generally the one more carefully articulated by writers on the topic, concerns the less idealistic side of man. Most people most of the time, the argument runs, are preoccupied with their own self-interest. (The parallel to Adam Smith's behavioral premise is striking.) In the realm of politics, this interest often includes the desire to control events and people and public expenditure – that "human frailty apt to grasp at Power," as Locke preferred to put it.[1] The inescapable implication is that factionalism is endemic to democratic processes. Ideals clash, as do the various personal interests of the participants. The problem is to prevent such intrinsic disharmony from getting out of hand.

Factionalism might be viewed as another form of competition. Theorizing akin to that of Adam Smith's is therefore often used by those concerned with how it should be managed. What is required for the functioning of good government, their argument runs, is a system of checks and balances. Although ultimately complex, this idea seems to have at its core two relatively simple notions. One concerns constituency representation. In the framing of legislation, for example, each concerned interest should have its spokesman in a debate that is deliberate and informed. Nor is the mere exchange of words sufficient. Each must have some possibility of affecting the outcome. Otherwise, debate becomes a sham. The other central notion of checks and balances involves the imposition of restraints. A propensity to grasp for power is also a propensity to encroach upon the domain of others. Power should therefore be confronted by power in a contest not hopelessly unequal. The executive and the different branches of the legislature, for example, can check each other by the mutual privilege of rejecting what the other has originated. An independent judiciary, precisely because it is independent, can restrain the actions of the executive and the legislative branches. The courts' primary role in this connection is that of policeman, ruling (upon request) when power encroachments appear to violate the law, particularly that most fundamental of laws, the constitution.[2]

Notice the marked similarity to Adam Smith's economic arguments about the merits of a competitive marketplace. Monopoly of production or monopoly of political power is sure to imperil the public good. Competition is the key. In the political arena, that competition should include, as it were, a "check" aspect and a "balance" aspect. Deliberate and informed debate among representatives elected to serve differing constituency interests should give to various factions a sense of meaningful participation. The resulting legislative output should also reflect the balancing of conflicting interests required to produce a majority vote. No less important, the competitive structure must also give to each participant the power to check the encroachment tendencies of others. Without such a division of power, the pursuit of self-interest by the powerful few could lead to nasty results for the many.

Typical of this line of reasoning was Madison's cautioning of the citizens of New York against "the accumulation of all powers, legislative, executive, and judiciary, in the same hands."[3] Possibly with a note of sadness he added, "It may be a reflection on human nature, that such devices should be necessary to control the abuses of government."[4] On the likelihood of abuses without a separation of powers he had no doubts whatsoever. And yet despite the cautioning words of Madison and others, this separation has always been somewhat tenuous in fiscal matters throughout the entire history of the Empire State. What has also been undermined, particularly in the twentieth century, is the priority of informed and deliberate debate among elected representatives of differing constituency interests. This curious emasculation of basic American principles of good government, more than any other factor, made possible the fiscal events of the Rockefeller years.

7.2. The executive versus the legislature

Consider first the division of powers between the legislature and the executive. Colonial New Yorkers hotly contested the right of the executive to originate money bills, as did many of their contemporaries throughout British North America. And yet when the first New York State Constitution was framed in 1777, the power to originate money bills was not made the exclusive right of the Assembly – an amazing oversight considering the tenor of the times. Quick to grasp at opportunities lurking in the vagueness of the Constitution's wording, the Senate successfully insinuated its influence into the determination of fiscal matters in the course of the nineteenth century.

The influence of *both* legislative bodies would be radically undermined, but only in the modern era. In matters of fiscal control, New York began the twentieth century roughly where it had begun the nineteenth: with the power to initiate money bills lodged firmly in the legislature. Although consistent with old republican ideals, this fiscal system was winning few laurels for coherence and efficiency as the modern era swept down upon it. Each state department, commission, or other administrative agency pleaded its case before legislative committees. Legislative committees then formulated proposals – often bearing little resemblance to initial pleas – and the legislature had the final say on appropriations. This was a chaotic annual ritual destined for destruction. The role of government in the new industrial economy was escalating at a whirlwind pace, at least by the standards of the previous century. Demands upon it were rising, tasks were multiplying, and the associated complexity staggered the nineteenth-century mind. Legislative control of money matters appeared, to an ever growing list of reformers, about as well suited to the modern era as a dinosaur. The call became ever more strident for consolidation under strong executive leadership, a plea that by 1919 had persuaded 24 of the 48 states to adopt some form of the modern executive budget. (The governor proposed, and the legislature reviewed, rather than the other way around.) New York was not among the 24. Its experiment with an executive budget beginning in 1913 had collapsed by 1915. In that latter year, a proposal at the state's constitutional convention to resurrect executive control of the budget went down to defeat. At the close of World War I, therefore, the legislators of the Empire State still had formal responsibility for preparing the state's budget. They would lose it – totally – within the decade.

Leading the charge was sometime Governor Alfred E. Smith, ably assisted in bill drafting by his young assistant, Robert Moses (ever an advocate of elitism in the functioning of good government). The landmark dates were three. In 1919 a Reconstruction Commission Report (initiated by Al Smith and directed by Moses) advocated a constitutional amendment introducing the executive budget system. The battle would rage unresolved for eight years. Triumph came in 1927, when the legislature passed and the voters ratified a constitutional amendment charging the governor with the responsibility of formulating annually "a complete financial plan." (The task of drafting the enabling legislation Al Smith gave primarily to his Secretary of State, Robert Moses.) Finally, in 1929, the first budget was submitted, consistent with the new constitutional amendment, from the office of Governor Franklin D. Roosevelt, a politician not averse to strong executive leadership in fiscal matters. Subsequent changes, from Roosevelt to Lehman to Dewey to Rockefeller, were merely refinements in organization and procedure. The monumental shift in fiscal responsibility and fiscal power – from legislature to executive – had been accomplished.[5]

By the advent of the Rockefeller years, control of money bills had therefore been placed squarely in the hands of the governor. The Executive Budget by that time was prepared annually by the Budget Division, which the governor controlled. Printed in December and released in mid-January, this document must be acted upon by the legislature before it can vote on any money bills of its own. Although the legislature may reduce items in the Executive Budget, additions or amendments must be listed separately, and are therefore subject to another New York curiosity: the line veto of the governor, whereby specific items in a bill (rather than the entire bill) can be struck down by the chief executive.[6] Not even the president of the United States can claim that power. Nor can the American president view a specific budget allocation as merely a ceiling placed upon his spending, to be approximated at his discretion. And with good reason. With this power in hand, any chief executive could strangle programs of which he disapproved, whatever dollar amounts were voted by the legislature. The mere threat of strangulation could also be used as a bargaining tool of immense power to coerce reluctant legislators – fearful for the survival of their pet projects – to vote for programs favored by the chief executive. Although denied to the president of the United States, this power is also granted to the governor of New York.

These powers over money matters are, in turn, indicative of a larger power structure that is nothing short of awesome. Political scientists have repeatedly emphasized what the public too often forgets: that if concentrating power imperils democratic processes, the density achieved in the Empire State is downright dangerous. In a study completed during Rockefeller's regime, for example, Joseph Schlesinger concluded that New York has a stronger chief executive than any other state in the union.[7] Schlesinger compared gubernatorial powers in all 50 states under such headings as tenure potential, powers of appointment, budget powers, and veto powers, in each case giving a numerical score deemed to be indicative of relative power. In the final ranking generated by the addition of all numbers so assigned, only New York's governor scored 19 out of a possible 19. (The nearest competitors were the chief executives of Illinois and New Jersey, each of whom was scored at 18.)

Damon Runyon once observed that while the race is not always to the swift nor the battle to the strong, that is the way to bet. In contests over fiscal matters in the Empire State, the odds generally favor, and often favor to an overwhelming degree, the policies and programs of the governor. The power here described is merely the tip of an iceberg of influence on which all but the most determined legislator (or the most suicidal) is sure to founder.

Never was this principal more in evidence than during the Rockefeller years. To begin with, there was the amassing of experience and influence that came with length of tenure. Rockefeller served as the chief executive of New York longer than anyone else except for George Clinton, the state's first governor. Long before the end of his tenure, Rockefeller had become, in the opinion of many, "an extraordinarily savvy operator, wielding the powers of the governership with a flair and cunning no predecessor since Al Smith had managed."[8]

Legislators could of course contest Rockefeller's recommendations by voting no. But how could they decide which proposals were unwise? The governor had at his command a large and expert staff. A single phone call could activate these minions into a frenzy of activity designed to inundate any and all challengers with data, reports, and documents. The plight of the typical legislator was well characterized by Senator Manfred Ohrenstein (D, Manhattan) when he openly confessed on one occasion, "We need information; we need to know what the hell we're doing, and we don't know what the hell we're doing."[9] The confession is appalling. That legislative scrutiny by the elected representatives of the people should have degenerated to such a level is enough to make the likes of Madison spin in his grave. In present-day fiscal matters, however, how could it be otherwise? As repeatedly emphasized elsewhere, the multiplicity of accounts and tortuous accounting procedures of the state are not conducive to understanding by the layman. And – a point too often forgotten by the public – legislators *are* laymen when it comes to most fiscal matters.

Into a great darkness Rockefeller deliberately shed as little light as possible. The Constitution requires that a bill be introduced at least three days before being acted upon. This provision can be waived, however, if in the opinion of the governor, the legislation in question qualifies as a "message of necessity." Nelson Rockefeller was frequently of that opinion. The net result was a repeated rushing of legislation through the Assembly and the Senate in a matter of hours, with the cooperation of the leadership in those two legislative bodies. (So flagrant was Rockefeller's use of this gambit that in 1971 the American Civil Liberties Union, in concert with other public interest groups, brought a suit charging that *in 79 cases that year* he had employed this emergency power when no emergency existed.)[10] With basic ignorance reinforced by haste, not a few legislators no doubt wondered from time to time, as Senator Ohrenstein put it, whether they knew what the hell they were doing. Rockefeller put the matter more discreetly: "In Albany it was sometimes easier for [the legislators] to pass my programs than to come up with alternatives."[11]

In fiscal matters, then, the battle lines usually featured the informed versus the uninformed, the powerful versus the weak. Legislators who fought the Governor's programs risked political suicide. For those who lent support, the list of possible favors was almost endless. Positions directly controlled by the Governor included 8,000 jobs exempt from the Civil Service merit system. Also subject to the Governor's influence to varying degrees were another 32,000 positions. The prospect of such rewards is only one of a multitude of pressures that the Governor could bring to bear on the recalcitrant legislator. A stark summary of those pressures is provided by one of the most astute observers of Albany politics, Warren Moscow. It is worth quoting in some detail.

> The governor could reward them with valuable job patronage that usually kept friends and constituents away from the unemployment lines and out of the poor houses. The governor could also turn over to favored and cooperative legislators bills that had been drafted by his staff so that they could get credit for developing programs about which they generally knew little or nothing. In addition, the governor could pass the word to his state agencies that certain legislators were in good standing

with the administration and thus should be afforded all the cooperation due an assemblyman or senator who was part of the governor's "team."

Intertwined with this gubernatorial power was the governor's potent influence in the dispensation of patronage to county party chairmen, whose own power came from their ability to deliver jobs to their local followers. These chairmen made sure that their state legislators did nothing to displease the governor. A phone call from the governor to a county chairman led to another from the chairman to his legislator, who was reminded he was not sent to Albany to be a statesman.[12]

Small wonder that Rockefeller would characterize the basic structure of Albany government as "the governor proposes and the legislature disposes."[13] In many instances, it seems, the Governor proposed and the legislature rubber-stamped. But not always. Acting as a brake on the initiatives of the chief executive are the considerable powers of the leader of each of the two legislative houses: the speaker of the Assembly and the majority leader of the Senate. A list of the men who have held these posts reads like an Albany *Who's Who*: Walter Mahoney, Joseph Zaretski, Earl Brydges, Warren Anderson (all majority leaders of the Senate in their day); Oswald Heck, Joseph Carlino, Anthony Travia, Perry Duryea (successive speakers of the Assembly in the postwar era).

To plow through the literature detailing the formal and informal powers of the two legislative leaders of New York is, for most, an unwelcome task. Despite the bracing tonic of examples, the assignment is sure to produce a certain glazing of the eye and fogging of the brain. The complexity of the structure, the subtle shifts that can be wrought by changing conditions and personalities – these are not the stuff to keep the average reader riveted to the page. The broad outlines, however, are simple enough. Consider the task of making a single legislative leader as powerful as possible. (That such an assignment is acrid smoke to democratic nostrils need not concern us here.) The requisite powers for achieving such a goal are almost self-evident. First, the legislative process generally requires that bills be acted upon by committees before being acted upon by the full legislative body. Rule (1): Concentrate control of all committee assignments in a single pair of hands. Second, which bills actually come to the floor of the legislature is determined by a set of rules, usually vested in a Rules Committee. Rule (2): Concentrate control of the rules (and the Rules Committee) in the same pair of hands. Third, the ability of the typical legislator to function effectively is to no small extent influenced by available staff and expense money. Rule (3): Give control of both to the same legislative leader.

If legislative leaders, like earthquakes, were scored according to the severity of the tremors that they could generate, the capacities of New York's Senate and Assembly leaders would read far up on the Richter scale. Under the three headings just noted, their powers include the following:

1. The power to appoint all committee members (including members of joint legislative committees)
2. The power to appoint all committee chairmen
3. The power to refer bills to committees
4. Control of the Rules Committee
5. Control of the expenditures of funds in each house; in particular, control of the allocation of additional staff grants and expense funds over and above the basic allocation made to all legislators

The manipulations made possible by these levers of power are more apparent in some cases than in others. The power to refer bills to committees, for example, is a useful tool in conjunction with the power to control committee membership. Alan Hevesi explains: "Having created a committee, the leader is, more often than not, in a position to predict the legislative action the committee is likely to take. A parallel power invested in him, that of the referral of bills to committees of his choice, further strengthens his ability to determine the destinies of any piece of proposed legislation."[14] Thus, for example, in 1966, Assembly Speaker Anthony Travia referred an abortion bill that he wished to kill not to the Public Health Committee – the obvious choice – but to the Codes Committee, 12 of whose 15 members were Catholics. Not surprisingly, the bill died in committee that year.

Perhaps most difficult to grasp, at least for the layman, are the manipulations by which the private bills of individual legislators can be advanced, retarded, or exterminated. This particular process the legislative leader has firmly by the throat through his control of which committee will consider the bill, when it will be considered, and whether it will ever emerge from committee.[15] In the blunt wording of former Senate Majority Leader Walter Mahoney, "On lesser bills the leader has life-and-death control, and this fact gives him leverage in attempting to influence men to cooperate on more important bills."[16] The same phrase – "life-and-death" – was used in a study by the State Education Department to describe the leadership's control of private members' bills. The study went on to point out that "a false step, an unsuccessful revolt, and the pet projects of the rebels would die in committee. To the average legislator such a fate would be political death, for he depends on cooperation for the passage of private or local bills that are vital to his constituency."[17]

To focus exclusively upon any single power, of course, does an injustice to the larger structure of which it is a part. All of the powers noted here matter, not just control of the fate of private members' bills. All of these are but constituent elements – albeit the central elements – in any legislative leader's attempt to weave a network of influence throughout the chambers and corridors of Albany. Predictably, some are better artisans than others. None can help but achieve a determining influence in the life of the typical New York legislator. As former Assemblyman Stephen J. Solarz (D, Brooklyn) noted, "When you combine the power to appoint, with patronage, and control over legislation, you get leadership strength."[18] Notice the choice of wording. The end product of this extraordinary amalgam of power is not "tyranny" or "bullying" but "leadership." The speaker of the Assembly and the majority leader of the Senate are, after all, elected by the legislators. This fact alone suggests that other factors besides the carrots and sticks at the leaders' disposal may encourage the would-be lawmakers to follow their lead. Stanley Steingut even went so far as to suggest that the Assembly speaker "mostly gets the men to go along with him through his personality and the friendships he develops, not the use of strong-arm techniques."[19] That statement would seem to confuse the importance of having power with the necessity of overtly applying it all the time. If personal charm and warm friendships are the main ingredients needed to get the many to follow the lead of the one, why have congressional legislative leaders fared so poorly compared with their counterparts in Albany?

The comparison is instructive. It is perhaps best amplified by those who have experienced the legislator's lot in both worlds. Two former New York assemblymen, one a Democrat and the other a Republican, each with six years experience in Albany, became congressmen in the early 1970s. Their verbal snapshots create the unmistakable impression that politics on the Potomac are considerably more democratic than those experienced in New York's capitol:[20]

> Here there is an attempt to convince – never the sledgehammer approach of mandating positions like we had in Albany.

> In Albany, the governor dealt directly with the leadership; here, the executive branch deals directly with the legislators, because the leadership can't deliver.

You have a great deal more power over bills in committee than you did in Albany. You have an opportunity to restructure a bill – 50 or 60 amendments are considered on a single measure. In Albany, a bill went to the committee, it was never changed, then it came out and was passed.

If the Ten Commandments were offered as an amendment to a bill in Albany, they'd be rejected on the grounds that they were a repudiation of the leadership.

There is much more time for reflection and deliberation on problems. There is none of the Mad Hatter scurrying around at the end of the legislative session, where a lawmaker has only one or two minutes to review a major bill. In Albany, you walk into the chamber in the morning and find a package of 40 to 50 bills and you don't know what many are about. Here the committees are well staffed, there is a great deal of preparation and each office is well informed on the pros and cons of a piece of legislation.

Sledgehammer tactics, negligible discussion and less amending, only a minute or two to review a major bill – these are not a characterization of the legislative process well calculated to please the founding fathers of the republic who took up arms over the issue of representative government. But are the impressions of these two legislators representative of the reactions of many? And if they are representative, to what extent do they signal a structure that contravenes the basic American ideals of good government?

The issue of the typicality of the impressions quoted is most easily settled by appealing to the powers outlined previously. Three men, and only three, have a virtual hammerlock on a system of rewards and punishments that, for most legislators, can make the difference between political success and political oblivion. Nor are these three reluctant to use their powers, as the history of New York politics demonstrates with a vengeance. In pursuit of legislators' votes, a determined governor in full flight is awesome to behold. When he is joined by the two legislative leaders, the force of the three borders on the irresistible.

Notice what the argument is not. This constellation of powers should not be taken to imply that the governor always gets his way or, in conjunction with the two legislative leaders, is the sole influence on legislation. Far from it. Logrolling with vested interests; bargaining now with the leadership, now with individual legislators; marshaling support from the public in general or from lobbyists in particular –

these are the daily fare of any occupant of the governor's mansion. What is being argued – and what is worth underscoring – is that in the contest over which fiscal measures will be passed, with what terms, and for whose benefit, the struggle is remarkably unequal. Legislators are not totally impotent, merely weak. Rebellions are not unheard of, merely unlikely. As Al Smith liked to point out, you don't shoot Santa Claus. By the same token, one is well advised not to kick Muhammad Ali. The average legislator will not always dance to the tune emanating from the governor's mansion or from the office of the man who leads in his legislative chamber. The tune of each, however, is sure to be infectious. Should both tunes merge as one, the tendencies for the feet to move and the hands to raise in accordance with the dictates of the music are irresistible for those who wish to make a career of Albany politics.

By no stretch of generosity, then, can the legislative process of Albany, particularly that concerned with fiscal matters, be viewed as government by the people, or even government by their elected representatives. The structure is elitist to the core. But if it is a small elite – and it is hard to imagine a shorter roster in any setting with pretensions to representative government – do the elite compete vigorously among themselves, and if they do, does that competition provide a structure of checks and balances that serves the public well?

Concerning the likelihood of a competitive struggle, three points are worth noting. First, even when governor and legislative leaders are from different parties and continually at loggerheads with each other, the net effect on the Executive Budget is usually far from dramatic. The task of overhauling that document is too complex and too time-consuming to admit of more than a few major changes. Thus in Harriman's regime, when the relationship among the power triumvirate reached a postwar low, the chief executive's budget was sometimes expanded by the legislature, sometimes contracted, with the final authorized version never more than a few percentage points different from what Harriman proposed (see Table 7.1). Second, the governor and the two leaders were all members of the same political party for 22 of the 30 years of New York legislative history since 1945 (see Table 7.2). With the power group so small and a similarity of party affiliation so pronounced, the odds were minimized for achieving that indispensable ingredient for checks and balances, an informed and deliberate debate among a range of strong competitors who collectively represent the interests of all major constituencies. Symptomatic of the absence of such competition under Dewey was the fact that the Executive Budget for 12 successive years was almost never cut, and when it was, the

Table 7.1. *Total expenditure for the New York State General Fund requested by the governor and approved by the legislature, 1945–78* (*$ millions*)

Fiscal year ending March 31	(1) Expenditure requested[a]	(2) Expenditure authorized[a]	(3) ([2] ÷ [1])
1945	380	360	0.95
1946	379	372	0.98
1947	556	600	1.08
1948	663	705	1.06
1949	754	725	0.96
1950	924	866	0.94
1951	852	891	1.05
1952	939	993	1.06
1953	1,054	1,054	1.00
1954	1,066	1,075	1.01
1955	1,123	1,320	1.18
1956	1,282	1,308	1.02
1957	1,501	1,437	0.96
1958	1,581	1,672	1.06
1959	1,821	1,793	0.98
1960	2,041	1,994	0.98
1961	2,035	2,092	1.03
1962	2,395	2,324	0.97
1963	2,591	2,595	1.00
1964	2,889	2,781	0.96
1965	2,920	2,894	0.99
1966	3,488	3,460	0.99
1967	3,987	4,022	1.01
1968	4,686	4,629	0.99
1969	5,494	5,519	1.00
1970	6,417	6,207	0.97
1971	7,257	6,748	0.93
1972	8,450	7,422	0.88
1973	7,900	7,785	0.99
1974	8,881	8,620	0.97
1975	9,383	9,677	1.03
1976	10,692	10,602	0.99
1977	10,764	10,978	1.02
1978	11,345	11,177	0.99

[a] Prior to 1957, excludes Capital Construction Fund.
Source: New York [State], *The Executive Budget,* 1945–78.

Table 7.2. *Political leaders and party affiliation in New York State,*
1945–77

Year	Governor	Majority leader, Senate	Speaker of Assembly
1945			
1946			
1947		Benjamin Feinberg (R)	
1948			
1949			
1950	Thomas Dewey (R)		
1951		Arthur Wicks (R)	Oswald Heck (R)
1952			
1953			
1954			
1955			
1956	Averell Harriman (D)		
1957			
1958			
1959		Walter Mahoney (R)	
1960			
1961			
1962			Joseph Carlino (R)
1963			
1964			
1965		Joseph Zaretski (D)	
1966	Nelson Rockefeller (R)		Anthony Travia (D)
1967			
1968			
1969		Earl Brydges (R)	
1970			
1971			
1972			Perry Duryea (R)
1973			
1974	Malcolm Wilson (R)		
1975		Warren Anderson (R)	
1976	Hugh Carey (D)		
1977			Stanley Steingut (D)

Source: The New York Red Book, ed. Ira Freedman, 1945–77 (Albany: Williams Press, 1977).

effect was trivial (see Table 7.1). Third, a difference in party affiliation is no guarantee of vigorous competition, as Nelson Rockefeller adroitly demonstrated in the 1960s. As described in more detail elsewhere, the Democrats were divided on who should become the legislative leaders following their sweep of both New York houses in 1964. Sensing opportunity in deadlock, Rockefeller threw his support behind Anthony Travia and Joseph Zaretski, thereby guaranteeing their ascension to the leadership posts in the Assembly and the Senate, and also guaranteeing an absence of hostile receptions for such Rockefeller proposals as the 1965 sales tax hike.

Again, notice what the argument is not. Loyalty to the same party by the powerful three, or loyalty won by favors given, does not preclude ideological differences, personal rivalries, or struggles over which dollars will be spent on what. But when the dust of battle settles – in the back rooms, in the committee hearing rooms, on the floor of the legislative chambers – the fiscal package ratified is almost always a slightly modified version of what the governor proposed, and that proposal, in turn, has become in the modern era primarily the governor's creation. The legislative leaders are still a party to the creation process, in part because of their control over the fiscal committees that hold hearings on suggestions in the formative stages and later scrutinize the finished document. The dominant pattern, however, is for the leadership to be consulted more on tactics than on substance, more on which maneuvers will facilitate passage in each house of the various items, framed primarily by the governor and his staff. The leaders can exploit this consultation to achieve a modification of terms, insisting that only with those modifications will passage be guaranteed, or at least a major fight avoided. Such changes, however, more often than not will constitute little more than minor variations on the grand themes orchestrated by the chief executive. Never was this more true than in the Rockefeller years. The potentialities for power inherent in his office he learned to exploit to the full. He was governor for so long. So many owed him so much. So few dared risk the slings and arrows under his command. The summary judgment of the best of his biographers bears repeating: that long before Rockefeller left office, he had become "an extraordinarily savvy operator, wielding the powers of the governorship with a flair and cunning no predecessor since Al Smith had managed."[21] In terms of dollars managed, Al Smith was not even in the same ball park as Nelson Rockefeller.

This, then, is the system of checks and balances that has characterized the legislative process in fiscal matters within the Empire State for much of the postwar era: a system where three men control an armory of weapons that in concert will overawe most of the legislators most of the time; a system in which cooperation more than competition has characterized the interaction of the three as they pursued fiscal targets established primarily by the chief executive; a system well characterized by Rockefeller as "the governor proposes and the legislature disposes"[22] – in short, a system of checks and balances distinguished for its absence of operative checks and the presence of a pervasive imbalance in the power politics of executive–legislator interaction, and of leader–follower interaction.

If balance has been lacking and checks have been ephemeral, what guardians of the public interest remain? The tempting answer is to claim that the public can protect its own interest through the discipline of the ballot box. If spending and/or taxes appear ill-advised or downright foolish, the voters can always throw out one set of politicians and replace them with another set more closely attuned to the public's views on fiscal matters, or so the argument runs. The difficulty is that the average citizen knows far too little far too late to make much of a difference to the budgetary process.[23] With one exception. The constitution of the Empire State requires that any increase in the debt of the state proposed by the legislature must be approved by the public in a referendum. The result is a New York curiosity. It is populist in spirit, rather than elitist. It runs counter to the twentieth-century tendency within the state to concentrate more and more fiscal powers in fewer and fewer hands. Perhaps most important of all, it reins in hard the politician's propensity to have expenditures outrun receipts. Whenever this does happen, the resulting shortfall in funds can only be covered by an expansion of debt. That proposed debt increase, when submitted for voter approval, must be explained and justified. If the public is dissatisfied, it can always vote no, sending chief executive and legislators back to the fiscal drafting board. In short, curiosity or not, this constitutional provision requiring voter approval for any debt increase is a formidable check in a structure of otherwise feeble checks and balances in the fiscal procedures of New York State. But has it worked? The answer, crudely put, is not when Nelson Rockefeller got his way. And in this particular matter, Rockefeller was determined to get his way.

In previous chapters the invention of the moral obligation bond was examined, first with respect to mechanical details, and then in terms of the political factors leading to its use.[24] Missing to this point are (1) the historical reasons for the constitutional provisions that the moral obligation bond was designed to circumvent, and (2) the reaction of the courts to what was clearly a constitutional question of the first importance. Billions hung in the balance. What would the courts say, and when would they say it?

7.3. The public versus debt escalation

New York State, the Comptroller announced, was on the "very brink of dishonor and bankruptcy."[25] The year was 1842. The language was strong stuff for the Comptroller of that or any other era. The causes for his concern were fiscal excesses of the past that threatened to imperil the very credit of the state. The problem had its origins, curiously enough, in the triumph of the Erie Canal. Toll receipts poured into state coffers at a prodigious rate, whetting the appetite of state decision makers for more. Their helter-skelter rush to build additional canals was relatively uninhibited by careful analysis of prospective revenues and costs. Fiscal ignorance harnessed to political ambition usually spells trouble, and New York's subsequent experience was no exception. Hard upon the heels of canal construction came credit extension to railroads and a host of other private companies. Hard upon the heels of this building and lending came the panic of 1837. By 1842 the burden of the debt so generated threatened to outrun the revenue-producing capabilities of the state.

If the problem was obvious, so was the solution. In pursuit of the latter, a Constitutional Convention assembled in Albany on June 1, 1846. When it adjourned four months later, it offered for popular ratification a constitutional amendment that, in the phrasing of the Convention, would place "strong safeguards against the recurrence of debt, and the improvident expenditure of the public money."[26] Those safeguards were centered in a single provision requiring that any future increase in debt proposed by the legislature must be approved by the voters of the state in a referendum.[27] The temper of the times was echoed in the indignation of the Chairman of the Finance Committee, who reviewed the matter in 1846. This amendment, he noted, "was saying that we will not trust the legislature with the power of creating indefinite mortgages on the people's property . . . Whenever the people were to have their property mortgaged for a State debt, . . . it should be done by their own voice, and by their own consent."[28]

That was the polite phrasing. The impolite phrasing was to suggest that the public could not trust any of the politicians any of the time when it came to issuing debt. Such a blanket condemnation was admittedly unfair for the public-spirited few as opposed to the grasping many. But it was still the way to bet, or so the citizenry of 1846 believed. Their fears and apprehensions were well summarized by the Chairman of the Finance Committee:

> If we look at home, at the neighboring states, or to foreign representative governments, we shall be obliged to acknowledge that their greatest infirmity is their disposition to contract

debts . . . It behooves those who were desirous of securing free and republican government to find some limitation safe in practice to this most dangerous power. In almost any case if a bad law is passed by the legislature it can be repealed . . . It is not so in relation to the subject of debts and compound interest. It is silent, creeps along, gets into the state, and when the act is once passed, the debt incurred, the obligation is as strong as death for its payment. That can only be wrung from the industry of the people by taxes, indirect and direct . . . They who vote the debt, vote to tax, although they cast the burden of the tax upon those who come after them.[29]

The problem can be recast in a framework of checks and balances. The politician's appetite for debt tends to be voracious. If he can borrow now, spend the funds on pet projects, and leave office before the bills come due, the advantages for the self-serving are overwhelming. The propensity to overissue debt is as old as the capacity of elected officials to issue promissory notes on the future. More than two centuries ago, David Hume underscored the dangers of debt creation in a structure of limited checks and balances: "It would scarcely be more imprudent to give a prodigal son a credit in every banker's shop in London, than to enpower a statesman to draw bills, in this manner, upon posterity."[30]

When it comes to monitoring debt creation – the drawing of bills upon posterity, in Hume's antiquated phrasing – the public is seldom a decent guardian of its own interests. As the Chairman of the Finance Committee noted, debt "is silent, creeps along." The reasons for the silence and the creep are not difficult to find. The public is slow to react if benefits from spending arise now while the burdens of taxation to pay for that spending arise later. Nor are they likely to be well informed about the issues. The politicians are unlikely to labor the public disadvantages of prospective spending that will operate to their personal advantage. Members of the financial community are unlikely to question the long-run merits of a debt expansion that enhances their immediate profits. Thus, should a debt issue of questionable public merit be proposed, the informed are likely to remain silent while the uninformed will almost surely be allowed to remain ignorant.

The constitutional provision requiring voter approval of a proposed debt issue can therefore provide a critical check in a system with precious little else in the way of checks and balances. Politicians are restrained sharply by the need for voter approval. The people become better informed as factions pro and con who seek their votes attempt to educate them on the issues. The casting of debt approval into such a capacious arena should also foster more intelligent debate in the popular press.

The end result, of course, is not perfection in the fiscal process. It is not even perfection in the issuance of debt. But what is guaranteed is a public scrutiny that should help to counter the "silence" and the "creep along" tendencies so endemic to the debt-creation process. The 1846 provision also guaranteed that never again would the Empire State be brought, as it had been brought in 1842, "to the very brink of dishonor and bankruptcy." The people would never stand for it. Or so the framers of the Constitution believed. They were wrong on several counts.

7.4. Rockefeller versus the Constitution

This restraint on the issuance of debt did not slow down Nelson Rockefeller any more than the Maginot Line slowed down Germany's advance into France in 1940. The evasion tactic was the same in both cases: the end run.

Rockefeller swept into office in 1959 with an announced policy of "pay-as-you-go" government. New Yorkers' response to that one should have been the same as the Duke of Wellington's response when addressed as Mr. Smith: "If you can believe that, you can believe anything." Rockefeller had barely adjusted to the novelty of the governor's mansion before he confronted the courts with a critical constitutional question. The response of the justices was to ignore it, at least while Rockefeller was in office. In this disregard can be found yet another slighting of checks and balances within the Empire State.

As noted in the previous chapter, the challenge arose as part of the chief executive's ravenous search for funds. Unsatisfied from the outset with the revenues generated by taxes, Rockefeller turned to the other logical source for dollars to spend: the issuance of debt. Like a terrier hot on the heels of disappearing prey, the Governor cannoned headfirst into the constitutional requirement that any increase in debt must be approved by the voters. Tolerating restraints was never one of Nelson Rockefeller's strong points. Tolerating this one was unthinkable. An elitist at heart, he did not take kindly to the need to explain every proposed debt increase to the voters. Worse, they might say no. They had said no several times to proposed bond issues in support of housing. The headlong pursuit of the grandiose therefore ran afoul of the need for popular approval. That of course was exactly what the framers of the 1846 provision had intended. They distrusted grandiose schemes generated in the back rooms of Albany. Government of the people, by the people, and for the people suggested the merits of popular scrutiny of high-priced proposals. So did the fiscal fiascoes generated in the wake of the Erie Canal's success. That scrutiny they had guaranteed by the provision noted. Grand schemes generally require a grand supply of dollars. Such funds are seldom generated by taxes alone. The other source is the sale of debt, and here the reins of restraint had been placed firmly in the hands of the voters.

Laws, however, are made of words. The implications of that obvious point usually escape the public but seldom escape the lawyers. A mastery of the words may permit manipulation of the laws to achieve ends quite different from those of the lawmakers who framed them. The constitutional provision under discussion applied to the "full faith and credit debt" of the state. (This wording was designed to signal to prospective creditors that these obligations would have a first claim, or first lien, against tax revenues.) If the issuance of this type of debt was inhibited by the necessity of gaining voter approval in a referendum, could not another kind of debt be devised that was free of such restraints? The answer was yes.

Just who had the initial creative insight is not entirely clear, but the man generally credited with solving this problem for Rockefeller is John Mitchell, then an attorney with the New York City firm of Nixon, Rose, Mudge. For New York State, Mitchell devised what became known as a "moral obligation" bond. Its central features have been spelled out previously. In brief, these involved (1) the establishment by the state legislature of a public authority to issue bonds, (2) the establishment by that authority of a special fund to meet all interest and principal payments due on its bonds, (3) the promise of the state to cover any shortfall in this public authority fund, and finally (4) the structuring of this state promise in words ("shall annually apportion") chosen deliberately to make that promise a moral, rather than a legal, commitment. Thus did Mitchell and Rockefeller hope to skirt one constitutional requirement while not violating another – the requirement prohibiting the state from extending its credit to any public corporation.[31] The state, the argument ran, was not extending its credit, only its moral backing. This may strike the layman as a blatant attempt by lawyers to undermine the intent of constitutional provisions. To the financial community, however, it proved eminently acceptable. In part this reflected the expectation that the state would not dare default on a given moral obligation debt issue and thereby imperil its credit standing in financial markets. Or, in the cautious phrasing of a major bond rating service, "It is expected that the State of New York will remain at all times under strong moral suasion to maintain its schedules of charges and programs of aid to the end that these [moral obligation] bonds will remain in good standing."[32]

Everybody seemed to gain. Rockefeller gained access to billions of dollars to finance a variety of New York State projects. Bond dealers gained the commissions on all the associated financing. Public authorities gained access to funds that otherwise would not have been available to them at such low rates of interest or, in some cases, would probably not have been available at all. The citizens, of course, were disenfranchised, and would remain so unless the courts reestablished their right to vote. But would they?

7.5. Silence in the courts

The important constitutional question, to review, was whether moral obligation debt violated the constitutional provision prohibiting the state from extending its credit to a public authority.[33] Only one source could supply the answer: the courts. What they supplied instead was a total silence from the moment that such bonds were issued in the early 1960s until two years after Rockefeller left the governor's office.

Why this curious inactivity for 15 years on a constitutional matter of the first importance? The problem was not indifference on the part of the general public. Efforts were made to challenge the constitutional legitimacy of moral obligation bonds. The difficulty was that the prospective plaintiffs were merely citizen-taxpayers.

For more than a century, New York courts had ruled "that a citizen-taxpayer, who cannot show any direct or personal injury, lacks standing to challenge the allegedly unconstitutional expenditure of state moneys."[34] In simple language, taxpayers were denied access to judicial review of any state legislation involving fiscal matters. The court's rationale for this denial is somewhat difficult to detect in the rarefied verbiage of a multitude of legal decisions. The classic argument was that a plaintiff must have a "direct and immediate" interest, and the interests of mere taxpayers were too removed to justify granting them standing in court on such issues. Probably more to the point and certainly more candid was Judge Gabrielli's statement that this banning of taxpayers from the courts was a "last protection against any nuisance or crackpot litigation,"[35] a sentiment echoed by another justice, who referred to the fear "that opening the doors of the court to taxpayers would cause a flood of actions by officious meddlers."[36] To put the matter somewhat differently, and perhaps too contentiously, this view expressed an intrinsic distrust of a democratic approach, at least with respect to citizen access to the courts for judicial review of the fiscal legislation of the state.

What this meant, in effect, was that any citizen-taxpayer who went to court to challenge the constitutionality of moral obligation bonds was told to get out. If citizens could not use the courts for this purpose, who could? The attorney-general could, but he was not likely to do so. As the court was quick to note, the customary role of an attorney-general is to defend the constitutional validity of governmental actions, not to attack them. (Justice Fuld put it more bluntly: "The suggestion . . . that the Attorney-General and other state officials may be relied upon to attack the constitutional validity of state legislation is both unreal in fact and dubious in theory.")[37] If the attorney-general would not, and the average citizen could not, who was left? No one.[38]

Notice the devastating implications for the operation of checks and balances. The state has a Constitution. The executive and the legislature are required to act in accordance with the terms of that Constitution. If they are suspected of violating those terms, the courts have the power to declare the actions in question unconstitutional and therefore "null and void," as the justices prefer to put it. But if no case ever reaches the courts because no citizen is allowed to sue for want of so-called standing, then the justices will remain silent. From their traditional role in the separation of powers among the executive, the legislature, and the judiciary, the justices are thereby relegated to no role at all, at least where the constitutional validity of state financing techniques are concerned. The legal issue at stake here is therefore not just some archaic curiosity limiting the ability of citizen-taxpayers to use the courts for certain purposes. What is at stake is nothing less than the effective functioning of one of the most revered principles of American government.

There were to be three moments of truth for the courts in the litigation over Rockefeller's attempt to escape constitutional restraints on the issuance of debt. The first came in 1963. *By the narrowest of possible margins,* four to three, the judges of the highest court of the state upheld this tradition of denying citizen-taxpayers access to judicial review of questionable fiscal practices.[39] Not surprisingly, the practice of issuing moral obligation bonds ballooned after 1963. To cite but one example, the Housing Finance Agency by the time of Rockefeller's resignation as governor had outstanding debt of $4.8 billion, a number surpassed by the *total* debt of only three states in the union.[40] Such extensive use was hardly surprising. Neatly sidestepping the need for voter referenda as it did, and with no apparent threat of judicial review of its constitutionality, this particular form of debt was welcomed with open arms by all directly concerned: the chief executive, the public authorities, and the financial community.

The day of reckoning in the courts, however, could not be postponed indefinitely. It came in 1975. The highest court of the state in that year finally gave to citizen-taxpayers what it had denied to them for more than a century: the right to sue the state on the constitutionality of money bills.[41] For at least some of the justices, this represented the overthrowing of a tradition that was not merely undemocratic in spirit, but perniciously undemocratic in practice. When the old tradition was upheld in 1963, at least one of the presiding judges was convinced that the court was making a mistake. "The apathy of the average citizen concerning public affairs has often been decried; under the court-made rule now reaffirmed, it is being compelled."[42] Twelve years later this line of reasoning apparently carried the day when a majority of the judges agreed that this barrier to judicial review must go. They readily conceded that to continue to deny citizen-taxpayers standing to sue the state on money matters "would be in effect to erect an impenetrable barrier to any judicial scrutiny of legislative action."[43] That scrutiny, in turn, has always been a vital part of the American tradition of checks and balances. Or, as the court preferred to put the matter, "The role of the judiciary is integral to the doctrine of separation of powers. It is unacceptable now by any process of continued quarantine *to exclude the very persons most likely to invoke its powers.*"[44]

By 1975, however, this smacked of an offer to lock the barn door after a decade and a half of alleged thievery. More cautiously, what the chief justices were now prepared to do at the request of citizen-taxpayers was to inspect the fiscal farmyard for constitutional deviants. Oddly enough, moral obligation bonds had been subjected to that inspection several months prior to this judicial decision in another landmark case from 1975. How was this possible? How could the court possibly pass judgment on the constitutionality of moral obligation bonds issued by public authorities of the state even before they granted citizen-taxpayers the right to sue on such matters?

The answer lay in a curious parallel between the fiscal activities of New York City and those of the state. In 1974 the Stabilization Reserve Corporation (SRC) had been created to help solve the fiscal crisis of the city. Its approach to issuing debt was reminiscent of the well-established tradition described previously for public authorities. A fund was established by SRC for the purpose of paying all principal and interest on its debt. Any shortfall in this fund the city agreed to make up by diverting to SRC certain state funds paid to New York City.[45] Through this arrangement the debt of SRC became, in effect, the moral obligation bonds of the city. The Constitution of the state established debt limits for all municipalities (including New York City), and – more dramatic for our purpose – expressly forbade the city from extending its credit to any public corporation.[46] Quick to seize the apparent opportunity to test the constitutionality of both municipal and state use of moral obligation bonds, Leon Wein brought suit against New York City.[47]

To even the most opaque of legal minds there was a striking parallel between the procedures whereby the city provided fiscal backing for SRC debt and those whereby the state gave its support to the bonds of public authorities. In both cases, a public authority established a fund for paying principal and interest on its debt. In both cases, provision was made to cover any deficiency in that fund by appropriations from either the city or the state. This extension of fiscal support, in turn, seemed to challenge constitutional provisions forbidding both municipalities and the state from extending credit to a public authority. Whatever the courts decided about the constitutionality of SRC debt was therefore almost sure to be the crucial legal precedent whenever the constitutionality of the state's moral obligation bonds was subjected to judicial review.

The stakes in *Wein* v. *City of New York* were therefore enormous. That puts the case too mildly. They were horrendous. Hanging in the balance was nothing less than the legitimacy of billions upon billions of debt issued by a variety of public authorities. Would the moral obligation gimmick, at long last subjected to judicial review, be declared in violation of the state's Constitution? The financial community, in a state of predictable nervousness, waited for the answer.

In Judge Jasen's opinion, the answer was a resounding yes. The debt-issuing arrangements of the Stabilization Reserve Corporation Act violated both "the letter and the spirit" of the state Constitution. In formulating his condemnation of these practices, Jasen zeroed in on the central legal issue: Was the debt of SRC also appropriately viewed as the debt of the city?

> No amount of words can disguise the simple fact that while liability of the city is disavowed, it effectively commits its sources of revenue from the State at the discharge of the obligations of the Stabilization Reserve Corporation . . . The fact is that while the city's sources of revenue from the State are not committed by existing law but only by annual appropriations, their continuance is economically and governmentally inevitable. The city has, therefore, committed its sources of revenue to the payment of these "debts"; that is tantamount to a com-

mitment of credit economically, practically, and therefore, legally.[48]

More simply put (and perhaps too simply put), the city would have no choice but to honor this commitment. If it had no choice, practically speaking, then its "moral" commitment was an irrevocable commitment and therefore a legal commitment. And the Constitution forbade such a legal commitment of the city's credit in support of a public authority.

The clear implication was that *all* moral obligation bonds were unconstitutional, whether issued by a municipality or by the state. Into the laps of the bureaucrats and the politicians Judge Jasen was therefore throwing a bombshell. The shattering fiscal implications he confronted head on. The central issue, Jasen argued, was not whether fiscal upheavals might follow the condemning of moral obligation debt, but whether the sanctity of the Constitution should be secondary to fiscal needs: "I am aware that constitutional limits upon debt contracting and taxing powers have been questioned as anachronistic and alternatives have been offered . . . A reappraisal of the need and the form of such limitations may be in order."[49] But if there is to be such a reappraisal, Jasen argued, let it be decided openly by the people and their elected representatives. To allow new fiscal devices to circumvent old constitutional provisions at the initiative of the few is clearly undemocratic. Worse, "the SRC and other techniques for debt ceiling avoidance erode the principle of constitutional supremacy."[50] If that principle is no longer sacred, the rule of law itself becomes imperiled. Chief Justice Breitel recognized the danger in a related case: "It is a Constitution that is being interpreted and as a Constitution it would serve little of its purpose if all that it promised, like the elegantly phrased Constitutions of some totalitarian or dictatorial Nations, was an ideal to be worshipped when not needed and debased when crucial."[51] In a word, any plea to temper enforcement of constitutional provisions because of pressing fiscal concerns was not merely wrongheaded. It was downright dangerous. Or so Judges Jasen, Breitel, and Jones staunchly insisted.

For all their pleas and closely reasoned arguments, no seismic rumbles struck the financial community as a result of *Wein* v. *City of New York*. At first glance, this is remarkable. How could three judges of the highest court in the state declare moral obligation bonds unconstitutional without imperiling the entire financial structure of both the city and the state? The answer is that once again *by the slimmest possible majority* (four to three) the Court of Appeals ruled that this type of debt did not contravene the Constitution.

The basic argument of the four judges appears to be anchored in a concern for fiscal needs. For guidance in their decision upholding moral obligation bonds these four judges appealed to – of all things – a 1955 decision involving the City of Elmira and a precursor of the moral obligation credit-extending technique.[52] The City of Elmira had established the Elmira Parking Authority and agreed to apportion annually any funds needed to cover deficits incurred by the Authority up to a maximum of $25,000. Did this arrangement contravene the constitutional provision against municipalities extending their credit to a public authority? In the Elmira case, the courts ruled that it did not, claiming that any funds transferred from the city to the Parking Authority were in the nature of a gift. New York City's promise to back up the moral obligation bonds of its public authority, SRC, was also analagous to a gift, the majority of the justices now argued in 1975, and – the crucial point – such a commitment was therefore not legally binding, whether or not dissenting Judge Jasen was correct that in practice the city would have no alternative but to honor that commitment. In writing the majority's decision in the 1955 Elmira case, Judge Desmond issued a cautionary word to all future judges concerning challenges to the legality of new fiscal devices in an era of growing fiscal needs: "We should not strain ourselves to find illegality in such programs. The problems of a modern city can never be solved unless arrangements like these . . . are upheld, unless they are patently illegal."[53] Two decades later, the four justices who framed the majority opinion in *Wein* v. *City of New York* not only heeded Desmond's cautionary words, but repeated them verbatim in justifying their own decision.[54] They too believed that one should not strain to find illegality in fashionable fiscal procedures of the city or the state. Whatever else, the justices could hardly be accused of straining.

The court had spoken. What was blatantly unconstitutional to three was acceptable to four. But majorities are what matter, however slim. That one of the four was subsequently investigated for transactions in New York City securities while hearing cases on the city's finances is hardly comforting. That discomfort is intensified by the realization that it was the first time in the 140-year history of the state's highest court that one of its members was subjected to disciplinary hearings. The result of those hearings – "censure and disapproval" but not removal from office – may strike the layman as somewhat lenient, given that the judge in question held more than $3 million in New York City notes at the time he was deciding the momentous fiscal issues in *Wein* v. *City of New York*.[55] Such reactions, however, are irrelevant. The legality of moral obligation bonds has been decided by the one body qualified to make that decision. And they are legal. About that there can be no dispute.

There could be dispute, and indeed should be dispute, over another matter. As noted at the outset of this section, moral obligation bonds raised two quite different legal issues. The obvious one concerned whether they violated the Constitution. Equally important, however, was whether citizen-taxpayers would be allowed to ask the courts to decide that question. The three moments of truth for the courts were three landmark cases separated by more than a decade: *St. Clair* v. *Yonkers Raceway* (1963), *Wein* v. *City of New York* (1975), and *Boryszewski* v. *Brydges* (1975). The tragedy of the situation – or at least, from the standpoint of checks and balances, the failure of the system – was that the question of the constitutionality of a debt instrument invented in the early 1960s was not decided until 1975. By that time, this suspect device (the moral obligation bond) had been used so extensively that arguments based on fiscal necessity had acquired an awesome weight – awesome enough to squash into near irrelevance, at least for some, such venerable principles as the primacy of the Constitution. The courts surely should have been called upon to decide the issue early in the 1960s, long before such a sorry state of affairs had come to pass. Or put another way, if that crucial ingredient of checks and balances, judicial review, is not readily brought to bear, the result – as unsurprising as it is disturbing – is very little check by the courts on the actions of the executive and the legislature.

7.6. While New York slept

On January 8, 1975, New York's first Democratic governor in sixteen years was preparing to deliver his State of the State message in the Assembly chamber, in formal terms, as the guest of the Assembly speaker. Other guests included the state's 60 senators, for whom chairs had been placed in the well of the chamber. As the senators filed in, veteran Assemblyman Louis DeSalvio of Manhattan called out, "Watch your pockets, fellows."[56] It was a bit late in the day for such advice, at least for New York taxpayers. The somber tones of the new governor's address – in marked contrast to the mirth provoked by DeSalvio's quip – reflected a 1975 setting of economic retardation and fiscal burdens that left little room for cheerfulness. But why, one might reasonably ask, had New Yorkers been such poor guardians of their own pockets? In a system characterized by few legislative restraints on the fiscal initiatives of the chief executive, and a protracted refusal of the courts to consider the constitutionality of novel debt techniques, the burden of watching pockets fell all the more heavily upon the citizens themselves. They were exquisitely unequal to the task.

Part of the reason was apathy. From William Smith's much-quoted

complaint in 1756 of "the torpor which generally prevails" to Judge
Fuld's 1963 observation that "the apathy of the average citizen concerning public affairs has often been decried," a recurring theme in
the Empire State has been the elephantine insensitivity of the electorate to issues of public policy. Interacting with this indifference are
several other traits, each with a lengthy history of its own. Dating from
colonial days was a crass commercialism that was at once the despair of
the moralist and the engine for economic progress. (To James Feni-
more Cooper, for example, New Yorkers were little better than "a
congregation of adventurers.") Harnessed to commercial drive was an
ongoing belief in progress, with the associated bias favoring activism
over inertia. Gracefully captured in the state's motto "Excelsior," this
sentiment was perhaps better characterized in the 1960s by the more
colloquial "let her rip." Finally, throughout America in general and in
New York in particular there was, in the twentieth century, a change in
public attitudes concerning what the government ought to do, and how
it ought to do it. The last of these proved to be particularly crucial, and
therefore requires a further word of explanation.

The modern age confronted both federal and state governments with
the problems of expanding jurisdiction in a world becoming progressively more complex. Increased efficiency became a compelling need,
and a shibboleth for reform. If the problem was to make government
more efficient, the solution was to make it more centralized, or so one
persuasive argument ran.[57] Dating from roughly the turn of the century, this mounting desire for energetic, decisive leadership in
government – for "getting things done" – inevitably brought a shift in
power from the legislature to the executive. If problems of efficiency
were to be tackled by reorganizing governmental decision making,
using organizational units structured as hierarchical pyramids of authority, tightly organized and strictly run, it followed that the men at
the top were sure to have increased authority and responsibility. (The
chief executive's duties in such a system one organizational theorist
attempted to capture in the acronym POSDCORB: planning, organiz-
ing, staffing, directing, coordinating, reporting, and budgeting.)[58]
Such ideas were to effect a radical transformation of American governmental processes in the twentieth century. Within the Empire
State, their ascendancy was apparent in the rise of the Executive
Budget, in the streamlining and consolidation of executive agencies, in
the growing reliance upon council-managers in cities, and in the proliferation of self-contained and self-directed bureaucracies called public benefit corporations.

But if government was to be more efficient, it was also to be more
active, particularly in the realm of social welfare. "If . . . you insist

that man's dignity requires a standard of living, in which his capacities are properly exercised," wrote Walter Lippmann in the 1920s, "the criteria which you then apply to government are whether it is producing a certain minimum of health, of decent housing, of material necessities, of education."[59] Lippmann's list did not end there, but this part was symptomatic of a vision that was to capture the imaginations of both the public and the politicians in the years ahead.

The rise to prominence of this penchant for social activism is commonly dated from Roosevelt's New Deal policies – policies that evoked responsive echoes at the time within New York, if not within many other states. Initial prominence did not, however, signal total victory. First came World War II, diverting the nation's energies elsewhere. Then came a postwar era in which fiscal conservatism and caution set the tone for much that governments were willing to attempt. By the early 1960s, however, a major resurgence was underway. Its disparate forces included, at the national level, the replacement of Eisenhower by first Kennedy and then Johnson, the election of a more liberal Congress, and a revamped welfare policy captured in a phrase that promised much: the Great Society. Reinforcing these political trends, and bolstered by them, was a veritable explosion in the public's expectations concerning what the government could do, and ought to do. New York was in the vanguard of the movement. As the expanded expectations of its public encouraged the social activism of Nelson Rockefeller, so Rockefeller's policies and pronouncements fostered a further rise in the public's expectations. Now was the time for "getting things done," because now, it was generally agreed, there was so much to do. Now was therefore also a time for strong leadership, by the Governor, and by public authority chiefs.

In the erosion of checks and balances, the public was therefore a significant part of the problem, and its contribution ran far deeper than indifference and apathy. Its rising expectations had bolstered the rising ambitions of its leaders. Its demands for energy and efficiency, for strong leadership and centralization, had contributed to an evolving governmental structure that became increasingly the plaything of the few.

The failures of the public, however, were not entirely of its own making. The media was strikingly silent about procedural changes that might have been a source of considerable concern. No clamor in the press was raised, for example, against moral obligation bonds or lease-purchase agreements. Public authorities tended to be vigorously endorsed as one means of circumventing red tape and meddling politicians. The media was not given to emphasizing that the meddling of politicians, from another vantage point, could be called scrutiny and supervision by the elected representatives of the people.

As the press had failed to alert the public to certain fundamental problems, so the political leaders labored to disguise others. The system at their command was well suited to that task. The torrents of data that continually flow from the governor's office are well calculated to dull all but the most determined mind. Worse, so labyrinthine are the state's finances that the likelihood of ignorance is raised to a near certainty, however alert the audience remains. The machinations of the state's financiers were described at length in Chapter 4.[60] Here it is perhaps sufficient to recall the growing potential for confusion inherent in the changing structure of the books. As early as 1964 the State Comptroller cautioned that "the full scope of the State's activities and financial condition is no longer disclosed in the General Fund accounts."[61] What was true in 1964 was overwhelmingly true by the end of the Rockefeller years. The General Fund by that time had become an account of almost secondary importance in the overall ebb and flow of public moneys in the state. How predictable it was that by 1971 the same Comptroller would complain that "there is an impression that the State is making gigantic expenditures, plunging into tremendous debt, beyond the control *or even the comprehension* of the electorate."[62] The way the books were kept, a failure of comprehension in the electorate was virtually guaranteed.

For most of the postwar era, the fog generated by tortuous accounting procedures was reinforced by near total inaccessibility of debates and hearings that accompanied the budgetary process. All documents and information on a piece of legislation submitted to the governor for his approval are contained in so-called bill jackets. These are likely to include "reports and letters from State departments, legislators (including the sponsoring legislator's introductory memorandum), standing or joint legislative committees, bar associations, lobbyists, and private citizens explaining why they are for or against the bill."[63] Until recently this invaluable source of information was "sealed" for five years, that is, made totally inaccessible to the public and the press.[64] Even Assembly and Senate debates – those most fundamental of all legislative records – are not readily available. There is no constitutional requirement that they be printed and made public. The one attempt to remedy this defect at the Constitutional Convention of 1915 prompted the sponsor of the proposal, Elihu Root, to observe: "As it is now, no one knows what the legislature is doing or why it is done except as the quite limited news articles of the public press are spread throughout the state . . . I see no reason, sir, why this great State . . .

should permit its legislature to do its business in such a way that there is no means of knowing the reasons for its actions."[65] Elihu Root saw no reason for this failure because there was none. And yet the permissiveness of the public allowed this tradition of a near total absence of official records of debates to persist for much of the period from 1915 to the present. (Transcripts of Senate debates were first made available on request in 1960; those for the Assembly, only in 1973.)

The absence of a printed record of debates is ultimately a minor barrier to the public's understanding of fiscal issues in New York. The major impediment is the apparent determination of most politicians to obfuscate the issues rather than inform. In this they are often ably assisted by the bureaucrats. Richard Dunham, Budget Director under Governors Rockefeller and Wilson, publicly endorsed the deception process, claiming that "any budget director who can't make $100 million appear and disappear isn't worth his salt."[66] The challenge to American ideals is both blatant and disturbing. Those who condone deceptive practices as an inevitable part of the governing process forget what Henry Adams stressed long ago:

> Money is the vital principle of the body politic; the public treasury is the heart of the state; control over public supplies means control over public affairs. Any method of procedure, therefore, by which a public servant can veil the true meaning of his acts, or which allows the government to enter upon any great enterprise without bringing the fact fairly to the knowledge of the public, must work against the realization of the constitutional idea.[67]

No one was more adept at furthering the public's ignorance than Nelson Rockefeller. To the traditions of convoluted accounting, inaccessible documents, and political smokescreens disguised as budgetary explanations he added a new and troubling dimension that was peculiarly his own. In 1966 he hired one of those masters of misdirection, a Madison Avenue advertising agency. Their assignment: Sell Nelson Rockefeller. That was a tall order in 1966. Rockefeller was confronting the toughest gubernatorial fight of his life. No New York governor had heretofore made such use of Madison Avenue in seeking reelection, and the ad agency chosen (Tinker and Partners) until that point had never marketed a candidate.

It was a fortunate marriage of interests, so fortunate that the same ad agency was given the identical selling assignment in 1970. To help detect the preferences of the public, Rockefeller provided the results of public opinion polls financed at his own expense. These attempted to identify pivotal voters: "those who were undecided or who favored

Rockefeller's opponents but gave to the governor a fairly good rating on a scale of 0–10 on his personal or political attributes."[68] From this constituency the polls attempted to elicit biases and concerns – however irrelevant to the substantive issues of the election – that could then be the target of mass media advertising. For the democratic process, the implications were, and are, alarming. The genius of Madison Avenue has been harnessed to the political self-interest of the politician, with the single objective of persuading rather than informing an all-too-gullible public. Tinker and Partners were well suited to the task. They had, for example, persuaded Braniff Airlines to end the "plain plane." If they could convince the public that several colors on the hull of an aircraft were good reasons for preferring one airline over another, designing a political advertising campaign that shied away from substantive issues should have required a minimum of mental realignment.

How much at variance this process was, and is, with the goal of an informed electorate evidencing "active, aggressive interest" in state politics, as Judge Jones phrased the matter in the landmark case that gave standing to the citizen-taxpayers of New York.[69] Thomas Jefferson put it better:

> In every government on earth is some trace of human weakness, some germ of corruption and degeneracy, which cunning will discover and wickedness insensibly open, cultivate, and improve. Every government degenerates when trusted to the rulers of the people alone. The people themselves therefore are its only safe depositories. And to render even them safe their minds must be improved to a certain degree.[70]

What New York politician could take to heart this modest urging to improve the public's mind on fiscal matters "to a certain degree" without a sense of failure? It may well be that the people do get the kind of government they deserve. Perhaps New Yorkers deserved no better than a structure that was elitist and inscrutable, the plaything of the few rather than the servant of the many. Their passivity, their indifference, and their bias for strong leadership had all contributed mightily to its creation. In this undemocratic enterprise, however, they received a lot of help along the way. Far too much help.

8

A city turned wastrel

8.1. Bankruptcy: the setting

New York City Council Chamber, Thursday evening, May 29, 1975. They were all there: the full 43-member City Council, the Board of Estimate, the city department heads, the leaders of the labor unions, and representatives of the news media. Front and center, perspiring in the glare of television lights, was an emotional Mayor Beame with a press release that, for believability, ranked with Chicken Little's statement about falling skies. The sky on this occasion was cloudy, the expected high for Friday was 80 degrees, and New York City was bankrupt. To its weather forecast that night the *New York Post* had added "Air: Unhealthful." It had no idea how apt that phrase would be when applied to the municipal bond market of the following day. The financial crisis of the city, in a nutshell, was that bills were coming due and it lacked the money to pay them. The state offered to help, but only in a small way. Welfare payments due the city in 1976 totaling $200 million would be made available immediately. This almost matched the $220 million in debt coming due the next day (Friday, May 30). The difficulty was that coming due in the next 30 days were bills totaling more than a billion. And no one in the private sector – absolutely no one – was about to lend the city that kind of money. As of that Thursday night, most financial institutions and private investors would not lend it a dime. Governor Carey offered a cautious diagnosis of the problem: "When you can't borrow because you're overcommitted, you have to get out of a borrowing situation."[1] As a characterization of bankruptcy, that phrasing was a masterpiece of discretion. No amount of polite wording could disguise one unpleasant fact: Debts running to hundreds of millions of dollars were about to come due, the city did not have the money to pay them, and it could not get the requisite funds – not from Albany, not from Washington, and not from Wall Street.

For the financial capital of America, it was the ultimate indignity. The city's economy had already received a thousand blows with no clear hand upon the cudgel: the flight of industry, the penalties of rising congestion and declining security, the influx of the poor and the unskilled, the exodus of the wealthy and the professional. Things are in the saddle, Emerson once complained, and ride mankind. Citizens of the Big Apple no doubt had similar thoughts as they contemplated the impersonal forces that seemed to make for deterioration all around them. Now the financial markets had slammed the door in their disbelieving faces. It was unthinkable. And yet it had happened. This was not merely adding insult to injury. This was an injury, potentially of grievous dimensions. What – or who – had ridden straight into the ground the credit rating of one of the world's greatest cities in one of the world's wealthiest nations?

The tempting starting point to find the answer is to refer to the impersonal forces underlying the deterioration noted previously: the rising congestion making for slower deliveries and a scarcity of space; the changing composition of the population that eroded the city's tax potential; the growing magnetism of other regions that tugged at the industry and commerce of the city to come away. Even these events were hardly the exclusive product of impersonal "things." Each featured in its causal fabric the twisted strands created by the conscious and unconscious decisions of politicians and bureaucrats. As documented at length in previous chapters, the inadequacies of the city's transportation system, for example, reflected the refusal of those with power and funds to address the problem. The exodus of the wealthy received a powerful prod from rising taxes. The flight of industry received something more akin to a clout than a prod from a taxation structure that was vigorously progressive. The reluctance of the poor and unemployed to leave the city in search of better opportunities was not unrelated to a welfare system distinguished for its generosity compared to that available elsewhere.

This list, if elaborated, would border on a restatement of much that has gone before. What matters here is that the focus is misdirected. The question is not why the economy of New York City was deteriorating. The question is why the city went bankrupt. The two are not totally unrelated. The exodus of business affected prospective tax receipts. The influx of the unskilled had implications for welfare spending. This was a setting that promised fiscal difficulties. It was not a setting that guaranteed bankruptcy. Something else was happening besides the economic retardation of the metropolis, something more unambiguously human in its origins, and for that reason, more reprehensible for the failures it precipitated. Firmly in the saddle and lashing the city toward financial chaos were not things – Emerson's focus – but people. But who?

The unraveling begins, predictably, with the escalation of total city debt. As illustrated in Figure 8.1, the numbers took off for the upper stratosphere in the 1970s. The picture as it stands, however, is deceiving. The ability of the city to pay its bills had surely changed over time. A rising population implies a rise in prospective tax revenues, especially in an era of growing per capita income. To help in gauging the changing ability of the city to repay borrowing, one must therefore convert that total debt to per capita debt. Inflation also affects the burden of promissory notes. Insofar as the incomes of the citizenry can keep pace with price inflation, so does the taxation potential of the city. Moreover, debtors gain when prices rise,[2] and the city has always been a debtor. It owed to its creditors of the past dollars of the present – depreciated dollars that would buy less in 1975 than in 1965 or 1955 or whenever they were initially borrowed. The real burden of the debt should therefore be expressed in constant dollar terms, or dollar totals owed, corrected for price inflation. The debt totals in Figure 8.1 were therefore corrected for these two factors; that is, corrected for price inflation and expressed on a per capita basis. The results appear in Figure 8.2. They are astonishing.

The one comparison that fairly leaps from the page is that per capita debt of the city, in real (or constant dollar) terms, was actually *lower* in 1970 than it was in 1910! And this despite the fact that real per capita income within America had almost tripled in the intervening 60 years.[3] This is hardly symptomatic of a city on the edge of bankruptcy, at least not as of 1970.

The second puzzle of Figure 8.2 is why the real per capita debt of New York City declined so sharply in the periods 1914–20 and 1940–48. The puzzle deepens when one notes that, as illustrated in Figure 8.1, total debt rose continuously throughout the twentieth century, interrupted by infrequent declines that were as trivial as they were short-lived. This apparent inconsistency is explained largely by two factors. The politicians who controlled the city's fiscal destiny, irrespective of party affiliation or historical circumstances, apparently have had a propensity to escalate the city's debt *throughout the entire twentieth century*. That propensity was severely restrained by two world wars. The civilian economy boomed, tax dollars rolled in, but expenditure ambitions ran afoul of wartime shortages. With a limited ability to push expenditures beyond receipts, the politicians could hardly increase borrowing to cover deficits that they were prevented from incurring. The rise in total (nominal) debt was therefore momentarily slowed.

But why the staggering decline portrayed in Figure 8.2? Why did real per capita debt in, say, the post–World War II era fall to levels *far below* those of the 1930s? The answer is inflation.[4] The sharp rise in

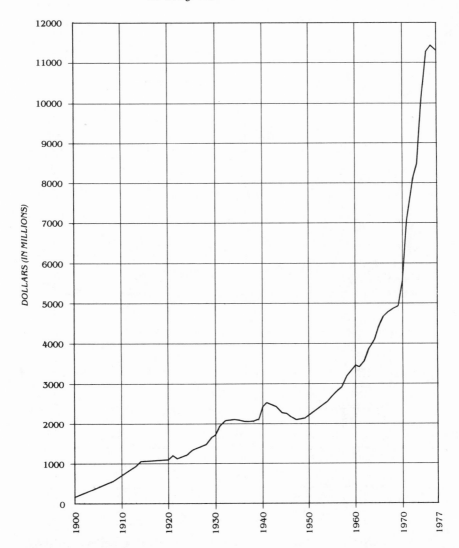

Figure 8.1. New York City net total debt, 1900–77. *Source:* See Table 8.1.

prices accompanying two world wars and their aftermath benefited New York City in the way that price inflation always benefits a debtor.[5] The commitment to repay is fixed at the time of borrowing. A sharp rise in prices is equivalent to a sharp fall in the value of money. Residents of the Big Apple were therefore big winners in the inflation–debtor sweepstakes in this century – not once, but twice. Despite the propensity of city politicians to spew forth notes and bonds

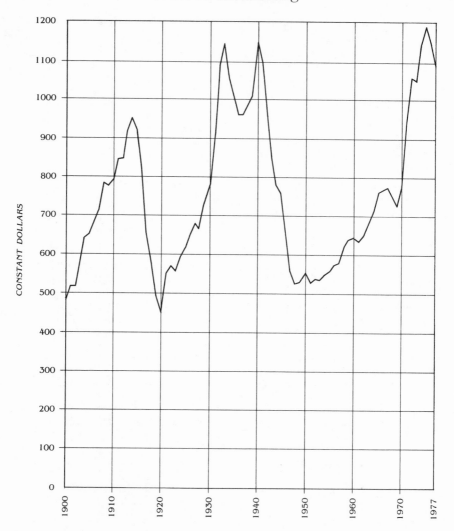

Figure 8.2. New York City per capita debt in constant dollars, 1900–77.
Source: See Table 8.1.

from 1900 onward, the real per capita debt of the metropolis by 1970
was no larger than it had been in 1944, or 1931, or 1909.

   If New York City gained in this way from inflation, who lost? The
unsurprising answer is all those who bought the city's notes and bonds,
and were subsequently repaid in depreciated dollars. Two groups
have therefore shared the burden of paying off the city's debt. The first
is the obvious target for the burden: the taxpayers whose dollars were

used to retire outstanding notes and bonds. The second group – no doubt amazed by the burden shifted to them – were all those creditors who received these taxpayers' dollars, only to discover that the purchasing power of money was far less than it had been when they initially loaned the money. There is perhaps a special irony that in a nation giving homage to frugality, the winners were the least frugal and the losers were those who saved and with those savings purchased New York City debt.

All of the discussion to this point is merely background to the question still unanswered: Why did the City go broke in 1975? The data of Figure 8.2 make crystal clear what the problem was *not*. In 1975, the year the financial markets said no, the real per capita debt of the metropolis was *less than 4 percent* higher than it was in 1940. Real per capita income within America had more than doubled between 1940 and 1975.[6] Presumably the income of New York City residents had risen by a roughly comparable amount. Certainly there was nothing in the argument that the burden of the debt per citizen or per taxpayer was getting out of hand. What then was getting out of hand?

A comparison of Figures 8.1 and 8.3 begins to bring the answer into focus. Two things happened in the late 1960s and early 1970s. First, the city's debt began to rise at rates that were remarkable, even relative to its own rapid expansions of the past (see Table 8.1). Second, more and more of that borrowing was in the form of short-term debt. The associated mathematics are both obvious and vicious.

If a man borrows $20,000 due in 10 years, and then lacks the funds to repay the debt when it comes due, he can always hope to renew the loan. If he has good prospects of repaying the $20,000 after a further 10 years, he might "roll the debt over" (i.e., renew it), gaining a second 10-year loan with the expectation of repaying it 20 years after the dollars initially changed hands. His refinancing problems become far more complicated if his borrowing contract is not for 10 years but for 1 year. This would imply in our example that 19 successive times (rather than once), he must return to prospective lenders asking that the $20,000 debt be rolled over.

Consider now a second scenario, in which the man in question does not borrow a single time, but annually runs a deficit of $20,000. If as before all loan contracts are for only 1 year, his financing problems shift from the merely difficult to the next to impossible. Every single year he must return to the credit market to ask prospective lenders for two amounts: the $20,000 to cover this year's deficit, and an amount sufficient to roll over all debts accumulated from previous years. The second dollar figure will grow at an alarming rate, as Table 8.2 indicates. Notice that while the annual deficit remains unchanged, annual

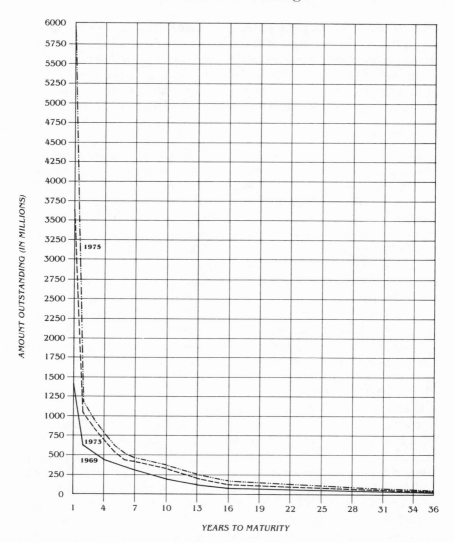

Figure 8.3. Maturity structure of New York City debt, 1969, 1973, and 1975. *Source:* See Table 8.2.

borrowing quickly becomes a *large* multiple of this annual deficit. These numbers merely illustrate a well-known law of finance: If deficits are run up every year and financed by short-term borrowing with no prospect of immediate repayment, total annual borrowing will rise at a rate that is virtually guaranteed to make creditors apprehensive sooner or later.

Table 8.1. *New York City temporary, total, and per capita debt,*
1900–77

Year	Net funded debt ($ millions)	Temporary debt ($ millions)	Net total debt ($ millions)	Estimated population (thousands)[a]	Per capita debt	
					Nominal	Real[b]
1977	6,930	4,445	11,374	7,330	1,552	1,098
1976	6,560	4,867	11,426	7,406	1,543	1,153
1975	6,798	4,540	11,338	7,482	1,515	1,192
1974	6,734	3,416	10,150	7,559	1,343	1,153
1973	6,007	2,518	8,525	7,637	1,116	1,054
1972	5,515	2,650	8,165	7,715	1,058	1,058
1971	4,714	2,319	7,033	7,795	902	940
1970	4,361	1,288	5,649	7,875	717	785
1969	4,229	747	4,977	7,887	631	728
1968	4,232	693	4,925	7,875	625	757
1967	4,254	635	4,888	7,864	622	787
1966	4,246	467	4,712	7,852	600	782
1965	3,920	526	4,446	7,841	567	763
1964	3,755	316	4,070	7,830	520	715
1963	3,620	231	3,851	7,819	493	688
1962	3,491	128	3,619	7,807	464	657
1961	3,342	100	3,443	7,796	442	637
1960	3,363	88	3,451	7,785	443	646
1959	3,290	74	3,365	7,790	432	640
1958	3,147	63	3,210	7,801	412	623
1957	2,880	85	2,965	7,812	380	584
1956	2,768	84	2,852	7,823	365	580
1955	2,646	70	2,715	7,834	347	568
1954	2,548	63	2,610	7,845	333	557
1953	2,455	54	2,509	7,856	319	542
1952	2,406	74	2,480	7,867	315	544
1951	2,332	85	2,417	7,878	307	536
1950	2,273	95	2,368	7,889	300	560
1949	2,134	85	2,219	7,858	282	537
1948	2,108	92	2,200	7,814	282	530
1947	2,114	69	2,183	7,769	281	565
1946	2,195	36	2,231	7,725	289	658
1945	2,285	46	2,331	7,681	304	761
1944	2,288	57	2,345	7,638	307	789
1943	2,385	85	2,470	7,594	325	858

Table 8.1. (*cont.*)

Year	Net funded debt ($ millions)	Temporary debt ($ millions)	Net total debt ($ millions)	Estimated population (thousands)[a]	Per capita debt	
					Nominal	Real[b]
1942	2,485	82	2,567	7,551	340	960
1941	2,520	83	2,602	7,508	347	1,100
1940	2,431	79	2,511	7,466	336	1,148
1939	2,074	84	2,158	7,414	291	1,011
1938	2,005	124	2,129	7,387	288	984
1937	1,980	125	2,105	7,334	287	967
1936	1,887	120	2,007	7,280	276	967
1935	1,864	219	2,083	7,227	288	1,015
1934	1,886	262	2,147	7,175	299	1,061
1933	1,897	245	2,142	7,123	301	1,148
1932	1,841	226	2,067	7,071	292	1,091
1931	1,807	107	1,914	7,020	273	912
1930	1,703	91	1,794	6,969	257	782
1929	1,606	77	1,683	6,894	244	722
1928	1,516	27	1,543	6,751	229	674
1927	1,446	56	1,502	6,611	227	680
1926	1,367	65	1,431	6,474	221	648
1925	1,292	69	1,360	6,340	215	618
1924	1,202	66	1,269	6,208	204	598
1923	1,130	49	1,179	6,080	194	565
1922	1,086	61	1,147	5,954	193	575
1921	1,065	114	1,178	5,830	202	555
1920	1,031	103	1,135	5,709	199	455
1919	1,028	42	1,070	5,597	191	499
1918	1,026	49	1,075	5,506	195	581
1917	1,020	55	1,075	5,416	199	664
1916	1,007	36	1,044	5,327	196	816
1915	974	52	1,026	5,240	196	915
1914	942	60	1,003	5,155	195	949
1913	892	40	932	5,071	184	915
1912	820	42	862	4,988	173	855
1911	757	53	809	4,906	165	850
1910	688	66	754	4,826	156	797
1909	648	60	708	4,728	150	785
1908	589	74	663	4,576	145	788

Table 8.1. (*cont.*)

Year	Net funded debt ($ millions)	Temporary debt ($ millions)	Net total debt ($ millions)	Estimated population (thousands)[a]	Per capita debt Nominal	Per capita debt Real[b]
1907	538	54	591	4,429	134	718
1906	475	51	526	4,286	123	689
1905	431	41	472	4,148	114	654
1904	401	35	435	4,015	109	638
1903	334	42	376	3,886	97	576
1902	312	12	324	3,761	86	518
1901	299	5	304	3,640	84	519
1900	278	2	280	3,523	79	490

[a] Estimated between census years by interpolation.
[b] Deflated by GNP implicit price deflator (1972 = 100).
Source: New York [City], Office of the Comptroller, *Annual Reports*.

Table 8.2. *Hypothetical example of effects of cumulative debt roll-overs (thousands of dollars)*

Borrowing during	(1) Borrowing for current deficit	(2) Borrowing to roll over all debts coming due	(3) Total borrowing ([1] + [2])
First year	20	0	20
Second year	20	20	40
Third year	20	40	60
⋮	⋮	⋮	⋮
Tenth year	20	180	200

This is exactly what the great city was doing in the late 1960s and early 1970s (see Table 8.3). Worst of all were the reasons for much of its borrowing. If a municipality sells bonds to acquire money to build, say, a toll bridge, the subsequent flow of toll receipts can be used to pay off the principal and interest on the debt in question. If instead that municipality borrows to finance current operating expenses, the chances of the expenditure items in question ever generating future receipts to help pay off that debt are trivial in the extreme. It is basically the difference between a man borrowing to buy a taxi and a man borrowing to buy a box of Kleenex. The latter may appear essential to the borrower, but its acquisition hardly brings in its wake the promise of prospective dollar earnings.

It was New York City's folly that its fiscal practices combined the worst of all possible worlds: booming debt, much of it to cover current operating expenses, much of it financed on a short-term basis, which guaranteed the need to refinance soon, because the city was plunging ever deeper into debt. The likelihood of a halt in debt escalation was about the same as the likelihood that the city could pay off its debts, with both probabilities in the same league as King Canute's chances of turning back the ocean with a broom. No respectable accounting firm in the country would approve of this kind of behavior by a private corporation. No banker with an ounce of sense would lend repeatedly to any individual with insatiable borrowing demands and no prospect of repayment. The remarkable fact is how similar behavior on the part of New York City was tolerated by so many lenders for so long. The day of reckoning, however, could not be put off forever.

8.2. The details of financial collapse

Part of the reason why the financial community took so long to slam the door on a profligate city was a certain reverence for the borrower. This was no inconsequential corporation or small municipality. This was a mighty city – for some, *the* mighty city, the financial capital of America. Part of the lag reflected questionable accounting procedures that helped to obscure just how serious the problem really was.[7] The press did not help matters, tending as it did to take the fiscal statements of City Hall at face value, including the blurred distinction between promised remedies and accomplished fact.[8] Compounding this was a naïve and pervasive faith that difficulties were only momentary, and that the underlying structure was as solid as a rock. In a curious way, John Lindsay helped to reinforce this faith by repeatedly insisting that it was not justified. Year after year he spoke of "fiscal crisis" and "threatened austerity," but nothing much seemed to happen. As Mayor Beame noted in retrospect, after eight years of his predecessor appearing to cry "wolf," the public tended to disregard purveyors of gloom and doom.[9] As for members of the financial community, one unanswered question is a variant of Senator Baker's key question concerning Nixon and the Watergate coverup: What did they know, and when did they know it? The issue is unlikely ever to be resolved. From first to last, members of that community have insisted that for all

Table 8.3. *New York City debt service on gross funded debt and temporary debt for selected years, 1961–77*
(*$ thousands*)

Type of debt and years to maturity	Fiscal year ending June 30					
	1961	1965	1969	1973	1975	1977
Debt in default	0	0	0	0	0	4,244,600
Temporary debt	100,400	525,690	747,255	2,517,510	4,540,175	200,000
Gross funded debt due in 1 year	425,395	522,548	680,380	1,085,944	1,401,306	1,428,410
Total debt service due in:						
1 year[a]	525,795	1,048,238	1,427,635	3,603,454	5,941,481	5,873,010
2 years	391,997	503,208	644,176	1,043,842	1,228,768	1,274,658
3 "	350,310	459,925	519,012	881,787	951,909	986,177
4 "	316,663	405,360	451,682	722,540	767,391	815,838
5 "	278,889	340,153	383,224	538,645	579,016	674,857
6 "	247,264	304,142	323,683	448,129	502,557	628,546
7 "	229,862	282,243	286,725	421,504	446,855	583,545
8 "	212,445	261,050	248,179	369,089	411,541	501,358
9 "	198,482	239,256	222,356	321,614	377,169	367,951
10 "	188,103	208,628	209,389	294,663	343,187	326,228
11 "	171,893	178,988	197,501	268,097	319,208	287,923
12 "	158,655	156,806	171,204	248,810	280,594	246,963
13 "	144,916	140,915	149,603	228,475	245,248	213,644
14 "	131,665	133,236	133,690	193,447	212,644	183,552
15 "	121,529	124,842	115,828	161,662	181,718	149,246
16	110,427	102,169	102,734	143,256	164,053	140,858

Table 8.3 (cont.)

Type of debt and years to maturity	Fiscal year ending June 30					
	1961	1965	1969	1973	1975	1977
17 "	100,876	90,942	93,072	134,297	149,347	132,057
18 "	94,679	85,772	83,618	119,332	140,885	123,872
19 "	87,195	76,869	75,433	106,081	132,084	116,681
20 "	65,747	66,690	69,690	99,073	123,898	109,220
21 "	55,800	58,601	63,275	91,726	116,707	99,352
22 "	51,506	52,161	55,208	85,286	109,247	90,252
23 "	47,947	45,828	49,095	79,468	99,352	82,485
24 "	45,425	40,873	44,037	73,377	90,252	75,581
25 "	43,025	35,251	39,752	64,809	82,485	65,286
26 "	39,819	29,118	35,190	57,202	75,581	57,057
27 "	36,250	24,540	31,652	51,025	65,286	48,660
28 "	31,450	20,529	27,578	45,480	57,057	38,327
29 "	26,203	17,766	22,619	36,338	48,660	36,521
30 "	20,217	14,072	17,126	29,263	38,327	35,535
31 "	16,259	11,540	12,514	26,029	36,521	34,532
32 "	14,028	9,551	9,751	25,325	35,535	33,580
33 "	12,125	8,249	8,689	24,788	34,532	32,596
34 "	10,062	6,847	8,324	24,217	33,580	31,202

35 "	8,195	5,524	8,350	23,629	32,596	27,883
36 "	19,548[b]	4,111	8,315	23,092	31,202	23,234
37 "	N.A.	3,048	8,333	22,514	27,883	16,031
38 "	N.A.	2,691	64,262[b]	21,526	23,234	6,468
39 "	N.A.	25,964[b]	N.A.	18,613	16,031	720
40 "	N.A.	N.A.	N.A.	14,370	6,468	665
41 "	N.A.	N.A.	N.A.	8,734	720	713[b]
42 "	N.A.	N.A.	N.A.	2,677	665	N.A.
43 "	N.A.	N.A.	N.A.	668	713[b]	N.A.
44 "	N.A.	N.A.	N.A.	1377[b]	N.A.	N.A.
All years	4,605,252	5,625,696	6,422,504	11,199,330	14,562,187	14,572,864

Note: Debt service includes interest payments, redemption of serial bonds, sinking fund installments, and earnings of sinking funds. Gross funded debt includes all debt that was issued to be due in "a period of years." (See New York [City], Office of the Comptroller, the *Annual Report*, 1960–61, p. 355). This includes virtually all debt outstanding more than one year. Temporary debt includes tax and revenue anticipation notes issued in anticipation of, and repayable from, real estate taxes and other revenue sources, such as State Aid to Education; bond anticipation notes; and budget notes, issued to cover a portion of expenses "unforeseen or not sufficiently provided for in the Expense Budget." (See ibid.) Budget notes may be outstanding two years. The others may be renewed indefinitely but count against the debt ceiling in the state Constitution after being outstanding five years. Dollar amounts (thousands) are nominal, undeflated for the price level.

[a] The sum of the three lines above it. Debt in default is assumed to be due in a year or less.
[b] Includes debt service due in all longer terms. The cutoff date is different in various *Annual Reports*.
Source: New York [City], Office of the Comptroller, *Annual Report*, 1960–61, pp. 375, 396; 1964–65, pp. 460, 481; 1968–69, pp. 484, 510; 1972–73, pp. 457, 483; 1974–75, pp. 485, 509; 1976–77, pp. 75, 81.

their expertise, and despite their access to information as underwriters of New York City securities, they knew almost nothing until collapse was at hand. William Simon's statement is typical: "No one questioned the assumptions that the city's budget would be balanced, that city officials could and would raise taxes, if needed, to honor debts, and that the city's government was fundamentally sound. I shared these assumptions, and so did all the 'hardheaded' bankers of New York."[10] Certainly, by their own admission, this was not a crew given to close scrutiny of the product. That American maxim of the marketplace, "Let the buyer beware," was taken very much to heart by those who peddled the securities of the city. Mayor Beame was less than kind when he likened the lot to a collection of used car salesmen:

> My view with respect to the banks – and I've told it to the leading bankers – is that they took no overt action to let the public know that they think our securities are good. Naturally, if you're a salesman selling cars and you don't talk up your product, or if you talk it down, you're not going to sell any cars. They just took the position that it wasn't their responsibility to say anything about New York securities.[11]

There was therefore about the impending collapse a special inertia, an innate tendency for the inner beams to rot and pipes to corrode to a point of no return while passers-by admired the unchanging porticos and columns of the exterior. Inevitably, however, cracks and crumblings surfaced that alarmed even the most casual observer. When that happened, a tornado of doubt and suspicion, as powerful as it was sudden, swept over the fiscal structure that had become so vulnerable. The effect was ruin.

The deterioration began to surface in the closing months of 1974. In that year New York City came to the market no less than 18 times, peddling a total of $8 billion in short-term notes. By the fall, the market was a trifle uneasy. In November, Mayor Beame and Comptroller Harrison Goldin of the city engaged in a public wrangle over the likely deficit in the upcoming year. Beame regarded a shortfall of $430 million as probable. The Comptroller argued for $650 million, a figure 50 percent above the Mayor's, and awesome in its absolute magnitude. It is hard to imagine a public disagreement better calculated to focus attention on the fiscal shenanigans and doubtful bookkeeping practices of the city. Despite their differences, the Mayor and the Comptroller continued to insist that investors who purchased New York City notes and bonds "are investing in the world's wealthiest and soundest city as far as these obligations are concerned."[12] Many believed them. As Abe Lincoln liked to insist, you can fool some of the people all of the time.

Others grew uneasy, and progressively so as the fall drew to a close. By December, the major New York City banks advised the Mayor that the market for city obligations was "drying up."[13] As the primary underwriters for the city, they knew what they were talking about. Their inventories of unsold bonds and notes were piling up as security prices plummeted and interest rates soared. On December 2, the city offered $600 million in securities. It received exactly one bid from a consortium of major banks, and paid an interest rate quite without precedent in the city's history: 9.5 percent. Because the securities in question were tax exempt, this was equivalent to a before-tax rate of almost 20 percent. The market was not yet saying no, but it was beginning to exact a higher price for playing a game in which the risks of participation were being reassessed upward.

After a momentary lull in January of 1975, the winds of suspicion were whipped into a full-fledged storm by two unrelated events. A prospective city offering was scrutinized in February by a law firm (White & Case) at the request of Banker's Trust. Apparently by accident, and to everyone's surprise, the firm discovered that the city did not have the tax receipts required by law to secure a $260 million note sale. Banker's Trust and Chase Manhattan therefore refused to go through with the underwriting. About the same time (late February), the Urban Development Corporation defaulted on $104.5 million in notes coming due. It was the first major government agency to default since the Great Depression. Within days, New York City was forced to pay an astronomical interest rate (8.69 percent) on a $537 million issue of bond anticipation notes. Mayor Beame, for one, was outraged. In a statement complaining about the high cost of borrowing, he noted that the recent default of UDC had created "an unwarranted climate of suspicion in the marketplace."[14] For New York City securities, that suspicion was about as unwarranted as Trojan distrust of wooden horses.

In the municipal bond market, March had come in like a lion, roaring with apprehension. It went out like a tornado. On the thirteenth and twentieth of that month the city offered short-term notes for sale, more than half of which went unsold. By April, when the city offered a $450 million note issue, no one – absolutely no one – wanted any part of it at any price. The roof had fallen in. Political and fiscal maneuvering tended to obscure the total collapse for more than a month, but the city's ability to borrow was, from that point on, in shambles. Frantic appeals to Albany brought some relief in the form of advances of welfare payments due later in 1975. Similar appeals to Washington brought nothing. With a few extra Albany dollars in hand, the city managed to limp along for a few weeks, eating into cash reserves. The day of reckoning was May 30, 1975. Some $220 million in notes were coming due on that Friday, and the funds were simply not available. On May 28, Comptroller Harrison Goldin asked for bids to underwrite a long-delayed $280 million note issue. If no bids were received, he warned, the city would have to default on the $220 million coming due in two days. No bids were received. As Abe Lincoln used to argue, you cannot fool all of the people all of the time. The result was the press conference described at the outset of this chapter. The time had finally come for honesty and austerity. It was also time for a candid scrutiny of the books. Looking back upon the wreckage from the vantage point of 1976, Mayor Beame spoke for perhaps most of the main participants in this fiscal and financial debacle: "I knew there were going to be problems, obviously, but . . . nothing like this."[15]

8.3. The reasons why: of wages and welfare

When the great city went under in financial markets, a frenzied search for the reasons why threw up two main contenders. Debt expanded too fast because spending expanded too fast, the reasoning went. This rapid expansion in expenditures, in turn, was linked primarily to increased payrolls for city employees and increased welfare payments. Depending upon which of the two was emphasized, the city was portrayed either as a victim of greedy unions extracting pound after pound of flesh from weak-kneed politicians or, alternatively, as a victim of its own generosity, giving away too much in the name of too many worthy causes.

From the standpoint of causal analysis, this dichotomy and the associated debate smack of an argument over which snowfall caused the roof to cave in. It was the combined weight that made the difference. The contribution of each of the two factors to the total reads: "Wages, first; welfare, second; both, a lot." In the ten years culminating in 1975 (the year of financial collapse), total operating expenditures of the city rose by $8.3 billion, of which 43 percent was attributable to an increase in labor costs, and 27 percent to increased welfare spending.[16] But why, the citizenry demanded to know, had these items gone up by so much? And could not some of these increases have been avoided? The answer to the second question is clearly yes, as will be argued in the next section. At this juncture the task is to sketch the reasons underlying the rise in wages and welfare spending.

A city's priorities are usually best revealed by the changing composition of its budget. Between 1961 and 1976, between Wagner and collapse, New York City devoted a progressively larger share of its

Table 8.4. *New York City percentage share of total
expenditure represented by seven major functions, fiscal
years 1961 and 1976*

Function	1961	1976	Percentage increase/ (decrease)
Welfare[a,b]	12.3	22.6	10.3
Hospitals[a]	8.2	9.7	1.5
Higher education	1.9	4.5	2.6
Subtotal	22.4	36.8	14.4
Police	9.5	6.4	(3.1)
Fire	4.9	2.8	(2.1)
Sanitation[c]	5.4	2.7	(2.7)
Education	25.6	18.4	(7.2)
Subtotal	45.5	30.3	(15.1)

[a] Expenditures for medical care, including Medicaid, appear in
both the welfare and the hospital categories because of the
city's accounting procedures.
[b] Welfare includes the budget of the Department of Social Services (DSS) and the child care portion of the charitable institutions budget of the city.
[c] As used here, sanitation refers to the costs of the agencies that
composed the Environmental Protection Administration (EPA).
Source: New York [City], Temporary Commission on City Finances, *An Historical and Comparative Analysis of Expenditures in the City of New York*, Eighth Interim Report, October
1976*f*, p. 15.

budget to welfare, and a progressively smaller share to public services,
particularly police, fire, sanitation, and education (see Table 8.4). A
comparison of the resulting per capita spending by function with that
of other cities is complicated by the various ways different cities keep
their books, with New York City winning first place for the bizarre.
Available evidence nevertheless does suggest that New York City per
capita spending is out of line on almost all counts, but more out of line
on some (welfare, higher education, health, hospitals, and housing)
than on others (primary and secondary education, police, fire, and
sanitation).[17] Welfare, it seems, deserves special scrutiny on several
counts. Priorities had clearly shifted in its favor in the decade culminating in the city's financial debacle. But whose priorities?

The background to the welfare story is quickly told. Demographic shifts interacted with a generous structure of social programs that became progressively more generous, with the bottom line reading ever more dollars spent. Emma Lazarus's words on the Statue of Liberty took on new meaning in the postwar years. "Give me your tired, your poor, your huddled masses" – and they came in droves: from Puerto Rico, from the urban slums of the South, from the depressed rural pockets that laced the cotton and tobacco lands from North Carolina to the Mississippi Delta. This was not quite what the city or Emma Lazarus had in mind. But come they did: the poor, the uneducated, the non-English speaking. Coincident with this influx, the wealthy, the skilled, and the educated fled the city for the suburbs. The resulting shift in population mix virtually guaranteed that even if welfare schemes were not enhanced, more would have to be spent. To cite only two numbers, but perhaps the most popular two in this context, between 1950 and 1970, the percentage of the city's population over the age of 65 rose from 8 to 12, and the proportion of the city's families with incomes below the nation's median income level rose from 36 to 49 percent, or by a staggering one-third.[18] It was an alarming distortion of the advertising slogan: "You're not getting older, you're getting better." New York City dwellers, on the average, *were* getting older, and they were getting worse, at least when it came to their ability to generate income.

Interacting with this changing composition of the population was, as one analyst put it, "New York's long tradition of providing enriched levels of public service."[19] That tradition was reinforced repeatedly in the postwar years, so that by the early 1970s, the city could boast a network of social services almost unrivaled in the country. The list included 19 municipal hospitals, a city university system with free tuition, low- and middle-income housing programs, free day-care centers, and a Medicaid program that was among the most generous in the country. When the city's spending for *all* social programs is added up and compared with the total welfare spending of other metropolitan areas, New York clearly stands out in welfare aid per capita.[20] In the modern era the Big Apple had become, as T. H. White chose to put it, not John Winthrop's City on the Hill, but the City of the Soft Touch.[21] Soft or not, that touch amounted to more than $2.7 billion by 1975, or 24 percent of the city's total budget.[22]

But expenditure for what? The answer is summarized in Table 8.5. Two numbers dominate: expenditures for Aid to Families with Dependent Children and for Medicaid and State Medical Assistance Program. The two combined amounted in 1976 to almost 60 percent of the total welfare spending of the city. A closer inspection of what was spent under these headings, and why, yields several improbable conclusions.

Table 8.5. *Social welfare and health expenditures in New York City, fiscal year 1976*

Program	Public Assistance ($)	Amount ($)
Aid to Families with Dependent Children	1,050,005,000	
Home Relief and Veteran Assistance	190,219,000	
Supplemental Security Income[a]	55,140,000	
Subtotal (Public Assistance)		1,295,364,000
DOSS[b] Miscellaneous Assistance Programs		48,215,000
DOSS Salaries, Debt Service, Fringe and Administrative Expenses		431,926,147
Day Care of Children		173,300,000
Child Care in Foster Homes and Institutions		200,035,740
Medicaid and State Medical Assistance Program		1,864,821,388
Health and Hospitals Corporation[c]		482,379,704
Mental Health Services		104,823,076
Public Health Service		98,017,272
Medical Examiner Service		3,463,537
Health Services Administration, Debt Service, and Fringe Benefit Expenses		37,204,544
Human Resources Program		166,822,184
Addiction Services Agency		77,959,598
Youth Services Agency		37,855,956
Total[d]		5,022,188,146

[a] The amount shown for Supplemental Security Income represents only the city's contribution to the program because the program is administered by the Social Security Administration. The amounts for the other programs, administered by the city, represent total benefit costs.
[b] DOSS is the Department of Social Services.
[c] Other than Medicaid.
[d] Tabulation does not include transit subsidies for the elderly, housing subsidies, and tax exemptions.
Source: New York [City], Temporary Commission on City Finances, *The Medicaid Program in New York City: Some Proposals for Reform*, Sixteenth Interim Report, June 1977e, p. 6.

First, the matter of public assistance programs. Why was so much being given to so many?

In a quagmire of bureaucratic details, only four points matter for purposes of this discussion. First, New York City has three major public assistance programs:

1. Aid to Families with Dependent Children (AFDC), designed primarily to help families where no father is present and a mother with children is head of the household
2. Supplemental Security Income (SSI), which provides relief for the aged, blind, and disabled
3. Home Relief (HR), a state program designed to help those in need of relief who do not meet federal requirements

Second, in total dollars spent, the city's public assistance program reduces to AFDC and "all others," with the latter trivial by comparison (see Table 8.5). Third, these welfare programs constituted a major drain on the city's budget mainly for three reasons:

1. Widespread eligibility (in 1975, one-sixth of the population of the city received some form of public assistance.)
2. Above-average payments per case. (New York State ranks first among all states in the average grant per AFDC case.)[23]
3. Above-average cost of each program borne by the municipality. (New York State is one of only six states that requires its local governments to share the cost of all three programs, and only one other state, Minnesota, begins to compare with New York for the percentage of total costs foisted upon the local municipalities.)[24]

Fourth, while the city helps to administer these programs, by and large it has no significant control over them, and therefore no significant control over the costs incurred because of them. All major decisions for all major programs are made by either the state or the federal government, or both. In the case of the AFDC program, for example – the giant of welfare spending in the city – the local government has virtually no control over eligibility criteria or benefit levels.[25]

An examination of the other major thrust of welfare relief, Medicaid, reveals a city caught in a vice by the same factors: widespread eligibility, atypically high costs per recipient, and negligible local control over spending. The Medicaid program was instituted in May of 1966 by the state in response to federal initiatives.[26] The instant and ongoing effect was a ballooning expenditure item in the city's budget for reasons not unlike those cited for the public assistance programs noted above:

1. Eligibility terms were generous. (In 1975, one-fifth of the city's residents were eligible to have some or all of their health care expenses paid for by Medicaid.)
2. Services provided were the most extensive in the nation. (Services offered under the Medicaid program consist of

seven basic services that, under the federal legislation establishing the program, must be offered by all states involved in the program, and seventeen optional services, the provision of any of which is up to the discretion of the individual states. Only Minnesota and New York State opted to provide all seventeen.)

3. Costs per patient are among the highest in the nation. (The cost per recipient for Medicaid services in New York is 88 percent above the national average.)[27]

4. The city is required by the state to pay an atypically high percentage of all Medicaid costs. (New York State's requirement that each county and New York City pay 25 percent of Medicaid costs is unique among the fifty states. Only seven other states require their local governments to pay more than 1 percent of all Medicaid expenditures; only four of those require more than 10 percent; none requires more than 16 percent.)

The soaring costs of the program are, surprisingly, not mainly the result of the extensive optional services provided in New York. In 1975, for example, the seven basic services mandated by the federal government accounted for 81 percent of total Medicaid payments. Of these seven, the two main culprits in the race to higher prices have been inpatient hospital costs and nursing home care. The absence of control of associated rates in these two areas has been nothing short of scandalous.[28] Finally, and perhaps most important of all, the control of these rates, like the control of the entire Medicaid program, is vested well beyond the city's borders. As the Mayor's Temporary Commission on City Finances put the matter, "The rules and regulations establishing eligibility requirements, service availability and reimbursement rates are established by the Federal and State governments, leaving the City almost no scope for reducing its Medicaid expenses."[29]

From this sketch of the major social welfare programs of the city emerge two frequently neglected conclusions. The first is that New York is not quite the City of the Big Heart after all, at least not insofar as these handouts are concerned. It can hardly be given credit for what it neither originated nor subsequently controlled. (In passing, it should be noted that city officials were clearly a party to the process, insofar as not once did they vigorously oppose any of the welfare schemes contrived by others.) By the same token, the Temporary Commission on City Finances was somewhat wide of the mark in its explanation of the shifting expenditure pattern noted at the outset (see Table 8.4). In its view, "Intergovernmental aid that is tied to City allocations leverages City resources, thereby shifting the City's resource-allocation decisions toward programs where the State and Federal governments provide matching funds and away from the traditional service areas of local government – police, fire, and sanitation –where State and Federal aid is minimal."[30] The city fathers can hardly be portrayed as responding to changing incentives to make decisions that, in fact, they never made. Much closer to truth would be a portrait of these officials having foisted upon them large expenditure items that, in their novelty and magnitude, necessarily changed the percentage allocation in favor of welfare, but hardly signaled a shift in City Hall's desires away from the public services noted. New York, on the average, continued to spend more on these conventional public services than did other cities. It was just that it spent even more on welfare.

A related conclusion concerns how decisions were made in the state capital and the costs shunted down the Hudson. The vigor with which Albany legislators embraced federally initiated welfare programs was equaled by their enthusiasm for shifting as much of the expense as possible onto other shoulders. Passing the buck is hardly confined to Empire State politicians, but in this instance they far outdistanced their counterparts in other state legislatures. To New York City fell the task of raising half the nonfederal funds for items sure to strain a budget already overstretched. To residents of City Hall that prospect must have been as welcome as a Saint Bernard in an overloaded lifeboat. But one is not inclined to refuse a Saint Bernard passage if higher authorities have mandated a seat for it.

What of the other accessory to overspending, rising wages? The escalation of wage payments is, by and large, a story of growing union strength against a backdrop of political weakness. The date most commonly singled out as the starting point for analysis is May 31, 1958: the day on which Mayor Wagner signed executive order number 49 giving to the city's 100,000-odd employees the right to join a union of their choice and the right to bargain collectively. Notice what was not granted. Strikes were specifically declared illegal. The unions nevertheless flouted this law, at first tentatively, and then vigorously when no serious penalties were suffered by the violators. This experiment in unlawful activity began on January 1, 1966, when 34,800 transit workers went on strike, the first major citywide strike in New York City's history. Mayor Lindsay capitulated, the resulting wage settlement was generous, and the associated penalties for violating the law were trivial. To at least one commentator, "The 1966 transit strike was John Lindsay's Bay of Pigs."[31] A rash of strikes followed, including in 1968 both the sanitation workers and the teachers. The following year, incumbent Mayor Lindsay faced a formidable reelection problem. He reacted in a predictable way, energetically courting union support, by and large by brandishing a checkbook. (He would win with only 42 percent of the vote.) Victor Gotbaum, head of District Council 37 of the State, County, and Municipal Employees' Union, no doubt exaggerated when he suggested, "We have the ability, in a sense, to elect our own boss."[32] Gotbaum nevertheless had a point. The city does have an exceptionally large number of municipal employees relative to its population. (Per 1,000 residents, New York City has 49 employees, whereas virtually every other major city has between 30 and 35.)[33] Their political clout is formidable. By one calculation, if every city employee were married, lived in the city, and had one close friend or relative whose vote could be influenced, the implied voting bloc would constitute 30 percent of all eligible voters, or close to half of those likely to vote in any given election.[34] With union officials flaunting this kind of political weaponry, elected officials were not given to excessive toughness at the bargaining table. Bargaining in the Lindsay era was anything but tough. But were the results scandalous?

At first glance, the answer appears to be no. A comparison of public employee wages in New York City with those in other metropolitan areas suggests that New York City wages were "not particularly out of line" once allowance is made for differences in the cost of living in different cities.[35] Two points, however, should be kept in mind. The first is that New York City *is* way out of line in the number of public employees per 1,000 residents. If exceptionally high wages were not wrested from the city, more jobs were. Second, wages and salaries are only part of the story.

The evidence suggests that New York City employees were way out of line in a second category: fringe benefits. To some analysts, such as the Congressional Budget Office, that evidence is tentative, prompting a cautious judgment: "What little reliable evidence there is seems to indicate that New York City provides its employees with considerably more in the way of fringe benefits – pensions, health insurance, etc. – than is offered the employees of other large cities."[36] To others, such as William Simon, the evidence is overwhelming, and caution gives way to outrage. Pensions, he thundered, "were appalling."[37] City payments for retirement and Social Security benefits rose from $261 million in 1961 to $1.3 billion in 1975, with the prospect that this figure will reach $3 billion by 1985. To generous retirement benefits have been added other fringe benefits, including "days off for giving blood, extra-long lunch hours, guaranteed 'rest' periods,"[38] and more conventional items, such as health and disability insurance. According to one estimate, the total cost of all fringe benefits combined amounted to 68 cents over and above every dollar paid in wages and salaries.[39] For federal employees, the comparable figure is 35 cents; for employees of private industry and other state and local governments, 30 to 33 cents.[40]

Buried in these numbers is a story largely untold and yet central to understanding how politics interacted with economics to bring the city down. The analysis to this point has sketched how union power grew in the 1960s, how that power could be brought to bear upon politicians at the bargaining table, and what the major concessions that unions wrested from the politicians were: exceptionally high fringe benefits. But which fringe benefits? Three numbers supply the answer. In fiscal 1976 the city paid out a total of $1,790 million for "Retirement Costs" and other fringe benefits, of which 83 percent went for retirement costs alone, and 17 percent for all other fringes.[41] In short, while union leaders may have stormed every hill, the one that they unambiguously captured and made their own was labeled "Pension Benefits." Few know the details of the storming, which border on the fiscally absurd. First, it was a repeated assault. Between 1960 and 1970, for example, 216 separate statutes were passed related to pension benefit changes.[42] Second, virtually every conceivable union was a party to the process. To touch upon only a few of the key battles in an ongoing war, major benefit liberalizations were granted to employee groups as follows:[43]

Sanitationmen	1963
Corrections	1964
Housing Police	1964
Uniformed Transit Police	1964
Teachers	1964
Higher Education Teachers	1965
Sanitationmen	1967
Transit Employees	1968
General City Employees	1968
Board of Education Employees	1968
Teachers	1970

Third, the number retiring was accelerated by granting, first to policemen and firemen, and then to others, the right to retire on half-pay after twenty years of service.[44] Fourth, payments were escalated by modifying the retirement benefit calculation. The usual scheme consists of computing retirement benefits as a percentage of the average of salaries earned during the retiree's three to five highest-paid years – usually his or her last years of employment. The New York City scheme (initiated in 1963) consists of using the salary earned in the year of retirement, or even the salary earned on the day of retirement. Fifth, last, and worst, the original funding philosophy by which the city and the employee split equally the cost of providing a retirement benefit has been totally destroyed. In the unemotional wording of the

Mayor's Temporary Commission on City Finances, "The five pension systems of the City of New York have been for some time . . . virtually noncontributory pension systems for all City employees."[45]

Higher benefits, earlier retirements, and the near obliteration of employee contributions – that is surely about as close to total victory as any union bargainer is likely to come. A city that makes excessive wage concessions can always consider reducing them in the future. A city that hires too many workers can always lay some off. A city that makes excessively generous pension commitments is locked in. One is reminded of the characterization of debt cited in the previous chapter: "It is silent, creeps along, . . . and when the act is once passed, the debt incurred, the obligation is as strong as death for its payment."[46] The parallel is instructive. Pension commitments are also as strong as death. Those made by the City of New York did creep along silently, almost totally unnoticed by the people. Had they bothered to pay attention, they would have been struck by what was being conceded, and by whom. Caught between union demands and their own ambitions to succeed at the ballot box, the politicians gave away the most where it cost them the least. Pension concessions were like expenditure increases financed by debt. The immediate benefits to those who made the concessions were considerable – in this case, union support at the polls – while the costs were shifted, by and large, to other politicians of the future. To the latter group will fall the unpleasant task of finding the revenues to pay retiring workers the generous rewards granted long ago at the bargaining table. Put another way, a forecast in early 1960 of likely political behavior in the face of growing union strength, had it been founded on nothing more than the single premise of crass self-interest, would have predicted with distressing accuracy the choices actually made by politicians in the subsequent decade.

The search for culprits and causes has yielded a short list featuring (1) an exceptionally generous welfare scheme and a population whose changing composition included a growing percentage of those eligible for welfare, and (2) an unusually large number of public employees receiving unexceptional wages but exceptional fringe benefits, primarily in the form of retirement benefits. That list, however, is only a part of the explanation of why the city went bankrupt, and a minor part at that. The focus that it encourages is also somewhat misdirected. The controlling question should not be why expenditures rose. The central issue is why a rise in expenditures was converted into debt. *Nothing* in this list of causal forces points toward bankruptcy. What it points to is a growing tension between scarce revenues to meet rising demands and the politicians' desire to survive and flourish.

But why was that tension resolved in such a peculiar way? No respectable accounting firm in the country would approve of borrowing year after year to finance current expenditures. The New York Constitution had been deliberately tailored to prevent municipalities from doing just that, not for subtle reasons grounded in political philosophy, but because such a process was universally recognized as the height of fiscal folly. And yet this particular city, for all its know-how as the financial capital of America, not only disregarded a well-known canon of financial management, but in doing so somehow managed to slip around constitutional restraints designed to prevent such disregard. How was it all possible?

8.4. The reasons why: of debt limitations and their circumvention

Debt: that was the problem. Spewing forth from City Hall in ever larger quantities, it cascaded down upon Wall Street with a rush that swept away the politician's inhibitions, the banker's common sense, and ultimately the credit rating of the city. Something had gone desperately awry. For more than a century, concerned citizens had attempted, at one Constitutional Convention after another, to head off a fiscal debacle such as this. They had devised, they thought, a system of restraints for both the municipalities and the state that would place a tight rein upon the profligate tendencies of politicians. What were those restraints, and why had they failed?

The state restraints were anchored in two provisions. One required an annual balancing of the budget, which precluded any borrowing for current expenses. The other required that all proposed debt issues be approved by the voters in referenda, which gave to the public the power to veto the unwise and the excessive. By writing both provisions into the Constitution, the framers made possible judicial review when either provision appeared to be violated by actions of the legislature and/or the executive. As documented in previous chapters, this system failed, partly because the device of moral obligation bonds circumvented the need for voter approval, partly because the constitutional legitimacy of this debt instrument was not tested in the courts for 15 years, and partly because when that review finally came, four of seven justices declared the new device legal for reasons that emphasized the fiscal necessities of the modern era.

The city took a different route. The provision on balancing the budget was ignored.[47] In its stead were two kinds of restrictions, one of which limited the length of time during which a bond or note could be outstanding. In summary form, these limits required (1) that short-term debt be retired very quickly (usually within a year), and (2) that the period of borrowing for long-term purposes correspond to "the probable useful life" of the project into which the borrowed funds would be channeled.[48] The short-term debt requirement reflected the belief that short-term borrowing should be used only to solve budgetary shortages that were temporary. The long-term limitation was designed to prevent such situations as the issuance of a 60-year bond to pay for a school that would be obsolete in 40 years. Taxpayers should not be paying off debt for benefits long since disappeared, the controlling rationale seemed to be. The other major constraint consisted of a ceiling on the total of long-term debt outstanding – 10 percent of the value of taxable real estate – whereby the issuance of debt was linked to the revenue-generating potential of the city.[49] (An attempt was also made to institute pay-as-you-go capital financing, which amounted to requiring a down payment from current funds for capital projects undertaken.)[50]

Notice that the budget is balanced by implication rather than by law (as is the case with the state). To take an extreme example, suppose that the mayor of the City of New York wanted to pay his secretary's salary by borrowing the funds. By any reasonable interpretation of the phrase "probable useful life," the benefits from this expenditure occur during the current year, as the secretary fulfills her duties. Long-term borrowing to pay for this short-term benefit is therefore precluded by the Constitution. The mayor could still float short-term notes to pay this bill, but since all short-term debt must be quickly redeemed, the clear implication is that a momentary deficit this year should be paid off next year (presumably by running a surplus large enough to retire the loan in question). The balanced-budget notion, then, seems to apply to an averaging across several years.

Notice further that the courts are in a position to decide very little. The state legislature was given the authority to decide what the "probable useful life" of a project would be, and was therefore the key decision-making body controlling the authorized life of various city bond issues. If the state made foolish decisions about the probable useful life of a project, thereby authorizing long-term debt to finance what was actually a current expense, who could challenge that decision? If the provisions limiting the maturity of short-term debt were violated by constant roll-overs of that debt, who could stop the process? The answer was certainly not the courts. As events unfolded in 1975, the ultimate check was provided by the financial community, when all of these practices were clearly out of hand. But by then it was too late. Far too late.

One can visualize the framers of the 1938 constitutional amendments, as the Convention drew to a close, folding their hands with a sense of satisfaction. There, they probably said, is a solid system sure to inhibit the excessive issuance of debt. Not a perfect system, to be sure. The limitation that tied total debt to likely revenue sources might have adopted a focus broader than revenues from real estate taxes. But given these legal restrictions upon the maturity structure and the absolute total of debt outstanding, fiscal excesses by municipalities of New York State were surely a thing of the past. How wrong they were.

If placing restraints upon the issuance of debt was a long-standing tradition in New York, so was evasion of such restraints. These limitations were something of a fiscal Maginot Line, doomed to ineffectiveness because of the ease with which they were avoided. The trumpet call to blitzkrieg was sounded by Mayor Wagner in the mid-1960s: "I do not propose to permit our fiscal problems to set the limits of our commitments to meet the essential needs of the people of this City."[51] If fiscal irresponsibility required a slogan, that would do admirably. John Lindsay took it to heart and the result was chaos. In fairness to Lindsay, the ensuing debacle was far from being his exclusive creation. To engineer a complex and thorough fiscal ruin required a lot of help. This Lindsay received, and with surprising ease. Part of that assistance came from the politicians of his day. Part of the requisite help came from politicians of an earlier era, who, by the time Lindsay took office, had firmly established a tradition of evading the fiscal constraints of the Constitution. They had established far more than a tradition. Their legacy to posterity was a thorough undermining of most of the restrictions here noted.

The 1938 effort to shift capital financing toward a pay-as-you-go basis was doomed from the start. By 1952, a Mayor's Committee on Management noted how it was being frustrated by increasing exemptions of large-scale borrowings from the provisions in question.[52] By the time John Lindsay swept into City Hall, so flagrant had these exemptions become that yet another Mayor's Committee on city finances noted that "the 1938 plan is now in fact a dead letter."[53]

The provision limiting debt to 10 percent of the value of taxable real estate was circumvented in two ways. One was to establish public authorities, such as the Triborough Bridge Authority, whose debt issues were not subject to this constitutional provision. A second was to amend the Constitution, early and often, so that by the postwar era the purpose of the original constitutional limitation had been battered almost to death. The process was as old as the provision, which dates from 1884. Debt issued to construct or acquire certain facilities, for example, was repeatedly exempted. The list includes water-supply facilities (1884), docks (1909), rapid transit facilities (1909, 1938), low-rent housing (1938),[54] hospitals (1949), and schools (1951). Also excluded from the 10 percent restriction is short-term debt, such as tax anticipation notes. This by no means exhausts the list. The end result, as suggested, is a fiscal structure that defies the spirit of the original constitutional restriction. With initial complexity furthered by amendments, it also defies the understanding of all save a handful of professional bureaucrats and politicians. Small wonder that by 1952, long before the debt excesses of the 1970s, experts were concluding that "the constitutional debt limit, as it applies to New York City, is a regulatory contrivance which has been so distorted by amendment as to deprive it of much resemblance to any well-rounded principle of control."[55]

The worst was yet to be. In the Wagner–Lindsay–Beame era, three devices dominated the incessant and widespread effort to circumvent constitutional limits on the issuance of debt. One was an elaboration of an old technique: the issuance of debt through public benefit corporations that were not subject to the same constitutional restrictions as was the city. The second and third became linked with financing the city's annual deficit, which quickly swelled to disturbing proportions. To borrow some of the needed funds, certain current expenses were judged to be not current expenses at all, but rather a kind of capital expense having a "probable useful life" extending well beyond the year in which the expenditure was made. These expenses were accordingly charged to the capital account, and debt was issued for the period during which their supposed benefits were imagined to flow. The other main device for financing the city's mounting deficit was short-term borrowing that, in effect, became long-term borrowing through the old technique of continually renewing that debt whenever it came due. Each of these three fiscal contraptions deserves closer attention.

Public benefit corporations, as described at length in earlier chapters, were a well-established technique for financing certain public projects. Also described at length previously were the various ways in which the state employed this device in the modern era to circumvent its own constitutional limitations. The city was not slow to follow the state's lead. Much of the city's capital construction was financed by public benefit corporations – unkindly labeled by some "dummy corporations" – particularly the construction of hospitals, schools, housing, and transit facilities by such entities as the New York City Transit Authority and the New York City Housing Development Corporation.[56] The process usually involved a city proposal, state legislative approval, the governor's signature, and then the issuing of debt by the corporation in question. The Transit Construction Fund was a typical case. It established a construction fund to float bonds in order to provide funds for new transit construction. From first to last, from city proposal to state Assembly debate to Rockefeller's signature on the bill, the issue was cast explicitly in terms of the need to circumvent the constitutional debt limit of the city.

In 1974 the city even tried to use this gimmick to solve a financial crisis of its own. The entity in question was to be called the Stabilization Reserve Corporation, or SRC. This was a dummy corporation with a difference. Designed to borrow $520 million and turn the proceeds over to the city, SRC had no revenue-generating potential of its own. All that it could claim was the moral obligation of the city to channel to it certain funds (notably the stock transfer tax).[57] By the time that the courts declared its prospective debt constitutional (May 1975), financial markets were closed to all city-related borrowing. SRC therefore never sold any securities. The legal decision giving it constitutional legitimacy was nevertheless of the first importance. It paved the way for the Municipal Assistance Corporation, in many ways the Goliath of public benefit corporations, designed to rescue the city's finances, and operating outside any limitations upon city debt.

If the city had one endemic problem in the late 1960s and early 1970s, it was a recurring annual deficit. This is what prompted the effort to establish the Stabilization Reserve Corporation, but that was something of a last gasp. Public benefit corporations were not the main solution for this problem. Part of the solution, as noted previously, was to reclassify certain current expenditures as capital expenses. These could then be charged to capital account, and the funds borrowed to cover the expense. The borrowing in question could only be for a period corresponding to the "probable useful life" of the benefits supposedly flowing each year from the initial expenditure. But if that expenditure really was a current expense, the benefits disappeared during the year in which the dollars were spent (or at least the vast bulk of those benefits). If this was the reality, any attempt at reclassification was obviously an exercise in imagination. The imaginations that mattered belonged to state legislators who responded to city requests by giving to various current expenses lives of "probable usefulness" well calculated to boggle the mind of any competent accountant. All of these came in the form of amendments to New York's Local Finance Law.[58] Examples of this exercise in legal fiction included giving an extended "probable useful life" to such current expenses as spending for vocational education[59] (30 years), for the cleaning and beautification of buildings (10 years), for social and technical assistance to tenants eligible for public assistance (5 years), for conducting a special census (3 years), and for codification of laws by municipalities (3 years). Again and again the State Department of Audit and Control objected to these reclassifications, and always for the same reason: They were current expenses according to all the canons of conventional accounting.[60]

The gimmick did not originate with Lindsay. So well established had it become that when he was elected mayor, a Mayor's Commission

Table 8.6. *Borrowing for current expenses in New York City, fiscal years 1965–78*

Fiscal year	Total city capital budget funds ($ millions)	Borrowing for current expenses	
		Amount ($ millions)	% of city capital budget funds
1965	720	26	3.6
1966	590	57	9.7
1967	538	68	12.6
1968	673	68	10.0
1969	619	84	13.6
1970	800	151	18.9
1971	1,004	195	19.4
1972	1,162	226	19.4
1973	1,342	274	20.0
1974	1,359	564	41.5
1975	1,376	724	52.6
1976	1,445	697	48.2
1977	713	572	80.2
1978	865	523($608)[a]	60.5(70.3)[a]

[a] The $523 million figure represents the amount of capitalized expense budget items under the earlier definition. The $608 million figure represents the amount under the new definition.
Source: Data provided by Citizens Budget Commission, reproduced in New York [City], Temporary Commission on City Finances, *The City in Transition: Prospects and Policies for New York,* Final Report (New York: Arno Press, 1978), 157.

for Better City Finance had already noted its existence with alarm.[61] What was new were the magnitudes involved. From a total of $26 million in 1965, this annual charging of current expenses to capital account had ballooned to $724 million by 1975, an increase of better than 2,500 percent in a decade (see Table 8.6).[62] As for the dangers inherent in the process, these were ably spelled out by the Mayor's Commission:

That borrowing for current expenses is an unsound practice is generally recognized. Its unfavorable influence in the case of New York City may be summarized as follows:
It encroaches on borrowing power needed for other purposes.

It is detrimental to the City's credit standing.
It results in unjustified interest cost.
It conceals and postpones the impact of current expenses
on taxes.
It increases annual borrowing significantly and expands
outstanding debt.[63]

What the Commission might have added, but did not, was that if the practice was pushed to absurd lengths, the city's ability to borrow might be terminated. But that possibility no doubt lay beyond the Commissioners' wildest nightmares in 1966.

Neither of these devices – borrowing through public benefit corporations and charging current expenses to capital account – could begin to compete in terms of sheer volume with the third gimmick: the short-term roll-over. Here too imaginations ran rampant: in forecasting tax revenues from defunct properties unlikely to yield a dime, in expectations of federal and state aid that were clearly overblown, in delaying the conversion from short-term notes into long-term bonds in anticipation of declines in interest rates that never came.

As indicated in Table 8.1, the temporary (or short-term) debt of the city exploded in the 1970s. From a quarter of a billion dollars in 1965, the total rose to three-quarters of a billion by 1969, and to four-and-a-half billion by 1975 – *an increase of almost four billion dollars in six years.* A word of explanation is required concerning the various debt instruments involved.[64]

TANS. Tax anticipation notes, as the name implies, are short-term debt instruments issued in anticipation of tax receipts.

RANS. Revenue anticipation notes can be issued in anticipation of other revenues, notably federal and state aid.

BANS. Bond anticipation notes, again as the name implies, are short-term notes issued in anticipation of their being refunded into longer-term bonds. In theory, these notes could be issued for any purpose for which bonds could be issued. In practice, New York City BANS were issued primarily in anticipation of bond sales to finance housing projects.

Budget notes. This debt instrument was issued, not in anticipation of anything, but in the event of unexpected expenditures causing an unforeseen deficit.

All of these short-term debt instruments were designed to be that and nothing more: notes that would be outstanding for a brief period of time, usually one year, and seldom for more than two years.[65] Three of the four could, by law, be renewed or rolled over, but only for a short period of time, usually three to five years.[66] If ever a set of legal provisions gave an unambiguous signal as to intent, these regulations accomplished that. Their controlling premise – as obvious as it was advisable – was that short-term notes should be used only to solve short-term problems. What other appropriate usage could there possibly be for debt instruments designed to anticipate impending revenues, or to solve momentary shortages produced by unexpected expenditures, or to facilitate the issuing of bonds?

Now for the abuses.

TANS. In pursuit of funds, probable tax receipts were consistently overestimated – one is tempted to say outrageously overestimated. Notes were issued, for example, against delinquent property taxes that had no hope of being collected. Perhaps the best indication of how flagrantly this process was abused was the State Comptroller's judgment that "the $502 million of real estate taxes receivable on the City's books at June 30, 1975, were overstated by approximately $408 million."[67]

RANS. The same technique of overestimating likely revenues led to the same results: notes issued, revenues not forthcoming, notes reissued. From Albany the city received both ongoing encouragement and legal changes that spurred the process. In 1965, for example, with the vigorous endorsement of Rockefeller and Wagner, the Local Finance Law was amended to allow the issuance of RANS in anticipation of tax revenues to be collected in the *subsequent* fiscal year. (The undisguised purpose was to finance an estimated $85 million deficit incurred by New York City in fiscal 1964–65.) In the same year, Albany legislators slaughtered the requirement that limited the total of RAN borrowing by the city to the amount of revenue actually collected during the previous fiscal year. Cut loose from any reference to receipts of the past, this borrowing would now be limited only by expectations for the ensuing budget year. Visions of sugar plums would dance in too many heads for too many years. The state legislature further muddied the waters in 1971 by authorizing the issuance of RANS on an overall basis, rather than against a specific type of revenue. This allowed the lumping together of all optimistic RAN forecasts, and thereby complicated the task of identifying which forecasts were excessive.

BANS. The rolling over of bond anticipation notes is doubly curious. It is clearly inconsistent with the spirit of the enabling legislation. Why not do what the law envisioned: float notes in anticipation of bonds, then sell bonds and use the proceeds to retire the notes? The debt would remain outstanding, but by converting it from a short-term instrument to a long-term one, problems of continually rolling that debt over would be avoided. Why did city officials prefer a recurring

headache to a long-term sedative? The answer appears to be the hope
that interest rates would fall. Why convert into high-interest long-term
debt now, the argument seemed to be, when cheaper borrowing rates
are just around the corner? That expectation flew in the face of all the
signals coming from financial markets, but optimism remained relatively untarnished by the facts. Interest rates failed to decline to "acceptable" levels, and consequently BANS – particularly those associated with housing – were repeatedly rolled over. Once again Albany
legislators and the Governor facilitated the process: in this case, by
repeatedly amending the Local Finance Law to authorize BAN extensions in 1966, 1968, 1970, 1972, 1973, 1974, and 1975.[68]

Budget notes. For the city, the 1970s did not begin auspiciously.
Caught short by a series of events including a downturn in the national
economy and congressional hedging over revenue sharing, the Big
Apple went to Albany, hat in hand, seeking the authorization for a
short-term loan to cover an undisguised deficit. At the state capital, the
door was always open, at least when the plea did not threaten to cost
state politicians any of their money. In 1971, the Governor and the
state legislators therefore responded by authorizing two provisions that
permitted a special form of deficit financing by the city. One increased
the limit for the issuance of budget notes from 1 percent to 4 percent of
the city's budget. The other allowed a delay in repaying these (supposedly short-term) notes until July 1974. The city responded by selling $308 million worth of budget notes, maturing in three years. When
the maturity date loomed in 1974, the city attempted to convert these
budget notes into the debt of a public benefit corporation that it
created specifically for that purpose: the Stabilization Reserve Corporation. This particular debt shuffle came to naught. As noted previously, a legal challenge to the constitutionality of SRC prevented it
from selling any debt until the court's approval was forthcoming in
May of 1975. By that time, no city debt, direct or indirect, could be
sold, whatever its constitutional merits.

On the road to ruin, some financial gimmicks contributed more than
others. The short-term roll-overs that contributed most, as indicated by
Table 8.7, were revenue anticipation notes and bond anticipation
notes. The two accounted for 96 percent of the increase in total temporary debt between 1970 and 1975, and 91 percent of temporary debt
outstanding when the city went under in 1975. Each of these debt
instruments, by law, could be rolled over only for a brief period of time
(three and five years, respectively). With special legislation from Albany and debt shuffles in City Hall (one RAN retired, but a second
issued whose receipts could be used to pay off the first), the roll-over
possibilities had, in practice, no clear time limit except the tolerance of

Table 8.7. New York City debt and MAC debt, 1953–78 ($ millions)

Outstanding as of June 30	Gross funded debt	Temporary debt[a]						Total city debt[a]	MAC debt
		TANS[b]	RANS[c]	Budget notes	BANS[d]	Other	Subtotal		
1978	7,381	—	—	—	—	—	—	7,381	5,106
1977[e]	7,697	280	252	—	496	—	1,028	8,725	4,139
1976	7,427	280	844	—	947	—	2,071	9,498	3,950
1975	7,767	380	2,560	—	1,570	30	4,540	12,307	—
1974	7,652	317	1,798	308	909	84	3,416	11,068	—
1973	6,917	265	887	308	958	100	2,518	9,435	—
1972	6,380	232	1,180	461	687	90	2,650	9,030	—
1971	5,635	206	1,096	308	587	122	2,319	7,954	—
1970	5,236	170	537	—	467	114	1,288	6,524	—
1969	5,080	155	129	—	405	58	747	5,827	—
1968	5,044	147	94	—	404	48	693	5,737	—
1963	4,428	63	—	34	114	20	231	4,659	—
1953	3,413	36	—	4	—	14	54	3,467	—

[a] Excludes city temporary debt held by MAC.
[b] Tax anticipation notes.
[c] Revenue anticipation notes.
[d] Bond anticipation notes.
[e] Revised figures.
Source: Citizens Budget Commission, Twenty-Five Year Pocket Summary of New York City Finances, Fiscal Year 1978–79.

the financial community. Therein lay the rub. Beginning in 1974, the national economy plunged into the worst peacetime recession since World War II. In a set of not entirely unrelated events, federal and state aid became more difficult to get. Forecasts of aid that were the rationale for New York City RAN issues remained obstinately optimistic. Expected funds failed to materialize, and RAN borrowing ballooned. (Between 1973 and 1975, it rose from $887 million to $2,560 million, or by 189 percent.) Recession should have brought in its wake lower interest rates and consequently more refunding of BANS into bonds. Instead, recession was accompanied by double-digit inflation and long-term interest rates that shot up in 1974 and remained high in 1975.[69] The arguments for delaying the conversion of BANS to bonds thus became even more compelling, and the total of this short-term debt outstanding rapidly increased. (From $958 million in 1973, it rose to $1,570 million in 1975, or by 64 percent.)

It was too much for financial markets to stomach. Symptoms of indigestion had long been apparent. In 1974 the city came to the market no less than 18 times to peddle its securities. By 1975 its short-term debt flotations were averaging $750 million a month; its long-term flotations, $500 million quarterly.[70] The city's looming debt needs for 1976 totaled some $8 billion, three-quarters of which involved short-term debt and therefore more roll-over problems in the immediate future.[71]

From the vantage point of the wreckage that ensued, it seemed reasonable to ask who had run the boat onto the rocks. The hands upon the debt controls were of two kinds. In the city proper, the budgetary process, in theory, consisted of extended interactions among three parties: the mayor (representing the executive), the City Council (representing the legislature), and the Board of Estimate (a mixture of the two).[72] In practice, during the Wagner–Lindsay years the budget, with its associated debt proposals, was very much the creation of the mayor, with the other two bodies lacking the time and the staff to offer more than minor amendments.[73] (The parallel with the budget procedures of the state, in the emasculation of legislative input, is striking.) Aiding and abetting this process every step of the way were Albany politicians whose amendments to New York's Local Finance Law were, as noted, nothing short of indispensable.

These, then, were the reasons that the great city went under. At first glance, it is a story of a sagging economy and escalating expenditure demands: for wages, for welfare, and for a multitude of other city services. These pressures caught the city politicians in a vice, as coalitions of city workers and welfare recipients managed to link expenditure proposals to prospective votes, the gathering of which seemed crucial to political survival. The politicians' response was to do what politicians usually do, which is to overdo, or so the argument runs. But how was it possible for them to overdo? The tendency of expenditure demands to outrun available revenues is hardly a problem peculiar to New York City. This is the daily fare of every politician in every municipality in America. What was special about the New York case was *not* how these tensions between demand and supply became intensified, but rather how that tension was resolved by the endless issuance of debt. On second glance, then, the city went under primarily because constitutional constraints were circumvented, the city repeatedly ran a deficit, and as a result, spewed forth an ever mounting supply of debt that ultimately strained and then overstrained the capabilities of the financial community. This particular fiscal folly required the collaboration of two sets of politicians. One resided in City Hall, generating proposals. The other resided in Albany, giving encouragement and approval to those proposals, frequently in the form of amendments to New York's Local Finance Law. None of the participants up and down the Hudson – or at least no one who was in a position of significant power – gave the slightest indication of any willingness to check the process. If they had a slogan, it was that no one ever won an election by promising the people less, and who cares if we have more debt? The entire sorry mess can hardly be viewed as a decline in fiscal morality within the Empire State in the postwar era. Fiscal morality has never been the strong point of city or state officials, as repeatedly demonstrated by the financial debacles of the past. What happened was that an old game was played for higher stakes. And that was the city's undoing. It had withstood in the past a number of evasions of constitutional restraints with their attendant escalation of debt. It could not withstand the fiscal excesses of the 1970s. Too much had been issued. Too much of that required frequent renewal. And the city's deficit, the monster that none would attack, made insatiable demands for more.

The citizenry, from first to last, had little sense of what was going on. The place to hide a dead leaf, Father Brown used to argue, is in a forest. The crippled and butchered constitutional restrictions that fairly littered the fiscal landscape of the city were almost impossible to detect in the thickets and underbrush of endless legal provisions and amendments that controlled what could be borrowed and by whom. Then, too, the books were kept in such a curious way that even the financial community was fooled, or so it has consistently maintained. "If you don't know the buck," boasted Abe Beame's campaign slogan, "you don't know the job," and few had the audacity to suggest that they did. Insulated from public queries by this complexity, the few who did know, as they pursued their own fiscal priorities, were not given to enlightening the many about the true structure of the whole.

The story is told of Babe Ruth emerging from a salary negotiation, only to have a reporter point out that he was now being paid more than President Hoover. Ruth thought for a minute, and replied, "I had a better year." What New York Yankee of the early 1970s, whatever his athletic fumblings, could not look the politicians of the city in the eye and reiterate that claim? Failures of the past, however, were not the issue, at least not in June of 1975. The single controlling priority of politician and financier alike was to keep the city from being declared legally bankrupt. But how?

8.5. MAC and other rescue operations

To follow the fiscal maneuverings of the city after the collapse of May 1975 is at once a simple and a complex task. Complexity is unavoidable, given the myriad of legal acts, informal agreements, and security issues contrived to solve three fundamental problems. Simplicity of approach and clarity of understanding are best attacked by keeping ever to the fore the three problems in question:
1. The city had to find huge sums annually to cover maturing debt *and* an operating deficit that annually ran to hundreds of millions of dollars.
2. Those dollars could not be raised by the city itself because it had been declared persona non grata in the municipal bond market.
3. Given the magnitude of the sums involved, and the jaundiced view that many investors brought to all securities linked with the fate of New York City, the total amount annually required could not even be raised by the institution deliberately manufactured to do the raising: the Municipal Assistance Corporation (or Big MAC for short).

The inescapable conclusion was that the city could avoid formal bankruptcy only if others would lend it large sums of money. There were three and only three possible sources: the state government, the federal government, and the pension funds of city and state employees. The city tapped all three. At one point, not even that was enough. The resulting shortfall was solved by a legal maneuver as curious as it was successful. The city simply refused to pay off certain maturing notes. Amazingly, that was not called bankruptcy. It was not even called default. It was called a moratorium. But this is to get ahead of our story.

The events in question began to unfold in June of 1975. The setting has been outlined in Section 8.1. Millions of dollars in city debt were about to come due. The city did not have the money to pay them, and it could not borrow. Formal bankruptcy was to be avoided at all costs. If neither the state nor the federal government would solve the problem directly, perhaps the state could solve the problem indirectly. Two ideas converged with a rush. Public benefit corporations had borrowed for years with only the moral obligation backing of the state. The courts had ruled in early 1975 that moral obligation debt did not violate New York's Constitution.[74] Why not have a public benefit corporation borrow what the city needed, back that borrowing by promising to funnel to this corporation certain state revenues due the city,[75] and underwrite all securities of the corporation in question with the phrase recently declared legal and long appended to so many security issues within New York: "moral obligation of the state"? That would surely fly. And it did, but falteringly.

The craft was labeled the Municipal Assistance Corporation. It was designed to solve, of all things, a short-run problem. Let MAC borrow several billion,[76] use the proceeds to fund short-term debt of the city into long-term debt, *and within three months,* the argument ran, the city would be able to return to the market on its own. The city found that it could do no such thing. Worse, MAC found that its security sales, sluggish in July and tenuous in August, had ground to a halt by the summer's end. The public apparently was not keen to lend the necessary billions to the city either directly or indirectly through the guise of a public benefit corporation. This was hardly surprising, given that MAC had no assets and no taxing powers, and no legal guarantee of state support (only a "moral" one), and finally, given the fact that none of the city's fiscal problems which necessitated the creation of MAC in the first place had been resolved.

Bankruptcy again hovered in the wings. Once more it was beaten back by the combined efforts of city and state politicians. In the early morning hours of September 9, 1975, bleary-eyed Albany legislators passed an 80-page piece of legislation that few had read and probably none understood. What they understood were threats such as that of Assemblyman Burton G. Hecht of the Bronx, who predicted "disaster and riots in the City of New York if this bill is not passed."[77]

The one clear result of the legislation was the Emergency Financial Control Board, set up by the state to review, control, and supervise the financial management of the city "during the period of financial emergency." In less polite wording, management of the city's budget was wrenched from city officials and transferred to a state agency.[78] To this structural change was appended a financial plan that kept changing because the investing public kept saying no. In October of 1975 a deal was worked out involving (1) short-term loans from the state, (2) moderate loans from the financial community (mainly New York City banks), and (3) the purchase of $950 million of MAC bonds by city and state pension funds.[79] Curiously enough, the entire second plan was based upon the same idiotic premise that underlay the first plan creating MAC: that what was to be tackled was a short-run problem, so the solution need only be short run. The expectation now was that this funding would carry the city for several months, after which the city (or MAC, or both) would reenter the bond market and borrow whatever was needed. The public would have none of it. Indeed, so perturbed had private investors become that the state itself encountered grave difficulties in borrowing. This did not augur well for plan number two. It did not take a financial genius to see trouble barreling down the road. Lest the point be missed by the arithmetically handicapped, David Rockefeller spelled out the bottom line to a U.S. Senate Committee on October 18: "According to data compiled by the office of the New York City Comptroller, in New York City alone, the cash flow situation in the next three and a half months is so acute . . . that even if the City could suspend all debt service payments . . . it would still have a cash flow short-fall in excess of $1 billion."[80] The ability of the state to solve this shortfall was virtually nil. Again Rockefeller labored the obvious: "The State of New York can do no more. Not only has the State itself lost market access, but its credit-worthiness, too, is in jeopardy."[81]

The list of possible rescuers had now been reduced to one. MAC had tried and failed. A combination of state aid and private sales to pension funds had been tried, but it was not enough. Only the federal government could save the day. Plan number three of necessity therefore included federal support, but once again several curious wrinkles were added that bordered on the ludicrous. On December 15, 1975, President Ford signed the New York City Seasonal Financing Act. The implication seemed to be that the lending in question was not designed to aid a city sinking ever deeper into debt, but rather to combat certain "seasonal imbalances" when expenditures momentarily outran receipts.[82] In this same Alice in Wonderland spirit, the city agreed to balance its budget by June 1978. (It would not come within half a billion dollars of that objective.) Finally, and apparently as one condition of enlisting federal support,[83] the city refused to pay off some of its maturing short-term notes. This was labeled by the state the Moratorium Act of November 15, 1975. Its terms were nothing short of a legal outrage. Holders of some $2.4 billion of maturing city notes were informed that payment would be suspended until November 15, 1978, with an option of converting to MAC bonds in the intervening three years. If ever an act was blatantly unconstitutional, this was it. A short-term note is a contract. Article 1, section 10, of the federal Constitution stipulates that no state "shall . . . pass any . . . law impairing the obligation of contracts." Now the New York State legislature had done exactly that. A full year would pass before the courts finally announced the self-evident, declaring the act unconstitutional. In the intervening 12 months, the state in general and MAC in particular would regain enough respectability that, with ongoing federal help, the city could find the dollars to pay off maturing debt and finance its annual deficit, which, like the poor, was always with it.[84]

8.6. A distant thunder

From first to last, it has been a perilous enterprise. Capitulation and compromise, frenzied brinkmanship, and not a little fiscal wizardry – these have become almost routine in a continuing salvage operation designed to disguise the obvious: that the city as a financial entity has gone broke. But the operation has been successful. There was, after all, only one criterion for success: that legal bankruptcy be avoided. The world must be spared this undraped spectacle of financial woe. The world, the argument ran, was not yet ready for the shock. The details of successive drapings, whereby plan three gave way to plan four and later variants, need not concern us here.[85] Five points and three ominous inferences are worth underscoring.

First, most of the major participants in the rescue operation have had an odd view of what basically has gone awry. The problem, they believe, is that investors will not lend. The solution is to devise new ways to persuade them to lend. Their creative energy has therefore been devoted almost exclusively to playing with financial erector sets – building, restructuring, and replacing – with city unions and financial institutions eager to aid and abet this inventive process.

Second, the basic problem is not a borrowing problem. It is not a cash flow problem. It is a deficit problem. Not all observers have been befuddled by the outpouring of data and double-talk from Albany and City Hall. Thirty-eight months after the 1975 collapse, for example, the *Wall Street Journal* complained about the misdirected focus of the rescue operation. "The doctors are concocting a patent medicine cure for anemia, but the patient has a severed artery. The fuss about financing only serves to obscure reality. New York's problem is a budget problem. The essential task is to stop spending more than it takes in."[86]

Third, the city continued to spend more than it took in throughout the latter half of the 1970s. The best measure of how seriously city officials and others have taken the matter of eradicating the city's operating deficit is the dimension of that deficit since emergency measures were first initiated with the creation of the Municipal Assistance Corporation in June of 1975. For the fiscal years ending June 30, the annual deficits (in millions of dollars) have been as follows:

1976	1,870
1977	1,039
1978	712
1979	422

The 1978 figure is illustrative of several problems. According to the city's accounting system, it ran a *surplus* of $32 million in 1978. That year, however, the city's books, for the first time in its history, were audited by independent public accountants. According to conventional practices, they noted, the city ran a *deficit* of $712 million. The very fact that the two numbers diverged by three-quarters of a billion dollars suggested that the financial house declared a shambles in 1975 was in less than perfect order three years later.[87] Even more disconcerting was the revelation that the city's books, when correctly tallied, were still awash in a sea of red ink.

Fourth, the possibilities of the city plunging into the black are not encouraging. Tax increases are ill-advised, given their linkage to economic retardation discussed in Chapter 3. The persistence of that retardation makes unlikely the swelling of revenues from a resurgence of industrial activity within the city. Expenditure cuts are difficult to make, partly because some items, such as welfare, are largely beyond the city's control, and other items, such as wages, are caught in a maelstrom of union power and political expediency. The unions, as one might expect, tend to be somewhat unenthusiastic about making sacrifices for the common good. (Greeted with the prospect of a reduction in the city's firefighters, Richard J. Vizzini, head of the Uniformed Firefighters Association, reportedly shouted at Mayor Beame, "What are you trying to do – burn down the whole [expletive deleted] city?")[88] The politicians show no signs of getting tough at the bargaining table. In July of 1978, for example, the Citizens Budget Commission noted with dismay:

> Unfortunately, the City also adopted an imprudent principle – that any positive balance left in the fund at a fiscal year's end would be tantamount to a budget surplus and thus spendable for purposes not included in the budget as adopted. This is illustrated by the City's using the Fiscal Year 1978 end-of-the-year balance in the Contingency Reserve Fund (which reportedly may have reached $400 million) to fund wage increases in Fiscal Year 1979. As a result, the City must

start its build-up of reserves all over again in the Fiscal Year 1979 budget. Presumably, the same "raiding" of reserves will occur at the end of every fiscal year provided, of course, there is something left in the fund to raid.[89]

More simply put, city officials and union negotiators seem bent upon implementing their own peculiar variant of Parkinson's second law: that expenditure rises to meet income. In this case, the expenditure (wages) rises to absorb extra income that could have been used to cut the operating deficit. So ingrained has this procedure become that city officials even cite it when justifying their failure to implement the kind of massive expenditure cuts needed to get the budget balanced. Deputy Budget Director Lou Friedrich explains: "There's no point cutting before we have to. For one thing, we won't be able to tuck a surplus away for a rainy day. Labor will just demand that if we have any extra money, we give it to them."[90] That rainy day is fiscal 1982, when by law the budget must be balanced, and the federal government will reassess its support of the city. If a failure to make large cuts well before that deadline arrives means an inability to balance the budget when it arrives, then Friedrich's rainy day is likely to become more akin to a typhoon, well capable of destroying a frail fiscal structure.

If tax receipts are unlikely to surge and expenditures show no sign of plummeting, the odds of the city's deficit persisting are disturbingly high. Mayor Koch was more accurate than he cared to admit when he pointed out in the summer of 1978 that "the struggle for a sound city is not over. It is just beginning."[91] The battle has yet to be seriously joined, while the prospective forces for bankruptcy remain awesome.

Fifth, and last, should legal bankruptcy occur, the fiscal holding actions of recent years have radically shifted the burden of default. At the center of bankruptcy is the notion that creditors will receive less than 100 cents on the dollar for every dollar owed. Had the city defaulted in the spring of 1975, the losers would have been all those who held New York City notes and bonds at that time. Just who those people were is difficult to determine, but it does seem clear that the financial community of the city would have taken a beating. Now a new cast of potential losers has emerged. Again, they are not easily identified, with one exception. The pension funds of city employees are now loaded down with city obligations, where previously they had been comparatively barren of such holdings, at least as of May 1975. The pension funds of state employees would also now be similarly burdened, had State Comptroller Levitt, as their sole trustee, bowed to the many pressures to make him use these billions to salvage the sagging fiscal fortunes of the city.[92]

Now the inferences. Against the backdrop of the points just made, they are as self-evident as they are disconcerting. First, if formal bankruptcy is to be avoided, federal support is critical. From the fire and brimstone of Abe Beame to the muted tones of the Congressional Budget Office, virtually every analyst has emphasized how dependent the rescue operation has become upon continued federal participation. Second, if the federal government withdraws its support, or even reduces that support in a big way, the state will probably not be strong enough to rescue the city on its own. This was demonstrated with a vengeance in the fall of 1975, when federal support was first enlisted as the only hope of averting bankruptcy. Third, if the federal government withdraws, the city founders, and the state takes on the role of rescuer of last resort, the state itself may become a victim of that salvage operation. Somewhat unfair was an Albany legislator's characterization of the fall 1975 rescue operation as "trying to keep an aircraft carrier from sinking by attaching it to a rowboat."[93] As a fiscal craft, the Empire State is surely far more than a rowboat. The city, however, with its awesome freight of debt, is hardly less than a nautical monstrosity, at least relative to the fiscal buoyancy of the state. If a leaky hull is subsequently torpedoed, the question is not whether it will go down. The question is what will go down with it.

8.7. Who was to blame?

It was an old story. The cast was different, the setting somewhat novel, but the dominant plot read "too much debt." But why?

Against the backdrop of arguments developed thus far, the thesis of this chapter should be readily apparent. The key is *not* to be found in forces underlying the surge in city expenditures, nor in the forces causing revenues to lag. The central explanation is to be found in the process whereby the pressures for expenditures to outrun receipts were converted into debt. The devices used were primarily short-term debt roll-over, the charging of current expenses to capital account, and borrowing under the guise of public benefit corporations. The politicians' recourse to these devices reflects a problem endemic to democracies. Their priorities emphasize self-interest and reelection more than the long-run good of the constituency they are ostensibly elected to serve. At least this appears to be depressingly true of most of the politicians most of the time. The New York City experience is but a case in point. Caught between a rock and a soft place, between hard choices and debt escalation, the New York politicians who mattered made the predictable choice. It was these choices, made over and over again, that led to fiscal ruin.

How could the entire sorry episode have been avoided? The question is instructive. It throws into sharp relief the principal failure of the system. If the problem at bottom was the politician's propensity to overissue debt, the solution was a system that monitored that issuance to squelch the excessive and the irresponsible. But monitored by whom? The executive and the legislature could hardly be part of the solution. They were the problem. The only possible answer is the third branch of government: the courts. What New York needed and did not have was a set of laws prohibiting such fiscal foolishness as the issuance of debt to cover current expenses, and ready access to judicial review by the citizenry when they had good reason to believe that those laws were being violated. In short, the problem was as old, as conventional, as a failure of checks and balances.

Had such a system been in place and worked, the likely course of events is difficult to specify in much detail. Several effects, however, would have been assured. Politicians who said yes too freely would have been forced to say no. The realities of the city's economic retardation of necessity would have been confronted earlier. The associated sluggishness in tax receipts combined with a tax structure already pushed to the limit clearly implied that the city could not do it all: not *all* of the pay increases and *all* of the welfare programs and *all* of the services demanded from it. Which cuts would have been made is difficult to say, but that some expenditures would not have been made is a certainty. The funds simply were not there to do it all. A sense of fiscal reality would therefore have dominated where it was too often absent: in union bargaining and in Albany debates concerning welfare programs and how the costs should be divided between the city and the state. The end result would hardly have guaranteed perfection. It would have guaranteed the making of harder choices sooner, and for that reason, those choices would almost surely have been superior to what was actually done. Above all, bankruptcy would not have been a possibility, because excessive short-term borrowing would not have been a possibility. When a man knows he is to be hanged in a fortnight, Dr. Johnson once observed, it concentrates his mind wonderfully. The tragedy of New York City is that the day of concentration – the day of confronting the fiscal realities implied by economic retardation – was put off until the attendant problems bordered on the insoluble.

If the central problem was as conventional as defective checks and balances, so were the associated failures. The history of New York City fairly reeks with fiscal excess. Immediately following the Civil War, for example, Boss Tweed almost tripled the outstanding debt of the city within the span of three years (1868–71). In the words of one commentator, "Borrowing was freely indulged in, even to pay the current expenses of government, and the loans were extended through refunding operations rather than paid off."[94] At the outset of World War I, so flagrantly did the city violate the canons of sound finance that in 1915 the local banks, as a condition for making further loans, tried to force the city to adopt a pay-as-you-go basis for all non-revenue-producing improvements.[95] The excesses of the 1970s were perhaps most clearly foreshadowed in the excesses of the 1930s, when the city issued short-term notes in anticipation of realty tax collections that clearly far outstripped what would actually be collected. Subsequent revenues, to no one's surprise, proved inadequate to pay off the notes and finance current expenditures. The response of city officials, as predictable as it was imprudent, was a repeated refunding that rapidly escalated the total of short-term debt outstanding. Investors became reluctant to lend, and banks became reluctant to underwrite more city borrowing. (How familiar that sequence now is.) Bankruptcy in this instance was avoided only by the so-called Bankers' Agreement of October 1933, whereby the city was forced to adopt more prudent fiscal practices, including provisions for short-term debt reductions and more realistic calculations of expected tax receipts.[96]

Time and again the concerned citizens of the Empire State have grappled at Constitutional Conventions with these propensities to overissue debt. Time and again they have legislated constitutional restraints – limiting total long-term debt, limiting the maturity structure of that debt, limiting the period during which short-term debt can be outstanding. Time and again the executive and the legislature have passed laws or devised new techniques that undermined these constitutional constraints in spirit and in fact.

That is the unsolved puzzle that almost none of the analysts of the city's debacle has confronted. Oliver Wendell Holmes, Jr., once suggested that for the legal case before him a page of history was worth a volume of logic. What is distressing about the New York City case is that neither history nor logic is being brought to bear upon a problem that cries out for recognition and resolution. How can laws be contrived to inhibit such fiscal folly as borrowing to finance current expenses? And once contrived, how can their subsequent undermining be prevented? What wording is necessary and what safeguards of the public interest will do the job? The failures of the past century underscore how difficult these problems are to solve. But solved they must be, or the forces of excess, so frequently marshaled in the past, are sure to rear their ugly heads in the future.[97] If the city's fiscal history has proven nothing else, it has proven that. It is a commentary on the democratic process that this delicate issue of redrafting checks and balances is almost never faced head on. On those rare occasions when it is, the controlling premise is all too frequently that politicians are more to be trusted than is the public, that constraints on the future issuance of debt must be minimized in the name of flexibility.[98] Down that particular road will not be found salvation. The only sure encounter will be a repetition of the past. And that prospect is hardly to be embraced with enthusiasm.

Finally, the question noted at the outset, the question that controls this chapter as it controls much of the discussion of the city's financial downfall: Who was to blame? The answer turns upon the conceptual framework that one brings to the causal processes at work. If everything is counted that either raised expenditures or slowed receipts – from economic retardation to federal welfare programs to the transit strike – the very size of the resulting list of causal forces and related personalities is sure to blur the question of responsibility. No one was to blame because everyone was to blame, the tempting conclusion seems to be. If instead, the focus is upon those forces that facilitated continual borrowing to finance recurring operating deficits, the list is shorter and the contributing personalities emerge in stark relief. Every city official who supported, actively or passively, proposals and policies for which the bottom line was more debt to finance current expenditures is, to use the legal phrasing, an accessory before the fact. So is every Albany legislator who was a party to the passage of laws that sanctioned this process. If the cast is large, the offense at least is well defined. The propensity of city and state officials to blame the unions, the banks, the federal government, is as predictable as it is misplaced. From a multitude of wellsprings came pressures for expenditures to outrun receipts. But theirs was the decision to give way, and in the giving way, to embark upon financial practices long recognized as the height of fiscal idiocy. They were the ones (again in legal phrasing) who had "the last clear chance" to stem a rising tide of red ink that would ultimately engulf nothing less than the financial capital of America. Their failure is both personal and professional. Their actions contravened the spirit of the Constitution if not the letter of the law, and well they knew that fact. "Things" were not in the saddle riding the city's fiscal might into the ground; people were – people elected or appointed to serve the public interest. Not their own interests, but the public's interest. The financial chaos they wrought is but one measure of how miserably they served that goal.

Indignation should perhaps be tempered with a sense of irony. There is about the entire venture an aura of the absurd. As Senator

Proxmire noted when yet another rescue operation was in the wind, "New York [City] should need credit like the Sahara needs sand."[99] The confidence that bristles forth from phrases such as the Big Apple or the Empire State is somewhat at variance with the fiscal facts of recent years. But irony is surely not enough. For New York residents who see the city's financial machinations for what they are – as farcical as they are dangerous, as endemic as they are unresolved – there is perhaps a symmetry of response to that of President Lincoln when confronted with disheartening New York election returns in the fall of 1862. He was reminded, Lincoln said, of the Kentucky lad who stubbed his toe: he was too big to cry, and far too badly hurt to laugh.

9

Conclusion

Nothing has changed. More cautiously, as this book goes to press, not one of the basic flaws in the structure of the political economy of the state is being seriously reviewed, much less resolved.

Consider the potential for excesses in the issuing of debt. The legislature did move in 1976 to "cap" the use of moral obligation bonds in some areas, although not in others (most notably, in the issuance of such debt by the Municipal Assistance Corporation). But every device whereby constitutional restraints upon the issuance of debt were circumvented in the past can still be used to circumvent those limitations in the future.

Consider the role of the chief executive. The legislature is now somewhat better staffed and therefore better informed. It also has become in recent years somewhat more capable of resisting pressures exerted by the chief executive as the power of political parties has waned and that of vested interest groups has grown. The budget wrangles, the veto overrides, the clashes between a Democratic governor and a Republican-dominated Senate all suggest that the pendulum of power is swinging back in favor of the legislature. But are such changes sufficient to prevent a Rockefeller-type dominance in the future? The governor of New York still has at his command the potential for extraordinary influence lurking in devices denied even to the president of the United States, including the line item veto, the manipulations made possibly by messages of necessity, and the accumulation of power that comes from repeated reelection to an executive position with no legal limits upon tenure in office. In short, the potential for a mismatch in power between the executive and the legislature is still there.

Consider the role of the courts. They should be the third branch of government, monitoring the fiscal activities of the other two for potential constitutional violations. In New York's case, which fiscal excesses of the past might the courts be able to prevent in the future? The highest court in the state has declared legal the main fiscal gimmick (the moral obligation bond) that effectively circumvented the one constitutional restraint of consequence inhibiting the excessive issuance of debt (the requirement that all proposed increases in state debt be approved by voters in a referendum). As for the escalation of debt by New York City or any other municipality, the role of the courts has been minimal, and will continue to be minimal, because the relevant constitutional restraints are vaguely specified and easily avoided. The debt defenses of the city and the state are down, assuring vulnerability to any politician whose large style, like that of Shakespeare's Henry VI, agrees not with the leanness of his purse.

Consider the problem of access to the courts. Citizen-taxpayers no longer have "standing" in the legal matter that matters most: the right to sue the state whenever its bond-issuing practices appear to violate the Constitution. A recent series of legal maneuvers and judicial decisions[1] have again barred from the courts the only people likely to request judicial review of suspected constitutional violations, should constitutional limitations upon the issuance of debt ever be tightened up enough to be worth invoking.

Consider New York public authorities. In some instances, their recent operations have been characterized less by drive and more by drift than in the Rockefeller years. They still retain, however, all of the powers, and all of the potential for insensitivity to public needs inherent in their remarkable insulation from the political process. Nor is there any move afoot to make their present structure and operations correspond more closely to an old ideal: the single-purpose, fiscally independent public benefit corporation whose life terminates when that single purpose is accomplished.

Consider the democratic ideal of deliberate and informed debate by elected representatives who carefully weigh conflicting constituency interests. Despite modest improvements in recent years, New York legislators still tend to have too little knowledge of the issues, too few staff members to remedy that ignorance, and too little time to remedy it themselves. The confusion and haste of the final days of a legislative session remain nothing short of scandalous. Events of 1980 illustrate the problem. The Assembly and the Senate, after approving almost no legislation since the session began in January, rushed through hundreds of bills in the final week in June. Bills were frequently approved at the rate of one every 30 seconds. Pages scurried to and from the podium with whole boxes of bills, while the legislators, as one newspaper noted, "scarcely seemed to know what they were voting for."[2] After lasting for better than 12 hours, the final session ended at 3:26 A.M., amid the debris of cookies, cheese, and apples used to sustain members, and the scattered remnants of legislation they had ostensibly considered. Complained Assemblyman Clark C. Wemple (R, Niskaguna), "It is legislation by ordeal."[3] This is hardly the image of a responsible elected body designed to inspire confidence. It is also hardly the ideal body to take over many of the tasks heretofore conducted by public authorities. If the insulation of these bureaucracies is to be shattered for the sake of making their policies more responsive to the will of the people, the elected representatives of those people must obviously do better – much better – in terms of informed, deliberate, and judicious debate. This will undoubtedly cost more money – for staff, for carefully researched reports, and for salary increases to compensate legislators for more time spent in Albany. The price of a first-rate government comes high, particularly in the modern era when so much is demanded from it.

Consider finally the question whether the state must ultimately face a crisis in the making. The principal ingredients are four: continued economic retardation, a continuing deficit in New York City's operations, the overstretched fiscal structure of the state, and congressional review of federal support for New York City in 1982.

The most reasonable forecast for the economy, unwelcome though it may be, is for economic retardation to persist. This dreary prospect some experts will resist, noting such statewide developments as employment growth in the late 1970s,[4] or alternatively noting signs of improvement at the heart of the problem: the sluggish performance of New York City. Most popular among such signs are the recent surge in foreign investment in the city; the slowing down of wage and price increases to growth rates below the national average; the selective recovery of a handful of industries (such as tourism and construction); and, until the national economy began to slump unmistakably in 1980, the hope that the national recovery of the late 1970s would persist well into the next decade and thereby stimulate continued New York recovery.[5] Also popular in certain quarters is a Darwinian view of the economic debacle of the 1970s. The weak firms have been eliminated, the argument runs, leaving only the hardy breeds more capable of adjusting to pressures in the economic environment.[6] The fittest have survived, and the survivors will stay put.

The Darwinian argument represents little more than the triumph of hope over experience. Nothing in data presently available suggests that the firms now in New York are more prone, or less prone, to remaining in the state than they were in the 1970s. The previous exodus of manufacturing firms, for example, may have weeded out the weak, but that exodus may also have weakened many service industries by creating in them excess capacity. No one knows the answer. What does seem clear is the limited prospect for change among the pressures causing in the past some firms to leave and others not to enter. None of these pressures is likely to be modified in a dramatic and positive way in the near future, for reasons documented at length in Chapters 2 and 3.[7]

Two issues must be carefully distinguished. One concerns long-run or secular growth prospects for the state. Under that heading the unanswered question is whether New York State retardation in the 1980s will be more akin to the sluggish growth of the 1960s or to the sharply worse performance of the 1970s. But continued retardation there will surely be. The second issue concerns cyclical or short-run growth prospects for the immediate future. If the national economy continues to be sluggish in the early 1980s, the timing for New York's impending fiscal crisis could not be worse. Admittedly, the economies of both the city and the state now appear to be less sensitive to cyclical downturns than those of many other regions, largely because both areas rely so heavily upon industries (such as services) that traditionally are less susceptible to cyclical swings.[8] The crucial issue, however, is not the ability to slump gracefully, but the ability to grow, and thereby generate more jobs, higher incomes, and larger tax receipts.

Were it not for New York City's fiscal problems, the state could unquestionably weather whatever storms are lurking in the 1980s. A sluggish economy will inhibit the growth of its tax receipts. Spending sprees of the past have created spending commitments of the present that are difficult to scale down dramatically. The net effect is little fiscal room to maneuver, or at least to maneuver on a grand scale. These problems by themselves, however, would promise inconvenience, not agony. The economic shoe would pinch, but the Empire State would hardly emerge a fiscal cripple.

The problem is New York City. The central frailty now is what the central frailty has been for better than a decade: The city has an operating budget running in the red. More deficits will mean more borrowing to cover those deficits. The city has limited ability to borrow, the state has limited ability to rescue the city on its own, and the federal government will review its support in 1982.

Will the city's budget be in balance by that date? The signs are not encouraging. From what attempts to be an optimistic survey of the city's economic prospects comes one of the most alarming statements:

> Despite the recent recovery in local business activity, as well as the reductions made by the municipal administration in manpower and services following the onset of the fiscal crisis, the city's operating budget continues to run at a substantial deficit. These deficits, moreover, are projected for future years even without taking into account the wage increases for the municipal labor force that are likely to be negotiated when the present contracts run out.[9]

That gloomy warning is difficult to reconcile with the dogged sunniness of Mayor Koch, who announced that the city's budget would be balanced a full year ahead of time (in fiscal 1981). The Mayor's assertions, however, must be taken with several grains of salt. First, he has failed to attack the deficit problem with any long-range master plan. Wage and salary savings have been achieved almost entirely through the random process of work-force attrition (a process that implements a budget cut any time a city employee retires, resigns, or dies, irrespective of where service cuts should be made). His various tax proposals have been stigmatized by experts as "quick-fix" packages, similar to those of his predecessors.[10] As for problems of improving labor productivity, Koch has done virtually nothing of consequence. ("We've wasted the last two to three years," complained MAC chairman Felix Rohatyn in late 1979, "when we should have been putting in management reforms, productivity improvements, and budget cuts.")[11] Second, the Mayor's forecast of a balanced budget in fiscal 1981 appears to be wildly optimistic, based upon the cheeriest of all possible assumptions concerning federal and state aid and a mild national economic slump destined to have only minor effects upon the city's tax receipts and welfare payments. Third, new wage contracts negotiated with the city's municipal employee unions in the late spring and early summer of 1980 implied a deficit for 1982 *well in excess of one billion dollars,* a number that could become noticeably worse should the national recession persist through 1981. To hope that the city will close this kind of budget gap by itself is to assume a willingness to face fiscal austerity that has been singularly absent in the past. Comer Coppie, Executive Director of the city's Emergency Financial Control Board, applied the verbal sledgehammer where it was hardly needed. The problem, he noted, was "very, very serious."[12]

The optimists often counter such concerns with what has become a popular article of faith: The federal government will take over welfare payments, thereby freeing the city from a major expenditure burden and allowing it to balance its books. But is that probable? The Twentieth Century Fund Task Force on the Future of New York City was not hopeful: "There is little likelihood of major increases in federal . . . contributions to the City's large welfare population in the immediate future."[13] Daniel Patrick Moynihan was less restrained: "The Carter Administration has actually reduced Federal aid to New York City. But this is trivial compared to the Administration's inability to grasp the problems of this city and state."[14]

The city's fiscal problems are not limited to an ongoing deficit in its operating budget. Two other complications loom on the horizon, promising predicaments. One is the maturing of debt previously issued. The other, is the need to repair and renovate much of the capital infrastructure of the great metropolis. New York City must maintain, among other things, some 1,200 elevated highway structures, 6,200 miles of paved streets, 6,300 miles of water main, 6,000 miles of sewers, 38 miles of water tunnel, and 100,000 water main valves. Even the most optimistic of city surveys concedes that many of these facilities are in a "dangerous state of disrepair . . . For many years, city administrations have allowed the roads, bridges, subways, sewers, water mains, and other basic facilities to deteriorate, sometimes dangerously, frequently stretching replacement cycles hundreds of years longer than the facilities could endure."[15]

Where will the dollars come from – to refurbish the deteriorating capital infrastructure of the city *and* to cover maturing debt issues *and* to balance a municipal operating budget still running in the red? The most optimistic characterization of the present is "alarming." The most optimistic characterization of the immediate future is "ominous." From two of the most expert academicians on New York City matters comes perhaps the best compact summary of the city's short-run prospects: "New York City has a balanced budget in fiscal year 1981 only in a technical sense that belies the continuing imbalance between *recurring* revenues and *recurring* expenditures. Even if the budget is balanced this year or next, it will become quickly unbalanced. The budget remains problematic because it has not reached a point of equilibrium with the local economy."[16] The prospect that these problems will be substantially alleviated by increased federal aid are not promising, as New York's Senator Moynihan has repeatedly emphasized: "It will be difficult, given the mood of Washington, to win either special aid for New York City or to enact federal urban programs of a more general scope that can relieve the city's fiscal strain."[17] President Carter also conceded that there was only "slender support" for the city in Congress.[18] Most disturbing of all was Moynihan's repeating of the Senate Banking Committee's warning issued in 1978, when it voted more fiscal aid for New York City: "This is the last time."

What are the possible solutions, or at least the partial remedies? A barrage of proposals can be expected in the immediate future. The problems are pressing and time is short. As the citizen struggles to make sense of these, eight rather different considerations should be kept in mind.

First, the powers of New York City and/or New York State to limit economic retardation are severely restricted by fiscal excesses of the past. Major cuts in taxes are difficult to implement because of spending commitments previously made. Major new programs to encourage some firms to enter the state and others not to leave are difficult to fund because the extra dollars needed are difficult to find. The most useful weapons presently in the government's armory are perhaps the ones that are now being relied upon so heavily: old-fashioned boosterism and a new-fashioned spirit of cooperation with the business community at every level of government. The best that can be expected from policies such as these, however, is a moderation in economic retardation, not a reversal.

Second, if the city must solve its fiscal crisis largely by itself, the city must balance its budget. If the economy remains sluggish, tax revenues will not grow to any significant degree, particularly real tax revenues corrected for inflation. If real revenues do not grow significantly, and a large deficit is to be eliminated, some expenditures must be cut. This can be accomplished through absolute reductions, or through expenditure increases that are below the rate of inflation. The effect of the latter is a cut in real, or constant dollar, spending.

Third, if city expenditures are to be cut, someone must sacrifice. The possibilities include fewer public employees, lower wage increases for the remaining employees, and cuts in certain city public services. This does not exhaust the list, but retrenchment must become the order of the day. At the moment the city, while rich in proposals, is relatively poor in policies designed to accomplish what should have been broached long ago: scaling down fiscal operations to mesh more realistically with the new constraints implied by economic retardation. For years the city has attempted to maintain a system of local government benefits that have exceeded local government revenues, covering the difference by running up debt and running down its capital infrastructure. What was needed in the 1960s and 1970s, and is still needed, is a revolution of diminished expectations. That fight, however, has yet to be seriously joined. Nor will it be seriously joined until the politicians, the public employees, their union leaders, and everyone else involved in determining the fiscal fate of the city become convinced that major sacrifices are unavoidable. The fiscal warriors of the present day are doing little more than attacking with paring knives a dragon vulnerable to nothing less than swords. And so the deficit remains.

Fourth, even if the city's operating deficit disappeared tomorrow, the city would still face fiscal challenges of the first magnitude. Preoccupation with the short-run problems of balancing the budget should not obscure such long-run needs as refurbishing the capital infrastructure of the metropolis, particularly its mass transit system, but also its highways, bridges, sewage systems, and water mains. Such needs the city can continue to neglect only at its economic peril.

Fifth, most elected politicians are almost sure to slight such long-run needs as they remain preoccupied with their own short-run ambitions. If the past presents a single convincing lesson, it is that. The two-stage problem yet to be resolved in this or any other state is how the citizens might be persuaded to abandon their own indifference to long-run economic problems, and how the citizens, once aroused, might force their elected representatives to address such long-run problems seriously, and on an ongoing basis.

Sixth, refurbishing the capital infrastructure of the city is only one of two major long-term priorities that politicians, state and local, are sure to slight. The other, ignored by many and forgotten by most, is ultimately more important. It is repairing the Constitution of the state. Whatever the strong points of New York's present Constitution, in matters of debt control and public authority regulation it is a twisted wreck compared to what the framers of the past believed they had constructed. It is also the source of gubernatorial powers that, under Rockefeller, made most fiscal contests between the executive and the legislature disturbingly unequal. If this document is to be, in Daniel Webster's phrase, "the people's Constitution," it is high time that the people reviewed the many modifications designed and implemented over half a century by a small elite. At the very least, the people must fashion new constitutional restraints upon the issuance of debt. If they shirk that duty, the lessons of the past make clear that they are sure to encounter excessive public borrowing in the future.

Seventh, in any discussion of whether the Constitution should be restructured, two conflicting points of view are sure to surface. They are as ancient, as respectable, and ultimately as irreconcilable, as Hamilton's clashes with Jefferson over what a government ought to do, and how it ought to do it.

One view favors the few and distrusts the many, favors strength and activism in government and disdains weakness and inertia. If government is to "get things done," its exponents argue, the executive must be powerful and decisive, the legislature must be relatively weak and compliant, and the people must be consulted as little as possible. The functioning of government is therefore to be dominated by elites – intelligent, educated, and informed, and with a sense of what is best for the general welfare. The electorate tends to be viewed with some distrust, and not a little scorn. The public, the argument runs, is too ill informed on the issues, too parochial in its outlook to assess the larger needs of the state, and too protective of its pocketbook. Indifference and apathy are thus not frailties of the citizenry to be decried, but critical ingredients for the effective functioning of democratic governments. These traits help still what otherwise would become a cacophony of demands, whose provincial diversity would intensify factionalism and defuse decisiveness. Supporters of such a view favor feeble checks and balances, as long as that feebleness favors elites in general and the executive in particular. Any constitutional provision requiring voter approval of proposed increases in state debt they regard as an intolerable constraint. To deny citizen-taxpayers standing in court to challenge the constitutionality of the state's fiscal actions is, for them, a desirable protection against nuisance or crackpot litigation.

Exponents of the opposing viewpoint distrust the activism of political and bureaucratic elites, cut loose from popular debate and popular control. From the days of Jefferson to the present, their emphasis has been upon the legislature as the body most sensitive to conflicting constituency needs, and most likely not to overdo in attempting to respond to those needs. It is a viewpoint that favors less decisiveness and more debate, less dominance by leaders and more participation by the many. To the claim that a government finely tuned to the popular will is sure to do too little, they reply that if the people choose less, the people ought to have less. The zealousness of the few, not the inertia of the many, poses for them the greater threat to the general good. The public, they assert, that very bedrock of democracy, is surely more deserving of trust than elites are willing to concede. The public, they might add, although far from perfect, does have qualities "which justify a certain portion of esteem and confidence," in Madison's phrase. More important, as Madison pointed out, "Republican government presupposes the existence of these qualities in a higher degree than any other form."[19] If the people tend to be ill informed, then educate them. If the people tend to be too parochial in their priorities, then lead them by exhortation and example to their own good sense of what is best for the republic.

Although both viewpoints have been much in evidence throughout New York's history, the elitist position has tended to gain the upper hand in the modern era. This is apparent in the exceptional powers granted to the governor, in the expanded reliance upon public authorities, in the dominant role of the leaders in both the Assembly and the Senate, and in the denial of standing in court to citizen-taxpayers. The question that must now be faced is not whether the elitist view is wrong and the viewpoint emphasizing popular participation is right. The question is whether, as New York's political institutions now function, the pendulum has swung too far in favor of one point of view, and if it has, whether the time has come to swing it back, not totally, but partially.

Eighth and last, galvanizing the citizens into taking on a wholesale reexamination of their Constitution will not be easy. Those with a vested interest in the status quo are sure to labor to subvert the process. The public for its part is usually inclined to sleep until catastrophe is pounding at the door. Then, too, their natural inertia is now reinforced by old political habits. So many have tolerated so much from so few for so long. If the citizenry should become aroused, however – if ever they become convinced that their interests are now badly served by a political and bureaucratic structure brazenly at odds with old American ideals – they can always reassert their right to re-fashion that document that specifies the rules by which they shall be governed. In such an enterprise they cannot hope to make the New York system a perfect replica of Daniel Webster's nineteenth-century paradigm: "The people's government, made for the people, made by the people, and answerable to the people."[20] They might however fashion a better approximation.

In January of 1794, Thomas Jefferson went home to Monticello, turning his back on politics forever, or so he thought. A Virginia plant-er's life was what he craved and what he reveled in. As the din of politics in the new republic became more distant, muted by the rhythm of the seasons and the farmer's instinct for the soil, he mused that Montaigne had a point: Ignorance was the softest pillow on which a man could rest his head. For all its insularity, Monticello did not keep entirely from his thoughts the injustices wrought by the powerful few on the unsuspecting many. "I am still warm when I think of these scoundrels," he confessed, but hastened to add that he thought of them as little as possible, "preferring infinitely to contemplate the tranquil growth of my lucerne and potatoes."[21] New Yorkers of today are not unlike Thomas Jefferson of Monticello, preferring to contemplate the immediate problems and gratifications of their own lives rather than agonizing over the activities of governments and bureaucracies so far removed from potatoes and lucerne, from bagels and baseball. This book for them is an exercise in discomfort. Its goal has been, in Jeffer-son's phrasing, to ring a firebell in the night. Whether such a call to action, however clamorous, will divert them from their daily lives to larger issues such as these is far from clear. The motto of their state, however, is still Excelsior.

APPENDIX A

The construction of New York fiscal data

A.1. Understanding New York State accounts

An understanding of how the state's books are kept is central to understanding the expenditure and indebtedness data published annually by the comptroller. That topic has two drawbacks. It is desperately complex, and for most, desperately dull. The following makes no pretense to solving the second problem, but does try to shed some light on the first.

A.1.a. Some preliminary concepts

The legal entity

The story begins in a harmless enough way. The starting point – really an aside to the lawyers – is to note that the state is a legal entity quite independent of the bureaucrats and elected politicians who act as its agents. It can own property, sue and be sued, assess and collect taxes, and make contracts. As a legal entity, the state collects and disburses dollars that run to billions. The devices that it uses for this rather obvious governmental function are what confound understanding and, when understood even partially, stagger the imagination.

Revenues

The procedures used by the state to collect its funds are fairly straightforward. As the layman would expect, the bulk of these are raised by taxes, mainly personal income taxes and consumption and use taxes (see Table A.1). The two combined yield about three-quarters of total revenues in any one year, the rest coming from general business taxes and Miscellaneous Revenues. (Again, consult Table A.1 for a more detailed list of the taxes involved.) The problem – and it is monumental – is to track down where these dollars go.

The first step is to clarify a few elementary accounting concepts. The second is to use these concepts to explain the nature of a fund. The

353

Table A.1. *New York State taxes and miscellaneous revenues, 1977 (dollars)*

	Fiscal year ending		Change
	March 31, 1977	March 31, 1976	
Personal income tax[a]	4,526,975,197	4,012,807,841	+ 514,167,356
General business taxes:			
Corporation and utilities taxes	447,507,593	392,809,912	+ 54,697,681
Corporation franchise tax, article 9A[b]	1,042,508,473	877,296,050	+ 165,212,423
Unincorporated business tax	69,035,881	64,699,600	+ 4,336,281
Bank tax[c]	177,945,562	190,866,352	− 12,920,790
Insurance tax	170,952,045	173,310,090	− 2,358,045
Total general business taxes	1,907,949,554	1,698,982,004	+ 208,967,550
Consumption and use taxes:			
Sales and use tax[c]	2,218,161,977	2,148,915,367	+ 69,246,610
Motor vehicle tax	255,496,245	259,530,779	− 4,034,534
Motor fuel tax[d]	491,572,352	461,026,148	+ 30,546,204
Alcoholic beverage tax	150,234,186	153,855,731	− 3,621,545
Alcoholic beverage control licenses	36,413,287	33,111,518	+ 3,301,769
Cigarette tax	334,172,685	337,466,124	− 3,293,439
Highway use tax	40,780,736	39,449,618	+ 1,331,118
Total consumption and use taxes	3,526,831,468	3,433,355,285	+ 93,476,183
Other taxes:			
Estate and gift taxes	199,273,611	147,567,788	+ 51,705,823
Pari-mutuel tax	172,298,266	180,298,702	− 8,000,436
Real estate transfer tax	8,590,662	6,892,872	+ 1,697,790
Racing and boxing exhibitions taxes	1,225,151	1,082,714	+ 142,437
Total other taxes	381,387,690	335,842,076	+ 45,545,614

Total taxes	10,343,143,909	9,480,987,206	+ 862,156,703
Miscellaneous Revenues:			
Revenues of general departments	83,159,468	79,444,296	+ 3,715,172
Sundry general revenues	634,808	709,034	− 74,226
Refunds and reimbursements^e	43,325,903	47,246,639	− 3,920,736
Federal grants and reimbursements	55,449,896	59,732,885	− 3,282,989
Lottery^f	90,763,928	27,418,430	+ 63,345,498
Land, buildings, and property sold	838,324	1,696,890	− 858,566
Abandoned property receipts^g	125,938,930	43,435,779	+ 82,503,151
Income from investments and bank deposits	24,729,081	26,634,561	− 1,905,480
Transfers from other funds^h	33,373,082	17,109,738	+ 15,263,344
Total Miscellaneous Revenues	458,213,420	303,428,252	+ 154,785,168
Federal revenue sharing^i	293,697,780	234,913,238	+ 58,784,542
Total taxes, Miscellaneous Revenues, and Federal Revenue Sharing	11,095,055,109	10,019,328,696	+ 1,075,726,413

---

[a] Reported personal income tax revenues for 1977 reflect approximately $230 million of 1976 personal income tax refunds, which were deferred to the 1977–78 fiscal year. In 1976, $64 million of net collections resulted because the Personal Income Tax Refund Reserve Account was reduced to $1 million on March 31, 1976, compared with $65 million on March 31, 1975.

[b] Reported corporation franchise tax revenues for 1977 were $5.7 million less than net collections because the Corporation Franchise Tax Refund Account was established at $5.8 million on March 31, 1977, compared with $0.1 million at March 31, 1976. A major tax rate increase affecting corporation franchise taxes was passed by the legislature during fiscal year 1975–76, but because of the late enactment of this legislation, the impact of the rate increase was reflected the first time in 1977 revenues.

[c] During the Special Legislative Session held in December 1975 a tax rate increase affecting bank taxes was passed. In addition, legislation was passed requiring monthly rather than quarterly remittance of sales tax levies from vendors with quarterly tax collections of $300,000 or more.

Notes to Table A.1. (cont.)

a Does not include $4.5 million (1977 and 1976) of additional motor fuel tax revenue deposited in the Outdoor Recreation Development Account; also does not include $16,638,691 (1977) and $14,872,479 (1976) additional motor fuel tax revenue deposited in the Emergency Highway Reconditioning and Preservation Fund. These taxes are deposited pursuant to Chapter 89 Laws of 1965 and Chapter 648 Laws of 1972, respectively.

e For 1976–77, includes $20.0 million repayment of loan from the City of Buffalo, $1.7 million in repayments from counties of loans for care of children with multiple handicaps and $0.9 million from the Housing Finance Agency pursuant to recovery agreements. For 1975–76, includes $23.2 million interest repayment from New York City and $5 million from the Metropolitan Transportation Authority.

f Lottery sales that had been suspended in October 1975 were resumed in August 1976 with the institution of a new "instant game" format.

g Effective December 31, 1975, the dormancy period for abandoned property held by stockbrokers and dealers was reduced from five to three years.

h During fiscal year 1976–77 legislation was enacted providing for several transfers from other funds to the General Fund:

	In millions
Outdoor Recreational Development Account	$15.0
State Housing Debt Fund	8.0
Housing Development Fund	2.5
Purchase of Services Account	$1.0
Youth Facilities Development Fund	0.8

Additional transfers were also made from the Unemployment Insurance Interest and Penalty Fund ($3.5 million), and the Community Mental Health and Mental Retardation Facilities Development and Revolving Fund ($0.3 million). During 1975–76, transfers from other funds included $10.1 million of interest income transferred from the New York State Property and Liability Insurance Security Fund.

i For 1976–77, includes $48.6 million in special Federal Revenue Sharing pursuant to Title 2 of the Public Works Employment Act.

Source: New York [State], Office of the Comptroller, *Preliminary Annual Report*, 1977, p. 5.

356

third will be to analyze the structure of New York funds – there are over 1,000 – and to explain how these are linked to that key expenditure document of the state: the Executive Budget. Readers familiar with accounting should of course ignore the next subsection and proceed directly to Section A.1.b.

A few basic accounting concepts

A fund, as a first approximation, may be thought of as a pot of money. Over any time period (say, a year), receipts flow in and expenditures flow out: concepts with which the layman is only too familiar. At any point in time (say, March 31, 1979), the net value of a fund can be evaluated by using a balance sheet. The value of what it owns (assets) minus the value of what it owes (liabilities) is equal to its net value or net worth. What may not be intuitively obvious are the items that count as assets and liabilities, and how those items are evaluated.

An asset is anything that has a marketable value. It may be a physical object such as a building, a paper asset such as a bond, or a legal right such as access to water. If it is owned by the state and could be sold for a price, it is an asset of the state, whether or not actual sale is ever contemplated. Difficulties arise in attempting to value such items, precisely because they often are not sold. Cash, of course, presents no problem. The relevant value is printed on the bill. Bonds, on the other hand, may be sold for amounts quite different from the numbers printed on them. (Their market value fluctuates as interest rates fluctuate.) The worth of a building must be estimated, using either initial cost or replacement cost as a guideline. The guideline is then modified to allow for deterioration (if any). Always the theoretical touchstone for evaluation is the same: For how much could this asset be sold? If the answer is zero, then the object in question has ceased to be an asset of the state.

Liabilities are promises to pay at some point in the future. These may be as formal as a bond (promising to repay the lender, say, $1,000 in five years plus interest) or as informal as the normal credit extension that accompanies routine purchases by any large organization (as when the state promises to pay within 30 days for writing paper delivered to it). The first will be listed under "Bonds and Notes," the second under "Accounts Payable." Notice incidentally that what is a liability to the borrower is an asset to the lender. In the example involving writing paper, if you were the supplier of this paper to the state, you would enter the amount owed by the state under "Accounts Receivable" (one of your asset categories).

Notice finally that a private individual cannot long survive if the value of all liabilities exceeds the value of all assets. Bills come due that cannot be paid, no prudent lender will supply more funds, and bankruptcy must be declared. Suppose however that the main lender is the state, the recipient of these borrowed funds is a public authority, and that the state never asks for repayment, or more cautiously, for more repayment of borrowed funds than the public authority can easily pay. In this situation, bankruptcy may be an accounting fact – liabilities exceeding assets – but not a legal inevitability. To this curious phenomenon the discussion will return in Section A.1.d.

A.1.b. *The mysterious funds of New York State*

Basic structure

The fund is the basic unit of analysis for New York State accounts. A fund might be thought of as a large pot containing cash, investments, IOU's (accounts receivable) from other funds, and bills (accounts payable) to other funds. Sometimes money is thrown into the pot, as when mental patients' fees are collected.[1] At other times, money is drawn out to pay a bill, or to buy a new hospital, or to give to a poor person. A bond may be taken out and sold and the money thrown back into the pot.

Number

New York State has more than 1,000 separate funds, and the question arises: Why so many? The answer clearly is not to make the comptroller's report more intelligible.

Legal requirements, convenience in keeping track of expenditures, or the desire to shift control may lead to the creation of a new fund rather than reliance upon an old one. When a bond is issued, for example, the law usually requires that a special fund be established to pay off the principal and interest on that particular bond. Thus sinking funds are used to accumulate the necessary assets to pay off a term bond when it comes due. If the bond is instead a serial bond (that is, it calls for the retirement of some of the principal throughout the life of the bond), a bond fund will be established to receive taxes or other revenues, including transfers from other funds. Almost all federal aid is received in so-called Special Revenue Funds, one for each program or purpose, thereby creating the appearance that all dollars received are spent only for the designated purposes.[2] (Highway aid can be spent only for highways, and so on.)

General classification: inside the Treasury and
outside the Treasury

The difficulty of the task ahead cannot be overstated. The twists and
turns of New York State bookkeeping can confound even the expert
accountant. The journey is therefore sure to be perilous for the layman.
What follows is therefore an attempt – really several successive
attempts – to lay bare the skeletal structure of New York funds.

The starting point is with a curious phrase: "in the Treasury."[3] All of
the more than 1,000 state funds are divided into two categories. Those
"in the Treasury" are not so designated because they share the same
common vault in some impregnable Albany building. That phrase
refers instead to the question of control: funds in the Treasury are
jointly controlled by the State Comptroller and the Commissioner of
Taxation and Finance. It therefore comes as no surprise that all other
funds (or funds outside the Treasury) are controlled by someone else.
These latter funds, about 900 in all, are often designated by the title
"Sole Custody Funds," that phrase signaling the fact that one person is
in charge. In the cumbersome phrasing of the Comptroller, "Each is
singularly administered by the applicable State departmental officials
outside the Treasury."[4]

The phrase "sole custody" in conjunction with the earlier phrase
"outside the Treasury" suggests a second obvious division. Funds inside the Treasury – and under the control of the two key financial
officers of the state – will be used for the daily operations of the state
government. Those outside the Treasury will not be so used, but will
instead serve some special function, depending upon which state official controls them. Though this is all perfectly logical, it is not quite
accurate. The manner in which the state keeps its books invariably
blurs such obvious distinctions. In this instance, some funds outside
the Treasury are used as part of the state's regular daily operations, and
some funds in the Treasury are not. To the confusions lurking in this
mixture the discussion will return in Section A.1.c.

As a prelude to that discussion, the next requirement is some analysis of the kinds of funds held inside the Treasury and outside the
Treasury. These are therefore the topics of the following subsections.

Funds inside the Treasury: the General Fund
and others

The first point to note is that these funds are composed of the General
Fund and about 175 others. The second point is that the 175 pale in

comparison with the importance of the one. Third, the General Fund used to be called "the General Fund and Related Accounts," in which the word "accounts" referred to other funds. (Which other funds will be discussed shortly.)

The General Fund. This is the key fiscal entity of the state. It is the topic of the Executive Budget, and the heart of the state's fiscal operations. It is "general" in contrast to all other funds, which are specific as to source of money, use of money, or both. At present, this one General Fund is merely the combined activity of three other funds:

1. The State Purposes Fund, designed to finance the operations of the state government, its agencies, and its departments (including the paying of debt dervice)
2. The Local Assistance Fund, designed to finance aid to localities in the state
3. The Capital Construction Fund, designed to finance the construction (or reconstruction) of various capital facilities of the state

The third of these handles long-term projects, such as highways, parkways, hospitals, schools, and prisons.[5] The first two finance daily operations, with the division between them determined by whether the expenditure in question is for the operation of the state government or for aid to localities within the state. The State Purposes Fund therefore pays for the activities of the three branches of state government: executive, legislative, and judicial. The Local Assistance Fund may channel state funds to localities in the form of state–local revenue sharing and other grants, or allocate funds for specific purposes, such as education, social services, highways, or mental health.

It was not always so. Given that this study covers the period since 1945, a few words of explanation are required concerning how the General Fund evolved into its present form.

In 1946 the General Fund was split into two of the three funds just noted: the State Purposes Fund and the Local Assistance Fund. The Capital Construction Fund was nowhere to be found, at least not under that title. What was to be found was the Postwar Reconstruction Fund, established in 1944,[6] which was merely the Capital Construction Fund with a different name. (The name was changed to the present one in 1949.) It was maintained as a separate entity until fiscal 1961, when it was merged with the other two. At that time the comptroller devised the phrase "General Fund and Related Accounts" to signal the inclusion in the General Fund of what had previously been separate from it.

This is only part of the evolution story. The rest concerns other "related accounts" – really other funds – that for part of the postwar era were separate from the General Fund, but that must be added to it to arrive at the expenditure totals that constitute the Executive Budget. There are three obvious funds and one curiosity:

1. The War Bonus Fund
2. The War Bonus and Mental Health Bond Account
3. The Highway Account
4. The Teachers' Salary Emergency Increase Fund

All require a word of explanation.

The *War Bonus Fund,* in existence from 1947 to 1958, collected the receipts of bond sales and distributed bonuses to returning veterans.[7] The bonuses were classified as a State Purposes expenditure.

The *War Bonus and Mental Health Bond Account,* in existence from 1947 to 1968, had its name changed several times,[8] but the function remained the same: to collect the taxes specifically levied to pay off the War Bonus Bonds. In this example, the reader confronts several New York State curiosities. The first is the puzzling split of functions between two funds. One sold bonds and paid the bonuses; the other collected revenues and paid off the bonds. The second curiosity is that the taxes passed to raise the money[9] proved to be far too generous. The dollars fairly cascaded in, the bonds were quickly retired, and the problem was then whether to repeal the taxes or to rechannel the revenues raised by them. The taxes had been announced in conjunction with the bonus and the associated bonds, and repeal was therefore the straightforward solution. The legislators thought otherwise. The taxes were preserved and the excess funds transferred to the Capital Construction Fund. In 1955 the activities of the fund were expanded to include financing Mental Health Construction Bonds. This explains the fund's curious name, which is, of course, no more (and no less) absurd than is the linkage of war bonus financing to mental hospital construction. One indication of how the end results diverged from initial intentions can be found in the aggregate flow of dollars. Between 1948 and 1968, a total of $2,050 million in revenues were received. Of this sum, War Bonus debt service payments took only $368 million. The remaining $1,682 million were distributed to the Capital Construction Fund ($998 million), the Local Assistance Fund ($546 million), and the State Purposes Fund ($13 million), with $128 million used for debt service payments on Mental Health debt.[10]

In short, in the two decades following the authorization of tax increases to pay for war bonuses, only 18 percent of the money raised was actually used for that purpose. In 1968 this account was merged with the General Fund, which makes it impossible to identify how much was raised after that year by war bonus taxes.

The *Highway Account,* in existence from 1959 to 1968, received certain tax revenues (notably the Motor Fuel Tax) and paid off certain highway bonds. Any excess funds could be transferred back to the Capital Construction Fund or to the General Fund. This account was also merged with the General Fund in 1968.

The *Teachers' Salary Emergency Increase Fund* existed only briefly between 1947 and 1950. Created in 1947 to effect a sharp increase in teachers' salaries,[11] it received its revenues from the Local Assistance Fund and transferred excesses back to that fund. In effect, it was merely a special subfund of the Local Assistance Fund, and as such, must be included in any totals for General Fund expenditure for this period. It is the only such subfund to be created since World War II.

To review: All New York State funds are either inside the Treasury or outside the Treasury; the funds inside the Treasury consist of one very large one – the General Fund – and about 175 others; the General Fund is now comprised of three parts: the State Purposes Fund, the Local Assistance Fund, and the Capital Construction Fund; and finally, the General Fund evolved into its present form by merging with the State Purposes Fund and the Local Assistance Fund various other funds directly involved with the financing of state activity – most notably, the Capital Construction Fund in 1961, and less notably, both the Highway Account and the War Bonus and Mental Health Bond Account in 1968.

Funds inside the Treasury other than the General Fund. But what of those 175 funds other than the General Fund that function inside the Treasury? These may be classified into seven broad categories:

1. Bond Funds
2. Debt Service Funds
3. Special Revenue Funds
4. Enterprise Funds
5. Intragovernmental Service Funds
6. Trust and Agency Funds
7. Other Custodial Funds

All but the seventh are part of the state government's regular operating funds. Again, a word of explanation is required about each.

Bond Funds: As the name suggests, these receive the proceeds of the sale of bonds and pass the dollars along to the General Fund (usually to the Capital Construction Fund). Given the constitutional requirement that the state borrow only for a specified purpose, each new borrowing (and newly specified purpose) tends to make for an associated new Bond Fund. The War Bonus Fund discussed previously is an example of such a fund.

Debt Service Funds: Again the name is suggestive. Outstanding debt must be serviced; that is, principal and interest payments coming due must be met. Each bond issue normally has its own Debt Service

Fund, and these funds usually receive revenues designated for that purpose. For example, fees received from users of state park and recreation facilities are funneled through such a fund to pay off the debt service on Park and Recreation Land Acquisition Bonds. The War Bonus and Mental Health Bond Account, as noted previously, was also a Debt Service Fund.

Special Revenue Funds: The largest number of Treasury funds fall into this category. Just as Bond Funds receive the proceeds of bond sales, so Special Revenue Funds receive other dollar inflows restricted as to use by law or by administrative regulations – mainly user fees (such as fishing licenses or State University tuition), which are earmarked for specific types of expenditures, and federal funds en route to local governments to support state-administered federal programs.

Enterprise Funds: The state occasionally operates the equivalent of a business, usually a self-supporting venture that finances the services it renders by charging its users. For example, hospitals and nursing homes must be inspected. They pay a fee for that service (inspection, supervision, and auditing) to an Enterprise Fund, which sets its inspection charges at levels designed to recover the cost of rendering these services. One special feature of such funds, therefore, is that their associated accounting makes it possible to show whether they are operated at a profit or a loss, that is, whether user charges do or do not recover the full cost of providing that service.

Intragovernmental Service Funds: These funds are similar to Enterprise Funds, with one notable exception. The prefix "intra" (meaning "between") is the key. The state is also in the business of selling services to itself, with fees designed to recover the cost of such services. One reason for this bookkeeping curiosity is to facilitate cost accounting analysis of such services. An example is the World Trade Center Rent Account Fund, which, as the name suggests, collects rental payments from the government agencies that have office space in the World Trade Center in New York City.

Trust and Agency Funds: These handle escrow-type transactions directly related to the activities of the state. That is, a legally binding agreement has been established whereby certain funds have been put in the care of a third party – in this case, the state – by individuals, private organizations, or other governmental agencies. Among the largest are the Social Security Contributions Fund and the Federal Withholding Tax Fund, both of which hold dollar inflows only temporarily before transferring them to the relevant federal agency.

Other Custodial Funds: All Trust and Agency Funds are clearly custodial funds in the sense that the state has custody of them. The puzzle is why a separate category "other" is required. The answer turns upon whether the funds in question should be considered as governmental operating funds and, as such, should have their receipts and expenditures incorporated into the consolidated financial statements of the state. It is a fine distinction that escapes any but the informed inner circle. Funds collected through federal withholding taxes are regarded as arising from transactions "directly related to the activities of the state" and, as just noted, are therefore classified under Trust and Agency Funds. The state's Common Retirement Fund is not so regarded, but is clearly involved with escrow-type transactions. As such, it is classified under Other Custodial Funds. Perhaps the simplest way to distinguish between the two types of custodial funds is this: Ask whether the transfer of its custody to some third party totally separate from the state would in any way affect state fiscal activity. If the Common Retirement Fund, for example, were managed by someone else, the effect would be negligible. Receipts flow in, payments to retirees are made, and surplus funds are invested, but all of these flows at no time impinge upon regular state fiscal activity. It is therefore not a Trust and Agency Fund (which does impinge on such activity), but rather an Other Custodial Fund (which does not).

To review, the funds inside the Treasury are composed of the General Fund and about 175 lesser funds. The General Fund, as its name suggests, is not specific as to source of money or use of money. All of the other 175 are.

Were these 175 to be assembled in a single location in the form of 175 pots, and the receipts and expenditures of those pots scrutinized for a number of months, several patterns would emerge. All collect money and make payments. Some collect the proceeds of bond sales (Bond Funds), whereas a far larger number collect earmarked revenues (Special Revenue Funds). Some collect fees for services rendered, either from other government agencies (Intragovernmental Service Funds) – a large set of small funds – or from other users (Enterprise Funds) – a small set of small funds. One set collects revenues from various sources to service the debt of the state (Debt Service Funds), a category roughly as numerous as the different number of bonds outstanding at any point. Finally, one set collects and holds money in trust, with the dollar flows arising either out of regular state activities (Trust and Agency Funds) or out of other kinds of activities (Other Custodial Funds).

There is a second, and ultimately more important, way of categorizing these funds by the ebb and flow of dollars that should and should not be counted when formulating the budget of the state. To these issues, the discussion will return in Section A.1.c.

Funds outside the Treasury

As noted previously, the distinction between "inside" and "outside" the Treasury is based exclusively upon control. Those funds inside the Treasury are jointly controlled by two state officials (the Comptroller and the Commissioner of Taxation and Finance). All funds outside the Treasury are controlled by a single individual (sometimes by *one* of the two state officials just noted); hence the name "Sole Custody Funds." Or as the State Comptroller prefers to put it, "Each is singularly administered by the applicable state departmental officials outside the state Treasury"[12] – normally the head of the agency that maintains the fund. Numbering in excess of 900, these funds can be divided into four major categories:

1. Revenue Funds
2. Service Funds
3. Quasi-State Agency Funds
4. Trust and Agency Funds

Revenue Funds: These are conduits for money destined for the state Treasury, usually the General Fund. In other words, the state has established one category of funds outside the Treasury whose main function is to receive dollars and shunt them to another fund inside the Treasury. Examples include the motorvehicle license and registration revenues collected by the Commissioner's Fee Fund (by the Department of Motor Vehicles) and stock transfer taxes collected by the Stock Transfer Tax Fund (administered by the Commissioner of Taxation and Finance), which are subsequently shunted via the General Fund to New York City for the support of local government activities.

Service Funds: These funds perform a function analogous to that of Intragovernmental Service Funds (which are inside the Treasury). The state is basically in the business of selling services to itself, in this instance, primarily the services of "service centers" (such as commissaries and community stores), which are operated on a self-sufficient, nonprofit basis. The purchasers are primarily state employees or wards of the state (prison inmates or mental patients). The commissaries, for example, sell personal care items to inmates of state prisons.[13]

Quasi-State Agency Funds: This is a small collection of relatively unimportant funds that defies any simple effort to categorize its members. The Comptroller's description is hardly helpful. These funds, he notes, "are either membership corporations whose operations are associated with a State agency, or agencies established by the State primarily for the purpose of assisting the State to carry out its function."[14] Most of the dollar flows are concerned with financing campus facilities such as bookstores and food services.[15] Most of the remaining money appears to be associated in some way with research activity: for example, Environmental Conservation Research, Inc., Health Research, Inc., Welfare Research, Inc., Research Foundation of the State University of New York, and the somewhat esoteric Agriculture and New York State Horse Breeding Development Fund.[16]

Trust and Agency Funds: Immediately the reader should be struck by a curiosity. The funds about to be discussed clearly involve the state in some fiduciary capacity. The comparable set of funds inside the Treasury was divided between those arising out of regular state fiscal operations (called by the same name: Trust and Agency Funds) and those in no way connected with those operations (Other Custodial Funds). Here both kinds are lumped into a single category with a name identical to one of the sets of funds inside the Treasury. For maximizing confusion, it would be difficult to improve upon these designated categories.

Trust and Agency Funds outside the Treasury consist of assets received and held by a single state official in some fiduciary capacity (trustee, agent, or custodian). The resulting collection is a mixed bag that ranges all the way from the Teachers' Retirement System Fund (which is huge and totally divorced from the state's fiscal operations) to the Abandoned Property Fund (which is not similarly divorced). The first, as its name suggests, administers the revenues, expenditures, and investments associated with a retirement fund. Its supervision could be transferred to (say) the doorman at the Waldorf and not affect the flow of dollars to and from the state. (Presumably the investment of surplus funds might be somewhat less prudent, but although of concern to retiring teachers, the deterioration of receipts would not affect the flow of funds into state coffers.) The Abandoned Property Fund, on the other hand, collects the proceeds from abandoned property and makes payments to claimants "who present satisfactory proof of their right to the abandoned property."[17] Claims, however, fall far short of receipts, with the residual – and a healthy sum it is – annually transferred to the General Fund.[18]

To review, the state has more than 900 Sole Custody Funds, designated as "outside the Treasury" because they are in the custody of a single official. Some of these are clearly split off from regular state operations, and service the receipts and expenditures associated with a specific function. Most, if not all, of the Service Funds fall in this category. One set of funds, Revenue Funds, is designed to collect money and funnel it into other funds inside the Treasury. One small set of relatively unimportant funds defies easy categorization: Quasi-State Agency Funds. One large set that includes some very important funds is also something of a hodgepodge, but it is a fiduciary hodgepodge called Trust and Agency Funds. In a narrow and unhelpful sense, these funds outside the Treasury are distinguished from comparable funds inside the Treasury on the basis of who controls them. The distinction with respect to whether or not they are appropriately linked to regular state activities – and therefore appropriately incorporated into the regular fiscal statements of the state – is one of several thorny topics for the next section.

A.1.c. From fund structure to state accounts

The bottom line for state budgeting is either the General Fund or All Operating Funds. The puzzle is how to get there from a structure that includes better than 1,000 separate funds: a fiscal jungle sure to repel all but the most determined explorer.

Suppose that your task were to take charge of New York State books, and establish total state spending for the previous year. The layman expects the state to be run much as an individual household is run. Money flows in and out, and the task of establishing expenditures should be as simple as monitoring outflows. This expectation collides with the reality of the 1,000 funds. Money does not flow in and out of a single pot. There are many pots, some of which are relatively self-sufficient, whereas others have a lot of dollars flowing among them. A second approach, it seems, is required.

This begins by asking what the basic functions of state government are. Partly they are to provide the normal services of any state government: the services associated with the running of the executive, the legislature, and the judiciary. Let us funnel all of the associated expenditures through a single fund appropriately labeled "State Purposes Fund." The other major function of the government of New York is to channel certain dollars – some from its own coffers and some from the federal government – to various localities to help them provide certain basic services such as education and welfare relief. Let us pass such dollars through a single fund with the similarly unsurprising title "Local Assistance Fund." Finally, it might be useful to split off long-run projects from the day-to-day flow of dollars. Some projects, such as highways, buildings, or bridges, take large sums of money, require some time to build, and once constructed, provide benefits to their users for many years. This is in sharp contrast to the dollars used to pay a judge, or to supplement the income of a disabled mother. Let us funnel all of the dollars required for capital construction projects through a third fund: the Capital Construction Fund. The net result is the three funds that in turn constitute the General Fund.

New York State operates under an executive budget system; that is, the chief executive prepares the document that details revenues and expenditures for the upcoming year (the Executive Budget), and the legislature reacts to those proposals. This detailing is nothing more than the net flows into, and out of, the three funds that comprise the General Fund. If that is all there is to state bookkeeping, wherein lies complexity and lurking confusion?

Even if New York had only the three funds noted, the task of disentangling what goes where would not be easy. Part of the reason is that whereas two funds do not have any flows between them – the State Purposes Fund and the Local Assistance Fund – these two do have a multitude of transactions with the third: the Capital Construction Fund. This complicates the task of detailing expenditures by purpose. How much did the state spend last year on, say, health and related activities? Some dollars would be funneled through the Local Assistance Fund in the form of Medicaid payments. Others would be diverted to such capital projects as the construction of mental health facilities. The question can therefore be answered only by scouring all three acounts for health-related spending and combining the results into a single total. That search, however, is made difficult by the lack of a single specific purpose associated with many of the headings used, and by the factor noted previously: the flow of dollars between funds.

This is, however, merely the edge of the underbrush. Many of the tangles and thickets are the result of the state's keeping not just 3 accounts, but well over 1,000. Each bond issue, for example, tends to have a separate fund to receive its proceeds when sold (a Bond Fund) and another to pay off its principal and interest when due (a Debt Service Fund). Revenues as they are received may flow initially into funds inside the Treasury (a Bond Fund or a Special Revenue Fund) or into funds outside the Treasury (a Revenue Fund). Any citizen determined to reconcile fund activity with, say, reported state spending is therefore in for a nasty time. Few entertain such aspirations. The more common desire is to know how much is spent for different state and local services in any given year. The critical issue might therefore be posed in slightly absurd terms. Consider all of the dollars that are actually spent by the state in any given year for any purpose appropriately called state spending. Think of these dollars as suddenly turning red to distinguish them from other money. The issue then reduces to this: Are all of the dollars flowing through the General Fund red and are there any red dollars that do not go through the General Fund? If the answer is yes to the first and no to the second, then General Fund spending, as reported by the State Comptroller, is what it appears to be: total state spending in a given year.

In fact, it is no such thing. Notice the startling implications if it is not. What the governor proposes, and what the legislature reacts to, are the expenditures – and only the expenditures – included in the Executive Budget. But the Executive Budget is confined to the activities of the General Fund. It therefore follows that whatever spending is not funneled through the General Fund is also not subject to legislative review. The incompleteness of the General Fund is therefore not just a bookkeeping problem. It raises the prospect of a breakdown in one of the fundamental principles of American democracy: legislative control over money matters.

To return to our flow of red dollars: What percentage pass through the General Fund? The comptroller's answer, at least at first glance, is less than crystal clear. "The General Fund contains only the expenditures which are financed from tax revenues, from miscellaneous revenues not earmarked for specific purposes, and from some of the bond and note proceeds."[19] The implication is that the same fund fails to include expenditures financed by earmarked revenues, or by some other bond and note proceeds.[20] Or as the Comptroller chose to put it: "These totals of receipts and expenditures represent only part of the State's financial operations. They do not reflect operations of the State accomplished through other funds. State activities – similar to those financed by the General Fund – are also financed by earmarked revenues, Federal funds, special bond funds, and agencies and authorities with power to issue bonds."[21]

The "earmarked revenues" problem is particularly crucial. Recall that the General Fund is just that: a fund detailing the activities of general (not specific) revenues. This means that *any* expenditure financed by an earmarked revenue will not pass through the General Fund, although the expenditure itself may be clearly part of the regular activities of the state. Examples are legion: fees from hunting licenses earmarked for the Conservation Fund; fees from users of state parks earmarked for the debt service charges on park and recreation land acquisition bonds; fees from college tuitions earmarked for debt service associated with State University construction projects; mental patient fees earmarked for debt service associated with the construction of mental hygiene facilities. Some of these revenues actually were once part of General Fund receipts before being earmarked and split off. All of the associated expenditures concern General Fund types of activities; that is, they all arise out of transactions conducted in direct support of regular state activities.

But precisely what is missing, and how can these omissions be remedied? The answer to both questions begins with the procedures used by the comptroller to construct a second and more comprehensive category: "All Operating Funds."[22] Let us start with the General Fund, and add to it any expenditure made from *any* fund inside the Treasury that did not at some point pass through the General Fund. Recall that there are potentially seven categories of funds involved: Bond Funds, Debt Service Funds, Special Revenue Funds, Enterprise Funds, Intragovernmental Service Funds, Trust and Agency Funds, and Other Custodial Funds. One category must immediately be dropped. All of the fiscal activity of Other Custodial Funds is the result of a strict fiduciary relationship that prevents these funds from being used for the regular operating needs of the state government. This reduces the relevant set to six. Much or all of the fiscal activity of some of these is invariably linked to the General Fund, particularly Bond Funds that pass along their receipts from bond sales, and Debt Service Funds that get from the General Fund the dollars needed to make principal and interest payments when due. As such, these dollar flows will be noted in General Fund activity. The most suspect category is Special Revenue Funds, precisely because the word "special" signals the fact that these funds, as noted previously, receive dollar inflows restricted as to use by law or by administrative regulations, mainly user fees earmarked for specific kinds of spending and federal funds en route to local governments. And it is earmarked revenues – because they are "specific" – that escape passage through the fund controlling only "general" revenues (the General Fund).

This procedure would add to General Fund spending all other relevant state spending by funds inside the Treasury, but what of omitted and relevant spending elsewhere? One gargantuan category *never* included in All Operating Funds is spending by statewide public authorities. The other obvious type of spending added in by the comptroller to get the totals for All Operating Funds comes from regular state funds outside the Treasury.

Again recall the categories: Revenue Funds, Service Funds, Quasi-State Agency Funds, and Trust and Agency Funds. The first is not a major problem. These funds merely act as conduits to channel receipts into the Treasury, usually to the General Fund directly. If the dollars go through the General Fund, they will be recorded in the Executive Budget. The second and third categories noted are trivial in size. The fourth is the puzzle. This is a mixed set of funds, all with some fiduciary relationship but – and this is the point – that relationship does not in all cases preclude use of those funds for regular state operations.

Two in particular are important – so important that their activities are added in by the Comptroller when he is constructing the totals for All Operating Funds "in order to report the total financial transactions in direct support of State operations."[23] These are the Mental Hygiene Program Funds of the Facilities Development Corporation and the Emergency Highway Reconditioning and Preservation Fund of the New York State Thruway Authority. The first of these collects patient fees that are used to pay for the construction of mental health facilities.[24] The second collects a portion of the motor fuel tax and uses the proceeds to reimburse the New York State Thruway Authority for repairs to state highways.[25] Both therefore receive types of revenue formerly deposited directly to the General Fund. Their inclusion thus assures that receipts reported under All Operating Funds capture all tax revenues of the state.

But surely this explanation is too facile. Something is missing. More precisely, the hundreds of millions that flow through hundreds of Sole Custody Funds (particularly Trust and Agency Funds) are missing. Why? The answer is *not* because they are unrelated to regular state operations. The answer is that the Comptroller does not control them, and lacking control, he is reluctant to include them in All Operating Funds. The two exceptions just noted he does control. The laws establishing these two included the key phrase "audit and warrant of the comptroller," which established that control. The danger at this point stems from a certain mental bludgeoning. The accounts are vast. They number in the hundreds. The subject is, for most, not well calculated to rivet attention to the page. The phrase "All Operating Funds" seems to signal a comprehensive task accomplished: All state expenditures and revenues have been listed in the associated totals. Nothing could be further from the truth. What has been listed are the flows over which the Comptroller has control. What has been omitted are the activities of a hoard of Sole Custody Funds over which he has little control, *and* the activities of a hoard of public authorities over which he has even less control. In a word, All Operating Funds is grievously deficient as a portrait of the total dollars annually flowing through the state, its agencies and departments, and statewide public authorities performing regular governmental services. In the realm of the blind, according to the old adage, the one-eyed man is king. Those who scrutinize state spending as reported under the General Fund or All Operating Funds admittedly have a better grasp of state operations than the uninformed, but their resulting perspective is as notable for what it omits as for what it includes.

A final review may be about as welcome as a final visit to the dentist, but at least in its favor is the promise that the ordeal is almost over.

1. New York State has over 1,000 funds, some of which are "inside the Treasury," and some "outside the Treasury." That distinction merely signals whether or not a fund is under the joint control of the

State Comptroller and the Commissioner of Taxation. As such, it is singularly useless in attempting to construct annual state spending from the activities of specific funds.

2. The linkage of fund activity to state fiscal activity begins with the General Fund, which on close inspection is a summary label for the activities of three funds: the State Purposes Fund, the Local Assistance Fund, and the Capital Construction Fund. The key fiscal document of the state, the Executive Budget, attempts to detail the receipts and expenditures of one and only one fund: the General Fund.

3. This detailing of receipts and expenditures is *not* identical with total state fiscal activity in any one year, in part because it fails to include hundreds of millions in dollars that never once pass through the General Fund. This defect the comptroller attempts to remedy by publishing data for All Operating Funds.

4. Those data for All Operating Funds are not in the least identical with total spending for all state-related activity. What this category details – to put the matter bluntly – is the activity of funds (*a*) involved in state activity and (*b*) under the control of the Comptroller. The incompleteness in All Operating Funds is therefore as pervasive as all those dollar flows over which the comptroller has little control.

5. To construct (say) total spending as reported for All Operating Funds, one must: (*a*) begin with total state spending reported under the General Fund (really the combined spending of three funds); (*b*) add to that total all spending from all funds inside the Treasury that did not pass through the General Fund (except the spending of those special fiduciary funds labeled Other Custodial Funds); and finally (*c*) add the spending activities of two Trust and Agency Funds outside the Treasury: the Mental Hygiene Program Funds and the Emergency Highway Reconditioning and Preservation Fund.

Three different kinds of overviews suggest three different levels of indignation. The first is comparatively mild. The General Fund covers about two-thirds of regular state fiscal activity. Of the remaining one-third, the vast bulk (about 75 percent) is the result of federal aid.[26] Most state-financed expenditures therefore seem to be captured by the General Fund and thus included in the Executive Budget. That document is therefore far less flawed by omissions than one might expect, or so the argument runs. Omissions there clearly are, but as a percentage of state activity, they seem to be comparatively minor. The second level of indignation is more strident. It is based not upon what is included in, or excluded from, the General Fund and the Executive Budget, but rather upon how the books are manipulated to confuse and mislead. These wheelings and dealings are therefore the topic of the next section. The third level of indignation stems from the realization that both the General Fund and All Operating Funds, however well they capture regular state activity, exclude entirely that irregular state activity conducted by public benefit corporations. Most of the related problems have been considered in Chapters 6 and 7. The question how public authority debt is linked to unwise debt escalation is reviewed briefly in Section A.1.e.

A.1.d. *Selected wheelings and dealings*

Introduction

Were a set of bookkeeping practices designed to maximize confusion, it would be difficult to improve upon those contrived for New York State. Part of the problem, as noted to this point, is a structure of multiple funds, with the flow of revenues and expenditures among them defying any simple logic, or any simple taxonomy. Part of the problem is that this structure is subjected to accounting manipulations that are – to use the kindest possible phrase – highly irregular. What follow are merely a few examples chosen to illustrate the kinds of manipulations employed. Perhaps the best warning of the treachery in the waters ahead was given in an unguarded moment by a budget director of Nelson Rockefeller's: "Any budget director who can't make $100 million appear and disappear isn't worth his salt."[27] That is not a joke. It is not an idle boast. As the following description suggests, it is merely an informed assessment of accounting possibilities.

Cash-basis accounting

Nothing better illustrates the politician's propensity to distort accounting in pursuit of political goals than the use – or more correctly, the misuse – of cash-basis accounting in New York State accounts. The alternative is accrual accounting. The difference lies in the point at which assets and liabilities are officially recorded. In cash-basis accounting, the chief concerns are sources and uses of cash, which is only one of many components of wealth. As long as a person or organization becomes wealthier, it should be indifferent to the form in which the wealth arises. In accrual accounting, the chief concern is calculating the assets and liabilities generated or destroyed within each reporting period, usually a year, in order to evaluate the operations for that year and address the question: Are we better or worse off?

This may seem like an innocuous distinction, but it is not. Consider the following example. An individual decides to estimate, as of December 31, whether he has operated at a surplus or a deficit in the previous year. Suppose that he has sold $50,000 worth of merchandise in the past 12 months, of which $5,000 has yet to be paid for. (He therefore has listed as an asset under "accounts receivable" an entry of $5,000, due, say, at the end of next February.) Suppose further that he had added $60,000 to his debts, but that none of that $60,000 must be paid until January. If these constitute all of his transactions for the previous 12 months, has he generated a surplus or a deficit? At first glance, the answer seems to be patently obvious. He gained $50,000 in sales but added $60,000 in liabilities, so he ran a $10,000 deficit. If he uses accrual accounting, that is the correct answer. If he uses cash-basis accounting, the results are changed dramatically. Under receipts, he would include only those sales for which he has received cash ($50,000 − $5,000 = $45,000). Under liabilities, he would include only those debts that have been a drain on cash. Because no debts in our example have yet been paid, the correct entry under liabilities is zero. A cash-basis view of his operations therefore suggests a surplus of $45,000.

Clearly, over an extended period of time these two systems should yield about the same results. Money due will ultimately be received and money owed will ultimately have to be paid. The problem is that when a state uses a cash-basis system, politicians are under pressure to delay payments and accelerate receipts. That is particularly so if the state has a constitutional provision requiring a balanced budget. The end result for New York is a continual juggling of the books that obscures what the real surplus or deficit is in any fiscal year (as opposed to the surplus or deficit indicated by a cash-basis accounting system). The legislature in 1980 passed an act that would have forced the state to abandon its irregular ways, and adopt generally accepted accounting principles (GAAP), including the principle of accrual accounting. The Governor vetoed the bill because it "would have required the executive branch to give the Legislature large amounts of new information in the generally secretive budgeting process."[28]

Balancing an unbalanced budget

The New York State Constitution requires that the Executive Budget be balanced every year. In many years, no such balance is actually achieved, at least not according to the usual norms of accounting procedures.

Part of the gimmickry involves the manipulations discussed in the previous subsection. Cash-basis accounting is combined with efforts to delay cash outlays and accelerate receipts. In fiscal 1976, for example, $25 million in refunds that would normally have been paid by March 31 were paid after that date. In 1977 the amount involved was $230 million. As for instances of accelerating receipts, in fiscal 1976, the state began requiring monthly remittances of the sales tax by those sellers collecting large amounts of this tax. In addition, these sellers must now pay an estimated tax for March by March 20. This money can therefore be counted as received in the current fiscal year (i.e., by March 31). Another instance that is perhaps less obvious concerns a change in the collection procedures of the Abandoned Property Fund. The state is entitled to collect such abandoned property as bank accounts, stock accounts (with stock brokers), and utilities deposits. In fiscal 1977 the collection of stock accounts was increased by reducing the period of abandonment from five years to three years.

A second possibility for spurious balancing of the budget arises because the Executive Budget is limited to receipts and expenditures flowing through the General Fund. Various funds that exist outside the Executive Budget (that is, outside the General Fund) can therefore be built up in fat years of actual surpluses and drawn down in lean years of actual deficits. The total balance of the Refund Reserve Accounts, for example, is called the Undistributed Receipts. This total rose to $166 million in fiscal 1961, and then dropped to $12 million by the end of fiscal 1962. Reflecting similar if more recent manipulations, Undistributed Receipts fell from $231 million on April 1, 1974, to $2 million on April 1, 1976. Examples involving specific funds are also not difficult to find. In fiscal 1973, the Personal Income Tax Refund Reserve Account – usually the largest one – became exceptionally large as the state funneled into it a surplus generated in that year. A recession followed, with the predictable raiding of funds to cover a deficit. In fiscal 1975, $185 million was transferred from this account into the General Fund, and in fiscal 1976, $64 million more.

First instance appropriations

Another illustration of the politician's propensity for suspect accounting practices is the extensive use of "first-instance" appropriations. In the Comptroller's more cautious phrasing, " 'First Instance' appropriation is one of the more confusing elements in our financial structure."[29]

This fiscal procedure is not intrinsically offensive. But then a camouflage net is also not intrinsically offensive. It depends upon how it is used. Advances are made initially ("in the first instance") from state moneys to pay for certain expenditures, with reimbursement for the advance when the revenues that would normally finance those expenditures are received. At first glance, the effect is simply to allow certain kinds of expenditures to be made before associated receipts are received. Or, put somewhat differently, it appears to be a variant of the popular "fly now, pay later" policy of airlines, with the state acting as short-term lender.

This all seems harmless enough. Admittedly the loans are interest free, but if, say, $20 million is advanced in July and repaid in November, the period is short, the transaction is "washed out" of the state's books, and reported receipts and expenditures at fiscal year end (March 31) are totally unaffected. Many of these advances, however, are not short term. Some are destined to remain outstanding for years – a few even to the year 2040! The Comptroller offers as examples[30] (1) advances to public authorities under long-term repayment agreements (with the ominous afterthought that "in some cases, timely repayments have not been made"), (2) advances to finance federal shares of various programs, and (3) advances to "pre-finance" construction projects of the State University (that is, loans are made pending repayment from bond sales, with construction proceeding in the interim).

One resulting defect is that the legislature tends not to scrutinize thoroughly – or as thoroughly as a regular expenditure – advances that amount to loans for an extended period to finance major kinds of expenditures by government departments, agencies, and public authorities. Because the funds will be repaid, the argument seems to be, the lending is hardly worth a second look. The public, for its part, is unlikely to be well informed on matters buried deep in the Comptroller's *Annual Report* under "First Instance Appropriations and Related Accounts Receivable." Another related defect is that many of those accounts receivable are never received.[31] In short, under the guise of a first instance appropriation the legislature is making what amounts to an outright gift. The gift aspect, of course, must only be confronted when the prospect of repayment is candidly appraised, and the account receivable written off as a bad debt.

For the reader now totally lost in the shuffle, the first entry is a debit to cash as the first instance advance is made, and a credit to accounts receivable. The second entry writes off the accounts receivable under bad debts. The straightforward transaction would be to record a decrease in cash and an increase in that expenditure category for which the first instance advance was used. In terms of the accounts discussed previously, if the state is in the business of making extensive loans and gifts to finance major expenditures – in 1977, expenditures from first instance appropriations totaled better than a billion dollars[32] – then such transactions should be recorded as part of regular (rather than irregular) General Fund activity. The State Comptroller concurs: "Such appropriations [should be] curtailed [and] the related expenditures should be financed through direct General Fund appropriations, to the extent feasible."[33]

Back-bonding

This is one of the more curious fiscal devices of New York. The state government proposes a capital improvement, and then (as required by the Constitution) acquires the approval of voters in a referendum for the issuance of full faith and credit debt to finance that capital improvement. The debt, however, is not issued immediately. Other funds are used to finance the project in question. At a later date, the debt approved by the voters is issued, but the dollars so raised are channeled not into the project for which the debt was originally authorized – that project has already been completed and paid for – but rather into some other use.

The maneuver is called back-bonding, the phrase suggesting that the bonds now being issued are for a project already constructed and financed. The reasons for using this device are most easily seen in a simple example. Suppose the state has a momentary surplus of $50 million, and wishes to construct a complex of bridges costing $50 million. Suppose further that the politicians believe that the voters would approve a debt issue for the bridges in question. Then instead of doing the obvious – using the surplus to build the bridges – in effect they preserve that surplus (to be spent at a later date) by paying for the bridges with the present surplus, and getting voter authorization to issue $50 million in debt at a later date. When the debt is issued, the $50 million so raised goes back into the General Fund.

The effect in this example is to avoid using surplus funds to build a capital project for which the voters would approve a debt extension. This is consistent with the desire to spend as much as possible, and to finance the maximum possible through the issuance of debt. It is far from clear that this is consistent with the spirit of the Constitution. That document requires voter-approved debt to be issued for a specific purpose: the purpose stated when the politicians seek voter approval for a specific debt issue. What happens with back-bonding is that surplus dollars finance the project approved by the voters, and the subsequent debt issue is used to recapture that surplus for some other use.

A.1.e. The dangers of debt and debtlike commitments

General

There are broadly three reasons for a government to issue debt. Two are eminently reasonable, and one is not. All three, of course, are unreasonable if they lead to bankruptcy. The key question therefore is when such a prospect seems likely, and when it seems relatively unlikely.

One reason for issuing debt is a mismatch between the flow of receipts and expenditures. This phenomenon is well known to most individuals. Bills must be paid now, and receipts to cover those bills will arrive later. The obvious solution is to borrow, pay the bills, and repay the loan when revenues are received. Governments, just like individuals, often find themselves in this position. Each spring, for example, New York State is confronted with a variety of expenditures, including much of its Local Assistance payments and its contributions to various retirement funds. The state therefore issues tax and revenue anticipation notes that are subsequently paid off when the taxes and revenues are collected later in the year.[34] Notice that this kind of fiscal operation implies no sustained increase in net debt. The debt actually issued is soon retired when revenues arrive to cover previous expenditures. There is therefore no prospect whatsoever that this type of borrowing can be accused of being "fiscally unsound." The controlling premise is that revenues will soon arrive to cover expenditures. When this premise is violated, expenditures outrun receipts, and the effect can be the highly suspect procedure of borrowing to finance current expenditures. Before that dubious procedure is considered, however, we should examine the other respectable reason – and the main reason – for governments to issue debt.

That reason, in a nutshell, is to finance capital improvements. The rationale is that the benefits from capital improvements, such as a bridge or a school, are spread out over the expected life of the improvement. Those who receive the benefits should be those who pay, or so the argument runs. The problem is how to raise the dollars from those who will benefit in the future to pay for the construction of a school or a bridge that must be built in the present. The solution is to issue debt, using the dollars so raised to pay for the capital improvement, and then repay that debt by taxing those who receive future benefits. This tax could take the form of an increment to the property tax, or in the case of a bridge, a toll collected from cars passing over it.

Borrowing to finance long-term capital improvements is a long-standing tradition in New York State. Roughly half of the state's debt presently outstanding was issued to pay for transportation improvements: highways, airports, and mass transit facilities. Housing and urban renewal debt is another major component (although it has declined slightly since 1969).[35]

This use of debt contrasts sharply with the previous case in that it usually brings in its wake a net addition to the government's debt that will last well beyond the present fiscal year. As with the previous case, all such projects are as sound as the prospect of repayment. If the revenues are sure to be available in the future – because the taxpayers' incomes have risen, or because toll receipts are sure to be adequate, or for some other comparable reason – then more debt now can hardly threaten bankruptcy later. The judgment of what is fiscally sound, however, is often complex. The matter is relatively easy in the case of a bridge that is to be paid for by abundant tolls. The cost of the bridge is known, the tolls can be forecast, and the source of revenue for repayment is quite specific. But what of a multitude of proposed capital improvements, such as highways, schools, and hospitals, all of which are to be repaid by an increase in general taxes levied in the future (that is, by higher income and sales taxes)? At what point do these projects, as a collective entity, become unsound? If the prospective tax burden far exceeds the ability of New Yorkers to pay, again the answer is obvious. But suppose that the prospective tax burden merely implies a tolerable rise in tax rates, but those higher rates will drive more industry out of New York State? In the latter case, the projects are fiscally sound in that they do not threaten state bankruptcy. The revenues will surely be available to repay the debt. But are they sound in some larger sense? As noted in the concluding chapter, the answer for New York State is far from clear. At this juncture, the remaining task is to elaborate a reason for issuing debt that is not sound even by the narrow criterion of fiscal propriety.

The motivation in this case is to cover current expenditures. This appears to be exactly like the first case, except that expenditures made now will not be covered – or covered entirely – by revenues received later in the year. The result is a deficit that must be financed by debt. Unlike the first case, this debt must remain outstanding long after the fiscal year is over. Admittedly, in certain circumstances, such a fiscal venture would seem reasonable. If a municipality could be sure that by spending more now it could attract firms sure to add significantly to tax revenues in future years, what mayor would not champion the cause of those expenditures (and the associated borrowing) as eminently sound? This is merely a variant of the first kind of borrowing – to cover a mismatch in the flow of expenditures and receipts – where the mismatch persists for more than several months. The case becomes unambiguously unsound, however, if borrowing to cover current expenses is repeated year after year, and there is *no* clear prospect of additional revenues being generated to pay off that additional debt.[36] This in essence is the fiscal folly of New York City, as elaborated in Chapter 8.

Debtlike commitments

The two major "debtlike" commitments of the state are lease-purchase agreements and moral obligation bonds. The nature of both has been described in more detail in the body of the text.[37] Suffice it to recall here their central feature, which is to allow the state to borrow funds indirectly, and thereby avoid the need for voter approval of debt increases in statewide referenda.

One must be careful to distinguish between devices used to circumvent constitutional provisions and those which threaten the fiscal viability of the state. Until the mid-1970s, almost all of the debt and debtlike commitments of New York State were issued for one of the two respectable reasons noted in the preceding subsection; that is, either to cover a temporary gap between expenditures and receipts or to finance long-term capital improvements. Lease-purchase agreements were made primarily with the Housing Finance Agency to finance the construction of mental hospitals and university buildings. A similar type of agreement with the County of Albany was contrived to finance the Albany South Mall or Empire State Plaza. Moral obligation debt was mainly issued by the Housing Finance Agency to finance hospitals, nursing homes, and housing.[38]

With the advent of the Municipal Assistance Corporation, a new and alarming item entered the state's debtlike commitments. New York City was shut out of the bond market in the late spring of 1975. The state and city combined to use an old institution (the public authority) and a relatively new fiscal gimmick (the moral obligation bond) to save the day, at least temporarily. The Municipal Assistance Corporation was created to borrow the funds needed by the city, with the state backing the debt of MAC with a moral obligation agreement. The striking new feature was the purpose for which debt was being created. MAC has been forced to borrow between one and two billion dollars annually *not* primarily because New York City needed funds to finance capital improvements – the old rationale for debtlike commitments by the state – but rather because the city was running an annual deficit and had to borrow to cover operating expenses. In short, at the heart of the process was the fiscal folly cited previously: borrowing continually to finance current expenses. The state has become progressively more involved in that folly because the debt of the issuing public authority (MAC) has progressively increased, and all of that increasing debt carries the state's moral obligation backing. Because the city has been incapable of balancing its annual budget, further increases seem inevitable. In short, the MAC venture is not just morally offensive because it involves a fiscal gimmick to circumvent a constitutional provision. It is downright dangerous. The end result may yet imperil the entire fiscal fabric of the state. The sums are vast – billions upon billions – the borrowing persists, and there is no sign of change in the central cause of that borrowing: the repeated tendency of current city expenditures to outrun current receipts.

A.2. Estimating All Operating Funds prior to 1964

Data for the General Fund and Related Accounts are available from 1946 on; those for All Operating Funds, from 1964 on. A critical statistical problem is therefore to estimate All Operating Funds for the earlier part of this study (1946 to 1963).

Part of the solution is to identify those items appropriately included in All Operating Funds for which data are available prior to 1964. These include:

1. Federal aid to localities
2. First instance appropriations[39]
3. Debt service paid from Treasury funds

If these three are added to totals for the General Fund and Related Accounts as a means of estimating All Operating Funds prior to 1964, how much is still left out?[40] An obvious check is to compare the results when the correct totals for All Operating Funds are available. In 1961 and again in 1962 the Comptroller estimated expenditures from all Treasury funds, which at that time were equivalent to All Operating Funds. If totals for these two years and those for 1964 on are compared with the totals resulting from adding to the General Fund and Related Accounts the three items just listed, the results are as shown in Table A.2.

In recent years, the fund structure has become more complex, as have the state's accounting procedures. It therefore seems reasonable to conclude that prior to 1964, an estimate of the total for All Operating Funds by this procedure (Budgetary Accounts plus three items) would

Table A.2. *All Operating Funds: percentage by which actual total exceeded estimated total, 1961–76*

Year	%	Year	%
1976	4.5	1968	6.4
1975	8.3	1967	5.4
1974	4.8	1966	3.1
1973	8.9	1965	4.5
1972	8.4	1964	4.7
1971	7.2	1963	N.A.
1970	6.4	1962	0.7
1969	5.6	1961	0.7

Note: General Fund and Related Accounts adjusted to include items noted previously; that is, federal aid to localities, first instance appropriations, and debt service paid from Treasury funds.

fall short of the actual total by 4 percent in 1963, and by 1 percent in years prior to 1961. The resulting estimates appear in Table C.12 (Appendix C).

A.3. Correcting New York fiscal data for changes in the aggregate price level

In the three decades following World War II, the total revenue, expenditure, and debt of the Empire State increased by almost astronomical amounts. In the same time period, however, the price level also shot up, particularly in the period since the mid-1960s. How should New York fiscal data be adjusted to allow for this rise in aggregate prices? The obvious answer is to deflate all data by some index that measures the rise in the general price level. But which index?

Most price indexes are calculated by using fixed weights. In the case of the Consumer Price Index (CPI), for example, the starting point is to define a market basket for the "typical" consumer. The term "market basket," while traditional, is a bit misleading. For a typical consumer what must be determined are the quantities consumed (in a year) of everything from apples to refrigerators, from automobiles to housing. By no stretch of the imagination can an automobile be viewed as being easily placed in a market basket. The next step is to multiply all of these (fixed) quantities by the prices in successive years. Suppose that this multiplication gives a total value for our mythical market basket of $4,000 in 1976 and $4,400 in 1977. Then the CPI is said to have risen by 10 percent in 1977.

This same procedure can be used to construct a price index for state and local governments rather than for consumers. Again the first assignment is to designate a typical market basket – in this case, the typical bundle of goods and services that a government would be likely to purchase in a year. These (fixed) quantities are then multiplied by their prices in successive years to calculate by how much prices rose, on the average, for state and local governments.

A variant of this approach is to calculate an "implicit price deflator," in particular, the implicit price deflator for the Gross National Product, or GNP. Assume that GNP was in 1976 $1,000 billion and in 1977, $1,200 billion. The first step is to calculate "real" GNP for 1977, that is, what the value of GNP would have been in 1977 if no inflation had occurred. Each subcategory of GNP is divided by the relevant price index. Total consumer spending, for example, is deflated by the Consumer Price Index. Similarly, the Wholesale Price Index is used to deflate some categories of capital goods. These deflated components of GNP are then added together to get an estimate of "real" (as opposed to "nominal") GNP in 1977. Suppose that the result of this addition is $1,100 billion. Then real GNP rose from $1,000 to $1,100 billion, or by 10 percent. Note that nominal GNP in 1977 was $1,200 billion while real GNP was only $1,100 billion. This implies that the general price level in 1977 rose by 9 percent $[(1,200 \div 1,100) - 1]$. The implicit price deflator for GNP for 1977 is therefore 9 percent. It is "implicit" because it is the product of a residual calculation based upon various deflations of GNP components by various price indexes.

Which of the many available indexes is most appropriate for deflating New York State fiscal data? The answer, of course, is something of a judgment call. State expenditures were deflated by the price index for state and local governments. Among all indexes available, this one seemed to be the best (although still an imperfect) measure of how the average price level was changing for those goods and services purchased by New York. For debt, a more general index seemed required. Whether the focus is upon the present owners of the debt (and by implication, the bundle of goods and services for which a given value of debt could be traded) or upon those whose taxes will ultimately repay it (and by implication, the bundle of goods and services they might have had if the taxes were not to be levied), the GNP deflator seemed most appropriate. Revenues are perhaps the most complicated issue to decide. If one wishes to focus upon what the money will buy for the state, the appropriate deflator would seem to be the same one used for state expenditures, namely, the price index for state and local governments. If instead the focus is upon the "real" value of what taxpayers gave up in surrendering these revenues, then the most appropriate index would seem to be either the CPI (if the taxpayers are exclusively consumers) or the GNP deflator (if the composition of the taxpayers cannot be identified).

The choice of index is far from trivial. Between 1946 and 1976, the price index for state and local governments rose at an average annual rate of 6.3 percent; the GNP implicit price deflator, by 4.2 percent. In short, the prices paid by the state for goods and services during this period rose much faster (almost 50 percent faster) than the general price index.

A.4. The War Bonus and the temporary tax increase that became permanent

On November 4, 1947, the voters of New York State ratified Article VII, Section 18, of the Constitution of the State of New York. This provided for a transfer payment from the people of the state to those persons who had been members of the armed forces of the United States between December 7, 1941, and September 2, 1945, and who had been residents of New York State before entering the armed forces. A constitutional amendment was required because the large sum of money involved – estimated to be up to $400 million – was to be borrowed using full faith and credit debt instruments of the state. Perhaps because of the patriotic nature of the request, the amendment was approved overwhelmingly by the people. (The vote was 2,221,800 to 805,826.) Had the voters been aware that they were approving a permanent tax increase, the vote might have been less resounding.

The War Bonus had two peculiar features: the nature of its debt, and the devices used to pay off that debt. Much of New York State debt is issued as 40-year serial bonds. The debt issued to raise the War Bonus was for 10 years only. A total of $300 million in 10-year serial bonds and $100 million in one-year notes was issued.[41] The original plan was to convert the $100 million into longer-term debt. The funds proved to be unneeded, however, and the $100 million issue was redeemed at the end of the year.

To raise the revenues required to redeem the longer-term debt, the legislature did the obvious: pass several taxes, notably a one cent-per-pack increase in the cigarette tax and an additional personal income tax amounting to 10 percent of the then existing statutory rates. What was perhaps not obvious, but should have been, was the absence of any clear provision to repeal these taxes once the debt had been paid off. The money poured in as the population increased, personal income rose, and cigarette consumption grew dramatically. The taxes were not reduced. In 1954, for the first time, a transfer was made to the Capital Construction Fund in the amount of $56.6 million. Every year thereafter a transfer was made to the Capital Construction Fund or to the General Fund. In 1958, when the last $30 million of debt was redeemed, $78 million in taxes was collected.

The War Bonus Account was then given the new task of paying off some Mental Health Construction Bonds. It was more than equal to the task. The annual payments in question were less than $15 million, whereas revenues quickly swelled to 10 times that figure. In 1964 they reached $150 million; in 1968, $221 million – a figure that was then equivalent to 5 percent of the total revenues of the General Fund. In the latter year, the fund disappeared as a discrete entity, even if the taxes did not. The War Bonus and Mental Health Bond Account merged with the General Fund in 1968, thereby making impossible the task of identifying how much money the old 1948 taxes were raising in each year after 1968. The amount raised between 1948 and 1968 was $2,050 million in revenues. Of this sum, War Bonus debt service payments required only $368 million. The remaining $1,682 million was distributed to the Capital Construction Fund ($998 million), the Local Assistance Fund ($546 million), and the State Purposes Fund ($13 million), with $128 million used for debt service payments on Mental Health debt.[42] In short, in the two decades following the authorization of tax increases to pay off the War Bonus, *only 18 percent* of the amount collected was actually used for that purpose. The taxes remained long after the debt was paid off as yet another tribute to the politician's reluctance to relinquish a revenue.

A.5. Shared Taxes

The Empire State from its inception has had a tradition of sharing its receipts with local communities. Beginning in the late eighteenth century, New York aided its localities in providing public schools (called common schools in the Constitution). In 1898 highway aid was added. Subsequently, health and welfare aid was granted. In 1916 the system of Shared Taxes came into being. This was to provide much of the local aid given by New York State until 1946. A portion of the receipts of certain state taxes was distributed directly to localities.[43] These taxes were the corporation franchise tax, the personal income tax, the alcoholic beverage control license fees, the motor vehicle tax, the motor fuel tax, the utilities tax, and the mortgage tax.[44] Since 1944, the mortgage tax, rather than being split evenly between the state and the localities, has been passed entirely to the localities.

In fiscal 1947 a new system was inaugurated. Because the system of Shared Taxes made the actual amount of local aid to be received quite uncertain (consequently making local budgeting difficult), the Local Assistance Fund was created to provide aid at a predictable level. The corporation franchise tax, however, was shared in small quantities until 1952, and the mortgage tax is still, in 1980, passed through, although the amount involved has never exceeded $68 million in one year.

Recently, two older taxes have been shared with New York City in the older, pre-1947 style. These are the stock transfer tax, which has been directed to the city since 1966 (with a deduction for the costs of collection since 1969) and the New York State Sales Tax for the Benefit of New York City, which was instituted in 1975 at the same time that the New York City Sales Tax was repealed. The New York State Sales Tax for the Benefit of New York City is given to the Municipal Assistance Corporation, which deducts the amounts, if any, that the city owes the state for loans secured by short-term state borrowing to be paid by the city through this tax, and remits the remaining amount to the city. The Municipal Assistance Corporation also receives and holds (for debt service) or remits to the city the stock transfer tax.

In the tables prepared for this study, the old Shared Taxes and the mortgage tax (at all times) are not counted as either receipts or expenditures of the state. The state simply functions in these instances as a collection agency, turning over directly to localities whatever dollars are collected. The associated receipts and spending are therefore appropriately viewed as local (and not state) activity. Similarly, the stock transfer tax and the New York State Sales Tax for the Benefit of New York City are treated as New York City taxes, and are not included in any of the tables of this study portraying state (as distinct from city) activity.

A.6. The Tax Revenue Stabilization Reserve Funds

When the State Purposes Fund and Local Assistance Fund were set up in 1946, two associated reserve funds were also established: the State Purposes Reserve Fund and the Local Assistance Reserve Fund. The two combined were called the Tax Revenue Stabilization Reserve

Funds. The purpose of the reserves was suggested by the title just noted. They were to be "a safeguard against possible future declines in revenues."[45] The basic idea was that postwar surpluses would be funneled into them, with the surplus of either fund transferred at year end to its counterpart reserve fund (for example, from State Purposes Fund to State Purposes Reserve Fund). The resulting balances "in reserve" could then be drawn down in deficit years, with the proviso that these be repaid in three of the next six years by moneys from the comparable part of the General Fund (that is, from the State Purposes Fund if the deficit occurred there and was temporarily covered by advances from the State Purposes Reserve Fund).

Each reserve fund has an effective floor – what was accumulated in the four or five years after 1946 (roughly $140 million for the two combined) – and a ceiling expressed as a percentage of the total spending of the relevant fund (for the State Purposes Reserve Fund, 35 percent of the expenditures of the State Purposes Fund; for the Local Assistance Reserve Fund, 45 percent of the expenditures from the Local Assistance Fund).

The intent of the original law, long outmoded, has been ignored since 1960. The establishment of these reserve funds reflected the flush fiscal conditions of the immediate postwar era. The actual balances now held are comparatively trivial (about $150 million). The Capital Construction Fund was incorporated into the General Fund in fiscal 1961, and the state budget director thereafter channeled all surpluses into it.[46]

The books of these two reserve funds are maintained in a curious way. For 364 days of the year, they lend their total reserves to their counterparts in the General Fund (either the State Purposes Fund or the Local Assistance Fund). For one day of the year, the fiscal year end (March 31), the General Fund "repays" these loans by transferring to each reserve fund the appropriate amount, not in cash, but in accounts receivable. The next day (April 1), the reserve funds "lend back" the accounts receivable, and receive in their stead an IOU from the General Fund, to be repaid in 364 days. In effect, then, a short-term loan (364 days) is a permanent loan, and interest free.

A.7. The flows of receipts and expenditures among federal, state, and local government units

In recent years, the State Comptroller has included in his *Annual Report* a section detailing the aggregate flows among the federal, state, and local governments. The resulting account is both informative on specifics and useful as a summary description of the fiscal linkages among the three. For readers unfamiliar with the linkages, the following description from the 1977 *Annual Report* (pp. 38–41) may prove useful.

The governmental framework

New York State residents receive services from all three levels of government – Federal, State, and local. The services a resident might receive on a given day could be services of, for example, national parks, state roads, or local schools. The financing, administration, and delivery of these services involve the intricate workings of the governmental system.

The development of the means to support government activities has brought us to the point where services performed by one level of government are often financed, wholly or in part, by the other levels. This involves the transfer of moneys from one governmental unit to another – usually in the form of governmental aid.

The cost of financing, administering, and delivering governmental services varies from one locality to another within any state. Many factors are likely to influence these costs including, among others: the capacity of the taxing jurisdiction to generate revenues, the level and composition of services expected by the residents, the prevailing wage rates in the area, and management efficiency.

Accordingly, a more comprehensive picture of the State financial operations described in this Report requires an overview of the Federal-State-local fiscal system within which New York State conducts its affairs.

The analysis which follows is based on data gathered and published by the U.S. Bureau of the Census – the official source of comparable data covering all 50 State-local governmental systems. Because of differences in terminology and definition from state to state, the figures reported in this section may not directly correspond with data contained elsewhere in this Report.

The money flow within the system

Charts I and II show the flow of moneys during 1974–75, both nationwide and within New York State. Each chart shows: (1) a one-way flow of Federal moneys to state and local treasuries; (2) a tendency of states to send the bulk of Federal aid, plus additional state-raised funds, on to the localities; and (3) the ability of localities to spend more than they raise because of the aid flows referred to in (1) and (2).

National Fiscal System – Chart I indicates that the Federal, State and local governments raised $403.2 billion of revenues during 1974–75, of which $181.2 billion was collected by the 50-State-local governmental systems ($96.8 billion by the states, $84.4 billion by local governments). The remaining $222.1 billion or 55.1% was raised by the Federal government, which funneled $47.1 billion (21.2% of total Federal revenues) back to state and local governments. When State aid to local governments is added to the Federal aid "passed through" by the States, the combined effect is to increase the amount available to local governments by $60.3 billion or 71.4%. (In other words, the $84.4 billion raised by local governments was increased by 71.4% to a total income available for spending of $144.7 billion.)

New York State Fiscal System – Chart II shows that Federal, State, and local governments collected $49.8 billion of revenues in New York State during 1974–75, of which $22.9 billion was collected by the New York State-local system ($10.7 billion by the State, $12.2 billion by local governments). The remaining $26.9 billion was raised by the Federal government which funneled $5 billion (18.6% of Federal revenues raised in New York State) back to New York State and its local governments. Federal aid had the effect of increasing the amount available for spending by the entire New York State-local system by 21.9%. Combined State and Federal aid to New York local governments had the effect of increasing the amount available for local spending by $10.9 billion or 89.6%.

In Chart II, New York State's system of local governments is shown as divided into two categories: (1) the City of New York, which provides all government services to its five-county area, and (2) the approximately 9,000 counties, cities, towns, villages, school districts, and special districts which together serve the 57 counties comprising the rest of New York State.

Although they are empowered to impose sales and other non-property taxes, local governments in New York obtained 69.1% of all local tax revenues in 1974–75 from the property tax.

Nature of the System – Although the New York State operations (Chart II) appear closely comparable to those of the nation as a whole (Chart I), the fiscal patterns are neither fixed over the years nor uniform among the States. Governmental fiscal systems are always in flux because of the actions of legislatures at all levels, the impact of economic factors, and other reasons. The most dramatic changes have occurred in the annual volume of dollars. The 1974–75 nationwide total of $403.2 billion (Chart I) is 46% greater than the comparable $275.7 billion of 1970–71; New York totals increased 34% in the same period.

Over the last 5 years, Federal direct general expenditures (excluding National defense and international relations) increased by 54%. During the same period, direct general expenditures by the 50-State-local systems increased by 52%. In New York, direct general State-local expenditures increased by 48%.

In the year 1974–75, the following major elements in intergovernmental flows of funds for the nation and for New York State are revealed by Charts I and II:

– The Federal government portion of total (Federal-State-local) government revenues was one percent less in New York than it was in the nation as a whole (54.0% vs. 55.1%).

– The Federal government returned less, as a percent of revenues collected, to the New York State-local system than it did to State-local systems nationally (18.6% vs. 21.2%).

– State government revenues in New York were 21.5% of the Federal-State-local aggregate; the comparable national average was 24.0%.

– A smaller portion as a percent of its own revenues was utilized by the New York State government for its own use, than by State governments nationally (44.7% vs. 86.3%).

CHART I
FLOW OF GOVERNMENTAL REVENUES: NATIONWIDE 1974-75
(In billions of dollars)

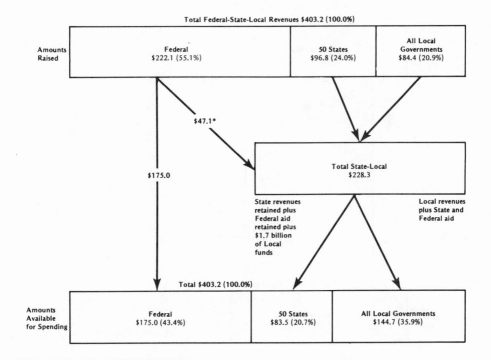

Total Federal-State-Local Revenues $403.2 (100.0%)

Amounts Raised

| Federal $222.1 (55.1%) | 50 States $96.8 (24.0%) | All Local Governments $84.4 (20.9%) |

$47.1*

$175.0

Total State-Local $228.3

State revenues retained plus Federal aid retained plus $1.7 billion of Local funds

Local revenues plus State and Federal aid

Total $403.2 (100.0%)

Amounts Available for Spending

| Federal $175.0 (43.4%) | 50 States $83.5 (20.7%) | All Local Governments $144.7 (35.9%) |

---

*21.2% of Federal revenues used to aid states and localities.

Source: Bureau of the Census, <u>Governmental Finances 1974-75.</u> Data comprises "general revenues" only (i.e., excludes utility, liquor stores, and insurance trust revenues.)

CHART II
FLOW OF GOVERNMENTAL REVENUES IN NEW YORK STATE 1974-75
(In millions of dollars)

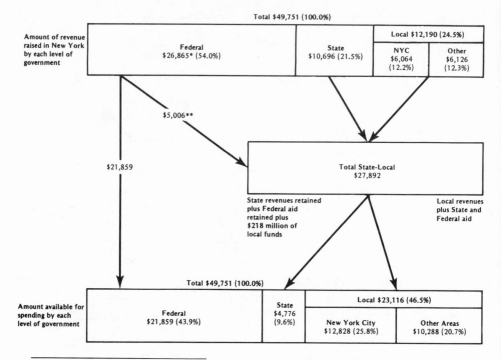

Total $49,751 (100.0%)

Amount of revenue raised in New York by each level of government

| Federal $26,865* (54.0%) | State $10,696 (21.5%) | Local $12,190 (24.5%) | |
| | | NYC $6,064 (12.2%) | Other $6,126 (12.3%) |

$5,006**

$21,859

Total State-Local $27,892

State revenues retained plus Federal aid retained plus $218 million of local funds

Local revenues plus State and Federal aid

Total $49,751 (100.0%)

Amount available for spending by each level of government

| Federal $21,859 (43.9%) | State $4,776 (9.6%) | Local $23,116 (46.5%) | |
| | | New York City $12,828 (25.8%) | Other Areas $10,288 (20.7%) |

*Represents Federal Tax Burden; from Tax Foundation, Inc.
**18.6% of Federal revenues raised in New York used to aid the State and its localities.

Source: Bureau of the Census, Governmental Finances in 1974-75.

APPENDIX B

Tax incentives for business in New York State and New York City, 1979

New York State

Job Incentive Program. An exceptional program which provides tax credits against the State's corporation franchise tax or unincorporated business tax to manufacturers, wholesalers, insurance companies and certain other firms for locating or expanding in the State, creating or retaining at least five jobs, and conducting an approvable training program. Under this program, tax credits can run for up to 10 years and could reach almost 100 percent. In addition to the credit against State taxes, Job Incentive Program legislation also permits local communities to offer real property tax exemptions to eligible companies.
Capital Investment Credit. A credit of 4 percent of new capital invested in buildings and/or depreciable tangible personal property used primarily for manufacturing, processing, assembling and certain other types of production is applicable against the franchise tax on business corporations, the unincorporated business income tax or personal income tax, as an alternative to the Job Incentive Program. The credit first applies to the tax payable for the year the investment is made. Any excess may be carried forward until depleted.
Employment Incentive Credit. An additional 2 percent credit is deductible by corporations making capital investments from the tax payable in each of the three years succeeding the year of the original investment, provided the firm's average number of employees in the State (excluding general executive officers) in each taxable year is at least 101 percent of the average of the year immediately preceeding the year of investment. Excess credits may be carried forward until wholly liquidated.
Business Property Tax Exemption. Construction, alteration, installation and improvement of industrial or commercial real property in the State (outside of New York City) costing more than $10,000 may be eligible for a graduated exemption from local real property taxation, special *ad valorem* levies and service charges. Exemptions can be as high as 50 percent of the increase in assessed valuation in the first year, and decline by five percentage points in each of the succeeding nine years.

Local taxing authorities are empowered to reduce the percentage of the exemption by local law.

New York City

A firm which relocates a minimum of 100 job opportunities to New York City from out of the state, and which moves into rented space, may be eligible for a tax credit based on any rent increases caused by rises in the rate of the city tax on real property.

The city also permits a deduction of depreciation at double the Federal rate to arrive at net taxable income for investment in depreciable tangible property to be used in manufacturing, research and development, and/or pollution control. Any such deduction unused in the tax year may be carried foward.

Commercial or industrial construction or reconstruction in New York City may be eligible for exemption from assessment for real property tax purposes at varying rates. To qualify, new facilities must be constructed on predominantly vacant land according to plans approved by the New York City Industrial and Commercial Incentive Board. The maximum exemption from assessment for new commercial facilities amounts to 50 percent of any increase in value in the year, and declines by five percentage points in each of the succeeding nine years.

New industrial buildings or commercial or industrial facilities reconstructed according to Board-approved plans may be granted an exemption beginning at 95 percent of any increase in value in the first year after completion, and declining by five percentage points in each of the succeeding 18 years.

Source: New York [State], Department of Commerce, *New York State: The Best Business Advantages in America,* 1979.

APPENDIX C

Statistical tables

Table C.1. U.S. employment by industry, 1946–78 (thousands)

Year	Total	Manufac-turing	Mining	Construc-tion	Transpor-tation and public utilities	Wholesale and retail trade	Finance, insurance, & real estate	Services	Government
1946	41,674	14,703	862	1,661	4,061	8,376	1,697	4,719	5,595
1947	43,881	15,545	955	1,982	4,166	8,955	1,754	5,050	5,474
1948	44,891	15,582	994	2,169	4,189	9,272	1,829	5,206	5,650
1949	43,754	14,441	930	2,194	4,001	9,264	1,828	5,240	5,856
1950	45,197	15,241	901	2,364	4,034	9,386	1,888	5,357	6,026
1951	47,819	16,393	929	2,637	4,226	9,742	1,956	5,547	6,389
1952	48,793	16,632	898	2,668	4,248	10,004	2,035	5,699	6,609
1953	50,202	17,549	866	2,659	4,290	10,247	2,111	5,835	6,645
1954	48,990	16,314	791	2,546	4,084	10,235	2,200	5,969	6,751
1955	50,641	16,882	792	2,839	4,141	10,535	2,298	6,240	6,914
1956	52,369	17,243	822	3,039	4,244	10,858	2,389	6,497	7,277
1957	52,853	17,174	828	2,962	4,241	10,886	2,438	6,708	7,616
1958	51,324	15,945	751	2,817	3,976	10,750	2,481	6,765	7,839
1959	53,268	16,675	732	3,004	4,011	11,127	2,549	7,087	8,083

1960	54,189	16,796	712	2,926	4,004	11,391	2,629	7,378	8,353
1961	53,999	16,326	672	2,859	3,903	11,337	2,688	7,620	8,594
1962	55,549	16,853	650	2,948	3,906	11,566	2,754	7,982	8,890
1963	56,653	16,995	635	3,010	3,903	11,778	2,830	8,277	9,225
1964	58,283	17,274	634	3,097	3,951	12,160	2,911	8,660	9,596
1965	60,765	18,062	632	3,232	4,036	12,716	2,977	9,036	10,074
1966	63,901	19,214	627	3,317	4,158	13,245	3,058	9,498	10,784
1967	65,803	19,447	613	3,258	4,268	13,606	3,185	10,045	11,391
1968	67,892	19,781	606	4,318	4,318	14,099	3,337	10,567	11,839
1969	70,384	20,167	619	4,442	4,442	14,705	3,512	11,169	12,195
1970	70,880	19,367	623	3,588	4,515	15,040	3,645	11,548	12,554
1971	71,214	18,623	609	3,704	4,476	15,352	3,772	11,797	12,881
1972	73,675	19,151	628	3,889	4,541	15,949	3,908	12,276	13,334
1973	76,790	20,154	642	4,097	4,656	16,607	4,046	12,857	13,732
1974	78,265	20,077	697	4,020	4,725	16,987	4,148	13,441	14,170
1975	76,945	18,323	752	3,525	4,542	17,060	4,165	13,892	14,686
1976	79,382	18,997	779	3,576	4,582	17,755	4,271	14,551	14,871
1977	82,256	19,647	809	3,833	4,696	18,492	4,452	15,249	15,079
1978	85,763	20,332	837	4,212	4,859	19,394	4,676	15,979	15,476

Note: Data are for employees on nonagricultural payrolls.

Sources: For 1946–48: U.S., Bureau of the Census, *Historical Statistics of the United States: Colonial Times to 1970* (1975), I, 137. For 1949–78: U.S., Department of Labor, *Monthly Labor Review*, September 1979, p. 77.

Table C.2. *New York State employment by industry, 1946–78 (thousands)*

Year	Total[a]	Manufac-turing	Mining	Construc-tion	Transpor-tation and public utilities	Wholesale and retail trade	Finance, insurance, & real estate	Services	Government
1946	5,325	1,986	9	169	534	999	365	646	618
1947	5,518	1,994	10	199	549	1,096	376	687	608
1948	5,596	1,977	11	213	544	1,139	383	709	622
1949	5,473	1,853	10	209	510	1,133	384	732	641
1950	5,576	1,916	10	231	504	1,136	391	737	652
1951	5,755	2,007	11	235	519	1,148	399	756	682
1952	5,828	2,045	11	220	519	1,151	407	762	714
1953	5,936	2,119	11	223	517	1,164	413	768	721
1954	5,828	2,006	10	327	492	1,161	423	776	725
1955	5,917	2,007	10	246	501	1,183	438	798	735
1956	6,093	2,042	10	258	517	1,219	449	834	763
1957	6,179	2,024	10	258	516	1,239	460	881	790
1958	6,027	1,867	9	253	491	1,228	469	900	810
1959	6,128	1,893	9	262	488	1,244	477	937	819
1960	6,182	1,879	9	262	482	1,251	483	978	838
1961	6,158	1,823	9	255	480	1,248	495	997	850

1962	6,261	1,838	9	271	472	1,269	500	1,028	876
1963	6,274	1,804	9	266	466	1,277	499	1,055	897
1964	6,371	1,795	9	263	475	1,305	501	1,099	924
1965	6,519	1,838	9	256	478	1,339	502	1,138	959
1966	6,710	1,895	9	259	480	1,363	510	1,181	1,012
1967	6,858	1,886	9	257	489	1,383	529	1,233	1,073
1968	7,002	1,879	8	260	488	1,409	559	1,274	1,124
1969	7,182	1,871	8	265	497	1,442	595	1,329	1,176
1970	7,155	1,761	8	267	501	1,446	596	1,360	1,218
1971	6,997	1,635	7	271	471	1,422	594	1,360	1,238
1972	7,028	1,602	7	268	473	1,445	595	1,396	1,243
1973	7,121	1,622	7	279	470	1,463	592	1,430	1,258
1974	7,070	1,574	8	258	457	1,442	585	1,450	1,299
1975	6,791	1,407	7	202	433	1,396	580	1,440	1,326
1976	6,779	1,439	7	189	428	1,416	575	1,456	1,268
1977	6,848	1,460	7	190	425	1,428	578	1,500	1,261
1978	7,025	1,483	6	198	429	1,453	585	1,569	1,302

Note: Data are for employees on nonagricultural payrolls.

[a] Numbers may not add owing to rounding.

Source: New York [State], Department of Labor, *Employment Statistics*, vols. III, VI, and X; New York [State], Department of Labor, *Employment Review*, 1971–79.

Table C.3. *Upstate New York employment by industry, 1952–78 (thousands)*

Year	Total[a]	Manufac- turing	Mining	Construc- tion	Transpor- tation and public utilities	Wholesale and retail trade	Finance, insurance, & real estate	Services	Government
1952	1,825	832	9	81	143	314	48	168	231
1953	1,895	879	8	83	142	324	49	169	240
1954	1,835	814	8	87	132	327	53	168	247
1955	1,874	816	8	88	135	338	58	176	255
1956	1,943	839	7	97	138	346	58	186	270
1957	1,982	831	7	98	137	347	60	211	287
1958	1,894	730	6	87	130	357	69	217	297
1959	1,919	734	6	88	129	359	70	231	303
1960	1,928	730	6	84	124	352	68	251	312
1961	1,898	706	6	78	119	348	69	257	313
1962	1,926	716	6	77	118	356	69	266	320
1963	1,930	707	6	76	115	360	69	272	323
1964	1,977	716	6	83	114	368	70	284	334

Year								
1965	2,059	751	6	90	115	381	72	297	347
1966	2,158	790	6	96	117	398	74	311	365
1967	2,217	789	6	95	118	409	78	326	396
1968	2,259	783	5	98	119	420	79	337	417
1969	2,316	786	5	100	121	432	83	352	437
1970	2,318	753	5	96	122	438	86	369	451
1971	2,294	705	5	97	117	438	89	384	461
1972	2,324	698	5	100	118	458	91	393	463
1973	2,386	728	5	102	118	472	94	405	463
1974	2,427	738	6	95	117	476	97	417	483
1975	2,340	663	5	75	108	464	96	415	514
1976	2,386	674	5	76	108	481	96	434	512
1977	2,436	687	5	79	109	494	99	446	517
1978	2,515	703	4	83	112	509	102	468	534

Note: This table excludes data for the counties covered by Table C.4.
[a] Numbers may not add owing to rounding.
Source: See Table C.2.

Table C.4. Downstate New York employment by industry, 1952–78 (thousands)

Year	Total[a]	Manufac- turing	Mining	Construc- tion	Transpor- tation and public utilities	Wholesale and retail trade	Finance, insurance, & real estate	Services	Government
1952	4,003	1,213	2	139	376	837	359	594	483
1953	4,041	1,240	3	140	375	840	364	599	481
1954	3,993	1,192	2	150	360	834	370	608	478
1955	4,043	1,191	2	158	366	845	380	622	480
1956	4,150	1,203	3	161	379	873	389	648	493
1957	4,197	1,193	3	160	379	892	398	670	503
1958	4,133	1,137	3	166	361	871	400	683	513
1959	4,209	1,159	3	174	359	885	407	706	516
1960	4,254	1,149	3	178	358	899	415	727	526
1961	4,260	1,117	3	177	361	900	426	740	537
1962	4,335	1,122	3	194	354	913	431	762	556
1963	4,344	1,097	3	190	351	917	430	783	574
1964	4,394	1,079	3	180	361	937	431	815	590

Year									
1965	4,460	1,087	3	166	363	958	430	841	612
1966	4,552	1,105	3	163	363	965	436	870	647
1967	4,641	1,097	3	162	371	974	451	907	677
1968	4,743	1,096	3	162	369	989	480	937	707
1969	4,866	1,085	3	165	376	1,010	512	977	739
1970	4,837	1,008	3	171	379	1,008	510	991	767
1971	4,703	930	2	174	354	984	505	976	777
1972	4,704	904	2	168	355	987	504	1,003	780
1973	4,735	894	2	177	352	991	498	1,025	795
1974	4,643	836	2	163	340	966	488	1,033	816
1975	4,451	744	2	127	325	932	484	1,025	812
1976	4,393	765	2	113	320	935	479	1,022	756
1977	4,412	773	2	111	316	934	479	1,054	744
1978	4,510	780	2	115	317	944	483	1,101	768

Note: Data for 1952–71 are for New York City plus Nassau, Suffolk, Westchester, and Rockland counties; thereafter data include Putnam County as well.

[a] Numbers may not add owing to rounding.

Source: See Table C.2.

Table C.5. *Consolidated Edison: revenue per kilowatt-hour for commercial–industrial customers, 1946–78 (cents)*

	Average charge	Charge deflated by	
		WPI[a]	Electricity index[b]
1946	3.07	4.93	3.41
1947	3.00	3.92	3.37
1948	3.11	3.76	3.47
1949	2.85	3.62	3.15
1950	2.77	3.39	3.05
1951	2.76	3.03	3.02
1952	2.76	3.12	2.99
1953	2.77	3.17	2.96
1954	2.75	3.14	2.93
1955	2.69	3.06	2.83
1956	2.69	2.97	2.82
1957	2.71	2.90	2.83
1958	2.68	2.83	2.76
1959	N.A.	N.A.	N.A.
1960	2.69	2.83	2.70
1961	2.68	2.84	2.68
1962	2.73	2.88	2.73
1963	2.67	2.83	2.67
1964	2.65	2.80	2.66
1965	2.73	2.83	2.75
1966	2.68	2.69	2.70
1967	2.77	2.77	2.77
1968	2.77	2.70	2.75
1969	2.73	2.56	2.66
1970	2.87	2.60	2.70
1971	3.46	3.04	3.06
1972	3.80	3.19	3.20
1973	4.27	3.17	3.42
1974	6.49	4.05	4.40
1975	6.93	3.96	4.15
1976	7.29	3.98	4.10
1977	8.09	4.17	4.27
1978	8.07	3.86	3.97

[a] Wholesale Price Index, all commodities (1967 = 100).
[b] Retail price index of electricity, composite (1967 = 100).
Sources: Consolidated Edison data from New York State Public Service Commission; price indexes from U.S., Bureau of the Census (1975), I, 199, 214; U.S., Bureau of the Census, *Statistical Abstract of the United States,* 1978, pp. 484, 499.

Table C.6. *Net tax revenues collected in New York State in four broad categories, 1946–77 ($ millions)*

Fiscal year ending March 31	Total taxes	Personal income tax	General business taxes	Consumption & use taxes	Other taxes
1977	10,364.2	4,527.0	1,907.9	3,547.9	381.4
1976	9,500.4	4,012.8	1,699.0	3,452.7	335.8
1975	8,842.9	3,753.6	1,456.3	3,300.9	332.1
1974	8,122.3	3,352.0	1,296.1	3,153.6	320.5
1973	7,666.2	3,065.2	1,282.6	2,985.1	333.3
1972	6,634.6	2,516.3	1,148.9	2,617.9	351.4
1971	5,949.5	2,550.2	869.6	2,220.6	309.1
1970	5,794.8	2,506.4	962.2	2,030.1	296.0
1969	4,981.0	2,151.6	858.4	1,662.8	308.2
1968	4,167.8	1,787.9	609.9	1,504.4	265.5
1967	3,852.7	1,527.1	632.0	1,429.9	263.7
1966	3,268.6	1,270.9	569.4	1,128.0	300.2
1965	2,820.0	1,131.7	695.6	666.6	326.0
1964	2,672.1	1,136.3	581.1	640.2	314.5
1963	2,482.5	1,018.7	579.8	613.1	270.9
1962	2,291.7	988.6	453.0	591.0	258.9
1961	2,051.8	803.7	425.3	573.9	248.8
1960	1,928.9	756.6	399.1	554.0	219.2
1959	1,555.0	565.8	386.9	427.1	175.3
1958	1,481.0	513.5	391.1	413.4	163.0
1957	1,416.8	476.3	374.2	402.2	164.1
1956	1,334.6	447.3	334.8	393.5	159.0
1955	1,178.7	367.5	312.4	370.4	128.4
1954	1,113.2	351.1	304.3	354.5	103.4
1953	1,099.6	337.0	319.8	348.5	94.2
1952	1,011.6	297.0	307.3	318.6	88.7
1951	899.3	247.7	244.6	313.6	93.5
1950	876.5	262.9	251.2	292.1	70.3
1949	744.4	160.8	236.9	272.5	74.2
1948	689.7	134.1	231.8	244.9	78.8
1947	633.1	114.6	190.6	249.0	78.9
1946	646.3	147.8	217.9	196.3	84.3

Note: In 1968–7 the lottery was classed as a tax; here it is reclassed as Miscellaneous Revenue. The 1964 motion picture tax was reclassed as Miscellaneous Revenue; here it is classed as a tax. Figures may not add owing to rounding.
Source: New York [State], Office of the Comptroller, *Annual Report* (hereafter *Annual Report of the Comptroller*), 1946, p. 32; 1947, p. 20; 1948, p. 140; 1949, p. 140; 1950, p. 150; 1951, p. 144; 1952, p. 144; 1953, p. 144; 1954, p. 144; 1955, p. 142; 1956, p. 142; 1957, p. 144; 1958, p. 144; 1959, p. 160; 1960, p. 171; 1961, p. 159; 1962, p. 59; 1963, p. 39; 1964, p. 43; 1965, p. 47; 1966, pp. 44, 47; 1967, pp. 44, 47; 1968, pp. 42, 45; 1969, pp. 43, 45; 1970, pp. 42, 45; 1971, pp. 40, 43; 1972, pp. 43, 47; 1973, pp. 43, 47; 1974, pt. II, pp. 7, 11; 1975, pt. II, p. 7, 11; 1976, pt. II, pp. 7, 11.

Table C.7. *Net tax revenues collected in New York State, 1946–77*
($ millions)

Year	Personal income tax	General business taxes					Consumption	
		Corpora-tion and utilities taxes[a]	Corporation franchise tax[b]	Unincor-porated business tax	Bank tax[c]	Insurance tax[a]	Sales & use tax	Motor ve-hicle tax
1977	4,527.0	447.5	1,042.5	69.0	177.9	171.0	2,218.2	255.5
1976	4,012.8	392.8	877.3	64.7	190.9	173.3	2,148.9	259.5
1975	3,753.6	332.1	763.5	64.2	140.0	156.6	2,000.9	244.5
1974	3,352.0	391.7	706.3	65.0	103.2	29.9	1,863.2	237.6
1973	3,065.2	373.2	694.1	73.1	107.5	34.6	1,734.1	241.0
1972	2,516.3	333.6	601.5	68.5	111.2	34.2	1,532.8	216.9
1971	2,550.2	272.7	433.8	63.2	75.3	24.7	1,175.9	217.7
1970	2,506.4	247.5	529.3	77.6	86.2	21.5	1,012.0	211.6
1969	2,151.6	228.9	465.8	67.0	77.5	19.2	698.8	202.1
1968	1,787.9	179.7	313.7	46.1	52.4	17.9	630.9	195.1
1967	1,527.1	171.9	357.1	46.6	39.9	16.4	604.3	175.4
1966	1,270.9	161.9	301.8	43.5	47.0	15.2	298.4	192.5
1965	1,131.7	152.8	404.5	59.6	64.6	14.1	0.0	142.8
1964	1,136.3	145.2	325.7	30.2	66.6	13.5	0.0	137.2
1963	1,018.7	139.3	316.9	37.3	70.3	16.0	0.0	130.9
1962	988.6	138.5	219.6	32.7	47.8	14.3	0.0	133.0
1961	803.7	133.5	209.7	37.7	32.5	11.9	0.0	125.3
1960	756.6	128.8	183.3	31.5	42.8	12.7	0.0	124.7
1959	565.8	121.4	190.4	30.8	34.0	10.3	0.0	125.5
1958	513.5	115.7	201.9	31.1	31.7	10.8	0.0	117.1
1957	476.3	109.3	196.6	33.1	25.6	9.6	0.0	114.2
1956	447.3	101.2	165.6	30.1	28.6	9.3	0.0	118.2
1955	367.5	95.1	166.2	19.7	22.3	9.1	0.0	105.7
1954	351.1	92.4	163.9	20.7	20.9	6.5	0.0	98.4
1953	337.0	86.0	187.0	21.1	17.3	8.5	0.0	95.0
1952	297.0	79.9	183.5	20.6	14.6	8.8	0.0	86.3
1951	247.7	71.0	138.2	16.3	13.4	5.6	0.0	80.5
1950	262.9	65.0	155.2	15.0	10.6	5.4	0.0	77.0
1949	160.8	62.3	141.2	16.3	11.4	5.6	0.0	67.7
1948	134.1	57.7	126.3	22.8	20.5	4.6	0.0	62.0
1947	114.6	52.6	84.3	29.6	20.0	4.1	0.0	66.1
1946	147.8	47.6	123.9	32.8	10.1	3.4	0.0	48.6

Note: Figures might not add owing to rounding.

[a] The corporation and utilities taxes are shown separately in the *Annual Reports of the Comptroller* until 1966. In 1974 about 30% of this group was added to the insurance tax, quadrupling it.

[b] The corporation franchise tax includes the tax on the organization of corporations until 1966 and the unrelated business tax since 1971.

[c] There were two types of bank taxes until 1966, which are combined here.

[d] Alcoholic beverage control licenses include the alcoholic beverage control price schedule listing fee until 1952.

406

	and use taxes				Other taxes[f]				
Motor fuel tax	Alcoholic beverage tax[d]	Alcoholic beverage control licenses	Cigarette tax[e]	Highway use tax	Estate & gift taxes[g]	Pari-mutuel tax	Real estate transfer tax	Racing & boxing taxes[h]	Stock transfer tax
512.7	150.2	36.4	334.2	40.8	199.3	172.3	8.6	1.2	0.0
480.4	153.9	33.1	337.5	39.4	147.6	180.3	6.9	1.1	0.0
498.9	154.6	32.8	330.5	38.8	146.2	177.4	7.5	1.1	0.0
498.8	155.5	32.6	328.5	37.3	145.1	164.7	8.8	2.0	0.0
462.5	154.8	32.9	322.8	37.0	164.8	157.0	8.3	3.3	0.0
408.4	122.3	33.0	273.3	31.2	177.3	163.3	6.8	4.1	0.0
365.3	116.8	32.9	262.6	29.4	130.1	169.9	5.2	3.9	0.0
374.8	112.6	33.2	256.6	29.3	127.9	158.5	5.9	3.7	0.0
375.2	93.4	50.2	257.8	25.4	149.4	151.7	3.5	3.6	0.0
291.8	71.7	66.6	226.3	22.0	119.7	142.3	0.0	3.6	0.0
275.8	68.2	65.1	218.5	22.7	116.0	144.0	0.0	3.6	0.0
269.3	66.2	64.3	216.3	21.0	132.1	140.9	0.0	3.3	23.9
250.8	63.2	63.0	127.0	19.7	106.5	135.6	0.0	3.6	80.8
243.2	61.3	56.3	123.0	19.2	111.1	123.3	0.0	3.4	76.6
244.8	61.6	23.7	134.1	18.0	91.3	110.6	0.0	3.1	65.9
231.9	60.8	23.8	125.1	16.7	81.7	95.3	0.0	2.9	78.9
221.9	58.4	23.9	127.9	16.6	87.5	93.2	0.0	3.2	64.8
215.2	57.2	24.2	116.4	16.3	71.6	86.9	0.0	3.0	57.6
140.4	55.4	24.0	67.4	14.5	39.6	78.1	0.0	2.9	54.7
140.2	52.9	23.9	63.5	15.9	47.1	74.6	0.0	2.8	38.4
132.6	55.0	24.0	61.4	15.0	51.9	71.2	0.0	2.4	38.6
125.4	51.5	24.1	59.9	14.3	53.7	61.2	0.0	2.4	41.6
119.0	49.2	24.0	58.3	14.1	28.0	57.0	0.0	2.5	40.9
110.7	49.2	24.1	59.9	12.2	29.3	48.7	0.0	2.5	23.1
108.3	46.9	23.9	61.2	13.2	30.0	38.5	0.0	2.3	23.3
102.5	46.3	23.8	59.8	0.0	27.9	33.8	0.0	1.7	25.3
97.2	52.9	24.4	58.6	0.0	32.4	28.3	0.0	1.5	31.2
90.1	45.1	23.5	56.4	0.0	22.4	26.6	0.0	1.5	19.9
83.8	45.0	23.7	52.2	0.0	27.3	27.2	0.0	1.6	18.1
76.9	47.0	23.0	36.1	0.0	34.5	26.9	0.0	1.7	15.7
73.6	54.4	22.1	32.8	0.0	24.6	30.1	0.0	1.9	22.4
53.8	47.4	20.5	26.1	0.0	24.7	31.4	0.0	1.5	26.6

[e] The cigarette tax includes the tobacco products tax from 1960 to 1964.

[f] The lottery was classified as a tax from 1968 to 1971; here it has been reclassified as Miscellaneous Revenue.

[g] The estate and gift taxes include two types of estate taxes in 1946–47, the transfer tax from 1946 to 1965, and the gift tax since 1972.

[h] The motion picture tax is included under the racing and boxing taxes from 1946 to 1964. In 1964, it was classified in the *Annual Report* as Miscellaneous Revenues.

Source: See Table C.6.

Table C.8. *Miscellaneous Revenues of the New York State General*

Fiscal year ending March 31	Miscellaneous revenues	Rev. of gen. depts. & sundry gen. revs.	Nonfederal refunds & reimbursements		Federal refunds & reimbursements
1977	458.2	83.8	43.3		55.4
1976	303.4	80.2	47.2		59.7
1975	280.5	71.0	19.6		47.0
1974	308.9	64.3	23.4		29.1
1973	221.8	55.8	14.6		10.1
1972	150.9	55.0	11.9		17.0
1971	171.3	56.7	15.9		30.9
1970	117.0	48.1	17.6		13.3
1969	111.0	38.4	20.4		1.0
1968	76.3	37.5	14.3		3.6
1967	55.8	35.4	8.2		0.5
1966	57.1	31.6	8.1		0.5
1965	45.9	30.8		6.9	
1964	80.2	53.9		6.3	
1963	73.7	60.1		5.7	
1962	74.6	54.4		4.6	
1961	65.7	52.3		6.5	
1960	69.9	56.6		8.3	
1959	60.4	47.0		7.7	
1958	56.7	42.4		8.5	
1957	52.6	38.8		8.4	
1956	47.5	36.1		7.8	
1955	48.4	33.8		6.9	
1954	66.7	29.7		6.5	
1953	38.4	26.8		6.3	
1952	45.3	24.4		13.0	
1951	40.8	22.9		6.5	
1950	36.6	21.5		5.1	
1949	35.1	20.4		5.2	
1948	30.1	18.4		4.7	
1947	28.7	19.6		6.1	
1946	24.9	15.0		6.4	

Note: The motion picture tax was classified in 1964 as Miscellaneous Revenues; here it is classified as a tax. The lottery was classified as a tax from 1968 to 1971; here it is classified as Miscellaneous Revenues. Figures may not add owing to rounding.

Fund and Related Accounts, 1946–77 ($ millions)

Lottery	Land, buildings, & property sold	Abandoned property receipts	Income from investments	Transfers & adjustments	Capital construction fund miscellaneous receipts
90.8	0.8	125.9	24.7	33.4	
27.4	1.7	43.4	26.6	17.1	
54.4	0.7	31.2	54.5	2.0	
52.8	3.0	25.8	83.9	26.7	
53.3	0.7	15.8	65.2	6.3	
34.3	1.1	14.8	7.9	13.9	
30.3	4.6	12.0	3.2	17.6	
26.0	0.9	8.1	3.1		
27.5	1.4	8.8	3.4	10.0	
8.9	0.8	7.3	2.0	2.0	
	1.0	9.1	1.5	0.1	
	1.5	7.4	1.3	6.8	
	1.1	5.8	1.2		
	0.4	18.1	1.4		
	0.9	5.5	1.5		
	0.4	12.3	2.8		
	0.4	3.1	3.3		
a		3.0	0.4	1.5	1.5
a		2.9	0.4		2.3
0.2		3.7	1.4		0.7
0.1		3.3	1.3		0.7
a		2.9	0.4		0.2
a		2.7	0.5	3.6	0.8
a		1.9	2.4	25.9	0.3
0.1		2.6	2.6		0.1
a		1.4	6.2		0.1
a		1.0	1.2	8.9	0.3
a		3.2	4.4	2.3	0.1
a		1.8	7.4	0.2	0.1
a		1.7	5.1		0.1
a		1.6	1.3		a
a		3.4	0.2		a

a Less than 0.05.
Source: See Table C.6.

Table C.9. *Revenues and other receipts of the New York State General Fund and Related Accounts, 1946–77 ($ millions)*

Fiscal year ending March 31	Net receipts of taxes	Effect of changes in the undistributed receipts	Tax revenue	Miscellaneous Revenues	Special federal aid	Total revenues	Other receipts	Borrowing for Capital Construction	Borrowing for State Purposes	Total receipts
1977	10,369.9	− 5.7	10,364.2	458.2	293.7	11,095.1		173.4		11,268.4
1976	9,417.0	+ 64.0	9,481.0	303.4	234.9	10,019.3		135.8		10,155.1
1975	8,658.3	+165.0	8,823.3	280.5	228.7	9,332.4	129.0	73.3		9,534.8
1974	8,182.1	− 80.0	8,102.1	308.9	224.3	8,635.3		0.0		8,635.3
1973	7,802.3	−147.0	7,655.3	221.8	392.4	8,269.5		56.4		8,325.9
1972	6,628.0	+ 2.0	6,630.0	150.9		6,780.9		158.3		6,939.2
1971	5,925.0	+ 20.0	5,945.0	171.3		6,116.3		608.0		6,724.3
1970	5,790.5	− 0.2	5,790.3	117.0		5,907.3		304.0		6,211.2
1969	4,996.0	− 19.5	4,976.5	111.0		5,087.5		436.3		5,523.8
1968	4,138.9	+ 24.4	4,163.4	76.3		4,239.6		389.7		4,629.2
1967	3,848.2	− 0.1	3,848.2	55.8		3,904.0		121.6		4,025.6
1966	3,282.5	− 15.0	3,267.5	57.1		3,324.6	20.8	118.6		3,463.9
1965	2,825.0	− 5.0	2,820.0	45.9		2,865.8	32.0	0.0		2,897.8

Year									
1964	2,679.1	− 7.0	2,672.1	80.2	2,752.3	29.0	0.0		2,781.3
1963	2,474.1	+ 8.5	2,483.2	73.7	2,556.3		0.0		2,556.3
1962	2,137.8	+153.9	2,291.7	74.6	2,366.3		0.0		2,366.3
1961	2,157.6	−105.8	2,051.8	65.7	2,117.5		0.0		2,117.5
1960	1,981.5	− 52.6	1,928.9	69.9	1,998.8		44.9		2,043.6
1959	1,556.4	− 1.4	1,555.0	60.4	1,615.7		196.2		1,811.5
1958	1,475.8	+ 5.2	1,481.0	56.7	1,537.9		90.4		1,628.2
1957	1,416.9	− 0.1	1,416.8	52.6	1,469.4		0.0		1,469.4
1956	1,334.4	+ 0.2	1,334.6	47.5	1,382.1		0.0		1,382.1
1955	1,178.5	+ 0.2	1,178.7	48.4	1,227.1		0.0		1,227.1
1954	1,113.3	− 0.1	1,113.2	40.8	1,154.0		0.0		1,154.0
1953	1,099.6	− 0.1	1,099.6	38.4	1,138.0		0.0		1,138.0
1952	1,011.7	− 0.1	1,011.6	47.1	1,058.7		65.0	0.6	1,124.4
1951	899.7	− 0.4	899.3	40.8	940.1		12.0	5.2	957.4
1950	877.1	− 0.7	876.5	34.3	910.8		0.0	17.0	927.8
1949	737.1	+ 7.3	744.4	35.1	779.5		0.0	15.0	794.6
1948	687.7	+ 2.0	689.7	30.1	719.8		0.0	420.0	1,139.8
1947	584.3	+ 48.8	633.1	33.2	666.2		0.0		666.2
1946	663.1	− 16.7	646.3	26.6	672.9		0.0		672.9

Source: See Table C.6.

411

Table C.10. *Adjusted expenditures from the New York State General Fund and Related Accounts, 1946–77 ($ millions)*

Fiscal year ending March 31	Local assistance	State purposes	Capital construction	Debt service	Total expenditures
1977	6,686.7	3,348.7	540.4	412.5	10,988.4
1976	6,318.7	3,319.9	617.4	395.0	10,651.0
1975	5,637.7	3,101.1	490.8	327.8	9,557.4
1974	5,110.8	2,741.7	360.2	295.3	8,508.1
1973	4,724.3	2,458.3	338.0	264.5	7,785.0
1972	4,290.6	2,344.9	563.7	223.1	7,422.3
1971	3,825.0	2,130.1	616.6	175.7	6,747.5
1970	3,687.9	1,853.2	526.2	139.2	6,206.6
1969	3,229.4	1,650.8	538.4	100.2	5,518.9
1968	2,686.0	1,418.5	461.1	63.6	4,629.2
1967	2,377.0	1,169.9	419.7	54.9	4,021.5
1966	2,121.4	1,005.8	293.4	39.4	3,460.0
1965	1,672.5	932.9	247.9	40.3	2,893.5
1964	1,542.1	872.7	327.9	38.1	2,780.8
1963	1,382.2	807.6	366.2	38.6	2,594.5
1962	1,264.7	718.5	291.7	49.3	2,324.3
1961	1,134.0	636.1	268.1	49.2	2,087.4
1960	1,040.7	624.7	274.0	53.1	1,992.6
1959	946.0	577.4	240.9	33.2	1,797.5
1958	864.5	544.3	222.8	55.1	1,686.6
1957	751.0	492.4	166.3	55.3	1,465.1
1956	686.9	453.2	142.3	59.4	1,341.7
1955	622.5	426.7	152.8	60.0	1,262.2
1954	586.7	397.2	134.9	60.3	1,179.1
1953	568.7	382.4	130.0	62.2	1,143.3
1952	541.2	355.8	105.7	60.8	1,063.7
1951	525.5	318.4	128.7	71.1	1,043.7
1950	505.1	320.2	122.0	74.1	1,021.4
1949	402.2	424.0	81.2	172.1	1,079.4
1948	406.3	418.7	75.5	51.4	951.8
1947	287.8	203.8	63.1	36.5	591.2
1946	267.8	172.2	13.7	39.9	493.6

Note: Includes Capital Construction Fund, War Bonus Fund, War Bonus and Mental Health Bond Account, Highway Account, and Teachers' Salaries Emergency Increase Fund. The transfers from the State Purposes Fund to the Broadway Office Building Fund are classified as State Purposes expenditures. The redemption of temporary debt by the War Bonus Fund is classified as Debt Service. All Local Assistance Fund expenditures not classified as Debt Service are classified as Local Assistance. All State Purposes Fund expenditures not classified as Debt Service are classified as State Purposes. The payments of bonuses by the War Bonus Fund are classified as State Purposes.

Table C.11. *New York State: expenditures from All Operating Funds, including first instance appropriations, 1961–62 and 1964–77* *($ millions [current])*

Fiscal year ending March 31	Expenditures				
	Local assistance	State purposes	Capital construction	Debt service	Total
1977	10,426.2	4,345.3	876.0	835.9	16,483.4
1976	9,982.8	4,245.8	1,152.1	699.2	16,079.9
1975	8,792.6	3,950.6	1,020.9	618.7	14,382.8
1974	7,874.9	3,538.2	1,013.6	557.3	12,984.0
1973	7,646.6	3,190.2	957.9	487.0	12,281.7
1972	6,731.1	3,010.9	1,344.7	398.6	11,485.3
1971	5,548.7	2,678.7	1,261.5	340.1	9,829.0
1970	5,129.9	2,298.2	997.2	297.8	8,723.1
1969	4,593.7	2,030.9	1,019.7	218.7	7,863.0
1968	3,563.2	1,755.5	946.8	173.1	6,438.6
1967	3,098.0	1,512.1	840.2	143.7	5,594.0
1966	2,559.9	1,277.3	630.5	110.9	4,578.6
1965	2,031.0	1,163.9	560.2	104.6	3,859.7
1964	1,834.9	1,082.1	575.7	95.9	3,588.6
1963	N.A.	N.A.	N.A.	N.A.	N.A.
1962	N.A.	N.A.	N.A.	N.A.	2,818.0[a]
1961	N.A.	N.A.	N.A.	N.A.	2,499.3

[a] The figure given on p. 37 of the *Annual Report* for 1962 is $2,858.5, but that includes both "General Fund and Related Fund and Accounts" of $2,369.3 and First Instance Funds of $221.8. Because the $2,369.3 includes $40.5 of "Net Cash Outgo from CC Fund for first instance appropriations," that $40.5 is counted twice. Compare the treatment in 1961, for which year there is no double counting.

Source: Each year's data are taken from the *Annual Report* dated four years later, which is the last time it appears, except 1961 and 1962, taken from the current year, and 1974 to 1977, taken from the *Annual Report* of 1977. *Annual Report of the Comptroller*, 1977, pt. I, pp. 15, 17, 20, 22; 1976, pt. I, pp. 16, 17, 20, 22; 1975, pt. I, pp. 12, 14, 17, 19; 1974, pt. I, pp. 11, 13, 14, 17; 1973, pp. 10, 12, 13, 16; 1972, pp. 10, 11, 13, 15; 1971, pp. 10, 11, 13, 15; 1970, pp. 12, 13, 15, 17; 1969, pp. 13, 14, 17, 19; 1968, pp. 13, 14, 16, 17; 1962, pp. 12, 37; 1961, pp. 16, 50.

Notes to Table C.10 (*cont.*)
Source: Annual Report of the Comptroller, 1946, pp. 16, 95; 1947, pp. 18, 55; 1948, pp. 33, 81, 86; 1949, pp. 25, 73, 78; 1950, pp. 25, 81, 86; 1951, pp. 23, 77, 82; 1952, pp. 23, 77, 82; 1953, pp. 23, 77, 82; 1954, pp. 23, 77, 82; 1955, pp. 23, 77, 82; 1956, pp. 23, 77, 82; 1957, pp. 23, 77, 82; 1958, pp. 23, 77, 82; 1959, pp. 37, 90, 96; 1960, pp. 47, 100, 106; 1961, p. 61; 1962, p. 55; 1963, p. 35; 1964, p. 35; 1965, p. 37, 1966, p. 37; 1967, p. 37; 1968, p. 37; 1969, p. 37; 1970, p. 37; 1971, p. 35; 1976, pt. II, p. 6; *Preliminary Annual Report of the Comptroller*, p. 2.

Table C.12. *New York State: expenditures from All Operating Funds estimated using quantities reported from 1946 to 1977 ($ millions)*

Fiscal year ending March 31	(1) Expenditures: General Fund and Related Accounts	(2) Federal aid to localities	(3) Expenditures: first instance appropriations	(4) Debt service not from the General Fund	(5) Subtotal of (1) to (4)	(6) Expenditures: All Operating Funds	(7) Actual or assumed[a] ratio of (5) to (6)
1977	10,988.4	3,053.1	1,392.3[b]	244.5[b]	15,678.3	16,483.4	0.9512
1976	10,651.0	3,041.2	1,444.3	227.1	15,363.6	16,079.9	0.9554
1975	9,557.4	2,589.4	820.5	221.6	13,188.9	14,382.8	0.9169
1974	8,508.1	2,763.4	893.0	202.4	12,366.9	12,984.0	0.9524
1973	7,785.0	2,497.6	733.0	173.0	11,188.6	12,281.7	0.9109
1972	7,422.3	2,047.5	921.0	135.8	10,526.6	11,485.3	0.9165
1971	6,747.5	1,441.9	798.4	108.5	9,096.3	9,802.6	0.9279
1970	6,206.6	1,245.3	594.4	114.4	8,160.7	8,714.5	0.9364
1969	5,518.9	1,212.6	589.0	92.5	7,413.0	7,852.0	0.9440
1968	4,629.2	741.8	561.0	83.2	6,015.2	6,425.5	0.9361
1967	4,021.5	648.0	558.4	78.5	5,306.4	5,610.0	0.9459
1966	3,460.0	412.0	510.3	65.9	4,448.2	4,591.6	0.9688
1965	2,893.5	336.5	410.4	60.2	3,700.6	3,872.9	0.9555
1964	2,780.8	272.0	326.2	54.4	3,433.4	3,601.8	0.9532
1963	2,594.5	248.7	294.4	40.8	3,178.4	3,310.8	0.9600[a]
1962	2,324.3	216.0	222.6	30.1	2,797.5	2,818.0[c]	0.9927
1961	2,087.4	159.6	202.6	29.2	2,483.1	2,499.3[c]	0.9935
1960	1,992.6	157.7	251.9	22.9	2,425.1	2,449.6	0.9900[a]
1959	1,817.5	146.0	212.4	22.1	2,198.0	2,220.2	0.9900[a]
1958	1,686.6	139.3	149.8	20.8	1,996.5	2,016.7	0.9900[a]

Year						
1957	1,465.1	118.5	78.1	19.8	1,681.5	1,698.5	0.9900[a]
1956	1,341.7	115.3	76.2	18.6	1,551.8	1,567.5	0.9900[a]
1955	1,262.2	110.9	76.3	17.2	1,466.6	1,481.4	0.9900[a]
1954	1,179.1	109.0	77.0	15.1	1,380.2	1,394.1	0.9900[a]
1953	1,143.3	98.2	81.2	14.5	1,337.2	1,350.7	0.9900[a]
1952	1,063.7	92.4	64.0	12.3	1,232.4	1,244.8	0.9900[a]
1951	1,043.7	82.4	46.2	10.8	1,183.1	1,195.1	0.9900[a]
1950	1,021.4	67.7	45.9	8.4	1,143.4	1,154.9	0.9900[a]
1949	1,079.4	58.8	29.5	6.0	1,173.7	1,185.6	0.9900[a]
1948	951.8	48.8	21.6	6.0	1,028.2	1,038.6	0.9900[a]
1947	591.2	35.8	12.8	5.9	645.7	652.2	0.9900[a]
1946	385.5	31.7	4.9	9.3	431.4	435.8	0.9900[a]

[a] The actual value of expenditures from All Operating Funds is unknown for 1963 and for 1946–60, inclusive. The figures in column (6) are derived from those in column (5) on the assumption that the known components of this expenditure amount to 96% of the total in 1963 and 99% before 1961. The actual ratios of the components used in the estimation process to the known totals for 1961, 1962, and 1964–77, inclusive, are shown in column (7). The "unknown" additions equal the differences between the numbers in column (5) and those in column (6) for the years concerned.

[b] In 1977, $95.7 million of debt service was paid by first instance appropriation, here subtracted from column (3) to avoid double counting.

[c] In 1962 ($4.3 million) and 1961 ($4.5 million), the expenditures from the Parks and Recreation Land Acquisition Account are included in the subtotal, column (5), but not in columns (1) to (4).

Source: Annual Report of the Comptroller:

(1) 1977, pt. II, p. 6; 1976, pt. II, p. 6; 1971, p. 35; 1970, p. 37; 1969, p. 37; 1968, p. 37; 1967, p. 37; 1966, p. 37; 1965, p. 37; 1964, p. 35; 1963, p. 35; 1962, p. 55; 1961, p. 61; 1960, pp. 47, 100, 106; 1959, pp. 37, 90, 96; 1958, pp. 23, 77, 82; 1957, pp. 23, 77, 82; 1956, pp. 23, 77, 82; 1955, pp. 23, 77, 82; 1954, pp. 23, 77, 82; 1953, pp. 23, 77, 82; 1952, pp. 23, 77, 82; 1951, pp. 23, 77, 82; 1950, pp. 25, 81, 86; 1949, pp. 25, 73, 78; 1948, pp. 33, 81, 86; 1947, pp. 18, 55; 1946, pp. 16, 95;

415

Notes to Table C.12. (cont.)

(2) 1977, pt. II, pp. 40–1; 1976, pt. II, pp. 40–1; 1975, pt. II, pp. 42–3; 1974, pt. II, pp. 42–3; 1973, pp. 78–9; 1972, pp. 78–9; 1971, pp. 74–5; 1920, pp. 84–5; 1969, pp. 88–9; 1968, pp. 72–3; 1967, pp. 74–5; 1966, pp. 70–1, 1965, pp. 92–3; 1964, pp. 86–7; 1963, pp. 83; 1962, p. 103; 1961, p. 93; 1960, p. 93; 1959, p. 83; 1958, p. 69; 1957, p. 69; 1950, p. 69; 1955, p. 69; 1954, p. 69; 1953, p. 69; 1952, p. 69; 1951, p. 69; 1950, p. 73; 1949, p. 69; 1948, p. 77; 1947, p. 29; 1946, p. 27;

(3) 1977, pt. II, pp. 52–9; 1976, pt. II, pp. 52–9; 1975, pt. II, pp. 54–61; 1974, pt. II, pp. 54–61; 1973, pp. 90–7; 1972, pp. 90–7; 1971, pp. 90–6; 1970, pp. 102, 108; 1969, pp. 112–18; 1968, pp. 116–22; 1967, pp. 106–11; 1966, pp. 92–7; 1965, pp. 114–19; 1964, pp. 109–13; 1963, pp. 108–11; 1962, pp. 127–31; 1961, pp. 119–21; 1960, pp. 70, 96, 101; 1959, pp. 60, 86, 92; 1958, pp. 46, 72, 78; 1957, pp. 46, 72, 78; 1956, pp. 46, 72, 78; 1955, pp. 46, 72, 78; 1954, pp. 46, 72, 73, 77; 1953, pp. 46, 72, 77; 1952, pp. 46, 72, 79; 1951, pp. 46, 72, 79; 1950, pp. 48, 76, 83; 1949, pp. 42, 43, 46, 75; 1948, pp. 50, 51, 54, 83; 1947, pp. 22, 23, 57, 60; 1946, pp. 19, 99;

(4) 1977, pt. II, p. 101; 1976, pt. II, p. 101; 1975, pt. II, p. 102, 1975, pt. II, p. 106; 1974, pt. II, p. 106; 1973, p. 134; 1972, p. 132; 1971, pp. 36, 125; 1970, pp. 38, 138; 1969, pp. 38, 148; 1968, pp. 17, 38, 148; 1967, pp. 40, 136; 1966, pp. 40, 122; 1965, pp. 40, 146; 1964, pp. 38, 139; 1963, p. 121; 1962, p. 141; 1961, p. 131; 1960, p. 115; 1959, p. 105; 1958, p. 59; 1957, p. 59; 1956, p. 59; 1955, p. 59; 1954, p. 59; 1953, p. 59; 1952, p. 59; 1951, p. 59; 1950, p. 61; 1949, p. 58; 1948, p. 65; 1947, p. 40; 1946, p. 45.

(5) 1977, pt. I, pp. 15, 17, 20, pt. II, p. 101; 1976, pt. I, pp. 16, 17, 20, pt. II, p. 102; 1975, pt. I, pp. 12, 14, 17, pt. II, p. 106; 1974, pt. I, pp. 11, 13, 14, pt. II, p. 106; 1973, pp. 10, 12, 13, 134; 1972, pp. 10, 11, 13, 132; 1971, pp. 10, 11, 13, 125; 1970, pp. 12, 13, 15, 38, 148; 1969, pp. 13, 14, 17, 38, 148; 1968, pp. 13, 14, 16, 17, 38, 148; 1967, pp. 17, 40, 136; 1966, pp. 19, 40, 122; 1965, pp. 12, 40, 146; 1964, pp. 18, 38, 39; 1962, pp. 36–8; 1961, pp. 49–51.

Table C.13. *Total debt and debtlike commitments of New York State,*
1946–77 ($ millions)

At end of fiscal year (March 31)	(1) Full faith and credit debt of the state	(2) Full faith and credit debt of authorities	(3) Lease-purchase agreements	(4) "Moral obligation" debt[a]	(5) Total
1977	3,706	537	3,406	8,786	16,435
1976	3,641	541	3,276	9,173	16,631
1975	3,509	560	3,147	5,197	12,413
1974	3,448	566	2,954	4,246	11,214
1973	3,451	582	2,702	3,079	9,814
1972	3,362	581	2,284	2,149	8,376
1971	3,130	558	1,836	1,596	7,120
1970	2,523	571	1,537	1,101	5,732
1969	2,258	547	1,270	842	4,917
1968	1,769	523	1,073	663	4,028
1967	1,323	505	777	462	3,067
1966	1,236	499	537	418	2,690
1965	1,089	503	433	410	2,435
1964	1,082	505	191	333	2,111
1963	1,072	504	46	254	1,876
1962	1,050	493	28	60	1,631
1961	1,035	495	19	60	1,609
1960	988	498	15		1,501
1959	897	499	14		1,410
1958	744	500	14		1,258
1957	715	400	11		1,126
1956	704	450	5		1,159
1955	691	250	1		942
1954	738	250			988
1953	727	60			787
1952	706	60			766
1951	736				736
1950	681				681
1949	675				675
1948	768				768
1947	360				360
1946	388				388

Note: Figures for debtlike commitments are based upon the classification
scheme of the comptroller. See, for example, *Annual Report of the Comptrol-*
ler, 1976, pt. I, pp. 24–9.

Table C.14. *Full faith and credit debt of New York State,*
1946–76 ($ millions)

As of March 31	Net full faith and credit debt	Canals	Highways	Mass transportation	Aviation	Total transportation	World War I and II bonuses	Forests
1976	3,641.5		1,256.7	472.7	87.8	1,817.2		
1975	3,508.9		1,347.3	433.3	90.5	1,871.1		
1974	3,448.4		1,422.1	389.5	84.5	1,917.1		
1973	3,451.3		1,528.8	342.6	60.2	1,931.6		
1972	3,362.2		1,601.2	276.2	37.0	1,914.4		
1971	3,129.6		1,587.0	159.0	14.0	1,760.0		
1970	2,522.6	0.1	1,218.2	68.5	4.0	1,290.8		0.1
1969	2,258.3	0.3	990.7	65.5		1,056.5		0.2
1968	1,769.1	0.4	663.7			664.1		0.3
1967	1,323.2	0.5	350.0			350.5		0.4
1966	1,236.1	0.8	295.2			296.0		0.5
1965	1,088.7	1.3	161.1			162.4		0.7
1964	1,081.6	2.7	174.4			177.1		0.8
1963	1,072.0	4.5	188.1			192.6		1.0
1962	1,050.2	6.3	202.4			208.7		1.1
1961	1,034.5	9.4	222.0			231.4		1.3
1960	988.1	12.4	241.6			254.0		1.5
1959	897.0	15.5	258.8			274.3		1.6
1958	743.5	18.3	211.2			229.5		1.7
1957	715.0	21.3	189.0			210.3	30.0	1.9
1956	703.5	23.9	200.2			224.1	60.0	2.0
1955	682.3	26.4	210.0			236.4	90.0	2.2
1954	737.8	29.0	219.0			248.0	120.0	2.3
1953	726.8	31.5	224.0			255.4	150.0	2.5
1952	706.4	32.9	217.1			250.0	180.0	2.6
1951	736.2	36.4	202.2			238.6	212.3	2.7
1950	681.0	38.5	154.2			192.7	250.0	2.9
1949	675.2	40.3	149.0			189.3	277.8	3.0
1948	665.5	42.1	154.4			196.5	303.6	3.1
1947	359.7	43.8	159.6			203.4	5.4	3.3
1946	387.8	45.6	164.9			210.5	7.2	3.4

Source: Annual Report of the Comptroller, 1946, pp. 119, 121; 1947, pp. 65, 67; 1948, pp. 89, 91; 1949, p. 80; 1950, p. 88; 1951, p. 84; 1952, p. 84; 1953, p. 84; 1954, p. 84; 1955, p. 84; 1956, p. 84; 1957, p. 84; 1958, p. 84; 1959, p. 98; 1960, p. 108; 1961, p. 124; 1962, p. 134; 1963, p. 114; 1964, p. 130; 1965, p. 136; 1966, p. 112; 1967,

---

Notes to Table C.13 (*cont.*)

[a] *Annual Report of the Comptroller,* 1976, pt. I, p. 26 n. See ibid., 1977, pt. I, p. 28, n. 1, for an explanation of the dates of the data in this column, namely, October 31, before 1971.

Source: Annual Report of the Comptroller:

(1) 1977, pt. II, p. 86; 1976, pt. II, p. 88; 1975, pt. II, p. 90; 1974, pt. II, p. 90; 1973, p. 120; 1972, p. 120; 1971, p. 113; 1970, p. 127; 1969, p. 137; 1968, p. 137; 1967, p. 127; 1966, p. 112; 1965, p. 136; 1964, p. 130; 1963, p. 114; 1962, p. 134; 1961, p. 124; 1960, p. 108; 1959, p. 98; 1958, p. 84; 1957, p. 84; 1956, p. 84; 1955, p. 84; 1954, p. 84; 1953, p. 84; 1952, p. 84; 1951, p. 84; 1950, p. 88; 1949, pp. 89, 91; 1947, pp. 65, 67; 1946, pp. 119, 121 (and a letter from John J. O'Connor to Peter D. McClelland dated July 26, 1977);

Parks and recreation	Housing and urban renewal	Mental health	Higher education	Other state construction	Environmental protection	Pure water	Railroad preservation & development	Emergency unemployment relief
171.2	779.1	117.6	170.0	0.3	42.2	537.7	6.4	
151.1	798.0	130.2	153.0	0.4	10.0	395.1		
139.2	790.5	143.0	152.7	0.5		326.5		
141.3	784.3	161.3	158.1	0.6		274.1		
129.4	802.2	168.3	155.3	0.7		192.0		
101.9	820.3	174.7	118.0	0.8		153.9		
80.2	838.2	159.7	67.1	0.9		85.6		
84.9	849.1	157.1	54.6	1.0		55.0		
73.6	815.1	126.9	38.1	1.1		50.0		
67.2	784.1	92.7	23.6	1.2		3.4		
71.9	756.2	83.5	26.1	1.9				
76.7	722.7	94.3	28.6	3.2				
49.4	713.1	105.1	31.1	4.9				
52.3	670.0	115.9	33.6	6.6				
23.5	645.3	126.7	36.1	8.7				
8.1	606.7	137.5	38.6	10.8				
4.1	526.1	148.3	41.1	13.0				
4.4	436.4	142.7	21.2	16.4				
4.8	382.3	104.2		20.8				
5.1	386.5	55.6		25.7				
5.4	352.9	27.9		31.2				
5.8	309.0			39.0				
6.2	314.5			46.8				
6.6	257.8			54.6				
6.9	203.7			63.3				
7.5	203.0			72.2				
8.0	146.3			81.2				
8.5	105.9			90.6				
9.0	53.2			100.1				
9.5	25.6			109.5				3.0
10.0	26.2			119.0				11.5

p. 127; 1968, p. 137; 1969, p. 137; 1970, p. 127; 1971, p. 113; 1972, p. 120; 1973, p. 120; 1974, pt. II, p. 90; 1975, pt. II, p. 90; 1976, pt. II, p. 88.

Notes to Table C.13 (*cont.*)

(2) 1977, pt. I, p. 28; 1960, p. 108; 1959, p. 98; 1958, p. 84; 1957, p. 84; 1956, p. 84; 1955, p. 14; 1954, p. 14; 1953, p. 14; 1952, p. 14;

(3) 1977, pt. I, p. 26; 1962, p. 146; 1961, p. 137; 1960, p. 145 ("Construction of Buildings");

(4) 1977, pt. I, p. 28;

(5) The sum of (1), (2), (3), and (4).

Table C.15. *Authority debt backed by the full faith and credit of New York State, 1955–76 ($ millions)*

Year ending March 31	Total outstanding debt	New York State Thruway Authority	Port Authority of New York and New Jersey	Job Development Authority
1976	541	385	83	73
1975	560	398	86	76
1974	566	409	88	69
1973	582	420	91	71
1972	581	430	93	58
1971	558	439	72	47
1970	571	447	74	50
1969	547	455	44	48
1968	523	463	12	48
1967	505	467	12	26
1966	499	476	14	9
1965	503	480	16	7
1964	505	485	17	3
1963	504	489	13	2
1962	493	493		
1961	495	495		
1960	498	498		
1959	499	499		
1958	500	500		
1957	400	400		
1956	450	450		
1955	250	250		

Source: Annual Report of the Comptroller, 1976, pt. I, p. 28; 1960, p. 108; 1959, p. 98; 1958, p. 84; 1957, p. 84; 1956, p. 84.

Table C.16. *Debt service expenditures of New York State, 1946–77 ($ millions)*

Fiscal year ending March 31	Direct state debt: principal and interest			Debtlike commitments: lease-purchase and "moral obligation"		Total debt service
	General Fund[a]	First instance appropriations[b]	Other operating funds	General Fund	Other operating funds	
1977	412.5	95.7	74.3	83.2	170.2	835.4
1976	395.0		73.0	77.0	154.1	699.2
1975	327.8		64.3	69.3	157.3	618.7
1974	295.3		66.8	59.6	135.6	557.3
1973	264.5		59.4	49.5	113.6	487.0
1972	223.1		64.7	39.8	71.1	398.7
1971	175.7		61.8	29.5	46.7	313.7
1970	139.2		66.3	20.0	48.1	273.6
1969	100.2		57.3	15.0	35.2	207.7
1968	63.6		56.4	13.2	26.8	160.0
1967	54.9		57.5	10.2	21.0	143.6
1966	39.4		55.2	5.6	10.7	110.9
1965	40.3		49.1	4.1	11.1	104.6
1964	38.1		50.9	3.4	3.5	95.9
1963	38.6		40.8	N.A.	N.A.	79.4
1962	49.3		30.1	N.A.	N.A.	79.4
1961	49.2		29.2	N.A.	N.A.	78.4
1960	53.1		22.9	N.A.	N.A.	76.0
1959	33.2		22.1	N.A.	N.A.	55.3
1958	55.1		20.8	N.A.	N.A.	75.9
1957	55.3		19.8	N.A.	N.A.	75.1
1956	59.4		18.6	N.A.	N.A.	78.0
1955	60.0		17.2	N.A.	N.A.	77.2
1954	60.3		15.1	N.A.	N.A.	75.4
1953	62.2		14.5	N.A.	N.A.	76.7
1952	60.8[c]		12.3	N.A.	N.A.	73.1[c]
1951	71.1[c]		10.8	N.A.	N.A.	81.9[c]
1950	74.1[c]		8.4	N.A.	N.A.	82.5[c]
1949	172.1[c]		6.0	N.A.	N.A.	178.1[c]
1948	51.4[c]		6.0	N.A.	N.A.	57.4[c]
1947	36.5		5.9	N.A.	N.A.	42.4
1946	39.9		9.3	N.A.	N.A.	49.2

[a] Includes interest on temporary debt, such as the annual spring borrowing.
[b] Interest on tax and revenue anticipation notes used to finance loans to New York City.
[c] Includes redemption of temporary debt, and administrative expenses, of the War Bonus Fund and War Bonus Account: 1952 – 3.1; 1951 – 13.0; 1950 – 13.0; 1949 – 110.4; 1948 – 0.6.

Source: Annual Report of the Comptroller, 1977, pt. II, p. 101; 1976, pt. II, p. 102; 1975, pt. II, p. 106; 1974, pt. II, p. 106; 1973, p. 134; 1972, p. 132; 1971, pp. 36, 125; 1970, pp. 38, 138; 1969, pp. 38, 148; 1968, pp. 17, 38, 148; 1967, pp. 40, 136; 1966, pp. 40, 122; 1965, pp. 40, 146; 1964, pp. 38, 139; 1963, p. 121; 1962, p. 141; 1961, p. 131; 1960, p. 115; 1959, p. 105; 1958, p. 59; 1957, p. 59; 1956, p. 59; 1955, p. 59; 1954, p. 59; 1953, p. 59; 1952, p. 59; 1951, p. 59; 1950, p. 61; 1949, p. 58; 1948, p. 65; 1947, p. 40; 1946, p. 45.

Table C.17. *New York State: the War Bonus and Mental Health Bond Account (1948–68) and the War Bonus Fund (1948–58) ($ millions)*

Fiscal year ending March 31	War bonus payments	Tax revenues	Administrative expenses	Debt service payments	Transfer to Capital Construction Fund	Transfer to Local Assistance Fund	Transfer to State Purposes Fund
1948	173.2	4.2	0.7	*a*	0.0		
1949	141.4	42.6	1.0	44.0	0.0		
1950	17.8	48.0	0.4	48.0	0.0		
1951	5.3	47.1	0.1	47.4	0.0		
1952	0.6	52.9	0.1	36.7	0.0		
1953	0.3	57.8	0.1	33.5	0.0		
1954	0.2	59.0	0.1	32.9	56.6		
1955	0.1	60.3	0.1	32.2	30.0		
1956	0.1	69.7	*a*	31.7	35.0		
1957	0.1	73.4	*a*	31.1	49.0		

Year							
1958	0.1	78.2	0.1	30.5	50.0		13.0
1959	a	85.3	a	6.2	56.0		13.0
1960	a	107.1	a	12.5	92.0		
1961	0.1	113.2	a	14.7	96.0		
1962	0.1	134.5	a	14.4	128.5		
1963	a	140.0	a	13.0	127.1		
1964	a	150.8	a	11.1	139.8		
1965	0.1	151.1	a	13.6	137.5		
1966	0.1	162.3	a	14.6	0.0	147.6	
1967	a	191.5	a	13.7	0.0	175.2	
1968	a	221.2	a	13.8	0.0	210.2	

Note: The War Bonus and Mental Health Bond Account was called the War Bonus Account from 1947 to 1953 and the War Bonus and Mental Health Construction Bond Account from 1954 to 1959.

a Less than 0.05.

Source: *Annual Report of the Comptroller*, 1948, p. 86; 1949, p. 78; 1950, p. 86; 1951, p. 82; 1952, p. 82; 1953, p. 82; 1954, p. 82; 1955, p. 82; 1956, p. 82; 1957, p. 82; 1958, p. 82; 1959, p. 96; 1960, p. 106, 1961, p. 110; 1962, p. 112; 1963, p. 92; 1964, p. 99; 1965, p. 105; 1966, p. 83; 1967, p. 97; 1968, p. 107.

Table C.18. Expenditures on mental hygiene institutions and by the Mental Hygiene Department in New York State, 1946–64 ($ millions)

Fiscal year ending March 31	Expenditures of Mental Hygiene Department			Expenditures of Capital Construction Fund[a]	Total[b]	Expenditures on mental hygiene institutions[c]
	State Purposes	Local Assistance	Capital Construction			
1964	255.3	16.1	33.6		305.0	248.3
1963	244.7	14.9	21.9		281.6	238.1
1962	229.7	14.0	23.2		266.9	223.3
1961	214.5	11.7	28.0		254.2	208.3
1960	207.2	11.7		35.7	218.9	201.3
1959	194.3	10.6		74.5	204.9	188.8
1958	180.3	8.6		72.1	188.9	175.3
1957	165.3	7.1		54.8	172.4	161.3
1956	155.9	5.0		44.5	160.9	152.3
1955	142.8	0.1		49.7	142.9	139.6
1954	130.3	[d]		40.8	130.3	127.2
1953	128.4	0.0		41.4	128.4	125.7

Year					
1952	119.8	0.0	40.2	119.8	117.4
1951	103.6	0.0	39.6	103.6	101.5
1950	97.5	0.0	17.8	97.5	95.6
1949	93.0	0.0	6.7	93.0	91.2
1948	80.7	0.0	7.1	80.7	79.1
1947	61.8	0.0	2.7	61.8	60.3
1946	50.5[e]	0.0[e]	4.2	50.5[e]	49.1

[a] Before 1961, the Capital Construction Fund was separate from the General Fund, and its expenditures were not divided among the state's departments. For 1960, the figure shown is "Hospitals, prisons, and welfare institutions"; for years before 1960, the figure shown is "Hospitals, colleges, schools, prisons, etc.," "Hospitals, colleges, schools, prisons, and other construction," or "Construction of State buildings, etc." The components cannot be identified until 1966. The figure in this column is not included in the total column next to it.

[b] Does not include the column immediately to the left. See note a.

[c] Part of the State Purposes expenditures, except in 1965, when the Mental Hygiene Services Fund is included.

[d] Less than 0.05.

[e] The Local Assistance–State Purposes classification did not exist in fiscal 1946, but a zero is assumed for the Local Assistance component in imitation of the seven zeros above it.

Source: *Annual Report of the Comptroller*, 1964, pp. 44, 62; 1963, pp. 40, 64; 1962, pp. 60, 84; 1961, pp. 64, 85; 1960, pp. 50, 75, 100; 1959, pp. 40, 65, 91; 1958, pp. 26, 51, 77; 1957, pp. 26, 51, 77; 1956, pp. 26, 51, 77; 1955, pp. 26, 51, 79; 1953, pp. 26, 51, 79; 1952, pp. 26, 51, 79; 1951, pp. 26, 51, 79; 1950, pp. 28, 53, 83; 1949, pp. 28, 51, 75; 1948, pp. 36, 59, 83; 1947, pp. 21, 34, 57; 1946, pp. 18, 39, 99.

Table C.19. *Mental hygiene expenditures from All Operating Funds in New York State, 1964–77 ($ millions)*

Fiscal year ending March 31	Expenditures on mental hygiene			
	State Purposes	Local Assistance	Capital Construction	Total
1977	906.3	141.9	23.0	1,071.2
1976	895.9	118.7	39.0	1,053.6
1975	827.4	121.1	47.8	996.3
1974	711.2	79.1	56.3	846.6
1973	630.2	55.2	93.7	779.1
1972	595.2	95.2	126.6	817.0
1971	562.8	44.4	105.3	712.5
1970	483.0	66.3	81.7	631.0
1969	424.9	59.1	89.7	573.7
1968	376.2	31.7	76.3	484.2
1967	333.9	36.9	45.6	416.4
1966	288.9	25.4	45.3	359.6
1965	263.6	16.9	40.0	320.5
1964	255.6	16.7	32.6	304.9

Source: Annual Report of the Comptroller, 1977, pt. I, pp. 15, 17, 20; 1976, pt. I, pp. 16, 17, 20; 1975, pt. I, p. 12, 14, 17; 1974, pt. I, pp. 11, 13, 14; 1973, pp. 10, 12, 13; 1972, pp. 10, 11, 13; 1971, pp. 10, 11, 13; 1970, pp. 12, 13, 15; 1969, pp. 13, 14, 17; 1968, pp. 13, 14, 16; 1967, p. 17; 1966, p. 19; 1965, p. 12; 1964, p. 18.

Table C.20. *Statewide public authorities of New York State: annual gross revenues as a percentage of bonds and notes outstanding, 1960–76*

Fiscal year ending March 31	(1) Bonds and notes outstanding at fiscal year end ($ millions)	(2) Gross revenues in the fiscal year ($ millions)	(3) (2) ÷ (1) (%)
1976	14,935	2,394	16.02
1975	14,150	2,067	14.60
1974	13,254	1,890	14.25
1973	12,057	1,844	15.29
1972	10,589	1,640	15.48
1971	8,875	1,572	17.71
1970	7,357	1,403	19.07
1969	6,502	1,187	18.25
1968	6,161	1,137	18.45
1967	5,108	1,059	20.73
1966	4,663	925	19.83
1965	4,536	836	18.43
1964	4,198	763	18.17
1963	3,744	727	19.41
1962	3,268	575	17.59
1961	3,131	552	17.63
1960	2,921	528	18.07

Source: Annual Report of the Comptroller, 1977, pt. I, p. 36; 1976, pt. I, p. 40; 1975, pt. I, p. 32; 1974, pt. I, p. 27; 1973, p. 23; 1972, p. 23; 1971, p. 22; 1970, p. 23; 1969, p. 24; 1968, p. 22; 1967, p. 30; 1966, pp. 27, 28; 1965, p. 27; 1964, p. 20; 1963, p. 30; 1962, pp. 48, 49; 1961, p. 53.

Table C.21. *Statewide public authorities of New York State: annual gross revenues as a percentage of bonds and notes outstanding, 1976*

Public authority	(1) Bonds and notes outstanding at fiscal year end ($ thousands)	(2) Gross revenues in the fiscal year ($ thousands)	(3) (2) ÷ (1) (%)
Albany Port District	3,526	1,031	29.23
Battery Park City	200,000	0	0.00
Buffalo and Fort Erie Public Bridge	2,480	3,479	140.28
Capital District Transportation	0	5,039[a]	∞
Central New York Regional Market	123	283	230.08
Central New York Regional Transportation	0	4,587[a]	∞
Dormitory Authority[b]	1,938,977	3,443	0.17
East Hudson Parkway	0	6,321	∞
Energy Research and Development	9,530	2,614	27.42
Environmental Facilities Corporation	23,408	454	1.93
Facilities Development Corporation[c]	0	59,860	∞
Genesee Valley Regional Market	1,212	405	33.41
Higher Education Services Corporation	0	83,383[d]	∞
Housing Finance Agency[c]	5,203,547	5,817	0.11
Industrial Exhibit	2,576	750	29.11
Jones Beach State Parkway	5,801	13,062	225.16
Lake Champlain Bridge	0	412	∞
Long Island Rail Road[e]	0	133,670	∞
Manhattan and Bronx Surface Transit Operating	0	130,403	∞
Medical Care Facilities Finance Agency	161,320	1	0.00
Metropolitan Transportation[e]	53,565	46,488[a]	86.78
Municipal Assistance Corporation[f]	0	0	—
Municipal Bond Bank	0	0	—
New York City Transit	113,750	643,461	565.68
New York State Bridge	22,995	8,203	35.67
New York State Job Development	77,860	1,296	1.66
New York State Thruway	762,212	136,364	17.89
Niagara Frontier Transportation	0	23,044	∞
Ogdensburg Bridge and Port[g]	920	1,066[a]	115.86
Port Authority of New York and New Jersey[h]	2,021,677	526,451	26.04
Port of Oswego	0	374	∞
Power Authority of the State of New York	2,402,343	231,879	9.65
Project Finance Agency[f]	0	0	—
Rochester–Genesee Regional Transportation	430	7,426[a]	1,726.97
Staten Island Rapid Transit	0	1,319	∞

Table C.21. *(cont.)*

Public authority	(1) Bonds and notes outstanding at fiscal year end ($ thousands)	(2) Gross revenues in the fiscal year ($ thousands)	(3) (2) ÷ (1) (%)
State of New York Mortgage Agency	362,611	31,673	8.73
State University Construction Fund[b]	0	0	—
Thousand Islands Bridge	0	1,738	∞
Triborough Bridge and Tunnel	255,990	195,839	76.50
United Nations Development Corporation	55,200	5,232	9.47
Urban Development Corporation	1,252,787	77,362	6.17

[a] Does not include revenues from operating assistance programs.

[b] The Dormitory Authority is partially supported by the State University Income and Dormitory Income Funds (operating funds), which had receipts of $378,803,000 in 1976. This sum produces totals of $1,938,977,000 and $382,246,000, and a ratio of 19.71%. The State University Construction Fund initially reserves the money but issues no financial statements.

[c] The Facilities Development Corporation helps support the Housing Finance Agency. The figures shown omit the $347,313,000 (in 1976) channeled through the Mental Hygiene Program Funds (an operating fund). The combined totals are $5,203,547,000 and $412,990,000, producing a ratio of 7.93%.

[d] Covers sixteen months; omits all operations except the Guaranty Student Loan Fund.

[e] The Long Island Rail Road is part of the Metropolitan Transportation Authority, although they are shown separately. The totals are $53,565,000 and $180,158,000.

[f] These are "special purpose authorities whose financial statements do not lend themselves to this schedule" (*Annual Report of the Comptroller,* 1976, p. 37). "MAC has assets of $576 million, liabilities of $4,068 million (of which $3,676 million is Bonds Outstanding), and a net funding deficit of $3,492. Its bonds are secured by a first call on New York City's share of" certain taxes. PFA "has assets of $527,741,000, liabilities of $318,959,000 (of which $302,209,000 represents Bonds and Notes Outstanding); contingent liabilities of $197,280,000; and a restricted fund balance of $11,502,000" (ibid.).

[g] Covers fifteen months.

[h] Omits Commuter Car program financed under state-guaranteed bonds. As of December 31, 1976, this program had assets of $103.7 million, $100.5 million of which were in commuter cars, and bonds outstanding of $80.9 million.

Source: Annual Report of the Comptroller, 1976, pt. I, p. 37, pt. II, pp. 69, 80.

APPENDIX D

Tables, figures, and maps

Tables

430

Figures

Maps

Notes

1. Introduction

1 Daniel Webster, *The Writings and Speeches of Daniel Webster* (Boston: Little, Brown, 1903), II, 50.

2 New York [State], *Report of the Debates and Proceedings of the Convention for the Revision of the Constitution of the State of New York, 1846* (W. Attree and W. Bishop, 1846), 946.

3 A second technique for circumventing the need for voter approval was the lease-purchase agreement. For a description of how it worked and where it was used, see Chapter 6.

4 David Hume, *Essays: Moral, Political and Literary* (Oxford: Oxford University Press, 1963), 357.

5 New York [State], Temporary State Commission on Coordination of State Activities, *Staff Report on Public Authorities under New York State*, by William Ronan, Legislative Document no. 46, March 21, 1956, p. 56.

6 Letter accepting the nomination for governor, October 7, 1882. (George F. Parker [ed.], *The Writings and Speeches of Grover Cleveland* [New York: Cassell, 1892], 6.)

7 James Ring Adams, "New York City's Legal Hangover," *Wall Street Journal*, March 24, 1980, p. 24.

8 Ibid.

9 Webster (1903), II, 63.

2. Economic structure and economic problems

1 *New York Times*, April 10, 1977, p. 1.

2 Ibid., February 15, 1977, p. 45.

3 Quoted in Timothy B. Clark, "The Frostbelt Fights for a New Future," *Empire State Report* II (October–November 1976), 332.

4 Employment data for 1965. See Section 2.4.a.

5 The qualifications mainly concern the prospect that a factor inflow will raise, rather than lower, factor returns through such mechanisms as the generation of economies of scale. A rising density of commercial and industrial activity, for example, could lead to specialization of services and other benefits loosely characterized in the development literature as "agglomeration effects."

6 Examples come readily to mind, such as a flight to avoid religious persecution or the forced migration of American Indians. Nevertheless, throughout most of American history, for most of its migrating people, the

hypothesis that the dominant motivation was higher prospective economic rewards seems to hold up reasonably well.

7   The combined population of Nassau, Suffolk, Rockland, and Westchester counties increased by 2.4 million, which is approximately 56 percent of the total state increase (outside New York City) of 4.3 million.

8   The counties are Erie (+316,000), Monroe (+274,000) and Onondaga (+178,000), respectively.

9   Calculated from data in U.S., Bureau of the Census, *Historical Statistics of the United States: Colonial Times to 1970* (1975), I, 243–4. If the growth rate in New York's per capita income (because of retardation factors) falls behind the growth rate in national per capita income, then per capita income within the Empire State must decline as a percentage of national per capita income.

10   If transfer payments are excluded, New York's average per capita income in 1978 was only about 3 percent higher than the national average. See Roy Bahl, "Fiscal Retrenchment in a Declining State: The New York Case," *National Tax Journal* XXXII (June 1979*a*), Supplement, 284. According to one estimate, when regional cost-of-living adjustments are made, New York real per capita income was 8 percent above the national average in 1969 and 6 percent below that average in 1978. (Frans Seastrand, New York Department of Commerce, private communication, July 1, 1980.)

11   To both employment and income data one must append a cautionary note that, although technically important, does not imperil any of the main conclusions cited in the text. Employment data are based upon place of residence. As such, they reflect the employment of New York State residents only. Out-of-state residents who work in New York tend to exceed the number of New York residents who work in other states (primarily because of New Jersey and Connecticut residents commuting to New York City to work). New York employment data as reported therefore tend to understate the "true" number of jobs in the New York economy. All of the conclusions noted in the text, however, deal with relative growth rates. As long as the ratio of reported employment to "true" employment did not shift dramatically during this period (which seems unlikely), the major conclusions survive unscathed. Similar if somewhat more complicated coverage problems arise with income data. Here, too, as long as the relative coverage did not change dramatically, the conclusions concerning the decline in New York's per capita income as a percentage of the national average survive. For further discussion of both problems, see Roy Bahl, "The Long Term Fiscal Outlook for New York State," in *The Decline of New York in the 1970's: A Demographic, Economic and Fiscal Analysis* (Binghamton: Center for Social Analysis, 1977), 97, n. 2, and 98, n. 1.

12   Output comparisons are precluded by a scarcity of reliable data. Gross State Product has been estimated by the New York Department of Energy, but only for the years following 1960.

13   Comparison based upon estimation procedures outlined in New York [State], Council of Economic Advisors, *Annual Report*, 1971, 11.

14   See David J. DeLaubenfels, "Soil," in John H. Thompson (ed.), *Geography of New York State* (Syracuse: Syracuse University Press, 1966), 109.

15   The fractions refer to calculations for the region that includes the following counties: Rockland, Westchester, Queens, Nassau, Kings, New York,

Bronx, Richmond, and Suffolk.

16   See New York [State], Department of Labor, *Labor Statistics Relating to the Economy of New York State*, Research Report 1975–25, November 1975*a*.

17   Ibid., 26.

18   The index used here is the result of simple division. If, say, New York employment in 1952 totaled 6 million jobs, and state employment totals in every year were divided by 6 million, the result would be an index of New York State employment, using 1952 as the "base" year, or with "1952 = 100." This last phrase signals two things: (1) all annual employment totals have been divided by the 1952 employment total, and (2) the results have been multiplied by 100, or expressed in percentage terms. Thus, if the number for 1970 resulting from this division were 150, this would indicate that 1970 employment was 150 percent of 1952 employment (or 6 million × 150/100 = 9 million). One advantage of such an index is that it facilitates the comparison of the growth performance among various numerical series that are not at all similar in absolute amounts. United States total employment in 1952 exceeded 41 million. New York employment in 1952 totaled roughly 2 million in the upstate region and 4 million in the downstate region. How can the growth in three such widely different numbers be compared? One solution is to convert all three to indexes and plot the results, using the same base year (that is, the same year as divisor). The choice of the base year is arbitrary, but for purposes of comparing growth performances, dividing by the first year in the series helps the visual comparison of relative growth rates.

19   This does not imply that retardation began in 1946. The choice of that year was dictated by data availability. The rate of growth of employment in New York's manufacturing sector first fell behind the comparable national growth rate before the turn of the century. This sluggishness was more than offset by rapid employment growth in other sectors, at least until the 1930s.

20   Government employment has been excluded from this index of nonmanufacturing employment.

21   Here too the implication is not that retardation began only in 1952. The choice of initial year was again dictated by data availability.

22   As this book goes to press, no reasonably accurate estimates of these multiplier effects are available on a statewide basis. See Section 2.7, "Of models and methodology."

23   These estimates are not easily derived, and all such estimates should therefore be viewed as approximations to the true value of export activity. For a description of how the estimates of Table 2.6 were derived, see Raymond D. Horton and Charles Brecher (eds.), *Setting Municipal Priorities: 1980* (Montclair, N.J.: Allanheld, Osmun, 1979), app. 1.

24   This statement (based upon conventional shift-share analysis) is true, whether one focuses upon broad industrial classifications, such as those of Table C.2 (Appendix C), or upon industrial divisions within manufacturing. See for example New York [State], Department of Labor (1975*a*), 23–46; Benjamin Chinitz, "Manufacturing Employment in New York State: The Anatomy of Decline," in *The Decline of New York in the 1970's: A Demographic, Economic and Fiscal Analysis* (Binghamton, N.Y.: Center for Social Analysis, 1977), 67, 73; Peter D. McClelland, "The Structure of the Unemployment Problem," in

Felician F. Foltman and Peter D. McClelland (eds.), *New York State's Economic Crisis: Jobs, Income, and Economic Growth* (Ithaca, N.Y.: New York State School of Industrial and Labor Relations, 1977), 41–4.

25 The following empirical assertions are based upon the Dun and Bradstreet file on employment and establishments. These data are available for four years – 1969, 1972, 1974, and 1976 – and cover between 50 and 80 percent of all private sector employment, with available information including the establishment's size, age, four-digit SIC code, corporate affiliation, location, and sales. Coverage apparently varies across regions, and across time. The empirical assertions discussed here, however, are of the most general sort, and therefore are unlikely to be seriously biased by changing coverage. Those assertions are based upon both published material by, and conversations with, those who have worked extensively with these data. For further discussion, see Roy W. Bahl, "The New York State Economy: 1960–1978 and the Outlook," Metropolitan Studies Program, Maxwell School, Syracuse University, Occasional Paper no. 37, October 1979*b*, pp. 63–72; David L. Birch, "The Job Generation Process," unpublished paper, M.I.T. Program on Neighborhood and Regional Change, Cambridge, Mass., 1979; Carol L. Jusenius and Larry C. Ledebur, *Documenting the "Decline" of the North,* U.S. Department of Commerce, Economic Development Research Report, June 1978.

26 A number of experts on the state's economy have privately expressed doubt to the authors concerning this finding, citing the unusually high bankruptcy rates of New York. All of the death rate data, however, are consistent with this assertion.

27 The one notable exception is New Hampshire.

28 The economic problems of New England, for example, appear to be quite unrelated to migration. Available evidence suggests that in recent years "the migration of firms in either direction [in or out] has not been significant." See Carol L. Jusenius and Larry C. Ledebur, *Where Have All the Firms Gone? An Analysis of the New England Economy,* U.S. Department of Commerce, Economic Development Research Report, September 1977.

29 The linkage between New York City as a port of disembarkation and the subsequent retention of immigrants appears to be obvious, but it is not. In the realm of pure theory, the arriving immigrant should contemplate all possible location options. In practice, this choice procedure appears to have been constrained in many cases by ignorance and by ethnic, religious, and family ties anchored in the New York City area. For such reasons, the city probably retained more of new arrivals than would have been the case had the location decision been made for strictly economic reasons and with perfect information.

30 The two main data sources on firm migration are (1) New York State Department of Commerce files, and (2) the Dun and Bradstreet files discussed in Section 2.4. These have been analyzed in New York [State], Select Committee on the Economy, *Industry in New York: A Time of Transition,* Legislative Document no. 12, 1974, app.; New York [State], Department of Commerce, "A Statistical Profile of Industrial Migration in New York State: 1975," unpublished paper, 1978*b*; Marilyn Rubin, Ilene Wagner, and Pearl Kramer, "Industrial Migration: A Case Study of Destination by City–Suburban Origin within the New York Metropolitan Area," *Journal of the American Real Estate and Urban Economics Association* VI (Winter 1978), 417–37; Birch (1979).

31 As for the characteristics of large corporations that moved, some evidence exists to suggest that the giant corporations that shifted their headquarters out of New York City were below-average performers in their industry in productivity, profitability, and rates of growth. See Regional Plan Association, "Business in the Region: Structure and Performance of the Region's Producer Economy in 1972–75," *Regional Plan News*, no. 103, April 1979*a*, p. 10.

32 In the postwar era, the commerce of the Port of New York continued to grow, but at rates well behind those registered for the nation as a whole. Between 1947 and 1977, for example, total (net) waterborne commerce of the United States rose by almost 250 percent, while that of New York advanced by less than 40 percent. The reasons for this declining importance are many, including the technological changes noted, but also (1) government policies that aided competitive shipping routes (such as the development of the St. Lawrence Seaway), (2) rising congestion on the city's main traffic arteries, plus deteriorating and defective rail linkages with the hinterland, and (3) mismanagement and neglect by New York City officials. See John I. Griffin, *The Port of New York* (New York: Arco, 1959); Mitchell L. Moss, "Staging a Renaissance on the Waterfront," *New York Affairs* VI, no. 2 (1980), 3–19. (Data from U.S., Corps of Engineers, *Waterborne Commerce of the United States, 1977*, pt. 1, pp. 5, 48.)

33 See Section 2.1. To this list of factors, the financial community might wish to add the interest rate ceilings of New York usury laws that recently have encouraged certain banks to move some of their consumer lending operations to states with higher usury ceilings. A proposal to modify this New York law was narrowly defeated in 1980. (See for example *New York Times*, June 15, 1980, pp. 1, 30.) Another factor occasionally mentioned is the deterioration of the capital stock, particularly in the New York metropolitan region. Net investment in that region lagged about one-third behind national levels in 1975 "and shrank drastically by 1975. That year, it barely exceeded depreciation. Indications are that large corporations made a net investment of over $2.0 billion in the [New York Metropolitan] Region in 1975. Because total net investment was barely $0.5 billion, the clear implication is that very substantial *disinvestment* took place in the rest of the private economy, mostly in the small business and residential sectors." (Regional Plan Association [1979*a*], 6.) Though a decline in the capital stock will affect future growth possibilities, this particular decline would seem to be an effect of the other causes listed in this section.

34 See for example Walter Isard, *Location and Space Economy* (Cambridge, Mass.: M.I.T. Press, 1956); Curtis C. Harris, Jr., and Frank E. Hopkins, *Location Analysis* (Toronto: D. C. Heath, 1972); G. B. Norcliffe, "A Theory of Manufacturing Places," in Lyndhurst Collins and David F. Walker (eds.), *Locational Dynamics of Manufacturing Activity* (New York: John Wiley, 1975), 19–57. A useful layman's introduction to the topic can be found in the two articles by William Alonso in John Friedmann and William Alonso (eds.), *Regional Policy: Readings in Theory and Applications* (Cambridge, Mass.: M.I.T. Press, 1975), 35–96.

35 *New York Times*, May 16, 1976, p. 52.

36 Differential tax rates are also less important than might be initially expected. "This is because corporate taxes are based not on the location of a

company's mailbox, but on the location of its employees, its sales, and its property. A company whose only facility in New York City is its headquarters office, for example, typically allocates a large percentage of its taxable income to other jurisdictions, beyond reach of the New York State and New York City tax collectors." (Herbert E. Meyer, "Why Corporations Are on the Move," *Fortune* XCIII [May 1976], 253.)

37   Meyer (1976), 254.

38   "What Management Needs to Know before Picking a Plant Site," *Dun's Review* CXIV (October 1979), 15.

39   *New York Times*, April 17, 1975, p. 43.

40   As of the writing of this book, there are three models of the New York City region, and three models for forecasting New York State employment. The New York City models are briefly reviewed in Horton and Brecher (1979), 31, n. 5. The statewide models are assessed in some detail in Bahl (1979*b*), 111–29. An excellent and recent survey of the state of the art is available in Roger Bolton, "Multiregional Models in Policy Analysis," paper presented at a Conference on Modeling the Multi-Region Economic System, Philadelphia, June 14–15, 1979. All of the models confront grave data problems. None can satisfactorily come to grips with firm relocation or branch expansion and contraction. At the most general level, Bolton notes, "One can only be distressed by how inadequately investment is specified even in models which are otherwise extremely complicated and sophisticated" (p. 15).

41   Forecasting the total impact upon employment would probably be a two-stage process. The first step would require estimating the initial impact of a particular policy – say, a tax break for manufacturing firms – upon employment in the firms directly affected. The second step would be to estimate the multiplied effect of this initial change, as more manufacturing employment stimulated demand in other sectors of the region.

3.   The causes of New York retardation

1   *New York Times*, February 7, 1971, p. 3.

2   Calculated from data in U.S., Bureau of the Census (1975), I, 12, 22.

3   More recently the black population has shown some signs, albeit modest signs, of drifting to the suburbs also, particularly to New York City's suburban ring.

4   In 1975, New York City had 55 percent of the total population in the U.S.A. of Puerto Rican origin. At 941,000, it was close to two-thirds the size of the entire population of Puerto Rico itself. (New York [City], Temporary Commission on City Finances, *Economic and Demographic Trends in New York City: The Outlook for the Future*, Thirteenth Interim Report, May 1977*b*, p. 91.)

5   See New York [City], Temporary Commission on City Finances (1977*b*), 87–92.

6   There is some recent evidence for New York suggesting that for certain classes of migrants, particularly upper-income groups and retirees, this linkage may be rather weak. See Calvin Beale's Discussion *of Manufacturing Employment in New York State: The Anatomy of Decline*, in *The Decline of New York in the 1970's* (1977), 40–1.

7   See for example Elizabeth F. Durbin, *Welfare Income and Employment* (New York: Praeger, 1969), 55–60; Larry R. Jackson and William A. Johnson, *Protest by the Poor: The Welfare Rights Movement in the City of New York* (New York: Rand Institute, 1973), 236; David M. deFerranti et al., *The Welfare and Nonwelfare Poor in New York City* (New York: Rand Corporation, 1974), R–1381–NYC; Miriam Ostow and Anna B. Dutka, *Work and Welfare in New York City* (Baltimore: Johns Hopkins, 1975), 75–6; Larry H. Long, "Poverty Status and Receipt of Welfare among Migrants and Nonmigrants in Large Cities," *American Sociological Review* XXXIX (February 1974), 46–56.

8   Estimate by Miles D. Storfer, New York State Department of Social Services, for mothers receiving AFDC payments. (Private communication, July 31, 1978.)

9   For an extended description of all of these programs, see New York [City], Temporary Commission on City Finances, *Public Assistance Programs in New York City: Some Proposals for Reform*, Twelfth Interim Report, February 1977f.

10   New York [City], Temporary Commission on City Finances (1977*b*), 86.

11   For a review of sources and evidence, see Peter A. Morrison, "New York State's Transition to Stability: The Demographic Outlook," in *The Decline of New York in the 1970's* (1977), 12.

12   Ibid.

13   The causes of this decline of course are not limited to the change in population mix, as indicated by the fact that the period of greatest decline (1929 to 1950) predates the period of heavy minority influx. The median income of minorities was nevertheless well below the regional average.

14   The city's trend toward an older population has far outpaced that of the nation. As of 1975, for example, 13 percent of New York City's population was 65 or older. The comparable national figure was 10.5 percent. (New York [City], Temporary Commission on City Finances [1977*b*], 75.)

15   The state's crude birth rate (number of births per thousand) fell from 18.6 to 13.0 between 1965 and 1975. The comparable national decline was from 19.4 to 14.2. (Morrison [1977], 9.)

16   See New York [City], Temporary Commission on City Finances (1977*b*), 90.

17   The one flow contrary to this marked outmigration is the sharp increase in the 1970s in New York City's foreign-born population, particularly its nonwhite foreign-born population. (See ibid., 92–5.)

18   The crude rate of natural increase (birth rate minus death rate) in 1970 was 5.6 per thousand for New York State's white population and 17.3 per thousand for its nonwhite population. Comparable rates for New York City were 3.9 and 16.7 per thousand, respectively. (Calculated from data supplied by the New York State Department of Health, Vital Statistics Division.)

19   See for example Morrison (1977), 10; New York [City], Temporary Commission on City Finances (1977*b*), 71.

20   New York [State], Department of Labor, *Annual Planning Information, Rochester Area*, BLMI Report FY78, no. 92, June 1978, p. 1. The pervasiveness of outmigration from all the inner cities is suggested by the following migration estimates for the city as a whole:

| City | Estimated net migration, 1970–77 | |
	No.	%
Albany	−2,400	−0.3
Binghamton	−8,600	−3.2
Buffalo	−68,800	−5.1
Elmira	−5,600	−5.6
New York City[a]	−814,100	−9.0
Rochester	−31,800	−3.3
Syracuse	−16,600	−2.6
Utica–Rome	−23,700	−7.0
Total state	−867,000	−4.8

[a] Bronx, Kings, New York, Putnam, Queens, Richmond, Rockland, and Westchester counties.
Source: Ibid., FY79, no. 52, p. 8.

21　This factor is particularly stressed in the optimistic pronouncements of Herbert Bienstock, former head of the New York office of the Bureau of Labor Statistics. See, for example, *New York Times,* April 17, 1975, p. 43; ibid., January 8, 1978, p. 75; Herbert Bienstock, "New York City's Labor Market: Past Trends, Current Conditions, Future Prospects," *City Almanac* XII (December 1977), 17–18.

22　Very recent and somewhat tentative evidence suggests that a larger percentage of minorities and low-income families may be leaving the state, but it is too early to determine whether this trend will persist and whether the volume will be significant. For a review of the evidence, see Bahl (1979*b*), 44–8.

23　See New York [City], Temporary Commission on City Finances (1977*b*), 79–84.

24　The rapid rise of younger migrants from the city in the early 1970s reflected, to no small degree, a rise in supply as postwar babies became would-be workers, and a slump in demand as the state's secular retardation was reinforced by a national downturn in the business cycle.

25　See, for example, Felician F. Foltman, "The Business Climate in New York State: A Survey of the Perceptions of Labor and Management Officials," in Foltman and McClelland (1977); New York [State], Legislative Commission on Expenditure Review, *Industrial Development in New York State,* Program Audit 12.1.74, November 25, 1974, p. 5.

26　New York [State], Select Committee on the Economy (1974), 38.

27　The other is Rhode Island.

28　Most analysts emphasize that the evidence does not support the hypothesis that this law has produced more frequent and longer strikes in the state. For example, data on time lost because of labor disputes per 10,000 potential man-days make clear that New York has a record almost identical to the national average. (See New York [State], Select Committee on the Economy [1974], 38.) The law may nevertheless have an effect on wages by strengthening union bargaining power.

29 As of 1972, for example, 36 percent of nonagricultural employees in New York belonged to a union, which placed the state in sixth place nationally, behind West Virginia (41), Michigan (38), Washington (38), Pennsylvania (38), and Hawaii (37). (*Directory of National Employee Associations,* 1973.)

30 *New York Times,* January 3, 1976, p. 30.

31 New York [State], Select Committee on the Economy (1974), 39.

32 See New York [City], Temporary Commission on City Finances (1977b), 46–51.

33 U.S., Department of Labor, *Industry Wage Survey: Women's and Misses' Dresses,* Bulletin 1783, August 1971 (1973).

34 New York [State], Select Committee on the Economy (1974), 38.

35 *Wall Street Journal,* March 31, 1976, p. 22.

36 New York [State], Select Committee on the Economy (1974), 39.

37 *New York Times,* April 7, 1973, p. 27.

38 New York [State], Legislative Commission on Expenditure Review (1974), 8.

39 For a review of the evidence, see Bahl (1979b), 19, 97–101.

40 "The more standard the product (corsets, brassieres, housedresses, nightgowns) the more likely it is to be made outside the City in a plant employing 100 or more workers and using the section method. Even within the industries making products generally lacking in individuality, the smaller shops making specialty items tend to be located within the City. Certainly, technological change, even in the extremely labor-intensive garment business, has speeded standardization and made individual skills less important. Synthetic fabrics, steam forming, computer-directed pattern making and sewing machines which go faster, need less oiling and come in new models for special purposes have all made it easier for manufacturers to migrate to states where the wages are lower and the space is cheaper and easier to use." (New York [State], Legislative Commission on Expenditure Review [1974], 22.)

41 One recent study suggests that the gap has narrowed appreciably since 1973. This conclusion, however, was reached using a technique that is somewhat controversial, based upon pay levels for comparable workers rather than upon wage rates for comparable jobs. (See Leonard G. Sahling and Sharon P. Smith, "Regional Wage Patterns: How Does New York Compare with the Rest of the Country?" *Federal Reserve Bank of New York Quarterly Review* V [Spring 1980], 5–11.) Most observers seem to agree that the growth rate of manufacturing wages in New York has been below the national growth rate for much of the 1970s. What remains a subject of dispute is how the absolute levels of wages (manufacturing and nonmanufacturing) compare across different industries among different localities. For evidence that New York labor is still perceived by many businessmen as relatively expensive, see Julia Vitullo-Martin, "The Real Sore Spot in New York's Economy" *Fortune* C (November 19, 1979), 92–105; Chemical Bank, *Looking toward the 80's in Upstate New York: A Chemical Bank Survey of Medium-Sized Businesses* (April 1980).

42 "Oil and natural gas production found principally in the western region amounts to 0.2 percent and 1.6 percent of the State's respective use of these fuels." (New York [State], State Energy Office, *New York State Energy Consumption and Supply Statistics, 1960–1976*, August 1978, p. 17.)

43 Coal supplies come primarily from Pennsylvania, Virginia, and West Virginia. (Ibid.)

44 See New York [State], Public Service Commission, "Opinion and Order Establishing Restrictions on Attachments of New Gas Customers . . . ," October 26, 1971; ibid., Opinion no. 77–19, October 31, 1977. (These and related opinions are often referred to as CASE 25766.)

45 See for example New York [State], Legislative Commission on Expenditure Review (1974), 8–10; see also Peter Slocum, "Natural Gas: A Lack of Policy Planning," *Empire State Report* II (April 1976), 98.

46 "At present, virtually every megawatt of the electric generating capacity located in that area [of New York City and Long Island] is petroleum-fired." (New York Power Pool, *Long Range Generation and Transmission Plan, 1979*, April 1, 1979, I, 8.)

47 New York [State], Council of Economic Advisors, *Annual Report*, 1974, p. 18.

48 For evidence of how electricity and gas charges vary across the state, see New York [State], Legislative Commission on Expenditure Review (1974), 7–8. This variation makes almost worthless such statements as "Steel companies already are paying 40 percent more for their power than comparable companies in Pennsylvania." (*New York Times*, February 2, 1976, p. 38.) A cost comparison depends critically upon where the steel company is located in New York State.

49 On the matter of taxes, a senior vice-president of Consolidated Edison (the largest utility in the state, serving the New York City area) noted, "Our taxes per kilowatt hour are more than twice that of the next most heavily taxed company and more than four times those of some upstate utilities." (*New York Times*, August 29, 1977, p. 30.)

50 Foltman (1977), 137–66. In footnote *c* of his key table on business perceptions, Foltman notes, "If the six items relating to 'energy' . . . are combined, this factor moves to fourth place" (p. 151).

51 New York [State], Legislative Commission on Expenditure Review (1974), 5.

52 Michael Sterne, "Lower Taxes and Better Government Called Keys for City to Hold Industry," *New York Times*, May 16, 1976, pp. 1, 52.

53 In 1975, Governor Carey asked the New York State Department of Commerce to produce examples of industries that had left New York "because of energy problems." The Department could not produce one. (Donald Gilligan, "Conservation vs. Development," *Empire State Report* II [October–November, 1976], 376.)

54 *New York Times*, January 29, 1976, p. 37.

55 New York Power Pool (1979), vol. I.

56 Ibid., I, 9.

57 As of 1979, the "Peak Load" was estimated by the New York Power Pool at 21,430 megawatts, which was only 70 percent of their capacity estimate of 30,410 megawatts. (Ibid., II, 20.) Juggle these numbers as one will, with margins for unforeseen breakdowns and regional disparities in supply, the inescapable conclusion is that capacity at present exceeds demand.

58 For a discussion of delays in the past, see James M. Kenney and

Thomas R. Kershner, "The Electric Utilities and Economic Development in New York State," in Foltman and McClelland (1977), 75–81; Lloyd L. Kelly, "Energy and Economic Development: Critical Decisions and Consequences," in ibid., 82–96. See also Steve Lawrence, "Only One Power Plant Has Been Approved in New York since the Legislature Created the Sitting Board in 1972," *Empire State Report* IV (January–February 1978), 14–17.

59   Some energy-intensive industries have been able to negotiate special utility rates. For examples, see Paul J. Browne, "PASNY's New Supply of Cheap Hydroelectric Power Could Confer Enormous Economic Benefits," *Empire State Report* IV (January–February, 1978a), 11–13. One development that could dramatically change the relative cost of energy in the New York City area is a shift from oil to coal for power generation. Such a prospect does not appear to be probable from a political standpoint.

60   Daniel Patrick Moynihan, "The Federal Government and the Economy of New York State," press release, rev. ed., July 15, 1977, p. 14. The plant in question was a proposed power plant, to be built on Staten Island to generate power by burning refuse.

61   Quoted in Betty Hawkins, "New York's Environmental Impact Tussle," *Empire State Report* I (February–March, 1975), 65.

62   The terms of the 1969 National Environmental Policy Act require all federal government agencies to include, in every recommendation or report on proposals for legislation and other major federal actions significantly affecting the quality of the human environment, a detailed statement by the responsible official on:

1. The environmental impact of the proposed action
2. Any adverse environmental effects that cannot be avoided should the proposal be implemented
3. Alternatives to the proposed action
4. The relationship between local short-term uses of man's environment and the maintenance and enhancement of long-term productivity
5. Any irreversible and irretrievable commitments of resources that would be involved in the proposed action should it be implemented

63   For a brief account sympathetic to Rockefeller that details his role in these two developments, see Robert H. Connery and Gerald Benjamin, *Rockefeller of New York* (Ithaca, N.Y.: Cornell University Press, 1979), 328–51.

64   Ibid., 353.

65   In 1972, Rockefeller vetoed a bill that would have given to the New York Department of Environmental Conservation review powers over impact statements to be required of state agencies.

66   Quoted in Hawkins (1975), 65.

67   Economists are inclined to regard environmental degradation as an "externalities" problem; that is, the decisions of one group (say, automobile drivers) create costs (pollution) which those making the decision do not bear personally, or at least do not bear entirely. Much of the early focus of environmental impact statements concerned government-related projects, where the externalities image does not quite fit. Presumably the government, as the agent of all the people, is supposed to consider (or "internalize") all relevant costs in deciding the merits of a given project. The necessity of preparing environmental impact statements for such proposals merely forced to the fore

considerations that previously might have been neglected, but should not have been neglected.

68 The basic purpose of this act, in its own words, was "to incorporate the consideration of environmental factors into the planning, review and decision making processes of state, regional and local government agencies . . . To accomplish this goal, SEQR requires that all agencies determine whether the actions they directly undertake, fund or approve may have a significant effect on the environment; and if it is determined the action may have a significant effect, to prepare or request an environmental impact statement." Sorting out who must prepare a statement and when is not a simple task. In general terms, SEQR applies to certain actions by state and local agencies, including:

1. Projects affecting the environment that (*a*) are directly undertaken by an agency, (*b*) are funded by an agency, or (*c*) require one or more permits or approvals from an agency
2. Planning activities that affect future choices
3. The making of rules, regulations, procedures, or policies

For a concise summary of the act and its application, see Cornell Center for Environmental Research, "Your Responsibilities under SEQR: A Local Guide," Extension Bulletin F. & OH–LA 79–2, August 1979.

69 New York [State], *Revised Record of the Constitutional Convention of the State of New York, April Fifth to August Twenty-Sixth, 1938* (Albany: J. B. Lyon, 1938), II, 1567.

70 New York [City], Temporary Commission on City Finances, *The City in Transition: Prospects and Policies for New York* (New York: Arno Press, 1978), 142. Elsewhere the Commission was somewhat more venturesome, suggesting that "manufacturing activities are particularly sensitive to local tax rates. Various business tax increases since 1966 have had a particularly negative effect on manufacturing activity in New York City." (*The Effects of Taxation on Manufacturing in New York City*, Ninth Interim Report, December 1976*a*, p. 1.)

71 See, for example, New York [State], Select Committee on the Economy (1974), 46–9; New York [State], Economic Development Board, *Taxation in New York State: A Comparative Study*, by Charles de Seve, Richard W. Richardson, and Thomas Vasquez, May 1977 (hereafter de Seve, Richardson, and Vasquez [1977]); Mark A. Willis, "Business Taxation in New York City," *Federal Reserve Bank of New York Quarterly Review* IV (Spring 1979), 22–8; and the various statements by New York [City], Temporary Commission on City Finances, especially (1976*a*), 1–2; (1977*b*), 4; (1978), 141–6; and *The Effects of the Bond Transfer Tax*, First Interim Report, November 1975, pp. 10–11.

72 See, for example, New York [State], Legislative Commission on Expenditure Review (1974), 5; Foltman (1977), 145–51; Sterne (1976), 1, 52.

73 For examples, see statements by an executive of Moog, Inc. (precision control devices, Buffalo) in *New York Times*, August 29, 1977, p. 45; by RCA Corporation officials in ibid., March 4, 1971, p. 39; by American Broadcasting Company officials in *Wall Street Journal*, May 13, 1973, p. 14; by the president of Eastman Kodak Co. (Rochester) in ibid., April 5, 1971, p. 15; by executives of Time–Life Books in ibid., March 25, 1976, p. 19; and by executives of Adams Express Co. (investment company) in ibid., March 31, 1976, p.22.

74 Perhaps the best of recent studies directed to the first question is de Seve, Richardson, and Vasquez (1977). In a covering letter to Governor Carey,

Richardson noted "the inadequacy of existing studies." Concerning the second question, he stated point blank that "there is no useful literature either at the state or federal level, which provides any real insight into the impact of taxation either on business or personal decisions to migrate internally in the United States." (Ibid., 9.)

75 Ibid., ii. This ranking can be modified – some might even say obscured – if we focus upon state taxes only, or upon the tax burden per $1,000 of personal income. New York's ranking among the 50 states has varied considerably under these different measures, as suggested by the following:

Tax measure for ranking	New York State's ranking	
	1965	1974
State and local taxes		
Per capita	1	1
Per $1,000 of personal income	10	1
State taxes only		
Per capita	12	4
Per $1,000 of personal income	39	12

76 For evidence of the near instant exodus resulting from these tax increases, see *Wall Street Journal,* December 17, 1975, p. 8; ibid., December 18, 1975, p. 2; ibid., February 9, 1976, p. 8; *New York Times,* September 18, 1975, pp. 1, 61; ibid., December 18, 1975, pp. 71, 72; ibid., February 5, 1976, p. 35; ibid., February 25, 1976, p. 65; ibid., April 13, 1976, p. 51.

77 The bond-transfer tax was repealed in March 1976. The stock-transfer tax could not be repealed, because it was pledged as part of the backing for the debt obligations of the Municipal Assistance Corporation. An effective (as opposed to a legal) repeal was achieved when, in August of 1976, the governor signed a bill allowing security dealers a credit against city and state income taxes for the amount of the stock-transfer tax they paid on sales executed for their own accounts.

78 See especially de Seve, Richardson, and Vasquez (1977); see also New York [State], Legislative Commission on Expenditure Review (1974), 11–20.

79 De Seve, Richardson, and Vasquez, for example, note that "New York City based multistate firms . . . pay higher combined state and city taxes than their competitors pay in nearly all other sites. These firms account for a majority of New York City corporate business activity." (De Seve, Richardson, and Vasquez, [1977], v.)

80 See for example New York [State], Department of Commerce, *Taxes and Plant Location in New York and Other Industrial States,* Research Bulletin no. 1, March 1976*b*; from the same state department, "Tax Incentives: New York State," September 14, 1977, and "Tax Incentives: New York City," September 30, 1977.

81 Advisory Commission on Intergovernmental Relations, *Significant Features of Fiscal Federalism,* Washington, D.C., Report M–79, April 1974, pp. 59–60. The measure was based upon average use among the 50 states of major revenue sources, weighted by the personal income of the residents.

82 As of 1976, New Jersey taxed unearned income, Connecticut taxed dividends and capital gains, and Pennsylvania taxed gross taxable personal income at a flat 2 percent. (New York [State], Department of Commerce, [1976*b*], 5, 12.)

83 For an individual earning $50,000 a year, Richardson calculates the total state tax bill (income, property, and sales taxes) net of all adjustments as follows: New York City, $5,652; New Jersey (Ocean County), $2,226; Connecticut (Middlesex County), $2,178; Pennsylvania (Indiana County), $1,979. (De Seve, Richardson, and Vasquez [1977], app. p. 6D.)

84 New York [State], Select Committee on the Economy (1974), 28, 85.

85 "Exodus of Corporate Headquarters," *Empire State Report* I (September 1975), 329.

86 The elasticity of the state income tax has been estimated at 1.2, with other elasticities estimated to run as high as 1.47. (See Bahl [1977], 29–31; and Bahl [1979*b*], 88.) Forecasting the future trend in state revenues is complicated by a number of unknowns, the most crucial of which would seem to be (1) the likely course of future state retardation and (2) the likely response of firm relocation decisions to different prospective tax changes.

87 See Bahl (1979*b*), 108.

88 Bahl (1977), 42.

89 Bahl (1979*b*), p. 105. Because recent cuts in the personal income tax have been particularly concentrated in the upper income brackets, these changes may have a disproportionate effect on industrial relocation. Whether large beneficial results will be forthcoming is still unclear.

90 See for example Bahl (1977), 20, and Bahl (1979*b*), 87–8.

91 See Chapter 7. See also Rona B. Stein, "New York City's Economy: A Perspective on Its Problems," *Federal Reserve Bank of New York Quarterly Review* II (Summer 1977), 49–59; Raymond D. Horton, "People, Jobs, and Public Finance in New York City: Implications of the Fiscal Crisis," *City Almanac* XII (August 1977), 1–13.

92 *New York Times*, January 22, 1980, p. 1.

93 Ibid., January 7, 1979, p. 74.

94 Ibid., December 29, 1977, sec. 4, p. 8.

95 See for example ibid., May 16, 1976, pp. 1, 52; New York [State], Select Committee on the Economy (1974), 9, 45, 46.

96 Foltman (1977), 150, 151.

97 *New York Times*, October 31, 1975, p. 13.

98 Ibid., February 2, 1976, p. 1.

99 Ibid., January 29, 1977, p. 22.

100 Ibid., May 26, 1976, p. 51.

101 Press Release, Tuesday, October 18, 1977, p. 3.

102 New York [State], Job Development Authority, *Annual Report*, March 31, 1979, p. 2. For a more detailed description of JDA lending powers and how they have changed over time, see Robert T. Dormer, "Another Round for Job Development," *Empire State Report* V (October–November 1979), 45–7.

103 The JDA was also authorized to issue bonds to finance pollution control facilities, but this activity was curtailed when legislation was enacted in 1976 "capping" moral obligation bonds. See Dormer (1979), p. 47.

104 Unlike most other public authorities whose bonds have only the "moral" backing of the state, the bonds of JDA have the "full faith and credit" backing of the state. Their authorization therefore requires voter approval. (See Chapter 5.)

105   New York [State], Department of Commerce, *Why It Pays to Do Business in New York State,* March 1979, pp. 19–20.

106   IDA bonds are not obligations of either the issuing agency or the host municipality. They are merely guaranteed by the credit of the business seeking the lease-purchase agreement.

107   In fact:

> Interest income derived from revenue bonds issued by local industrial development agencies is exempt from the New York State tax on personal income and, subject to certain limitations under Federal IRS regulations, from Federal income tax. Under these limitations, issues of $1 million or less are tax exempt and, under certain circumstances, an issue of up to $10 million may be tax exempt. However, no limitation is imposed upon issues whose proceeds are to be used for the acquisition and site development of an industrial park or to provide facilities for sewage or solid waste disposal and air- or water-pollution control.

(New York [State], Department of Commerce [1979], 20.)

108   For a more detailed description, see Appendix B.

109   Michael P. McKeating, "New York Losing the Race for New Industry," *Empire State Report* I (October 1975*a*), 378.

110   New York [State], Legislative Commission on Expenditure Review (1974), 33.

111   Ibid., S–5.

112   New York [State], Office of the Comptroller, *Public Authorities in New York State,* December 31, 1974, p. 53.

113   See Section 3.6.

114   For a description of this kind of borrowing, see Chapter 6.

115   Foltman (1977), 153–4.

116   Ken Auletta, *The Streets Were Paved with Gold* (New York: Random House, 1979), 76–7.

117   For recent evidence that government is still viewed as something of a problem by the New York business community, see Vitullo-Martin (1979), 92–105; Chemical Bank (1980); New York [State], Assembly, Office of the Speaker, *Small Business: New York's Forgotten Majority,* February 21, 1980.

118   The states usually included in the Sunbelt are Virginia, North and South Carolina, Georgia, Florida, Tennessee, Alabama, Mississippi, Arkansas, Louisiana, Oklahoma, Texas, New Mexico, Arizona, and (as the region is usually defined) the southern portion of California. Which states are included at the margin is, of course, something of a judgment call.

119   See for example the six-part study of the Sunbelt by the *New York Times,* February 8–13, 1976.

120   Population movements and industrial relocation interact in a variety of ways. For example, the migration of individuals is influenced by the prospects of better jobs. As more people move into an area, the size of the labor pool and the local market expand, drawing more industry in and thereby improving job prospects, which in turn draw more people in.

121 *New York Times,* February 9, 1976, p. 24.

122 "The Second War between the States," *Business Week,* no. 2432, May 17, 1976, p. 95.

123 See Rubin, Wagner, and Kramer (1978), 430.

124 Moynihan (1977), 6. See also by the same author "The Politics and Economics of Regional Growth," *Public Interest,* no. 51, Spring 1978, pp. 3–21.

125 For this and the following Tax Foundation estimate, see Michael J. McManus, "Issues Facing the Northeast," Fund for the City of New York, June 16, 1976c, pp. 23–4.

126 "Federal Spending: The North's Loss Is the Sunbelt's Gain," *National Journal,* no. 26, June 26, 1976, p. 881.

127 In subsequent revisions of his original estimate, Moynihan changed the collections figure from $33.7 to $36.9 billion to allow for IRS refunds, and modified the net deficit from $7.4 to $17.1 billion by allocating to New York a share of the federal government's deficit in 1976. See Moynihan (1977), 6 n and app. C, p. 3.

128 The "Foreign Economic and Financial Assistance" of $1 billion was excluded because it "evidently consists of foreign aid transactions handled through New York banks." (Ibid., p. 10.)

129 As the distribution records are actually kept, the Community Services Administration allocates these total interest payments to New York, northern New Jersey, and western Connecticut.

130 Moynihan (1977), 9.

131 "Federal Spending" (1976), 880.

132 CONEG Policy Research Center, Inc., and the Northeast–Midwest Research Institute, *A Case of Inequity: Regional Patterns in Defense Expenditures, 1950–1977,* August 1977, p. 3.

133 Ibid.

134 A similar case can be made for ignoring corporation tax payments. If the question is in which region the burden falls, then a tax of, say, $100 million on General Motors should be distributed according to the location of car and truck buyers (to the extent that the tax is passed on to consumers) and the location of stockholders (to the extent that the tax cuts into profits).

135 "The Politicization of Research at the Fed," *Business Week,* no. 2594, July 16, 1979, p. 110.

136 Ann R. Markusen and Jerry Fastrup, "The Regional War for Federal Aid," *Public Interest,* no. 53, Fall 1978, p. 88.

137 *New York Times,* March 20, 1976, p. 1.

138 Ibid., August 28, 1977, p. 1.

139 Ibid., July 29, 1977, p. 22.

140 For details of these company moves and commentary on them, see ibid., January 27, 1974, p. 42; ibid., May 22, 1976, p. 29; ibid., March 12, 1976, p. 21; "More Companies Send New York a Message – 'Goodbye,' " *Fortune* XCIII (May 1976), 272.

141 *New York Times,* December 25, 1975, p. 42.

142 Ibid.

143 See for example the following from the *New York Times:* March 4, 1971, p. 39; July 20, 1971, p. 23; November 3, 1971, p. 65; April 9, 1972, p. 17; June 9, 1972, p. 39; May 13, 1973, p. 73; October 15, 1975, p. 20; December 25,

1975, p. 42; June 23, 1978, p. 3. See also New York [State], Select Committee on the Economy (1974), 8, 42, 43; New York [State], Legislative Commission on Expenditure Review (1974), 5, 6, 28; Foltman (1977), 149–51.

144 Data are for 1977, quoted in Auletta (1979), 194.

145 *New York Times,* July 20, 1971, p. 23.

146 Ibid., June 9, 1972, p. 39.

147 Ibid., December 25, 1975, p. 42.

148 New York [State], Select Committee on the Economy (1974), 42.

149 *New York Times,* May 16, 1976, pp. 1, 52.

150 See the sources cited in Table 3.14. For the upper-income group, New York City ranked third behind Anchorage and Honolulu.

151 In the mid-1960s, for example, the average number of workers per unit in New York manufacturing firms was 47 (the smallest number among the major industrial states), compared with 65 for the nation as a whole. New York City averaged only 32, whereas upstate firms averaged 93. (New York [State], Department of Commerce, *Manufacturing in New York State,* Research Bulletin no. 23, November 1968, p. 5.)

152 New York [State], Select Committee on the Economy (1974), 32.

153 See for example *Wall Street Journal,* March 31, 1976, p. 22; *New York Times,* October 22, 1970, p. 50; ibid, August 2, 1971, p. 27; ibid., August 27, 1971, p. 30; ibid., February 20, 1976, p. 1; ibid., May 7, 1978, p. 31; New York [State], Legislative Commission on Expenditure Review (1974), 5, 22, 24, 27; New York [State], Select Committee on the Economy (1974), 31–5.

154 Consumer price comparisons must be approached with caution on two counts. Comparison across cities at a point in time are meaningless. (One cannot say, for example, that because the New York City figure in 1974 was 5 percent higher than the all-city average, therefore New York City was 5 percent more expensive to live in.) Each index reflects only relative changes from the same base year, such as 1967. One can compare rates of change. The New York City CPI, however, is constructed to reflect changes in living costs for urban wage earners and clerical workers, a relatively low-income group. The changes for higher income groups may be somewhat different, particularly insofar as rent control benefits them less.

155 *New York Times,* May 16, 1976, pp. 1, 52.

156 In the mid-1970s, Amtrak carried roughly 46,000 passengers per day. The New York Metropolitan Transportation Authority carried nearly 4 million people a day on its subway and commuter trains (plus well over 2 million bus riders). See "New York's David Yunich: Building toward a Dream," *Railway Age* CLXXVII (October 11, 1976), 16.

157 Estimate by the Regional Plan Association, *New York Times,* July 28, 1969, p. 20.

158 See for example *New York Times,* February 28, 1971, p. 36; ibid., September 23, 1972, p. 35; ibid., October 16, 1973, p. 86.

159 New York [State], Select Committee on the Economy (1974), 43.

160 "Eight Trade Groups Are Leaving City," *New York Times,* February 20, 1970, p. 1.

161 The one dramatic exception is the PATH link (formerly the Hudson and Manhattan), which is a model of efficiency. Run by the Port Authority of New York and New Jersey (the initials PATH stand for Port Authority Trans-Hudson), it has received lavish funding from a public authority that has consistently refused to support other forms of mass transit. For an elaboration of its refusal, and the reasons why PATH became an exception to that policy, see Chapter 6, Section 6.6.a.

162 As obvious as this point is, it is too often forgotten in the heat of political debate. It makes no sense, for example, to pay an annual subsidy of $100 million a year to maintain a transit line whose annual external benefits are far below $100 million.

163 The State Comptroller, for example, has found through various audits of the Transit Authority "gross examples of overtime abuses, absenteeism, loafing and poor productivity and supervision that add up to the waste of millions of dollars." (*New York Times*, October 20, 1975, p. 40.)

164 Roughly 75 percent of rapid transit trips are estimated to originate in, or be destined for, the central business district. (Regional Plan Association, "The State of the Region: 1977," *Regional Plan News*, no. 101, November 1977*b*, p. 12.)

165 William Vickrey, "Improving New York's Transit Service: An Economist's View," *City Almanac* VIII (April 1974), 10.

166 See Chapter 6, Section 6.6.a. Symptomatic of the Port Authority's intransigence in these matters is its refusal to create direct freight access to the City. New York is the only major city in America that still floats railroad cars across the river on barges. The Port Authority was established in 1921, in part for the express purpose of building one or more rail freight tunnels to eliminate such a primitive arrangement. After more than half a century, it still has not done so. The New York City region's share of the nation's rail shipments has fallen catastrophically since World War II (from 40 percent in 1950 to 10 percent in 1975), reflecting both the dilapidated state of its rail freight system and the limited access to the city. "In terms of rail freight," observed Anthony M. Riccio, planning director of the city's Office of Economic Development, "New York City is still operating with a 19th-century system." (*New York Times*, July 8, 1980, p. A1.)

167 As of 1977. (Ibid., January 3, 1978, p. 33.)

168 See for example the 1977 report of the Committee for Better Transit, ibid., March 11, 1977, sec. 2, p. 2.

169 For a careful review of MTA forecasts, see Edward S. Seeley, Jr., "The Financial Outlook for the New York City Transit Authority: Problems and Solutions," *City Almanac* XIV (June 1979), 1–14.

170 The 2 percent tax on the gross receipts of oil companies included a provision barring the oil companies from passing the tax along to consumers, a provision that is almost sure to be challenged in the courts. See *New York Times*, June 20, 1980, p. B2.

171 See for example Seeley (1979) and Michael Rosenbaum, "Transit Talks Seem Headed for a Crisis," *Empire State Report* VI (January 14, 1980), 1, 8–12. Even if the federal formula for mass transit subsidies is revised, the probable revisions will not begin to solve the problem. See *New York Times*, August 25, 1980, p. 88.

172 *New York Times*, January 21, 1979, sec. 4, p. 6.

173 Estimated for Governor Carey by the State Department of Transportation in 1976. Even if this figure is off by a factor of two (and in the era of double-digit inflation, it may now actually be too low), all of these conclusions concerning the inability of the city and the state to generate such funds stand. For a review of various estimates, see Michael S. Belluomo, "Travelling into the Future with the VHST, PRT, VTOL . . . and the BTM?" *Empire State*

Report V (April 1979*b*), 38. For a more recent estimate, and a comment on how preventive maintenance has become worse, see *New York Times,* March 30, 1980, p. E6.

174 The current planning by the city and the state for capital replacement so flagrantly underestimates the need that in June of 1980 the federal Environmental Protection Agency threatened to withhold federal highway and sewage treatment funds unless the dollars destined for public transit were radically revised upward. According to Charles Warren, a regional EPA administrator, the "real capital needs" are roughly twice what is being planned for. (*New York Times,* June 26, 1980, p. B1.)

175 Harvey S. Perloff et al., *Regions, Resources and Economic Growth* (Lincoln, Nebr.: University of Nebraska Press, 1960), 151.

176 (Cambridge, Mass.: Harvard University Press, 1960), chap. 11.

177 *New York Times,* January 27, 1965, p. 21.

178 Also obscuring secular problems in the private sector at this time was the rapid growth in public sector employment.

179 New York [State], Department of Commerce, *Area Indexes of Business Activity: New York State, 1957–1969,* Research Bulletin no. 27, February 1970.

180 See Dick Netzer, "New York City's Mixed Economy: Ten Years Later," *Public Interest,* no. 16, Summer 1969.

181 New York [State], Office of Planning Coordination, *New York State: Economic Outlook for the Seventies,* December 1969, p. 2.

182 New York [State], Council of Economic Advisors, *Annual Report,* 1972, pp. 11–12.

183 Ibid., p. 12.

184 *New York Times,* May 16, 1976, pp. 1, 52.

185 Ibid., January 9, 1972, p. 39.

186 Ibid., December 16, 1976, p. 94.

187 Ibid., May 7, 1978, p. 31.

188 Ibid., February 7, 1971, sec. 5, p. 3.

189 Ibid., December 20, 1975, p. 39.

4. Fiscal structure and fiscal problems

1 Other logical possibilities include federal subsidies and gifts. For massive spending, however, these sources are unlikely to provide most of the requisite funds.

2 For a detailed description of the distinction between the General Fund and All Operating Funds, see Appendix A.1.

3 Described in Appendix A.1.

4 See Appendix A.1.d.

5 Comment of Albert Roberts, fiscal analyst for the Republican minority in the Assembly, quoted in Lois Uttley, "The Executive Budget: Political Gamesmanship," *Empire State Report* V (June–July 1979), 31.

6 New York [State], Office of the Comptroller, *Annual Report* (hereafter *Annual Report of the Comptroller*), 1977, pt. I, p. 37.

7 As of March 31, 1977, the Housing Finance Agency had $5.2 billion outstanding in bonds and notes; all statewide authorities combined had $14.9 billion; New York State had $3.7 billion. (Ibid., pp. 24, 37.)

8 As of March 31, 1980, the Municipal Assistance Corporation had a total of $6.2 billion in bonds outstanding. (Municipal Assistance Corporation for the City of New York, *Report for the Third Quarter Ending 3–31–80*, p. 5.)

9   For the history of this provision, see Chapter 7.

10   All data for March 31; see *Annual Report of the Comptroller*, 1978, pt. I, p. 29; Municipal Assistance Corporation, *Report for the Third Quarter Ending 3–31–80*, p. 5.

11   The curiosity under Dewey – rapid spending increases and slow growth in debt and taxes – is to be explained by the availability in the immediate postwar years of a generous surplus generated during World War II. See Chapter 5.

12   For fiscal 1976, the relevant totals are as follows (in $ millions):

Full faith and credit debt of state	3,642
Lease-purchase agreements	3,276
Guarantees for public authority debt:	
Full faith and credit guarantee	541
Moral obligation guarantee	9,714
Total	16,631

Almost all of the lease-purchase agreements are with public authorities, the one notable exception being the agreement with Albany County for the rental of the Albany Mall. (See *Annual Report of the Comptroller*, 1976, pt. I, pp. 24–9.)

13   The total is comprised of the following (in $ millions):

State-guaranteed debt outstanding:	
Full faith and credit guarantee	541
Moral obligation guarantee	9,173
Other debt outstanding	4,436
Total	14,150

Of this, about half of the full faith and credit–guaranteed debt has been issued by the New York Thruway Authority; roughly four-fifths of the moral obligation debt has been issued by the Municipal Assistance Corporation (42 percent), the Housing Finance Agency (32 percent), and the Urban Development Corporation (12 percent). (See *Annual Report of the Comptroller*, 1976, pt. I, pp. 28, 29, 41.)

14   See Table 4.3. The average for all states is computed by dividing the recorded total (72,127) by 50.

5. The political economy of the governors

1   The total budget for HEW in Carter's 1979 budget proposal was $182 billion.

2   The categories are those used by the comptroller of the state. Expenditure figures are for All Operating Funds. Details of how these calculations were made are provided in the notes to Table 5.1.

3   In the case of Dewey, the calculations date from fiscal 1946 – the year ending March 31, 1946 – as the first annual period relatively free of wartime constraints.

4   The reader may be confused by the fact that the fiscal year for the state ends on March 31, whereas governors depart on December 31. Harriman's last year was 1958. The last budget that Harriman controlled was for the fiscal year ending March 31, 1959.

5   "Higher Education," "Aid to Public Schools," and "Other Education."

6   "Health," "Mental Hygiene," "Medicare/Medicaid" (state and federal).

7   "Local Administration"; see note (c) to Table 5.1.

8   One of the major cash disbursements undertaken under Dewey and not discussed here was the distribution of bonuses to all New York residents who served in the armed forces during World War II ($50 for those who served 60 days or less within the United States, $150 for those who served more than 60 days within the United States, and $250 for those who served outside the United States). A $400 million bond issue received voter approval to meet these payments. The ultimate cost was to be paid by a 10 percent income tax increase and a one-cent-per-pack cigarette tax. Typical of New York finances, these increments in the tax structure persisted long after the bond issue in question was completely paid off. For further details, see Appendix A.4.

9   See Chapter 7, Section 7.2.

10   Alan G. Hevesi, *Legislative Politics in New York State* (New York: Praeger, 1975), 104.

11   Only three times between 1946 and 1957 did New York borrow for capital construction.

12   Determining the annual rate at which this $457 million surplus was dissipated is complicated by injections into the Capital Construction Fund from three other sources of funds: (1) transfers from the General Fund, (2) transfers from other funds, such as the Abandoned Property Fund, and (3) transfers from bond sales. Any reasonable variation of assumptions concerning which dollars were used first still leaves unscathed the basic conclusion noted in the text: that by the time Dewey left office, almost all (if not all) of the immediate postwar surplus had been spent.

13   New York State Thruway Authority, *Annual Report*, 1951, p. 1.

14   The final construction cost of $962 million was almost twice this revised figure.

15   See Section 6.2.

16   Democrats charged Republicans with political opportunism – state and congressional elections were in the offing – and cited other construction needs as more pressing. The statement by Paul E. Fitzpatrick, Democratic State Chairman, was typical: "The Republican state administration has not yet learned that first things must come first. First needs of the state at this time are schools and hospitals, particularly additional hospitals for our mentally ill." (*New York Times*, March 13, 1950, p. 1.) Dewey was quick to note the limited relevance of this attack. "The Thruway is to be self-liquidating and self-supporting and makes it possible for the state to maintain itself so as to support its schools and hospitals as it now does." (Ibid., March 10, 1950, p. 22.) Such arguments helped to justify the building of a highway in the early 1950s based upon the concept of user costs. They left totally unexplored the issue of why control of that highway should be turned over to a public authority.

17   *New York Times*, March 21, 1950, p. 21.

18   The prospective annual financial benefit from such backing was far from trivial, as the Thruway Authority was quick to emphasize:

Ordinarily, an independent authority embarking on a new venture such as this and with no assets, except anticipated revenue, to support a bond issue, would be required to pay an interest rate of, let us say, 3¼ percent. Assuming a bond issue of $450 million to construct the Thruway, this would mean an annual payment for interest and amortization of about $20 million over the 40-year life of the bonds. In addition, however, in order to satisfy the potential investors that their investment was adequately protected, the authority would be required to demonstrate that it could earn more than the minimum requirements. This extra coverage could easily amount to more than 35 percent of the actual debt service cost. Even at 35 percent it would amount to another $7 million. This would mean that if the Authority issued straight revenue bonds, the average annual cost to the user to pay the principal and interest of the bonds plus coverage would amount to something like $27 million.

A state guarantee, however, would not only lower the interest rate from 3¼ percent to 2 percent or less, but would obviate the necessity for coverage. This would mean that the Authority would be able to reduce its estimates of revenue needs by approximately $12 million annually.

(New York State Thruway Authority, *Annual Report,* 1951, p. 7.)

19   The initial tenement house act appears to date from 1867. See Lawrence Veiller, *Tenement House Legislation in New York, 1852–1900* (Albany: Brandow, 1900), p. 188.

20   *New York Times,* January 6, 1938, p. 14.

21   Ibid., November 7, 1938, p. 3.

22   The dates and amounts authorized were as follows: 1947, $135 million; 1949, $300 million; 1954, $200 million. With the original $300 million authorized under Lehman in 1938, this brought the total to $935 million.

23   For a description of how state funds were channelled into low-income housing in the Dewey–Harriman years, see New York [State], Temporary State Commission on Coordination of State Activities (1956), app. B.

24   The middle-income range in New York State was $4,500 to $9,000. The desired rent range, according to the *New York Times,* was $22 to $25 per room. (February 15, 1956, p. 1.) A plan for middle-income housing was also conceived independently by Warren Moscow while he was acting as an "idea man" for Mayor Wagner. According to Moscow, the details were worked out in conferences called by him with Robert Moses and representatives of the New York City Housing Authority, then taken to Albany, reworked, and incorporated into the 1954 and 1955 legislation. (Warren Moscow, private communication, March 24, 1980.)

25   *New York Times,* February 15, 1956, p. 1.

26   The margin was considerably less narrow outside New York City, where 55 of 57 counties turned in a negative majority.

27   New York [State], Joint Legislative Committee on Housing and Multiple Dwellings, *Report,* Legislative Document no. 39, 1955, pp. 1–2.

28   Harriman's statements were also singularly devoid of content. For example, he noted that "families whose incomes are only slightly above the level of [low-income] public housing tenants often find themselves in a no-man's-land of housing – with incomes too low for adequate private housing but too high for public housing. (Governor's Message to the Legislature Recommending 8-Point Program, McKinney's Session Laws of New York 1638

[March 28, 1955].) This amounted to little more than the observation that wherever the cutoff income level was established, those just above that level would have difficulty. This might be an argument for redefining the cutoff. It hardly justified pouring millions of dollars into housing projects designed to help many whose income was well above that cutoff.

29 See for example, January 4, 1952, p. 1, or January 28, 1953, p. 1.

30 The failure of these numbers to add to the same total is explained by the presence in 1948 in both the Senate and the Assembly of one member of the American Labor Party.

31 January 25, 1949, p. 8.

32 *New York Times,* April 7, 1949, p. 36. The 1925 formula was part of Al Smith's pioneering program to assist local school districts in meeting education costs. The original formula was based upon the cost of theoretical teacher units. Under the new 1949 law, the formula was based upon an estimated cost per student.

33 Of this total increase, $91 million or 74 percent was attributed by the *New York Times* to "recommendations of the State's Temporary Commission on Education Finance," with the remaining $32 million the result of "mandatory increases . . . due to anticipated increases in pupil enrollment." (April 19, 1956, p. 1.)

34 February 26, 1958, p. 1.

35 *New York Times,* April 24, 1958, p. 27.

36 Rupert Hughes, *The Story of Thomas E. Dewey, Attorney for the People* (New York: Grosset and Dunlap, 1944), 391.

37 The best the Empire State could boast was a limited number of state teachers colleges.

38 *New York Times,* April 5, 1948, p. 1. Two bills were signed, the first relating to the establishment and operation of a state university and the appointment of trustees, the second authorizing the establishment of two-year community colleges and state-aided four-year colleges. "Governor Dewey explained that the bills . . . followed the recommendations of the [Young] Commission in all major particulars." (Ibid., 42.)

39 Ibid., January 24, 1955, p. 1.

40 The measure passed the legislature first in 1956, then in 1957, and was ratified by the voters of the state in November of that year.

41 Deflated to constant (1972) dollars, these annual spending totals for 1955 and 1959 are $50.4 million and $65.4 million. See Table 5.1, line (1).

42 Converted to constant 1972 dollars, $1,052 million becomes $993 million.

43 See Table 5.2.

44 See Chapter 6.

45 Frank Gervasi, *The Real Rockefeller* (New York: Atheneum, 1964), 60.

46 That Nelson's mother was less than enthusiastic about his propensity to exceed his monthly allowance is suggested by the note that accompanied her financial aid. "A notice came from the bank that you had overdrawn . . . and I had Miss Kelly deposit $10 for you . . . I haven't mentioned it to Papa, thinking that it was better for you to do so, and also because I know that it would disappoint and grieve him." (Joe Alex Morris, *Nelson Rockefeller: A Biography* [New York: Harper, 1960], 72.)

47 Later renamed the Office of the Coordinator of Inter-American Affairs, or CIAA.

48 Peter Collier and David Horowitz, *The Rockefellers: An American Dynasty* (New York: Signet, 1976), 229.

49 James Desmond, *Nelson Rockefeller: A Political Biography* (New York: Macmillan, 1964), 144.

50 To those who suggested that he switch parties, Rockefeller had a standard reply: "I don't believe in party switching. I really would rather pull people forward than hold people back. If I was in the Republican party I was pulling the party forward. And if I'd have been in the Democratic party I would have been in the position of holding people back." (Michael Kramer and Sam Roberts, *"I Never Wanted to Be Vice-President of Anything!": An Investigative Biography of Nelson Rockefeller* [New York: Basic Books, 1976], 62.)

51 The objectives of AIA were "to give leadership in bringing about cooperation which will result in helping people in other lands to help themselves in combatting poverty, disease and illiteracy; to strengthen, through the dissemination of technical knowledge, modern equipment and managerial experience, the self-sufficiency and independence of the individual, the basic forces which make possible the growth and development of the democratic system." (Letter from Nelson Rockefeller to his father, quoted in Gervasi [1964], 127.) The purposes of IBEC – aside from making a profit – were "to promote the economic development of various parts of the world, to increase the production and availability of goods, things and services useful to the lives and livelihoods of their people and thus to better their standards of living." (Alvin Moscow, *The Rockefeller Inheritance* [New York: Doubleday, 1977], 168.)

52 J. A. Morris (1960), 234–5.

53 Rockefeller's competitiveness was legendary, as his brothers repeatedly learned in their boyhood years. Others would learn it too. At Dartmouth, for example, his roommate was known as a brilliant student. Rockefeller's response was typical: "He was brilliant but I was damned if I was going to let him take me. So I worked." (Ibid., 31.)

54 Ibid., 137.

55 The suit was never brought to court.

56 J. A. Morris (1960), 210.

57 Collier and Horowitz (1976), 238 n.

58 Ibid., 454.

59 Ibid., 323.

60 Former governors who received their party's nomination for the presidency since the Civil War make up (as Rockefeller well knew) an impressive list: Horatio Seymour, Samuel Tilden, Grover Cleveland, Theodore Roosevelt, Charles Evans Hughes, Alfred E. Smith, Franklin D. Roosevelt, and Thomas Dewey.

61 Desmond (1964), 85.

62 A. Moscow (1977), 153.

63 "Nelson Rockefeller has no recollection of ever saying any such thing. In fact, he had even considered issuing a personal denial to the editors of *Newsweek*, where the quote appeared on September 2, 1974, shortly after his nomination [for the vice-presidency]. The authors traced the quote back to a

profile by *New York Times* reporter Francis X. Clines, then to another story by
James Clarity (who had since been assigned to the *Times'* Moscow Bureau),
and finally to Robert Phelps, a respected former *Times* man and now an editor
of the *Boston Globe.* 'About a week after Christmas 1963,' Phelps recalled, 'I
had asked for a private interview. We were on an airplane, and I sat down and
talked to him. I remember the plane circling over Washington and seeing the
lights. I asked him that, and that's the quote. I'll stand by it. It's accurate' "
(Kramer and Roberts [1976], 379, n. 1).

64 James Poling (ed.), *A Political Self-Portrait: The Rockefeller Record*
(New York: Thomas Y. Crowell, 1960), 37.

65 Desmond (1964), 183.

66 Collier and Horowitz (1976), 357.

67 Ibid., 227.

68 Gervasi (1964), 26.

69 Collier and Horowitz (1976), 454.

70 Ibid., 337.

71 Art. 11, Sec. 1.

72 Converted to constant dollars, these figures become $301 million,
$815 million, and $2,381 million, respectively. (*New York State Statistical
Yearbook,* 1977, p. 201; ibid., 1967, p. 99; *The Book of the States,* 1948–49, p.
400; price indexes from the *Survey of Current Business,* nominal figures deflated by GNP deflator, 1972 dollars.)

73 Converted to constant dollars, these figures become $164, $302, and
$685, respectively, with the multiplication reduced from 11.9 to 4.2. (For
sources and deflator, see previous note.)

74 In 1974 the term was reduced from 15 to 7 years.

75 Mike M. Milstein and Robert E. Jennings, *Educational Policy-
Making and the State Legislature* (New York: Praeger, 1973).

76 Quoted in "The Board of Regents: History and Functions," *Empire
State Report* I (December 1974), 41.

77 *New York Times,* April 25, 1962, pp. 1, 24. The committee in question
was the Joint Legislative Committee on School Finance, headed by Charles
Diefendorf.

78 Cited in Amy Plumer, "Perfect Politics in Imperfect School Aid,"
Empire State Report I (April 1975b), 108. Samter, at the time of his study, was
Executive Secretary of the Conference of Large City Boards of Education of
New York State.

79 Milstein and Jennings (1973), 108.

80 Quoted in ibid., 112.

81 Thus, for example, the ceiling on state aid (frozen in 1969) was raised
by $100 million, and the state's share of primary and secondary education
spending was restored to its previous level of 49 percent (rather than being
reduced to 46 percent, as heretofore proposed).

82 Milstein and Jennings (1973), 115.

83 *New York Times,* December 31, 1959, p. 16.

84 Ibid., October 16, 1960, p. 69.

85 From 401,000 in 1959 to 804,000 in 1970.

86 These stand for, respectively, Search for Education and Evaluation
through Knowledge, Full Opportunity Program, Educational Opportunity
Program, and Higher Education Opportunity Program. The Open Admissions

Program (1969) and SEEK (1967) were both aimed at minority groups, the latter providing special testing, counseling, and remedial services. FOP, EOP, and HEOP were designed to provide tutorial aid, counseling services, and financial assistance for students in community colleges, the State University, and private colleges and universities, respectively.

87   Tuition had been charged at SUNY since 1961. In the same year, the public colleges of New York City were authorized to institute tuition fees, but none did.

88   Construction was to be financed by borrowing through the State University Construction Fund, a source not available to CUNY.

89   In another November development having no clear linkage to the Rockefeller announcement of proposed building, Chancellor Albert Bowker of CUNY first announced a proposal to institute tuition at CUNY (with offsetting scholarships), which he subsequently withdrew; then he announced his resignation, which he also subsequently withdrew. These events seemed to be less concerned with the tuition issue at CUNY than with an administrative fight over control of policy. (See, for example, *New York Times*, November 16, 1965, pp. 1, 27; ibid., November 21, pp. 1, 58; ibid., November 22, pp. 1, 45; ibid., December 15, 1965, pp. 1, 51.)

90   November 21, 1965, sec. 4, p. 9.

91   *New York Times*, November 16, 1965, p. 4.

92   Another related development in May that came to naught was the fumbling effort of Republicans to frame alternative legislation that would put CUNY under SUNY control.

93   *New York Times*, May 11, 1966, p. 36.

94   Ibid., May 13, 1966, p. 64.

95   No specific limit was set on the total borrowing, but it was "generally agreed" that the amount in question would be "about $400 million" through 1970. (*New York Times*, June 22, 1966, p. 1.) Bonds were to be issued through the State Dormitory Authority.

96   *New York Times*, July 2, 1966, p. 8.

97   Ibid., July 6, 1966, p. 33.

98   New York [State], Legislative Commission on Expenditure Review, "Construction of Dormitories and Other University Facilities," Program Audit 5.2.71, December 1, 1971, p. S–2.

99   CUNY debt consisted of bonds and notes issued on its behalf by the Dormitory Authority ($256.1 million for the senior colleges and $17.5 million for the community colleges). SUNY debt consisted of bonds and notes issued on its behalf by the Dormitory Authority ($482.2 million) and by the Housing Finance Agency ($1,551 million). (*Annual Report of the Comptroller*, 1974, pt. I, p. 20; New York State Dormitory Authority, Audit by Haskins & Sells, May 29, 1974, p. 35.)

100   Expressed in constant (1972) dollars, these figures become $65 million and $993 million, reducing the multiplication from 24 to 15. (See Table 5.1.)

101   See note 98.

102   The forecast drop in full-time undergraduates is from 549,374 in 1975 to 365,000 by 1993; in total undergraduate enrollment (including part-time as well as full-time), from 805,460 to 604,650 in the same time period, a drop of 25 percent. (New York [State], Education Department, *The Regents 1978*

Progress Report on their 1976 Statewide Plan for the Development of Post-secondary Education, University of the State of New York, October 1978*b*, p. 8.)

103 See for example Donald Axelrod, "Higher Education," in Robert H. Connery and Gerald Benjamin (eds.), *Governing New York State: The Rockefeller Years* (New York: Academy of Political Science, 1974), 133–4.

104 *New York Times,* March 5, 1967, p. 1. The committee was comprised of McGeorge Bundy from the Ford Foundation, James Bryant Conant, former President of Harvard, John Hannah, President of Michigan State, Theodore Hesburgh, President of Notre Dame, and Abram Sachar, President of Brandeis. After Conant declined the chairmanship for reasons of poor health, it was accepted by Bundy, and the resulting report therefore tended to be referred to as the Bundy Commission report.

105 The Bundy Commission had attempted to meet this problem by advocating a system of quality controls that do not appear to have been implemented. In fiscal 1973, for example, "All chartered institutions that met existing standards and constitutional requirements were eligible, the money going equally to rich and poor, outstanding and mediocre, efficient and inefficient, socially responsible and indifferent. Bundy's admonition that aid should not be channeled to marginal and low-quality institutions seems to have been overlooked." (Axelrod [1974], 141–2.)

106 Excluding honorary degrees.

107 See, for example, *New York Times,* December 21, 1959, p. 16; ibid., October 16, 1960, p. 69; ibid., March 12, 1961, p. 1; New York [State], *The Public Papers of Nelson A. Rockefeller: Fifty-Third Governor of the State of New York* (hereafter *Public Papers of Rockefeller*), 1961, p. 6.

108 Perhaps the best summary of the Rockefeller blueprint for attacking health problems in the state was the outline given by the Governor in 1967: See *New York Times,* February 2, 1967, pp. 22–3.

109 In constant (1972) dollars, these figures are $403 million and $2,589 million, respectively. Totals are for "Health," "Mental Hygiene," and "Medicaid/Medicare" in Table 5.1.

110 Arthur L. Levin, "Health Care," in Connery and Benjamin (1974), 177–8; U.S., Congress, House, Committee on the Judiciary, *Report on the Confirmation of Nelson A. Rockefeller as Vice President of the United States,* 93rd Cong., 2nd sess., November 21, 1974*c*, pp. 59–60. Mental health facilities constructed included 5 new state schools, 1 new state hospital, 6 new children's hospitals, and 11 new rehabilitation centers. Initiated but not completed under Rockefeller were 6 new state schools and 4 new state hospitals.

111 See for example *Statement of Governor Nelson A. Rockefeller before the Joint Legislative Committee on Problems of Public Health and Medicare,* Albany, New York, May 24, 1966.

112 New York [State], Temporary Commission to Revise the Social Services Law, *The Administration of Medicaid in New York State,* Interim Study Report no. 6, Albany, February 1975 (hereafter *Administration of Medicaid in New York*), 27.

113 Part A of the new Medicare law (available to all) was designed to cover hospitalization costs for the elderly through funds accumulated in the Social Security Fund. Part B (available on a voluntary basis) was designed to cover a percentage of other medical costs, with part of the funds generated by individual contributions by participants in the program and the rest of the funds contributed by the federal government.

114 "The percent of federal participation for expenditures for medical care and services is based on a formula related inversely to the per capita income of the state in comparison with the per capita income of the United States. However, the Federal Medical Assistance for any state 'shall not be less than 50 percentum or more than 83 percentum.' New York State is reimbursed on a 50 percent matching basis." (*Administration of Medicaid in New York*, 21.)

115 A state had to provide at least five basic services by July 1, 1967, to qualify: inpatient hospital services, outpatient hospital care, laboratory and X-ray care, nursing home benefits, and physicians' services.

116 The more generous provisions tended to carry the day. The final compromise in organizational structure included these elements: (1) the State Board of Social Welfare was given the authority to set income eligibility levels, (2) the State Department of Social Welfare retained responsibility for drawing up and supervising Title XIX plans, and (3) the State Department of Health retained responsibility for "developing standards of medical care plans."

117 *New York Times*, May 1, 1966, p. 1.

118 Quoted in Hevesi (1975), 118.

119 *Report of the Special Actuarial Committee of the New York State Conference of Blue Cross and Blue Shield Plans*, June 6, 1966, p. 4.

120 These legislative changes were:

    1969. A prohibition against program reduction was changed to indicate that while state financial support must be maintained, optional items of care could be dropped if necessary because of inflated prices.

    1972. The requirement that each state show it was making efforts in the direction of broadening the scope of services in its Medicaid program and liberalizing eligibility requirements for Medicaid was repealed. Additionally, the 1969 "maintenance of effort" amendment, under which a state could not reduce its aggregate expenditures for the state share of its Medicaid program from one year to the next, was repealed.

(*Administration of Medicaid in New York*, 25.)

121 In 1968, for example, Rockefeller proposed a reduction in the state's contribution to Medicaid of $200 million, the Senate raised the figure to $300 million (by tightening eligibility requirements), the Assembly after some scuffling concurred, and the Governor "immediately" signed the more restrictive bill. (See Hevesi [1975], 121–2. See also *New York Times*, February 8, 1968, p. 35; ibid., March 5, 1968, pp. 1, 22; ibid., March 12, 1968, pp. 1, 33; ibid., March 27, 1968, pp. 1, 34.)

122 The optional services are (1) clinic services, (2) prescribed drugs, (3) dental services, (4) prosthetic devices, (5) eyeglasses, (6) private-duty nursing, (7) physical therapy and related services, (8) other diagnostic, screening, preventive, and rehabilitation services, (9) emergency hospital services, (10) skilled nursing facility services for patients under 21, (11) optometrists' services, (12) podiatrists' services, (13) chiropractors' services, (14) care for patients 65 or older in institutions for mental diseases (15) care for patients 65 or older in institutions for tuberculosis, (16) care for patients under 21 in psychiatric hospitals, and (17) institutional services in intermediate care facilities. (See *Administration of Medicaid in New York*, 24.)

123   Ibid., 8.

124   The figure is a state estimate, quoted in Janice Prindle, "New York's $3 Billion Medicaid Boondoggle," *Empire State Report* II (July 1976), 211.

125   Quoted in ibid.

126   *Administration of Medicaid in New York*, 1.

127   Building of facilities, of course, did not originate with Rockefeller, but was merely greatly accelerated by him. Thus, for example, in 1954 Dewey proposed and the legislature and the public approved a $350 million bond issue for the construction of mental hospitals. The striking contrast with later developments is not just the smallness of the sum, but more importantly, that voter approval for an increase in debt was sought as the Constitution intended. (See *New York Times*, November 3, 1954, p. 14.) Mental health was also a leading priority of Rockefeller's. His public statements endorsed the cause, his budgets repeatedly raised allotments for it, and these requests apparently breezed through the legislature with a minimum of controversy. (See for example ibid., January 18, 1966, p. 26; ibid., January 18, 1967, p. 1; ibid., February 2, 1967, p. 22; ibid., January 22, 1969, p. 31.)

128   *Administration of Medicaid in New York*, 4.

129   See for example New York [State], Health Planning Commission, *Proposed State Health Plan*, March 1979. In 1978 the State Division of Health Care Planning and Resource Management forecast for 1981 excess capacity of 9.8 percent. ("Monthly Inpatient Need Satisfaction Profiles by County," *Bureau of Facility and Service Review*, March 1, 1979, p. 10.) Perhaps predictably, analyses of current hospital difficulties by members of that industry give very little emphasis to previous overbuilding as a central cause of current economic pressures. See for example Hospital Association of New York State, *Seventh Annual Fiscal Pressures Survey: 1977*, December 1978.

130   *Public Papers of Rockefeller*, 1960, p. 1562.

131   U.S., Congress, House, Committee on the Judiciary, *Nomination of Nelson A. Rockefeller to Be Vice President of the United States*, Hearings, 93rd Cong., 2nd sess. (Hereafter House, *Vice President Hearings* [1974]), November 21, 1974, p. 62.

132   *Public Papers of Rockefeller*, 1960, p. 1562.

133   The three attempts were made in 1961, 1969, and 1971. See U.S., Congress, Senate, Committee on Rules and Administration, *Nomination of Nelson A. Rockefeller of New York to Be Vice President of the United States*, Hearings, 93rd Cong., 2nd sess. (Hereafter Senate, *Vice President Hearings* [1974]), November 1974, pp. 1172–9.

134   Ibid.

135   House, *Vice President Hearings* (1974), 297.

136   The latter two reasons were repeatedly emphasized by Rockefeller. See for example *Public Papers of Rockefeller*, 1968, pp. 1298–300; ibid., 1969, p. 1015; ibid., 1971, pp. 1116–17.

137   The figure of $1,325 million represents the total of items 8 through 18 in Table 5.2. The total increase for these same categories under Dewey and Harriman was $275 million.

138   This, in turn, was "equal to what a wage earner working a thirty-five-hour week at $3.80 an hour would earn," which prompted the originator of the estimate to conclude that it "therefore can be considered a fairly generous

standard of welfare." (Blanche Bernstein, "The State and Social Welfare," in Connery and Benjamin [1974], 158.)

139 Of the $7.2 billion spent in New York State in 1976 for "State-Aided Public Assistance and Services Program," 41 percent went for "Medical Assistance" and 30 percent for "Income Maintenance." AFDC spending, in turn, accounted for 82 percent of total income maintenance spending. (See also Table 5.2.) AFDC provides subsistence aid to a parent or relative for the benefit of a child. The main objectives, as Rockefeller put it, are "to preserve his home and enable him to remain with his family." (*Public Papers of Rockefeller,* 1969, p. 159.)

140 Curiously enough, the greatest explosion was not in New York City but in its suburbs. See for example *New York Times,* December 7, 1967, pp. 1, 37.

141 See for example *Public Papers of Rockefeller,* 1968, p. 26; ibid., 1969, p. 52.

142 We are indebted to Eleanor A. Sochocki, Associate Commissioner for Income Maintenance, who raised with us in private correspondence most of the factors considered in this paragraph.

143 The basic needs allowances were increased on September 1, 1966, by 2.3 percent; on July 20, 1967, by 3.2 percent; on January 1, 1968, by 3.7 percent.

144 *New York Times,* May 10, 1969, p. 24.

145 In the late 1960s, these factors were reinforced by newly created Welfare Rights Organizations. These advocacy groups encouraged application and assisted in the process. Also contributing to the publicity effort were the "federally financed antipoverty agencies [that] were informing more of the poor of their rights to receive aid." (Ibid., December 7, 1967, p. 1.)

146 Until 1969. Beginning in that year, the field investigation was replaced by an affidavit from the applicant declaring his or her need for assistance.

147 U.S., Congress, Joint Economic Committee, Subcommittee on Fiscal Policy and Intergovernmental Policy, *Income-Tested Social Benefits in New York: Adequacy, Incentives, and Equity,* by Blanche Bernstein, Studies in Public Welfare, Paper no. 8, 93rd Cong., 1st sess., July 8, 1973, p. 29.

148 Janet Ruscoll, quoted in ibid., p. 29.

149 Senate, *Vice President Hearings* (1974), 1177.

150 It might be argued that the attack had a third aspect consisting of residency requirements for welfare recipients. As previously noted, Rockefeller did endorse the implementation of such requirements repeatedly (1961, 1969, and 1971). This could hardly be viewed as part of an assault intended to succeed, however, since the Governor apparently expected from the outset that the resulting laws would be declared unconstitutional. (See House, *Vice President Hearings* [1974], 297.)

151 A related but minor development preceded the main assault by more than a decade. In 1959, Rockefeller signed two bills, one to reenact permanently a lapsed work relief program allowing localities to require fathers to work for their Home Relief checks, and a second requiring local districts to refuse aid to any employable person who fails to register with the nearest employment agency or who refuses suitable employment.

152 In 1967, Congress enacted the Work Incentive Program (WIN) that required work or work training for every "appropriate" person in families

receiving AFDC. In 1971, "appropriate" was redefined to include any welfare mother whose youngest child was six or older.

153 New York [State], Legislative Commission on Expenditure Review, *State Job Placement Programs,* Program Audit 11.1.75, December 30, 1975*b*.

154 Ibid., 68.

155 The actual percentage placed was 1.58; the percentage of those placed who stayed more than three months, 28. The product of the two (0.0158 × 0.28) is 0.4 percent. (Ibid., 63–4.)

156 Bernstein (1974), 154.

157 Gerald Astor, "Nelson Rockefeller Talks about the Gap between the People and the Politicians," *Look* XXXII (September 17, 1968), 59.

158 *Arizona Republic,* October 26, 1973, p. 1, quoted in Senate, *Vice President Hearings* (1974), 1174.

159 The wording is Rockefeller's. See House, *Vice President Hearings* (1974), 62.

160 Ibid.

161 New York [State], Legislative Commission on Expenditure Review (1975*b*), 65–6.

162 Between Harriman's last year and Rockefeller's last year, total annual AFDC payments rose by $982 million in nominal terms, or by $875 million in real terms. (See Table 5.2.)

163 The abandonment rate estimates tend to vary from 30,000 to 50,000 per year. See for example "How to Save New York," *Time* CVI (October 20, 1975), 16; *Wall Street Journal,* May 28, 1975, p. 18.

164 Robert M. Bleiberg, "Rotten Boroughs: New York City Has Been Undermined by Rent Control," *Barron's* LV (October 27, 1975), 7.

165 Quoted in *Wall Street Journal,* May 28, 1975, p. 18. The organizations in question were the Citizens Housing and Planning Council, the Citizens Budget Commission, and the Citizens Union.

166 James Grant, "Disaster Area: Rent Control Has Helped Turn Gotham into One," *Barron's* LV (April 21, 1975), 5.

167 Although silent on the linkage between rent control and the need for housing subsidies, Rockefeller was not silent on the merits of continuing rent control. He was driven to publicizing this view by the election tactics of his opponent in 1958. Accused of being against rent control, Rockefeller counterattacked with his customary vigor: "Radio and television spots were bought in wholesale lots to preach the message that Rockefeller promised to continue and improve rent control. To make sure that nobody missed the message, ads appeared even in the sports pages of the New York City papers." (Desmond [1964], 189–90.)

168 Senate, *Vice President Hearings* (1974), 1086.

169 New York State Limited Profit Housing Companies Act (1955).

170 See for example *New York Times,* January 7, 1960, pp. 1, 20; ibid., March 11, 1960, p. 16; ibid., March 25, 1960, p. 15.

171 New York [State], Housing Finance Agency, *Annual Report,* 1963–64, p. 9.

172 *Annual Report of the Comptroller,* 1976, pt I, pp. 24, 41. (The full faith and credit debt of the state at this time totaled $3.6 billion.)

173

A growing disenchantment was developing among private entrepreneurs with the extraordinary amount of time (from three to six years) that was required to work through the labyrinth of state, local, and federal requirements to process a housing development, whether on urban renewal or privately owned land, and with the city or state housing agencies. This unhappiness was matched by disaffection of public development agencies with private developers because of their unwillingness to undertake any serious expenditures (in itself a source of delay) prior to obtaining a guarantee that a proposed project would be processed to a satisfactory conclusion. The public agency could not give this guarantee, because of the seriatim nature of statutorily required approvals by other public bodies involved in the development process.

(Frank S. Kristof, "Housing" in Connery and Benjamin [1974], 192.)

174   Robert H. Connery, "Nelson A. Rockefeller as Governor," in Connery and Benjamin (1974), 12.

175   *New York Times,* April 10, 1968, p. 73.

176   Ibid., April 11, 1968, p. 41.

177   Kristof (1974), 193. "Subject only to the consent of its board of directors, UDC could exercise the following powers in carrying out its functions: condemn real property; override local building codes, zoning ordinances, building permits, and occupancy certificate requirements; substitute the state's building code and issue its own building permits and certificates of occupancy, acquire sites and finance the planning and construction or rehabilitation of residential, industrial, commercial, or civic projects; create subsidiary corporations, lend or give them funds, and enter into contracts for the purchase, lease, sale or mortgage of property; and borrow up to $1 billion (subsequently increased to $2 billion) in the open market." (Ibid., 194.)

178   See Chapter 6, Section 6.6.b.

179   See Table 3.12.

180   Rockefeller's behavior during the infighting has been a subject of dispute. The interpretation advanced here – the "kid gloves" approach, as the *New York Times* phrased it – is supported by various articles in that paper and by our interviews with some of the participants. (See for example *New York Times,* March 8, 1959, p. 59.) According to a different view, Rockefeller fought viciously from the first, using the classical weaponry of the politician in power, including patronage, appointments, and support for local bills. (See for example Desmond [1964], 207; Hevesi [1975], 98–9; "Rockefeller's First Test," *New Republic* CXL [April 13, 1959], 5.) In no case, however, are these assertions supported by examples, an omission particularly striking in the Hevesi book, which is otherwise so well documented.

181   Harriman was quick to respond by emphasizing that during his administration the Republican-controlled legislature had repeatedly increased his budget recommendations without adequately providing for revenues to cover prospective higher costs. The question of fault, however, does not appear to have captured the popular imagination in this instance.

182   *New York Times,* February 21, 1959, p. 12.

183   The broad outlines of this trade were well recognized at the time. See for example ibid., February 4, 1965, pp. 1, 20; ibid., February 5, 1965, p. 1.

184   Ibid., April 2, 1965, p. 31.

185   April 2, 1971, p. 44.

186   The evidence suggests that Rockefeller had considerable influence in the paring process. See for example *New York Times,* March 16, 1971, p. 41; ibid., April 4, sec. 4, pp. 2–3.

187   With the loan, the prospective transit fare increase was 5 cents; that for the commuter rail fares, no more than 20 percent. Without the loan, the prospective transit fare increase was 15 cents, and commuter fares would have to be raised 50 percent. (Ibid., December 15, 1971, p. 68; ibid., December 28, 1971, p. 33.)

188   Ibid., January 5, 1972, p. 46.

189   See Table 3.12.

190   Gerald Benjamin, "Patterns in New York State Politics," in Connery and Benjamin (1974), 38.

191   For personal reminiscences about this transformation by a legislator whose Albany career spanned the process, see Jack Bronston, "The Legislature in Change and Crisis: 1958–78," *Empire State Report* IV (October–November 1978), 40–1.

192   *New York Times*, January 2, 1959, p. 1.

193   As of 1973. Enrollment data refer to full-time students. The state had also helped to finance an expansion in two-year community colleges in the same time period, from 14 to 38.

194   *New York Times*, January 8, 1959, p. 18.

195   New York [State], Governor, National Housing Research Foundation, press release, July 13, 1968, p. 1.

196   *New York Times*, October 7, 1973, p. 35.

197   *Empire State Report* V (February 1979), 4–5.

198   *New York Times*, December 12, 1973, p. 53.

199   Quoted in Jack Newfield, "The Case against Nelson Rockefeller," *New York Magazine* III (March 9, 1970), 26.

200   *Olmstead et al.* v. *United States*, 48 S. Ct. 564 at 573 (1928).

6. Public authorities in New York State

1   New York [State], Office of the Comptroller, *Statewide Public Authorities: A Fourth Branch of Government?* Comptroller's Studies on Issues in Public Finance, Study no. 1, vol. I, November 1972a, p. 1.

2   The state debt was $3.4 billion.

3   Data for 1962 from *Annual Report of the Comptroller*, 1963, pp. 19, 28–9; for 1974 from ibid., 1975, pp. 22–3, 33; ibid., 1977, pp. 24, 33, 36; New York [State], Office of the Comptroller (1974), 1.

4   See, for example, Ronald Forbes, Alan Frankle, and Christopher Carter, "Public Debt in the Northeast: The Limits on Growth," in *The Northeast: Managing a Way Out*, Proceedings of a Symposium on Legislative Actions for Survival in Credit Markets, Boston, February 10–11, 1977, p. 126; Annmarie Hauck Walsh, *The Public's Business: The Politics and Practices of Government Corporations* (Cambridge, Mass: M.I.T. Press, 1978), 357–60.

5   Public authorities may also (1) sue and be sued, (2) have a corporate seal, (3) make by-laws for the management and regulation of their affairs, (4) borrow money and issue evidence of indebtedness, (5) fix rates and collect fees, charges, or tolls for the use of facilities, and (6) exercise the power of eminent domain wherever granted by specific legislation. Since 1938, public authorities cannot levy taxes.

6   New York [State], Office of the Comptroller (1972a), 2.

7   New York [State], Temporary State Commission on Coordination of State Activities (1956).

8   Under the state's Constitution (Art. VIII, Sec. 4), local governments – with a few exceptions – are allowed to contract indebtedness up

to 7 percent of the average full valuation of their taxable real estate; for cities over 125,000, the limit is 9 percent; for New York City and Nassau County, it is 10 percent.

9 This provision applies to full faith and credit debt, but not to "short-term borrowing in anticipation of revenues or [to] debts to meet forest fire, insurrection, war or invasion emergencies." (New York [State], Temporary State Commission on Coordination of State Activities [1956], 47–8.)

10 Ibid., 47.

11 Ibid., 46.

12 Under the heading of "also ran" one should mention the stimulus given to the formation of public authorities by the rise of federal programs offering "grants and long-term, low interest loans for public works and public housing developments." The federal government "encouraged the states to create public corporations empowered to issue revenue bonds to finance revenue-producing improvements so that the states might participate more fully in the federal public works program." (Ibid., 50.) There is no reason in theory why the desire of a given state to participate in such programs should lead to the creation of public authorities. In practice, federal programs did stimulate the creation of such authorities because (1) state participation involved the borrowing of funds, and (2) public authorities offered a convenient way to circumvent constitutional provisions restricting the amount of local debt and requiring a referendum for state debt. In short, the critical factor was not what the federal government was initiating, but the way certain state politicians were responding to those initiatives by actively circumventing constitutional limitations on the issuance of debt.

13 Ibid., 49.

14 Ibid., 54.

15 Ibid., 56.

16 New York [State], Office of the State Comptroller (1972*a*), 2.

17 Here too there is an entry under "also ran." Ronan argues that another reason for favoring public authorities over state agencies is that the former may be more flexible, insofar as public authorities are independent of "the traditional procedures and controls which are found in regular government." (New York [State], Temporary State Commission on Coordination of State Activities [1956], 56–7.) This smacks of solving a leaky faucet by replacing the entire sink. If the procedures are the problem, then it is the procedures that should be overhauled.

18 Ibid., 53.

19 Ibid., 54.

20 March 8, 1978, p. B-3.

21 The complexity of the Moses empire at its height almost defies description. The following gives some idea of how a small part was interconnected as of 1956:

The Jones Beach State Parkway Authority and the Bethpage Park Authority are closely associated with the Long Island State Park Commission whose members comprise the boards of the two authorities. The affiliation of these two authorities with this State park commission form but one part of the vast network of authority affiliation with regular government, both State and local, that has resulted from the appointment of one man to numerous authority and government positions. This individual is President of the Long Island State

Park Commission by gubernatorial appointment. As the President of this State park commission he is: (1) a member of the State Council of Parks of which he has been elected Chairman; (2) President of the Jones Beach State Parkway Authority; and (3) President of the Bethpage Park Authority. In addition he is also the Chairman of the State Power Authority by gubernatorial appointment. In this capacity he has undertaken the construction of park facilities which have been coordinated with other State park facilities by virtue of his position as Chairman of the State Council of Parks.

In New York City he is (1) City Construction Coordinator; (2) City Commissioner of Parks; (3) a member of the City Planning Commission; and (4) the Chairman of the Triborough Bridge and Tunnel Authority. He has been appointed to all of these positions by the Mayor of the City of New York. As a result of all of these offices he has been in a position to coordinate the work of a large number of State, city and authority operations.

(New York [State], Temporary State Commission on Coordination of State Activities [1956], 557–8.)

22   Most of the ideas developed here in an attempt to answer this question are treated more fully in Robert A. Caro, *The Power Broker: Robert Moses and the Fall of New York* (New York: Vintage Books, 1975), esp. chap. 28.

23   It should perhaps be noted that longevity for New York public authorities was not the outright invention of Robert Moses. At the time of his legalistic machinations with the Triborough Act, for example, at least three New York public authorities were conceded perpetual existence by law: the Port Authority of New York and New Jersey, the Albany Port District Commission, and the Lake Champlain Bridge Commission. What Moses invented was a device for converting temporary authorities into near-permanent authorities.

24   Caro (1975), 625.

25   Sec. 2527, p. 660.

26   Moses became even more vulnerable when he reached the age of 65 in 1954. New York law required that all officials retire at this age unless a specific extension was granted by the governor. Moses nevertheless retained his major positions until 1962, when a mismanaged fight with Rockefeller culminated in his resignation from a variety of executive positions.

27   Robert Caro would seem to overstate the independence of Moses from the threats of politicians. In his discussion of La Guardia's position, for example, he conveys an aura of near helplessness of the mayor in any confrontation with the powerful bureaucrat. (Caro [1975], 636.) As Caro himself notes in the case of Roosevelt, however, major clashes with chief executives could be followed by major concessions on Moses' part (see ibid., 303–4).

28   Ibid., 623.

29   Ibid., 472

30   New York [State], *Report of the New York State Constitutional Convention Committee*, vol. IV (1938), 191.

31   Ibid.

32   Ibid., 192

33   In a few instances, the state has extended its full faith and credit backing to the debt of a public authority. In each case, however, the voters must approve the associated constitutional amendment authorizing such a

guarantee. Because the main purpose of moral obligation debt is to circumvent voter approval, this type of alternative to the state issuing its own debt has not been widely used by the politician.

34   The basic legal notion was that (1) if the public authority fund ran short, and (2) the state refused to make up the difference, resulting in (3) default by the public authority, then (4) holders of public authority debt could sue the authority, but they could not also sue the state as a guarantor of authority debt, precisely because the guarantee was "moral" and not legal.

35   Quoted in Maureen D. Griess, "Empire State Plaza: Does 'Nelson's Folly' Have a Future?" *Empire State Report* III (February 1977), 43.

36   Quoted in Kramer and Roberts (1976), 159.

37   Alfonso A. Narvaez, "Levitt Says Cost of Mall Will Exceed $1.5 Billion," *New York Times,* June 7, 1971, p. 48.

38   The *Fortune* estimates of $230 for the Mall and $40 for an adjacent building are quoted in Nicholas von Hoffman, "Rock of Ages, Deft You See," *Washington Post,* December 19, 1970, p. Bl. Arthur Levitt determined that the cost per usable square foot was $94 for the Office Tower, $106 for the Swan Street Building, $165 for the four Agency Buildings, $138 for the Legislative Building, and $199 for the Justice Building. The cost per usable square foot (converted to 1970 price levels) for the five office buildings constructed at the uptown State Campus Site between 1963 and 1966 he estimated to range between $35 and $46. (New York [State], Office of the Comptroller, *Audit of New York State, New York City, and Public Authorities for the Two Years Ended March 31, 1972,* April 25, 1973, p. 22.)

39   The Mayor of Albany at the time, Erastus Corning II, claimed that Rockefeller went for the idea "like a trout for a fly." (Eleanore Carruth, "What Price Glory on the Albany Mall?" *Fortune* LXXXIII [June 1971], 94.)

40   The original idea was for the City of Albany to undertake the project, but the county was quickly substituted in order to lower the prospective interest charges on borrowed funds.

41   Two of the marked contrasts between UDC and HFA are (1) one was targeted at "low-income" housing, the other at "middle-income" housing, and (2) the financing methods used to sponsor housing are different. In broad outline, HFA reviews building projects proposed by private developers, determines which will be self-supporting, and then finances those projects by selling bonds. Each bond issue is tied to a specific project, with revenue from that project pledged to pay the interest plus redemption costs of the bonds in question. UDC, in contrast, issues general-purpose bonds tied to no specific project, and actively engages in the planning of projects. The direct participation of this authority in project development helps explain the range of extraordinary powers initially granted to UDC, including (1) the power to acquire land by condemnation, purchase, or lease, (2) the power to develop its projects without regard to local zoning ordinances or building codes, and (3) exemptions of its projects (partial or full) from local real estate taxes.

42   Quoted in U.S., Congress, House, Committee on the Judiciary, *Analysis of the Philosophy and Public Record of Nelson A. Rockefeller, Nominee for Vice President of the United States,* 93rd Cong., 2nd sess., October 1974a, p. 20.

43   The main form that the federal subsidy took was an interest rate subsidy, lowering the effective costs of borrowed funds to almost zero.

44   Many of the complexities of UDC's defaulting on its notes are de-

scribed in New York [State], Moreland Act Commission, *Restoring Credit and Confidence,* a Report to the Governor on the Urban Development Corporation and Other State Financing Agencies, March 31, 1976. The basic point made there is the one made here: that "the notion of self-sufficiency was particularly inappropriate for UDC" (ibid., 10). The major risks undertaken by UDC are listed by the Moreland Commission as follows: "Some were inherent in the type of projects which UDC undertook; namely, location in marginal areas for families who could not afford to pay market rent. Some were inherent in UDC's rapid accumulation of construction commitments which got too far ahead of its ability to go to the market with its bonds to finance such commitments. Some resulted from the elimination of the normal lender scrutiny of project feasibility, as a result of UDC's combining the roles of developer and lender." (Ibid.) Implied by the word "risks" is the other major point emphasized in the text: that prospective receipts would almost surely fall short of expenses, necessitating an outside source of funds to avoid bankruptcy. The conclusion of the Moreland Commission in this regard is fraught with condemnation: "Neither UDC nor the State made provisions for *any* of these risks." (Ibid., emphasis added.)

45 Quoted in Timothy B. Clark, "UDC Crisis: Future Fallout on N.Y. Bonds?" *Empire State Report* I (May 1975*b*), 171.

46 Quoted in Timothy B. Clark, "The Rapid Rise and Fast Fall of the UDC," *Empire State Report* I (April 1975*a*), 110.

47 As of July 1980.

48 In 1974, for example, the legislature voted that $100 million in subsidies be allocated as follows (in $ millions):

Metropolitan Transportation Authority	
(for the New York City Transit Authority and	
other New York City systems)	70.0
Metropolitan Transportation Authority	
(for the Long Island Rail Road and other MTA	
commuter activities)	20.0
Capital District Transportation Authority	0.7
Central New York Regional Transportation Authority	0.6
Rochester–Genesee Regional Transportation Authority	1.0
Niagara Frontier Transportation Authority	1.8
Other public transportation systems	5.9
Total	100.0

(New York [State], Office of the Comptroller [1974], 17.)

49 Ibid., 18.

50 Ibid., 14.

51 Ibid., 9.

52 Data on debt outstanding as of December 31, 1974, from ibid., 14. Details of MTA loans from ibid., 10–11; of Ogdensburg Bridge Authority loans, from ibid., 12; New York [State], Office of the Comptroller, *Statewide Public Authorities: Individual Authority Summaries,* Comptroller's Studies on Issues in Public Finance, Study no. 1, Vol. II, November 1972*b*, pp. 8–9; New York [State], Office of the Comptroller, *Public Authorities in New York State: A Financial Study,* Comptroller's Studies for the 1967 Constitutional Convention, Study no. 4, June 1967, p. 52.

53 New York [State], Office of the Comptroller (1974), 9.

54 New York [State], Office of the Comptroller, Division of Audits and Accounts, "Financial and Related Practices, Facilities Development Corporation," March 31, 1977 (Audit Report AL–Auth–2–77); "Audit Report on the New York State Thruway Authority Relative to a Proposed Toll Increase Effective June 1, 1975" (Audit Report AL–Auth–15–75); "Audit Report on Financial Condition of New York State Bridge Authority, Poughkeepsie, New York, for the Calendar Year 1970" (Audit Report NY–Auth–7–72); "Financial and Operating Practices, Metropolitan Surburban Bus Authority" (Audit Report NY–Auth–11–77); "Procurement Practices in the Construction and Operation of the World Trade Center, Port Authority of New York and New Jersey" (Audit Report NY–Auth–24–78); New York [State], Office of the Comptroller (1974).

55 Prior to 1973.

56 Walsh (1978), 221.

57 Only Maine and New York require special acts of the legislature to establish a public benefit corporation. Other states have general laws that authorize their creation by counties and municipalities.

58 As outlined in Section 6.2, public benefit corporations in New York State are not subject to two key constitutional limitations upon the issuance of debt: (1) unlike the state, they require no approval of proposed debt issues in a referendum, and (2) they operate outside all of the limitations upon total municipality debt.

59 At the end of the Rockefeller era, authorities operating with no debt limit included the Environmental Facilities Corporation, the Power Authority, the Capital District Transportation Authority, the Central New York Regional Transportation Authority, the Metropolitan Transportation Authority, the Niagara Frontier Transportation Authority, the Rochester–Genesee Regional Transportation Authority, the Port of Oswego Authority, the Albany Port District Commission, the Lake Champlain Bridge Commission, the Triborough Bridge and Tunnel Authority, and the Atomic and Space Development Authority. The State University programs of the Housing Finance Agency were also not subject to any debt limit.

60 The list included Edward J. Logue (Urban Development Corporation), Paul Belica (Housing Finance Agency), Alton G. Marshall (Urban Development Corporation and Sports Authority), William J. Ronan (Metropolitan Transportation Authority, Power Authority, Port Authority), Charles J. Urstadt (Housing Finance Agency, Battery Park City), and William A. Sharkey (Dormitory Authority). (See Walsh [1978], 267.)

61 Ibid., 274.

62 Quoted from an interview in Kramer and Roberts (1976), 145.

63 Quoted in Caro (1975), 173.

64 One should note in passing that the top bureaucrat may have only limited control of the policies and practices of middle-level management. The executive director of the Port Authority, for example, does have exceptional in-depth control, whereas his counterpart in the Metropolitan Transportation Authority has a far more tenuous grasp of the operation of that authority's several parts.

65 Based on "Bonds and Notes Outstanding," the 11 largest are (1) Battery Park City Authority, (2) Dormitory Authority, (3) Housing Finance Agency, (4) New York City Transit Authority, (5) Port Authority of New York and New Jersey, (6) New York State Thruway Authority, (7) Power Authority of the State of New York, (8) Medical Care Facilities Agency, (9) State of New York Mortgage Agency, (10) Triborough Bridge and Tunnel Authority, (11) Urban Development Corporation. The first five are not subject to any pre-audit; the next two (numbers 6 and 7) have their maintenance and operating expenses pre-audited, but not their payrolls.

66 Effective June 7, 1977, the head of an audited authority must respond in writing to the comptroller's recommendations "for corrective action," noting "what steps were taken to implement such recommendations, and, where recommendations were not implemented, the reasons therefore." Copies of the response are to be sent to the governor; the president, president pro tem, and minority leader of the Senate; the speaker, majority, and minority leaders of the Assembly; and the chairman and ranking minority members of the Senate Finance Committee and the Assembly Ways and Means Committee of the State Legislature. (N.Y. Exec. Law § 170 [McKinney Supp. 1972–78]).

67 Quoted in New York [State], Office of the Comptroller, (1967), 22.

68 See *Annual Report of the Comptroller,* 1977, pt. I, p. 37.

69 In theory, the Port Authority is subject to an exceptional range of controls. In practice, most of them fail to make the Authority responsive to the public's needs. The three major controls are the following:

All resolutions enacted by the board of commissioners are subject to gubernatorial veto; all requests for new projects, powers, and duties must be authorized by two state legislatures; and any taking of property requires the consent of the land-owning municipality, compliance with local zoning, or use of local government to condemn land on behalf of the authority. The authority is subject to legislative investigations by committees of two state legislatures and the U.S. Congress. Both states have the right to undertake audits of the authority's internal books and other documents whenever they choose. (Walsh [1978], 261.)

70 Ibid., 181.

71 In 1972, Tobin resigned in a huff because some of the newly appointed members did have the audacity to resist being a rubber stamp for his management.

72 For details and further sources on this fiasco, see Walsh (1978), 294–5.

73 Quoted in ibid., 339.

74 The proposal also involved the building of the World Trade Center, discussed later in this section.

75 The judgment of one of the best studies of public benefit corporations concerning the nature and merits of this legal device is worth quoting in some detail:

A covenant is a provision in the bond indenture approved by a corporation's board of directors that commits the corporation to do or not to do certain things. Insofar as they are incorporated into legislation, covenants may be treated as contracts entered into by the government and may thus freeze policy options. Authority managements maintain that bondholders require stringent covenants, although the bondholders seldom participate with the underwriters and bond attorneys in drafting indentures. Hence it is difficult to determine whether bondholders require definitive covenants or whether skillful authority managements merely invoke bondholders as an excuse to obtain covenants which they seek for their own purposes. These two sources of motivation are usually mixed. (Walsh [1978], 95.)

76   Ibid., 99.

77   In addition to rail links to the airports noted, the project included a link into Union County, New Jersey, and from Hoboken into Penn Station.

78   In the five-year period 1967–71, for example, net income totaled $579 million. (New York [State], Office of the Comptroller [1972b], 60.

79   See *Annual Report of the Comptroller*, 1977, pt. I, p. 34.

80   New York [State], Office of the Comptroller, "Procurement Practices in the Construction and Operation of the World Trade Center, Port Authority of New York and New Jersey" (Audit Report NY–Auth–24–78).

81   J. Kevin Murphy, "New York City's Port Authority Bus Terminal," *Empire State Report* IV (September 15, 1978), 14.

82   New York [State], Moreland Act Commission (1976), 257.

83   Ibid., 257.

84   Ibid., 244.

85   Ibid., 257.

86   Ibid., 258.

87   Ibid., 257.

88   Until 1975.

89   New York [State], Moreland Act Commission (1976), 245.

90   Ibid.

91   Ibid., 253.

92   Ibid., 251–2,

93   The Division could also have requested more information to accompany the drawing down of any first instance appropriation. Instead, they settled for "a description of each project to be funded by the appropriation, the total cost of each project, and the specific number of units planned for each site, documented by studies demonstrating sufficient demand for the units." (Ibid., 253.)

94   "In its final form, the March 1972 audit report recommended among other things that the Legislature impose a dollar limitation on the amount of money that can be expended by UDC on projects which have not been certified as feasible by the Board of Directors, and that UDC establish a properly controlled cost system to identify and allocate the costs of its projects and programs. In addition, the report noted that the Corporation had under consideration projects totaling $1.7 billion and that other projects under study would increase total project costs to over $3 billion." (Ibid., 262–3.)

95   "When asked whether any of the recipients of the 1972 UDC audit report reacted to the findings or recommendations, Mr. Ives [former Deputy State Comptroller in charge of the Division of Audits and Accounts] testified that he did not recall receiving any reaction from either the Executive offices or the Legislature." (Ibid., 263.)

96   Ibid., 261.

97   Mark Twain, *Pudd'nhead Wilson* (Leipzig: Bernhard Tauchnitz, 1895), p. 63.

98   Speech in the Virginia Convention, June 5, 1788, in Gaillard Hunt (ed.), *The Writings of James Madison* (New York: G. P. Putnam, 1904), V, 126.

99   This and the previous figure are from the *Annual Report of the Comptroller*, 1977, pt. I, p. 37.

100　New York [State], Office of the Comptroller (1974), 5.

101　See for example New York [State], Office of the Comptroller (1972*a*), 2; (1974), 2.

102　Walsh (1978). For her conclusion on this point, see p. 10.

103　In December of 1975 the state formulated a "Build-Out Plan" to help four financially troubled authorities (the Housing Finance Agency, the Medical Care Facilities Finance Agency, the Dormitory Authority, and the Environmental Facilities Corporation) acquire the requisite funds to complete (build out) construction already in process. Part of that plan involved limitations upon the future use of moral obligation debt by public authorities. (For details, see the comptroller's 1976 *Annual Report*, pt. I, pp. 39–40.) Nothing in this plan prevents the legislature from voting in the future to escalate the use of moral obligation funding by public benefit corporations.

104　Walsh (1978), 133.

105　Ibid., 6.

7. Of feeble checks and balances

1　John Locke, *Two Treatises of Government*, ed. Peter Laslett (Cambridge: Cambridge University Press, 1960), bk. II, sec. 143, p. 409.

2　More rigorously put, the courts' function is to police the boundaries of lawful power, to assure adherence to procedures specified in the law for the exercise of lawful power.

3　"The Federalist, No. XLVII," *The Federalist* (New York: Tudor Publishing Co., 1937), 329.

4　Ibid.

5　The state currently has two budgets in addition to the Executive Budget: the Supplementary Budget, usually small in magnitude, framed by the legislature but heavily influenced by the governor; and the Deficiency Budget, introduced by the governor in January, usually small and noncontroversial in substance, requesting appropriations not covered in either of the other two budgets.

6　The governor's veto can be overridden only by a two-thirds vote of both Assembly and Senate, an event that never occurred in the twentieth century prior to Governor Carey's veto of the Stavisky bill in 1976.

7　Joseph A. Schlesinger, "The Politics of the Executive," in Herbert Jacob and Kenneth Vines (eds.), *Politics in the American States* (Boston: Little Brown, 1965), 220–8.

8　Collier and Horowitz (1976), 457.

9　"The New York State Bar Association Pushes the Legislature to Mend Its Ways and Means," *Empire State Report* I (August 1975), 298.

10　Ultimately the suit was dismissed by the state supreme court. *Norwick* v. *Rockefeller*, 70 Misc. 2d 923 (S. Ct. Spec. Term, N.Y. Co., 1972); aff'd. 40 A.D. 2d 956 (1st Dept., 1972); aff'd. 33 N.Y. 2d 537 (1973).

11　Quoted in "New York State Bar Association Pushes the Legislature to Mend Its Ways and Means" (1975), 298.

12　Warren Moscow, "The Spectre of More Veto Overrides," *Empire State Report* II (August 1976), 254.

13　Quoted in Humphrey S. Tyler, "The Legislature: A Profile of Rancor," *Empire State Report* II (May 1976), 131.

14　Hevesi (1975), 16.

15 The main devices used by the majority leader of the Senate were summarized by a former New York senator as follows:

> The Majority Leader controls the calendar; he can star a bill (the placement of a star on a bill already on the calendar means that it cannot be acted upon unless and until the star is removed; starring a bill is the exclusive prerogative of its sponsor and of the leader). He can also "lay aside" a bill, which means temporary postponement of action. Thus he can determine when controversial bills will come up for debate. He also decides whether unanimous consent motions are, or are not, in order. (Such motions are usually aimed at the interruption of the debate for the purpose of raising a subject matter that is not strictly related to the business pending before the House.) He can even hold secret Saturday and Sunday meetings to "age" bills he supports. (Under the Constitution, a bill must age, that is, sit on the desk of the legislators for three days before it can come up for a final vote.)

(Former Senator Clinton Dominick, quoted in Hevesi [1975], 9–10.)

16 Hevesi [1975], 207.

17 Ibid., 208.

18 Clay Richards and Carol Richards, "From Albany to Washington with Love," *Empire State Report* III (January 1977), 36.

19 Hevesi (1975), 29.

20 All of these quotations are from Richards and Richards (1977), 35–6.

21 Collier and Horowitz (1976), 457.

22 Tyler (1975), 131.

23 For further discussion, see Section 7.6.

24 See Chapter 4, Section 4.4, and Chapter 6, Section 6.4.

25 New York [State], Department of Audit and Control, *Annual Report*, 1843, p. 13. For an extensive and scholarly review of the legal issues raised in this section, the definitive work is still William J. Quirk and Leon E. Wein, "A Short Constitutional History of Entities Commonly Known as Authorities," *Cornell Law Review* LVI (April 1971), 521–97.

26 New York [State], *Journal of the Convention of the State of New York, 1846* (Albany: Carrol and Cook, 1846), 1547.

27 Art. VII, Sec. 11, reads in part: "No debt shall be hereafter contracted by or in behalf of the state, unless such debt shall be authorized by law, for some single work or purpose, to be distinctly specified therein. No such law shall take effect until it shall, at a general election, have been submitted to the people, and have received a majority of all the votes cast for and against it at such election." The provision concerning a single purpose is a natural complement to the referendum requirement. Without it, the voters would often be hard pressed to assess the merits of a proposed debt increase. Also, frequent authorizations for vague general purposes could undermine the purpose of the referendum, insofar as a general-purpose authorization approved now might subsequently be used to raise funds for a specific purpose that voters would have vetoed, had they been given the chance.

28 New York [State], *Report of the Debates and Proceedings of the Convention for the Revision of the Constitution of the State of New York* (1846), 946.

29 Ibid., 943–4.

30   Hume (1963), 357.

31   Art. VII, Sec. 8, reads in part: "Nor shall the credit of the state be given or loaned to or in aid of any individual, or public or private corporation or association."

32   Quoted in *Annual Report of the Comptroller*, 1966, p. 23 n. Another example of how pervasive this belief has been in the financial community was the reply of a vice-president of Moody's Investors Service, Inc., when asked why the bond rating of the Urban Development Corporation (AA) was higher than that of New York City (Baa): "The Urban Development Unit's better rating resulted from its guarantees by New York State." (Quoted in William J. Quirk, "Standing to Sue in New York," *St. John's Law Review* XLVII [March 1973], 435, n. 17.)

33   The constitutional provisions allegedly violated by moral obligation bonds are not confined to the single issue cited. For a careful review of all of the relevant issues see Quirk and Wein (1971), 585–96.

34   *St. Clair* v. *Yonkers Raceway*, 13 N.Y. 2d 77 (1963). A review of the legal history on standing in New York before and after this case can be found in Quirk (1973), 429–82.

35   *Boryszewski* v. *Brydges*, 37 N.Y. 2d 370 (1975).

36   *St. Clair* v. *Yonkers Raceway*, 13 N.Y. 2d 80 (1963). One should hasten to add that the justice who noted this fear did so as part of a dissenting opinion that advocated an overturning of the long tradition that denied taxpayers standing. With respect to this particular fear, he noted that the evidence from other states was overwhelmingly to the contrary.

37   *St. Clair* v. *Yonkers Raceway*, 13 N.Y. 2d 79 (1963).

38   Some analysts have argued that the State Comptroller, Arthur Levitt, could have (and should have) forced the issue into the courts by refusing to turn over certain funds to public authorities that used moral obligation bond financing. This would have forced state officials to sue Levitt to get the money transferred. Levitt was one of the earliest and most vociferous critics of this type of financing, but he consistently maintained that such an action on his part, predicated on the assertion that this financing was unconstitutional, was inappropriate. It would have required him to begin with a premise that had to be decided not by the state comptroller but by the courts: that moral obligation bonds were indeed unconstitutional.

39   *St. Clair* v. *Yonkers Raceway*, 13 N.Y. 2d 72.

40   This $4.8 billion included $2.5 billion in moral obligation bonds and $2.1 billion in lease-purchase agreements. The three states whose total debt exceeded $4.8 billion in 1973 were New York ($13.0 billion), California ($6.1 billion), and Pennsylvania ($4.8 billion). All debt data were estimated as of December 31, 1973, from published sources. (See U.S., Bureau of the Census, *State Government Finances*, 1973; *Book of the States*, 1976–77, p. 262; *Annual Report of the Comptroller*, 1973 and 1974.)

41   *Boryszweski* v. *Brydges*, 37 N.Y. 2d 361. In the same year, the New York State legislature passed an act (several months after the case in question) that also gave this right to citizen-taxpayers. What the citizen-taxpayers gained first from the legal case and then from the new law, however, was far less than the right to sue the state on all money matters. See note 1 to Chapter 9.

42   *St. Clair* v. *Yonkers Raceway*, 13 N.Y. 2d 81 (1963).

43   *Boryszewski* v. *Brydges*, 37 NY 2d 364 (1975).

44   Ibid. Italics added.

45 The state was also involved in the support of SRC debt. If the city for any reason failed to make up the deficiency in SRC's Capital Reserve Fund, the state agreed to transfer to this debt fund of SRC various funds due New York City, such as Stock Transfer Taxes and per capita aid. This added a second line of defense against SRC default, presumably with the aim of strengthening creditor confidence in the viability of the enterprise.

46 Art. VIII, Sec. 4, prohibits the city from contracting debt in excess of 10 percent of the valuation of real estate. Art. VIII, Sec. 1, prohibits any municipality from giving or lending its credit in aid of any public or private corporation. These were not the only constitutional provisions allegedly violated by SRC debt, but they are the most crucial for purposes of this discussion.

47 *Wein* v. *City of New York*, 370 NYS 2d 550 (1975). Because the suit was brought against the city (not the state), Wein gained standing as a citizen-taxpayer, but not without a fight.

48 Ibid., 559.

49 Ibid., 561.

50 Ibid.

51 *Flushing National Bank* v. *MAC*, 40 NY 2d 739 (1976).

52 *Comereski* v. *City of Elmira*, 308 NY 248, 125 N.E. 2d 241.

53 Ibid.

54 *Wein* v. *City of New York*, 370 NYS 2d 558 (1975).

55 At the beginning of January 1975, the judge in question (Jacob D. Fuchsberg) held $3.4 million in New York City notes. He continued to purchase additional city notes from January through May, 1975. In May of 1975, *Wein* v. *City of New York* was argued. For this and other actions he received, as noted, "censure and disapproval." In a dissenting opinion arguing for stronger disciplinary action, Judge J. Simons argued that "we have before us evidence of a continuous pattern of trading in New York securities during a period when appeals closely affecting those securities were coming before the court regularly and we also have evidence of the respondent's [Fuchsberg's] participation in many of those appeals." As for the effective operation of checks and balances, Judge Simons went on to observe: "The evidence presented raises issues going directly to the heart of the judicial system, the impartiality of its Judges and the integrity of the court's decisions." For all these fulminations, the decision of the four (including Fuchsberg) in *Wein* v. *City of New York* stands: Moral obligation bonds have been judged not to violate the Constitution of the state. (*Matter of Fuchsberg*, 43 NY 2d [a], [z, qq, bbb, ccc] [Ct. on the Jud. 1978].)

56 Reported in Humphrey S. Tyler, "The Government Troupe Debuts," *Empire State Report* I (January 1975a), 4.

57 Some political theorists also argued that more centralized power tended to be more responsible power. See for example Woodrow Wilson, *Congressional Government: A Study in American Politics* (Boston: Houghton Mifflin, 1885), 93, 283–5.

58 Luther Gulick, "Notes on the Theory of Organization," in Luther Gulick and L. Urwick (eds.), *Papers on the Science of Administration* (New York: Institute of Public Administration, 1937), 13–14.

59 *Public Opinion* (New York: Harcourt, Brace, 1922), 313.

60 See also Appendix A.1.

61 *Annual Report of the Comptroller*, 1964, p. 30.

62 *Preliminary Report of the Comptroller*, 1971, p. 9.

63 New York State Library, *Source Material Related to Legislation in the State of New York and Annotated Bibliography of Legislative History and Legislative Intent* (rev., April 1977), 4.

64 At the end of the five-year period, bill jackets were forwarded to the State Education Department Library, where they were finally made available to the public. In September of 1975 the five-year secrecy tradition was dropped by Governor Carey. At the same time, all bill jackets from the years 1959 through 1973 were also opened to the public.

65 Quoted in New York State Library (1977), 1.

66 Quoted in Amy Plumer, "The Bottom Line Is the Budget Division," *Empire State Report* I (December 1975a), 483.

67 Henry C. Adams, *Public Debts: An Essay in the Science of Finance* (New York: D. Appleton, 1887), 23.

68 Benjamin (1974), 38.

69 *Boryszewski v. Brydges*, 37 NY 2d 364 (1975).

70 Thomas Jefferson, *Notes on the State of Virginia* (New York: Harper Torchbook ed., 1964), 142

8. A city turned wastrel

1 *New York Times,* May 30, 1975, p. 8.

2 This assumes that inflation is not perfectly anticipated and thus built into the interest rates paid by borrowers. The evidence is clear that much of the wartime inflation about to be discussed was not foreseen in this manner.

3 Real per capita income (1958 prices) was $1,299 in 1910 and $3,555 in 1970. (U.S., Bureau of the Census [1975], pt. I, p. 224, ser. F4.)

4 Population increase also served to reduce the per capita burden. This factor, however, is a trivial consideration in explaining the wild reversals of Figure 8.2.

5 Here too the key empirical point is that inflation was imperfectly foreseen by lenders, and therefore imperfectly reflected in interest rates. See note 2.

6 Real per capita income in 1958 prices rose from $1,720 in 1940 to $3,555 in 1970. (U.S., Bureau of the Census [1975], pt. I, p. 224, ser. F4.) Real per capita income in 1972 prices rose from $5,248 to $5,580 between 1970 and 1975. (U.S., Bureau of the Census, *Statistical Abstract of the United States,* 1977, p. 431.)

7 Much has been written about the bizarre bookkeeping practices of the city, most of it unintelligible to the layman. Designed almost half a century ago, and with no substantive updating since then, its major defects included (1) no conformity with generally accepted accounting principles, (2) no separate fund structure, and (3) no fund balance to show the results of its operations. Small wonder that from the most expert of sources would come the most scathing of condemnations: "The City's accounting and budgeting system, although lawful and uncritically accepted for many years, accomodated what [otherwise] would have been exposed as deficits." *Annual Report of the Comptroller,* 1974–75, foreword, p. xii.) See also Charles R. Morris, *The Cost of Good Intentions: New York City and the Liberal Experiment* (New York: W. W. Norton, 1980), 238–40.

8 According to one report, "In November 1974 the [*New York*] *Times* declined to publish a piece accurately noting that the real projected deficit for the fiscal year 1975–76 was at least $1 billion, and probably between $1.5

billion and $2 billion – a fact confirmed almost 16 months later by Felix Roha-tyn." (Edward N. Costikyan, "New York City's Bicentenial Revolution," *Empire State Report* II [August 1976], 258.)

9 Steven Marcus, "Cutting NYC's Enormous '75 and '76 Budget Deficits," *Empire State Report* I (February–March 1975), 61.

10 William E. Simon, *A Time for Truth* (New York: McGraw-Hill, 1978), 130–1. That Simon, of all people, should have acted on these premises is somewhat surprising, as he is the first to emphasize:

> It was particularly ironic in my case, for in the late sixties and early seventies, when I worked at Salomon Brothers, I had been a member of the Technical Debt Advisory Committee set up by Abraham Beame when he was Comptroller of New York. We supplied the city market advice on its financial transactions, but at no point during any of these sessions did any one of us seriously question the underlying fiscal condition of New York. We all worked with the numbers given to us by the city itself, just as do the advisory committees to the federal government. It never occurred to us to disbelieve those figures, which always indicated that New York would be able to repay its debt. (Ibid., 130.)

11 Abraham Beame, "Financing New York City," *Challenge* XVIII (September–October 1975), 41.

12 Letter from Abraham Beame and Harrison Goldin to the *New York Times,* November 11, 1974, p. 28.

13 As several analysts have emphasized in detailing the road to collapse, the market for New York City securities is concentrated largely in New York State, where the interest is exempt from not only federal but also state and local taxes. As this market became more restive and somewhat saturated, another factor making for rising interest rates was the need to offer higher compensation to nonstate residents whose earnings on New York City securities would not be exempt from state income tax. See for example Congressional Budget Office, "The Causes of New York City's Fiscal Crisis," *Political Science Quarterly* XC (Winter 1975–76), 665–6. For details on the financial community's growing sense of unease, see C. R. Morris (1980), 222–31.

14 Quoted in Ken Auletta, "Who's to Blame for the Fix We're In?" *New York Magazine* VIII (October 27, 1975*b*), 41.

15 Steven Marcus, "A Battered Beame Looks Back on a 'Tough Year,' " *Empire State Report* II (January–February 1976), 22.

16 Calculated by taking the percentages given for "Labor" and "Social Welfare Contribution" in "Total Expenditures by Object" for the fiscal years 1961 and 1975, and multiplying these percentages by "Operating Expenditures of the City of New York" for fiscal 1961 and 1975, in New York [City], Temporary Commission on City Finances, *An Historical and Comparative Analysis of Expenditures in the City of New York,* Eighth Interim Report, October 1976*f*, pp. 5, 23. Given the bookkeeping practices of the city, these percentages should be regarded as approximations only.

17 See Edward M. Gramlich, "The New York City Fiscal Crisis: What Happened and What Is to Be Done?" *American Economic Review* LXVI (May 1976), 415–29.

18 Congressional Budget Office (1975–76), 668.

19 Ibid., 670.

20 See for example Gramlich (1976), 418, 421.

21   Theodore H. White, "An Open Letter to the Democratic Majority: New York City Is the Test," *New York Magazine* VIII (November 10, 1975), 39.

22   Calculated from data in New York [City], Temporary Commission on City Finances (1976*f*), 5, 23.

23   "New York State ranks first among all states in the average grant per AFDC case. The State's average grant per case is 54 percent above the national average, 3 percent above that of Alaska, the second-ranking state which also has a very high cost of living, and 19 percent above that of third-ranking Wisconsin. If maximum payment levels are used as a basis for comparison, New York State ranks fifth among all states if the payment in New York State is based on average rents, and ranks second if maximum rents are used as the basis of comparison." (New York [City], Temporary Commission on City Finances, *Public Assistance Programs in New York City: Some Proposals for Reform*, Twelfth Interim Report, February 1977*f*, p. 71.)

24   "The share that must be paid by local governments in New York State, 25 percent of the cost of the AFDC program and 50 percent of the costs of the SSI supplementary and general assistance (Home Relief) programs, is the highest of any state. Of the twelve urban areas with the highest incidence of AFDC recipients, only one other, Newark, is located in a state that requires any local cost sharing for its AFDC program; however, localities in New Jersey pay only 12.5 percent of the costs of AFDC benefits compared to 25 percent in New York." (New York [City], Temporary Commission on City Finances [1977*f*], 76.)

25   The city does have discretion on how to administer the program.

26   "Prior to the introduction of Medicaid, New York City's indigent had two means of access to health care. The first was through the City's public health clinics, the municipal hospitals, and to a limited extent, the voluntary hospitals. These institutions provided some free health care for those unable to pay. The second was through the Kerr–Mills program for the aged, and the public assistance programs under which the recipients could seek permission to obtain private medical care for specific purposes. Thus, medical care was available to the indigent in New York City prior to Medicaid but it was of a limited nature, relying heavily on publicly provided services. With the introduction of the Medicaid program in 1966, the poor were able to select the services they received." (New York [City], Temporary Commission on City Finances, *The Medicaid Program in New York City*, Sixteenth Interim Report, June 1977, p. 16.)

27   Ibid., 66. (Data are for 1973.)

28   The cost per recipient for Medicaid services in New York is 152 percent above the national average for inpatient hospital services, and 134 percent above the national average for skilled nursing homes. (Ibid.)

29   Ibid., 67.

30   New York [City], Temporary Commission on City Finances (1976*f*), 32.

31   Auletta (1975*b*), 34.

32   Quoted in ibid., 31.

33   See Simon (1978), 135; Congressional Budget Office (1975–76), 672.

34   The estimate is by Raymond Horton, cited in Gramlich (1976), 417.

35   Congressional Budget Office (1975–76), 671.

36   Ibid. 672.

37   Simon (1978), 136.

38   Ibid., 137.

39   Ibid., 136. See also New York [City], Temporary Commission on City

Finances, *The Fiscal Impact of Fringe Benefits and Leave Benefits: Some Proposals for Reform*, Seventh Interim Report, June 1976*d*, p. 1.

40 Simon (1978), 137.

41 Calculated as follows: Total city payments for all fringe benefits (excluding retirement costs) in fiscal 1976 were $310.4 million; total payments for retirement costs alone were $1,479.98 million. (New York [City], Temporary Commission on City Finances, *The Fiscal Impact of Retirement Benefits: Some Proposals for Reform*, Sixth Interim Report, May 1976*e*, p. 5; New York [City], Temporary Commission on City Finance [1976*d*], 4.)

42 New York [City], Temporary Commission on City Finances (1976*e*), 3.

43 Ibid., 20.

44 One indication of the orders of magnitude involved is the estimate that the establishment in 1970 of the 20-year service, half-pay retirement plan for teachers immediately increased the liability of the Teachers Retirement System by $1.2 billion. (Ibid.)

45 Ibid., 17.

46 Statement characterizing New York State debt in 1846 by the Chairman of the Finance Committee. (See New York [State] [1846], 943.)

47 A number of analysts of New York City's crisis have argued that the city was under the same legal compulsion as the state to balance its budget. (See for example Congressional Budget Office [1975–76], 670.) The New York State courts have subsequently ruled that this is incorrect, that the city's Charter did not include any terms, explicitly or implicitly, requiring a balanced budget. (*William L. Quirk and Leon E. Wein* v. *Municipal Assistance Corporation for the City of New York and the City of New York*, 41 NY 2nd 644 [1977].)

48 By a state constitutional amendment in 1938, the maximum life was set at 40 years, with a few minor exceptions. The provision reads: "No indebtedness shall be contracted for longer than the period of probable usefulness of the object or purpose for which such indebtedness is to be contracted . . . and in no event longer than forty years" (Art. VIII, Sec. 2). (Water bonds, which may be issued for 50 years, are an exception.)

49 This limitation on the city's total net funded debt dates from 1884, when property tax receipts dominated total revenues. In 1938, by a constitutional amendment, the basis of calculation was changed to a five-year average of the value of taxable real estate as determined by the last complete assessment rolls and the four preceding rolls.

50 This provision was also instituted in 1938. Citing pay-as-you-go financing as the ultimate objective, the framers of this constitutional change instituted a requirement whereby an increasing percentage of capital outlays was thenceforth to be charged to the expense budget.

51 *Mayor's Executive Budget Message*, 1965–66, p. 2.

52 New York [City], Mayor's Committee on Management Survey, *The Financial Problem of the City of New York*, by Robert M. Haig and Carl S. Shoup, Item no. 5, June 1952, p. 473.

53 New York [City], Temporary Commission on City Finances, *Better Financing for New York City*, Final Report, August 1966*a*, p. 217.

54 Public housing has its own debt limit: 2 percent of the value of real estate.

55 Frederick L. Bird, *The Municipal Debt: A Description, Analysis and Appraisal of Debt Policy and Administration of the City of New York*, Mayor's Committee on Management Survey of the City of New York, Item no. 6, October 1951, p. 112.

56 Associated with the extensive use of public benefit corporations has been the extensive use of lease-purchase agreements. Many of the latter were undertaken in the name of the city by quasi-independent agencies, such as the Board of Education or the Board of Higher Education.

57 The state was also involved in the support of SRC debt. If the city for any reason failed to make up the deficiency in SRC's Capital Reserve Fund, the state agreed to transfer to this debt fund of SRC various funds due New York City, such as stock transfer taxes and per capita aid. This added a second line of defense against SRC default, presumably with the aim of strengthening creditor confidence in the viability of the enterprise.

58 Part of this kind of borrowing conducted by the city did not require the special authorization of the state legislature, but proceeded, in the words of the 1966 Mayor's Commission, by pushing "the definition of capital improvements to its furthest limit." Thus, for example, salaries and expenses of the Board of Water Supply were funded with water-supply bonds, and salaries of many departmental employees working on capital plans were funded with bonds issued for particular capital projects. (New York [City], Temporary Commission on City Finances [1966a], 79.)

59 The original wording was "job and business opportunity expansion programs of municipalities."

60 Items appropriately charged to capital account are primarily those expenses which result in the acquisition of a fixed asset with a useful life well beyond one year. The New York State Comptroller thus defines capital projects as "those capital outlays other than special assessment and enterprise fund projects, which involve the construction of major, permanent facilities having a relatively long life. These projects do not include fixed assets with a comparatively limited life, such as various types of machinery and office equipment. The latter are not generally appropriate objects for long-term borrowing by state and local governments and consequently are financed by current revenues." (New York [State], Division of Audits and Accounts, "Audit Report on the Planned Elimination of Operating Expenses from New York City's Capital Budget," Report no. NYC–45–76, app. [2/17/76], p. 2.)

61 New York [City], Temporary Commission on City Finances (1966a), 79–80.

62 Data from New York [City], Temporary Commission on City Finances (1978), 69. Much of this increase occurred in the years immediately prior to 1975. The annual totals were as follows:

Fiscal year ending June 30	Current expenses charged to capital account ($ millions)
1972	226
1973	274
1974	564
1975	724
1976	697

Source: New York [State], Division of Audits and Accounts, "Audit Report on the Planned Elimination of Operating Expenses from New York City's Capital Budget," Report no. NYC–45–76, Managerial Summary, p. 2.

63 New York [City], Temporary Commission on City Finances (1966*a*), 79–80.

64 Under Art. II of the State's Local Finance Law, municipal obligations are limited to seven basic types:
1. Serial bonds
2. Sinking fund bonds or corporate stock (the latter being the title New York City traditionally has applied to bonds redeemable from its sinking funds)
3. Bond anticipation notes (issued in anticipation of issuing long-term bonds)
4. Tax anticipation notes (issued in anticipation of taxes)
5. Revenue anticipation notes (issued in anticipation of revenues other than taxes)
6. Capital notes (usually with a maturity of one or two years, issued as a short-term alternative to bonds)
7. Budget notes issued for unforeseeable emergencies and for purposes for which insufficient provision or no provision is made in the annual budget. (These must be redeemed in the year following the year of issue.)

65 The limit on the maturity date of TANS and RANS was one year; on BANS, two years. Budget notes generally were viewed as being appropriately retired within a year of their issue.

66 The renewal terms were as follows:
1. TANS could be renewed for a period of one year or less, with roll-over not to exceed five years.
2. BANS could be rolled over for a period up to five years (provided partial redemptions were begun within two years from the date on which the original BAN was issued).
3. RANS could be rolled over for a period up to three years (not beyond the end of the second fiscal year following the fiscal year in which they were originally issued).

These terms were modified by the New York State Emergency Act (Sec. 5413).

67 New York [State], Division of Audits and Accounts, "Summary of Audit Reports Relative to Central Budgetary, Accounting and Finance Systems and Reporting Practices of New York City," Audit Report NYC–63–78, p. 8.

68 1966 N.Y. Laws, ch. 205, *amending* N.Y. Local Fin. Law 23.00b; 1968 N.Y. Laws, ch. 135, *amending* N.Y. Local Fin. Law 23.00b; 1970 N.Y. Laws, ch. 4, *amending* N.Y. Local Fin. Law 23.00b; 1972 N.Y. Laws, ch. 202, *amending* N.Y. Local Fin. Law 23.00b; 1973 N.Y. Laws, ch. 645, *amending* N.Y. Local Fin. Law 23.00b; 1974 N.Y. Laws, ch. 885, *amending* N.Y. Local Fin. Law 23.00b; 1975 N.Y. Laws, ch. 367, *amending* N.Y. Local Fin. Law 23.00 codified at N.Y. Local Fin. Law 23.00b (McKinney Supp. 1975).

69 Long-term interest rates on Moody's Aaa State and Local Bonds, for example, rose from roughly 5 percent to almost 7 percent in 1974, and remained slightly under 7 percent in 1975. (See Board of Governors of the Federal Reserve System, *Monthly Chart Book,* March 1978, p. 73.)

70 Calculation by the Municipal Assistance Corporation; see its *Annual Report,* 1976, p. 7.

71 Estimated by Congressional Budget Office (1975–76), 663.

72 The Board of Estimate (as of 1968) was composed of the mayor, comptroller, and president of the Council, each having 4 votes, and the five borough presidents, each having 2 votes, for a total of 22 votes. The mayor, comptroller, and president of the Council are elected by city-wide vote on party nominations that usually give geographical representations to the three largest boroughs. The borough presidents are elected in each borough. All members of the Board of Estimate have four-year terms.

The City Council (as of 1969) was composed of 37 members: 27 elected from individual districts and 10 elected at large (two per borough).

73   For a description of the budget-formation process and how it tends to be dominated by the mayor, see New York [City], Mayor's Committee on Management Survey (1952), 435–7, 492–500; New York [City], Temporary Commission on City Finances, *Financing Government in New York City*, Final Research Report of the Graduate School of Public Administration, New York University, June 1966*b*, pp. 228–47; Robert H. Connery and Demetrios Caraley (eds.), *Governing the City: Challenges and Options for New York* (New York: Praeger, 1969), 34–9.

74   See above, Chapter 7, Section 7.5.

75   The sales tax and the stock transfer tax due the city were to be funneled through MAC, but that funneling was a "moral obligation," not a law binding all future state legislatures to maintain the practice. The state also transferred to MAC certain per capita aid due the city.

76   Initially the debt ceiling of the Municipal Assistance Corporation was $3.0 billion (effective June 10, 1975). This figure has subsequently been revised upwards as follows:

	From	To
September 9, 1975	3.0	5.0
December 5, 1975	5.0	5.25
June 19, 1977	5.25	5.8
September 28, 1978	5.8	8.8
June 28, 1980	8.8	10.0[a]

[a] Exclusive of debt issued for refunding purposes.

77   Quoted in Rinker Buck, "State Swallows the Big Apple," *Empire State Report* I (September 1975*b*), 357.

78   The Emergency Financial Control Board was to consist of the governor, the state comptroller, the mayor, the city comptroller, and three members appointed by the governor with the consent of the state Senate. The mayor was therefore demoted in fiscal matters from chief executive to consultant. The Board was to set spending ceilings, supervise fiscal operations and planning, conduct audits, and review all proposed borrowings. The city treasurer was also demoted, insofar as all revenues (except those already pledged to bondholders) were to be funneled through an Emergency Financial Control Board Fund.

79   The state was to lend $750 million: $250 million in direct loans to the city and $500 million to MAC. Banks and other private investors were to put up $800 million. City and state pension funds were to purchase MAC bonds as follows (in $ millions):

City Teachers Retirement System	200
City Employees Retirement System	225

City Police Pension Fund	55
City Fire Department Pension Fund	10
City Board of Education Retirement System	10
State Policemen's and Firemen's Retirement System	125
State Employees Retirement System	125
State Teachers' Retirement System	100
State Insurance Fund	100
Total	950

80 U.S., Congress, Senate, Committee on Banking, Housing and Urban Affairs, *New York City Financial Crisis*, Hearings, joint statement of Ellmore C. Patterson, David Rockefeller, and Walter B. Wriston, October 18, 1975, 94th Cong., 1st sess., pp. 652–3.

81 Ibid., 661.

82 Federal loans to June 30, 1976, were to be for a maximum of $1.3 billion. In the subsequent two fiscal years, the city could borrow up to a maximum of $2.3 billion. Because seasonal loans almost by definition must be repaid at the end of the fiscal year, the city was compelled to borrow from the state to pay off the federal "seasonal" loan. A few days later it then borrowed a new "seasonal" loan from the federal government, and used part of the proceeds to repay the temporary state advance.

83 The linkage between the Moratorium Act and federal willingness to participate has been documented at length. See for example Special Counsel to the City of New York, "A Report to the Securities and Exchange Commission," November 23, 1976, pp. 7–9. The terms of the agreement also included a tax increase of trivial dimensions ($200 million).

84 The city itself attempted to return to the bond market in November of 1977, but it received such a miserable rating from Moody's (MIG–4) that the issue was withdrawn.

85 For a compact summary, see C. R. Morris (1980), 232–6.

86 "New York's June Showdown," *Wall Street Journal*, May 25, 1978, p. 24.

87 By law the city must now keep its books according to GAAP: generally accepted accounting principles.

88 Quoted in Marcus (1975), 63.

89 Citizens Budget Commission, *New York City's Fiscal Future*, vol. 45, no. 3, August 1978a, p. 11.

90 Quoted in Vitullo-Martin (1979), 100.

91 *New York Times*, August 9, 1978, p. B2.

92 See for example *New York Times*, May 7, 1980, p. B10.

93 Quoted in Buck (1975b), 338.

94 Frank LeRoy Spangler, *Operation of Debt and Tax Rate Limits in the State of New York*, Special Report of the State Tax Commission, no. 5, Albany, 1932, p. 45.

95 The chairman of the Joint Legislative Committee appointed to inquire into New York City's finances in 1915, Senator E. R. Brown, observed with some alarm, "While State officials are subject to the penalties of the law for incurring expenditure for any purpose in excess of moneys appropriated therefor, I find in the City of New York unlimited authority to exceed appropriations by making temporary loans." (*New York Times*, July 23, 1915, p. 18.)

96 For an extended discussion of the fiscal excesses and the subsequent terms with the bankers, see Herbert J. Ranschburg, "The Role of a Civic

Agency in the Decision Making Process at the Local Government Level,"
unpublished doctoral dissertation, Economics Department, New York University Graduate School, July 1957, chap. 2.

97 The New York State Financial Emergency Act does include new provisions inhibiting the issuing and rolling over of short-term debt (Sec. 5413). Whether these will prevent a recurrence of old abuses in the use of short-term debt remains to be seen. What is certain is that many of the old devices for issuing long-term debt can easily be abused in the future.

98 See for example the majority opinion in Association of the Bar of the City of New York, Committee on Municipal Affairs, *Local Finance Project: Proposals to Strengthen Local Finance Laws in New York State*, November 1978.

99 *New York Times*, July 30, 1978, p. 6E.

9. Conclusion

1 The maneuvering has been as remarkable as it has been unnoticed. The first step was to include in the 1975 revisions of the State Finance Law (1) a provision explicitly granting citizen-taxpayers the right to sue the state on *expenditure* matters, (2) a provision claiming that the law "does not apply" to bonds or bond anticipation notes (because these are *revenue* matters), and (3) a provision stating that where the new law does not explicitly apply, standing questions "must be resolved by the courts under common-law principles." (N.Y. State Finance Law § § 123-b, 123-i [McKinney 1979]). All this seemed innocuous enough, insofar as the question of whether the citizen had standing to sue on questions of debt was thrown back into the laps of the justices. This was sure to guarantee standing, because the citizen-taxpayer had already gained standing in a 1975 case (*Boryszewski* v. *Brydges* [37 N.Y. 2d 361]), and that standing right had subsequently been confirmed in a 1977 case (*Wein* v. *Carey* [41 N.Y. 2d 498]). Two years later, however, with a hairsplitting ability as deft as it was effective, the justices of New York's highest court insisted that standing had not been granted where it mattered most. In a landmark case in 1979 (*Wein* v. *Comptroller of the State of New York* [46 N.Y. 2d 394]), the court ruled that the citizen-taxpayer did not have standing to sue the state on matters relating to the sale of bonds and bond anticipation notes, because "there is a reasonably clear legislative intent to prevent taxpayer challenges in these cases" (395). As for earlier precedents that seemed to contradict this ruling, the court argued that the 1975 case related to the right to sue on expenditure issues, and the 1977 case applied only to tax and revenue anticipation notes. The inference that the courts drew was that the citizen-taxpayer did not have standing in matters relating to the issuance of any form of debt called a bond (or bond anticipation note). In sum, the 1975 legislation granted standing where it mattered least, carefully avoided granting it where it mattered most, and from that avoidance the court in 1979 inferred that the intention of the legislators was to deny it to citizen-taxpayers in matters relating to the state's use of bonds and bond anticipation notes.

2 *New York Times*, June 13, 1980, p. B3.

3 Ibid., June 16, 1980, p. B1.

4 See for example New York [State], Governor, *Annual Budget Message*, 1980–81, p. A4. New York employment did recover in the latter part of the 1970s. Total growth, however, remained quite modest (slightly under 6 per-

cent between 1976 and 1979) and heavily concentrated in the service sector. The critical issue is not whether New York can register short-run growth during an upswing in the national economy, but whether it is able to achieve long-run growth. The three available models that project employment totals for the state forecast an even slower employment growth in the 1980s than in the 1970s. See Bahl (1979*b*), 120–5.

5 See for example Peter C. Goldmark, Jr., "Foreign Business in the Economy of the New York–New Jersey Metropolitan Region," *City Almanac* XIV (August 1979), 1-14; Jane S. Little, "Locational Decisions of Foreign Direct Investors in the United States," *Federal Reserve Bank of Boston: New England Economic Review* July–August, 1978, pp. 59–62; Rona B. Stein, "The New York City Economy: Is the Worst Finally Over?" *Federal Reserve Bank of New York Quarterly Review* III (Summer 1978*b*), 24–9; and various articles emphasizing recovery, or near recovery, in selective industries in *New York Affairs* VI, no. 2 (1980). A recent survey also suggests that New York City businessmen are more optimistic than they were. See Chemical Bank, *Looking toward the 80's: A Chemical Bank Survey of Small and Medium Sized Businesses in New York*, conducted by Louis Harris and Associates, Inc., November 1979.

6 See for example *New York Times*, January 6, 1980, sec. 12, p. 89.

7 Evidence that has surfaced in recent years supporting this more negative view of New York City's economic prospects includes the Regional Plan Association's finding that investment has continued to decline in the New York City area (*New York Times*, June 1, 1980, p. 38); the Port Authority Committee on the Future's finding that the city's recovery has occurred primarily in the Manhattan central business district, while in "Brooklyn, Queens and the Bronx, the manufacturing and commercial sectors are still ailing" (ibid., July 24, 1979, p. B4); and the supporting conclusion from a study of a range of older American cities that "the overall pattern that emerges is one of isolated improvements in a few 'pockets of plenty,' accompanied by continued decline elsewhere" (ibid., July 7, 1980, pp. Al, B7).

8 See for example *New York Times*, August 31, 1980, p. F12; ibid., September 17, 1980, p. B3; Matthew Drennan and Georgia Nanopoulos-Stergiou, "The Local Economy and Local Revenues," in Charles Brecher and Raymond D. Horton (eds.), *Setting Municipal Priorities: 1981* (Montclair, N.J.: Allanheld, Osmun, 1980), 11–44.

9 Twentieth Century Fund Task Force on the Future of New York City, *New York: World City* (Cambridge, Mass.: Oelgeschlager, Gunn and Hain, 1980), 7.

10 Charles Brecher and Raymond D. Horton, "Fulfilling the Promise of Koch's Budget Goal," *New York Times*, February 2, 1980, p. 21.

11 Quoted in Vitullo-Martin (1979), 100. See also *New York Times*, October 22, 1979, p. B4; ibid., June 22, 1980, pp. E1, E6; ibid., July 4, 1980, pp. Al, B2.

12 *New York Times*, June 20, 1980, p. B4. Mayor Koch subsequently revised his 1982 deficit forecast to a mere half billion. The revision also appears unduly optimistic, as does the Mayor's plan to eradicate that deficit by some combination of federal and state aid, higher taxes, and work-force attrition.

13 Twentieth Century Fund Task Force on the Future of New York City (1980), 2.

14 "What Will They Do for New York?" *New York Times Magazine*, Janu-

ary 27, 1980, p. 30. Yet another bleak indicator in this context is the fact that federal revenue-sharing funds seem destined to disappear. The 1980 Democratic platform does include the promise that the federal government will take over local costs of Medicaid and welfare. The 1976 platform had similar promises of aid that were largely unfulfilled. As for this most recent promise, New York's Senator Moynihan conceded that it would be "difficult" to get such a bill passed. (*New York Times*, August 14, 1980, p. B3.)

15　Twentieth Century Fund Task Force on the Future of New York City (1980), 20–1. See also Bahl (1979*b*), p. 108; *New York Times*, October 22, 1979, pp. B1, B4; ibid., February 10, 1980, pp. A1, A26; David A. Grossman, *The Future of New York City's Capital Plant* (Washington, D.C.: Urban Institute, 1979); Tom Boast, "Debt and Capital Management," in Brecher and Horton (eds.) (1980), 113–42.

16　Brecher and Horton (eds.) (1980), 5.

17　"Washington and New York," press release, April 1979, p. 2.

18　*New York Times*, September 30, 1980, p. B1. For evidence of considerable animosity in Congress toward New York City, see Martin Wald, "Hard Times on the Hill for N.Y.," *Empire State Report* VI (June 16, 1980), 265, 267–8.

19　"The Federalist, No. LV," *The Federalist* (New York: Tudor Publishing Co., 1937), 383.

20　Webster (1903), VI, 54.

21　Letter to Tench Coxe, May 1, 1794, quoted in Bernard Mayo (ed.), *Jefferson Himself* (Charlottesville: University Press of Virginia, 1976), 195.

Appendix A. The construction of New York fiscal data

1　A fund in government accounting is defined as

> an independent fiscal and accounting entity with a self-balancing set of accounts recording cash and/or other resources together with all related liabilities, obligations, reserves, and equities which are segregated for the purpose of carrying on specific activities or attaining certain objectives in accordance with specific regulations, restrictions, or limitations . . . It should be pointed out that the concept of the fund as employed in governmental accounting is not synonymous with the term "fund" as it is sometimes employed in commercial accounting. In the latter, "fund" refers to an earmarked sum of cash or other assets, and no self-balancing group of accounts is provided therefor.

(National Committee on Governmental Accounting, *Governmental Accounting, Auditing, and Financial Reporting* [Ann Arbor, Mich.: Cushing–Malloy, 1968], 6–7.)

2　The appearance is often something of an illusion. If, for example, the state would have undertaken the activity in question anyway (say, building a highway), and if federal aid for that highway now enables the state to shunt its own dollars elsewhere, the net effect is that the federal government, by its contribution to highways, has enabled the state to bolster some sector other than highways.

3　The funds of New York State have been structured, by and large, according to the classifications and procedures spelled out in National Committee on Governmental Accounting, *Governmental Accounting, Auditing, and Financial Reporting.*

4   *Annual Report of the Comptroller,* 1977, p. 1.

5   "In addition, the costs of rehabilitation and improving existing facilities, payments for shore protection, canal improvements, flood control, certain State aid payments to localities in connection with the construction of Community Colleges and Public Safety Shelters, and rental occupancy payments for State office buildings are paid from this fund." (Ibid., pt. II, p. 45.)

6   The Postwar Reconstruction Fund was initially set up as a repository for the large surpluses of the war years. At the conclusion of hostilities, these funds were to be used to "provide a vast program of public improvements embracing highways, public buildings, parks and parkways, conservation of natural resources, and other projects which have been necessarily deferred because of wartime conditions." (Ibid., 1945, p. 2.)

7   In November of 1947, the voters of the state authorized a bond issue to finance the payment of a bonus to each person from New York State who was a veteran of the United States forces in World War II. Initially applicants had to be residents when applying, but that provision was eliminated in 1949.

8   The War Bonus Account (1947–55), the War Bonus and Mental Health Construction Bond Account (1955–59), and the War Bonus and Mental Health Bond Account (1959–68).

9   A one-cent-per-pack increase in the cigarette tax and a 10 percent income surtax. For a more complete description, see Appendix A.4.

10   The separate items do not add exactly to $2,050 million because of rounding.

11   Payments were made in the form of a grant to each school district of $300 per teacher, or an amount per teacher sufficient to increase the salary of each teacher to $2,000, whichever was greater. (See *Annual Report of the Comptroller,* 1948, p. 13.)

12   Ibid., 1977, p. 1.

13   Also included under this category of funds are those specifically designed for the rehabilitation of the residents at the mental, correctional, and other institutional facilities of the state (such as occupational therapy funds, hobby shop funds, and art and craft funds).

14   *Annual Report of the Comptroller,* 1977, pt. II, p. 116.

15   For example, see ibid., 128, 130, 131.

16   See ibid., 128.

17   Ibid., 114.

18   More correctly, all money in excess of $750,000 is so transferred. (See ibid.)

19   Ibid., 1971, p. 3.

20   More carefully defined, the General Fund "does not incorporate expenditures financed from all bond proceeds, from indirect financing sources, or from the majority of Federal funds and other earmarked revenues." (Ibid., 1975, pt. II, p. 43.)

21   Ibid., 1964, p. 14.

22   The phrase "All Operating Funds," and the associated aggregate revenues and expenditures, date from 1964. For a description of how these totals were estimated prior to 1964, see Appendix A.2.

23   *Annual Report of the Comptroller,* 1977, pt. II, p. 79.

24   The actual functioning of the fund is somewhat more complex. The Comptroller explains:

The Facilities Development Corporation is a corporate government agency, whose purposes are to provide for the design, construction, acquisition, reconstruction, rehabilitation or improvement of mental hygiene facilities, health facilities and certain community mental health and retardation facilities within the State of New York. The financing of these projects is by contract with the New York State Housing Finance Agency. All related debt service expenses (rental installments to H.F.A. and reserve requirements) along with the Corporation operational expenses are paid from patient care fees collected at the State's mental hygiene facilities. These fees are deposited directly to the Mental Hygiene Program Funds and amounts remaining in the funds, over and above the foregoing expenses, are available for transfer to the Mental Hygiene Services Fund (a special revenue fund in the State Treasury) for financing operations at certain facilities.

(*Annual Report of the Comptroller*, 1977, pt. II, p. 79.)

25   The fund also pays some debt service, and retains any excess funds.

26   Of the remaining 25 percent, much is accounted for by mental patients' fees used to build and maintain mental hospitals and by dormitory residents' fees used to build and maintain the State University.

27   Richard Dunham, quoted in Plumer (1975a), 483.

28   *New York Times*, July 4, 1980, p. B2.

29   *Annual Report of the Comptroller*, 1968, p. 32.

30   Ibid.

31   As of March 31, 1976, for example, New York City owed the state $750 million, and other accounts receivable totaled more than $450 million, of which $42 million had been outstanding for more than four years.

32   *Annual Report of the Comptroller*, 1977, pt. II, p. 52.

33   Ibid., 1969, p. 31.

34   In the late 1970s these "Spring Notes" amounted to $3 to $4 billion. The state has also borrowed $800 million to advance to New York City, which repays the interest and principal later in the year. Excluding this loan to the city, the state borrows each spring about 25 percent of the amount it subsequently collects in taxes.

35   The statements in this paragraph refer to full faith and credit debt only. The question of debtlike commitments is taken up subsequently.

36   The wealth transfer aspect of this operation is from future generations (those who must repay the debt) to the present generation (those who benefitted from the additional current expenditures financed by debt). This may or may not be objectionable, depending upon one's view of present needs and the ability of future generations to pay compared with that of the present generation.

37   See especially Chapter 6, Section 4, and Chapter 7, Sections 3 and 4.

38   Similar agreements with the Urban Development Corporation proved to be somewhat more precarious, because the capital projects so financed were less likely to yield the revenues needed to pay off the principal and interest on the debt. The default of UDC, however, was a default on notes only, which did not carry the moral obligation backing of the state.

39   "Before 1974–75, the net results of first instance advances and related reimbursements were excluded for budgeting and reporting purposes from the

operating statements of the General Fund." (*Annual Report of the Comptroller, 1977,* pt. I, p. 5.)

40   This addition should not include the mortgage tax. See Appendix A.5 on Shared Taxes.

41   This amount was temporarily exceeded, in that a total of $420 million was issued (between March 2 and March 10 of 1948), including $20 million in two-week notes.

42   The components do not add exactly to $2,050 million because of rounding.

43   *Annual Report of the Comptroller,* 1947, p. 4.

44   Ibid., 1946, p. 25.

45   *Annual Report of the Comptroller,* 1946, p. 5. The Capital Construction Fund (at that time called by a different name) had no comparable reserve fund.

46   Thus, for example, the Comptroller noted in 1977 that "while year-end balances in the funds for state purposes and local assistance are required to be transferred to their respective stabilization reserve funds, revenues of these funds during the fiscal year ending March 31, 1977, were so allocated as to leave no balance for transfer to the reserve funds." (Ibid., 1977, pt. II, p. 61.)

Bibliography

Adams, Henry C. 1887. *Public Debts: An Essay in the Science of Finance*. New York: D. Appleton.

Adams, James Ring. 1980. "New York City's Legal Hangover." *Wall Street Journal*, March 24, p. 24.

Advisory Commission on Intergovernmental Relations. 1973. *City Financial Emergencies: The Intergovernmental Dimension*. Washington, D.C.: U.S. Government Printing Office.

1974. *Significant Features of Fiscal Federalism*. Washington, D.C., Report M–79, April.

1976. *Significant Features of Fiscal Federalism*. Washington, D.C., Report M–106, June.

1977. *Trends in Metropolitan America*. Washington, D.C., M–108, February.

Alealy, Roger E. and David Mermelstein (eds.). 1977. *The Fiscal Crisis of American Cities*. New York: Vintage.

Alonso, William, 1975*a*. "Industrial Location and Regional Policy in Economic Development," in John Friedmann and William Alonso (eds.), *Regional Policy: Readings in Theory and Applications*. Cambridge, Mass.: M.I.T. Press, 64–96.

1975*b*. "Location Theory," in John Friedmann and William Alonso (eds.), *Regional Policy: Readings in Theory and Applications*. Cambridge, Mass.: M.I.T. Press, 35–63.

Association of the Bar of the City of New York, Committee on Municipal Affairs. 1978. *Local Finance Project: Proposals to Strengthen Local Finance Laws in New York State*, November.

Astor, Gerald. 1968. "Nelson Rockefeller Talks about the Gap between the People and the Politicians." *Look* XXXII (September 17), 58–9.

"Attacking the Mass Transit Mess." 1972. *Business Week*, no. 2231, June 3, pp. 60–5.

Auletta, Ken. 1977. "A Reporter at Large." *New Yorker*, August, pp. 28–48.

1975*a*. "Should These Men Go to Jail?" *New York Magazine* VIII (December 1), 36–41.

1979. *The Streets Were Paved with Gold*. New York: Random House.

1975*b*. "Who's to Blame for the Fix We're In?" *New York Magazine* VIII (October 27), 30–41.

Axelrod, Donald. 1974. "Higher Education," in Robert H. Connery and Gerald Benjamin (eds.), *Governing New York State: The Rockefeller Years*. New York: Academy of Political Science, 131–45.

Bahl, Roy W. 1979*a*. "Fiscal Retrenchment in a Declining State: The New York Case." *National Tax Journal* XXXII (June), Supplement, 277–87.

1977. "The Long Term Fiscal Outlook for New York State," in *The Decline of New York in the 1970's: A Demographic, Economic and Fiscal Analysis.* Proceedings of a Conference Held at State University of New York at Binghamton, November 8–9, 1976. Binghamton: Center for Social Analysis, 95–142.

1979*b*. "The New York State Economy: 1960–1978 and the Outlook." Metropolitan Studies Program, Maxwell School of Citizenship and Public Affairs, Syracuse University. Occasional Paper No. 37, October.

Bahl, Roy W., Alan K. Campbell, and David Greytak. 1974. *Taxes, Expenditures, and the Economic Base: Case Study of New York City.* New York: Praeger.

Bahl, Roy W. and David Greytak. 1976. "The Response of City Government Revenues to Changes in Employment Structure." *Land Economics* LII (November), 415–34.

Bauer, David. 1980. "The Question of Foreign Investment." *New York Affairs* VI, no. 2, 52–8.

Beale, Calvin L. 1977. "Discussion of Manufacturing Employment in New York State: The Anatomy of Decline," in *The Decline of New York in the 1970's: A Demographic, Economic and Fiscal Analysis.* Proceedings of a Conference Held at State University of New York at Binghamton, November 8–9, 1976. Binghamton: Center for Social Analysis, 37–42.

Beame, Abraham. 1975. "Financing New York City." *Challenge* XVIII (September–October), 37–43.

Belluomo, Michael S. 1979*a*. "Commuting: All Aboard!" *Empire State Report* V (April), 36–7.

1979*b*. "Travelling into the Future with the VHST, PRT, VTOL . . . and the BTM?" *Empire State Report* V (April), 38–40.

Benjamin, Gerald. 1974. "Patterns in New York State Politics," in Robert H. Connery and Gerald Benjamin (eds.), *Governing New York State: The Rockefeller Years.* New York: Academy of Political Science, 31–44.

Berle, Peter A. A. 1974. *Does the Citizen Stand a Chance? Politics of a State Legislature: New York.* Woodbury, N.Y.: Barron's Educational Series.

Bernstein, Blanche. 1974. "The State and Social Welfare," in Robert H. Connery and Gerald Benjamin (eds.), *Governing New York State: The Rockefeller Years.* New York: Academy of Political Science, 146–60.

Bienstock, Herbert. 1970. "Manpower Directions in New York City in the 70's." *City Almanac* V (December), 1–11.

1977. "New York City's Labor Market: Past Trends, Current Conditions, Future Prospects." *City Almanac* XII (December), 1–18.

"A Billion-Dollar Boost for Transit." 1967. *Railway Age* CLXII (April 3), 21–4, 52.

Birch, David L. 1979. "The Job Generation Process." Unpublished paper, M.I.T. Program on Neighborhood and Regional Change, Cambridge, Mass.

Bird, Frederick L. 1951. *The Municipal Debt: A Description, Analysis and Appraisal of Debt Policy and Administration of the City of New York.* Mayor's Committee on Management Survey of the City of New York. Item no. 6, October.

Bleiberg, Robert M. 1975. "Rotten Boroughs: New York City Has Been Undermined by Rent Control." *Barron's* LV (October 27), 7.

"The Board of Regents: History and Functions." 1974. *Empire State Report* I (December), 41.

Boast, Tom. 1980. "Debt and Capital Management," in Charles Brecher and Raymond D. Horton (eds.), *Setting Municipal Priorities: 1981*. Montclair, N.J.: Allanheld, Osmun, 113–42.

"A Bold Proposal for Mass Transit." 1966. *Railway Age* CLX (May 2), 14–18.

Bolton, Roger. 1979. "Multiregional Models in Policy Analysis." Paper presented at a Conference on Modeling the Multi-Region Economic System, Philadelphia, June 14–15.

Brackett, Jean C. 1969. "New BLS Budgets Provide Yardsticks for Measuring Family Living Costs." *Monthly Labor Review* XCII (April), 3–16.

Bradbury, Katherine L., Anthony Downs, and Kenneth A. Small. 1980. "Some Dynamics of Central City–Suburban Interactions." *American Economic Review* LXX (May), 410–14.

Brecher, Charles and Raymond D. Horton. 1980. "Fulfilling the Promise of Koch's Budget Goal." *New York Times*, February 2, p. 21.

Brecher, Charles and Raymond D. Horton (eds.). 1980. *Setting Municipal Priorities: 1981*. Montclair, N.J.: Allanheld, Osmun.

Bronston, Jack. 1978. "The Legislature in Change and Crisis: 1958–1978." *Empire State Report* IV (October–November), 40–1.

Brown, Betsy. 1976. "Assessing New York's Need for Housing." *Empire State Report* II (August), 261–5.

1977. "Co-opting a Dream: The Making of a Financial Nightmare." *Empire State Report* III (March), 105–10.

Browne, Paul J. 1978a. "PASNY's New Supply of Cheap Hydroelectric Power Could Confer Enormous Economic Benefits." *Empire State Report* IV (January–February), 11–13.

1978b. "State Purchases Total $1/2 Billion a Year – Is New York's Law Giving an Edge to New York Businessmen?" *Empire State Report* IV (December), 20–2.

Buck, Rinker. 1975a. "Keeping the Big Apple Afloat: The Panel Approach: Swimming in the Dark." *Empire State Report* I (November), 411–13, 440.

1975b. "State Swallows the Big Apple." *Empire State Report* I (September), 338–9, 357.

1975c. "The State's Indigestion from a Bad Apple." *Empire State Report* I (October), 371–3, 401–3.

1980. "How Am I Doing? An In-Depth Look at Mayor Koch's Record." *New York* XIII (September 8), 18–32.

Caro, Robert A. 1975. *The Power Broker: Robert Moses and the Fall of New York*. New York: Vintage Books.

Carruth, Eleanore. 1971. "What Price Glory on the Albany Mall?" *Fortune* LXXXIII (June), 92–5, 165–7.

Chartock, Alan S. 1976. "Why Legislators Don't Return to Albany." *Empire State Report* II (January–February), 17–21.

Chemical Bank. 1979. *Looking toward the 80's: A Chemical Bank Survey of Small and Medium Sized Businesses in New York*. Conducted by Louis Harris and Associates, Inc., November.

1980. *Looking toward the 80's in Upstate New York: A Chemical Bank Survey of Medium-Sized Business*, April.

Chinitz, Benjamin. 1977. "Manufacturing Employment in New York State: The Anatomy of Decline," in *The Decline of New York in the 1970's: A Demographic, Economic and Fiscal Analysis*. Proceedings of a Conference Held at State University of New York at Binghamton, November 8–9, 1976. Binghamton: Center for Social Analysis, 57–78.

Citizens Budget Commission. 1977a. *Citizens Budget Commission Recommendations on the Final Report of the Temporary Commission on City Finances.* vol. 44, no. 4, November.

1976. *Compendium of Major New York City Social Service Programs.* vol. 43, no. 3, September.

1978a. *New York City's Fiscal Future.* vol. 45, no. 3, August.

1978b. *New York City's Fiscal Prospects: Forecasts of New York City Revenue and Expenditure Patterns for FY 1979 through FY 1983.* vol. 45, no. 1, February.

1980a. *Policy Issues Raised by New York City's Proposed Financial Plan for Fiscal Years 1980–1984.* vol. 47, no. 2, February.

1977b. *A Review of Real Estate Tax Incentive Programs in New York City.* vol. 44, no. 2, March.

1977c. *Short-Term Options for Financing the City University.* vol. 44, no. 1, February.

1980b. *Statement on New York City's Financial Situation.* vol. 47, no. 1, January.

1978–79. *Twenty-Five Year Pocket Summary of New York City Finances.*

1977d. *Wanted: Solutions to Seven Major Problems.* vol. 44, no. 5, December.

Clark, Timothy B. 1976. "The Frostbelt Fights for a New Future." *Empire State Report* II (October–November), 332, 335–40.

1975a. "The Rapid Rise and Fast Fall of the UDC." *Empire State Report* I (April), 110–11, 132–4.

1977. "Rockefeller's Legacy." *Empire State Report* III (April), 141–63.

1975b. "UDC Crisis: Future Fallout on N.Y. Bonds?" *Empire State Report* I (May), 170–3, 191–3.

Collier, Peter and David Horowitz. 1976. *The Rockefellers: An American Dynasty.* New York: Signet.

Collins, Lyndhurst and David F. Walker (eds.). 1975. *Locational Dynamics of Manufacturing Activity.* New York: John Wiley and Sons.

Comes, Frank. 1976. "Has Carey Kept His Promise to Business?" *Empire State Report* II (September), 292–5.

CONEG Policy Research Center, Inc., and the Northeast–Midwest Research Institute. 1977. *A Case of Inequity: Regional Patterns in Defense Expenditures, 1950–1977,* August.

Congressional Budget Office. 1975–76. "The Causes of New York City's Fiscal Crisis." *Political Science Quarterly* XC (Winter), 659–74.

Connery, Robert H. 1974. "Nelson A. Rockefeller as Governor," in Robert H. Connery and Gerald Benjamin (eds.), *Governing New York State: The Rockefeller Years.* New York: Academy of Political Science, 1–15.

Connery, Robert H. and Gerald Benjamin (eds.). 1974. *Governing New York State: The Rockefeller Years.* New York: Academy of Political Science.

1979. *Rockefeller of New York.* Ithaca, N.Y.: Cornell University Press.

Connery, Robert H. and Demetrios Caraley (eds.). 1969. *Governing the City: Challenges and Options for New York.* New York: Praeger.

Cornell Center for Environmental Research. 1979. "Your Responsibilities under SEQR: A Local Guide." Extension Bulletin F. & OH–LA 79–2, August.

Costikyan, Edward N. 1976. "New York City's Bicentennial Revolution." *Empire State Report* II (August), 257–60.

The Decline of New York in the 1970's: A Demographic, Economic and Fiscal Analysis. 1977. Proceedings of a Conference Held at State University of New York at Binghamton, November 8–9, 1976. Binghamton: Center for Social Analysis, May.

deFerranti, David M. et al. 1974. *The Welfare and Nonwelfare Poor in New York City.* New York: Rand Corporation, Report R–1381–NYC.

DeLaubenfels, David J. 1966. "Soil," in John H. Thompson (ed.), *Geography of New York State.* Syracuse: Syracuse University Press, 104–10.

de Seve, Charles, Richard W. Richardson, and Thomas Vasquez. 1977. *Taxation in New York State: A Comparative Study.* New York State Economic Development Board Report, May.

Desmond, James. 1964. *Nelson Rockefeller: A Political Biography.* New York: Macmillan.

Dormer, Robert T. 1979. "Another Round for Job Development." *Empire State Report* V (October–November), 45–7.

Drennan, Matthew P. 1980. "New York's Airlines Industry Flies High." *New York Affairs* VI, no. 2, 80–4.

Drennan, Matthew P. and Georgia Nanopoulous-Stergiou. 1979. "The Local Economy and Local Revenues," in Raymond D. Horton and Charles Brecher (eds.), *Setting Municipal Priorities: 1980.* Montclair, N.J.: Allanheld, Osmun, 6–33.

1980. "The Local Economy and Local Revenues," in Charles Brecher and Raymond D. Horton (eds.), *Setting Municipal Priorities: 1981.* Montclair, N.J.: Allanheld, Osmun, 11–44.

Durbin, Elizabeth F. 1969. *Welfare Income and Employment.* New York: Praeger.

Dutka, Anna B. and Marcia Freedman. 1980. "Where the Jobs Are." *New York Affairs* VI, no. 2, 20–36.

Ehrbar, A. F. 1980. "Financial Probity, Chicago Style." *Fortune* C (June 2), 100–6.

Epstein, Jay Edward. 1975. "The Great Rockefeller Power Machine." *New York Magazine* VIII (November 24), 44–73.

"Exodus of Corporate Headquarters." 1975. *Empire State Report* I (September), 329.

Fantus Company. 1975. *A Study of the Business Climate of the States.* Prepared for the Illinois Manufacturers' Association, August.

"Federal Spending: The North's Loss Is the Sunbelt's Gain." 1976. *National Journal*, no. 26, June 26, pp. 878–91.

Ferretti, Fred. 1976. *The Year the Big Apple Went Bust.* New York: Putnam.

Foltman, Felician F. 1977. "The Business Climate in New York State: A Survey of the Perceptions of Labor and Management Officials," in Felician F. Foltman and Peter D. McClelland (eds.), *New York State's Economic Crisis: Jobs, Income, and Economic Growth.* Ithaca, N.Y.: New York State School of Industrial and Labor Relations, 137–65.

Foltman, Felician F. and Peter D. McClelland (eds.). 1977. *New York State's Economic Crisis: Jobs, Income, and Economic Growth.* Ithaca, N.Y.: New York State School of Industrial and Labor Relations, Cornell University.

Forbes, Ronald, Alan Frankle, and Christopher Carter. 1977. "Public Debt in the Northeast: The Limits on Growth," in *The Northeast: Managing a*

Way Out. Proceedings of a Symposium on Legislative Actions for Survival in Credit Markets, Boston, February 10–11.

"A Free Ride for New York's Subway Users?" 1971. *First National City Bank Monthly Economic Letter* (September), 13–15.

French, J. H. 1860. *Gazetteer of the State of New York.* Syracuse: R. D. Smith.

Friedmann, John and William Alonso (eds.). 1975. *Regional Policy: Readings in Theory and Applications.* Cambridge, Mass.: M.I.T. Press.

Fuchs, Victor R. 1962. *Changes in the Location of Manufacturing in the United States since 1929.* New Haven: Yale University Press.

Gervasi, Frank. 1964. *The Real Rockefeller.* New York: Atheneum.

Gilligan, Donald. 1976. "Conservation vs. Development." *Empire State Report* II (October–November), 376–85.

Ginzberg, Eli. 1979. "New York City: Next Turn of the Wheel." *Empire State Report* V (February), 36–9.

Glickman, Norman J. 1977. *Econometric Analysis of Regional Systems.* New York: Academic Press.

Goldmark, Peter C., Jr. 1979. "Foreign Business in the Economy of the New York–New Jersey Metropolitan Region." *City Almanac* XIV (August), 1–14.

Gramlich, Edward M. 1976. "The New York City Fiscal Crisis: What Happened and What Is to Be Done?" *American Economic Review* LXVI (May), 415–29.

Grant, James. 1975. "Disaster Area: Rent Control Has Helped Turn Gotham into One." *Barron's* LV (April 21), 5, 20, 21, 24.

Greenhut, Melvin L. 1956. *Plant Location in Theory and in Practice.* Chapel Hill: University of North Carolina Press.

Griess, Maureen D. 1977. "Empire State Plaza: Does 'Nelson's Folly' Have a Future?" *Empire State Report* III (February), 43–7.

Griffin, John I. 1956. *Industrial Location in the New York Area.* New York: City College Press.

1959. *The Port of New York.* New York: Arco.

Grossman, David A. 1979. *The Future of New York City's Capital Plant.* Washington, D.C.: Urban Institute.

Grumet, Barbara R. 1975. "Mental Health Program Flounders." *Empire State Report* I (January), 14–18.

Gujarati, Damodar. 1978. *Pensions and New York City's Fiscal Crisis.* Washington, D.C.: American Enterprise Institute.

Gulick, Luther. 1937. "Notes on the Theory of Organization," in Luther Gulick and L. Urwick (eds.), *Papers on the Science of Administration.* New York: Institute of Public Administration, 1–45.

Haggberg, Marie. 1980. "Changing Patterns in the Garment Industry." *New York Affairs* VI, no. 2, 85–7.

Haider, Donald and Thomas Elmore, Jr. 1975. "New York at the Crossroads: The Budget Crisis in Perspective." *City Almanac* IX (February), 1–14.

Hallett, E. Bruce. 1979a. "Carey's Death-Defying Feat." *Barron's* LIX (August 20), 12.

1979b. "Good Money after Bad? The Urban Development Corp. Is Wheeling and Dealing Again." *Barron's* LIX (August 20), 4, 5, 12, 18, 20.

Hamilton, Alexander, James Madison, and John Jay. 1937. *The Federalist.* New York: Tudor.

Harris, Curtis C., Jr., and Frank E. Hopkins. 1972. *Location Analysis*. Toronto: D. C. Heath.

Hawkins, Betty. 1975. "New York's Environmental Impact Tussle." *Empire State Report* I (February–March), 64–7, 93–5.

Hevesi, Alan G. 1975. *Legislative Politics in New York State*. New York: Praeger.

Holcomb, Charles R. 1975. "The Pension Balloon Is About to Burst." *Empire State Report* I (May), 158–65, 182–4.

Horton, Raymond D. 1979. "Economic Development," in Raymond D. Horton and Charles Brecher (eds.), *Setting Municipal Priorities: 1980*. New York: Basic Books, 112–33.

    1977. "People, Jobs, and Public Finance in New York City: Implications of the Fiscal Crisis." *City Almanac* XII (August), 1–13.

    1974. "Public Employee Labor Relations under the Taylor Law," in Robert H. Connery and Gerald Benjamin (eds.), *Governing New York State: The Rockefeller Years*. New York: Academy of Political Science, 161–74.

Horton, Raymond D. and Charles Brecher (eds.). 1979. *Setting Municipal Priorities: 1980*. Montclair, N.J.: Allanheld, Osmun.

Hospital Association of New York State. 1978. *Seventh Annual Fiscal Pressures Survey: 1977*. December.

"How to Save New York." 1975. *Time* CVI (October 20), 9–17.

Hughes, James W. and George Sternlieb. 1978. *Jobs and People: New York City, 1985*. New Brunswick, N.J.: Rutgers University, Center for Urban Policy Research.

Hughes, Rupert. 1944. *The Story of Thomas E. Dewey, Attorney for the People*. New York: Grosset and Dunlap.

Hume, David. 1963. *Essays: Moral, Political and Literary*. Oxford: Oxford University Press.

Hunt, Gaillard (ed.). 1904. *The Writings of James Madison*. New York: G. P. Putnam.

Isard, Walter. 1956. *Location and Space Economy*. Cambridge, Mass.: M.I.T. Press.

Jackson, Larry R. and William A. Johnson. 1973. *Protest by the Poor: The Welfare Rights Movement in the City of New York*. New York: Rand Institute.

Jefferson, Thomas. 1964. *Notes on the State of Virginia*. New York: Harper Torchbook ed.

Jusenius, Carol L. and Larry C. Ledebur. 1978. *Documenting the "Decline" of the North*. U.S. Department of Commerce, Economic Development Research Report, June.

    1976. *A Myth in the Making: The Southern Economic Challenge and Northern Economic Decline*. U.S. Department of Commerce, Economic Development Research Report, November.

    1977. *Where Have All the Firms Gone? An Analysis of the New England Economy*. U.S. Department of Commerce, Economic Development Research Report, September.

Kalish, Richard J. 1974. "Environmental Protection," in Robert H. Connery and Gerald Benjamin (eds.), *Governing New York State: The Rockefeller Years*. New York: Academy of Political Science, 250–62.

Kelly, Lloyd L. 1977. "Energy and Economic Development: Critical Decisions and Consequences," in Felician F. Foltman and Peter D. McClelland (eds.), *New York State's Economic Crisis*. Ithaca, N.Y.: New York State School of Industrial and Labor Relations, 82–96.

Kenney, James M. and Thomas R. Kershner. 1977. "The Electric Utilities and Economic Development in New York State," in Felician F. Foltman and Peter D. McClelland (eds.), *New York State's Economic Crisis*. Ithaca, N.Y.: New York State School of Industrial and Labor Relations, 75–81.

Kerker, Robert P. 1979. "The Battle for Control of the Budget." *Empire State Report* V (June–July), 20–7.

Kramer, Michael and Sam Roberts. 1976. *"I Never Wanted to Be Vice-President of Anything!": An Investigative Biography of Nelson Rockefeller*. New York: Basic Books.

Kristoff, Frank S. 1974. "Housing," in Robert H. Connery and Gerald Benjamin (eds.), *Governing New York State: The Rockefeller Years*. New York: Academy of Political Science, 188–99.

Kroft, Steve. 1975. "The Magic and Myth of the Big Lobbyists' Influence on New York State's Government." *Empire State Report* I (April), 116–27.

Lawrence, Steve. 1978. "Only One Power Plant Has Been Approved in New York State since the Legislature Created the Sitting Board in 1972." *Empire State Report* IV (January–February), 14–17.

Leone, Robert A. and Raymond Struyk. 1976. "The Incubator Hypothesis: Evidence from Five SMSAs." *Urban Studies* XIII (October), 325–31.

Levin, Arthur L. 1974. "Health Care," in Robert H. Connery and Gerald Benjamin (eds.), *Governing New York State: The Rockefeller Years*. New York: Academy of Political Science, 175–87.

Lichtenberg, Robert M. 1960. *One-Tenth of a Nation: National Forces in the Economic Growth of the New York Region*. Cambridge, Mass.: Harvard University Press.

Lippmann, Walter. 1922. *Public Opinion*. New York: Harcourt, Brace.

"LIRR Drama Rolls toward Climax." 1969. *Railway Age* CLVII (August 18), 30–1.

Lirtzman, Sidney and David Bresnick. 1978. "The New Integrated Financial Management System Brings New York City's Fiscal System Out of the Dark Ages." *Empire State Report* IV (October–November), 42–5.

Little, Jane S. 1978. "Locational Decisions of Foreign Direct Investors in the United States." *Federal Reserve Bank of Boston: New England Economic Review* (July–August), 43–63.

Locke, John. 1960. *Two Treatises of Government*. Ed. Peter Laslett. Cambridge: Cambridge University Press.

Long, Larry H. 1974. "Poverty Status and Receipt of Welfare among Migrants and Nonmigrants in Large Cities." *American Sociological Review* XXXIX (February), 46–56.

Lowi, Theodore J. 1964. *At the Pleasure of the Mayor*. New York: Free Press of Glencoe.

McClelland, Peter D. 1977. "The Structure of the Employment Problem," in Felician F. Foltman and Peter D. McClelland (eds.), *New York State's Economic Crisis: Jobs, Income, and Economic Growth*. Ithaca, N.Y.: New York State School of Industrial and Labor Relations, 39–74.

McKeating, Michael P. 1975a. "New York Losing the Race for New Industry." *Empire State Report* I (October), 378–81, 390–2.

1975b. "New York's Tired Economy Going Flat." *Empire State Report* I (September), 327–9, 351–3.

McManus, Michael J. 1976a. "How the Northeast Finances Southern Prosperity." *Empire State Report* II (October–November), 347–52.

1976b. "In the Face of Dire Economic Necessity." *Empire State Report* II (October–November), 333, 343–5.

1976c. "Issues Facing the Northeast." Fund for the City of New York, June 16.

1976d. *The Need for a Northeast Coalition.* Fund for the City of New York, June 16.

McManus, Michael J. and Frank A. Weil. 1976. "No One Is in Charge: The Need for a System of Metropolitan Governance." *Empire State Report* II (October–November), 364–75.

Marcus, Steven. 1976. "A Battered Beame Looks Back on a 'Tough Year.'" *Empire State Report* II (January–February), 22–3.

1975. "Cutting NYC's Enormous '75 and '76 Budget Deficits." *Empire State Report* I (February–March), 61–3, 90.

Markusen, Ann R. and Jerry Fastrup. 1978. "The Regional War for Federal Aid." *Public Interest*, no. 53, Fall, pp. 87–99.

Mason, Bert, Richard N. Boisvert, and Lois M. Plimpton. 1978. "Financing New York's Governments." Unpublished paper, Department of Agricultural Economics, Cornell University, A. E. Res. 78–6, July.

Mathewson, Kent. 1974. *The Regionalist Papers.* Detroit: Metropolitan Fund, Inc.

Mayo, Bernard (ed.). 1976. *Jefferson Himself.* Charlottesville: University Press of Virginia.

Meyer, Herbert E. 1976. "Why Corporations Are on the Move." *Fortune* XCIII (May), 252–4, 270–2.

Miller, Ronald H. 1977. "Environmental Programs and the State Economy," in Felician F. Foltman and Peter D. McClelland (eds.), *New York State's Economic Crisis.* Ithaca, N.Y.: New York State School of Industrial and Labor Relations, 97–124.

Milstein, Mike M. and Robert E. Jennings. 1973. *Educational Policy-Making and the State Legislature.* New York: Praeger.

"More Companies Send New York a Message – 'Goodbye,'" 1976. *Fortune* XCIII (May), 272.

Morris, Charles R. 1980. *The Cost of Good Intentions: New York City and the Liberal Experiment.* New York: W. W. Norton.

Morris, Joe Alex. 1960. *Nelson Rockefeller: A Biography.* New York: Harper.

Morrison, Peter A. 1977. "New York State's Transition to Stability: The Demographic Outlook," in *The Decline of New York in the 1970's: A Demographic, Economic and Fiscal Analysis.* Proceedings of a Conference Held at State University of New York at Binghamton, November 8–9, 1976. Binghamton: Center for Social Analysis, 3–36.

Moscow, Alvin. 1977. *The Rockefeller Inheritance.* New York: Doubleday.

Moscow, Warren. 1976. "The Spectre of More Veto Overrides." *Empire State Report* II (August), 254–6.

1967. *What Have You Done for Me Lately? The Ins and Outs of New York City Politics.* Englewood Cliffs, N.J.: Prentice-Hall.

Moss, Mitchell L. 1980. "Staging a Renaissance on the Waterfront." *New York Affairs* VI, no. 2, 3–19.

Moynihan, Daniel Patrick. 1977. "The Federal Government and the Economy of New York State." Press release, rev. ed., July 15.

1978. "The Politics and Economics of Regional Growth." *Public Interest*, no. 51, Spring, pp. 3–21.

1979. "Washington and New York." Press release, April.

1980. "What Will They Do for New York?" *New York Times Magazine*, January 27, pp. 30–4, 38–40.

"MTA's Man from Macy's Maps a Marketing Approach." 1974. *Railway Age* CLXXV (August 12), 26–32.

Mueller, Eva and James N. Morgan. 1961. "Location Decisions of Manufacturers." *American Economic Review* LII (May), 204–17.

Muller, Thomas. 1975. *Growing and Declining Urban Areas: A Fiscal Comparison.* Washington, D.C.: Urban Institute.

Municipal Assistance Corporation for the City of New York. *Annual Report.*

Municipal Finance Officers Association. 1968. *Governmental Accounting, Auditing and Financial Reporting.* Ann Arbor, Michigan: Cushing-Malloy.

Murphy, J. Kevin. 1978. "New York City's Port Authority Bus Terminal." *Empire State Report* IV (September 15), 12–15.

National Committee on Governmental Accounting. 1968. *Governmental Accounting, Auditing, and Financial Reporting.* Ann Arbor, Mich.: Cushing-Malloy.

"Nation's 'Finest' Comes Up Short." 1969. *Business Week*, no. 2093, October 11, pp. 44–5.

Neches, Amy J. and Philip E. Aarons. 1980. "The City Approaches Industrial Development." *New York Affairs* VI, no. 2, 43–6.

Netzer, Dick. 1977. "The New York City Fiscal Crisis," in *The Decline of New York in the 1970's: A Demographic, Economic and Fiscal Analysis.* Proceedings of a Conference Held at State University of New York at Binghamton, November 8–9, 1976. Binghamton: Center for Social Analysis, 159–66.

1969. "New York City's Mixed Economy: Ten Years Later." *Public Interest*, no. 16, Summer, pp. 188–202.

Newfield, Jack. 1970. "The Case against Nelson Rockefeller." *New York Magazine* III (March 9), 26–33.

New York [City], Mayor's Committee on Management Survey. 1952. *The Financial Problem of the City of New York.* By Robert M. Haig and Carl S. Shoup. Item no. 5, June.

1951. *The Municipal Debt: A Description, Analysis and Appraisal of Debt Policy and Administration of the City of New York.* By Frederick L. Bird. Technical Monograph Number One, Item no. 6, October.

New York [City], Office of the Comptroller. 1977. *New York City's Hidden Debt: Lease-Purchase Agreements with Public Authorities.* October 17.

New York [City], Tempory Commission on City Finances. 1966a. *Better Financing for New York City.* Final Report, August.

1978. *The City in Transition: Prospects and Policies for New York.* Final Report. New York: Arno Press.

1977a. *The City University of New York: Proposals for the Future.* Tenth Interim Report, January.

1977b. *Economic and Demographic Trends in New York City: The Outlook for the Future.* Thirteenth Interim Report, May.

1977c. *The Effects of Personal Taxes in New York City: Some Proposals for a More Rational System.* Eleventh Interim Report, February.

1977*d*. *The Effects of Rent Control and Rent Stabilization in New York City*. Fifteenth Interim Report, June.

1976*a*. *The Effects of Taxation on Manufacturing in New York City*. Ninth Interim Report, December.

1975. *The Effects of the Bond Transfer Tax*. First Interim Report, November.

1976*b*. *The Effects of the New York City Estate Tax*. Fifth Interim Report, April.

1966*b*. *Financing Government in New York City*. Final Research Report of the Graduate School of Public Administration, New York University, June.

1976*c*. *Financing Mass Transit in New York City*. Fourth Interim Report, March.

1976*d*. *The Fiscal Impact of Fringe Benefits and Leave Benefits: Some Proposals for Reform*. Seventh Interim Report, June.

1976*e*. *The Fiscal Impact of Retirement Benefits: Some Proposals for Reform*. Sixth Interim Report, May.

1976*f*. *An Historical and Comparative Analysis of Expenditures in the City of New York*. Eighth Interim Report, October.

1977*e*. *The Medicaid Program in New York City: Some Proposals for Reform*. Sixteenth Interim Report, June.

1977*f*. *Public Assistance Programs in New York City: Some Proposals for Reform*. Twelfth Interim Report, February.

1977*g*. *The Role of Intergovernmental Fiscal Relations in New York City*. Fourteenth Interim Report, May.

1976*g*. *State Assumption of Court, Probation, and Correction Services in New York*. Second Interim Report, January.

1976*h*. *Synchronizing State and Federal Aid to New York City*. Third Interim Report, January.

New York City Transit Authority. *Annual Report*.

New York Power Pool. 1979. *Long Range Generation and Transmission Plan, 1979*. April 1.

"New York's David Yunich: Building toward a Dream." *Railway Age* CLXXVII (October 11), 16–20.

"New York's MTA Puts Railroads in the Picture – in a Big Way." 1970. *Railway Age*. CLXIX (October 12), 26–31.

New York [State]. 1846. *Journal of the Convention of the State of New York, 1846*. Albany: Carrol and Cook.

1959–73. *The Public Papers of Nelson A. Rockefeller: Fifty-Third Governor of the State of New York*.

1846. *Report of the Debates and Proceedings of the Convention for the Revision of the Constitution of the State of New York, 1846*. Albany: W. Attree and W. Bishop.

1938. *Report of the New York State Constitutional Convention Committee*.

1938. *Revised Record of the Constitutional Convention of the State of New York, April Fifth to August Twenty-Sixth, 1938*. Albany: J. B. Lyon.

New York [State], Assembly, Office of the Speaker. 1980. *Small Business: New York's Forgotten Majority*, February 21.

New York [State], Assembly Standing Committee on Corporations, Authorities and Commissions. 1972. *Public Authorities in New York State: Their Legal and Financial Status*. Legislative Document no. 32, April 24.

New York [State], Council of Economic Advisors. 1970–74. *Annual Report.*

New York [State], Department of Commerce. 1970. *Area Indexes of Business Activity: New York State, 1957–1969.* Research Bulletin no. 27, February.

1966. *A Century of Population Changes in Counties of New York State.* Research Bulletin no. 15, March.

1968. *Manufacturing in New York State.* Research Bulletin no. 23, November.

1972. *Manufacturing in New York State.* Research Bulletin no. 32, March.

1979a. *New York State: The Best Business Advantages in America.*

1965. *Personal Income in Areas and Counties of New York State.* Research Bulletin no. 9, March.

1976a. *Personal Income in Areas and Counties of New York State.* Research Bulletin no. 42, August.

1978a. *Personal Income in Areas and Counties of New York State.* Research Bulletin no. 46, November.

1979b. *Personal Income in Areas and Counties of New York State.* Research Bulletin no. 47, August.

1978b. "A Statistical Profile of Industrial Migration in New York State: 1975." Unpublished paper.

1976b. *Taxes and Plant Location in New York and Other Industrial States.* Research Bulletin no. 1, March.

1979c. *Why It Pays to Do Business in New York State.* March.

New York [State], Department of Labor. 1978. *Annual Planning Information, Rochester Area.* BLMI Report FY78, no. 92, June.

1977. *Annual Planning Report, Fiscal Year 1978: New York City.* Labor Research Report 1977–no. 81, July.

Employment Review.

Employment Statistics.

1975a. *Labor Statistics Relating to the Economy of New York State.* Research Report 1975–25, November.

1975b. *Manpower Projections: New York State, 1970–1980.* Publication B–204, January.

New York [State], Department of Social Services. *Statistical Supplement to Annual Report.*

New York [State], Department of State. 1976. *Local Government Handbook.* 2nd ed.

New York [State], Division of the Budget. *New York State Statistical Yearbook.*

1967. *Statistical Series of New York State.* Rev., August.

New York [State], Economic Development Advisory Committee. 1979. *Report.* May 30.

New York [State], Economic Development Board. 1977. *Taxation in New York State: A Comparative Study.* By Charles de Seve, Richard W. Richardson, and Thomas Vasquez, May.

New York [State], Education Department. 1978a. *College Participation Rates in New York State: Historical Statistics and Influential Factors.* University of the State of New York, Office of Postsecondary Research, October.

1978b. *The Regents 1978 Progress Report on Their 1976 Statewide Plan for the Development of Postsecondary Education.* University of the State of New York, October.

New York [State], Energy Office. 1978. *New York State Energy Consumption and Supply Statistics, 1960–1976.* August.

New York [State], Governor. *Annual Budget Message.*

1977a. *Economic Development Bond Issue.* Special Message to the Legislature, May 24.

1977b. *Governor's Five-Year Projection of Income and Expenditures, General Fund, Fiscal Years 1977–78 through 1981–82.* February 17.

New York [State], Health Planning Commission. 1979. *Proposed State Health Plan.* March.

New York [State], Housing Finance Agency. *Annual Report.*

New York [State], Job Development Authority. *Annual Report.*

New York [State], Joint Legislative Committee on Housing and Multiple Dwellings. 1955. *Report.* Legislative Document no. 39.

New York [State], Legislative Commission on Expenditure Review. 1971. *Construction of Dormitories and Other University Facilities.* Program Audit 5.2.71, December 1.

1977. *Health Planning in New York State.* Program Audit 1.1.77, January 3.

1974. *Industrial Development in New York State.* Program Audit 12.1.74, November 25.

1975a. *Programs for the Aged.* Program Audit 1.1.75, March 31.

1975b. *State Job Placement Programs.* Program Audit 11.1.75, December 30.

New York [State], Moreland Act Commission. 1976. *Restoring Credit and Confidence.* A Report to the Governor on the Urban Development Corporation and Other State Financing Agencies, March 31.

New York [State], Office of the Comptroller. *Annual Report.*

1973a. *Audit of New York State, New York City and Public Authorities for the Two Years Ended March 31, 1972.* April 25.

1976. *Audit Report on the Planned Elimination of Operating Expenses from New York City's Capital Budget.* Interim Report no. 5 on New York City Central Budgeting and Fiscal Practices, NYC–45–76.

1973b. *Debt-Like Commitments of the State of New York.* Comptroller's Studies on Issues in Public Finance. Study no. 2, January.

1973c. *Discipline in the Fiscal Process: "What Is the State of the State?"* Comptroller's Studies on Issues in Public Finance. Study no. 3. September.

1975. *Impact of the New York City Financial Crisis on New York State Borrowing.* Studies in Public Finance, October 15.

1970. *Principles of Accounting and Standards of Reporting for Public Authorities.* October.

1974. *Public Authorities in New York State.* December 31.

1967. *Public Authorities in New York State: A Financial Study.* Comptroller's Studies for the 1967 Constitutional Convention. Study no. 4, June.

1972a. *Statewide Public Authorities: A Fourth Branch of Government?* Comptroller's Studies on Issues in Public Finance. Study no. 1, vol. I, November.

1972b. *Statewide Public Authorities: Individual Authority Summaries.* Comptroller's Studies on Issues in Public Finance. Study no. 1, vol. II, November.

1978. *Summary of Audit Reports Relative to Central Budgetary, Accounting and Finance Systems and Reporting Practices of New York City.* Report NYC–63–78, April 19.

New York [State], Office of the Comptroller, Office of the Special Deputy Comptroller for New York City. 1980. *Tax Revenues and the City Economy*. Report FCB–103–80, May 7.

New York [State], Office of Planning Coordination. 1969. *New York State: Economic Outlook for the Seventies*. December.

New York [State], Office of Planning Services. 1972. *New York State Economic System: The Interindustry Structure of the New York State Economy: 1963*. By Frans Seastrand, April.

New York [State], Select Committee on the Economy. 1974. *Industry in New York: A Time of Transition*. Legislative Document no. 12.

New York [State], Senate. 1975. *Balanced Growth for the Northeast*. Proceedings of a Conference of Legislative Leaders on the Future of the Northeast, Albany, December 11–13.

New York [State], State Energy Office. 1978. *New York State Energy Consumption and Supply Statistics, 1960–1976*. August.

New York [State], Tax Department. 1975. *Background Paper on Taxes and Job Climate for Task Force on Unemployment*. October.

New York [State], Temporary Commission to Revise the Social Services Law. 1974. *Background for Action: Legislative Proposals for Restructuring Public Welfare and Social Services in New York State*. Legislative Document no. 26, February.

1975. *The Administration of Medicaid in New York State*. Interim Study Report no. 6, Albany, February.

New York [State], Temporary State Commission on Coordination of State Activities. 1956. *Staff Report on Public Authorities under New York State*, by William Ronan. Legislative Document no. 46, March 21.

"The New York State Bar Association Pushes the Legislature to Mend Its Ways and Means." 1975. *Empire State Report* I (August), 298–9.

New York State Dormitory Authority. 1974. Audit by Haskins and Sells, May 29.

New York State Library. 1977. *Source Material Related to Legislation in the State of New York and Annotated Bibliography of Legislative History and Legislative Intent*. Rev., April.

New York State Thruway Authority. *Annual Report*. 1976.

Norcliffe, G. B. 1975. "A Theory of Manufacturing Places," in Lyndhurst Collins and David F. Walker (eds.), *Locational Dynamics of Manufacturing Activity*. New York: John Wiley, 19–57.

The Northeast: Managing a Way Out. 1977. Proceedings of a Symposium on Legislative Actions for Survival in the Credit Markets, Boston, February 10–11.

Ostow, Miriam and Anna B. Dutka. 1975. *Work and Welfare in New York City*. Baltimore: Johns Hopkins.

Ostrom, Vincent. 1973. *The Intellectual Crisis in American Public Administration*. University, Ala.: University of Alabama Press.

Padula, Fred. 1977. "The New York State Budget Charade." *Empire State Report* III (January), 22–8.

Parker, George F. (ed.). 1892. *The Writings and Speeches of Grover Cleveland*. New York: Cassell.

Pellish, Harold. 1976. "The 'Moral Obligation' to Regain Credit." *Empire State Report* II (April), 91–3, 107.

Perloff, Harvey S. et al. 1960. *Regions, Resources and Economic Growth*. Lincoln, Nebr.: University of Nebraska Press.

Pierce, Neal R. 1972. *The Megastates of America.* New York: Norton.
  1976. "The Northeast Maps Battle Plan for Economic Revival." *Empire State Report* II (December), 406–13.
Plumer, Amy. 1975a. "The Bottom Line Is the Budget Division." *Empire State Report* I (December), 455–8, 483.
  1974. "Education in Flux: Whither the Board of Regents?" *Empire State Report* I (December), 4–7, 40–3.
  1975b. "Perfect Politics in Imperfect School Aid." *Empire State Report* I (April), 107–9, 135–8.
Poling, James (ed.). 1960. *A Political Self-Portrait: The Rockefeller Record.* New York: Thomas Y. Crowell.
"The Politicization of Research at the Fed." 1979. *Business Week,* no. 2594, July 16, pp. 106–15.
Port Authority of New York and New Jersey. 1979. *Regional Recovery: The Business of the Eighties.* June 1.
Prindle, Janice. 1976. "New York's $3 Billion Medicaid Boondoggle." *Empire State Report* II (July), 211–12, 233–7.
  1975. "Taxpayers Granted Day in Court." *Empire State Report* I (July), 265.
Puryear, David and Roy W. Bahl. 1977. "Economic Problems of a Mature Economy," in Felician F. Foltman and Peter D. McClelland (eds.), *New York State's Economic Crisis.* Ithaca, N.Y.: New York State School of Industrial and Labor Relations, 17–38.
Quirk, William J. 1973. "Standing to Sue in New York." *St. John's Law Review* XLVII (March), 429–82.
Quirk, William J. and Leon E. Wein. 1969. "Homeownership for the Poor: Tenant Condominiums, the Housing and Urban Development Act of 1968, and the Rockefeller Program." *Cornell Law Review* LIV (July), 811–70.
  1975. "Rockefeller's Constitutional Sleight of Hand." *Empire State Report* I (November), 429–31.
  1971. "A Short Constitutional History of Entities Commonly Known as Authorities." *Cornell Law Review* LVI (April), 521–97.
Ranschburg, Herbert J. 1957. "The Role of a Civic Agency in the Decision Making Process at the Local Government Level." Unpublished doctoral dissertation, Economics Department, New York University Graduate School, July.
Regional Plan Association. 1979a. "Business in the Region: Structure and Performance of the Region's Producer Economy in 1972–75." *Regional Plan News,* no. 103, April.
  1977a. "Power for the MTA." *Regional Plan News,* no. 126, June.
  1979b. *The Region's Money Flows.* Bulletin 128, April.
  1975. "The State of the Region." *Regional Plan News,* no. 97, March.
  1977b. "The State of the Region: 1977." *Regional Plan News,* no. 101, November.
  1980. *Regional Accounts: Structure and Performance of the New York Region's Economy in the Seventies.* By Regina B. Armstrong. Bloomington: Indiana University Press.
Reir, Sharon. 1978. "The Urban Development Corporation: Back In Business." *Empire State Report* IV (December), 5–8.
Richards, Clay and Carol Richards. 1976. "The Fiscal Crisis: Who Dunnit?" *Empire State Report* II (January–February), 40–1.

1977. "From Albany to Washington with Love." *Empire State Report* III (January), 35–7.

Rickles, Robert N. 1979. "Mass Transit in New York State: Where Do We Go from Here?" *Empire State Report* V (February), 17–25.

Rockefeller, Nelson A. 1966. *Statement of Governor Nelson A. Rockefeller before the Joint Legislative Committee on Problems of Public Health and Medicare*. Albany, May 24.

"Rockefeller's First Test." 1959. *New Republic* CXL (April 13), 5–6.

Ronan, William. 1956. *Staff Report on Public Authorities under New York State*. Prepared for New York State Temporary Commission on Coordination of State Activities. Legislative Document no. 46, March 21.

Roniger, George. 1976. "Economic Review of the New York Region: Catching the National Upswing." *City Almanac* XI (June), 1–14.

1975. "The Economy of the New York Region: Lessons from the 1974–75 Recession." *City Almanac* X (June), 1–15.

1974. "New York's Economy – into the Late 1970's." *City Almanac* IX (June), 1–12.

Rosenbaum, Michael. 1980. "Transit Talks Seem Headed for a Crisis." *Empire State Report* VI (January 14), 1, 8–12.

Rossant, M. J. 1976. "How Rockefeller Destroyed New York." *Harper's Magazine* CCLII (January), 62–74.

Rubin, Marilyn, Ilene Wagner, and Pearl Kamer. 1978. "Industrial Migration: A Case Study of Destination by City–Suburban Origin within the New York Metropolitan Area." *Journal of the American Real Estate and Urban Economics Association* VI (Winter), 417–37.

Sahling, Leonard G. and Sharon P. Smith. 1980. "Regional Wage Patterns: How Does New York Compare with the Rest of the Country?" *Federal Reserve Bank of New York Quarterly Review* V (Spring), 5–11.

Salins, Peter D. 1976. "Is There a Metro Government in New York's Future?" *New York Affairs* III (Spring), 53–65.

Samuels, Howard. 1976. "The Uses of Default: The Inevitable Is Now Desirable." *New York Magazine* IX (March 15), 42–50.

"Saving New York from Strangling." 1968. *Business Week*, no. 2010, March 9, pp. 64–7.

Sayre, Wallace S. and Herbert Kaufman. 1960. *Governing New York City: Politics in the Metropolis*. New York: Russell Sage Foundation.

Scanlon, Rosemary. 1980. "Tooling Up for Regional Marketing." *New York Affairs* VI, no. 2, 47–51.

Schlesinger, Joseph A. 1965. "The Politics of the Executive," in Herbert Jacob and Kenneth Vines (eds.), *Politics in the American States*. Boston: Little Brown, 207–37.

Schwartz, Gail Garfield. 1978. "New York City in Transition: Economic Development." *City Almanac* XII (February), 1–12.

Seastrand, Frans. 1972. "The Interindustry Structure of the New York State Economy: 1963." Unpublished paper, New York State Office of Planning Services, April.

"The Second War between the States." 1976. *Business Week*, no. 2432, May 17, pp. 92–7.

Seeley, Edward S., Jr. 1979. "The Financial Outlook for the New York City Transit Authority: Problems and Solutions." *City Almanac* XIV (June), 1–14.

Shaffer, David. 1975. "Legislature Still Groping for Direction." *Empire State Report* I (April), 290–1, 294–5.

Shefter, Martin. 1977. "New York City's Fiscal Crisis: The Politics of Inflation and Retrenchment." *Public Interest,* no. 48, Summer, pp. 98–127.

Silverman, Eli B. 1976. "U.S. Federalism: A Bad Recipe for NYC." *Empire State Report* II (April), 110–14.

Simon, William E. 1978. *A Time for Truth.* New York: McGraw-Hill.

Slocum, Peter. 1976. "Natural Gas: A Lack of Policy Planning." *Empire State Report* II (April), 98–101.

Spangler, Frank LeRoy. 1932. *Operation of Debt and Tax Rate Limits in the State of New York.* Special Report of the State Tax Commission, no. 5, Albany.

Spitznas, Thomas. 1980. "New York City's Financial Industry: Just How Captive Is It?" Paper presented at the Conference on New York City's Economic Base, City College of the City of New York, May 15.

Stein, Rona B. 1978a. "The Economy of Upstate New York." *Federal Reserve Bank of New York Quarterly Review* III (Autumn), 26–30.

　　1978b. "The New York City Economy: Is the Worst Finally Over?" *Federal Reserve Bank of New York Quarterly Review* III (Summer), 24–9.

　　1977. "New York City's Economy: A Perspective on Its Problems." *Federal Reserve Bank of New York Quarterly Review* II (Summer), 49–59.

Sterne, Michael. 1976. "Lower Taxes and Better Government Called Keys for City to Hold Industry." *New York Times,* May 15, pp. 1, 52.

Sternlieb, George and James W. Hughes (eds.). 1976. *Post Industrial America: Metropolitan Decline and Inter-Regional Shifts.* New Brunswick, N.J.: Rutgers University, Center for Urban Policy Research.

　　1978. *Revitalizing the Northeast: Prelude to an Agenda.* New Brunswick, N.J.: Rutgers University, Center for Urban Policy Research.

Stevens, Rosemary and Robert Stevens. 1970. "Medicaid: Anatomy of a Dilemma." *Law and Contemporary Problems* XXXV (Spring), 348–425.

"A Summer of Discontent for Commuters." 1969. *Business Week,* no. 2083, August 2, pp. 74–6.

Sveikauskas, Geddy. 1978. "New York Utilities Claim They'll Need $100 Billion to Keep the Lights Burning – the Next 30 Years." *Empire State Report* IV (January–February), 6–10.

Thompson, John H. (ed.). 1966. *Geography of New York State.* Syracuse: Syracuse University Press.

Thompson, Joseph D. 1976. "What Is It with the Railroads?" *Empire State Report* II (September), 303–5, 316–22.

Tobier, Emanuel. 1977. "Manhattan's Central Business District: Key to New York City's Future." *City Almanac* XII (October), 1–13.

Tobier, Emanuel and Mark A. Wills. 1980. "Has New York's Printing Industry Bottomed Out?" *New York Affairs* VI, no. 2, 59–69.

Twentieth Century Fund Task Force on the Future of New York City. 1980. *New York: World City.* Cambridge, Mass.: Oelgeschlager, Gunn and Hain.

Tyler, Humphrey S. 1975a. "The Government Troupe Debuts." *Empire State Report* I (January), 4–8.

　　1976. "The Legislature: A Profile of Rancor." *Empire State Report* II (May), 131–3, 156–8.

1975*b*. "The Legislature Edges towards Openness." *Empire State Report* I (February–March), 56–9, 84–7.

1975*c*. "The Steady Growth of Backdoor Financing." *Empire State Report* I (June), 211–13, 222–3.

"Urban Transit Picks Up Some Speed." 1969. *Business Week,* no. 2090, September 20, pp. 66–73.

U.S., Bureau of the Census. 1975. *Historical Statistics of the United States: Colonial Times to 1970.*

State Government Finances.

Statistical Abstract of the United States.

U.S., Congress, House, Committee on Banking, Finance and Urban Affairs, Subcommittee on Economic Stabilization. 1978. *New York City's Fiscal and Financial Situation.* 95th Cong., 2nd sess., February and March.

U.S., Congress, House, Committee on the Judiciary. 1974*a*. *Analysis of the Philosophy and Public Record of Nelson A. Rockefeller, Nominee for Vice President of the United States.* 93rd Cong., 2nd sess., October.

1974*b*. *Nomination of Nelson A. Rockefeller to Be Vice President of the United States.* Hearings. 93rd Cong., 2nd sess., November and December.

1974*c*. *Report on the Confirmation of Nelson A. Rockefeller as Vice President of the United States.* 93rd Cong., 2nd sess., November 21.

U.S., Congress, Joint Economic Committee. 1975*a*. *Impact of New York City's Economic Crisis on the National Economy.* 94th Cong., 1st sess., November 10.

1975*b*. *New York City's Economic Crisis.* 94th Cong., 1st sess., September and October.

U.S., Congress, Joint Economic Committee, Subcommittee on Fiscal Policy and Intergovernmental Policy. 1979. *Central City Businesses: Plans and Problems.* 95th Cong., 2nd sess., January 14.

1973. *Income-Tested Social Benefits in New York: Adequacy, Incentives, and Equity.* By Blanche Bernstein. Studies in Public Welfare, Paper no. 8, 93rd Cong., 1st sess., July 8.

1967. *Revenue Sharing and Its Alternatives: What Future for Fiscal Federalism?* 90th Cong., 1st sess., July.

U.S., Congress, Senate, Committee on Banking, Housing and Urban Affairs. 1975. *New York City Financial Crisis.* Hearings. 94th Cong., 1st sess., October.

U.S., Congress, Senate, Committee on Government Operations, Subcommittee on Intergovernmental Relations. 1967. *Creative Federalism.* 90th Cong., 1st sess., January 31 and February 1, 2, and 6.

U.S., Congress, Senate, Committee on Rules and Administration. 1974. *Nomination of Nelson A. Rockefeller of New York to Be Vice President of the United States.* Hearings. 93rd Cong., 2nd sess., September and November.

U.S., Corps of Engineers. 1977. *Waterborne Commerce of the United States, 1977.*

U.S., Department of Commerce, Bureau of Economic Analysis. *Survey of Current Business.*

U.S., Department of Labor. 1979*a*. *Employment and Earnings, United States, 1909–1978.* Bulletin 1312–11.

1973. *Industry Wage Survey: Women's and Misses' Dresses*. Bulletin 1783, August 1971.

1979b. *The Job Future in New York–Northeastern New Jersey: Occupational Employment Projections to 1985*. Regional Report 60, February.

Monthly Labor Review.

Usdan, Michael D. 1974. "Elementary and Secondary Education," in Robert H. Connery and Gerald Benjamin (eds.), *Governing New York State*. New York: Academy of Political Science, 225–38.

Uttley, Lois. 1979. "The Executive Budget: Political Gamesmanship." *Empire State Report* V (June–July), 28–32.

Veiller, Lawrence, 1900. *Tenement House Legislation in New York, 1852–1900*. Albany: Brandow.

Vernon, Raymond. 1960. *Metropolis 1985: An Interpretation of the Findings of the New York Metropolitan Region Study*. Cambridge, Mass.: Harvard University Press.

Vickrey, William. 1974. "Improving New York's Transit Service: An Economist's View." *City Almanac* VIII (April), 1–10.

Vitullo-Martin, Julia. 1979. "The Real Sore Spot in New York's Economy." *Fortune* C (November 19), 92–105.

1980. "Why New York City Can't Help Itself." *New York Affairs* VI, no. 2, 37–42.

Wald, Martin. 1980. "Hard Times on the Hill for N.Y." *Empire State Report* VI (June 16), 265, 267–8.

Walsh, Annmarie Hauck. 1978. *The Public's Business: The Politics and Practices of Government Corporations*. Cambridge, Mass.: M.I.T. Press.

Webster, Daniel. 1903. *The Writings and Speeches of Daniel Webster*. Boston: Little, Brown.

Weinstein, Bernard L. 1976. "Why Texas Outdraws New York for Business." *Empire State Report* II (October–November), 334, 346.

Weinstein, Bernard L. and Robert E. Firestine. 1978. *Regional Growth and Decline in the United States: The Rise of the Sunbelt and the Decline of the Northeast*. New York: Praeger.

Weinstein, Bernard L. and George Keller. 1975–76. "The Startling Changes in New York's Economy." *Search 2*, State University of New York, I (Winter), 5–19.

Weintraub, Arthur E. 1978. "Clean Air and Smokestacks: New York State Needs Both." *Empire State Report* IV (October–November), 19–23.

Weisman, Steven R. 1975. "Nelson Rockefeller's Pill: The UDC." *Washington Monthly* VII (June), 35–44.

Welles, Chris. 1975. "The Day New York City Defaulted." *New York Magazine* VIII (June 2), 30–6.

"What Management Needs to Know before Picking a Plant Site." 1979. *Dun's Review* CXIV (October), 14–16.

White, Theodore H. 1975. "An Open Letter to the Democratic Majority: New York City Is the Test." *New York Magazine* VIII (November 10), 39–43.

Willis, Mark A. 1979. "Business Taxation in New York City." *Federal Reserve Bank of New York Quarterly Review* IV (Spring), 22–8.

Wilson, Malcolm. 1979. "Nelson A. Rockefeller: Man of Balance." *Empire State Report* V (February), 4–5.

Wilson, Woodrow. 1885. *Congressional Government: A Study in American Politics*. Boston: Houghton Mifflin.

Winkleman, Michael. 1980. "Why the Apple Beckons: The Return of Tourism." *New York Affairs* VI, no. 2, 70–6.

Young, Janet S. 1979. "New York's Insurance Industry: Perspective and Prospects." *Federal Reserve Bank of New York Quarterly Review* IV (Spring), 9–19.

Zimmerman, Joseph F. 1974. "Public Transportation," in Robert H. Connery and Gerald Benjamin (eds.), *Governing New York State: The Rockefeller Years.* New York: Academy of Political Science, 214–24.

Index